THE GREAT STAGE
DIRECTORS

THE GREAT STAGE DIRECTORS

100 DISTINGUISHED CAREERS OF THE THEATER

Samuel L. Leiter

Foreword by Simon Callow

Facts On File®

AN INFOBASE HOLDINGS COMPANY

The Great Stage Directors: 100 Distinguished Careers of the Theater

Facts On File, Inc.
460 Park Avenue South
New York NY 10016

Library of Congress Cataloging-in-Publication Data

Leiter, Samuel L.
    The great stage directors : 100 distinguished careers of the theater / Samuel L. Leiter.
      p.   cm.
    Includes bibliographical references and index.
    ISBN 0-8160-2602-5
    1. Theatrical producers and directors—Biography—Dictionaries.
I. Title.
PN2205.L44 1994
792′.0233′0922—dc20   93-33380

Facts On File books are available at special discounts when purchased in bulk quantities for businesses, associations, institutions or sales promotions. Please call our Special Sales Department in New York at 212/683-2244 or 800/322-8755.

Text design by Grace M. Ferrara
Jacket design by Carla Weise
Printed in the United States of America

RRD VC 10 9 8 7 6 5 4 3 2 1

This book is printed on acid-free paper.

For Briar Autumn Falvo

CONTENTS

FOREWORD

LIKE IT OR loathe it, to a large extent the history of the theater in the second half of the 20th century is the history of its directors. It is now common to be able to buy a ticket for Jonathan Miller's *Hamlet* or Peter Brook's *A Midsummer Night's Dream* without having the slightest idea which actors are in it or who designed it, and although you probably know who wrote those plays, you would be hard pressed to discover the fact from the posters. Directors' interpretations are discussed in exhaustive detail; indeed, in many reviews, theirs are the only names mentioned. The distinguished critic of the London *Sunday Times* wrote a long and enthusiastic notice of a recent Old Vic production of Isaac Babel's *Mavra* without naming a single one of the 34 actors in the cast, nor the designer, nor the composer, nor the lighting designer. I wrote to the newspaper to warn innocent theatergoers that when they went to the show, they must not actually expect to see Roger Michell, the director in question, on stage, though his name was the only name apart from Babel's to be mentioned in the review (eight times, to be precise). This is a very good thing for a profession that barely existed at the beginning of our own century, an unheard of *prise de pouvoir*, which could not have been accomplished without the parallel rise of the make-or-break critic. Directing is so much easier to write about than acting or writing.

Or so it would seem. In fact, most writing about directing is a stab in the dark. After the success of the Edward Gordon Craig Adolphe Appia propaganda hailing the arrival of the Puppetmaster Director, it is assumed that everything that appears on the stage is there because the director has put it there; that it is part of a master plan. Without pausing to inquire, critics casually write of Mr. W or Ms. X "drawing a fine performance out of Sir Henry Y or Dame Madge Z." How do they know? For me, the millennium will have arrived when we read of Sir Henry or Dame Madge having drawn a fine production out of Mr. W and Ms. X. The designers, too, are frequently responsible for the triumph so automatically attributed to the director. This is not to suggest that his or her work is negligible, simply that more needs to be known about it. For the most part, it is swathed in mystery. This is partly intentional (to create the indispensable aura), partly because it is unquantifiable. Though there have been studies of directors, they have for the most part been of "great directors," and they have set out to demonstrate the greatness of their great subjects. The author sits in on rehearsals, carefully noting down the obiter dicta of the great man-woman and politely detailing the growth of the production. None of these volumes approaches the work in a properly anthropological spirit, analyzing the hierarchies, the ritualized games, the framework of custom and observance that is the substance of the daily life of the rehearsal, nor has any given a convincing account of the enormously complex structures of the process of artistic creation. Such a book, when it is written, may result in the falling of scales from certain critical eyes.* Perhaps not; it will certainly make their jobs a lot harder. The discovery that the director is both the most important and the most impotent figure in the setup will be rather dismaying. How, in a review, can you write about that?

Meanwhile, Sam Leiter, that unexampled and indispensable toiler in the vineyards of the history of the living theater of our century, has written a series of highly informative and perceptive profiles of the leading members of this fledgling profession since its inception, just over 100 years ago; for good measure, he has thrown in a couple of seminal figures, like Goethe (who would certainly be surprised to find himself reading a review of Peter Stein's *Faust*). Leiter has, with his habitual clarity and precision, given accounts both of the directors' careers and of the guiding ideas behind them. Taken overall, his book offers the best history of directing currently available, and much food for thought about this puzzling profession of being a director, umpire, therapist, trainer, ringmaster, sergeant-major, nanny, and audience of one, whose greatest achievement is—or should be—to make him or herself invisible and, ultimately, redundant.

—Simon Callow
London, England

* See, however, the books by Susan Letzler Cole and Shomit Mitter, listed in the bibliography, that appeared after this was written.

INTRODUCTORY NOTE

THE GREAT STAGE DIRECTORS provides brief, alphabetically arranged descriptions of 100 stage directors through history. It ranges from such early examples as Garrick and Goethe, who directed before the art itself had achieved formal recognition, to several of today's finest young artists. The coverage is international, although the majority are American and British. Despite the extremely limited space, an attempt has been made to include career achievements, capsulized accounts of representative productions, and an idea of the respective directors' concepts and working methods. Film and opera directing are mentioned but not described.* In cases of directors well known for other theatrical accomplishments (writing, performing, etc.), only their directing work is considered.

Many other directors easily could have been included. Queries have already come from those who have seen the manuscript. You have John Gielgud, why not Laurence Olivier? Joseph Chaikin is included, so where are Julian Beck and Judith Malina? This kind of thing can go on indefinitely. If Serban and Ciulei, why not Pintilie? If Suzuki, why not Ninagawa? If Strehler, why not Visconti, Zeffirelli, Costa, Ronconi? If Planchon, why not Chérau, Vitez? If Stein, why not Zadek, Grüber? And where are Bogdanov, Hytner, Warner, Hands, Lepage, Bogart, McAnuff, Efros, Hands, Barton, Garcia, and, on and on. The subtitle of this book mentions 100 directors and its purpose is to be representative, not all-inclusive. Those chosen represent every facet of the profession, from the radical avant-garde to the comfortably conventional; from the overtly commercial to the holiest of holies; from director-choreographers to classical revivalists; from bourgeois reactionaries to committed communists; from actor-managers to those who never acted; and from text

worshipers to auteurs and deconstructionists. Gordon Craig aside, important artists better known as theorists than practitioners have been excluded.

Apart from one or two exceptions, the "Further reading" lists accompanying each entry are limited to five major citations, unless more are referred to in the text itself. A general bibliography of titles covering more than one of my selections concludes the book. These works are mentioned in many of the "Also" citations following the "Further reading" lists.

I wish to thank the Research Foundation of the City University of New York for two grants supporting this project; Pamela Cobrin, my research assistant; the staff of the Gideonse Library of Brooklyn College, CUNY; the Lincoln Center Library for the Performing Arts; and the Museum of the City of New York. Institutions and photographers who helpfully provided illustrations are credited with their pictures, but I would like to thank the following for their help in gathering photos: Elzbieta Wrzesinska of the Stary Teatre, Krakow; Anna Pease of the Guthrie Theatre; Laura Davis of the American Conservatory Theatre; Nancy Lindeman of the Hartford Stage Company; Jeff Fickes of the Long Wharf Theatre; Ulrik Skeel of the Odin Teatret, Holstebro, Denmark; Ikuko Saito of SCOT, Japan; Tatiana Pohle of the Berliner Ensemble; Ann-Christine Jernberg of the Royal Theatre of Sweden; Mark Rasdorf of the Arena Theatre; Gordon Davidson's office at the Mark Taper Theatre; Marie-Josephe Fromond of the Théâtre National Populaire, Villeurbanne; Margaret Melozzi of the Trinity Repertory Company; and Katalin Mitchell of the American Conservatory Theatre. Every effort has been made to locate copyright holders for material reproduced in this book. The author would be grateful to learn of any omissions for correction in future editions. Thanks also to Glenn Loney, who provided me with a helpful draft of an unpublished article on Peter Stein; to Gary M. Krebs, my editor at Facts On File; my son, Justin; and my wife, Marcia.

—Samuel L. Leiter
Howard Beach, New York

---

*There are one or two exceptions to this limitation on opera descriptions, notably in the case of Gordon Craig, whose ideas on staging plays were first evolved during a sequence of operatic productions with amateurs. The restriction does not apply to operettas or comic operas, so, for example, Gilbert and Sullivan productions are occasionally discussed.

GEORGE ABBOTT (1887–   )

GEORGE FRANCIS ABBOTT was born in Forestville, New York, and was educated at Rochester University, later studying playwriting under George Pierce Baker at Harvard. During the longest and most continually productive career in American theater history, he was a successful actor, producer, director, and playwright, remaining active until well past the age of 100.

Abbott, a Broadway actor from 1913, began directing in 1924, beginning with *The Fall Guy*, which he coauthored with James Gleason. He shot to fame with *Broadway* (1926), cowritten with Philip Dunning. It established his slick, fast-paced, energetic directorial style, subsequently applied to comedies, farces, melodramas, and musicals. Although he was responsible for a string of melodramas through the twenties and thirties (among them Maurine Watkins's popular *Chicago* in 1926), he was especially in demand for comedies and farces, notably after his and John Cecil Holms's *Three Men on a Horse* (1934). Abbott's comic brilliance was noteworthy in his thirties' directorial hits, among them Sam and Bella Spewack's *Boy Meets Girl* (1935), John Monks Jr. and Fred F. Finklehoff's *Brother Rat* (1936), John Murray and Allen Boretz's *Room Service* (1937), and Clifford Goldsmith's *What a Life* (1938).

Dunning and Abbott's Broadway. *Directed by George Abbott. (1987)* (Photo: Martha Swope)

By 1934, Abbott was concentrating on writing, producing, and directing. Musical comedy increasingly occupied his directing time in the late thirties, when he staged Rodgers and Hart shows such as *On Your Toes* (1936), *The Boys from Syracuse* (1938), *Too Many Girls* (1939), and *Pal Joey* (1940). Musicals dominated his output in the forties, when Broadway saw *Best Foot Forward* (1941), score by Hugh Martin and Ralph Blane; *On the Town* (1944), score by Leonard Bernstein, Betty Comden, and Adolph Green; *High Button Shoes* (1947), score by Jule Styne and Sammy Cahn; and *Where's Charley?* (1949), score by Frank Loesser. Subsequent hit musicals in his debt were *A Tree Grows in Brooklyn* (1951), score by Dorothy Fields and Arthur Schwartz; *Wonderful Town* (1953), score by Bernstein, Comden, and Green; Rodgers and Hammerstein's *Me and Juliet* (1953); *The Pajama Game* (1954), score by Richard Adler and Jerry Ross; *Damn Yankees* (1955), also by Adler and Ross; *Once Upon a Mattress* (1959), score by Mary Rodgers and Marshall Barer; *Fiorello!* (1959), score by Jerry Bock and Sheldon Harnick; and *A Funny Thing Happened on the Way to the Forum* (1962), score by Stephen Sondheim. The latter won Abbott a Tony as best director of a musical.

Abbott's success ratio plunged in the sixties, when, apart from *A Funny Thing*, he was represented by only two other hits, both comedies, Phoebe and Henry Ephron's *Take Her, She's Mine* (1961) and Sumner Arthur Long's *Never Too Late* (1962). He remained active, but with less regularity than before. In 1973, he ventured into the regional theater with a revival of Howard Lindsay and Russel Crouse's *Life With Father* for the Seattle Repertory Theater, and in 1978 did his first Off-Off-Broadway play, Lee Kalcheim's *Winning Isn't Everything*, for the Hudson Guild Theater. In 1983 he won his second directing Tony with a revival of *On Your Toes*. Abbott subsequently focused on workshop productions of new musicals whose books he had written; a New Jersey revival of *Damn Yankees* (1986); and a Cleveland revival of *Broadway* (1987) that flopped when it moved to Broadway.

Clearly, Abbott staged some of the most popular works of the modern American theater, having directed 13 productions running over 500 performances. He was honored in 1965 by having the Fifty-fourth Street Theater (since razed) named after him.

Abbott's directorial style is often referred to as the "Abbott touch," a dazzling show business pizzazz and professionalism. The Abbott touch implies rapid and rhythmic pacing, doors that open and close swiftly for split-second entrances and exits, hilarious stage business, and machine-gun dialogue, all within a matrix of complete believability established by the actors and mise-en-scène.

Abbott attributed his actors' success to his insistence on their behaving honestly and speaking clearly. He required that actors always be truthful, no matter how farfetched the situation, and he stomped out all traces of artificiality or overacting. Seeking complete audibility, he demanded excellent diction (especially the ends of lines).

Because of his businesslike taciturnity and laconic aloofness, the very tall, impeccably dressed director was referred to as "Mr. Abbott." He knew just what the public would buy in the theater. In Abbott's terms this proved to be noncerebral material, with straightforward situations, colorful—and frequently very youthful—characters who are more types than individuals, and immediately comprehensible dialogue. He never staged a classic or literary drama, seeking instead works of wide appeal, often with some timely feature to which the average spectator could relate.

For all his conventionality, however, he could set trends, especially in his musicals, as when he introduced Shakespeare to musical comedy in *The Boys from Syracuse*; injected harsh cynicism into the normally saccharine musical genre in *Pal Joey*; used musical comedy to tackle the topic of labor relations in *Pajama Game*; directed a dark-toned musical about a prostitute, *New Girl in Town* (1957), based on Eugene O'Neill's *Anna Christie*; or conjoined Roman comedy to the musical stage in *A Funny Thing Happened on the Way to the Forum*.

Abbott, terrified of boring an audience, constantly revised and cut if there was any chance of losing attention. This often meant the extraction of excellent material, because he always thought in terms of the play as a whole and not of particular scenes. One cause for boredom, Abbott believed, was actors who, during a run, began to revise their timing to make the most of pauses, including the delaying of cue pickups. He thus kept a close eye on his shows after they opened, and gave warnings to actors guilty of disrupting the ensemble. "Take out those air spaces!" he would command.

Probably no aspect of Abbott's productions is as well known as his rapid pacing. He insisted that fast pacing was not the same as uncontrolled speed. Morton Eustis capsulized the Abbott touch:

What the director actually does to establish the desired tempo is to emphasize contrast both in speech and movement; to make the audience, instead of the actors, supply movement, by turning their eyes from one portion of the stage to another; to build up the volume, the speed, the intensity of the tone of voice here, chop it there; accelerate the motion of the actor, both in movement and gesture; speed up the rhythm of the company as an ensemble; slow it down, then build again; in short, to approach every problem related to everything the audience sees, hears or thinks about with variety, inventiveness and still more variety.

Abbott believed in typecasting, wherein actors resemble closely their role in temperament and appearance. He did not support repertory, which allows actors to play parts outside their type. Such a situation may eventually make an actor more versatile but it will also weaken a production, thought Abbott, who claimed he could tell the quality of a director by the actor cast as the butler. Throughout his career, he kept detailed casting information on file on all the actors he auditioned or interviewed, and employed casting directors to keep him up to date.

Abbott was courteous to auditioners, but forbade them from going on too long. In his opinion, an experienced director could tell the suitability of an actor immediately. However, unusually interesting actors were given additional time, and would even be asked to try different things to determine their range. He fulminated against Method-trained auditioners who engaged in private preparations while the director waited patiently for them to begin. Nevertheless, his type of audition forced Abbott to overlook some excellent actors, who either could not adjust to such a cold, businesslike method or simply were inept at sight readings.

When acting as his own producer, Abbott preferred lesser-known, and hence less expensive, talents to stars. He preferred actors who did not detract from the writing and whose personal problems did not involve him. Stars were acceptable when paid for by another producer.

Abbott often took a chance on fresh and untried actors, but he also liked to use certain players over and over. Thus, a pool of actors eventually became known as the "Abbott Stock Company," although no such formal body existed.

Whenever possible, he had the author attend rehearsals so that problems could be dealt with at once. A writer himself, he always asked the playwright for his approval before making any changes. He believed that production problems stemmed from the writing and not the acting. He resisted replacing actors, feeling that a strong enough script could survive with any competent cast. His rehearsal ability in revising scripts made him a popular play doctor, called in to assist productions floundering in previews or out of town.

Abbott's rehearsals began with several days of readings, as he determined what help the actors would require and what they could offer. He then began blocking, which, earlier in his career, was based on careful planning; later, he created in the crucible of rehearsal, having found that he normally discarded most of his prepared ideas. He started sketchily and worked to find a completely natural means of expressing the text, continually revising until the moves seemed right. The instant he made a mistake he fixed it, showing no embarrassment at having erred.

Abbott worked rapidly, wasting no time, and making instant decisions as things fell into place. He was quiet, intense, polite, and completely concentrated. Outbursts were rare. Commentary was brief and precise; blather was anathema. Productions were often staged in one week's time, followed by about a week of relative leisure as the actors focused on learning their words accurately. Abbott absolutely refused to accept paraphrasing.

Abbott gave the type of result-oriented directions that some find uncomfortable but that others appreciate for their uncanny appropriateness. Maureen Stapleton said, "He would tell you to walk behind the third pillow, wait two beats, and then say the line. Lou Jacobi and I used to look at each other and shake our heads—he was always exactly right."

Despite his distaste for psychological exploration of characters and situations, Abbott's directions were always rooted in motivation. Everything had a reason, nothing was done purely for effect. He listened carefully, constantly seeking internally justified, natural, and unforced readings.

Abbott ruled tightly but diplomatically. Only in the most extreme circumstances did he demonstrate his autocracy overtly. Stars did not intimidate him and he faced down some of the biggest when they chose to put on airs. He refused to become engaged in arguments with temperamental players and would sooner walk out than engage in a demeaning quarrel. For all his coolness, however, he used a whistle to gain attention when rehearsing a musical in a large theater; veteran Abbott actors could tell how upset he was by the volume of his blast.

To Abbott, a show was a business operation; it had to open on schedule. This meant absolute punctuality from all concerned. No sooner did he walk into the room than the rehearsal was underway.

Few stars dared to come late. Abbott simply refused to wait for them, choosing to work with their understudies instead. Because he hated to lose time, he often demonstrated movements for his actors or gave line readings if it moved things along more quickly.

Note-giving was before the entire company, not separately to individuals. He argued that any actor given a note before his peers was placed under a greater constraint to carry out the direction than if spoken to privately. This was especially true for notes that related to another's work, such as "Please don't make that move because it hurts so-and-so's performance."

Abbott was not especially gifted in the area of design, and he made no important visual breakthroughs. He wanted his sets, like his actors, to be straightforward, attractive, and effective in terms of the material being performed. There was nothing fancy about his lighting, the chief objective being visibility, especially in comedy.

George Abbott is a Broadway legend, both because of his fabulous longevity (in 1993, aged 106, he was revising the book of *Damn Yankees* for a new production) and because of the enormous number of his outstanding contributions in multiple realms of play production. His no-apologies commercialism, his ability to gauge the popular taste, his pacing and rhythm, and his unflappable professionalism were not intellectually challenging or aesthetically pathbreaking, but they offered immeasurable quantities of sheer pleasure on the Great White Way.

Further reading:

Abbott, George. *"Mister Abbott."* New York: Random House, 1963.

Eustis, Morton. "The Director Takes Command." *Theatre Arts Monthly* 20 (February 1936).

Millstein, Gilbert. "Mr. Abbott: One-Man Theater." *New York Times Magazine,* October 3, 1954.

Zolotow, Maurice. "Broadway's Most Successful Penny-Pincher." *Saturday Evening Post,* January 29, 1955.

Also: Laufe, *Broadway's Greatest Musicals*; Leiter, *From Belasco to Brook*; Mordden, *Broadway Babies.*

JOANNE AKALAITIS (1935–   )

JOANNE AKALAITIS, whose father was a factory worker, was born in Cicero, Illinois. She switched from premed to philosophy at the University of Chicago and attended graduate school at Stanford, but left to act in San Francisco. After sampling acting schools in New York, she and her then husband, composer Philip Glass, lived in France, where they met San Francisco theater friends Lee Breuer and Ruth Malaczech. In 1970, they and others founded Mabou Mines, the acclaimed, collaborative, avant-garde theater troupe, in New York.

Mabou Mines encouraged all members "to think conceptually about the text, design and structure of a piece," Akalaitis told Jonathan Kalb. Her directing debut was her adaptation of Beckett's two-character radio play, *Cascando* (1975), expanded to an eight-actor work with a cello score by Glass, who created most of Akalaitis's music. This visually metaphoric piece about the difficulty of artistic creation toured Europe in 1976. For each of her next three works she adapted other persons' writings; she created the scripts and, alone or in collaboration, the decor. Her early productions were staged either Off-Off or Off-Broadway, but she later worked in major regional theaters.

Dressed Like an Egg (1978) was inspired by a photo of the French writer Colette, leaning against parallel bars. It demonstrated a feminist perspective and commented on received ideas of gender definition. A book about an Antarctic explorer sparked *Southern Exposure* (1978), set in an all-white, bedroomlike environment, and using slides, film clips, and live action to contrast romantic conceptions of existence in the bleak world of the South Pole with the harsh facts of reality.

The dark satire *Dead End Kids* (1980) emerged from fears concerning nuclear holocaust in the wake of the Three Mile Island incident. Material came from many sources, ranging from Faust and Marie Curie to contemporary journalism. In a representative scene, a 1950s government movie about nuclear power was projected behind actors dressed in contamination suits handling radioactive isotopes. "Miss Akalaitis has found a way to make us think about the unthinkable all over again," praised the *New York Times.*

In 1981, Akalaitis began directing plays by other authors, beginning with West German Franz Xavier Kroetz's *Request Concert,* a photorealistic, wordless depiction of a lonely woman's coming home to her

Dead End Kids. *Directed by JoAnne Akalaitis. (1980)* (Photo: Carol Rosegg)

efficiency apartment and busying herself—in detailed activity collaboratively developed by Akalaitis and actress Joan MacIntosh—before ending her futile life. Akalaitis moved the play from Bavaria to Queens and converted the original's German "worker" to a middle-class working woman. Her intention was to make the play's politics more pertinent for a New York audience and, she told Jonathan Kalb, to emphasize the feminist theme of how such women "have no access to any kind of emotional or social life" in their urban isolation.

Request Concert contrasted strikingly with Akalaitis's nonlinear conceptualizations, designed to work subconsciously and provoke thought by combining music, sound, lights, decor, unusual costumes, stylized movement, slides, film, simultaneous action, cross-gender and -ethnic casting, dialectically conflicting words and images, and collage-like texts.

Michael Hurson's *Red and Blue* (1982), was a poorly received, abstract, hour-long fragmentary conversation, set in an intricately designed, nine-room doll house-like wall sculpture. It concerned "the passage of time" in terms of a pair of flickering lightbulbs, blue (male) and red (female), provided with offstage voices.

Following *The Photographer* (1984), a dance-theater-concert piece based on Edward Muybridge's photography, Akalaitis did Kroetz's *Through the Leaves* (1984), about a female butcher and her abusive boyfriend. A stylized, simultaneous setting of a butcher shop and apartment interior was used imaginatively with a combination of live action and taped monologues backed by Muzak and New Wave German music. The result was superrealism mingled with TV-like freeze-frames. Critics disliked the transposition to Queens, but Kroetz approved it.

Considerable controversy was generated by Samuel Beckett's *Endgame* (1984) at Cambridge's American Repertory Theater (ART) when Akalaitis—who usually ignores a playwright's scenic description and stage directions—placed it in a dismal subway tunnel, backed by electronic music. Hamm and Nagg were black. The dismayed playwright sued, claiming artistic desecration. The settlement saw his name removed from ads and programs.

ART also sponsored Akalaitis's revival of Jean Genet's *The Balcony* (1986), its setting now in Latin America and its score by Rubén Blades. One vivid image was a tableau in which, as a film of a revolution in progress was projected, Chantal flew on a wire above the revolutionaries like "Liberty Leading the People."

Green Card (1986), premiered in Los Angeles, represented a return to Akalaitis's 1970s collage work. Intended as a revuelike attack on America's immigration policies, and favoring an open door for all desiring entry, it was thought directorially exciting but politically naive and incohesive.

Akalaitis's reputation as a Kroetz interpreter was hampered by *Help Wanted* (1986), a brief anthology of six satirical sketches (from an original 15) that began at 10:30 P.M. The work, said the *Times,* "presents a bleak portrait of degrading familial and sexual relationships that . . . reflect the brutality and dehumanization inflicted by the industrial state." Akalaitis was again chastised for Americanizing Kroetz.

Len Jenkin's eccentric *American Notes* (1988) was Akalaitis's first full-length American play. The same year, Georg Büchner's *Leon and Lena (and Lenz)* was mounted at Minneapolis's Guthrie, its mythical Germanic background shifted to the American Southwest; a pastiche of country western music accompanied it. Most controversially, a major Guthrie backer known for making cluster bombs was parodied. The production satirized ethnic stereotypes: Leon was a flashy Hispanic, his friend Val a black breakdancer, and Lena an Asian. A film based on Büchner's introspective character Lenz was projected as a warning about the dangers of Leon's becoming similarly introspective.

A riveting five-hour revival of Genet's *The Screens* (1989), was also at the Guthrie. In preparation, Akalaitis traveled to North Africa, where, wrote Andrea Nouryeh, she "studied aspects of death, near-death experiences, and Islamic death rituals as a way of finding a gestural and auditory language that would evoke Genet's Land of the Dead." The eclectically costumed 50-member cast performed in the aisles as well as on stage and a world of decadence and doom was effectively captured.

Akalaitis's first Shakespeare, 1989's *Cymbeline*, in Central Park, was "A Romantic Fantasy in Victorian England" that viewed Victorian images from a 20th-century perspective in order to explore the text as a commentary on topical issues, from racism to misogyny. Nontraditional casting commented on colonialist attitudes. Despite such memorable scenes as the fog-enshrouded, slow-motion, freeze-frame battle, many thought the campy production disunified and undigestable. Defenders complained about the critics' obtuseness to Akalaitis's postmodern aesthetic, specifically designed to emphasize the play's disparate elements. Nevertheless, Shakespeare reinspired Akalaitis to work in theater, which she was on the verge of quitting.

Chicago's Goodman Theater hosted Akalaitis's revival of John Ford's *'Tis Pity She's a Whore* (1989), a violence- and sensuality-filled production restaged at New York's Public Theater in 1992. Fascist Italy replaced the original's Carolinian setting. "Its fascism and futurism championed the misogyny, the decadence, the cult of youth and athleticism, and the war-mongering attitudes that had direct parallels in contemporary America which Akalaitis envisioned when she read Ford's play," observed Nouryeh. The directorial choices contrasted biases against women in a male-dominated world.

Akalaitis returned to Shakespeare with a complex, six-hour production of both parts of *Henry IV* (1991) at the Public. Her staging, which used slides and film, blended an Elizabethan look with present-day props, including beer cans and *Playboy* magazine. One image tying Shakespeare's world to ours was a Hispanic thief with a stolen TV. An image especially liked by the *Times's* Frank Rich was in Part 2, when the director used "subtle design adjustments, whiteface makeup and a hedonistic dumb show to remake the Bruegelesque, relatively bucolic Boar's Head tavern of Part 1 into a metaphor for an old civilization splintering into modern decadence and the savagery of the charnel house."

Akalaitis's Public revival of Büchner's antiheroic *Woyzeck* (1992), in a dismal setting reminiscent of Anselm Kiefer's paintings, was praised and attacked. Critics debated the reordering of the fragmentary play's scenes, the increased emphasis on Woyzeck's common-law wife, a scene of soldiers showering while Woyzeck shaved the captain, the use of a filmed insert, and an ending in which a naked Woyzeck died in a gas chamber.

An uncompleted project on which Akalaitis has been working is *The Mormons,* an exploration of Mormonism. It had a 1990 workshop staging in Florida. Most recently, Akalaitis staged a revival of Jane Bowles's *In the Summer House* (1993) at Lincoln Center.

Akalaitis works from mental images passed on to her actors. Potential pieces that do not trigger these pictures are abandoned. Instead of doing dramaturgical research on the critical history of a play, she concentrates on visual research, even visiting places like those depicted in the action. She insists on social and political relevance but never lectures her actors about a play's meaning because she discovers it herself only in the process of rehearsals.

Reading rehearsals bore her, so she gets the actors moving at once, although a scene is likely to be read before being staged. Preoccupied with physicalization, she begins by having the actors do various exercises, usually with taped music from a wide variety of international sources. Production images occasionally stem from these sessions. Moreover, her innovative use of music is of vast importance to her aesthetic. She also stresses exercises in slow motion, which she believes are crucial for getting the actor to see himself clearly in space and to more effectively comprehend physical relationships. She often asks the company to consider themselves part of a painting so that they learn to view themselves compositionally in relation to their fellows; this evokes a sense of unity. Or she will remind the actors to remain in the same "world" when she notices disparities. This connects to her pre-runthrough appeals for actors to focus on what she calls the physical and emotional "geography" of the work.

She considers blocking "the mark of a real director," and tackles it early in order to capture the physical look right away. With the blocking done, but subject to change, she can concentrate on the work's inner life. Akalaitis strives to make the working process both collaborative and nonmanipulative.

Her work involves what she calls "character mudras," *mudras* being the gestural language of classical Indian theater, and she is determined to find a Western psychological equivalent "which," she told Arthur Bartow, "could hit the audience in a nonintellectual, almost Jungian way." She prefers actors to keep themselves under observation while acting, but not necessarily in the Brechtian manner of commenting on the role.

Another Akalaitis method—borrowed from Genet—is to avoid transitions and direct each unit of a scene as a play unto itself, making no attempt to tie it to what precedes or follows it. Actors, however, resist this technique in order to work in a more logical, causal sequence. But Akalaitis observed to Bartow that "It gives a kind of jerky, 'vortexy' rhythm to performance that I find exciting."

Akalaitis, who avoids psychologizing, prefers to ignore how an actor does his job. She admits that her refusal to cajole and nurse actors may be a drawback. She told Kalb, "If an actor has some problem, or comes to rehearsal in a bad mood, I tend not to take the actor aside and talk, but to go on with the rehearsal." She has a reputation for being aloof and unpleasant, although many defend her. She informed Bartow that "women directors have to be better behaved than men," or else they are labeled "bitchy or unfeminine." Ruth Malaczech, though, told Simi Horwitz, "She is comical, intense, frank, and sometimes harsh. But there's always integrity. And her goal is clarity. Of all the directors I've worked with . . . she is the most prepared, the most workmanlike." Nevertheless, Akalaitis states that she can only create in the interactive crucible of rehearsals, which she begins by waiting to see what the actors are ready to show her. While her goals are always visually precise, she allows the actors great freedom within that frame.

In 1991, when Joseph Papp died, Akalaitis inherited his leadership of the Public Theater; Papp himself had selected her. Many wondered if her uncommercial, avant-garde, intellectually challenging tastes, perceived dissatisfaction with subscription audiences, arguable failure to discover new playwrights, and unpopular politics (she supports the Palestine Liberation Organization) would alienate the audiences Papp had developed. In March 1993, in a widely debated decision, the Public's board of directors fired her—despite her three-year contract and advocates who claimed she had not been given sufficient time—and replaced her with George C. Wolfe.

Director Robert Falls declares, "JoAnne loves to push buttons and probe and poke and prod." A too-complacent theater needs such voices. At the Public, Akalaitis pushed the wrong buttons. It is doubtful that this setback will stop her or that she will not continue to be every ounce as provocative in the work she does hereafter.

Further reading:

Horwitz, Simi. "JoAnne Akalaitis." *TheaterWeek*, March 18, 1991.

Kalb, Jonathan. "JoAnne Akalaitis." *Theatre* 15 (Spring 1984).

Nouryeh, Andrea. "JoAnne Akalaitis: Post Modern Director or Socio-Sexual Critic." *Theatre Topics* 1 (September 1991).

Also: Bartow, *Director's Voice*; Cole, *Directors in Rehearsal.*

ANDRÉ ANTOINE (1858–1943)

ANDRÉ ANTOINE was born in Limoges to bourgeois parents and moved with them in 1869 to Paris. He took elocution lessons at Le Gymnase de la Parole, where he staged and starred in his first play (1874). He worked at the Comédie Française—whose Conservatoire rejected him—as an extra and a *claqueur*. He joined an amateur group, the Cercle Gaulois, which played on a tiny stage in a 343-seat Montmartre playhouse, but grew dissatisfied with their antiquated plays and methods. A number of writers, however, Émile Zola in particular, were seeking to shed the rigid conventions of romanticism and Scribean dramaturgy in favor of realism and naturalism. Zola believed social conditions could be improved by using the stage as a laboratory to scientifically study human behavior. Antoine arranged—by paying for it with one month of his gas clerk's salary—to take over the Cercle Gaulois for a night of one-acts.

Antoine's opening bill, produced on March 30, 1887, with amateurs calling themselves the Théâtre Libre, consisted of Paul Alexis's *Miss Apple* (based on a work by Edmond Duranty), Jules Vidal's *The Vain One*, Arthur Byl's *The Prefect*, and Léon Hennique's *Jacques Damour*, adapted from Émile Zola. The latter, produced with Antoine's mother's dining room furniture, was the most impressive. The company's unusual realism soon gained them renown. Despite Antoine's impecunious state (debt pursued him relentlessly), a second program was quickly arranged. The company opened their second bill, Oscar Méténier's naturalistic one-act, *In the Family*, about Paris slum life (staged without footlights and with the houselights dimmed—revolutionary gestures), and Émile Bergerat's commedia-inspired *Night of the Bergamasque*, to a celebrity-packed house. The program succeeded and Antoine gave up his job to devote full time to the theater; to economize he slept in the company's offices. The first program of his second season was the company's last at the Élysée-des-Beaux-Arts. The Théâtre Montparnasse, an out-of-the-way 800-seat theater (small by contemporary standards) in the Latin Quarter, became the troupe's home in 1887.

Antoine, avoiding revivals, attracted many new plays, often getting dramas rejected by Paris's major theaters, which frequently produced them after they were successfully shown at the Théâtre Libre. The latter was essentially a showcase for new work—by

the known and the unknown—that could not find an outlet elsewhere. Antoine insisted that he fully respected the playwright and that his role was to direct the plays, not to revise them (although he sometimes did). From 1887 to 1894, Antoine offered 112 new plays, far more than any of his contemporaries. Those that left the most lasting impression were in the naturalistic or "slice of life" style first used to describe Jean Jullien's *The Serenade* (1887). Jullien represented the viciously ironic naturalistic style called *comédie rosse* associated with the Théâtre Libre. Although in the early years Antoine was forced to rely on stock scenery, sometimes with props painted on the walls, the company increasingly employed lifelike settings, as when (to critical horror) they used real hunks of beef to depict a butcher shop. Antoine frequently achieved considerable verisimilitude by arranging the furnishings asymmetrically to resemble real-life interiors.

His atmospheric lighting was directly influenced by that of the English actor-manager, Henry Irving, including the latter's device of isolating elements of the mise-en-scène with spotlights to heighten their presence. He was a pioneer in French stage lighting, noting that "light alone, intelligently handled, gives atmosphere and color to a set, depth and perspective. . . . To get excellent effects from light, you must not be afraid to use and spread it unevenly."

Despite his tendency to stage all plays realistically, Antoine's repertory was eclectic, and included plays in a variety of styles, including symbolist and poetic, such as the works of Villiers de l'Isle-Adam, Théodore de Banville, Emilé Bergerat, and Catulle Mendès. He willingly served as paterfamilias to new and untried dramatists.

The world premiere of Leo Tolstoy's Russian peasant tragedy, *The Power of Darkness* (1887), banned in Russia, marked the introduction into the xenophobic Paris theater of the most challenging new foreign plays, especially those of Russia, Scandinavia, and Germany. In addition to Tolstoy, Gerhart Hauptmann (*The Weavers*, 1893; *The Assumption of Hannele*, 1894), August Strindberg (*Miss Julie*, 1893), and, most notably, Henrik Ibsen (*Ghosts*, 1890; *The Wild Duck*, 1891) were staged by Antoine before they were given elsewhere in Paris, although they were often condemned for their lack of French artistic values. These showings stimulated the regular staging of foreign plays in Paris.

A crucial influence on Antoine's art was the performances of the Duke of Saxe-Meiningen's company, which Antoine witnessed in Brussels in 1888. Antoine carefully studied the Duke's drawings, his deployment of actors, and the devices he used to gain his effects. The historical accuracy of the Meiningen work was especially impressive, as was the unique ensemble quality (particularly in the brilliant crowd scenes) and fundamental honesty of the acting (despite the lack of outstanding performers). The Meiningen historical approach was apparent in Antoine's direction of Hennique's *The Death of the Duke of Enghien* (1888), staged with photographic verisimilitude, with costumes copied from paintings, and sets founded on historical documents. Again, footlights were abandoned, while even more noteworthy was the chiaroscuro lighting of one scene solely by the use of lanterns. Antoine had his first opportunity to use the Meiningen's crowd principles in the Goncourt brothers' historical drama, *The Nation in Danger* (1889), in which he deployed several hundred closely drilled extras to indelible effect. His manipulation of large crowds was even more impressive in *The Weavers,* where unforgettable sound effects accompanied the mob's actions.

Antoine's company often borrowed professionals from the leading companies (which also lured many of his own actors away). Lesser players held day jobs, since Antoine paid them but a pittance. He was forced to rehearse after work at night, frequently without sufficient time for adequate polishing. Still, Antoine's actors gradually mastered his demands for realistic performances, even turning their backs on the audience. (Antoine had introduced this much criticized technique in his own acting.) Voices spoke in conversational tones and gestures were subdued and untheatrical. Actors studied nature closely and avoided conventional mannerisms, tricks, and poses. Moreover, the ensemble ruled and the star system was abolished, although certain actors, including Antoine, were applauded for their mastery.

The noncommercial company survived solely on subscriptions, offering very limited showings of each program. At the start of its first subscription season (1887–1888), Antoine himself hand delivered 1,300 subscription advertisements, but the success of their first program led over 3,000 to subscribe. The Théâtre Libre became the quintessential antiestablishment, "independent" theater, set up in some off-the-beaten-path location, operating on a shoestring, doing plays no one else dared to touch by declaring itself private and selling subscriptions, and establishing a uniquely individualistic, influential style.

In 1888, the company moved to the Right Bank's Théâtre des Menus-Plaisirs, to accommodate their growing audience. The ensuing years featured such important dramatists as François Curel (*The Other Side of a Saint*, 1892; *The Fossils*, 1892), Georges Courteline (*Lidoire*, 1891), Eugène Brieux (*Artists' Ménages*, 1890; *Blanchette*, 1892); and Georges de Porto-Riche (*Françoise's Luck*, 1892).

In 1895, Antoine, broke and in need of rest, turned the direction over to someone else and left to tour Europe with a group of actors. The Théâtre Libre was closed in 1896. Antoine served briefly as codirector of the state-supported Odéon with Paul Ginisty, resigned after a dispute, toured France and South America, and returned to take over the Théâtre des Menus-Plaisirs, renamed the Théâtre Antoine, in 1897. During this debt-plagued decade (1896–1906) his repertory consisted principally of his former works, but a wider public was now able to see them. Among important additions was a revival of Henri Becque's *La Parisienne* and several classical revivals, beginning with a notable *King Lear* (1904). In 1906, he succeeded Ginisty as sole director of the Odéon, which he renovated, and where he annually produced five major new productions and 10 minor ones. In 1914, financial problems forced him to resign.

At the Odéon, Antoine continued to encourage new dramatists, including avant-gardists. He also staged many classics, including Aeschylus, Euripides, Plautus, Shakespeare, Pedro Calderón de la Barca, Richard Brinsley Sheridan, Niccolo Machiavelli, Carlo Goldoni, Johann Wolfgang von Goethe, Friedrich Schiller, Molière, Pierre Corneille, Jean Racine, and even a series of medieval plays. Often these plays were produced in academically titled series (for example, "History of Realism and Romanticism in the Theater") that, together with accompanying lectures, reflected Antoine's educational mission. Most Théâtre Libre plays of French authorship were overlooked, while revivals of Tolstoy, Ibsen, and Hauptmann were offered. There was a place, however, for such native writers as Honoré de Balzac, Zola, Alphonse Daudet, l'Isle-Adam, and Becque.

At the Odéon he practiced his growing belief that the playwright was the dominant theatrical artist and that productions should adhere to each play's inherent stylistic requirements. He dismissed those who sought to demonstrate directorial virtuosity and respected those who were faithful to the writing. Antoine commissioned accurate translations, beginning with his Théâtre Libre version of *The Power of*

Darkness, in opposition to the usual French practice of liberal adaptation. Thus, his Shakespeare productions were unusually faithful and consequently often puzzled his audiences. He wanted sets that were organic reflections of the script and its style, not independent inventions of the designer. Music and sound also played important roles, and new scores were frequently commissioned.

Among Antoine's five Shakespeares were *Julius Caesar* (1906), *Coriolanus* (1910), and *Romeo and Juliet* (1910). Seeking to capture the rhythmic flow of the multiscened plays, Antoine alternated between scenes by incorporating small scenic areas within the fixed background, usually at the center, allowing the locale to be suggested by the actors' playing in reference to it; he then closed the curtains upon the inset scene while effecting a change behind them. This device, which rarely required a complete set change, allowed Antoine to use just one intermission. Still, though considerably simplified, Antoine's Shakespeare sets did not look much different from earlier romantic-realistic ones.

Equally significant were Antoine's revivals of French classics, which he sometimes played in their original manner, as when his version of Corneille's *Le Cid* (1907) mirrored its 1636 premiere at the Théâtre du Marais. For Racine's *Andromache* (1909), he placed spectators on stage dressed in court fashions and used chandelier and footlight candles to suggest antique methods. Similar efforts were expended on 19th-century *vaudevilles* and other genres. To capture the essence of farce in certain Molière plays, popular comedians from Parisian café-concerts played leading roles. Novel casting also figured in *Brittanicus* (1911), which cast young actresses as leading juveniles, to emphasize their adolescent qualities. Sometimes, he used such idiosyncratically personal approaches as abandoning the single traditional set of Orgon's home in *Tartuffe* (1908) in favor of a variety of locales inside and outside the house.

Antoine was aware that he was a pioneer in the new field of directing. He had to provide a conception of the whole play that was usually absent when a leading player did the staging. The director has to be a diplomat able to deal with all sorts of personalities and, when necessary, to wheedle performances out of temperamental artists without drawing attention to the fact. His role falls into two divisions: making decisions regarding the physical look and interpreting the dialogue to express its ideas. Antoine began by establishing the scenic environment without regard to the action, allowing the setting to determine the actors' behavior, an approach to which he attributed the Théâtre Libre's success. Although not always able to achieve his wishes, he believed an interior setting should first be designed with all four walls intact and the play rehearsed in this room before deciding which wall to remove and which angle to display. He appreciated the asymmetricality of English stage design and took the classical symmetry of the French theater to task. In designing such a set, he wanted the adjacent rooms and passageways to be indicated in the artist's plans, so that the company knew exactly how the specific room fit into the structure of the entire house. Experience taught him, however, that authentic fabrics, wallpapers, leathers, and the like are often less theatrically effective under the lights than substitute stage versions.

In creating the blocking, he wrote, the director should continually walk about the constructed set—replete with all its props—while imagining the movements. He appreciated a plethora of bric-a-brac in interiors in order to create a lived-in quality and to stimulate believable and interesting acting.

After the Odéon, Antoine devoted himself to writing screen plays and film and dramatic criticism. During his life he had singlehandedly founded the independent theater movement, opened the Paris stage to the best in advanced international drama, fostered the cause of truthfulness to life on stage while not restricting himself to any one school of dramaturgy, provided a platform for numerous plays that could find no other home, and advanced the theory of directorial eclecticism.

Further reading:

Antoine, André. *Memories of the Théâtre Libre.* Translated by Marvin Carlson. Coral Gables: University of Miami Press, 1964.

Chothia, Jean. *André Antoine.* Cambridge, England: Cambridge University Press, 1991.

Waxman, Samuel. *Antoine and the Théâtre Libre.* Cambridge, Mass.: Harvard University Press, 1926.

Also: Cole and Chinoy, *Directors on Directing;* Knapp, *Reign of the Theatrical Director.*

WILLIAM BALL (1931–1991)

WILLIAM GORMALY BALL was born in Chicago, Illinois. The son of a successful executive in the construction industry, he was raised in New Rochelle, New York. Ball studied at Fordham University, transferred to Pittsburgh's Carnegie Institute of Technology, and graduated with a B.A. in theater in 1953. In 1955, after he returned from a year studying foreign repertory theaters, Carnegie granted him a master's in directing. He was already well established as an actor on the regional theater and Shakespeare festival circuit.

Ball's directing debut was *As You Like It* (1955) at the San Diego Shakespeare Festival. In 1956, he did *Twelfth Night* (1956) at Antioch, but he did not specialize in directing until staging an award-winning, Off-Broadway version of Anton Chekhov's *Ivanov* (1958). He was soon directing in Houston, San Francisco, Washington, D.C., San Diego, and Stratford, Ontario. Most of these regional productions were of classics or semiclassics: Shaw, Turgenev, and Shakespeare. He staged five operas (including *Porgy and Bess* [1964]) for the New York City Opera and offered stunning Off-Broadway mountings of Dylan Thomas's *Under Milk Wood* (1959) and—a major achievement—Luigi Pirandello's *Six Characters in Search of an Author* (1963), which racked up 529 performances; he repeated it in London with Ralph Richardson.

The ingenious production began by creating an off-handedly natural atmosphere that made it seem as if the audience was going to observe not a play but a rehearsal. Actors and crew spoke in barely audible tones as they casually carried out their duties. Suddenly, observed John Simon,

> the lights go out, as though a fuse had blown, there is protestation and cursing, then one light goes on again. There, dressed in black, undulating in eerie unison, in an uncanny, penumbral, as it were, underwater lighting, is an at first indeterminate number of presences compressed into a kind of living cube—rather like some deep-sea fish pressing hungrily against the glass of their aquarium.

The interplay between the family and the actors was handled with remarkable skill. Action occurred constantly, on stage and in the auditorium and lobby. Simon said that Ball's fertile imagination turned the drama into "an intellectually disturbing,

emotionally tugging three-ring circus in which the funny, the frightening, and the unbearably sad are enacted simultaneously to our delight and awe." For the Lincoln Center Repertory Company, Ball offered a controversial version of Molière's *Tartuffe* (1965), in which Tartuffe was seen well before his famous late entrance.

Despite tempting commercial offers (he turned down *Fiddler on the Roof,* among others), Ball abandoned freelancing to found one of America's premiere nonprofit, resident companies, the American Conservatory Theater (ACT), begun in 1965 in Pittsburgh with $115,000 in grants. ACT occupied two theaters and produced 10 plays. Ball's manifesto called for the development of an actor-centered American national theater on the lines of the great European troupes, with a flamboyantly individualis-

William Ball directing at the American Conservatory Theater. (Photo: American Conservatory Theatre)

tic performance style that avoided the introspection of Method acting.

By late 1966, the ACT and Pittsburgh had reached an impasse. For 18 months, ACT turned nomad, appearing in various cities. For various reasons, it settled in San Francisco where, occupying two theaters (the large Geary and the more intimate Marine Memorial), it opened dramatically in 1967 with 16 plays in 22 weeks. From then on, it gained plaudits not only for its versatility and imaginative stagings—by others as well as Ball—of a repertory unrivaled in eclecticism and abundance (produced for years in a continental rotating system), but for having established one of America's finest actor-training programs. Of much importance to Ball's movement-oriented approach was the Alexander technique, designed to rid the body of muscular tension.

For years, the average annual repertory presented approximately 10 main stage productions, of which there were usually two revivals of earlier shows. The 50-actor company was kept tremendously busy, and some roles were double-cast to allow for flexibility. At first, Ball's own entries included restagings of his New York work. Ball's mountings averaged about two new works a season, avoided new scripts, and focused mainly on modern and ancient classics, including Shakespeare's *Twelfth Night* (1968), *Hamlet* (1968), *The Tempest* (1970), *King Richard III* (1974), and *The Taming of the Shrew* (1973); Anton Chekhov's *The Three Sisters* (1968) and *The Cherry Orchard* (1974); Sophocles' *Oedipus Rex* (1970); George Bernard Shaw's *Caesar and Cleopatra* (1971); Edmond Rostand's *Cyrano de Bergerac* (1972); Arthur Miller's *The Crucible* (1973); and Molière's *The Bourgeois Gentleman* (1977). Contemporary dramas included Edward Albee's *Tiny Alice* (1967) and *The American Dream* (1968); David Storey's *The Contractor* (1972); Tom Stoppard's *Rosencrantz and Guildenstern Are Dead* (1969) and *Jumpers* (1975); and Peter Shaffer's *Equus* (1976). Ball leaned toward plays that offered opportunities for theatricalist pyrotechnics. He declared that he would only direct plays whose "general beauty," meaning thematic and moral values, moved him; plays with overt political subjects rarely interested him.

In the late 1970s, Ball's productivity declined under managerial pressures. From mid-1976 to 1984, he directed only Shakespeare's *The Winter's Tale* (1978). In 1984, when money troubles were forcing ACT to concentrate on small-cast, skimpily mounted plays, he returned with Harold Pinter's *Old*

Times and Bill C. Davis's *Mass Appeal* (1985). He ended his ACT career with an ambitious, but unsuccessful, *The Passion* (1986), based on the anonymous Wakefield cycle.

Ball's later productions often estranged critics, some of whom were accused of having a bias against him. His most admired productions were from his early years, when he gained renown for his attention to ensemble; stylish, nonphotographic theatricality (including slow motion, freeze-frame, acrobatic, and dancelike touches); abundant energy; visual opulence; imaginative sound and music; carefully staged supernumeraries in scenes in which, conventionally, they would not have appeared; relatively spare scenic environments in which costumes, overt physicality, and movable props were the preeminent visual forces; and clearly spoken dialogue.

Ball's productions often took more pride in his virtuosity than in the play. Sometimes, Ball's proclivity for dynamism, nonstop bustle, rapid pacing, clever—and frequently comic—business, reliance on tableau effects, tendency to underline the obvious, use of vocal effects at the expense of verbal meaning, and insistence on decorative and performative unity was destructive to tone and meaning and to the establishment of the characters' individuality and psychological depth. An example of Ball's inventiveness was having Tartuffe use holy water to bless people, fling at antagonists, simulate tears, and wash his face. Ball frequently went over the top; he spent lavishly, regardless of the inevitable deficits. Even his curtain calls, called "walkdowns," were attention-grabbing.

Examples of Ball's milestones were *Tiny Alice* and *The Taming of the Shrew*. *Shrew* was a commedia delight, done in outrageously acrobatic style, with the wooing scene staged like a TV wrestling match in a ring; at its end, the muscular Petruchio lifted the 125-pound Kate straight over his head. Ball's *Tiny Alice*, which offered an unauthorized revision of the ending (and led to legal threats), did not clarify the play's murkiness, but dazzled with theatrical coups. Julius Novick recalled:

A fat Cardinal sprawling in his sleep—a great blob of red on a huge throne—made an arresting image to begin the play with. Later on, the Lawyer flung down the Butler belly upward across the huge model of Miss Alice's palace . . . ; the Butler's head was dangling over the edge of the model toward the audience; his arms were spread wide; the Lawyer was leaning fiercely over him, about to commit who knew what? . . . At the end, when Brother Julian, having finally been shot, takes an unconscionable time a-dying, . . . Ball saved the occasion by arranging a veritable orgy of light and sound to accompany Julian's throes.

Ball was energetic, driven, sometimes obstreperous, but charismatically colorful, known for his personal theatricality (particularly a black gaucho hat he once affected), managerial imperiousness, dictatorial authority, and the pressure cooker atmosphere he created; his soubriquets ran from genius to madman.

A crucial Ball technique was the need to discover a metaphor for a play. He might select a painting or photo that captured his concept and then limit the production's color palette to that in the picture. He was thus able to exercise artistic discipline over the production and to create harmony.

He was an idealist preoccupied with artistic unity, beauty, and spirituality. Ball strived to stimulate the activities of the actor's right brain (intuition, imagination) rather than his left (logic, rationality), putting a positive spin on everything contributed at rehearsals and—despite his reputation as a puppetmaster—treating his company as creative collaborators. Cynthia Robins said he had the power to infuse "his charges with the belief that they were capable of anything." The actor could leave the critical thinking to the director and enjoy great creative freedom. Ball termed his upbeat theatrical and personal philosophy "positation." To Ball, the ability to "say yes to every creative idea," as he noted in a textbook he authored, was a practical way to achieve success.

He wrote that a director must demonstrate love and respect for his actors, and must support their self-esteem and eliminate their fears of failure. If a disagreement arose, Ball recommended yielding, regardless of the issue. Ball insisted that every director should do some acting to understand the actor's fragile ego. He considered it unprofessional to fire an actor; the director must live with his mistakes.

Demonstrations and line readings were anathema. "Suggest it, coax it, cartoon, but never *do* it for the actor," he cautioned. It was acceptable, though, to suggest a proper reading by mentioning the "operative word" in a sentence, by paraphrasing, or even whistling the inflection. He elicited organic performances by asking questions, but never answering them, allowing the actors to arrive at the answers for themselves. Despite his focus on physicality and his disdain for the Method, he was a confirmed Stanislavskian and focused intensely on such concepts as beats (action-oriented divisions of the text)

and objectives (the characters' goals): the latter was Ball's "golden key," which he phrased with stimulating active verbs. Lengthy discussions were rejected; "speak as little as possible," he cautioned beginning directors.

Ball's performers were permitted to take chances and to stretch by playing challenging roles; some, however, accused him of frequent miscasting, made even more apparent when he placed handsome young favorites in roles for which they were not suited.

Ball prepared assiduously, even reading all of the playwright's writing. When necessary, he cut or altered scripts, but always before, not during, rehearsals. His alterations, usually made to clarify the narrative and speed up the action, were often debated; critics argued with his extensive editing of classical texts, from which familiar speeches and characters were excised.

He preblocked with tiny soldiers, but entered rehearsals having abandoned all notes and charts, allowing the actors either to find what he had foreseen or to revise his ideas. Rehearsals began with several days of reading the script "at table," focusing on objectives and character biographies. When he began blocking he prevented chaos by suggesting the initial moves himself, but meant these only as a springboard. Because he believed in the need to bind the company together, he commenced every rehearsal by touching (a handshake or hug) each performer, repeating the ritual at the end.

Improvisation was important, although Ball used it only when a play—usually realistic—required it. Most improvisations were designed to explore the characters' offstage lives. Improvs sometimes proved helpful in directing supernumeraries, each of whom was given a chance to develop a three-dimensional character; Ball often wrote words for them to say.

One of the strongest influences on Ball's staging was Alexander Dean and Lawrence Carra's textbook, *Fundamentals of Play Direction,* which lists specific rules of composition and picturization (many are repeated in Ball's own book), although a number of directors consider many of these rules questionable.

Ball's increasingly autocratic behavior revealed an undercurrent of psychological stress. In 1986, a power play erupted with ACT's board; the result was Ball's forced ouster. He occupied his remaining years in Los Angeles, and did some film and stage acting. He either rejected the directing offers he was made or quit those he accepted. In the end, he committed suicide, his loss symbolizing the difficulties faced by genius directors in the American theater. He had been crucial to the development of some of America's finest actors, including Richard Dysart, Peter Donat, René Auberjonois, Annette Bening, and Michael Learned, not to mention the many top directors who were under his spell. Despite his reputation as one of the greatest figures in the American resident theater, he was virtually ignored once he had left ACT. The company he created still survives, although no longer with the aura it bore during the heyday of William Ball.

Further reading:

Ball, William. *A Sense of Direction.* New York: Drama Book Publishers, 1984.

Robins, Cynthia. "Final Curtain: The Life and Death of a Theater Legend." *San Francisco Examiner,* November 10, 1991.

Wilk, John R. *The Creation of an Ensemble: The First Years of the American Conservatory Theatre.* Carbondale and Edwardsville, Illinois: Southern Illinois University Press, 1986.

Also: Novick, *Beyond Broadway;* Simon, *Uneasy Stages;* Ziegler, *Regional Theatre.*

EUGENIO BARBA (1936–   )

EUGENIO BARBA was born and raised in Gallipoli, in southern Italy, where his father, who was later killed in World War II, was in the military. Barba attended a military school from 1951 to 1954; lived in Norway between 1954 and 1960, although he worked on an Israeli kibbutz in 1959; and earned a master's in literature and religious history at Oslo University.

In 1961, after several months at the Warsaw Theater School, Barba became Jerzy Grotowski's assistant at the latter's new Opole theater. Through his publications, Barba was largely responsible for introducing Grotowski to the West. Barba, after traveling to India, familiarized Grotowski with Asian theater, which became an important part of each man's artistic methods.

The Odin Teatret, founded by Barba in Oslo in 1964, began as a small experimental troupe composed of unsuccessful applicants to the Oslo School of Dramatic Art. By 1965, it offered *The Bird Lovers,* based on a play by Norwegian Jens Bjørnboem. Ian Watson wrote that the propless, sceneryless work dealt with "the conflict between local villagers and an ecologically conscious group of developers to explore the horrors of a Nazi occupation of the village some twenty years earlier."

Odin settled down in the small, culturally enlightened town of Holstebro, where Barba himself designed the company's home. Composed of actors from several countries, Odin promoted Barba's unique "third theater" blend of social and artistic concerns. By "third theater," Barba means theater that is neither mainstream nor avant-garde but that involves previously untrained artists "whose entire day is filled with theatrical experiences, sometimes by what they call training, or by the preparation of performances for which they must fight to find an audience." At this theater's core is the actor who performs as a means of self-determination and expresses himself artistically without concern for commercial success. Despite his fame, Barba has never directed outside of this noncommercial framework.

Odin is a laboratory where Barba guides the actors in a process-oriented approach. Works are publicly shown only after a slow and lengthy gestation sometimes requiring several years. Occasionally, the creations of many months will be discarded before public presentations. Although his methods have driven off some actors, Barba likes to disrupt potential complacency by creating "earthquakes" that turn the group in new directions.

The first important Holstebro period comprised a series of ritualistic, environmentally daring, collaboratively created collages: *Kaspariana* (based on the tale of Kaspar Hauser, 1967); *Feraï* (1969); and *My Father's House* (based on Fyodor Dostoyevsky's life and writing, 1972). *Feraï,* their first international success after it opened in Paris, led to a government subsidy.

Part of their income derives from international tours, which last from nine months to longer. The intimate nature of Odin's work limits much of it to tiny venues seating between 60 and 100. Odin is widely known through the articles and books of Barba—a scholar and theoretician—and others and through workshops and seminars. Much of this is subsumed by the International School of Theater Anthropology (ISTA), founded in 1979 for the study of transcultural performance elements, especially the relation between Eastern and Western techniques.

In 1974, Barba and Odin temporarily transferred to a southern Italian town that had practically no

Eugenio Barba directing Theatrum Mundi *members of the Dharma Shanti Company of Bali. ISTA session, Bologna, Italy. (1990)* (Photo: Odin Teatret/Fiora Bemporad)

experience of theater. Here they developed "barter," whereby the company performed—usually outdoors—for the local residents. The latter, in lieu of paying with money or goods (although those were sometimes accepted), responded by performing local songs, stories, music, dances, or religious ceremonies.

Between 1974 and 1982, Odin traveled widely, promoting barter in rural Africa, Latin America, and Asia. Their activities led to the creation of several outdoor presentations, including spectacular parades and clown shows. (*The Book of Dances* in 1974, *Johann Sebastian Bach* in 1974, and *Anabasis* in 1982 were the major presentations.) The company's work, hitherto inward directed with the self as object, became aimed more toward the community. Instead of the earlier archetypal characters, specific characters and types became important. Major new productions included *Come! And the Day Will Be Ours* (1976); *The Million* (1979); *Brecht's Ashes 2* (1982); *Marriage with God* (1984); *Oxyrhyncus Evangeliet* (*The Gospel According to Oxyrhyncus*, 1985); *Judith* (1987), a one-woman piece about the biblical heroine; *Talabot* (1988); *The Castle of Holstebro* (1990); and *Itsi-Bitsi* (1991), a recent work, described on a flyer as follows:

> *Two young people experience the beginning of the '60's together: political activities, travel and drugs. What did they believe during that time? Why did it go wrong for so many? One of them, Eik Skaløe, the first beat-poet and singer performing in Danish, committed suicide in India in 1968. The other, Iben Nagel Rasmussen, actor*

with the Odin Teatret since 1966, sees her life today confronted by the visions and events from that time through the characters from her past performances.

Odin's training is carried out on what Barba calls a psycho-physiological level, employing exercises and techniques—including acrobatics and yoga—adapted from many cultures. The goal is to create a highly disciplined instrument that is alive with presence. Such presence is especially notable in moments of "pre-expressivity," when the actor is not performing overtly. In the early years, all actors trained uniformly; since *My Father's House* they have trained individually (although in the same room with one another), autonomously researching their own interests.

Productions emerge from an improvisatory process in which the actors are stimulated by images provided by Barba. Rehearsal videos are made so that the company can study them. The actors work on theme-related actions which are eventually set and learned completely so that they may be repeated. Ian Watson notes:

> *Barba uses these various fragments, which are rarely causally connected, much as rough drafts of scenes to which he adds texts that he and the actors have collected . . . from various sources. . . . He then gradually combines these vocal and physical montages into a cohesive whole, the production. The actor's own private images and emotions in the improvisations often have little to do with Barba's choices, which are combined because of the meaning they evoke for him through the montage effects produced when combined with others' images. He usually does not know where a production is heading until it is revealed to him during the painstaking, trial-and-error period of preparation, during which the technical work on design, music, and so on is simultaneously improvised.*

Each work—typically lasting about 90 minutes—uses an environmental configuration different from the others, but these arise organically as the actors materialize the production. (The actors also participate in the construction of the scenic means.) Normally, rehearsals began with a theme in mind. When he started work on *Oxyrhyncus*, however, Barba had none, demonstrating a move toward greater anarchy in the creative process.

Odin provides a highly physicalized, ritualistic performance style; it uses minimal props, basic but beautiful costuming, functional but expressively manipulated lighting, and spare sets to create a densely layered collage of images expressed in a nonlinear, centrifugally organized framework, often using several languages. The images transform themselves with theatrical if not conventional logic into other images. Barba's pieces can be engrossing and moving, but incomprehensible. Multiple viewings are necessary to unravel the thematic threads and associations. Barba expects that each spectator will derive a different meaning, none of them incorrect. The images speak on the level of the Jungian collective unconscious. Because of Barba's constant search for new ideas and expressive methods, each work differs strikingly from its predecessors, despite a certain stylistic consistency. The actors—influenced by Barba's preoccupation with Oriental forms—perform with remarkable agility and precision, using their bodies and voices unconventionally; normally, they play multiple roles in a single work. Most are accomplished musicians and they often perform on various instruments.

A representative early work is *Feraï*, inspired by Euripides' *Alcestis*. Barba's fascination with mythical structures led him to go beyond the story of a woman's sacrifice for her husband into a concern

Roberta Carreri in Judith. *Directed by Eugenio Barba.* *(1987)* (Photo: Odin Teatret/Tony D'Urso)

with what Marc Fumaroli calls "the dynastic aspects of the primitive legend." Euripides' tale was crossed with one from ancient Scandinavian lore and a scenario was written by a Danish ethnologist. The only scenic props were a knife, an ivory egg, and a blanket, but they were employed emblematically to suggest multiple thematic resonances within the shifting contexts. The intimate space, rendered shadowless by six overhead spotlights, was a rectangle with the small audience divided into two sections, seated opposite each other on a pair of long benches; the action transpired in front of and behind them. Audience members were an integral part of the proceedings, treated in different ways according to the needs of the characters and events. Whereas the earlier *Kaspariana* had been a hallucinatory series of images, *Feraï* had a fairly logical structure, and used dialogue as well as song to reveal the actors' vocal talents.

To date, only two full-scale Barba productions, *The Million* and *Brecht's Ashes 2*, have been seen in America. More comedic than many Barba pieces, the first (used in barter situations) was a musical collage set in a circuslike environment, with a constantly shifting focus. Centered on the travels of an English-speaking Marco Polo dressed as a Protestant pastor, it allowed the actors to demonstrate the theme of cultural imperialism—seen as Polo's vision following his journey—by having them perform in a variety of Asian and Latin American styles while recognizable Western music accompanied them. William Beeman commented:

> Decapitation of a fantastic golden-horned ram is accomplished to "The Stripper." Carnival stilt-walkers prance to "Oh Susanna." Brecht/Weill-style cabaret is mixed in with Indonesian gender and gongs. Costumes too are hybrid in degrees with shreds and visions of different cultures all woven into a single piece.

More somber was *Brecht's Ashes 2*, presented in English and German, which mingled and juxtaposed Brecht (who sometimes wore a Balinese mask); various Brecht characters, such as Galileo, Arturo Ui, and Kattrin; and actual persons, such as Brecht's wife, Helene Weigel, and Walter Benjamin, Brechtian commentator and collaborator. A single actor might play several roles, not separately but all as aspects of the same shifting persona. "The work," wrote Beeman, "deals with the parallels and disparities between Brecht's life and his literary work, taking the audience on a tour of Brecht's [contradictory] mind. . . ."

Talabot. *Directed by Eugenio Barba. (1988)* (Photo: Odin Teatret/Tony D'Urso)

Two more recent works are *Oxyrhyncus* and *Talabot,* both inspired by Latin America. The former was suggested by Latin American writings, but in its final form it included characters derived from early Christian manuscripts discovered in the town of Oxyrhyncus, the Bible, Gnostic mysticism, medieval history, Jewish lore, and tales of Brazilian bandits, etc. A Hasidic tailor, the Golem, Joan of Arc, the Prodigal Son, Sabbatai Zevi, and the Grand Inquisitor were the dramatis personae. Performed in a detached, objective manner (unlike the warmth of *Brecht's Ashes 2*), it used images of pain and destruction to ponder questions regarding the true or false presence of the Messiah and of "revolt being buried alive." Each of its six actors became the focus of any particular spectator's interpretation.

Free association was expected of audiences attending *Talabot* as well. As David Shoemaker notes of this complex work, created in Mexico, "The action . . . is characterized by unexpected changes of direction, breaks in the text's linear development, and a composition based on montage and the interweaving of two or more simultaneous actions." Among Barba's intentions was the destruction of conventional attitudes toward *commedia dell'arte* characters; the enactment of a fractured biography of Danish anthropologist Kirsten Hastrup, who was confronted with crises in her perception of reality following her alleged mystical encounter with an Icelandic folk figure; and the layering of her dualistic experiences with those of other 20th-century figures, such as Antonin Artaud, "Che" Guevara, and polar explorer Knud Rasmussen, all of whose stories are interwoven with Hastrup's. For example, to suggest the simultaneity of experience, Hastrup's character trembled in inarticulate mental distress, while across the space Artaud lectured at the Sorbonne in 1933 on "The Theater and the Plague"; sometimes he was in her nightmare and sometimes he was real (although widely separated in time and space). The actors, speaking English, Italian, or Norwegian, wore broken masks held together by rawhide. A "trickster" character in a Balinese mask, wrote Shoemaker, acted as "catalyst and commentator—the spectators' advocate who sets the scene, steps away to watch, prod, and provoke, and finally offers up her derision." Various images suggested the futility of revolt against authority. Also present was another Barba theme, "the loss or destruction of culture, both personal and collective."

Although barely known in America, Barba's work has had an international impact not unlike that of Grotowski's. Beeman argued that Barba's company "can lay claim to being one of the finest, if not *the* finest ensemble acting troupe in the world." Barba has created a community of dedicated artists whose contributions are as creatively vital as those of their director (they now practically direct their own performances). To Barba, using theater as culture is just as important as using it as art.

Further reading:

Barba, Eugenio. *Beyond the Floating Islands.* New York: PAJ Publications, 1986.

Beeman, William O. *"Brecht's Ashes 2; The Million." Performing Arts Journal* 8, no. 2 (1984).

Fumaroli, Marc. "Eugenio Barba's *Kaspariana." The Drama Review* 13 (Fall 1968).

———. "Funeral Rites: Eugenio Barba's *Feraï." The Drama Review* 14 (Fall 1969).

Shoemaker, David. "Report from Holstebro: Odin Teatret's *Talabot" New Theatre Quarterly* 6 (November 1990).

Watson, Ian. "Eugenio Barba: the Latin American Connection." *New Theatre Quarterly* 5 (February 1989).

————. "Eastern and Western Influences on Performer Training at Eugenio Barba's Odin Teatret." *Asian Theatre Journal* 5(Spring 1988).

Also: Roose-Evans, *Experimental Theatre.*

*Note: The following appeared too late to be used for this essay:

Christoffersen, Erik E., *The Actor's Way.* Translated by Richard Fowler. Cambridge, England: Cambridge University Press, 1993.

Watson, Ian. *Towards a Third Theatre: Eugenio Barba and the Odin Teatret.* Cambridge, England: Cambridge University Press, 1993.

HARLEY GRANVILLE BARKER
See GRANVILLE-BARKER, HARLEY.

JEAN-LOUIS BARRAULT (1910–1994*)

JEAN-LOUIS BARRAULT was born in Vesinet, near Paris, and studied painting before becoming an actor, training between 1931 and 1935 under the guidance of Charles Dullin. Dullin's advanced ideas introduced the young player to the world of Konstantin Stanislavsky, Gordon Craig, and Jacques Copeau, while also opening his eyes to the joys of *commedia dell'arte,* mime, and the beauties of Asian theater. Mime, especially as taught him by Etienne Decroux, was especially important to Barrault.

Among Barrault's many other inspirations was the visionary actor-director-theorist Antonin Artaud, prophet of the "Theater of Cruelty." Barrault eventually succeeded in realizing many of Artaud's notions concerning the place of ritual in theater, the use of masks, found spaces, incantatory speech and sounds, and the use of a hieroglyphic form of physical expression.

Barrault's directorial debut was his adaptation of William Faulkner's 1930 novel, *As I Lay Dying* (1935), using a chorus that chanted or sang a minimalist text, a musical accompaniment confined to the beating of a tom-tom, and a style emphasizing mime and incantatory vocalizations. This first example of what became Barrault's trademark style of "total theater" allowed the actors to portray not only human characters but animals and inanimate objects, including climactic forces, the result being more in the nature of a dance-drama than a conventional play.

In 1936, Barrault left Dullin and became active as a film and stage actor, using his earnings to explore his emerging directorial ideas. His most notable efforts in the late 1930s were his dancelike stagings of an adaptation of Miguel de Cervantes's late-16th century *The Siege of Numantia* (1937) and

his version of Norwegian author Knut Hamsun's novel *Hunger* (1939).

Barrault joined the Comédie Française in 1940, where he soon directed such plays as Jean Racine's *Phaedra* (1942), which he viewed as a symphony, orchestrating every speech as if it was part of a score, casting each role for its musical values. Meanwhile, Barrault directed a pair of spectacular outdoor productions at the Roland-Garros Stadium, one of them being Aeschylus' *The Suppliants* (1941), Barrault's first Greek tragedy.

In 1942, Barrault began his close association with the profoundly philosophical and symbolic plays of Paul Claudel, some of whose works were considered unstageable until Barrault took command of them. Barrault's first Claudel was *The Satin Slipper,* a verse play set in the Spanish Golden Age and replete with mystical overtones mingling many moods and styles and ranging freely through time and space. Mime solved many problems, allowing the actors' corporal expressivity to evoke the appropriate backgrounds and to move the play swiftly from locale to locale. Barrault's four-and-a-half-hour production was a masterpiece; he subsequently went on to direct half a dozen other Claudel works, which he appreciated for their mystical, spiritual themes and myriad theatrical possibilities.

Barrault left the Comédie Française in 1945, his last directorial assignment being a memorable version of Shakespeare's *Antony and Cleopatra.* Barrault and his wife, Madeleine Renaud, a brilliant actress, formed the Compagnie Renaud-Barrault (CRB), which opened at the Théâtre Marigny in 1946 with André Gide's adaptation of *Hamlet,* Barrault directing and starring in what became one of his greatest productions. The CRB was an unsubsidized repertory company, staging three or four plays a season, and producing classics and moderns, many of them pre-

*Barrault died shortly before publication of this book.

mieres. Barrault did farces (he was responsible for the revival of interest in Georges Feydeau), melodramas, classical tragedies, comedies, and avant-garde dramas, all staged in the repertory system, which Barrault believes is the best way for an actor to develop versatility.

A decade was spent at the Marigny and on tour to many countries. This was followed by three years of touring and playing at miscellaneous Paris theaters until the company was situated in the venerable Odéon in 1959, given a government subsidy, and named the Théâtre de France. Barrault productions mingled an assortment of advanced French drama with major revivals, and established a rivalry with the more conservative Comédie Française. To balance the main stage productions, an intimate theater was created and called the Petit Odéon. Unfortunately, Barrault lost his theater and subsidy in 1968 when the minister of culture was offended by the director's having allowed radical students to occupy the place during the year's political uprisings.

Barrault began to explore the possibilities of nonproscenium venues, seeking flexible spaces not necessarily intended for performances. The company first moved to a converted boxing arena, the Elysée-Montmartre, the site of Barrault's famed *Rabelais* (1968), his own adaptation of that writer's work. *Rabelais*, a countercultural paean to the hippie youth culture of the time, was eventually staged in an English-language version in England and America. A cruciform-shaped acting area was placed at the center of the large space, with the audience surrounding it. Rope arrangements cleverly simulated the outline of a circus tent and the riggings of a ship.

More such work continued in *Jarry on the Mound* (1970), a montage of Alfred Jarry's writings, produced in the arena, and *Before the Wind of the Balearic Islands* (1972), a previously unproduced part of Claudel's *The Satin Slipper*, given in a tent set up in a disused train station, the Gare d'Orsay.

From 1970 to 1974, Barrault's troupe was ensconced at the Théâtre Récamier. The Gare d'Orsay became its next home, being converted to the Théâtre d'Orsay, a twin-theater complex, in 1973. Barrault now directed only about one work a year, among them his adaptation of writings by Friedrich Nietzsche, *Thus Spake Zarathustra* (1974).

In 1981, Barrault moved to the Théâtre du Rond Pont, where he employed a 930-seat playhouse in conjunction with the 190-seat Petit Rond-Pont. Here he continued with his challenging productions, among them a circuslike interpretation of Aristophanes' *The Birds* (1985).

No repertoire as vast as Barrault's can lay claim to any one directorial method. Thus, Barrault has been as eclectic as any modern director, using whatever means he felt appropriate for the work at hand. Plays that required a "total theater" approach received it, but farces or realistic works were staged in styles appropriate to their writing.

Barrault belongs to France's "man of the theater" tradition wherein a true theater artist must have multiple artistic skills. He is a writer, theorist, director, actor, lighting designer, and producer. Although not a playwright, he adapted many of the works he staged and he worked closely with those dramatists with whom he came in contact, Claudel in particular. Technical skills in lighting, props, and music are also of use to a director, he claims, so that he can successfully guide every area of production and make them conform to a unified vision.

Barrault's focus on physical expression was something of an anomaly in the French theater, which had long been dominated by a love for the spoken word and where the actor's choreographic patterns were of secondary importance. Barrault's actors use their bodies to represent rivers, fires, men on horseback, and the like, and their voices can be instruments for speech as well as for a range of sounds, such as a saw cutting through wood. Thus, Barrault wrote that in Claudel's *Christopher Columbus* (1953), the total-theater actors,

> alternatively spinning wool, playing the guitar, becoming waves, walking, running, undulating on the sea, receiving the wind, dead, living, assuming reality, becoming shade, bellowing as Indian gods, howling like the tempest, murmuring like the breeze, prattling like gossips, indignant as mutineers, singing their joy, shouting their enthusiasm . . . motionless as a picture, stamping like maniacs, . . . spectators, commentators, actors, . . . conjure up . . . our dream of complete theatre.

In total theater, even the scenic and musical elements come alive to play their roles. Props produce sound effects, scenic units take on lifelike attributes, costumes assume multiple possibilities, lighting responds to everchanging emotional developments, and "as for the music . . . it proposes, it intervenes, it traces lines of joy or of distress," wrote Barrault.

Barrault prepares his scenic approach by searching for a "catalyst object" or "signifying object"—some metaphorical property which will sum up in itself the heart of the presentation. Examples are the throne in *Hamlet*, the screens used for hiding and eavesdropping in Pierre de Marivaux's *The False*

Confessions, or even the rhino-shaped walking stick carried by Dudard in Eugène Ionesco's *Rhinoceros.* He has made considerable use of masks, employing them in such works as Aeschylus' *The Oresteia, The Satin Slipper, Christopher Columbus,* and *Rabelais.*

He works intimately with his designers to capture the play's feeling, and often engages in extensive research for period plays to discover exactly what can be recovered to communicate the drama's core. The research serves to illuminate historical essences that can then be creatively transformed into living artistic expressions of the play.

Similarly intense is Barrault's preoccupation with music and sound, and he has worked with many of France's finest composers in developing scores. He sometimes reads and rereads the play to the composer as he explores his ideas and feelings. He also has been known to use highly innovative methods, such as the banging of wooden spoons to suggest copulation in *Rabelais.*

He will read everything he can find about a play and its author, and take extensive notes. When his intellectual preparation has fermented sufficiently he will prepare a detailed prompt book, setting down every detail, including the moves and gestures. The range of his preparation—including metaphysical and philosophical speculation—can be gauged by reading his analysis of *The Oresteia* in *The Theater of Jean-Louis Barrault.* Although he can be flexible and ready to make changes in rehearsal, he believes actors trust the director more when his preparation has been this thorough.

Before he casts, Barrault reads the entire play to the company and discusses their reactions with them so as to help uncover problems that audiences may later confront. His reading conveys as closely as possible how he wants the play performed. It is only after a week of "at table" readings and discussion that he casts, a method that would be impossible without a permanent troupe.

During week two the blocking commences and continues for two weeks. He cautions his actors against too quick a learning of their lines, fearing that memorizing the words too soon can hamper creativity. The moves are dictated and the actors follow them without discussion. Barrault hopes this will allow the actors to concentrate on character work instead of being distracted by questioning of their movements. He moves around with his actors as he blocks, adjusting them physically and demonstrating unhesitatingly when necessary. His actors

have to take what he gives them, as he is rarely interested in drawing out their performances from them. Actors are free to be as creative in developing their roles as they wish, providing their ideas are compatible with Barrault's framework.

Barrault is willing to find a balance between autocracy and laissez-faire. He does not interfere too much, for instance, in his actors' characterizations, focusing more on the specifics of movement and voice. Long-range familiarity with his actors allows him to understand their strengths and weaknesses. He and Renaud create a family atmosphere in which each player feels wanted and important, and where strong parental figures provide strength and security. His company is dedicated to disciplined work where the artistic results are more important than the individual's ego.

In the final weeks of the typical six-week rehearsal process, Barrault removes the fetters and allows his actors considerable freedom, even if it means tossing out much of his written mise-en-scène. The play begins to take on a life of its own and to change in subtle ways from earlier conceptions. The actors and director tap into the drama's lifeline and discover its final form, making this period the toughest yet also the most exciting. When Barrault is himself acting, this period can be unusually fruitful because of the example he sets.

Jean-Louis Barrault is generally considered the finest French director of his generation. Like Copeau before him, he views the theater almost as a religion and has dedicated his life to achieving in it artistry on the highest levels. He has brought the finest French theater to audiences on every continent in a series of grueling tours and in this way has been the most international modern French director. Barrault has broken new ground in the exploration of the potentialities of the actor as a total medium of expression and has continued to move forward in the search for new theatrical forms.

Further reading:

Barrault, Jean-Louis. *The Theatre of Jean-Louis Barrault.* Translated by Joseph Chiari. New York: Hill and Wang, 1961.

———. *Memories for Tomorrow.* Translated by Jonathan Griffin. New York: Dutton, 1974.

Also: Bradby, *Modern French Drama;* Innes, *Holy Theatre;* Leiter, *From Stanislavski to Barrault;* Whitton, *Stage Directors in Modern France.*

GASTON BATY (1885–1952)

GASTON BATY was born in Pélussin, not far from Lyon, France, and grew up in his well-to-do family's country home. He was educated at a Dominican *collège,* where he was deeply influenced by the teachings of St. Thomas Aquinas. When Baty graduated from the University of Lyon in 1906, he already had become fascinated by the city's *guignol* puppet theater. He studied art history in Munich from 1907 to 1908, becoming preoccupied with the German theater, especially the advanced work being done to "retheatricalize the theater" by Georg Fuchs and Fritz Erler. The writings of Adolphe Appia and Gordon Craig were also influential.

Baty worked in his father's lumber business, traveled to Germany and Russia, and grew familiar with the work of directors Max Reinhardt, Konstantin Stanislavsky, and Vsevelod Meyerhold. He was a passionate student, making frequent trips to Paris to observe productions there and doing extensive historical research. Ultimately, he became a prolific author, developing a coherent philosophy concerning theater's social and aesthetic functions. His pursuit of learning, including the fields of set, costume, and lighting design, was in preparation for becoming a director. Baty even wrote up detailed plans for possible productions. His first stagings were with amateur players in Lyon.

From 1914 to 1919, he was in the army, eventually staging folk plays in connection with a program to reintroduce native culture to the provinces. In 1919, at 34, Baty so impressed producer-director Fermin Gémier with his ideas that he was put under a five-year contract to design and direct.

After several design assignments for Gémier, Baty staged his first play, a spectacular version (with 200 extras and a menagerie of animals) of Charles Hellem and Pol d'Estoc's nativity drama, *The Grand Pastoral* (1920). He then did Saint-Georges de Bouhélier's smaller scale tragedy, *The Slaves* (1920), designing the entire production, before proceeding to a season (1920–1921) of six plays at the Comédie des Champs-Élysées (renamed the Comédie Montaigne-Gémier). The authors included Henri Lenormand (his *Simoon,* about incest in a Saharan environment, was a major success), Molière, Eugène Labiche, Fernand Crommelynck, George Bernard Shaw, and Paul Claudel. Baty either designed himself or employed the services of artists such as Charles Sanlaville and Émile Bertin. Baty's visual style at this time has been characterized as a simplified realism touching on surreality.

Although he continued to refine, revise, and supplement them throughout his career, Baty had published his basic aesthetic formulations by 1921. Using his knowledge of theatrical history, he argued that the French theater had to be rescued from its debilitating enslavement to literature, and that it was necessary to provide an artistic experience in which the text—while still retaining its fundamental importance—was fully enhanced by all available theatrical means. Theater was no longer to be literary and cerebral, but totally involving (he used the word "integral"), employing lights, sets, costumes, and acting to evoke those values typically dependent on the spoken word. Only thus can the audience regain the sense of collectivity that it held in ancient periods. Because his ideas (especially as expressed in the 1920 article "His Majesty the Word" ["Sire le Mot"]) went so strikingly against the grain of French theater aesthetics (exemplified by Copeau's "naked stage"), Baty's frequent reliance on exceptional visualizations led many to attack his productions for their presumed deemphasis of the text in favor of mise-en-scène. Still, no writer directed by Baty ever had anything other than praise for his treatment of their work.

In 1921, Baty formed the Compagnons de la Chimère (Companions of the Chimera), and directed another half-dozen plays. The most outstanding was Jean-Jacques Bernard's *Martine* (on a bill with Jean-Victor Pellerin's *Intimacy*). It exemplified Baty's experiments with a "theater of silence" (or "of the unexpressed"). Influenced by his Thomist beliefs, Baty felt that the entire universe, that which is apparent to the senses and that which is not, including the supernatural and the subconscious, is as real as man himself, that all are part of God, and thus are deserving of artistic representation. He found in a number of plays (especially those of Lenormand, Simon Gantillon, and Pellerin) an opportunity to use symbolic props, physical business, meaningful looks, and pauses as a way of expressing the unexpressed, mystical portion of existence. In *Martine,* for example, designed in a style of simplified realism, such devices as the absence of leaves on an apple tree, or the ticking of a clock, conveyed the emotional state of the inarticulate heroine. Thus, Baty committed himself to exploitation of theater's plastic and auditory means as a way of illustrating what was not apparent to the senses.

In 1923, the Compagnons built their own theater, the externally picturesque, but internally uncomfortable, 340-seat Baraque de la Chimère. The stage's unique feature was a sunken portion in front of the semicircular rear wall used as a cyclorama; actors could appear or disappear by the use of steps leading from the visible stage. Something similar was also used in Baty's later venues. Although Baty gained fame as a scenic master, his sets here were fairly simple, being arranged of blocks and cubes. Two new programs were staged at the Baraque before it closed.

Baty directed another six or so plays (including Eugene O'Neill's *The Emperor Jones*) for Gémier, this time at the Odéon, from 1923 to 1924, before taking on a new theater, the tiny Studio at the Comédie des Champs-Élysées (Louis Jouvet and Georges Pitoëff shared another space in the same building). Here he directed 16 plays from 1924 to 1928, including Gantillon's *Maya* (1924; new version, 1927); Lenormand's *In the Shadow of Evil* (1924) and *The Romantic Magician* (1926); August Strindberg's *Miss Julie* (1925); Pellerin's *Spare Heads* (1926); Elmer Rice's *The Adding Machine* (1927); and S. Anski's *The Dybbuk* (1928). *Maya* (in its second version), a poetically atmospheric drama about a Marseilles prostitute who becomes all things to all men, was one of Baty's greatest successes, and was often revived. One of the most unusual of Baty's stagings was of Pellerin's *Spare Heads*, which employed expressionistic means to explore a man's daydreams.

Baty was very active in the twenties: his company occasionally toured; he published a journal called *Masques*, devoted to his ideas; he directed at other theaters; and in 1927, he joined Charles Dullin, Pitoëff, and Jouvet in the loose confederation of directors called the Cartel des Quatre, designed to present a united artistic front and to provide mutual support. Of the four, he was the only one who was not also an actor, it being his belief that to mingle the two professions was to deprive the director of his required objectivity. His productions differed from theirs as well in his great reliance on scenic investiture.

From 1928 to 1929, Baty was at the Théâtre de l'Avenue, where he offered six productions, including *Hamlet* and Molière's *The Imaginary Invalid*, both in controversial stagings. Shakespeare's play starred the outstanding Marguerite Jamois, Baty's leading lady, as the prince. It aroused attention not only because of its cross-gender casting and interpreting Hamlet as younger than 20, but because Baty chose to employ the earliest known (more melodramatic) script of the play, the 1603 quarto, which he defended as being clearer and more emotionally gripping than its better-known later version. His staging revealed the considerable use of spectacle inherent in Elizabethan conventions.

Molière's comedy stirred debate because it was viewed not as a satire on the medical profession but (taking a hint from the dramatist's own life) as a depiction of a truly suffering Argan. Baty's surprisingly original attitude toward the classics became an important part of his work despite critical attacks for desecrating, sentimentalizing, or romanticizing them.

After directing briefly at the technically advanced but unwieldy Théâtre Pigalle, he settled in 1930 into the theater he was associated with for 17 years, the mid-sized, 19th-century Théâtre Montparnasse. His last complete season there ended in 1943, after which his participation was sporadic, Jamois having assumed control. Following his opening with Bertolt Brecht's *The Threepenny Opera*, Baty went on to stage 29 other plays at the Montparnasse. Between 1936 and 1948, he also provided six major stagings at the Comédie Française.

At the Montparnasse, which he renovated extensively (including converting the proscenium stage to a thrust), Baty felt more in command of the scenic side than ever. Here, with an outstanding ensemble, he made the theater a place not of confrontation with reality but of escape into fiction, poetry, and romance. Baty abandoned some of the more abstract tendencies he had experimented with earlier, and gave his imagination free rein as he or other designers created scenic environments that combined lushly colored, texturally dense, three-dimensional representationalism with poetic and symbolic overtones made possible through creative lighting. He used a panoply of technical means, including a turntable and wagon stages that allowed for episodic works to move cinematically from one lavishly designed scene to another without shifting breaks.

During the thirties and forties he staged a good many contemporary plays by authors such as Pellerin, Bernard Zimmer, Gantillon, Luigi Pirandello, Marcel Maurette, and Lenormand (a revival of his *The Failures* [1937]). Far more noteworthy, though, were Baty's revivals of Alfred de Musset, Johann Wolfgang von Goethe, Jean Racine, Eugène Labiche, and Shakespeare. In these works, closely akin to his romantic visions, he was able to exercise his considerable imagination more freely than with newer pieces. Also remarkable were his own adaptations of two 19th-century novels, Dostoyevsky's *Crime and Punishment* (1933) and Flaubert's *Madame Bovary* (1936), his collaboration with Maurette on *Manon Lescaut* (1938), and his original play, *Dulcinea* (1938), inspired by an episode in *Don Quixote*.

Baty's stagings incorporated a wide body of innovative ideas and often provoked attacks. His inclination to see dramas in terms of sin and redemption was frequently evident, as when, underplaying the murder mystery element, he infused *Crime and Punishment* with an aura of piety and morality, or when, far less defensibly, he depicted Emma Bovary as a sympathetic creature who achieves salvation by being carried off to heaven. To explain Emma's inner life, Baty provided a quartet of "Beauties" who acted as a chorus and were actually Emma's imaginary projections. (One of Baty's most famous decors was used in this production when Emma flirts in a provincial theater box while an opera is performed in the background, seen through the box's opening.)

If necessary, Baty updated a play's period, as when he moved Alfred de Musset's *The Caprices of Marianne* (1936) from the 15th to the 19th century, which helped it to become the most popular version yet produced of this romantic comedy. For Jean Racine's *Phaedra* (1940), Baty suggested a theatricalized antiquity as seen in 17th-century paintings, combining elements of ancient Greece and neoclassical France. When he staged de Musset's *The Candlestick* (1936) at the Comédie Française, he added the novel touch of two mimed scenes, one at the end, to extend the action of the play and strike an ironic note. In Baty's hands, Labiche's vaudeville-farce, *An Italian Straw Hat* (1938), became a surrealistic vaudeville-phantasmagoria, seemingly happening in a nightmare. Musset's *Lorenzaccio* (1945) was controversial because of its casting of a woman (Jamois) in the male lead, its extensive cutting of the protracted original, and its avoidance of using the text to highlight contemporary political parallels. Racine's *Bérénice* (1946) raised the loudest storm, because it shifted sympathy from the title character to Titus, suggested Roman religious practices through familiar

Christian ones, and revealed a huge crowd on stage to underline that Titus' duty to his people was the reason for his abandonment of Bérénice.

In the 1940s, disillusioned with the living theater and in failing health, Baty devoted considerable time to the development of a (hand) puppet company performing plays of his own composition and intended for provincial touring. He also became active in the postwar effort to decentralize the French theater and was instrumental in the establishment of the Centre Dramatique du Sud-Est (later, the Comédie de Provence), although he died just before it opened.

Baty was a strict authoritarian who came to rehearsal with a very thorough idea of his visual aims. At first, he was not considered an actors' director, as he used them to fulfill his preconceived ideas. He was more adept at manipulating the scenic means than he was at making his company create convincing performances (thus his fondness for puppets), but he eventually improved in this area. Annie Ducaux, the leading actress in *Bérénice*, even considered him more inspiring than any director she had ever worked with because he had such command of every textual nuance and knew how to make his actors understand them.

Gaston Baty was not only a major director and designer; he was also a principal theorist who sought consistently to employ his ideas in an eclectic range of plays. Given his pronouncements, Baty's mise-en-scènes were sometimes too explicit; his religious proclivities did not always prove amenable in their dramatic contexts; and his escapist view of theater could be argued. Baty's modern sensibility was apparent in his daringly personalized views of the classic repertoire, in his explorations of the theater of silence, and in his desire to create an integral synthesis of theatrical means so as, in Fuchs's words, to "retheatricalize the theater."

Further reading:

Guicharnaud, *Modern French Theater*; Hobson, *French Theatre Since 1830*; Knowles, *French Drama of the Inter-War Years*; Whitton, *Stage Directors in Modern France*.

DAVID BELASCO (1853–1931)

DAVID BELASCO was born in San Francisco and raised in Victoria, British Columbia. Beginning as a child actor, he accumulated a tremendous amount

of practical theater experience by working as an actor, director, playwright, play adaptor, stage manager, and producer in California. His frequent involvement with spectacular melodramas helped him develop considerable expertise in the areas of lighting and special effects. One of his most notable San Francisco productions was of Salmi Morse's *The Passion Play* (1879), which created a scandal because of its onstage depiction of Christ. A flock of real sheep also caused a stir. During his California period, Belasco was involved in over 300 productions.

Although he had acted in New York as early as 1879, he did not take a steady position there until he was hired by the Madison Square Theater in 1882, where he began by directing Bronson Howard's *The Young Mrs. Winthrop*, and continued to stage plays for several years, including his own *May Blossom* (1884). He left the Madison Square in 1885, worked with Steele MacKaye and Lester Wallack for a time, and then established himself at the Lyceum Theater where he worked for producer Daniel Frohman from 1886 to 1890, doing a variety of contemporary works including Henry C. De Mille and Charles Barnard's *The Main Line, or Rawson's Y* (1886) and Belasco and De Mille's *The Charity Ball* (1889).

In 1889, Belasco undertook the training for the stage of Mrs. Leslie Carter, a titian-haired Chicago socialite whose divorce was one of the major scandals of the day. He put Mrs. Carter through an unusually difficult period of preparation and then, beginning in 1890, began to star her in a series of plays, among the most successful of which included *The Girl I Left Behind Me* (1893), *The Heart of Maryland* (1895), and *DuBarry* (1901); Belasco either wrote or adapted each of these. Belasco wanted total control over his star's life; when she married without his approval, he angrily ended their relationship in 1906.

Belasco became famous as a "star maker" because of his success in the development of such players as Blanche Bates (in such plays as Belasco and John Luther Long's *Madame Butterfly*, 1900; Paul M. Potter's *Under Two Flags*, 1901; Belasco and Long's *The Darling of the Gods*, 1902; and Belasco's *The Girl of the Golden West*, 1905); Frances Starr (in such plays as Edward Knoblock's *The Easiest Way*, 1909; Edward Locke's *The Case of Becky*, 1912; Knoblock's *Marie-Odile*, 1915; and Hubert Osborne's *Shore Leave*, 1922); David Warfield (in such plays as Lee Arthur and Charles Klein's *The Auctioneer*, 1901; Klein's *The Music Master*, 1904; Pauline Phelps, Marion Short, and Belasco's *A Grand Army Man*, 1907; Belasco's *The Return of Peter Grimm*, 1911; and Shakespeare's *The Merchant of Venice*, 1922); and Lenore Ulric (in such plays as Belasco's adaptation of André Picard's *Kiki*, 1921; Avery Hopwood's ver-

sion of Ernest Vajda's *The Harem*, 1924; Edward Sheldon and Charles MacArthur's *Lulu Belle*, 1926; and Belasco's version of Ferenc Molnár's *Mima*, 1928).

During these years Belasco became one of the most outspoken adversaries of the Theatrical Trust, a monopoly of theater owners and managers who virtually controlled the nation's playhouses and dictated restrictive terms to prospective tenants. He therefore opened his own Broadway theater, the Belasco, previously the Republic, in 1900, replacing it in 1906 with the newly built Belasco (the Republic reverted to its original name). The new theater was provided with excellent technical features, and included a private office-studio which became famous for its eccentric atmosphere, including the presence of liveried servants. Meanwhile, a 1903–1904 lawsuit Belasco brought against the Trust was instrumental in weakening that organization.

At his own and other theaters, Belasco became increasingly well known for his detailed naturalism; his sets were filled with the minutiae of daily life. Fourth-wall illusionism remained his dominant style, no matter when the play was set. Even his one Shakespearean production was notably realistic. He often used real props and materials, from the wallpaper to the food. Whenever possible, walls were solid instead of being made of canvas-covered frames.

Despite his lavish care, Belasco's plays were assailed for their literary shallowness. When choosing a play he was normally more interested in its scenic opportunities or in those offered to its actors than he was in advancing the state of dramatic writing. He was renowned for the unusual lengths to which he resorted to create realistic backgrounds for second-rate plays, as when he reproduced the interior of a Child's restaurant for Alice Bradley's *The Governor's Lady* (1912), purchased the furnishings and wallpaper of a Tenderloin district boarding-house flat for *The Easiest Way*, or sent to Japan for the costumes and accessories to adorn *The Darling of the Gods*. Whenever possible, Belasco had rooms built off the main set so that the action seemed to continue into the wings. The extensive scenery frequently necessitated lengthy shifts that greatly stretched running times. Because of the inordinate care taken in obtaining all the proper details, the results were generally effective in their combination of colors and textures.

Belasco oversaw every facet of his productions, and he was known as a gifted lighting designer. Working with his chief electrician, Louis Hartmann (inventor of the baby spotlight), Belasco spent considerable time and money perfecting his lighting, even creating a special lab where effects and instruments could be developed. Footlights were abandoned in favor of front, side, and overhead lighting. He believed a director should be knowledgeable about the psychological and symbolic values of light and color; he should understand even the types of light one is likely to find in specific geographical locations. Endless hours—many of them with the actors forced to remain on stage—were spent illuminating his shows. For example, three months and $5,000 were spent in capturing a California sunrise for *The Girl of the Golden West.*

Nearly as important was the music and sound he employed. He once hired 30 stagehands to produce the precise sound of a storm. For all his love of musical atmosphere, he was careful not to allow the music to draw attention to itself.

Regardless of his technical achievements, Belasco's greatest strength may have been his ability to elicit strong performances. His actors were known for powerful emotional effects, not for subtlety. Belasco was a puppeteer, manipulating actors in every detail, leaving little to chance or imagination. He was outstanding at creating detailed activity to create the illusion of life.

Belasco projected an air of kind paternalism, fostered by his prematurely white hair, Napoleonic size, and propensity for dressing as a Christian cleric (despite his Judaism), but he ruled with an iron hand. Actors called him "Mr. Dave," "the Governor," "the Wizard," or "the Master." He utilized every psychological ploy possible, coaxing or bullying as the need required. Although he had reservoirs of patience, he might explode and then soften a moment later, his rage spent. A famous device to inspire an emotional response was to smash a supposedly cherished watch in frustration; the watch, of course, was a cheap one of which he kept a stock on hand. When polishing a play, Belasco thought little of keeping his actors rehearsing until the early morning hours, and forced them to repeat readings or business endlessly until he was satisfied. Hours might be spent on a single sentence. When directing crowd scenes, he drilled every extra, giving them an individualized character with a name and making sure they each understood their contribution.

For all his emphasis on creating stars, Belasco favored the idea of ensemble, as he wanted nothing to distract from the production's overall quality. Actors who were not already stars were pliable and capable of being shaped to the director's whims. Although he considered casting an instinctive art,

he sought actors who demonstrated ability, imagination, industry, patience, and loyalty. On occasion, a play's production was delayed up to a year as Belasco sought the perfect match between actor and role. Type casting was a firm belief, as was the need to cast with an appropriate blend of voices.

Before beginning rehearsals, Belasco studied the play and its requirements assiduously, usually ignoring the author's stage directions in favor of his own ideas. In concert with the designer he first worked out a ground plan and then, over a period of several days, decided where all the exits and entrances had to be as well as what the major tableaux were, so that no unwelcome surprises lay in store. To further guarantee smooth rehearsals, scenic models and renderings were provided. The sets were built in Belasco's own shops under his supervision. Belasco pondered deeply the specifics of period costumes, beards, and the like, even before he met with his designer. For modern plays, Belasco sometimes purchased clothes from people he met in the street if their garments suited his characters.

The average rehearsal period lasted six weeks. It began with the entire cast meeting and getting to know one another in the most cordial of atmospheres. They were exhorted to work in a cooperative, unselfish way. Belasco read the play himself, then the actors did so. The first week was "at table," with the play being read and the director commenting on vocal approaches as well as attending to necessary rewrites. When blocking began in week two, the stage manager supervised a procedure in which the actors were encouraged to use their imaginations to find their own movement patterns. When this was well under way, Belasco appeared and put into effect his carefully prearranged moves, ignoring most of the actors' discoveries. Learning their lines was not something Belasco's actors considered imperative in the early rehearsals, as he liked them to have a solid character grounding before they worried about their precise words. Shortly before the opening, the actors marched in a "dress parade" to display their costumes; dress rehearsals—frequently all-night affairs—followed. Several weeks of out-of-town tryouts and polishing were provided, with rehearsals often proceeding directly after a performance. When the play ultimately arrived in New York, Belasco stood on opening nights in the wings, encouraging his performers by his proximity.

The Merchant of Venice (1922), Belasco's sole classic, illustrates many of his methods. In attempting to make Venice a palpable reality, Belasco and his designer undertook extensive historical research before choosing to set the work in early 16th-century Venice, and employing heavy, slow-to-shift, three-dimensional sets to recreate that period and milieu. Some rearrangement of the action was necessary to reduce the amount of shifting, including placing the casket scenes (one of which was cut) one after the other in act two. The stage was filled with panto-mimic action to suggest a locale brimming with life. Among the more effective devices Belasco created was the arrival of Shylock (David Warfield) at his home following Jessica's elopement. As the lights dimmed, he crossed in silence to his door. When the lights came up again, the scene was inside the house and Shylock's knocking was heard as if from outside. The door opened to reveal Shylock standing there, surprised to find the house deserted. He en-tered, searching for Jessica, as the faint sound of revelers outside was heard. Still searching, Shylock went out and then reentered, this time finding his daughter's keys and ring on the floor. Noticing that the strong box had been rifled, he cried aloud, spotted a letter and veil left by Jessica, and began to read as the revelers' noise grew louder.

Belasco continued to direct until 1931, when he grew ill during the rehearsals of *Tonight or Never*, adapted by Frederick and Fanny Hatton from a Lili Hatvany play. He was then a legend, although a faded one, as his excessive emphasis on realism caused him to be considered an outdated throwback to the 19th century at a time when a far more imaginative style was being fostered. He was now considered facile, shallow, and sensationalistic; his usual play was sentimental, romantic, and melodra-matic—often with an overtly sexual theme. Plays profited greatly from Belasco's infusion of his special brand of theatrical life. Belasco established the role of the American régisseur, gaining worldwide recog-nition for his directorial contributions.

Further reading:

Marker, Lise-Lone. *David Belasco: Naturalism in the American Theatre.* Princeton: Princeton University Press, 1975.

Timberlake, Craig. *The Bishop of Broadway: The Life and Work of David Belasco.* New York: Library Pub-lishers, 1954.

Winter, William. *The Life of David Belasco.* 2 vols. New York: Moffat, Yard and Co., 1918.

Also: Leiter, *From Belasco to Brook.*

MICHAEL BENNETT (1943–1987)

MICHAEL BENNETT DIFIGLIA, whose father was a machinist for General Motors, was born in Buffalo, New York. Bennett studied dance from age two and became a local teenage celebrity. He dropped out of

Michael Bennett rehearsing A Chorus Line. *(1975)* (Photo: Martha Swope)

high school to join a touring company of *West Side Story*. In New York, Bennett danced in the choruses of Broadway shows (contributing many ideas of his own) and on TV's "Hullabaloo," where he met Donna McKechnie, his future wife (they were later divorced) and frequent lead dancer.

From 1962 to 1967, Bennett choreographed in stock, TV, some film sequences, and on Broadway. Robert Avian became an indispensable adjunct, bal-ancing Bennett's jazz and tap abilties with his own balletic strengths and acting as an ideal editor.

Bennett made his first big splash with his Tony-nominated choreography for Neil Simon's *Promises, Promises* (1968), its score by Burt Bacharach and Hal David. McKechnie was the lead dancer. Bennett's unique ability to make every member of the chorus a clear-cut character signaled his ability to blend directorial functions with those of dance creator. His dancers appreciated being treated as actors. The show was Bennett's first with designer Robin Wagner. Once Bennett became a director, Wagner became a permanent member of his team, which, from *A Chorus Line* (1975) on also included costumer

Theoni V. Aldredge and lighting specialist Tharon Musser. Bennett loved to use movable scenery that could be choreographed into the fabric of a show, creating a cinematic progression that barely used the curtain.

The success of André Previn and Alan Jay Lerner's *Coco* (1969) stemmed mainly from star Katharine Hepburn, a non-dancer and -singer, who played Paris designer Gabrielle "Coco" Chanel. Bennett's perfectionism was exemplified by the two weeks he spent in Chanel's Paris salon researching the show's background, and the extensive study he made of modeling publications and photography. Bennett actually directed much of the show because director Michael Benthall was having serious problems. Bennett, who gained a reputation as a Machiavellian "manipulator," realized that to get the headstrong Hepburn to follow his instructions, he had to tell her the opposite of what he wanted, and then allow her to have "her way" when she resisted.

In 1970, Bennett choreographed Stephen Sondheim's *Company*, directed by Harold Prince. For this chorus-less, stylistically revolutionary, fully integrated "concept musical," based on themes of urban alienation and marital malaise, Bennett furthered his penchant for giving performers (many in *Company* were not dancers) logical reasons for all their movements. Dance or dancelike behavior in a Bennett show always stemmed from character foundations rather than purely aesthetic reasons. Thus, it was difficult to tell that a show was Bennett's. His mode was eclectic, bringing out the special qualities of each piece, unlike the more idiosyncratic Bob Fosse.

Bennett's first directing credit was shared with Prince on another nonlinear, Sondheim concept musical, *Follies* (1971), about a bittersweet reunion of unhappy former showgirls on the crumbling stage of their old theater, the subject matter being intended as a metaphor for national disillusionment. Prince staged the acted scenes and Bennett directed and choreographed the musical sequences and dances, tying everything together in a seamless unity. Prince contributed the notion of having the faded showgirls shadowed by the exquisitely black and white-costumed ghosts of their youthful selves, but Bennett's psychologically probing sequences, especially "Who's That Woman" and "Loveland," remain among the highlights of modern musical staging. Artistic disagreements with Prince marred the experience for Bennett, who felt the show should have been less cynical and the characters more appealing. Although Bennett and Prince shared a di-

recting Tony (Bennett's choreography also won), Bennett henceforth demanded total power over his projects. As his thirst for control grew stronger, his self-destructive dependence on artificial stimulants—cigarettes, drugs, and alcohol—increased, and he began seeing a psychoanalyst.

Hoping that work with nonmusical actors would deepen his skills with musical performers, Bennett directed a non-musical, George Furth's *Twigs* (originally titled *A Chorus Line*; 1971), a tour-de-force for Sada Thompson who, following Bennett's inspiration, played four different, but related, characters. For the tour, Bennett allowed Thompson to make all her costume, wig, and makeup changes on stage where the audience could see them.

Bennett returned to musicals for *Seesaw* (1973), based on William Gibson's *Two for the Seesaw*, which Bennett was persuaded (despite great reservations) to take over during its disastrous tryouts. Bennett demanded dictatorial control and displayed his ruthlessness when, thinking star Lainie Kazan was wrong for her role, fired her. The librettist quit and the overhauled Tony-nominated script was technically credited to Bennett, but contributions were made by most of the cast with some assistance from Neil Simon. The show flopped but Bennett won a Tony.

Two comedies occupied Bennett in 1974, Herb Gardner's *Thieves*, which he quit during tryouts, and Simon's *God's Favorite*, a commercial failure. Meanwhile, Bennett had begun what became one of the peaks of American theater history. He conceived *A Chorus Line* as a tribute to chorus dancers or "gypsies." Early in 1974, Bennett, wanting to explore the anguish and joy of the gypsy, convinced about 18 to attend an emotionally purgative rap session at which he tape-recorded their often painful histories. Another session with a slightly different group was held a bit later. The hours of tapes were synthesized under Bennett's aegis into a perfectly melded series of semi-documentary-like, comic and sad monologues, songs, and dances, presented as if part of an audition being held by a Bennett-like director seated in the audience. One of the dancers, whose poignant story eventually became that of the gay Hispanic named Paul, was Nicholas Dante, who became the librettist; he was joined by James Kirkwood. Marvin Hamlisch and Edward Kleban wrote the music and lyrics, respectively.

Instead of following the usual procedure of going into rehearsal with a script and score, the show was created during a series of workshops (interrupted by breaks) over a nine-month period, subsidized by producer Joseph Papp's Off-Broadway organization.

A Chorus Line. *Directed by Michael Bennett. (1975)*   (Photo: Martha Swope)

Bennett, an excruciatingly painstaking worker, had never felt he had the time to perfect his work; the workshops were his solution. During them, characters became composites of those on the tapes, and new material was often added. The show went through frequent, sometimes drastic, changes. Bennett got many of his staging ideas from experimenting with the dancers, and he profited from their ability to improvise. Most of the final ensemble did not perform the stories they themselves contributed, and many at the rap sessions were not cast because of Bennett's need to vary the physical types he used.

The workshop idea was common to certain Off-Broadway groups, but was new for a Broadway-bound project; many shows later attempted to follow its path. The collaborative process led to frequent legal and personal hassles, as there were conflicting claims about who created what, but it also helped create a

show that was not only artistically ground-breaking but the longest-running hit in Broadway history (6,137 performances).

A *Chorus Line* opened at Papp's Public Theater in April 1975 and officially reopened at Broadway's Shubert in October. Of its nine Tonys, Bennett won two (sharing the choreography award with Avian). McKechnie, who played Cassie, also garnered one. The piece, with its fluid, cinematic blend of acting and musical performance, all within the context of Bennett's passion for revealing universal truths through a show business metaphor, was the quintessential concept musical, a show that could never have been created without the genius of a single artist combining the skills of director and choreographer. Bennett's brilliance drew from all collaborators not only their finest material but pointed their multifaceted talents toward a common goal.

The deceptively simple decor consisted of a white line behind which the dancers stood before a seemingly bare stage, with a series of swiveling periaktois (prismlike units) upstage; on one of the three sides of these were dazzling mirrors (a motif found in most of Bennett's work). The decor was marvelously enhanced by the unusually complex lighting design (one of the first on Broadway to be computer-operated). The apparently conventional costumes required months of planning to make them appear precisely like those the characters would wear.

Bennett periodically returned to get the show into shape when one of its many casts suffered burnout. When *A Chorus Line* hit its record-breaking 3,389th performance (1983), he staged an unforgettable, logistically mind-boggling gala in which most of those who had appeared in the show made a return appearance.

In 1978, Bennett directed *Ballroom,* with a score by Billy Goldenberg and Alan and Marilyn Bergman, based on a 1975 TV script about a lonely middle-aged widow's love affair with a man she meets at a Roseland-like ballroom. The $2.2-million piece was developed in four months of workshops at 890 Broadway, a complex Bennett had converted into rehearsal studios, office space, and a 299-seat theater. Despite its promise and frequent beauty, the intimate material was overblown and it flopped.

Much more impressive was Bennett's Motown musical hit (1,522 performances), *Dreamgirls* (1981), about a Supremes-like black singing trio from Chicago, scripted by Tom Eyen (its original director). After two six-week workshops, Bennett took over the direction for two more workshops, sharing the choreography with Avian and Michael Peters. The scenic solution to the multi-scened script was an elaborate, computer-operated, high-tech set of five huge, movable towers, capable of being slid into configurations that—with the aid of dramatic lighting and hydraulic bridges—could turn a basically empty stage into wherever the action needed to be. The set was as much a part of the choreography as the performers (some critics faulted the $3.6-million show for its preoccupation with stylish technology). A simplified version that returned to Broadway (1987) with manually operated towers was considered an improvement.

With *Dreamgirls* Bennett's Broadway career was effectively over. Most of his multiple projects had to be abandoned. In 1983 he did direct a short play, *Third Street,* for the Young Playwrights Festival, Off-Off-Broadway. Among others was the British musi-

cal, *Chess,* by Tim Rice and the Swed Abba, which Bennett gave up midstrea covering in January 1986 that he had AIDS. also invested an extraordinary amount of tale energy into a daring, sexually oriented show c *Scandal,* by Treva Silverman and Jimmy Webb about a woman's discovery of her libidinous potential; it was written and rehearsed extensively in nine months of workshops in 1984 but Bennett decided to abandon it, one of many reasons offered being his conviction that so explicit a show was irresponsible in the age of AIDS.

Bennett became a Broadway legend, loved by some, hated by others, and inspiring mixed feelings in many. He was extraordinarily manipulative, yet his ability to seduce actors into giving exceptional performances was part of his Svengaliesque genius. He always sought reality from his performers, coaching them to speak their lines conversationally and not to act them, and to behave with total honesty. He sometimes went to extraordinary lengths to get the right response, and could use psychological cruelty when he deemed it necessary. An example was when—to the shock of the company—he faked a serious injury during a rehearsal of *A Chorus Line* in order to show them by their own behavior how they should react to the injury sustained by a character in the show. Many were angered, but he only cared that the deception worked. On another occasion, to get nondancer Vincent Gardenia in *Ballroom* to feel comfortable dancing, he had the rehearsal studio decorated as a nightclub; after visiting it daily for a couple of drinks and some dancing with a couple of girls, Gardenia dropped his inhibitions.

To get the proper readings from actors, Bennett preferred to suggest images, or even to change a line to make it sound better, and worked closely with an actor until satisfied with his progress. When pressed for time, he gave line readings. He might also act the parts himself to show his goals. Many of his problems were solved by his gift for casting the right people. He could be brutal, cold, and mean, or loving, protective, and paternal. His neurotic screaming, ranting, and egotistical demands became notorious, yet many respected his quiet, intimate, tensionless, nurturing methods. His arsenal included getting results by making actors (male or female) fall in love with him.

Bennett's shows typically had happy, even sentimental, endings because he believed an audience should depart on a note of hope. His work was more gut-level emotional than cerebral, partially because

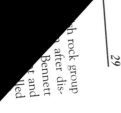

or well read. He was
lmost preturnatural
was limited to ex-
in dynamic theatri-
have called a limited
nagination. Bennett
ware of how to get
rtists, regardless of
shows he actually
will always be remembered for *A Chorus Line*.

Further reading:

Flinn, Denny Martin. *What They Did for Love: The Untold Story Behind the Making of "A Chorus Line".* New York: Bantam, 1989.

Kelly, Kevin. *One Singular Sensation: the Michael Bennett Story.* New York: Doubleday, 1990.

Mandlebaum, Ken. *"A Chorus Line" and the Musicals of Michael Bennett.* New York: St. Martin's Press, 1989.

Also: Gottfried, *Broadway Musicals*; Kislan, *Hoofing*; Laufe, *Broadway's Greatest Musicals*; Mordden, *Broadway Babies*.

INGMAR BERGMAN (1918–   )

INGMAR BERGMAN was born in Uppsala, Sweden. His father was a curate—and later, parish priest—in Stockholm, where the family moved in 1920. He

Ingmar Bergman directing Peer Gynt. (Photo: Royal Dramatic Theatre of Sweden/Bengt Wanselius)

began directing amateurs in the late 1930s, around the time he was attending Stockholm University. By 1944 he had staged 17 amateur and professional productions, including his own works (Bergman eventually wrote half a dozen dramas). He also had begun making inroads in Swedish films and eventually became one of the world's leading filmmakers (*Smiles of a Summer Night*, 1955; *Wild Strawberries*, 1957; *Persona*, 1966; *Fanny and Alexander*, 1982; etc.).

Bergman's early career saw him directing classical and modern drama at the Hälsingborg City Theater (1944–1946), the Gothenburg City Theater (1946–1950), and Stockholm's Intima Theater (1950) and Royal Dramatic Theater (Dramaten, 1951). In the 1950s, he was the mainstay of the Malmö City Theater (1952–1958), where his broad repertory included the leading foreign and Scandinavian dramatists. He assumed a permanent position at Dramaten in 1959, and from 1963 to 1966 headed the company, which acted in his often controversial productions ranging from Edward Albee to Shakespeare. He also sometimes guest-directed abroad.

In 1976, Bergman was arrested on a tax charge (from which he was later exonerated) and went into voluntary exile, taking a position at Munich's Residenz Theater, where he remained until 1981. In Munich he mounted plays by Anton Chekhov, Molière, and Witold Gombrowicz. Most impressive was his ambitious three-part 1981 Bergman Project, comprising Henrik Ibsen's *A Doll's House* and *Miss Julie* (in a four-hour production called *Nora and Julie*) and his three-hour stage adaptation of his television film, *Scenes From a Marriage*, staged simultaneously at a smaller space nearby. The three works in combination established the exciting resonances of male and female relationships within specific social

Peer Gynt. *Directed by Ingmar Bergman. (1991)*   (Photo: Royal Dramatic Theater of Sweden/Bengt Wanselius)

contexts. At Dramaten in the 1980s, he presented, among other works, two outstanding Shakespeare revivals and one of Eugene O'Neill; abroad he staged Molière and Ibsen, although he recently offered Ibsen's *Peer Gynt* (1991) and Yukio Mishima's *Madame de Sade* (1992) for Dramaten; both were seen in America in 1993.

Although his repertory of close to 80 productions has been eclectic, Strindberg, Ibsen, Molière, and Shakespeare have preoccupied him. He has staged several works in multiple productions (four of Strindberg's *A Dream Play*, for instance), each one demonstrating a new approach toward the material.

Although Bergman went through a period of considerable diversity in the 1940s and 1950s, alternating between austerity and spectacle, he gradually evolved a distinctive "chamber play" style. From the 1960s on, his work partook increasingly of a puritan aesthetic revolving around the three-part concept of text-actor-audience. Anything that obstructed the interplay of these elements was eliminated, the principal burden being on the actor's need to bring the text to the audience. Even the most naturalistic

plays were given minimalist stagings, becoming dependent on suggestion, not representation.

He first fully realized this technique's power with Strindberg's *The Crown-Bride* (1952), when he staged the clash between millfolk and outsiders, presumably taking place on an icy lake during a storm, by combining choreographic movement with evocative lighting on a practically bare stage. It was not until his staging of Georg Büchner's *Woyzeck* (1969), however, that Bergman made his sharpest turn away from what he calls the "theater of circumstances" toward a radically spare technique dominated by a relatively empty stage and an economical use of properties. He boldly located the attic in *The Wild Duck* (1972) far down stage (as opposed to its usual position upstage) and used only imaginative lighting and acting to suggest its presence.

Bergman's method permits him to stage technically complex, potentially expensive plays with the simplest means, including the 1970 *A Dream Play*, done with little more than lights and projections. Occasionally, a few isolated, but nonillusionistic, screenlike wall units are used to suggest a space, and actors may carry out scene changes in view of the audience. Bergman wants audience members to remain aware that they are watching a performance, hoping to intensify their involvement by bringing them briefly out of the action before immersing them in it again.

Bergman believes that every stage has a "magic point" at which the actors are at their most potent; the director must locate this point and stage the play in relation to it. Consequently, many Bergman productions feature a limited acting area carved out of the most dominant position, normally by the erection on it of a low platform that separates the area from the rest of the stage proper. Sometimes a platform variant is used, such as the large circle on the mostly empty stage for *Hamlet* (1988). A selective number of atmospheric pieces may enhance the decor, such as the pastiche of baroque scenery surrounding Molière's *The Misanthrope* (1973).

Interiors represented by relatively complete environments are noticeably unadorned and are thematically conceptualized. Notable was the stark set for Ibsen's *Hedda Gabler* (1964), a shallow arrangement backed by a wall of undecorated eight-foot-high screens (sans General Gabler's portrait) covered in dark red velvet, with a movable screen bisecting the space into two rooms, one on stage right for Hedda's usually hidden "inner room," the other on stage left for the main action. This arrangement kept Hedda in view continually, thereby relentlessly displaying her feeling of entrapment. On several recent occasions, Bergman employed more detailed investitures, one being the latest version of *A Dream Play* (1986), previously given austere stagings, and now mingling complex projections with a stage broken into a downstage outer room for the Poet, complete with ceiling, and an upstage inner one for his visions.

From the 1970s on, Bergman regularly allowed the off-platform areas to be seen by the audience and had cast members not involved in the action proper visible in the dim light quietly preparing for their entrances. The actor moving from one reality level into another displays the theater's transformational magic.

One reason for the impressiveness of Bergman's scenic spareness is his brilliant use of lighting and projections. His preference for strong, white, frontal lighting thrown by low-angle projectors hung from the first balcony has given rise to the term "Bergman lights." Projections give him the flexibility to establish multiple locales easily and swiftly; the projections are often connotative but also can be representational, as was the Stockholm house and church facade in the first scene of Strindberg's *Ghost Sonata* (1973). The technique allows him cinematically to open up plays that hitherto have been confined to interiors, as in O'Neill's *Long Day's Journey into Night* (1988).

Bergman's productions employ novel conceptualizations that express previously unrealized ideas in sometimes controversial images as they focus on a single overarching theme tying all parts of the play together. A small example was his use of the same actress to play the Mummy and the Young Girl in the 1973 *Ghost Sonata* to express his belief that the girl was becoming like her mother. At times he prefers to unify a heretofore realistically produced work by viewing it in dreamlike terms, as in his *Hedda Gabler* and *Long Day's Journey*.

His reductive method frequently leads to cuts. When the original dialogue obstructs a thematic point and cannot be removed, Bergman may redistribute it to other characters. He had the Student's closing lines in *The Ghost Play* spoken by the Colonel and the Mummy because the sympathetic words did not match the Student's unsympathetic behavior toward the Young Lady.

Bergman might underscore thematic concerns through such means as adding to the beginning of *Long Day's Journey* a pantomimic sequence of his own, showing the family members lovingly interlocked, possibly in order to set up a contrast to their ultimate estrangement. Similarly, he often ignores stage directions; Løvborg's manuscript became a mere pamphlet in *Hedda Gabler*, and the vision of Böcklin's "Island of the Dead" was eliminated from the end of *The Ghost Sonata* (1954), replaced with a tableau of the Student cradling the girl's head in his lap.

Bergman tends to isolate a minor character and to build up the role as a thematic linking device between stage and auditorium or one scene and another. Such, among others, was his employment of the mute court fool in Strindberg's *Erik XIV* (1956), the Poet in the 1970 *A Dream Play*, Laurent in *Tartuffe*, and Basque in *The Misanthrope*. Bergman attempts to be faithful to the inner spirit of the plays and rarely seeks to subvert the authors' intentions, especially not to introduce topicality.

Bergman believes that only if his preparation is complete and he feels both certain and content with his vision can he undertake to direct a play. Such preparation provides him with a nondogmatic foundation on which he and the actors, working in

Peter Stormar in Hamlet. *Directed by Ingmar Bergman. (1988)*   (Photo: Martha Swope)

harmony, can build, expand, and, if necessary, revise. The director requires absolute clarity in his total understanding of the play before he can rehearse.

A major consideration in preparing is an awareness of who is in the cast. His work has benefitted from his ability to work repeatedly with such actors as Gertrud Fridh, Ingrid Thulin, Liv Ullmann, Bibi Andersson, Anders Ek, and Max von Sydow.

During rehearsals, which may last two to three months (or more), Bergman moves actors about physically and even demonstrates, but he gives no line readings. Stanislavskian acting is dismissed as psychological masturbation. He abhors talkfests and prefers actors to view their performances technically. Musical images and rhythms are key methods of stimulating them. He considers rhythm the *sine qua non* of theatrical technique. Rhythm figures importantly in his work with actors on their lines, as it does with his blocking, what he calls his "choreog-

raphy." There is a dancelike quality to many Bergman productions.

All of the principal movements are indicated in a promptbook containing scenic and movement sketches and diagrams. Also preplanned are physical relationships, including whether or not characters are listening to what others are saying.

Although he often demonstrates, he also will encourage an actor to develop his own ideas. He stresses the close, almost erotic, nature of collaboration. Bergman's rehearsals are hermetically sealed events in which no undue distractions are allowed to intrude. He insists that "self-discipline, cleanliness, light and quiet prevail." There is usually an instantaneous communication with his actors, many of whom praise the creative freedom he inspires. One way that he gets actors to relax is to have them concentrate on their partners. He tells them that "acting is never an *I*, it is always a *you*. Because the minute two actors forget themselves and take everything from the other one, then you have the great moments of performance." He describes his goal as complete clarity:

Haziness in emotions and intentions must always be eliminated. Signals from all actors to the audience must be simple and lucid. Always one at a time, preferably rapid; one suggestion may contradict the next but intentionally, *then an illusion of simultaneousness and depth-effect arises, a stereo-effect. Events on the stage must reach the spectator at every moment, truth in the expression coming second; good actors always have resources to act as intermediaries for the reflected truth.*

Since 1969 Bergman has allowed the public to attend rehearsals, which he has found productive because the actors learn to accept the audience as a contributing factor. He declares the idea is for the actors' benefit although he admits that the audience reaps great benefit in learning that while there is no magic in the process, magic nonetheless plays a great part. These rehearsals are run-throughs showing the production at varying stages of completion, and are invariably preceded by Bergman's requesting the audience's imaginative assistance. Later, the company discusses the audience's reaction.

Bergman may be best known as a genius film director, but he has been equally as accomplished in the theater. His productions have made a unique contribution, through their unusually expressive actor-centered minimalism as well as through his brilliantly original, intensely humanistic conceptualizations of classical and modern texts.

Further reading:

Bergman, Ingmar. *The Magic Lantern: An Autobiography.* New York: Alfred A. Knopf, 1988.

Marker, Lise-Lone, and Frederick Marker. *Ingmar Bergman: A Life in the Theater.* 2d ed. Cambridge, England.: Cambridge University Press, 1992.

————. *Ingmar Bergman: A Project for the Theater.* New York: Ungar, 1983.

ROGER BLIN (1907–1984)

ROGER BLIN was born in Neuilly, near Paris, where his father was a physician. He studied literature at the University of Paris and became friendly with the surrealists. Before turning to directing, he was a film critic and a stage and film actor. A stutterer, Blin learned to overcome it when acting, as he did when directing actors. Poet, actor, director, and theorist Antonin Artaud was instrumental in guiding him into a theatrical career, which began with his assisting Artaud on and acting in Artaud's *The Cenci* (1935). He later appeared in a number of plays he directed himself. It was not until the two years (1949–1951) he spent at the small Théâtre Gaîté-Montparnasse that he began directing, beginning with Denis Johnston's *The Moon in the Yellow River* (1949), August Strindberg's *The Ghost Sonata* (1949), and Jean Silvant's *The Executioner Is Impatient* (1950). Arthur Adamov's *Parody* was staged elsewhere in 1952.

The Gaîté-Montparnasse venture was a financial disaster, but it was there in 1949 that Samuel Beckett asked him to consider a pair of plays, one of them Beckett's revolutionary *Waiting for Godot*, in which no one else seemed interested. Blin loved the unusual play but did not direct its premiere until 1953. The tragicomic *Godot*'s unconventional structure, spare, evocative, and lyrical colloquial language,

humorous coarseness, actionlessness, lack of sentimentality, and existential characters seemed radically untheatrical, but Blin sensed its genius. *Godot*, after rehearsing for a year, debuted at the tiny, ill-equipped Théâtre de Babylone, with the lanky Blin as Pozzo, usually played in later productions (including Blin's) by fleshier actors. Beckett's attendance at some rehearsals guaranteed the work's integrity, although he accepted several cuts and revisions. Blin sought fundamental human behavior, Beckett something more stylized. Critics and audiences were puzzled but Blin's contributions were acknowledged. Eventually, Blin's perspicacity in perceiving its worth was applauded. Blin staged seven French and non-French revivals of the play, including a freshly conceived 1978 mounting at the Comédie Française.

Blin had an extraordinary sensitivity to language. His love of words prevented him from taking undue liberties with a text; *Godot* demonstrated his fidelity, from dialogue to stage directions. Working with limited means, Blin and his designer created the austere but potent imagery of the nearly bare stage, mound, and scraggly tree (designed by Blin, a gifted visual artist) which have since seen numerous manifestations. In 1978, the set, built on a rake or incline to increase visibility, came closer to Beckett's "country road" description. Also used now were a pair of side curtains operated—for the entrances and exits of Pozzo and Lucky—like those in circuses. Beckett had frowned on Blin's idea for a circus-oriented production, but Blin retained the circular movement of an arena, paralleling the plot's circular structure.

The original actors had many difficulties playing such unfamiliar material, and Blin, who hated to talk metaphysics in rehearsal, insisted that they would succeed if they played as concretely as possible,. concentrating on their corporeal woes. Although many later versions have played up the farcical angle, in 1953 the tone was sober, underlining Blin's sensitivity to the cruelty of Beckett's vision, with the comedy underplayed.

Blin ultimately directed other Beckett masterpieces in their French premieres, including *Endgame* (1957), *Krapp's Last Tape* (1960), and *Happy Days* (1963), starring Madeleine Renaud. Unable to get a Paris production for the first, he performed it, by invitation, at London's Royal Court Theater. Its success led to a Paris production. In *Endgame* Blin played Hamm, whom he viewed as a King Lear-like character, although Beckett did not concur with that interpretation. Blin also had trouble in agreeing to Beckett's purely musical vision of the play, wherein the actors passed from one feeling to another without emotional transitions. Blin and his actors, despite Beckett's wishes, were unable to avoid infusing psychological overtones into their playing.

In 1959—following Jean Duvignaud's *Low Tide* (1956) and a black version of J. M. Synge's *In the Shadow of the Glen* (1958) for the amateur Griot Company—Blin was applauded as a major interpreter of another modern titan, Jean Genet, when he directed the world premiere of *The Blacks* at the 200-seat Théâtre de Lutèce; this was his first collaboration with designer André Acquart. *The Blacks*, the first of three Blin-directed Genet plays, opened after a year and a half of rehearsals. (Blin later did two other versions, one in English in 1961.) This linguistically knotty, violent, ritualistic, antiwhite theatricalist play employed an all-black company, some of them amateurs. Blin had to soothe several actors who were disturbed by the sometimes shocking nature of the material. Unlike Blin's usual invisible mise-en-scène, that for *The Blacks* was deliberately self-conscious and employed daringly exaggerated, even grotesque, methods of vocal and physical expression, including the dancing of "The Death of the Swan" by the Valet to signify his execution. The sculpturelike set consisted of multitiered, nonillusionistic tubular scaffolding wrapped in asbestos and swathed

in atmospheric lighting that gave it different shapes and colors.

Blin, who acted in Peter Brook's Paris production of Genet's *The Balcony* (1960), later directed it himself in the Netherlands (1966). Far more significant was the first French staging of Genet's *The Screens* (1966) at Jean-Louis Barrault's Odéon-Théâtre de France. This poetic but virulently antiestablishment play met with opposition because of the political sensitivity of its subject (French colonial oppression of the Algerians), its profanity, its murkiness, its bleak point of view condemning both Arabs and colonists, its celebration of degradation, and its technical complexity. Genet himself, despite his radicalism, insisted that the play be performed apolitically, with the focus on the story of Saïd, the Arab thief. Nevertheless, it became a political *cause célèbre*, was attacked by right-wingers, and had some performances disrupted. Most controversial was the scene in which a dying French lieutenant is honored by each of his soldiers' farting in his face (a scene Blin moved from offstage to on). Genet took an active part in the production, seeking a hieratic, oriental style of acting. Sixty-five actors played 110 roles, but before the regular rehearsals began, Blin worked privately with the principals for three months to explore nonrealistic, ritualistic acting approaches.

The unusually long play, trimmed to four hours, employed a three-tiered arrangement of portable standing screens—moved laterally by actors—on which designs were painted to suggest locales, and which, when required by the action, allowed the Arabs to paint violent revolutionary events on them. Various nonillusionistic techniques were employed, such as having a paper sun pasted on a screen so that ripping it off could represent night. The exaggerated makeups suggested Japanese techniques.

Other important works of the 1960s, some of them in other countries, included plays by Amos Kenan, Ramon Maria del Valle-Inclán, Jean-Pierre Faye, and Eduardo Manet. In the seventies, he directed such authors as José Triana, Shakespeare, Roland Dubillard, Slawomir Mrozek, August Strindberg, Athol Fugard, Manet, Osamu Takahashi, François Billetdoux, Thomas Bernhard, and Max Frisch.

Most of these works were new, densely written, formalistically difficult, thematically disturbing, and politically anti-establishment. Blin undertook intellectually challenging projects most others would have rejected as unproducible. A play had to "enthrall" him. He was difficult to pin down to one school or another. The invisible mise-en-scène was his trademark. "The more [the director's work] is effaced," he claimed, "the better."

Several productions demonstrated his exceptional ability to transfer a radio text to the stage. Others were done mainly to encourage a promising new writer. A radio play that accomplished the latter purpose was Jean-Louis Bauer's *Name's Isabelle Langrenier* (1979), an unconventional work that was developed from a 29-page, often incomprehensible, radio monologue. (This was Blin's first use of a musical background, his earlier preference having been to use human voices to create musical and sound effects.) Several plays demonstrated Blin's social commitment, although he normally avoided polemical plays. His most "propagandistic" work was Osamu Takahashi's ecology-minded *Minamata and Co.*, a true-life docudrama based on the effects of mercury pollution caused by a factory in Japan; the play was produced by the Roger Blin Company, a young group he allowed to use his name. Blin staged it in graphically imagistic terms, including the use of marionettes to show the victims of mercury poisoning. In order to stress its universality, only the slightest reminders of its Japanese origins were utilized. His productions were invariably overtly theatrical pieces that required the presence of a razor-sharp mind and a powerful visual sense before they could be staged.

Macbeth (1972), Blin's sole venture with Shakespeare, avoided a political reading and sought to explore its inner life. The ominous black and red setting was covered with a spongy material suggesting decay that was also used in the costuming. Movable scenic units on castors combined with resourceful lighting suggested the many locales. Blin's asexual witches were represented by three actors, one of them a dwarf, whose heads and legs protruded from a single garment. Banquo's ghost appeared when a servant wearing a mask on the back of his head turned around. When Lady Macbeth descended the staircase, her candle was handed along by arms extending from behind black drapes. Such touches, including the creation of all sound effects by vocalizations, evoked a hallucinatory world of evil and pain in which Macbeth was manipulated by forces beyond his control.

Blin did careful prerehearsal research, reading books, studying art works, and even traveling to a locale depicted in a play to soak up its atmosphere, as when he went with his designer to Galicia before staging *Divine Words* (1963). He worked closely with the writer, giving the same respect and attention to the untried as to the veteran. He normally respected stage directions and dialogue, and suggested only minor changes.

In rehearsal, he nervously smoked a thin black cigar as he watched or listened (with eyes closed). When he interrupted, he very politely demonstrated his aims physically, including speaking the lines, but with the intention that the actor would get the general idea and then follow through on his own. His manner was withdrawn and shy and never visibly authoritarian; he hated to give orders. Blin enjoyed it when actors came up with interpretations better than his own. At times he knowingly let an actor go wrong so that when an impasse was reached, the right way could more readily be discovered. He expressed the meaning of scenes in metaphors drawn from life, but sometimes couched his comments in jokes; actors occasionally had the notion that they had been barely directed at all and that their performances were stimulated by osmosis. Blin said that his poking fun at a scene not only relaxed the cast but helped them uncover hidden subtleties. He believed that the actor could uncover in the text all the inspiration necessary for his moves and gestures, and that his own role was to shape the actor's discoveries. He added ideas in small increments, day by day, so that fully rounded performances were shaped subliminally.

Blin discovered the play through trial and error in rehearsal, and did not arrive with everything planned. Thus he did not use a prepared production book. Little time was spent "at table," Blin preferring to get the actors on their feet right away. Lengthy theorizing was avoided.

Blin sought to tap inner resources of which the actors were unaware. He liked to cast people with unusual qualities, especially those with deep waters beneath still surfaces.

He was not addicted to any shape or size of theater, and worked in tiny as well as grandiose venues, even adapting the same work for radically different stages. He normally disdained machinery, although he occasionally resorted to such devices as a series of five small revolving stages in *Triptych* (1983). He worked intimately with his designers, preferring architects or sculptors to painters. Lighting was his personal domain.

Despite lacking an easily identifiable style, Blin made a considerable impact in his predilection for "unplayable" scripts, his explorations of ritualistic staging, his faithfulness to the writer, and his belief in the director's self-effacement.

Further reading:

Aslan, Odette. *Roger Blin and Twentieth-Century Play-wrights.* Translated by Ruby Cohn. Cambridge, England: Cambridge University Press, 1988.

Fletcher, John. "Roger Blin at Work." *Modern Drama* 8 (February 1966).

Knapp, Bettina. "An Interview with Roger Blin." *Tulane Drama Review* 7 (Spring 1963).

Also: Bradby, *Modern French Drama.*

OTTO BRAHM (1856–1912)

OTTO ABRAHAMSON, who changed his name to Brahm to mask his Jewish origins during a time of increasing anti-Semitism, was born in Hamburg, Germany, to a merchant family. He was educated in Hamburg and Perleberg. After working in a Hamburg bank, he quit to study literature at the University of Berlin, although, for technical reasons, he received his doctorate from Jena University. He gained renown as an author, editor, and theater critic.

Brahm's critiques sharpened his perceptions, not only of dramatic literature but of theatrical possibilities. Despite later being a pioneer of naturalism, he was originally not well disposed to the evolving realistic movement. He criticized actors who showed themselves off to the disadvantage of the playwright's language and intentions. Moreover, he believed in harmonious ensembles rather than histrionic virtuosity.

At the start of the 1880s, Brahm recognized the genius of Henrik Ibsen, whose penetrating and fearlessly honest works shocked many of his staid contemporaries. The widely censored *Ghosts*—given its Berlin premiere at a Sunday matinee in 1886—had a powerful effect on him. Brahm's first exposures to the working theater came with his assisting the director of this production and another who staged Ibsen's *The Wild Duck* (1888).

Related to Ibsen's influence on Brahm were other decisive forces, particularly the growing importance of France's naturalistic movement as expressed through the ideas of Émile Zola, and the realization of plays in the new manner at Paris's Théâtre Libre. With Zola as his model, Brahm found the artificiality and lack of psychological depth of most modern theater appalling. His preoccupation was not so much with the generally understood definitions of realism and naturalism as it was with the degree to which a play, no matter how painfully, truthfully reflected the reality of its times and avoided the romantic platitudes. Ugliness was acceptable if it mirrored reality. He saw most classics as lacking in psychological truth and rejected them in favor of modern works.

Brahm wanted to view truth not only through playwriting but in acting and directing. At a time when production was often dominated by sham theatrics, Brahm's demands had a revolutionary ring. The medium for the convergence of these ideas and influences was the founding by Brahm (the elected leader) and a group of Berliners of the Théâtre Libre-inspired Freie Bühne (Free Theater) in 1889. Their purpose was to circumvent intrusions of the law by creating a private subscription club to support the performance of worthy but little-known and often censored modern plays, many in the naturalistic mode. Although he handled the managerial responsibilities—from hiring actors to selecting the plays—the direction was done by others, whose work he oversaw. Instead of obtaining its own theater, the group rented available theaters for Sunday matinees (plays had only one performance), using paid actors who were involved during the week in commercial efforts. Backed by 634 members, the Freie Bühne opened with *Ghosts* (1889) and followed it up with the premiere of Gerhart Hauptmann's *Before Sunrise* (1889). Some of the season's nine plays were failures, and subscriptions slackened.

Brahm used the journal he founded in 1890, the weekly *Freie Bühne für Modernes Leben* (its name later was changed), to promote his pronaturalist beliefs. Moreover, similar noncommercial groups, but with somewhat different agendas, also cropped up.

In season two, the Freie Bühne's menu included Zola, August Strindberg, and Hauptmann, but only one premiere (by Otto Erich Hartleben). Despite shrinking membership, the society's purpose was being accomplished as the playwrights they championed became accepted in the regular theater world. A total of three plays were seen in seasons two and three, although the latter included Hauptmann's censored *The Weavers* (1893). (Brahm was an indefatigable foe of censorship throughout his career.)

At the season's close, Brahm resigned from the chairmanship. During its remaining 15 years, the society did only six more plays.

Brahm succeeded Adolf L'Arronge as manager of the Deutsches Theater in 1894, even though L'Arronge, the theater's owner, knew that the new lessee would present a different policy than his own by emphasizing new plays. Cord Hachmann of the Freie Bühne was retained as a director, but Brahm himself began to direct. Finances forced Brahm to employ a small company, somewhere between 30 and 40, half as many as other important theaters.

Brahm began with a classic, Friedrich Schiller's *Love and Intrigue* (1894), hoping to demonstrate the difference in the natural acting style he favored from the more conventional one employed by his predecessor for the same drama. An inconsistency in style among the leading players and a clash between the too-rational interpretation and the emotionally charged content led to failure. Fortunately, success arrived with the next presentation, *The Weavers,* in its first public performance in Berlin after Hauptmann managed to overturn its suppression. Despite (or because of) political controversy, including the cancellation of his expensive box by the emperor, the drama—about exploited textile workers—achieved 94 showings.

Brahm's emphasis on modern drama was introduced gradually, his first season presenting 10 classics, his second five, his third two, and his fourth five, while—apart from two works in the eighth season—no classics or standards were given new productions during his management's remaining six years. Not having a gift for bringing stage reality to such works, Brahm turned them over to his "head stage director" Hachmann and his successor, Emil Lessing, although they, too, failed to produce any important successes, even with such leading classical actors as Josef Kainz and Agnes Sorma. Brahm restricted his involvement in these productions to script revisions.

Brahm's powers flourished in the restricted medium of modern, realistic plays, especially those by such favorites of his as Arthur Schnitzler, Hauptmann, Georg Hirschfeld, and Ibsen. In order to remain solvent, however, he also had to resort to what he deemed second-rate realistic pieces that the public found appealing, among them the works of Hermann Sudermann, Max Dreyer, Hartleben, and Ludwig Fulda. Their plays were his biggest hits. Edmond Rostand's *Cyrano de Bergerac* (1898), a play for which Brahm did not have great esteem, was also very successful.

Under Brahm's baton, Schnitzler's *Light O' Love* (1896), *Free Game* (1896), *The Legacy* (1898), *The Green Cockatoo* (1899), *The Veil of Beatrice* (1903), and *The Lonely Way* (1904), among other works, were produced. Hauptmann became intimately associated with Brahm through stagings of *The Weavers, Florian Geyer* (1895), the nonnaturalistic verse fantasy *The Sunken Bell* (1896), *The Assumption of Hannele* (1897), *The Beaver Coat* (1897), *Drayman Henschel* (1898), *Michael Kramer* (1900), and many others. The less prolific and important Hirschfeld was also regularly produced by Brahm. More significant was Ibsen, who was represented in 1894–1895 by *A Doll's House, Ghosts,* and *Little Eyolf;* in 1895–1896 by *Pillars of Society;* in 1896–1897 by *The Wild Duck* and *John Gabriel Borkman;* in 1897–1898 by *Hedda Gabler;* in 1899–1900 by *Rosmersholm* and *When We Dead Awaken;* and in 1900–1901 by *An Enemy of the People.* In addition, Brahm also offered a home to such respectable dramatists as Maurice Maeterlinck, Hermann Heijermans, and Hugo von Hofmannsthal.

Brahm's ensemble was renowned for its compelling authenticity and harmonious unity in modern drama. Although it eventually lost Kainz and Sorma, the company, which ignored the traditional system of casting by role categories and accepted small roles as well as leads, could draw on such important players as Max Reinhardt, Friedrich Kayssler, Emanuel Reicher, Albert Bassermann, and Else Lehmann.

Brahm's collaborative methods were unusual in that he left the technical elements of the staging, including the various aspects of the mise en scène (decor, blocking, etc.), to Hachmann or Lessing, while he worked on the play's inner life, its thematic and character development. Brahm was concerned with the technical components only insofar as they were not harmful to the playwright's purposes. Hachmann and Lessing had little impact on the spiritual side of a play's realization, and merely carried out Brahm's wishes concerning externals. Direction was officially credited to the head stage director, however, not to Brahm.

Brahm's new plays usually relied on sets depicting specific locales, in keeping with naturalism's stress on the importance of environment in determining people's actions. Thus, although uncredited to particular artists, the sets were freshly designed rather than being pulled from stock, which was still being done with classics. They were created to serve the play, but not to draw undue attention away from the production's unity. Outdoor sets employed perspective drops and cut wings and borders, with three-dimensional furnishings as needed. Indoor scenes were played in ceilinged box sets with practical doors and windows and with enough furnishings to suggest the clutter of reality.

Brahm invited the playwrights to attend rehearsals and, on occasion, even to run them. They also participated in casting decisions. Brahm preceded rehearsals by working on the script with the dramatist. Despite his critical pronouncements on behalf of naturalism, his sensibilities frequently forced him to excise material he considered offensive, no matter how true to life. Inner reality predominated over external verisimilitude.

Rehearsals began with blocking. Then followed a week of the actors' scrutinizing the entire script (not only one's own role) to understand meanings and relationships. For about five days after this, Brahm worked on an act a day, focusing on the details of character and situation, while the head stage director corrected technical acting elements (timing, exits, entrances, cues, etc.). For three days the company worked on two acts a day, and a final two days were for run-throughs. Brahm sat in the house, never interrupting the actors nor demonstrating how to correct their errors. He talked to the actors one by one at the end of an act, explaining their problems. He could be cuttingly sarcastic, often asking rhetorically, "Do you attach much importance to this nuance?" and then quickly follow up with, "Then leave it out!"

The result of this unorthodox approach was what Horst Claus refers to as the "Brahm Style," a method of stage behavior that resembled the way people spoke and behaved in real life, although filtered through the artistic taste of the playwright and director to heighten and refine reality's rougher edges. Its subtlety and lack of overt theatricality marked it off from the typical methods of the day. In keeping with naturalistic dramaturgy, a great deal of dialogue was expressed in pauses, unfinished sentences, and vocal exclamations. Asides and monologues were normally eliminated by Brahm. He was a master at eliciting the subtextual bases of naturalistic speech and at

exploiting its resonances to express the character's inner life.

Brahm ran the Deutsches for a decade, making it a model of sound management and genial relationships; artistic rivalries were minimal or nonexistent. However, a dispute with L'Arronge led to the cancellation of Brahm's contract and his 1904 move to the Lessingtheater, to which he took practically his entire company and staff. Max Reinhardt, however, left to become Brahm's major rival when he took over the Deutsches in 1905.

At the Lessingtheater the new play policy stayed in effect, but even more attention was placed on box-office certainties. Ibsen's *The Lady From the Sea* was Brahm's opening production. The coming seasons also saw plays by the other mainstays, while Leo Tolstoy, Björnstjerne Björnson, Hermann Sudermann, Hugo von Hofmannstahl, Ferenc Molnár, George Bernard Shaw, Heinrich Mann, and others made important contributions. In 1909, Brahm began his 13-play Ibsen subscription cycle. Brahm's continuing focus on his favorite authors—especially Ibsen and Hauptmann—instigated criticism of his narrowness of vision.

As critic, director, and producer, Otto Brahm championed his own view of theatrical naturalism. He fostered plays of nonnaturalist writers as well, his principal goal being to find plays that honestly reflected life, whatever their aesthetic purposes. Writers of the symbolist and new romantic movements were staged under his guidance, and poetic fantasy was given a hearing as well. The theater world became familiar with the possibilities of ensemble-oriented, restrained, and lifelike acting, with perfectly articulated speech, through his stagings.

Further reading:

Claus, Horst. *The Theatre Director Otto Brahm.* Ann Arbor, Mich.: UMI Research Press, 1981.

Newmark, Maxim. *Otto Brahm, the Man and the Critic.* New York: G. E. Stechert, 1938.

Also: Cole and Chinoy, *Directors on Directing.*

BERTOLT BRECHT (1898–1956)

EUGEN BERTHOLD (later Bertolt) FRIEDRICH BRECHT was born in Augsburg, Germany, where his father worked at a paper company. Brecht briefly studied medicine at the University of Munich and settled in Munich after the war, becoming

known as an unconventional poet and playwright. He was fired from his first directorial job, Arnolt Bronnen's *Patricide* (1922), for a tryout group called the Junge Bühne when his methods proved unpopular.

Bertolt Brecht directing Kleist's The Broken Jug. *(1952)*
(Photo: Berliner Ensemble/Hainer Hill)

He picked up experience in Munich, Berlin, and Leipzig assisting others on his own plays, including *Baal* (1923), and codirecting Hans Henry Jahn's *Pastor Ephraim Magnus* (1923). He frequently codirected; only a small number of works list him as sole director. In 1924, he staged his and Lion Feuchtwanger's adaptation of Christopher Marlowe's *Edward II* (1924) in Munich. Among the elements he introduced, later associated with his "epic theater" theories, was the chalk-white makeup worn by the soldiers to suggest their fear and loneliness. The production was designed by Caspar Neher, who became a significant collaborator. In Brecht's adaptation of Marlowe's *Edward II*, Neher introduced such Brecht insignias as a half-curtain strung across the stage and many expository projections.

Berlin became Brecht's base when he staged a controversial revision of *Baal* (1926). Helene Weigel, Brecht's future wife and leading lady, was in it. Brecht also staged two Marielouise Fleisser plays, done anonymously for the Junge Bühne.

In 1927, Brecht first collaborated with composer Kurt Weill, beginning with *The Little Mahagonny*, a brief cantata (later expanded into *The Rise and Fall of the City of Mahagonny*) staged in a boxing ring at the Baden-Baden festival. Brecht achieved widespread success with his and Weill's musical satire on capitalism, *The Threepenny Opera* (1928); he participated (without credit) in its direction with Erich Engel.

Marxism had a powerful influence on Brecht, especially in view of Nazism's imminent threat, although he rarely interpreted Marx in a way that satisfied the Communist Party. Also influential were the complex epic theater stagings of Erwin Piscator, for whom Brecht worked in 1927. Brecht's politics were incorporated in a number of works that he wrote and directed, beginning with a series of short, propagandistic "teaching plays."

He and Engel codirected the unsuccessful *Happy End* (1929), but he rebounded with a staging of his 1926 Kiplingesque satire, *Man Is Man* (1931), at Berlin's Staatstheater. The Brechtian half-curtain and decorative minimalism were accompanied by grotesquerie in which two British soldiers were played on stilts and a third was thickly padded. Galy Gay was transformed from a milquetoast to a chalk-faced war machine covered with weapons, including a bayonet in his teeth.

Before Brecht fled into exile, he costaged an agit-prop adaptation of Maxim Gorky's novel about revolutionary consciousness, *The Mother* (1932), produced on temporary stages in working-class neighborhoods. Projections displayed slogans, scene titles, and photographs to punch the message across.

Brecht remained in exile for 14 years, residing in Europe and the U.S. He participated in the production of his plays by others in Paris, New York, Los Angeles, Copenhagen, and Stockholm. He also wrote the masterpieces that ultimately made him the century's premier German playwright. His most memorable collaboration was *The Life of Galileo Galilei*, premiered in Los Angeles (1947) before coming to Broadway (1948). Joseph Losey was the credited director, but most of the ideas stemmed from Brecht's close work with star Charles Laughton.

Brecht saw the theater as a didactic tool in the class struggle. He sought to alert audiences to the need for social change expressed in his work by introducing devices designed to break emotional involvement that might interfere with rational thought. These "anti-Aristotelian" methods were referred to as the "estrangement effect" (*Verfremdungseffekt*). He wanted familiar things to be viewed in a new light that would reveal their contradictions. The director must introduce scenic, technical, and acting methods that enhance the overt theatricality of the play and reduce emotional identification. But, as he admitted, his plays rarely achieved his theoretical estrangement. "Fun" was more important than academic expectations, and he struck a balance between thinking and feeling.

Brecht's postexile career began in 1948 when he staged his version of Sophocles' *Antigone* in Chur and Zurich, Switzerland. Creon was a Hitlerian dictator who hanged Antigone's brother for his resistance activities. Abstract choral masks on poles allowed for choreographic movement. Also in Zurich came Brecht's *Herr Puntila and His Man, Matti* (1948), although legal problems prevented him from taking directing credit.

By now Brecht had begun having hundreds of photos taken of his productions. Beginning with *Antigone*, this record, accompanied by notes, was intended for publication. Brecht's "model books" subsequently became vital tools for reconstructing or understanding his contributions. He liked to use rehearsal photos as references while he was still directing a production.

East Berlin's Deutsches Theater produced Brecht's *Mother Courage* (1949). This significant success— codirected with Engel—became Brecht's prototypical production, touring abroad and having a tremendous influence, even on Shakespearean staging. Exposition was projected onto the half-curtain, rough-hewn signs were used to identify locales, some characters wore masks, and the stage—suggesting the barren landscape of the Thirty Years War—was a nearly bare expanse backed by a cyclorama with the decor supplied largely by Courage's realistic sutler's wagon, pulled about by her offspring in the direction opposite to the revolve's movement. The highly selective gestures expressed the social and dramatic essence of each scene. The final image of the battered, stubborn Courage continuing to pull her wagon was indelible.

Mother Courage opened in the same month that Brecht, Weigel, and Engel cofounded East Berlin's subsidized Berliner Ensemble. After several productions staged or costaged by Brecht at other venues, chiefly the Deutsches, the company moved permanently to the Theater am Schiffbauerdamm. Here, Brecht provided his final masterwork, the folk-parable play, *The Caucasian Chalk Circle* (1954), which used half-masks, elaborate costumes, a combination of backgrounds resembling Chinese watercolors and Breugelesque groupings, an inventive use of the re-

Helene Weigel (c) in Mother Courage. *Directed by Bertolt Brecht. (1949) Pulling the wagon are Erwin Geshonnek and Angelika Hurcwicz.* (Photo: Berliner Ensemble/ Percy Paukschta)

volve, and a cast of 50 playing thrice as many roles. Brecht was in the midst of reviving *Galileo* when he died.

Brecht, knowledgable about all technical areas of theater, created one of the most influential theatrical styles of the century. His sets combined naturalism with symbolism. The highly selective props and furnishings were normally veristic and used-looking, while various background elements were shown only in impressionistic terms, including patently artifical moons and suns. His beautiful, predominantly earth-colored sets showed only what was essential; functional components were primary. As with all other contributing factors, the set added its own comment on the play, requiring designers who were socially, politically, and intellectually aware. Scene changes were often charmingly incorporated into the staging. Brechtian lighting was preponderantly white, bright, and sculptured but nonatmospheric. Before the Berliner Ensemble era, the instruments were exposed so as to reveal the lighting sources. At the Ensemble they were hidden because their presence had come to seem aesthetically intrusive.

Brecht employed a number of outstanding German composers, some of them, like Weill, Paul Dessau, Hanns Eisler, and Paul Hindemith, frequently. He participated closely in the composing and created many melodies that were refined by his composers. Music was especially useful as a critical commentator. Brecht's musicians often appeared on stage, as in Asian theater.

An important technique was what Brecht called the *gestus*, the actors' physicalization of their characters' relationship to their social circumstances; it had to be capable of being summed up in a simple sloganlike sentence or paragraph, such as "Pierpont Mauler Humbles Himself and Is Exalted." Brechtian acting stemmed from the actor's understanding of the character's social circumstances; the choice of movement, gesture, and vocalization was a response to those circumstances. Thus, in *Mother Courage,* Weigel had to say "Let the war be damned!," expressing her disgust for war—which had robbed her daughter of a chance to find a spouse—while simultaneously communicating her mercantile concerns, suggested by passing her hands over her goods. At other times, more spectacular thematic methods were used, as when a bizarre, carnival-like procession using a giant effigy of Galileo suggested Galileo's triumph over the church in *Galileo.* Lengthy rehearsal periods, sometimes lasting up to a year, permitted the time for the explorations required to uncover the social subtext.

Brechtian acting was conversationally realistic and earthy, and the characterizations three-dimensional, yet economical. In theory, the performer was to demonstrate his attitude to the character, to act, so to speak, in "quotes." Brecht wanted his characters to demonstrate the alterability of human nature, so his actors were to show that behavior stemmed from social and economic conditions. One rehearsal method used to get this effect had the actors speak in the third person and past tense, as well as reading the stage directions. However, Brecht did not wish to draw attention to such techniques in performance, which had to be seamless. Regardless of his pronouncements, players revealed that he had no objections to emotional identification, provided the actor did not forget the role's social dimensions or its place in the fabric of the play. Despite his pride in the actors' reality, Brecht wanted larger-than-life portrayals.

Brecht allowed even the visitors to his rehearsals to proffer comments. Following each day's rehearsal he met with his staff to explore their mutual feelings about the work accomplished and to map out the next day's goals. He sought to avoid a single, unified directorial vision in favor of a disjunctive style in which each of his collaborators displayed their own critical attitudes. Multiple viewpoints were to confront the spectator, not just the director's. Nevertheless, Brecht, the "Boss," invariably ended up dominating the process.

Brecht prepared by thoroughly studying the play for its social insights. He divided the story into those episodes that progressed the action and determined the relationship of each episode to the others. Rehearsals concentrated on polishing these independent episodes before they were linked in the final work.

Rehearsals often began with no specific setting planned in the hope that the design would evolve organically. Neher preferred to work this way and his sketches—based upon his attendance at rehearsals—often demonstrated groupings and characterizations that were adopted by the production.

Brecht liked to cast against type since he could thus use actors able to embody the social characteristics rather than the stereotypical physical aspects of their roles. He wanted his actors to be able to embody the complex and often contradictory aspects of their characters, not to concentrate on one side only.

Rehearsals—usually six days a week—began with a reading of the play that avoided overt "acting." Brecht analyzed the play for the company. Blocking—which occupied three months or more—ensued without "at-table" discussions (reserved for designers and codirectors). Rehearsals were pragmatic exercises dealing concretely with actor and technical problems. Actors were asked to demonstrate their ideas, not talk about them. Revisions were frequent up to and including dress rehearsals. Actors were given considerable freedom at first, Brecht being open to anything they could discover on their own. Rehearsals were a process of discovery. Gradually, he formalized the actors' choices, making each moment as impressive as a frame in a movie. He sometimes used famous paintings to inspire his compositions. The meaning of the picture had to be immediately clear and the sequence of events fully understood by the actors. Occasionally, he physically demonstrated what he wanted—with a slight exaggeration—or gave a line reading. He asked his actors not to work with scripts in hand and to improvise if necessary. They had to concentrate not on words but on telling the story.

Brecht was generally quiet and unobtrusive. He dressed in workman's attire and smoked smelly cigars. Rehearsals did not bog down when problems arose and the atmosphere was always light and friendly. On occasion, his temper blew, especially when there was a technical snafu. Timing was of extreme importance to him and he directed with a stopwatch. Rhythm was also pivotal, and toward the end he held a "marking" rehearsal in which the basic rhythm was emphasized by having the actors maintain it while moving rapidly through the play as in a silent film. Brecht stayed away from openings to take pressure off the cast.

Brecht was not only the greatest German playwright of the century, he was also one of Germany's best directors. Had he not been forced into exile, his career might have been studded with many more triumphs. His collaborative methods, epic theater theories, and use of the stage as a medium of social change were only some of his many memorable directorial contributions.

Further reading:

Fuegi, John. *The Essential Brecht*. Los Angeles: Hennessy and Ingalls, 1972.

————. *Bertolt Brecht: Chaos According to Plan*. Cambridge, England.: Cambridge University Press, 1987.

Weber, Carl. "Brecht as Director." *The Drama Review* 12 (Fall 1967).

Willett, John. *The Theatre of Bertolt Brecht: A Study from Eight Aspects*. London: Methuen, 1959.

Also: Leiter, *Stanislavsky to Barrault*.

BREUER, LEE (1937–   )

LEE BREUER (*né* Asher Leopold Breuer), whose father was an architect, was born in Philadelphia, Pennsylvania. The family settled in California when Breuer was 14. He attended UCLA, was active in film and theater, and won prizes for his existentialist-influenced dramas. In 1957, he met actress Ruth Malaczech, who became an integral part of his personal and artistic life.

They moved to San Francisco, where Breuer struggled to be a writer. Through Malaczech, Breuer directed a group of Actors Workshop actors in *The Caucasian Chalk Circle,* which so impressed Alan Schneider that he got him a salaried directing position with the company, for whom Breuer staged Samuel Beckett, Jean Genet, and Harold Pinter. He became familiar with the city's theatrical avant-gardists, among them JoAnne Akalaitis and Bill Raymond.

In 1965, Breuer and Malaczech traveled, ending up in Paris where they joined forces with Akalaitis (and her then husband, composer Philip Glass) and actors Frederick Neumann and David Warrilow. Breuer did some directing, most notably Beckett's *Play*, with Malaczech, Akalaitis, and David Warrilow, with music by Glass. During this period Breuer studied briefly at the Berliner Ensemble and the Polish Lab Theater.

In 1970, the Paris group formed a New York company called Mabou Mines, named for a Nova Scotia mining town Breuer never actually visited. Breuer was the *de facto* leader although, as the balance of power shifted, dissensions arose (especially between Akalaitis and Breuer, who had difficulty conceding authority in the interests of collaboration). Nevertheless, their work emerged from a collective spirit and blending of talents. One person was the designated director, and the others collaborated on the directing, producing, technical elements, design, and writing. Their methods became so well known, however, that Breuer—who is proud of his literary accomplishments, and considers his directing "tangential"—complained about the erroneous perception that his plays were written cooperatively.

Mabou Mines combined the visuals of conceptually oriented imagist theater with a psychologically penetrating, motivational acting method. Unlike imagists who use the actor as a merely decorative element, Breuer has always employed Stanislavskian methods, although he likes to add Brechtian "estrangement" devices in order to set up a dialectic and to help remind the audience that they are watching a performance.

Working under the ensemble's collaborative shelter, he evolved a piece over many months. When Breuer directed elsewhere, the lack of rehearsal time irritated him. With Mabou Mines productions, workshops were given in different venues until a final version was presented. Most pieces—kept alive by foreign and domestic tours—remained in the repertory. At first, they normally played in museums, galleries, or similar spaces.

Mabou Mines, based in New York's Soho, was in contact with the best "postmodern" painting and sculpture talents, as reflected in their designs. Breuer was fascinated by technical gadgetry. Some of his pieces—structurally influenced by films (particularly Jean Luc Godard's)—blended video, mirrors, sculpture, painting, lights, puppetry, ritualistic and choreographic movement, and amplified sound (including the use of body mikes).

The company made its first impact with a series of Breuer-written and -directed works called "animations." *The Red Horse Animation* (1970), *The B.*

Beaver Animation (1975), and *The Shaggy Dog Animation* (1978), in each of which the central characters are animals, provided material for the evolution of a performance style that moved from the largely physical *Red Horse* to the densely verbal methods of the later pieces. The animals are metaphors representing the plight of contemporary human beings, and their natures are linked to aspects of human psychology, especially those relating to the artist's creative problems. They contain a largely autobiographical streak, and the trilogy has resonances that convey themes and characters from piece to piece.

Harking back to Brecht's epic style, Breuer has said that he is chiefly concerned in exploring narrative modes; his nonlinear texts move freely among the past, present, and future; containing little dialogue, they are alive with literary mannerisms and depend on a variety of choral and monologue techniques. The animations are essentially plotless and conflictless; their literary richness, comic surprises, and poetic tone (Breuer calls some works "performance poems") suggest a variety of influences.

Breuer's Obie-winning *Shaggy Dog* was the best received animation; it was also the longest and most technically sophisticated. Centered on the dog, Rose, it employed amplified music and speech, a complex choral presentation of Rose's words, and, in addition to human actors, expressive three-quarters-life-size *bunraku*-like puppets, a significant influence on Breuer. (He received a 1983 grant to study in Japan.) *Shaggy Dog* is structured like a traditional shaggy-dog story to convey the enactment of a "Dear John" letter written by Rose to her former lover/master from whom she has finally achieved liberation—making the piece a tract about male-female power relationships. Set against a huge radio frequency band, the style varied according to where the needle happened to land—soap opera, rock and roll, country-western, Latin, jazz, etc.

Some of Breuer's work has been minimalist-conceptualist, as for example, *Red Horse*, which used three plainly dressed actors standing and lying on a stage backed only by wooden planks as they formed and reformed themselves into abstract and recognizable patterns suggestive of a horse and rider. Breuer's *Prelude to Death in Venice* (1979) used a single actor manipulating an alter-ego puppet and employing two adjoining phone booths.

Equally valuable minimalist work was represented by the three Beckett pieces (*Play* in 1971, *Come and Go* in 1971, and *The Lost Ones* in 1974). In the

Bill Raymond in Prelude to Death in Venice. *Directed by Lee Breuer. (1979)*   (Photo: Carol Rosegg)

latter Warrilow brought the nontheatrical script to startling life as, with surgical instruments, he manipulated many tiny figures (spectators were given opera glasses to help see them) in a miniature vision of Beckett's microcosmic, cylindrical universe of lost souls. By means of lighting, Warrilow and the audience were then transformed into the lost souls and the cylindrical theater became Beckett's hell.

Equally minimalist, but more technologically complex, was his dreamlike *Hajj* (1982), an hour-long, one-woman journey into herself using mirrors and unusual closed-circuit and prerecorded video techniques to project changing images of her face—past and present—as she put on makeup while speaking (in a complexly amplified and multiplied score) with her back to the audience.

Breuer is just as noted for his more elaborate presentations, beginning with his *The Saint and the Football Players* (1973). Like many other Breuer works, it envisions his concern with an American mythos, here isolated in the aesthetics of football. It included a regulation-sized team of 11 fully equipped players and a Glass score—substituting musical signals for those of the quarterback—in a choreographic piece about making yardage. A longer version was staged on a football field lit by truck lights, with music coming from Volkswagen radios.

An eclectic assortment of music, traditional and contemporary, avant-garde and popular, American and foreign, has played an increasingly important role; after Glass, Breuer's most important composer has been Bob Telson. Breuer's employment of music from diverse cultures, his use of exotic theatrical techniques, notably Asian, and his selection of iconographic pop culture features derives from his desire to abandon imitation of European forms and to create a crosscultural "American classicism."

One of his favorite styles is rhythm and blues, which inspired his and Telson's 20-minute "doo-wop" opera *Sister Suzie Cinema* (1980) set in a movie theater balcony and performed by an a capella black singing group expressing their love for the goddesses of the silver screen. His greatest achievement in the use of black-originated music is *The Gospel at Colonus* (1983), a brilliant adaptation of Sophocles' *Oedipus at Colonus* into a spectacular, 60-performer gospel music presentation performed as if in a Pentecostal church. It gave each main character its own chorus backup, and had Oedipus played by blind gospel singer-pianist, Clarence Fountain, while his chorus was composed of a blind quintet, the Five Blind Boys. Breuer's aim was to find a contemporary correlative to the ecstatic, semireligious experience of seeing a play in ancient Greece. His production, partly inspired by *kabuki*, even used *hanamichi*-like runways, although not through the audience. This piece, originally conceived to accompany *Sister Suzie*, came to Broadway in 1988.

Since 1980, Breuer has worked both with Mabou Mines and independently (he has also cochaired the directing program at Yale); his first independent venture was an iconoclastic staging at the American Repertory Theater in Cambridge, Massachusetts, of Frank Wedekind's "Lulu" plays, compressed by Michael Feingold into a single evening called *Lulu*. In his radically Americanized approach, the man-eating Lulu was turned into a black punk rock star, the play was performed as if it were a movie being dubbed in a postsynch studio, and it ended in the film *Psycho*'s Bates Motel. The theater lost many offended subscribers.

Time constraints damaged *Lulu* and Breuer's next, equally disastrous, outside venture, his Central Park version of *The Tempest* (1981), inspired by American mythic images. It was set in Disneyland, made near-continual use of a revolve, had a Mae West-like

Trinculo, dressed the shipwrecked characters like white-suited mobsters, employed five children as Ariel's voice, used Latin music, and so on.

His very ambitious recent works again met with resistance. *Lear* (New York version, 1990) used Mabou Mines actors and began its development in 1987. It was Breuer's remythologized version of *King Lear*, set among beer-swilling Southerners in Smyrna, Georgia, in the conservative late 1950s (seen as a parallel to the eighties), reversed all the roles' genders, and made the Fool a transvestite. Breuer hoped to provide a view of sexual politics by seeing traditional male displays of aggression as expressed in female characters, thus demonstrating that violence results not from gender but from power. He also examined racial attitudes in making Gloucester—the matriarchal Lear's devoted servant—and her legitimate daughter black, but the bastard white. A dog house, chicken coop, and pink Cadillac were important elements in this "Sam Shepardish" milieu, and everyone wore face mikes to amplify their slightest whispers.

Breuer's most extravagant work was his *The Warrior Ant* (1988), coproduced with Mabou Mines and in the making since 1984. Also called the *Insectiad*, Breuer intended it as a 12-part, three-evening presentation, although it remains a work-in-progress that has been seen in two installments. Before the first one was given a full presentation in Brooklyn, it had gone through numerous partial showings at a variety of venues. The work, which satirized themes in Plato, Virgil, Beckett, and Dante, incorporated over 100 performers, a Telson score played by African, Latin, Caribbean, and American groups, three authentic *bunraku* puppeteers, an aerialist, break dancers, belly dancers, Mabou Mines actors, and so on. Its fantastical story comments on the relationship of the individual human to his culture through the metaphor of a samurai drone-ant's relationship to his. Human and nonhuman puppet characters (the samurai ant was a traditional *bunraku* puppet, the others were specially built) had their words spoken by visible actors. Unusually vivid was the birth of the samurai ant from the belly of an 18-foot-high queen ant puppet with movable legs, wings, and antennae.

In 1992, another installment was presented at an Off-Broadway theater. Dubbed the *Ma Ha Bhar ANT A* (labeled Part 7C of the cycle), this political satire (striking out at, among other targets, the antiart Washington establishment, nonprofit leftwingers, and academia) employed the services of an authentic

Balinese shadow puppet master. The puppets were a visual delight.

Breuer is an impulsive director who operates with tremendous enthusiasm when carried away by his ideas. Susan Cole observed his *Warrior Ant* rehearsals, and found him always on the move, using vivid body language to demonstrate his desires. He allowed creative input by all concerned while nonetheless coordinating it to achieve his evershifting vision of the result. Breuer constantly rehearsed material and then questioned its validity, regardless of his initial enthusiasm. When he is the author, he does not hesitate to do rewrites on the spot. Restless and never satisfied, he continues to improve on a work even after it has opened.

Lee Breuer has many loyal acolytes, but just as many who find his volubility, manic energy, and apparent disorganization hard to take. His most recent work has not pleased the critical mainstream (Breuer attributes this to self-interest among the cultural elite). Although he said he would not direct

again, he offered *Peter Pan and Wendy* (called "act 1 of a work-in-progress," 1991), an adaptation of James M. Barrie's book by Liza Lorwin, and a year later, his addition to the *Insectiad*.

Further reading:

Breuer, Lee. "Lee Breuer on Interculturalism." Interview with Gabrielle Cody. *Performing Art Journal* 11/12 (1989).

Neely, Kent. "Lee Breuer's Theatrical Technique: From *The Animations* to *Gospel at Colonus.*" *Journal of Dramatic Theory and Criticism* 3 (Spring 1989).

Shewey, Don. "The Many Voices of Mabou Mines." *American Theatre* 1 (June 1984).

Wetzsteon, Ross. "Wild Man of the American Theatre." *Village Voice*, May 19, 1987; May 26, 1987.

Also: Cole, *Directors in Rehearsal*; Gontarski in King, *Contemporary American Theatre*; Savran, *In Their Own Words*.

BROOK, PETER (1925–   )

PETER STEPHEN PAUL BROOK was born in London, England, to immigrant Russian scientists. Before he graduated, at 19, from Oxford University, he established his own amateur theater, the Torch. Brook's first professional production was Jean Cocteau's *The Infernal Machine* (1945). Not long after, he joined the Birmingham Repertory Theater, where

Peter Brook rehearsing The Mahabharata *in Brooklyn. (1987)* (Photo: Martha Swope)

his first mounting was George Bernard Shaw's *Man and Superman* (1945). Stratford's Shakespeare Memorial Theater enjoyed Brook's services in 1946, among his offerings being a Watteau-inspired *Love's Labour's Lost* and a passionate *Romeo and Juliet* with controversial textual alterations. London saw Brook's work in various modern plays, including several by Jean-Paul Sartre. In 1948, he began directing operas. He scored a West End success with Howard Richardson and William Berney's folk-play, *Dark of the Moon* (1949). In 1950, Brook offered notable productions of Jean Anouilh and André Roussin as well as a notable *Measure for Measure* with his own Bosch- and Breugel-inspired sets and costumes.

Brook, who is fluent in French, staged plays in Brussels, Paris, and New York, in addition to London and Stratford-upon-Avon. His modern offerings, many with great stars, included Christopher Fry's *The Dark Is Light Enough* (1954), Truman Capote and Harold Arlen's Broadway musical *House of Flowers* (1954), Anouilh's *The Lark* (1955), T. S. Eliot's *The Family Reunion* (1956), Friedrich Dürrenmatt's *The Visit* (1958), an adaptation of the French musical *Irma la Douce* (1959), and Anouilh's *The Fighting Cock* (1959). There were such classics as *Venice Preserv'd* (1953), *Titus Andronicus* (1955), *Hamlet* (1955), and *The Tempest* (1957). *Titus*, his most famous revival of the period, starred Laurence Olivier and Vivien Leigh, and employed Brook's own designs and "concrete music" (electronic music composed of musical and other sounds). He evoked the grisly play's power by judicious adaptation and ritualistic devices: Lavinia's hacked-off hands were scarlet ribbons.

Jean Genet's *The Balcony* (1960) was a transitional piece. Brook's work became more and more experimental. In 1961, he became one of a triumvirate heading Stratford's Royal Shakespeare Company (RSC). A selective list of his memorable RSC work might include his existentialist, Beckettian *King Lear* (1962), done in a dispassionate Brecht-like fashion; an imaginatively stripped-down Artaudian staging of Genet's epic-proportioned *The Screens* (1964); Peter Weiss's *Marat/Sade* (1964); the collaboratively created, anti-Vietnam War, Living Newspaper, *US* (1966); a ritualistic, modern-dress version of Seneca's *Oedipus* (1968); *The Tempest* (1968), done in an environmentally experimental production with an internationally diverse cast, and a rearranged collagelike text; and a landmark *A Midsummer Night's Dream* (1970).

During the decade he helped lead the RSC's Theater of Cruelty workshops (1964). These laid the foundation for his later collaborative and improvisational activities. He also experimented with discovering a ritual-based language of sound and movement.

Marat/Sade combined techniques of Antonin Artaud and Bertolt Brecht to both play upon and distance the spectators' emotions. Set in a French insane asylum in 1808 and essentially a philosophical and political play-within-a-play debate, the play was turned into a phantasmagoria that conveyed a frighteningly real spectrum of madness. An abundant use was made of pantomimic expression, such as when Charlotte Corday whipped the Marquis de Sade by lashing him with her long hair. At the conclusion, the rioting inmates seemed intent on taking over the auditorium.

Brook's *Dream*, while faithfully rendering Shakespeare's words, removed its traditional romantic veneer and placed it in a white box topped by a gallery reached by slender ladders. Bright colors adorned the satin costumes, and numerous circus images infiltrated the action, including having the fantastical personnages perform while seated on trapezes. The forest was suggested by large metal coils suspended by fairies with fishing polelike props. Brook explored the play's sensual underside, and moments of striking eroticism were occasionally employed.

In 1970, Brook established the subsidized International Center for Theater Research (ICTR) in Paris. ICTR is dedicated to the creation of an internationally mixed company working collaboratively toward the creation of a universal theater language. Their first significant offering was the group-created *Orghast* (1971), presented at an Iranian arts festival, and performed in a language created from ancient Greek, Latin, and Avestan, designed to provoke emotional responses when used as sound and incantation rather than for literal meaning. The ritualistic production, which dealt with various ancient myths, was given amid spectacular surroundings of hills and ancient tombs, and at one point required the audience to move from one locale to another.

Other noteworthy activity included a 1972 tour of African villages, with the ICTR company laying down a carpet in village squares and performing improvisationally in an effort to discover the theater's fundamental nature; the development of *The Conference of the Birds*, a performance based on an allegorical Sufi poem; continued work on *Conference* in America (1973; a more formalized version emerged in 1979); an idiosyncratic, frequently acrobatic, politically pointed adaptation of *Timon of Athens* (1974), performed at Brook's renovated 500-seat theater, the Bouffes du Nord; *The IK* (1975), inspired by an anthropological study of a Ugandan tribe, and done in "poor theatre" style; *Ubu* (1977), a conflation of four texts by Alfred Jarry; the brief, group-created allegorical fable, *The Bone* (1977); a chamber-style *Antony and Cleopatra* (1978) for the RSC; and a modern-dress, ICTR *Measure for Measure* (1978).

Brook's Paris productions were stripped to bare essentials, using white light and few illusionistic props (many were "found" objects) or scenic units, with audiences and actors in intimate proximity to one another. Much of the work was shown on foreign tours.

In the 1980s and early 1990s, Brook provided a hit revival of François Billetdoux's *Tchin-Tchin* (1983) in Paris; an intermissionless *The Cherry Orchard* (1981; in French but seven years later shown abroad in English) at the Bouffes, with period costumes, acting in the house and on stage, and conventional sets replaced by carpets, cushions, and screens; a theater-oriented, hour-and-20-minute, ritualistic adaptation of Georges Bizet's *Carmen* (1981) that pared the orchestra down to a small onstage ensemble, used an alternating sequence of singers, and utilized a bullringlike sceneryless set; an adaptation of the anonymous Indian epic, *The Mahabharata* (1985);

The Mahabharata. *Directed by Peter Brook. (1985)*   (Photo: Martha Swope)

his third *The Tempest* (1991), and two 1992–1993 season pieces—the operatic *Impressions of Pelleas*, by Claude Debussy, and *The Man Who*, which Jean-Claude Carrière scripted from improvisations developed by a four-member company under Brook and Marie-Hélène Estienne's supervision.

The Tempest was a comically rich, whimsically dreamlike production given a minimalist realization, with the storm-tossed ship evoked by shouting actors manipulating bamboo sticks. Ariel and Prospero were played by black Africans, the former heavyset, and Caliban by a dwarflike, feral, white boy. The *Village Voice* reported:

> Everything is suggestion, everything is whimsy; butterflies swing on sticks carried by fairies; clothes for the two drunken butlers are thrown in from the wings; forest sounds are evoked by music; Miranda's wedding gown is a gauze veil; the "invisible" fairies play with sandpiles, hoops, and ropes to irritate the lost crew;

> characters jump, skip, romp in [a] sandbox, and climb the ladders at the side of the theatre.

Brook's major creation was his extraordinary, nine-hour *The Mahabharata* (1985), developed over a 10-year period. Within a fundamentally bare space Brook introduced inventive, ritualistic elements, including water and fire effects. Brook underscored the thematic threads concerning human conflict that made the work philosophically appropriate to the contemporary world. Originally seen at the Bouffes, it played on many other stages, including a limestone quarry. Its movement was suggested by Oriental martial arts and theater. Props served multiple purposes, and symbolic devices like using large, rolling wheels to represent chariots were common. Much of the music, played onstage, was improvised.

Brook's diverse career ranges from imaginatively staged but straightforward productions to expressions of the most advanced ideas, sometimes for new works and sometimes for familiar ones. He constantly seeks answers to basic questions concerning the nature of theater. He has employed a far-flung assortment of international methods, including commedia, nō, Living Newspaper, circus, music hall, and improvisation. His work has sought to define the theater's parameters and discover the nature of the audience-actor relationship. Since the 1960s he has increasingly preferred a three-quarters round deployment with many spectators, as at the Bouffes, on the same level as the actors, and with the occasional incursion of the players into the auditorium or with the audience allowed to invade the acting space. On several occasions he has worked in spectacular, natural locales.

When staging Shakespeare, he often has cut, added words, and rearranged bits and pieces, always in the interests of clarification; he believes that one may alter plays that will continue to thrive regardless. His earlier productions stemmed from visual concerns, but his later ones were preoccupied with ideas. Consequently, his selections are now based primarily on contemporary significance, although he disagrees with "using" a play to the detriment of its other values. He prefers to avoid pinning a play down with period costumes, and uses whatever eclectic, but unified, blend can best express its ideas.

Because he has often designed his own productions, and written their music, Brook exemplifies Gordon Craig's ideal of a total theater artist. Brook, however, has relied increasingly on such designers as Sally Jacobs and Chloé Obolensky for his innovative style. He prefers flexible designers who can alter their conceptions during rehearsals, which is probably one reason for the minimalism of so much of his work, in that revisions do not require major conceptual overhauls.

Equally striking is the musical and sound accompaniment to a Brook production, which may draw upon the widest range of sources—avant-garde, pop, and classic. Asian influences are strong. Many productions employed the imaginative creations of Richard Peaslee and Toshi Tsuchitori, who worked collaboratively with the actors, with whom they often shared the stage.

Brook favors open-ended rehearsal periods, and even after a play has opened keeps developing it, sometimes for years. He worked from six to eight weeks on a play with the RSC, but up to a year with the ICTR. Although he began his career by detailed preplanning, even using models and tiny figures, he soon abandoned that method and allowed his ideas to crosspollinate with those of the actors. He worked

in a trial-and-error manner toward a strongly felt but vaguely defined result (a "formless hunch").

Brook often discusses a point at length, but trusts that, in the long run, the actors know the answer better than he. He keeps experimenting, chipping away at the stone of the play to find the form revealed within. A wide range of techniques are used, from verbal explanations to improvisations, a specialty. His charisma and articulate expression of his thoughts work wonders, and he is noted for his ability to squeeze good performances from unlikely sources. Brook's placidity is widely acknowledged, but he is known as well for rarely complimenting his players. Although his perfectionism irks some actors, many praise him for leading them to a higher consciousness in understanding what it is to be human.

Brook seeks actors with "open" temperaments like his own, those who will constantly develop and improve their findings. He likes to cast against type and unconventionally. His ICTR casting has consistently been multinational and multiracial, with little concern for the ethnic origins of the dramatis personae.

Whereas in his early period he followed the usual pattern of a cast reading, analytic interjections, and blocking sessions, for over two decades most Brook rehearsals have begun with the actors seated in a circle on the floor and with exercises and discussion taking the place of reading and blocking. Company research into a play's background is essential, and there is a considerable amount of reading and perusal of visual aids. Also frequent is training in a production's special requirements, such as circus techniques for *A Midsummer Night's Dream*.

Brook prefers improvisations as a way to discover truths that prevent actors from being phoney. His exercises are multifarious; in rehearsing Seneca's *Oedipus*, an actor was asked to portray a snake in an imaginary situation, the goal being to enhance physical expressiveness by communicating through changing body rhythms. He draws upon a wide variety of breathing, vocal, and physical exercises culled from numerous disciplines; t'ai chi chuan and Oriental stick exercises, for example, have been used frequently. His company often provides material for further investigation from their multicultural background. The actors may play other actors' roles as a way of strengthening the ensemble.

Brook is the leading British director of the post-1950 period. He is admired, among other things, for his collaborative creativity, for his eclecticism, for his experimentation in uncovering the theater's roots and premises, for his devotion to theatrical interculturalism, and for some of the most unorthodox theatrical conceptions of the century.

Further reading:

Brook, Peter. *The Empty Space.* New York: Avon, 1968.
————. *The Shifting Point: 1946–1987.* New York: Harper and Row, 1987.
Heilpern, John. *Conference of the Birds: The Story of Peter Brook in Africa.* Rev. ed. New York: Methuen, 1989.
Trewin, J. C. *Peter Brook: A Biography.* London: Macdonald, 1971.
Williams, David, comp. *Peter Brook: A Theatrical Casebook.* London: Methuen, 1988.
Also: Croyden, *Lunatics, Lovers and Poets;* Innes, *Holy Theatre;* Leiter, *From Belasco to Brook.*

ARVIN BROWN (1940–   )

ARVIN BROWN was born in Los Angeles, where his father was a hardware contractor. He attended Stanford University, intending to be a writer. After graduating in 1961, Brown studied on a Fulbright at the University of Bristol, England, where, with no previous theatrical experience, he successfully directed August Strindberg's *The Stronger.* Brown loved the collaborative experience of directing; moreover, his writing background had taught him how to appreciate plays. As he told Lee Alan Morrow and Frank Pike, "I understood about reading for motivation, for undercurrents, for subtext, for language as a reflection of character, for atmosphere." After obtaining a master's from Harvard in 1963, he entered the Yale School of Drama.

New Haven, already home to the Yale Repertory Theater, became the site in 1965 of the Long Wharf Theater, a resident theater begun in a former meat market warehouse. Brown was hired to run the children's company, but before the first season had ended made his professional directing debut with Eugene O'Neill's *Long Day's Journey into Night* (1966), starring Mildred Dunnock and Frank Langella. In 1967, Brown became the artistic director, a position he has held ever since.

It was initially feared that the Long Wharf could not compete with the Yale Rep, but Brown demonstrated that New Haven could support two major theaters. For years, Long Wharf's seasons were largely devoted to what Brown calls "chamber theater," meaning small-cast, realistic plays given strongly acted, essentially traditional productions, while Yale tended to emphasize more experimental projects emphasizing directorial virtuosity.

The Long Wharf employs a 484-seat thrust-stage and a 199-seat workshop theater (opened in 1978). Brown has managed to keep the Long Wharf thriving, not only because of local patronage but because no other regional director has moved so many shows to Broadway and Off-Broadway. Brown's staging of Arthur Miller's *All My Sons* (1987) won a Tony as best revival.

Brown, who employs other directors to fill out his seasons, has been prolific, doing from two to four or five plays a season, including occasional jobs elsewhere, in cities such as New York. It has been his good fortune that the plays he chooses are usually appreciated by his audiences; he insists that he makes his selections to please himself before considering whether an audience will like them too. His choices range from revivals to originals, and he and his guest directors have made a significant impact by American premieres of a number of fine European, especially British, plays. Avant-gardism has been conspicuously absent.

Apart from John Webster's *The Duchess of Malfi* (1969), Brown has left the older or more unusual classics alone and concentrated on well-known plays by such modern authors as O'Neill, Miller, Anton Chekhov, George Bernard Shaw, Slawomir Mrozek, Tennessee Williams, Jean Anouilh, Henrik Ibsen, Noel Coward, George S. Kaufman and Moss Hart, Kaufman and Edna Ferber, Maxwell Anderson and Laurence Stallings, Sean O'Casey, Lillian Hellman, Harold Brighouse, Philip Barry, Edward Albee, James Goldman, James Kirkland, Thornton Wilder, Harley Granville-Barker, David Mamet, and William Inge. Best known of his revivals are those played in New York, most of them being transfers, but a couple were produced independently. Among them are Mamet's *American Buffalo* (1980; 1981; 1983); O'Neill's *Long Day's Journey into Night* (1972) and *Ah! Wilderness* (1976; 1988); Miller's *All My Sons* (1986) and *A View from the Bridge* (1983); Hellman's *Watch on the Rhine* (1980); and a double bill of Miller's *A Memory of Two Mondays* and Williams's *27 Wagons Full of Cotton* (1976), with Meryl Streep.

Brown's first new play was Thomas Murphy's *A Whistle in the Dark*, an excellently performed English play that transferred to Off-Broadway. He subsequently staged important premieres of Murphy's *On the Inside* and Murphy and Noel O'Donaghue's *On the Outside* (1976), Peter Nichols's *Forget-Me-Not Lane* (1973) and *The National Health* (1974)—as well as separate revivals (the second for Broadway) of Nichols's *A Day in the Death of Joe Egg* (1980, 1985)—Bernice Ruben's *I Sent a Letter to My Love* (1978), and David Edgar's *Mary Barnes* (1980). D. H. Lawrence's mostly forgotten *The Widowing of Mrs. Holroyd*, never staged before in America, proved a deft drama in 1974.

American plays premiered by Brown include Robert Anderson's *Solitaire/Double Solitaire* (1971), which moved to Broadway from the Long Wharf, and *Free and Clear* (1983); Richard Venture's *You're Too Tall, But Come Back in Two Weeks* (1975); Arthur Miller's *The Archbishop's Ceiling* (1977), produced in Washington, D.C.; Leigh Curran's *The Lunch Girls* (1977); Conrad Bromberg's *Two Brothers* (1978); Sherman Yellen's *Strangers*, produced on Broadway (1979); the full-length version of Shirley Lauro's one-act, *Open Admission* (1982); Rod Serling's stage version of his famous TV script, *Requiem for a Heavyweight*, transferred to Broadway (1984); Joe Cacaci's *Self Defense* (1987), transferred from New Haven to Off-Broadway; Austin Pendleton's *Booth is Back* (1990); Ira Lewis's *Chinese Coffee* (1992), starring Al Pacino and produced on Broadway; and Jonathan Tolin's *Twilight of the Golds* (1993), which opened in Washington, D.C., and played elsewhere before arriving on Broadway to weak reviews. A Canadian play, Joanna Glass's *Artichoke*, premiered in 1975. In 1970, Brown also made an impact with two important Maxim Gorky plays given their English-language debuts at the Long Wharf, *Yegor Bulichov* and *Country People*. Moreover, he has directed for TV, made a film, and mounted several operas and musicals, including *Regina* (1988), *Lost in the Stars* (1986), *Daarlin' Juno* (1976), and another Peter Nichols work, *Privates on Parade* (1979). A measure of Brown's stature is his having been invited to direct a dramatization of Amy Tan's novel, *The Joy Luck Club*, in Shanghai for the Shanghai People's Art Threatre (1993).

Brown's productions are noted for their realism, lack of conceptual fireworks, and powerful ensembles. When reading a new play, he looks for it to be honest, not overtly literary, and to come "right from the writer's gut" (quoted in Morrow and Pike). About the furthest he has gone in adapting a play is

Nichols's A Day in the Death of Joe Egg. *Directed by Arvin Brown. (1985) Clockwise from left: Margaret Hilton, John Tillinger, Joanna Gleason, Stockard Channing, and Tenney Walsh.*   (Photo: Martha Swope)

to change the locale from England to America, as he did on Brighouse's *Hobson's Choice* (1977) and Granville-Barker's *The Voysey Inheritance* (1990).

The Long Wharf's size is perfect for creating the kind of small-scale intimacy he believes necessary to evoke theatrical truth. Brown rarely reaches for striking theatricalism. His production of *Joe Egg*, in which the parents of a spastic child cope with their tragedy by breaking into fantasy music hall bits, was notable for his having detheatricalized these interruptions to make them more reflective of the couple's actual behavior. This preference for realism, considered by some a limitation, has been belied by his increasing interest in musicals and cinematically structured plays, a manifestation of his desire to become more stylistically eclectic. Regarding musicals, he wishes to place realistic behavior in larger-than-life theatrical contexts from which it is normally absent.

Brown feels he has done his job best when he has been most invisible. He told David W. Grogan,

I . . . feel the greatest compliment . . . is when people say my work looks undirected, in the best sense of the word. I love creating a sense of reality onstage that doesn't seem to have a ringmaster behind it. When that happens the play is alive.

Nevertheless, he manages to bring considerable insights to his work, as indicated by the way his version of *American Buffalo* elicited much more of its comic qualities than had been true of the original staging by Ulu Grosbard.

Because of his preoccupation with plays about characters and their relationships, and his belief that other media are superior to theater in expression of ideas, Brown considers his an actor's theater. He told Janice Paran and Joel Schechter, "What I believe the theater can do is flesh out ideas in human terms and relationship terms." One of the few overtly political plays he has done is Larry Kramer's *The Normal Heart* (1985), about AIDS.

Because of New Haven's proximity to New York, top stars often come to the Long Wharf, and there are others who belong to a sort of floating but nonpermanent repertory company. Among the many who have appeared in numerous Brown productions is Joyce Ebert, Brown's wife. A Brown production is often marked by riveting ensemble performances, although several of his works have profited from brilliant star turns. Glenn Loney claimed that Brown has a nose for talent and "a real gift for gathering about him players who seem to perform with abilities they only hinted at previously."

Before rehearsals commence, Brown reads the play over and over and does extensive research on its social and historical background. When he first began directing, he prepared beforehand with tiny figures, but failed to consider the motivations behind the moves. When Mildred Dunnock asked the reason for her blocking, he realized the inadequacy of his method and abandoned it for one that—stemming from his affection for actors—relied on intuitive procedures and allowed his company creative freedom in a nurturing atmosphere. Brown, who has himself never acted professionaly, hopes to draw the part out of the actor, rather than forcing the part on him. Wherever possible, Brown tries to uncover those features of a character that the actor shares, and then assists him in bringing these out. Actors find him trusting, supportive, sensitive, and controlled. At times, however, Brown will call upon

specific means to stimulate an actor as when, in order to get Geraldine Fitzgerald (as Mary Tyrone) worked up to a proper pitch at a climactic moment in the New York version of *Long Day's Journey*, he chased her around a table; the actress said that this produced feelings of hysteria and entrapment.

Over the years, Brown has become progressively freer and now enters a rehearsal with few preconceptions. Whereas he used to sit for an hour before rehearsals studying the upcoming scene, he now does so only sporadically. "That hour that I sit alone with the script, forming judgments, might prevent me from seeing a moment of fresh discovery," he told Arthur Bartow. Brown prefers to be totally immersed in the play and its meaning and then to let the actors reveal how they are going to realize his ideas.

A familiar Brown touch is his practice of never ending rehearsals on a negative note, but always finding something positive to say to shore up potential losses of confidence. He must be careful to find the right balance of praise; some actors are as uncomfortable with compliments as with criticism.

First rehearsals are usually a reading of the play, an explanation of the visuals, and a few words about his aims. Brown quickly begins his blocking, avoiding "at table" sessions and lengthy discussions. The only kind of questions he encourages are those related to problems of emotional understanding. He wants actors to trust their instincts, not their intellects. His lack of acting experience prevents him from demonstrating and forces him to find other ways to help actors over rough spots.

Being one who works often with new dramas, Brown collaborates closely with writers, but realizes that he must protect actors from those whose desire for results threatens to disrupt the creative process. The playwright's presence is tolerated to that point at which the actors begin their deepest explorations; he is then asked not to attend rehearsals for a week so that the cast, liberated by the writer's absence, can freely question a scene's viability. When a dramaturgic problem arises, the author may be asked to go home for several days, discover the difficulty by writing down everything that he knows about the scene, and then return so that Brown and he can fix the problem together.

Lighting designer Ron Wallace has been Brown's longest design collaborator, having worked with him from *Long Day's Journey* on. Their working relationship is so close that, after discussing conceptual ideas at the beginning of a project, Brown leaves the designer to work around him and then makes only minor adjustments before the play opens.

Joyce Ebert and Len Cariou in O'Neill's A Touch of the Poet. *Directed by Arvin Brown. (1992)* (Photo: Long Wharf Theater/T. Charles Erickson)

Brown's concepts are often phrased in images borrowed from painting, a formative influence on his visual style. One of his most interesting design-related ideas is to work against a script's most obvious tone. Instead of underlining a play's claustrophibia with a claustrophobic set, he might choose a con-

trasting feeling, allowing the play's life to emerge from the actors' expression of the dramatic world.

Julius Novick once described Arvin Brown as the kind of man who does not "stand out in a crowd; there is nothing show-bizzy about him. His manner is calm, relaxed, pleasantly ordinary." There is nothing ordinary, however, about Brown's success in sustaining the Long Wharf for over 25 years, his record of Broadway transfers, his establishment of a home for new plays and American premieres of foreign ones, his commitment to serving the author at the expense of directorial bulldozing, and his talent for giving outstanding realizations to the type of plays in which he has specialized.

Further reading:

Grogan, David W. "Leading Man of the Long Wharf." *Connecticut's Finest* (Autumn 1988).

Loney, Glenn M. "Long Wharf Theater." *Players* 45 (June/July 1970).

Novick, Julius. "He Trusts Plays, He Trusts Actors." *New York Times* October 12, 1975.

Paran, Janice, and Joel Schechter. "Long Wharf: An Interview with Arvin Brown." *Theatre* 10 (Summer 1979).

Also: Bartow, *Director's Voice*; Morrow and Pike, *Creating Theatre*; Ziegler, *Regional Theatre*.

JOSEPH CHAIKIN (1935–   )

JOSEPH CHAIKIN was born in Brooklyn, New York; his immigrant father was a Hebrew scholar. Chaikin was plagued by a chronically weak heart from childhood on. At one point, he spent two years in a Florida charity clinic. After the family moved to Des Moines, Iowa, Chaikin acted in amateur theater, an interest he pursued at Drake University before leaving in 1955 for a New York acting career. Chaikin helped found a short-lived, ensemble-oriented group, the Harlequin Players, for whom he directed—at a Lower East Side loft—a well-received bill of Sean O'Casey's *Bedtime Story* and Edna St. Vincent Millay's *Aria da Capo* (1957).

In 1959, he joined Judith Malina and Julian Beck's politically committed Living Theater, where he gained notice as an actor, turned against commercial theater, and grew convinced of the need for theater's social and political engagement.

While still with the Living Theater, he began—in 1963—his own laboratory, hoping to develop an

ensemble method, but circumstances prevented this work from going too far. Chaikin then joined a workshop started by a group of acting teacher Nola Chilton's students, who were looking to continue their studies after Chilton emigrated to Israel. The group engaged in exercises and improvisations, with no specific leader at first; Chaikin's investigations into nonnaturalistic theater, however, diverged from their other work. Those who disagreed with his nondogmatic, flexible, and experimental ideas departed. The remaining core called themselves the Open Theater in view of their receptivity to process and change. They sought to explore a world of internal states, including dreams and myths, to develop a truly integrated ensemble method, to discover means to make the theater experience as immediately "present" as possible, and to work outside the commercial system. Although they considered themselves democratic and collaborative, Chaikin was their spiritual and artistic guru. He was, though, unwilling to openly accept his position as the leader, even after fame beckoned. He later admitted to having invented a self-sacrificing persona while inwardly aware that this was little more than a manipulative guise.

The move from workshop to performance came gradually, beginning in 1963 with public demonstrations in its loft, and progressing to Off-Off-Broadway showings. These normally consisted of warmups, exercises, improvisations, and short plays. Chaikin continued to present such programs—at places such as the Martinique Theater, the Sheridan Square Playhouse, and Café LaMama—until 1967, when he directed the company's first full-length, collaboratively created project, *The Serpent,* with a Jean-Claude van Itallie text based on the actors' improvisations.

By the time it disbanded in 1973, the Open Theater had created four such works. During this time Chaikin, who continued to accept outside acting jobs—mainly noncommercial—for several years, also acted in several Open Theater productions directed by others; moreover, he staged some short plays under Open Theater auspices, among them the "Interview" segment of the commercially produced, three-piece *America Hurrah* (1966), van Itallie's *The First Fool* and *The Hunter and the Bird* (1964), Maria Irene Fornes's *Successful Life of Three* (1964), Megan Terry's *Calm Down Mother* (1964), and Bertolt Brecht's *Clown Play* (1966).

The collaborations often took a year or more to complete and were frequently revised after public showings. Goals often remained vague and the preparation process was a constant and painful whittling away, with brilliant moments discarded in the search for an ultimate form. Chaikin took a nonjudgmental attitude toward his actors, hating to interfere with their creativity, although this frustrated insecure players seeking feedback. Projects might be aborted after months of work. Chaikin was accused of hating to open a work, both because he was so enamored of rehearsals and because he often found it difficult to consider his work finished enough to be seen publicly. Sometimes the audience seemed an intruder on his research.

The group's range extended from essentially nonverbal, highly physicalized works to pieces employing equal amounts of verbal and physical material; however, the words and movements were so closely blended in their imagistic, nondiscursive nature that one was, in a sense, the expression of the other. Most characters were not naturalistic, representing types or concepts, with the actors moving swiftly from role to role according to need. The characterizations' open nature allowed for crossgender casting, without the effect of campy humor.

To develop the choreographic fluidity of their style, and to find expressive means that went beyond the bounds of realism, the company worked on thousands of games and exercises devised mainly by Chaikin, but often adapted from Viola Spolin. Most exercises were discarded, but many remained part of his methods for years. Functioning intuitively, he often made these up on the spur of the moment, moving from one to the other as the actors' ideas stimulated him. His aim was to get the performers to move with ease from character to character or idea to idea without the intrusion of abrupt transitions. Improvisation in performance was used rarely, if at all. Chaikin believed in the value of a well-crafted performance composed of perfectly polished and "inevitable" images that remain internally alive. He wanted actors to have the widest life experiences to deepen their sensitivity and sense of engagement with important subjects.

The Open Theater was recognized as the leading American force in the search for new approaches to the actor's art. Chaikin's actors conveyed feelings, moods, and ideas in vocal and physical ways the realistic theater had rarely explored. He aimed to establish a manner in which the actor, while feeling his part, was able to stand outside of it, thus crossing Stanislavskian empathy with Brechtian alienation. Much of his work was influenced by Jerzy Grotowski, Peter Brook, and Eugenio Barba, with each of whom he studied; equally influential was the Chinese theater, an inspiration in the distillation of effects to their most expressive essentials. Important thinkers and artists were often invited to participate in the lab sessions.

Although there was humor in the Open Theater's work—Chaikin insisted on the importance of entertainment value—the troupe seemed utterly serious. They would select a theme of shared importance, and then closely scrutinize each of their responses to the theme as it affected their lives. The group's life grew out of a fundamental dissatisfaction with the social/political environment, but they never became overtly propagandistic. Process preceded product and the group strove to discover the play as an end in itself, not to please an audience or make money.

Such writers as Sam Shepard, van Itallie, Susan Yankowitz, and Terry, participated in the Open Theater. Yankowitz described her job as "To observe what was happening in workshops, to distill and focus ideas, and to create original material which would elucidate the themes with which we were working."

Most Open Theater pieces were staged in an end-stage arrangement, the actors on one side, the spectators on the other, because such a disposition was the easiest to realize in the diverse environments (including prisons) the group used, both in the United States and abroad. Their style suggested Grotowski's "poor theater," with barely any scenery or props, only a few abstract wooden units, and simple, unadorned costumes. Occasionally, the actors' well-worn street clothing was used. Stage makeup was rarely worn. Music was used extensively, as were unusual sounds, and unconventional musical instruments created what someone called "bruitage" (from the French for "noise").

Chaikin, a music fanatic, has sought to make his pieces correspond with themes and leitmotifs, like good musical compositions. No attempt was made to hide the musicians or, for that matter, the actors who were "offstage" waiting to make an entrance. Lighting was usually nongelled and nonillusionistic.

Chaikin's Open Theater pieces, all of them nonliteral, nonlinear, were *The Serpent, Terminal* (1969), *The Mutation Show* (1971), and *Nightwalk* (1973). *The Serpent*, which premiered in Rome, was inspired by the biblical tale of Genesis; the 18-actor piece contrasted the loss of Eden with contemporary images of violence, notably the assassination of John F. Kennedy (enacted in a mimic sequence based on the Zapruder film). A highlight was when a group of actors entwined themselves to portray a many-tongued serpent. Roberta Sklar, Chaikin's codirector on *Terminal*, first given in Bordeaux, called it a "confrontation with mortality," since it investigated feelings toward death.

In 1970, Chaikin pared the company down to six, and the following works employed from six to eight actors. *The Mutation Show*, also codirected with Sklar, and lacking the input of a resident dramatist, took for its subject the processes of human and social change, and the related topic of the mutability of identity; it was partly inspired by the story of a girl raised among wolves and by that of Kaspar Hauser, a 19th-century boy confined to a tiny space for 16 years until he was suddenly released into the streets of Nuremberg. The piece premiered (as a work in progress called *Mutations*) in Algeria. The state of sleep and its multiple levels were explored in *Nightwalk*, premiered as an untitled work in progress

in New York; several playwrights offered material. Each of these award-winning pieces was widely seen.

The group split up at the peak of acceptance. Chaikin said that outside pressures were preventing them from advancing. They found themselves institutionalized and pigeonholed. This outside interest was leading to a derailment of their original impulses, thus suggesting the possibility of their moving into areas that might weaken their mission. After they dissolved, many members worked in similarly experimental circumstances.

Chaikin continued his explorations with the Winter Project. After two seasons of intense work the company began to show its work, but under restrictive circumstances, and not to the press. Their first fully public offering—using a reduced company—was *Re-Arrangements* (1979), a collage concerned with the rearrangments and adjustments people make in their relationships with others. Some of its material had been influenced by two poetic monologues Chaikin (who acted them) and Shepard cowrote and codirected in San Francisco, *Tongues* (1978) and *Savage/Love* (1979). With the company numbers once more diminished, the Winter Project gave its second collage, *Tourists and Refugees* (1980), dealing with themes of home and homelessness; it was revised as *Tourists and Refugees No. 2* (1981). *Trespassing* (1981), mostly written by Chaikin, was concerned with a dying woman's thoughts after suffering a stroke. Before folding, the Winter Project concentrated on the three-actor *Lies and Secrets* (1983) and, in London, a revision called *Trio* (1983).

Chaikin was also occupied staging a series of Off- and Off-Off-Broadway productions during these years, beginning with *Electra* (1974), a collaborative work based on Sophocles and crafted with writer Robert Montgomery and three actors; it told the story through two-character scenes; Agamemnon's spirit possessed Electra at the climax. In 1975, he staged a collaborative piece called *A Fable Telling a Journey*, using the theme of the quest to confront modern problems. The same year saw Anton Chekhov's *The Seagull* and a "documentary musical," *Chile, Chile*, about the toppling of the Allende regime. His workshop production of Adrienne Kennedy's *A Movie Star Has to Star in Black and White* arrived in 1976, and in 1977, he offered Beckett's *Endgame* (he redirected it in 1980). S. Ansky's *The Dybbuk* was his 1977 production; taken ill during its last week of rehearsal, Chaikin could not complete the show. While convalescing he listened to tapes of the performances and sent directing notes to the cast. Chaikin also staged the work in Hebrew for Tel Aviv's Habimah Theater in 1979.

Apart from his Winter Project offerings, his directing assignments in the early 1980s were Sophocles' *Antigone* (1982), stressing both the political and mourning themes, and *Imagining the Other* (1982), a politically inspired ensemble piece created in Israel with native actors. In 1983, he suffered a stroke during open-heart surgery and was unable to direct until 1985; it would be a few more years before he could resume acting. Chaikin went on to direct productions in New York (Kennedy's *Solo Voyages* in 1985; Eugène Ionesco's *The Bald Soprano* in 1987, codirected with Nancy Gabor; Yankowitz's *Night Sky* in 1991, and Beckett's *Texts for Nothing* in 1992); in Tel Aviv (*Out* in 1986); in San Francisco (untitled work in progress in 1987, Vaudeville Nouveau's *The Detective* in 1986, Ed Gueble's *Utterance in the Firmament* in 1989, the latter pair codirected with Larry Russell, and Yankowitz's *Utterances* in 1990); Larkspur, California (Ken Prestinzini's *Touch Me* in 1988, codirected with Tracy Ward); and in Los Angeles (*Waiting for Godot* in 1990).

Chaikin is responsible for introducing the collaborative method into American theater. His philosophy of process over product, and his commitment to ensemble work with a company of engaged actors, demonstrates his respect for the theater as an art. He expanded the actor's expressive vocabulary, demonstrated the viability of an imagistic style, and created exercises and widely influential concepts with names such as "sound and movement," "conductor," "perfect people," "worlds," "jamming," and "the chord." His emotional creations remained entertaining while being concerned with the human/social/political condition.

Further reading:

Blumenthal, Eileen. *Joseph Chaikin: Exploring at the Boundaries of Theater.* Cambridge, England: Cambridge University Press, 1984.

Gildzen, Alex, and Dimitris Karageorgiou. *Joseph Chaikin: A Bio-Bibliography.* Westport, Conn.: Greenwood Press, 1992.

Pasolli, Robert. *A Book on the Open Theatre.* New York: Avon, 1974.

Also: Croyden, *Lunatics, Lovers and Poets;* Shank, *American Alternative Theatre.*

GOWER CHAMPION (1920–1980)

GOWER CARLYLE CHAMPION was born in Geneva, Illinois. His father was an ad executive and his mother a well-known Los Angeles custom dressmaker (they divorced when Champion was two). At

Gower Champion directing 42nd Street. *(1980)* (Photo: Martha Swope)

Los Angeles's Fairfax High School he created a dance act with Jeanne Tyler and quit school.

In 1947, after serving in the Coast Guard, Champion married Marjorie Belcher, a childhood friend and daughter of a ballet master under whom he had studied (they divorced in 1973). As Marge and Gower Champion (originally Gower and Bell), they became America's most popular dance duo in nightclubs, television, and movies.

In 1948, Champion choreographed his first Broadway revue, *Small Wonder* (1948), its music by Baldwin Bergersen and Albert Selden, and both choreographed and codirected the hit revue *Lend an Ear* (1948), score by Charles Gaynor, that made Carol Channing a star and won Champion a Tony for his athletic, hilarious routines. His rise to fame as a director-choreographer continued with another revue, *3 for Tonight* (1955), score by Walter Schumann and Robert Wells, in which he, his wife, and Harry Belafonte appeared, but he did not have a hit until Charles Strouse, Lee Adams, and Michael Stewart's *Bye Bye Birdie* (1960), starring Dick Van Dyke and Chita Rivera. This 607-performance, rock-

and-roll satire, landed him two Tonys. Many later Champion shows also had show business backgrounds, mostly set in the past. One did not go to a Champion show for provocative content. They usually featured lightheartedness and nostalgic charm. *Birdie* received a fast-paced, comically inventive staging, its most memorable number being a sequence in which a bunch of teenagers talking on the phone kept moving about in various amusing positions in a honeycomb composed of individual cubicles.

Another hit was Bob Merrill and Stewart's sentimentally romantic *Carnival* (1961), based on the movie *Lili*, and with Jerry Orbach and Anna Maria Alberghetti as the lame puppeteer and the waif who loves him. Champion's innovations included a unit set, a colorful carnival that was created at the opening by the gaily clad actors on a bare stage backed by a painted drop. The carnival atmosphere was underlined by actors dressed as souvenir vendors walking through the aisles. At the end, the carnival was struck in full view, and the opening vista reappeared.

Champion directed his first straight play with Lillian Hellman's *My Mother, My Father, and Me* (1963), a flop on which, though he retained the credit, he was replaced by Arthur Penn. He rebounded with the megahit, *Hello, Dolly!* (1964), in which he reteamed with Channing in Stewart and Jerry Herman's musical version of Thornton Wilder's *The Matchmaker.* During a troubled out-of-town period, Champion and the writers did a thorough overhaul. The result won him a pair of Tonys. He later restaged it in London. *Dolly*'s 2,844 performances put it in the top 10 of the longest Broadway runs. Unique was a curved runway that surrounded the orchestra pit and allowed the star to approach the audience. Abe Laufe described how the director built up Dolly's grand entrance into the Harmonia Gardens. First came a number, "The Waiter's Gavotte," combining

slapstick, hijinks, and nimble footwork, with the waiters racing across stage carrying trays loaded with dishes, dueling with enormous skewers of shish kebab, and jostling, bumping, and running into each other. Yet . . . the waiters . . . never dropped a . . . tray or dish. . . . With the announcement that Dolly Levi has arrived . . . the spotlight focused on the entrance at the top of a center stairway, with the waiters lined up on both sides. Suddenly Channing appeared . . . in a red gown and jewels, and came down the stairs to sing "Hello, Dolly!" As the boys took up the second chorus, Channing went through a shuffle routine on the stage,

on the runway, and back on stage to make the song one of the biggest show-stoppers in the history of musical theater.

His next effort was Jerome Chodorov's flop farce, *3 Bags Full* (1966). Shortly afterward came Harvey Schmidt and Tom Jones's musicalization of Jan de Hartog's *The Fourposter*, renamed *I Do! I Do!* (1966), and starring Robert Preston and Mary Martin as a couple whose 50 years of married life are shown in stages. It retained de Hartog's two-character structure, which made it unusual and demanded great ingenuity to keep it from flagging. One of Champion's brainstorms was having the couple, sitting at dressing tables on a runway over the pit, put their old-age makeup on before the audience prior to the last scene. This effort struck gold for 584 showings; Champion also directed the London version.

Less successful was John Kander and Fred Ebb's *The Happy Time* (1968), based on a play about a French-Canadian family, and starring Robert Goulet. As often with Champion's shows, there were major tryout problems. This time he was unable to solve them but still managed to win two Tonys. Conceptually interesting was making Goulet's character a photographer whose memories—his pictures—were surrealistically projected onto a screen.

Champion turned to a nonmusical comedy, Georges Feydeau's French farce, *A Flea in Her Ear* (1968), at San Francisco's American Conservatory Theater. (New York saw it, briefly.) It had a striking black-and-white decor, but Champion's choreographic business damaged the play's realistic foundation.

During the 1970s, Champion slumped. While his own work was often praised, his shows failed to make money. In 1972, he directed and choreographed Jule Styne, Bob Merrill, and Peter Stone's risible *Sugar* (1972), based on the movie, *Some Like It Hot*, about two male musicians who hide from gangsters by joining an all-girl band. Despite out-of-town troubles, Champion's staging saved the day. John Simon said that Champion was a master of integrating dances into the overall movement of a show, having

done more than anyone to break down the barrier between the prose of mere blocking and the poetry of dance. . . . Here the connections between machinegun salvos and tap-dancing, between oldsters and being wheeled about in armchairs on casters and a veritable Dodgem ballet are jubilantly exploited.

Champion, noted Simon, was able to meld large numbers of dancers into "one flesh-and-muscle kinetic sculpture, a pullulating, polypoid mechanism

Lee Roy Reams (c) in 42nd Street. *Directed by Gower Champion. (1980)*   (Photo: Martha Swope)

shaping and reshaping itself before your eyes but remaining fixed around one pulsating center." Finally, Simon said, came Champion's brilliance at using props, *Sugar*'s dance routines using "everything from instrument cases to wicker chairs, newspapers to ear horns, spotlights to Pullman berths and their curtains."

Champion assumed the direction (Peter Gennaro choreographed) of a Debbie Reynolds vehicle, Harry Tierney and Joe McCarthy's *Irene* (1973), a much-revised 1919 musical that was dying on the road under John Gielgud's direction. Mordden states: "He cut the book, speeded the scene-to-scene transitions, expanded the title song from a duet into a production numbo [sic], and, basically, made Reynolds look good." The show had a long run, but lost money, possibly due to mismanagement.

It was followed by Jerry Herman's musical about the love affair of silent film figures Mack Sennett and Mabel Normand, *Mack and Mabel* (1974), which flopped despite an excellent score and stars Robert Preston and Bernadette Peters; a Los Angeles revue,

Who Could Ask for Anything More?, celebrating Ira Gershwin's lyrics (1976); a flawed rock-musical version of *Hamlet* called *Rockabye Hamlet* (1976) in which every word was sung; and a terrific Los Angeles revival of *Annie Get Your Gun* (1977) starring Debbie Reynolds. Although he cut a couple of songs, he greatly enhanced the acting-to-singing continuity of what remained and added a ballet to "There's No Business Like Show Business," which earlier productions had rarely given extensive staging. Mordenn said Champion made it "a surrealistic masque on a bare stage against a cyclorama in which the cast, made up as freak versions of themselves, welcomed Reynolds into the fraternity of the theater, and she too emerged in *commedia dell'arte* makeup."

Following a hiatus of several years, Champion made a victorious comeback with the nostalgia-laden *42nd Street* (1980), a dance-oriented musical (tunes by Al Dubin and Harry Warren) with a wobbly book based on a 1933 film about how the show must go on, and starring Orbach and Tammy Grimes. Champion refused to abandon the production although suffering from what proved a fatal blood disease; the seriousness of his condition was kept secret from the company. Ironically, he passed away on the very night the 3,485-performance hit opened to raves. The announcement of his death, news of which had been withheld from the cast, was made during the curtain calls by Champion's frequent producer and antagonist, David Merrick. The parallels between real life and the show's tale of a director's tribulations and the rise of a young star did not pass unnoticed. Champion was having a romance with ingenue Wanda Richert.

The *New York Times* review observed that the show's dances resembled a homage to Champion's career.

> For "The Shadow Waltz," he has sent his uncommonly graceful legions of chorus people gliding gaily in silhouette across a near empty stage. (It's the "Dancing" number from Hello, Dolly! with an added layer of wit.) For "You're Getting to Be a Habit with Me," he's done his own, showbiz version of Jerome Robbins' ballet, "The Concert." There's a chorine-filled castle of mirrors for "Dames," the requisite larger-than-life silver dollars for "We're in the Money," a break away train (shades of Sugar) for "Shuffle Off to Buffalo." That tribute to the jungle-jim opening of Bye, [sic] Bye Birdie opens Act II; singers occupy three stories of back stage dressing rooms to deliver "Sunny Side to Every Situation."

For the climax, Champion had the entire company perform "a tap-and-blues fantasy that simultaneously joshes and celebrates such an unlikely duo as George Balanchine and Busby Berkeley."

Champion was showbiz incarnate, the answer to a tired businessman's daydreams. Some, like William Goldman, thought him superficial: "his work looks gorgeous in the shop window, but take it home, and the seams start showing." But Simon called him a "Berkeley with brains and taste." Most agreed that he lacked the innovative magic of some of his contemporaries and that he did not have the easily recognizable choreographic idiosyncracies of a Bob Fosse. Still, his work was distinctive. Harold Clurman called him "the Tyrone Guthrie of musical comedy direction":

> He has humor and an unfailing sense of what will surprise, move and strike home on stage. His choreography is not particularly original or beautiful in itself, but with limited dance means it always manages to make a telling theatrical effect. If Gower Champion were to run a nightclub it would be the most "romantic" spot in town, because he knows how to combine elements of a

traditional glamour with the tension and hectic beat of metropolitan festivity.

Richard Kislan added:

> Champion asked that his dancers transform themselves to fit his vision as well as such idiosyncracies in his style as the "very tight torso," the tension in the arms, and the angular use of shoulders and knees harnessed to the demands of precise movement. The 42nd Street principal Lee Roy Reams confessed: "When I'm on that stage, it's still me, but I have to wear his body."

Champion was capable of combining the roles of director and choreographer within the same artistic vision. He relished his dual task because it allowed him to unify a show and to bring acting to dance and vice versa. Each dance number was created from an impetus to tell a story or to help advance the narrative through what he termed "musical staging." Kislan quotes him telling a *Times* interviewer in 1978:

> I use dancing to embellish, extend or enlarge upon an existing emotion. None of it could really stand alone. Being director and choreographer, the reason for me, anyway, is control. If you do both, the style is the same; one concept that you try to fold in on so there is a constant flow.

He prepared by doing extensive research. Before rehearsals commenced he had a sharp conceptual image in mind designed to unify all components. A visual idea, such as the walkway in *Dolly!*, had to get his motor running. His familiarity with all the technical crafts was of great assistance in this process and he often worked with the same team of backstage collaborators.

Time was rarely wasted at rehearsals, as the dances were worked out in advance. Performers loved working for him because, being good-natured, kind, and witty, he showed them affection and respect, while rarely displaying a temper. A relaxed atmosphere prevailed, although tight control was never relinquished.

Prior to tackling the musical numbers, he worked on the book so that the routines stemmed from character concerns. Being a performer himself, he often demonstrated movement and business, but hoped the actor would offer creative ideas as well. As rehearsals progressed, he eliminated whatever was not working, even entire scenes, and kept refining even after the opening.

Champion's double-barreled talents gave him a power that many relished. When he demanded Goulet for *The Happy Time* despite objections, insiders knew he would get his way. Goldman quotes a sarcastic observer:

> The second I heard the Goulet rumor, I knew it would be Goulet. You've got to understand why. Champion is always asking himself, "Am I really God?" His answer is, "Yes." . . . Everybody has always called Goulet an eight-by-ten glossy. Champion asks himself, "How can I . . . prove I'm God this time? I'll make Robert Goulet a star."

Champion was one of a fast-vanishing breed of director-choreographers who were responsible over the past four decades for making the American musical an almost seamless art in which dance and movement became predominant, not secondary,

components. Frank Rich summed up his accomplishments: "By applying an unstoppable imagination, galvanizing enthusiasm and a taskmaster's professionalism to a series of unpretentious, empty-headed entertainments, he almost single-handedly kept alive the fabled traditions of Broadway's most glittery and innocent past."

Further reading:

Rich, Frank. "Gower Champion Was a True Believer." *New York Times*, August 31, 1980.
Also: Clurman, *The Naked Image*; Goldman, *The Season*; Gottfried, *Broadway Musicals*; Kislan, *Hoofing on Broadway*; Laufe, *Broadway's Greatest Musicals*; Mordden, *Broadway Babies*; Simon, *Uneasy Stages*.

PING CHONG (1946–   )

PING CHONG was born in Toronto, Canada, but in 1948, his family moved to New York's Chinatown, where they ran a restaurant and took part in amateur Chinese opera. Chong studied art at Pratt Institute and film at the School of Visual Arts. During the sixties, he became active in "happenings," studied dance with Meredith Monk, and collaborated with her on several creations. Monk's multimedia style—using music, lighting, slides, film, dance, and even puppets—greatly influenced Chong.

Chong's use of media is more postmodern than Monk's since it allows each element to express its own discreet viewpoint rather than being blended with the others in the interests of unity. He began to develop this aesthetic with his early 1970s conceptualizations. Much of his inspiration derived from his feelings, as an Asian-American, of being an outsider in mainstream America. A number of works included a central figure representing Chong's alienated status as the "other." This tendency shifted from a focus on his own otherness to that of societies and cultures that are, in their mutual relationships, often marred by conflict.

Financial limitations caused Chong's early work to be minimalist, using little music, considerable silence and stillness, and only essential, heavily symbolic, props. Chong not only directed and choreographed his pieces, he also sometimes designed them and performed in them. His unconventional, usually plotless, collaboratively written, imagistic work leaned in the direction of nondramatic theatricalist poetry. Actors exhibited their sculptural qualities as

well as performance talents. Audiences were puzzled by the challenging nonlinear structures and evocative yet baffling visual ideas.

His first decade included *Lazarus* (1972; revised 1977); *I Flew to Fiji; You Went South* (1973); *Fear and Loathing in Gotham* (1975); and *Humboldt's Current* (1977). Most were seen Off-Off-Broadway, on tour, and occasionally abroad. In 1975, he formed the Fiji Company, later changed to Ping Chong and Company. Many actors have been with him for years.

Lazarus, sparked by a passage in the New Testament, included slides of city buildings and tenement stairways; a table and chair brought on and removed by visible stagehands, as in Chinese opera; an amplified offstage commentator; a zombielike, corned-beef sandwich eating Lazarus (symbolizing an alien or outsider presence in the land of the living), dressed in shirt and slacks but with mummy face wrappings; an edited sci-fi movie about a monster (another alien) who comes to earth in an egg and becomes a terror until shot down; a cut-out effigy of Lazarus pulled to heaven on a pulley arrangement; and a final image of a desolate, leaf-strewn city street, with light streaming through a manhole.

Fear and Loathing was Chong's quirkily minimalist version of Fritz Lang's film about a child murderer, M. With only three characters (the child, the detective, and the murderer), and a score by Monk, its fragmentary, elliptical style used ritualistic slow motion to enact a story about a troubled stranger to the urban landscape whose communication problems

Ping Chong (r) directing Nosferatu. *(1985)*   (Photo: Martha Swope Associates/Carol Rosegg)

lead to murder and suicide. Memorable scenes were played in silhouette behind a white screen and looked more like a movie than live theater.

Humboldt's Current, a determinedly multimedia piece, made greater use of performance to tell the anticolonialist tale of 19th-century explorer Charles Humboldt, who represents the harmful intrusion of one culture into others as he scours the globe in search of a mythical animal. At one point, the progress of oldtime adventurers was evoked by a stagehand manipulating a string of tiny, candlelit model ships across the darkened stage. Slides, newsreels, amplified voices and eclectic sound effects, silhouettes, and film were put to expressive use.

Chong's first important work of the eighties was the dream play *Nuit Blanche* (1981), which he called a "bricolage," meaning "a new world created out of any and all available materials from an old world" but also suggesting "bricole," a billiard carom shot resulting in an "indirect action or unexpected

stroke." Bricolage has been used to define most of Chong's subsequent work. The *New York Times* said the abstract but fascinating work "sifts the white night of dreams and memories and catapults verbal, visual, musical and photographic images into a kind of archaeological collage." Meditative in atmosphere, it combined images of the historical past extending from cave dwellers to Neil Armstrong's moon landing (on videotape) and mingled projections with live action. Unlike earlier works, *Nuit Blanche* included dramatic and comical segments dealing, said the *Times,* "with such subjects as repressive Old World paternalism and the threat of violence faced by visitors to emerging nations."

Chong's other 1980s works were *Rainer and the Knife* (Chicago, 1981); *A.M./A.M.—The Articulated Man* (New York, 1982); *Anna into Nightlight* (New York, 1982); *A Race* (Seattle, 1983); *Astonishment and the Twins* (Lexington, New York, 1983); *The Games* (Berlin, 1983), a collaboration with Monk;

Nosferatu. *Directed by Ping Chong. (1985)* (Photo: Martha Swope Associates/Carol Rosegg)

Nosferatu (New York, 1985); *Angels of Swedenborg* (Chicago, 1985); *Kind Ness* (Boston, 1986); *Without Law, Without Heaven* (Seattle, 1987); *Maraya—Acts of Nature in Geological Time* (Montclair, New Jersey, 1988); *Quartetto* (Rotterdam, 1988); *Snow* (Minneapolis, 1988); *Skin: A State of Being* (New York, 1989); *Noiresque: The Fallen Angel* (New York, 1989); and *Brightness* (New York, 1989). In the nineties he has offered *Deshima* (Utrecht, Holland, 1990); *4AM America* (Milwaukee, 1990); and *Elephant Memories* (Boston, 1990). The majority of the works came to New York . . . none of them exceeded an hour and a half.

An example of his work from this period is the nightmarish *A.M./A.M*, derived from a Jorge Luis Borges poem, "The Golem," itself about the 16th-century Jewish Frankenstein story. Chong told *Other Stages* that it was "about dreaming and the importance of being psychically connected to ourselves, which we're not. That's scary. When human beings in a society fail to have a rich psychic life then it's ripe for fascism." Live action occurring in a stark-white room was sandwiched between two films. One portrayed an idyllic garden existence. The second revealed the robotlike golem learning proper behavior; unable to assimilate this alien knowledge, he kills someone, runs away, and becomes a spiritually questioning member of the city. Between the films were five fables concerning the struggle between good and evil.

Another example is *Nosferatu*, based on F. W. Murnau's famed old vampire film. The movie was intercut with the action, set in the Manhattan apart-

ment of a yuppie couple, the Harkers, intended to stand for the darkness of the modern world because of the soulless, emotionless natures of these essentially undead persons. When they leave with another couple, the apartment harbors a dance of death by various figures, including skeletons. On their return, the couples fall into the vampire's power. Horror and comedy cohabited in the staging, designed, according to the *Village Voice*, "to keep us alive while we watch our city slowly giving way to the living dead, and maybe prod us to fight back a little." Chong's preoccupation with the enhancement of spiritual life was also behind another major work of the decade, *Angels of Swedenborg*, based on a Borges book about the Swedish philosopher.

More accessible than most Chong works was *Kind Ness*, played in a comedic vaudevillian style and, other than two slide sequences, using minimal technical support. Concerned again with otherness, this bare-stage piece began with a slide lecture on amusing, if strained, analogies (Richard Burton and Tupperware share "nesting" qualities); moved on to material about teenagers growing up in the 1950s, the anguish experienced by one of them, a gorilla named Buzz, and their memories of Buzz 10 years later; and a final scene in a zoo where Buzz has so become assimilated into human society that he is puzzled by a gorilla in a cage.

Chong's fondness for transposing literature into theater was visible in *Noiresque*, a playful film noir view of *Alice in Wonderland* that placed Lewis Carroll's classic in the context of an absurdist detective story. Performed with an Asian-American cast, it had Alice boarding the All Points Far East Local for Terminal City, an Orwellian technocracy inhabited by the dehumanized, machinelike Terminites, where she met Herr Hassenpfeffer (the White Rabbit). Protected by her guardian angel, she became enmeshed in a plot about a femme fatale and other colorful figures. A Big Brother-like loudspeaker now and then announced the time and asked "Are *you* where you should be?" Vaudevillian bits were sprinkled through the conversations. Signal lights suggested moving trains and a chorus danced in outsized top hats.

Chong often derives his ideas from his voracious reading, and he keeps a clipping file of articles and images he finds provocative. He enjoys placing his action in diverse, exotic locales. Creating a piece involves his crossbreeding of his research in surprising ways. When asked to do a piece based on Van Gogh, his investigations led him to create *Deshima*, a work combining such elements as the recent Japanese purchase of the "Irises" painting, the fact that Japan was opened to the West in the year of Van Gogh's birth, the previous restriction of foreigners to the island of Deshima, the influence of Japanese art on Van Gogh, and Chong's own concerns about anti-Asian racism.

Although not especially political, Chong is likely to be inspired by social themes, such as his dismay about the repression of the individual in the industrialized world, which triggered *Elephant Memories,* and which was supported by his readings of George Orwell and Franz Kafka. The greed of the Reagan years instigated *Nosferatu,* which also derived from the AIDs epidemic and a book about postwar Germany's bourgeoisie. The locale was transposed to America to confront yuppiedom's inability to deal with life's unpleasant aspects. On the other hand, *Brightness,* which had no particular theme, stemmed from purely aesthetic concerns when Chong took his inspiration from sets, costumes, masks, and music created by his collaborators.

Typically, Chong eschews causality in favor of a nonnarrative, discontinuous, sequence-by-sequence method. The effect may seem random, although the

Nosferatu. *Directed by Ping Chong. (1985)* (Photo: Martha Swope Associates/Carol Rosegg)

scenes are thematically connected. Unifying images and words are scattered throughout. Occasionally, there is an actual narrator, as in *Deshima,* where a black-suited black performer kept shifting identities, from a Japanese businessman to Van Gogh, and provided historical and cultural commentary. Time and place shift frequently with no apparent relation and characters are rarely stable entities. In the 11-scene *Snow,* for instance, the parts were connected by the image of snow. The achronological scenes in *Deshima* were united by the theme of that Japanese island's place in European-Asian-Japanese historical and cultural relations. A piece's meaning may not emerge until all the parts are viewed, as when, in *Anna into Nightlight,* the nature of a painful relationship between two sisters remained elusive until the ending.

Chong relies considerably on music and sound, his multifarious choices including the familiar and the idiosyncratic. The music is as likely to come from medieval times as from Russian punk rock. Sounds are frequently used more for atmospheric than literal qualities. One aspect of sound is Chong's language, which often includes passages from foreign tongues mixed with English, with no attempt at translation, thereby forcing the audience to sharply experience the presence of otherness. *Noiresque,* which uses four or five languages, is highly verbal, while the largely visual and musical *Brightness* barely uses any speech.

Chong uses films, slides, and TV, aiming to provide images that will resonate in relation to the actors, with whom they may create striking contrasts. The actors often use dancelike movement and gestures, and their inspiration may come from Oriental dance, jitterbugging, modern dance, and so on.

He likes to create collaboratively, depending on trial and error, and employing improvisation; the path a work will take is not clear from the outset. He contemplates the general direction of the piece while its relative dependence on visual or verbal elements remains unclear. He may have only a hazy notion of a theme or may actually have certain images—including slides and film—in mind. These ideas are discussed with his acting, design, and technical collaborators. Much gets written down, if only temporarily. The actors, who are able to dance, sing, and act, are asked to begin improvising around these ideas and Chong makes decisions based on what he sees and hears. He suggests reading and visual research to help stimulate the actors' imaginations. Chong's actors feel they are creative artists, not puppets. The designers also feel like creative components, developing their effects in the crucible of rehearsal. Apart from a few exceptions, the texts and performances are the product of contributions by all involved, although Chong is the final arbiter or editor, as he prefers to consider his role. He told *TheaterWeek*:

> *The structure, the architecture of a piece is always mine, but different cast members combine text, some devise movements. We all work together in a process of cross-pollinization. Performers have to understand that it is the overall concept that's important, that the costumes, the lighting, the sound, the masks are all equally important.*

Time constraints usually force the company to work quickly; pieces sometimes open before they are ready. Chong polishes even after the opening, making major revisions until he is satisfied.

Ping Chong is one of the most innovative American conceptualists. His work, though deliberately obscure, is thematically rich and theatrically original. One of the only Chinese-American directors to achieve widespread acclaim, he has reached such a high plateau that in 1991 he was able to present a retrospective of two decades of work.

Further reading:

Abbe, Jessica. "Chong's Simplicity: Sounds of Silence." *Other Stages*, January 28, 1982.

Banes, Sally. "The World According to Chong." *Village Voice*, February 28, 1984.

Hulser, Kathleen. "Electric Language." *American Theater* 4 (June 1987).

Kalb, Jonathan. "Ping Chong: From *Lazarus* to *Anna into Nightlight.*" *Theatre* 14 (Spring 1983).

Sandla, Robert. "Practical Visionary: Ping Chong." *TheaterWeek*, January 23, 1989.

LIVIU CIULEI (1923–   )

LIVIU CIULEI was born in Bucharest, Rumania, where his father was a prominent architect. He attended both the Bucharest Faculty of Architecture and the Academy of Music and Drama, graduating from them simultaneously in 1945. Ciulei's background prepared him to serve as architect, designer, director, and actor. When he made theater his career, his father built him the Odeon, where he gained attention as an actor.

In 1948, Ciulei joined Bucharest's Lucia Sturdza Bulandra Theater, practicing his multifaceted talents on many plays. He served as artistic director from 1963 to 1972, and his various tours helped make the Bulandra an international artistic force. Ciulei's exceptional abilities were on frequent display in European theaters, especially Germany's, since 1957, and in films.

The domination of communism and Soviet power over Rumanian cultural life became concrete in the year that Ciulei joined the Bulandra. Rumanian directors were expected to follow the dogma of socialist realism in their play selections and production methods. Those, like Ciulei, who wished more liberal means of expression learned how to subtly circumvent official requirements. New plays raised suspicions, so an increased emphasis on allusively subversive interpretations of the classics became widespread. Audiences became attuned to ferreting

out possible meanings. Ciulei exemplified those progressives who became experts at scrutinizing old plays, line by line, for provocative ideas.

One of his first steps in this direction was a 1957 article he wrote calling for socialist realism to be replaced by the "retheatricalization of the theater." This plea for a return to anti-illusionistic, stylized theater in which poetic techniques offered a deeply personal view of the play's implications had a catalytic effect on Rumanian theater. Among the techniques—reminiscent of Evgeni Vakhtangov's "fantastic realism"—he and his fellows developed were a reliance on metaphorical visual concepts in sets, props, and costumes; cinematic montage effects highly dependent on lighting; and grotesquerie that underscored the absurdist side of serious concerns. Ciulei began to explore his ideas in such outstanding productions as George Bernard Shaw's *Saint Joan* (1958) and Shakespeare's *As You Like It* (1961).

As You Like It was influential in its revolutionary antirealistic methods. Ciulei removed the vestiges of traditional romanticism by doing the comedy as an Elizabethan fairground show and introducing such theatricalist touches as a ballet corps to mime the Forest of Arden. Satirical grotesquerie in acting and design mocked the aristocracy: the usurping duke watched the wrestling match from a bathtub. The characters were divided into four groups, their make-

The Inspector General. *Directed by Liviu Ciulei. (1978) Clockwise from left: Max Wright, Theodore Bikel, Helen Burns, Pamela Payton-Wright.* (Photo: Martha Swope)

ups ranging from realistic to masklike according to how heavily they were satirized.

Ciulei's international reputation flowered after Georg Büchner's *Danton's Death* (1966) was restaged in Berlin in 1967. The individualistic attitude toward the French Revolution shown by Danton (played by Ciulei) made Rumanian officials uncomfortable. Another of his virtuosic Büchner productions (also toured through Europe) was *Leonce and Lena* (1970), inspired by the Bread and Puppet Theater. The audience observed the actors preparing as the latter warmed up and mingled with the spectators. A bare stage (the back wall remained exposed) supported a strolling player platform, and stagehands remained visible. Through the director's inventions and a remarkably cohesive ensemble that seemed at times to be improvising despite Ciulei's control, the problematic play came to surprising life, its theme of disaffected, rebellious youth demonstrating present-day relevance.

In 1972, Ciulei was stripped of his artistic directorship at the Bulandra after producing Lucian Pintilie's

politically touchy version of Nikolai Gogol's *The Inspector General.* He thereupon worked in Germany, Australia, and Canada; he also returned occasionally to the Bulandra. He began his American career in 1975 by restaging *Leonce and Lena* at the Arena Stage in Washington, D.C. The play, which he said (according to Hans-Gert Pfafferodt and Sloane Bosniak) contained "realism, expressionism, epic theater, absurd theater and documentarism," had a production reminiscent of its Rumanian one. The *Village Voice*, objecting to the replacement of narrative clarity by "spliced-together images," observed:

> the actors engage in cubist hi-jinks, hashing the action to bits, and stepping in and out of their roles quicker than one normally shucks an overcoat. There is a wild, and faintly benumbing prologue, full of comic shtick and firing squads and apparently random lines from all three Buechner plays. There is a Keystone Kops-style chase under strobe light, and a peek-a-boo slow-motion chase. There [is] . . . manic repetition of some lines to the point of near-insanity, and a giant old-fashioned squeeze-bulb camera that spews wedding photos of Princess Lena, which are then distributed among the audience. There's a giant and genuinely grotesque, drag-ball sequence at the end, and the front row of the house is called into play as a forest for the wedding procession to pass through.

Ciulei, who also mounted the work in Vancouver, soon provided the Arena with Maxim Gorky's *The Lower Depths* (1977), Shakespeare's *Hamlet* (1978), Molière's *Don Juan* (1979), and Slawomir Mrozek's *Emigrés* (1980). His Bucharest version of *The Lower Depths* had used a vertical set requiring the characters to climb to their cubicles. At the Arena, the sleeping spaces were laid out horizontally on the circular stage, where they resembled coffinlike crates, suggesting that the people were refuse.

Hamlet, set in a Bismarckian 19th-century world, reminded many of the conspiratorial atmosphere of Nixonian Washington. Ciulei intimated that beneath the polished surface of court life teemed an army of termites. Although the production drew both compliments and disparagement, most admired Ophelia's mad scene, which interrupted a formal dinner party. The *New York Times* commented, "The rupture that Hamlet made in the life of the Court could not be more agonizingly portrayed than by the fierce chanting of this girl in evening dress whose collapse disrupts a world of starched shirt-fronts, cut-glass and guilt."

Ciulei's Bulandra stagings of Paul Foster's *Elizabeth I* and I. L. Caragiale's *The Lost Letter* briefly visited

The Tempest. *Directed by Liviu Ciulei. (1981)*   (Photo: Guthrie Theater/Bruce Goldstein)

the Arena and New York's La Mama. The former was restaged in English for the Acting Company (1979), for whom he also did Carlo Goldoni's *Il Campiello, a Venetian Comedy* (1981).

He made a formidable debut in New York with his Off-Broadway staging of Frank Wedekind's *Spring Awakening* (1978), transferred from a student production at the Juilliard Theater Center to the Public Theater. Ciulei's design—a mesh fence dividing upstage from downstage—metaphorically captured Wedekind's criticism of the sexual repression forced on adolescents. Henry Popkin reported, "The only scenes outside [the fence] are those showing the only ways to get out—a funeral and the last piece of action, in which one of the boys finally liberates himself." The production—which borrowed music from Franz Schubert and Robert Schumann to

heighten the nuances—mixed realism with surrealism. A striking moment was the sight of four girls in blue tights slinking over a professor's desk as the latter unjustly reprimanded Melchior. Ciulei later explained that the image had been mentioned earlier by Melchior's recently deceased friend Moritz; its popping into the boy's head has no apparent reason except that people often think of the unexpected in trying circumstances.

In 1980, Ciulei became artistic director of Minneapolis's Guthrie Theater, which was then undergoing serious problems concerning its artistic identity. He remained for five years, offering productions by various important experimental directors, but balancing them with commercial fare. His own much talked-of mountings included *The Tempest* (1981), the world premiere of German playwright Thomas Bernhard's

Eve of Retirement (1981), *As You Like It* (1982), Bertolt Brecht's *The Threepenny Opera* (1983), Henrik Ibsen's *Peer Gynt* (1983), *Twelfth Night* (1984), and *A Midsummer Night's Dream* (1985). *The Tempest* pictured Prospero's island as surrounded by blood and strewn with the detritus of Western civilization, such as the *Mona Lisa*, armor, handless clocks, the head of a Venetian equine statue, and a legless grand piano supported by books. According to Mike Steele:

> *Ciulei's production . . . was teeming with references to its director's cultural journey. His Prospero, dressed in a casual cardigan sweater, was an artist-scientist-philosopher pulled from his native land and swept to an alien shore where he would be changed by a new environment, refreshed by new challenges, forced to reconcile Caliban-like primal drives with the Ariel-like magical inspiration of the artist.*

Ciulei endeavors to make the classics contemporary. He argues that no one knows how the plays were originally staged. "Even if we did," he told Frank Lipsius, "two factors have changed since that time: the audience and the performers. The play may be the same, but it has to suit our time."

Peer Gynt employed three different actors to portray Peer at separate life stages. Rustom Bharucha, who found that Ciulei had only sporadically been able to convey the play's social criticism, was impressed by the director's theatricality. Especially vivid was Ciulei's sense of the macabre as depicted in the troll scene (possibly influenced by Peter Stein's German production), in which the trolls wore swinish masks and—in one of the more revealing socially critical effects—underscored their monstrosity by dressing and behaving like Victorian *petits bourgeois*. Bharucha described the difficult-to-stage Threadballs scene:

> *Black, ethereal silhouettes emerge from the billowing smoke and mist to remind Peer of his wasted life. Apart from Aase's ghost, there are representations of a Thought, a Tear, and a Deed, which are projections of Peer's nebulous feelings of guilt and regret.*

Ciulei's Guthrie directorship ended with an interracial, scenically black, white, and red, "bitter" and "frightening" *A Midsummer Night's Dream*. Don Shewey wrote that it was

> *dominated by images of cruelty and humiliation—inflicted by gods on mortals, men on women, aristocracy on peasants, society on artists. The captured . . .*

> *Hippolyta is immediately stripped of her leather armor, which is burned before her eyes while servants cloak her in an insultingly feminine toga. Oberon's interference with the other characters' love lives . . . comes off as blatantly sadistic. Puck's love potion, administered while its victims are blindfolded, causes them to scream and writhe like tortured political prisoners.*

Ciulei's interpretation may have reflected his own disillusion at the Guthrie, from which he resigned under pressure despite reviving its artistic reputation. Subsequently, he freelanced in regional theaters and abroad, also staging operas. In the U.S., he offered a restaging of *Hamlet* (1986) at the Public, with a brilliant performance by Kevin Kline; a failed version of *The Inspector General* (1978) at Broadway's Circle in the Square; Shakespeare's *Coriolanus* (1987) at the McCarter; Euripides' *The Bacchae* (1987) at the Guthrie; and Anton Chekhov's *Platonov* (1988) at the American Repertory Theater. At the Arena, he directed Luigi Pirandello's *Six Characters in Search of an Author* (1988; also in Seattle, 1990), *A Midsummer Night's Dream* (1989), Victor Slavkin's *Cerceau* (1990), and William Saroyan's *The Time of Your Life* (1991), which the director characterized as "a fable about reality—the wishful thinking about how we would like people to be but not how they truly are."

Ciulei's staging has been considered as visually expressive and technically precise as mime. He works out all movements in detail and insists on exactitude in their execution. He has been kidded as resembling one who might ask an actor to leap into the air and pause briefly before landing.

In Rumania, he often depended on developing his ideas improvisationally, not in a prepared promptbook. This was modified in the American theater because of shorter rehearsal periods and his often having directed the same plays before. Still, even when doing *Leonce and Lena*, he allowed for improvisational rehearsals.

When working with experienced actors, he creates an unusually collaborative atmosphere, accepting input patiently and sensitively, although demonstrating his objections to certain ideas. Despite his sometimes being criticized as one whose architectural and design training leads him to focus excessively on decor and choreography, he has frequently succeeded in extracting unforgettable performances. An example of his taking the actor's problems into consideration occurred during *Leonce and Lena*, when an actor felt constrained by Ciulei's demands. The director told him that "it will not have the comedy or the importance it needs until the actor instills his own personality into it. . . . It is very important that the actor not feel restricted by anything" (Pfafferodt and Bosniak). Ciulei is not reticent about discussing the historical and social background of a work, and informs actors of significant things concerning the playwright. He might also sketch in character biographies for the cast.

Ciulei's American career has been erratic and his work subject to accusations of gimmickry and egocentricity. He has, however, retained his international reputation as the leading figure from a nation that, since the 1970s, has produced a string of great directors skilled at visualizing, in audaciously theatrical presentations, the hidden currents in classical works.

Further reading:

Bharucha, Rustom. "Ciulei's *Peer Gynt:* Under the Sign of the Onion." *Theatre* 15 (Winter 1983).

Lipsius, Frank. "Ciulei's Way: 'What Is this Tradition Thing?'" *Connoisseur* 214 (August 1984).

Pfafferodt, Hans-Gert, and Sloane Bosniak. "Büchner's 'Leonce and Lena' at the Arena Stage, Washington." *Theatre Quarterly* 16 (November-January 1975).

Popkin, Henry. "Another Rumanian Theatrical Master Gets a Showing." *New York Times*, July 2, 1978.

Shewey, Don. "Shaping a 'Dream' Far More Bitter Than Puckish." *New York Times*, July 6, 1986.

Steele, Mike. "The Romanian Connection." *American Theatre* 2 (July/August 1985).

Also: Leiter, *Shakespeare Around the Globe.*

MARTHA CLARKE (1944–   )

MARTHA CLARKE was born in suburban Baltimore where her father was an affluent jazz musician *cum* attorney and her mother a chamber pianist. She studied dance, entered the Juilliard School, and began performing with Anna Sokolow's company. She also studied painting at the Art Students League. In 1972, after a brief period of retirement following her marriage, she joined the acrobatic dance troupe Pilobolus. In 1978, she cofounded her own company, Crowsnest, and soon found a sponsor for her dance-theater pieces in Lyn Austin of the Music-Theater Group.

Her first program was Maria Irene Fornes's *Cabbages* and *Dr. Kheal* (1979), starring Linda Hunt, produced in Stockbridge, Massachusetts. Then she did George W. Trow's *Elizabeth Dead* (1980) Off-Off-Broadway, with the diminutive Hunt as Queen Elizabeth. This was an obscure, 75-minute, blank verse, memory monologue spoken by the queen just before dying. *A Metamorphosis in Miniature* (1982), which Clarke conceived, adapted, and directed, was a "work in progress" (a term given to the premieres of most of her subsequent work) and marked her as an imaginative, collaborative conceptualist. For this 45-minute, two-actor interpretation of Franz Kafka's *Metamorphosis*, Clarke trained actor David Rounds to suggest through movement and facial expressions alone the insect that Gregor has become. Hunt played all of the other roles. "It is remarkable how many art forms Clarke has compressed into her exquisite miniature," declared the *New York Post*.

In 1984, after a lengthy gestation, Clarke's breakthrough work, *The Garden of Earthly Delights*, premiered Off-Broadway and subsequently toured internationally, revised, and revived through 1988. *Garden* was a theatricalization of Hieronymus Bosch's 15th-century tryptich painting revealing the pleasures of heaven and the horrors of hell. Clarke combined visual, auditory, and performing arts to create a wordless, image-filled event in which seven dancer-actors (including herself) depicted the numerous medieval hallucinations in Bosch's crowded landscape. The pictures were animated through choreographic movement, including acrobatic, wire-supported aerial dancing against a sceneryless, but expressively lighted, void. Visions of comic and cruel grotesquerie mingled with the sublimely beautiful and tenderly erotic. The actors—dressed in flesh-colored tights—passed through the Garden of Eden and the Garden of Earthly Delights, then encountered the Seven Deadly Sins, and ended in Hell. They impersonated not only characters such as Adam and Eve, but objects including floating islands, trees, and mythological creatures. Masks were employed as well. Three musicians not only played their instruments but were part of the action. Characters could hide behind a glockenspiel or be tortured by a bass drum. The production began Clarke's ongoing collaboration with composer Richard Peaslee and lighting designer Paul Gallo.

As with most of her work, some felt the 60-minute piece was more dance than theater. Mel Gussow

The Garden of Earthly Delights. *Directed by Martha Clarke. Clarke is at the extreme right.* (Photo: Martha Swope Associates/Carol Rosegg)

declared, "In Martha Clarke's work, theater and dance are inseparable, unified into a style that lacks a name but not a dimension. Her pieces, marked by their precision and visual beauty, are performance art objects." Clarke described her work to Jennifer Dunning:

> There is a look of distilled images to it, a kind of cinematic accuracy. . . . I think of moving paintings. Or the house that you pass in a train at night. You never forget the moment you see someone move through the lighted window. I want my work to be endless windows.

Clarke confirmed her presence with Off-Broadway's 60-minute *Vienna: Lusthaus* (1986). (An earlier version, *Fromage Dangereuse*, was seen at Stockbridge in 1984.) Inspired by an exhibition about Vienna, she was engaged with capturing the essence of the morally decaying, fin-de-siècle city, which she did by beautifully coordinating performance and visual artistry to create a densely surreal experience. The images—alluding to figures such as

Sigmund Freud, Arthur Schnitzler, Adolph Hitler, Ludwig Wittgenstein, and Gustave Klimt—lap dissolved like a film from one into another, demanding considerable concentration.

This extensively researched production, its 157-word, fragmentary text by historian-dramatist Charles L. Mee Jr. (whose dreams provided him with inspiration), its gorgeous costumes and minimalist set by Robert Israel (beginning his collaboration with Clarke), were viewed through a scrim on a white box set with expressionistically tilted, towering walls built in perspective. It was a nonnarrative collage of dreamlike impressions capturing Vienna's cultural highlights, decadent hetero- and homosexuality, and political and military dread. Behind the pictures of beauty lurked terror or madness. An anti-Semitic undertone forecast the Nazi death camps. One indelible image revealed an actor wearing boots on his hands and miming two people having innumerably varied sexual experiences; an equine image revealed a soldier transmogrifying into a Lippizaner stallion. At the conclusion, snow fell as the male waltzers were transformed into jackbooted soldiers marching inexorably toward World War I.

Vienna: Lusthaus. *Directed by Martha Clarke. (1986)* (Photo: Martha Swope Associates/Carol Rosegg)

In 1987, Clarke returned to Kafka to stage an Off-Broadway, mixed-media version of Richard Greenberg's collage-text, *The Hunger Artist.* It was based on various Kafka writings. As abridged portions were read, actors performed them on a set composed of what the *Times* called "an expansive graveyard of dark earth in the foreground, a pinched room out of Beckett in the rear." The often ambiguous evening—designed, Clarke told Mel Gussow, to explore ideas of "emotional and literal starvation"—had Fellinesque and Beckettian touches, and moments of great interest. Although some scenes evoked Kafka's dark psyche, the piece was generally considered inaccurately Kafkaesque.

In 1988, Clarke turned to *Miracolo d'Amore,* developed at three festivals before arriving at the Public Theater, and sparked by Italo Calvino's Italian folk tales. Unlike its predecessors, it eschewed dancing and comprehensible text, and used an idiosyncratic pidgin Italian that was sung, as well as bird and dog sounds, sounds of wind and sea, and Latin passages from Dante and Petrarch. Considerable nudity was employed. The play wandered away from Calvino into autobiographical concerns with male violence toward victimized women, and was Clarke's first work without a specific world (Bosch, Vienna, etc.) as a foundation. This led to thematic ideas considered negligibly secondary to what were emotionally superficial aesthetic devices; in fact, Clarke was accused of displaying empty mannerisms. Although less innovative than earlier Clarke works, *Miracolo*—using slow motion for scenes of murder and rape—was expertly staged and contained pretty images. These extended from 19th-century Grandvillian women-as-flowers to those involving 17th-century Tiepolo-inspired figures of Pulcinella—the hunchbacked, wife-beating *commedia dell'arte* clown—in tall, conical hats, who maltreat women they encounter on a piazza. The set was a pie-shaped wedge with walls and floor painted Venetian red and with doors and windows through which musicians and others could be seen.

The Music-Theater Group (not involved with *Miracolo*) produced Clarke's 1990 work, the expensive, circus-influenced *Endangered Species,* which premiered at a tent in Pittsfield, Massachusetts, before coming to Brooklyn. She started the project after viewing a PBS special about animal preservation and elephant poaching. The text consisted of bits and pieces of Walt Whitman, and the Civil War provided a background motif. A circus elephant named Flora became a hopefully mysterious centerpiece, but there were other animals as well, including several horses. The animals, in their innocence, created a contrasting impression to the shifting images of human deception, warmaking, domination, and oppression (sexual and racial). The animals, actors, dancers, and singers performed on a spare set dressed with a large iron bed and oversized upstage doors that periodically opened to reveal the mist-enshrouded pachyderm. The movement of the animals and of several acrobatic performers provided fascinating interludes, but the textual interpolations were thought simplistic. In an arresting image, a female performer hid beneath one of the prostrate Flora's ears before emerging to slither over its body. For all its daring, the 65-minute show was bombarded (the *Times* termed it "elephantine" and "literal-minded"), although it had strong defenders. Scheduled for five weeks, it closed after two.

Most recently, Clarke created a stunning eleven-minute work called *Dämmerung* (1992) that premiered in the Netherlands and received its American debut at the American Dance Festival in Durham, North Carolina the following year. Set against a moody background of clouds, and accompanied by the music of Alban Berg, it featured dancer Gary Chryst in a tour-de-force performance depicting, wrote Anna Kisselgoff in the *Times,* "a man in the twilight of his life. His death onstage is so visibly a metaphor for Death in general that the end comes across as particularly brutal. Miss Clarke has outdone herself in this coup de théâtre." Chryst entered in a dark business suit and performed various dynamic actions that displayed the character's uncertainty and fear before the only other character, a woman dressed in black with a lace collar and symbolizing "the beloved or Death" entered. Finally, "Mr. Chryst goes rigid (as if shot) and takes off his jacket. The audience sees his back and for the first time, a bloodstain on his shirt." According to Kisselgoff, the ambiguity of the piece allowed for it to evoke images of Bosnia as well as of an AIDS victim.

Clarke heavily researches her backgrounds, including looking at art and viewing relevant films. In preparing *The Hunger Artist* she studied paintings by Chagall and Goya, viewed photos by Sander, and watched Fellini's *8½,* among other films. When images stick in her "mental filing cabinet," they often end up in a production, although the connection between result and source may seem vague. A photograph of a man with boots on his hands was used for the well-known sex sequence in *Vienna: Lusthaus.*

Clarke creates improvisationally. She is extremely collaborative and open to ideas. Some of her best ideas may come from her designers, who do their work in the maelstrom of rehearsals. The performers—chosen because of their individualistic appearances and qualities as well as technical ability—commit themselves on a deep level to achieve her process-oriented goals; she considers them extremely brave to do so. Clarke always makes the final choices herself. To generate images, she may simply tell her cast to entertain her; she will select from their discoveries. In *Miracolo*, she set them going by giving them a book by Charles Darwin. Her rehearsals look chaotic to outsiders, and her own uncertainty is worn like a badge. She may say nothing all day long except now and then to express approval. In this atmosphere, even accidents may be a fruitful source. Discoveries are put down in a notebook. Pulling the piece together is what she calls its "curve," but others might call it the spine. "I stumble the piece into shape," she said to Arthur Bartow, "and often don't get a vision until late in the process." Some actors—as opposed to dancers—reportedly have found Clarke's dependence on intuition too trying.

She told Bartow that, when her actors attempt ideas, "I don't want to see transitions or well-developed characters, and I tell my dancers that I don't want what they do to look like choreography." She notices fragments and puts them together with others, thus constructing an image which produces resonances when combined with other, similarly created, images. She has been greatly influenced by Milan Kundera's novels in which narrative explanation is minimalized, if provided at all.

Clarke has less confidence working with texts than movement, which can depend on abstractions. Words that introduce subtext and motivation provoke the actor's thinking. As she informed Bartow, she will ask the actors, "What do you *feel* about this, and what do you *need* to . . . whatever?," or say, "Why don't you try it that way?," or even "Just read it and we'll see."

Clarke's composer and designers and many performers go from work to work with her. The creation of a piece may take from six months to two years. Using a system of trial and error made possible by workshops, she struggles to create physically beautiful associative images revelatory of her concerns. She constantly revises and changes; the process often concludes with something far different from what was there at the beginning. Because her method is instinctive, she often finds herself midway in rehearsals frightened to death and without a clue as to where the work is going. *Miracolo* began as a work with text and was altered to pure pantomime six

weeks later. *Endangered Species* began as a work about the Holocaust, but—apart from some fleeting moments—became about the Civil War despite research and writing with the former background in mind. Many tricks arduously taught to the elephant were removed. In *The Garden*, she discarded an entire set in favor of a bare stage when she realized the obtrusiveness of the exquisite original.

She whittles, refines, and replaces until a pristine form emerges, stripped of everything extraneous. The last days before an opening, when she feels her objectivity is at its sharpest, see her working in a frenzy to finalize and polish; many outstanding notions—often her favorites—get tossed out. This helps cut the running times for her productions. "I have a terrible fear of things going on too long," she informed Gussow.

Clarke's most frequent theme is what she calls "battered love," which stems from her own life and experiences. "Each piece I choose," she told Gussow, "is a way for me to explain myself to myself." However, her most recent productions have caused complaints that, regardless of her aesthetic achievements, her creations are increasingly hollow, didactic, and self-important. She herself has wondered whether her contributions are not an example of the emperor's new clothes.

Prior to the debacle of *Endangered Species*, Clarke, the recipient of a generous MacArthur "genius" award, was planning to retire from the field of *auteurist* direction because of worries over funding and the anguish of bringing her personal demons to artistic life. She wants to work on films, operas (she directed *The Magic Flute* at Glimmerglass in 1992), and well-structured texts not of her own devising. Her three sequential catastrophes, as well as the tribulations that forced the closing of her last piece, could only have furthered this inclination.

Further reading:

Anderson, Porter. "Wild Kingdom." *TheaterWeek*, October 15–21, 1990.

Bennetts, Leslie. "Dream Imagery of *Vienna: Lusthaus*." *New York Times*, April 23, 1986.

Dunning, Jennifer. "Bosch's *Garden* Is Brought to Life." *New York Times*, November 18, 1984.

Gussow, Mel. "Clarke Worke." *New York Times Magazine*, January 18, 1987.

Hafrey, Leigh. "By Candlelight, Martha Clarke Creates Three-Ring Theater." *New York Times*, July 21, 1990.

Also: Bartow, *Director's Voice*.

HAROLD CLURMAN (1901–1980)

HAROLD CLURMAN was born in New York City, where his father was a physician. He was educated at Columbia University but left in 1921 to study in Paris at the Sorbonne, where he received the Diplome. Clurman attended the theater lectures of Jacques Copeau, who influenced him by his emphasis on the importance of the text.

Back in New York in 1924, Clurman became involved in the professional theater, first with the Experimental Theater (on what would soon be known as Off-Broadway) and then with the Theater Guild, where, until 1931, he served in various capac-

ities. Clurman took classes with ex-Stanislavsky actor Richard Boleslavsky and, in 1928, took his first stabs at directing when he and fellow employee Lee Strasberg staged two studio works.

Clurman made a crucial leap forward in the summer of 1931 when he, Strasberg, and Cheryl Crawford (another Guild worker) founded the Group Theater, begun as a Guild offshoot. They prepared for their first season by spending the summer at a Connecticut country resort. The Group soon became the nation's most important company, although Clurman was mainly an administrator and teacher;

Odets' Awake and Sing! *Directed by Harold Clurman. (1935) L to r: Morris Carnovsky, John Garfield, Art Smith, Stella Adler, Phoebe Brand.*   (Photo: Theater Collection, Museum of the City of New York)

he later became a renowned acting and directing instructor. He only began directing when Strasberg rejected Clifford Odets's *Awake and Sing* (1935).

The Group stressed the importance of a relatively permanent, nonstar ensemble, the production of socially aware plays, and the employment of a Stanislavsky-based, company acting style. Strasberg gave this theory his own idiosyncratic interpretation ("the Method"), emphasizing above all the technique of emotional memory, which requires an actor's feelings to be called forth by specific memories. Clurman (and Group member Stella Adler, whom he married in 1943), however, met Stanislavsky in 1934 and discovered that he had altered his ideas in favor of a method of physical actions in which emotion arises unconsciously, and therefore organically, from the actor's commitment to the play's given circumstances. This presumably leads to less self-indulgence, because the actor concentrates on the character, not himself.

The Group tried operating as an anticommercial entity in the commercial rat race, and by 1941 succumbed to financial and internal pressures, although it did enjoy a few hits. From 1937, Clurman was in sole command. By the time it ended, the Group had given the American theater a tremendous surge of energy through the works of several playwrights, most notably Odets. Influential artists such as Robert Lewis, Elia Kazan, John Garfield, Franchot Tone, Luther Adler, Sanford Meisner, Mordecai Gorelik, and Morris Carnovsky were vitalized by the Group.

The Group was political only in a very broad sense; despite the public perception, and even the existence of a communist cell, its plays avoided narrow ideology and expressed a liberal humanism. Clurman remained true to this vision. The Group's choices were dictated by the ethical, social, and moral dilemmas concerning their authors and not by specific political goals.

Following the significant success of *Awake and Sing,* about a middle-class Jewish family suffering the effects of the Depression, Clurman's Group projects included four more Odets plays: *Paradise Lost* (1935), *Golden Boy* (1937), *Rocket to the Moon* (1938), and *Night Music* (1940). Clurman also staged Irwin Shaw's *The Gentle People* (1939) and *Retreat to Pleasure* (1941), the Group's final production.

During the early forties, when he was writing an account of the Group, he directed two failures: Odets's adapation of Konstantin Simonov's Soviet play, *The Russian People* (1942), and Theodore

Reeves's *Beggars Are Coming to Town* (1945). The second half of the decade, during which he was also active as a producer and critic, saw him direct Maxwell Anderson's *Truckline Café* (1946), with Marlon Brando; another Simonov play, *The Whole World Over* (1947); the road version, with Anthony Quinn, of Tennessee Williams's *A Streetcar Named Desire* (1948); N. Richard Nash's *The Young and the Fair* (1949), which was the first of four plays he directed starring Julie Harris; and one of his greatest achievements, Carson McCullers's delicate but offbeat tale of a lonely young Southern girl's budding maturity, *The Member of the Wedding* (1950), with brilliant performances by Harris, Ethel Waters, and Brandon de Wilde. The play's plotlessness puzzled many, but Clurman's sensitive direction made it consistently compelling. The same year saw Arthur Laurents's *The Bird Cage.*

Now began a productive decade during which he staged 18 plays. The most significant were Lillian Hellman's *The Autumn Garden* (1951); a revival of Eugene O'Neill's *Desire Under the Elms* (1952); Laurents's *The Time of the Cuckoo* (1952); William Inge's *Bus Stop,* with a triumphant Kim Stanley performance; his only musical, Richard Rodgers and Oscar Hammerstein II's unsuccessful *Pipe Dream* (1955); Williams's *Orpheus Descending* (1957); O'Neill's posthumous *A Touch of the Poet* (1958); S. N. Behrman's *The Cold Wind and the Warm* (1958); George Bernard Shaw's *Caesar and Cleopatra* (1959), for Tel Aviv's Habimah Theater; and Shaw's *Heartbreak House* (1959). Moreover, Clurman became a major interpreter of French drama via his stagings of three Jean Anouilh plays, most notably *The Waltz of the Toreadors* (1957; revived in 1958), as well as Jean Giraudoux's intellectual comedy about the Trojan war, *Tiger at the Gates* (1955), starring Michael Redgrave, and staged in London before transferring to Broadway.

Clurman's directing declined in the sixties. His most outstanding productions were Marcel Achard's French comedy-mystery, *A Shot in the Dark* (1961), adapted by Harry Kurnitz and starring Harris; Giraudoux's *Judith* (1962); Arthur Miller's *Incident at Vichy* (1964), at the new Lincoln Center Repertory Theater; two O'Neill productions in Tokyo; Inge's *Where's Daddy* (1966); Anton Chekhov's *Uncle Vanya* (1969) in Los Angeles; and O'Neill's *Long Day's Journey into Night* (1978) in Washington, D.C. During this period Clurman taught college, lectured, served as Lincoln Center's dramaturge during the brief Elia Kazan-Robert Whitehead tenure (1963–

1964); wrote criticism for *The Nation;* and authored books.

Clurman's over 40 productions reveal high standards of selection, although his record in the classics is minimal. Most of his authors represented high literary and theatrical values; many received more than one production at his hands. The oldest play he ever did was *Uncle Vanya.* He believed deeply in only doing plays that spoke to current concerns; apart from certain exceptions, he thought that most old plays were not especially relevant to modern audiences. Although his repertoire included plays in a variety of styles, most were at least superficially realistic (although often with a poetic sensibility) in contemporary settings, with a theme of some social pertinence, and with a generally optimistic outlook. His stylized staging of *The Waltz of the Toreadors* revealed his ability to employ less realistic approaches when necessary. For all his realism, however, Clurman was noted for his ability to evoke poetically nuanced performances rather than busily naturalistic ones. The script always came first, and his goal was to be faithful to it.

Clurman believed that the best theater could only originate from the community created by a company with a distinct identity working closely together and sharing similar social and artistic ideas. The best results were obtained when the company was trained in a common method. Following the Group's demise, the closest he came to finding a similar situation was the short-lived Lincoln Center company. Whenever he directed, however, he cast with an ensemble concept in mind and used whatever means he could to establish a family feeling among the actors.

Clurman wrote a thoroughly detailed promptbook, having spent much time contemplating the script, researching its background, and making comments on it. He claimed that he wrote directorial "notes" and that the actors, like musicians, played them. He was the author (or composer) of the production and the playwright that of the script. He pondered questions relating to the impulses that led to the writing of the play, its meaning, and what made it moving or important. Knowledge of the playwright was crucial to comprehending his writing. He wrote down his impressions during repeated readings, including his formulation of the style and visual look. This sometimes conflicted with the author's directions, as when he revised Miller's description of the set for *Incident at Vichy* as a police station to one expressive of a Kafkaesque detention room, with more theatrical opportunities for entrances and exits than in the original. His objective was to evoke,

not so much a specific place, as a metaphorically appropriate environment.

His notes (many of which have been published) were refined into definitions of the play's "main action" or "spine," and the spines of all the characters (ideas developed from Stanislavsky's concern with objectives and superobjectives). The spine for *The Member of the Wedding,* for instance, was "to get 'connected'." Each character's spine had to connect to that of the play as a whole. Clurman's notes also commented on each character's qualities, style, business, and even "psychological gestures." Couching his spine discoveries in terms of "action" verbs, he might tell the actress playing Bessie in *Awake and Sing* that she always wants "to take care of everything." Frankie's in *The Member of the Wedding* was "to get out of herself." This helped the actress choose actions that made her character live actively and convincingly, and thus she was able to eliminate generalities, such as "to be strident." Characters have desires or "wants"; the desires are actions (or "beats") and carrying them out leads to further actions, with the entire play being a sequence of such desires interconnecting with those of the other characters; conflicting desires by others create obstacles that have to be overcome. As one "beat" concludes, another begins, even if the actor has no lines. Although Clurman noted all such "beats" in his prompt book, he was undogmatic and did not dictate them, using them instead as his guideline, to be called on only when needed.

On the blank page facing the text, Clurman entered three columns in which comments keyed to specific lines were written. One was for the basic action, another for the attitude or adjustment to that action (the manner in which it would be enacted), and the third for the physicalization of the action (the "business").

Clurman was one of the few Broadway directors who, during the first week or so of rehearsals, had the actors sit and read the script. At first he was silent, but as they read it again and again, he increasingly interrupted to offer advice about meanings and characters and to explain where the beats were. (Group actors called these "talking rehearsals.") He was brilliant at these sessions, and his literary and psychological perceptions, combined with his passionate way of expressing himself (he might get carried to the point of inarticulateness), made his analyses—liberally seasoned with metaphors and similes—exciting. Because of Clurman's preoccupation with social relevance, these discussions made the actors aware of the play's meaning for themselves and society. Actors became imbued with the play's wider importance beyond its entertainment value.

He used suggestive means to stimulate the actors and had a keen ability to sense what an actor needed to spark his imagination, but he refused to impose himself and hated to push for results. Sometimes he read the lines himself, hoping to incite an understanding of the action behind them, but he asserted that the actor was not to imitate him. He was acclaimed for his ability to draw out performances vastly superior to those the same actors provided under others. When, on rare occasions (such as Ralph Richardson in *The Waltz of the Toreadors*), an actor insisted on specific direction, Clurman provided it, but reluctantly.

Once the actors were sufficiently familiar with the play, he got them up on their feet; however, he declined to block, apart from setting exits and entrances and the like, believing that the best staging comes from the actors themselves making their choices organically on the basis of character needs. If the actor understood his spine, then he could create his own business and determine his own activities. Clurman felt that with actors who had an instinct for self-blocking, a play could be blocked in two days. He saw himself more as an editor than a "stager." His productions, therefore, were theatrical-

ized or obviously "directorial," and exemplified the "invisible director" school. Early in his career, he employed improvisations to induce lifelike behavior, but he gave this up because of the time it consumed and because it often proved counterproductive, leading the actor to play himself rather than the role. Although his promptbook had a column for business, its comments were notably sparse.

Harold Clurman's contributions to the Group and to the principles established there of honesty in acting and social commitment in play selection made him one of the modern American theater's most distinguished personages.

Further reading:

Clurman, Harold. *The Fervent Years: The Story of the Group Theatre and the Thirties.* Rev. ed. New York: Hill and Wang, 1957.

———. *All People Are Famous (Instead of an Autobiography).* New York: Harcourt Brace Jovanovich, 1974.

———. *On Directing.* New York: Macmillan, 1974.

Eustis, Morton. "The Director Takes Command, III: Murray Anderson and Harold Clurman." *Theatre Arts* 20 (April 1936).

Also: Johnson, *Directing Methods.*

JACQUES COPEAU (1879–1949)

JACQUES COPEAU was born in Paris, where his father ran an iron foundry. His formal education at the Sorbonne was interrupted in 1901 because of family problems. After living briefly in Copenhagen, he began to claim attention in Paris through his criticism. In 1909, he cofounded the *Nouvelle Revue Française,* an influential periodical, and he became known as a theatrical reformer.

His 1911 experience in codirecting (with Arsène Durec) a production of his and Jean Croué's adaptation of *The Brothers Karamazov* convinced him that the complacent French theater needed a visionary director to shake its foundations. This led to his 1913 founding of the revolutionary Théâtre du Vieux-Colombier located in an out-of-the-way street. Copeau set out to rid the theater of its commercialism and restore it to a plane of high artistic worth. His goal raised economic problems, as Copeau wanted to offer a subscription program of repertory at popular prices in a theater that sat only 500 (later reduced to 360).

"Ensemble" was vital to Copeau, who viewed his company as a troupe of actor-priests who placed their unselfish devotion and high moral standards at the service of art. He hated the word *cabotin,* which suggests the ham who puts himself before his art. Copeau believed that acting had declined from a once noble art and had been overrun by *cabotins.* He wished to restore it to a position of respect. He believed it would be helpful to raise his troupe's artistic and moral consciousness by removing them from the city's decadence and working with them in the countryside. They repaired to his home at Limon to prepare their first season, rehearsing and practicing out of doors in a strict regimen of physical and acting exercises, including sports, improvisation, sight-reading, and the study of plays and theories.

They began with Thomas Heywood's Elizabethan drama, *A Woman Killed with Kindness* (1913), which was followed by a varied repertory of classics and moderns, including Molière, Paul Claudel, and Shakespeare (*Twelfth Night,* which was a hit), as well as *The Brothers Karamazov.* Several actors became outstanding figures on the French stage, among them Louis Jouvet and Charles Dullin.

The outbreak of World War I cut short their plans and the theater had to close down for the duration. Copeau planned for the future, developing the idea of an actor-training school as an adjunct to the theater. He was inspired by a sojourn in Florence with designer-director Gordon Craig at the latter's theater school, and from meetings in Switzerland with eurhythmic master Emile Jacques Dalcroze and pioneer designer Adolphe Appia. Their ideas on the mise-en-scène, stage rhythm, and lighting proved invaluable. From 1915 to 1917, much of his energy was devoted to setting up and running his school.

In 1917, Copeau went to lecture in America and soon brought over his company, which he ensconced at New York's Garrick Theater for two arduous years. They opened with Molière's *The Tricks of Scapin,* with Copeau in the title role. This highly successful piece employed a practically bare stage, the most notable feature of which was an unadorned, two-and-one-half-foot-high rectangular platform set up on the stage floor, and reached by steps on each side. The vivid staging had the actors leaping on and off the platform with their slapstick antics. The naked platform (*trèteau nu*) became an important feature in Copeau's work. Though well received, the company was forced by economic pressures to stage many of the commercial plays which Copeau disliked. The schedule was tortuous, producing close to 50 plays in two seasons.

The company returned to Paris in 1919 and resumed production at the Vieux-Colombier (newly redesigned by Jouvet) with *The Winter's Tale,* which opened in 1920. Many productions followed, averaging three a week in rotating repertory, all of them employing with great imagination the flexible but highly simplified architecture that Jouvet had created. The company achieved worldwide fame for its brilliant acting and staging. Plays by Molière, Charles Vildrac, Prosper Merimée, Jules Romains, Henri Ghéon, Pierre de Beaumarchais, and many others were staged, the total for Copeau's seven seasons, including those in New York, reaching 85. The plays included medieval, Elizabethan, neoclassic, symbolist, romantic, and realistic examples.

A key factor in play selection was its emphasis on character over situation, because Copeau considered plays emphasizing the opposite to be farces or melodramas, in which he was uninterested. His new plays were infrequently successful; they tended to be more

literary than theatrical, many being the work of novelists.

The inexorable schedule took its toll on the sensitive Copeau, whose health began to suffer. By 1924, he had lost Dullin and Jouvet; after the painful failure of his own play, *The Birthplace,* he disbanded the company and moved with a contingent of actors, family, and students to a farmhouse in the Burgundy countryside. He hoped to create a group of highly moral, dedicated, and disciplined artists devoting their lives to experiments in theatrical style and truth. Masks and improvisation became important, and the work was aimed for the enjoyment of the local populace. Economics depleted the troupe until only a core of six remained, including Suzanne Bing, his nephew Michel Saint-Denis, and Copeau's son Pascal. They were known as "the Copiaus." Their offerings were mainly short musical and comic pieces, several by Copeau himself, and a number related specifically to harvesting.

Their work increasingly bypassed the literary in favor of commedia physicality and humor, training in which continued after they moved to Pernand-Vergelleses, Côte d'Or, in 1925. The company would arrive at a fairground or similar venue and set up a naked stage. In 1927, Copeau left the company, which lasted two more years. Saint-Denis took over the remaining disciples in 1930 and founded the influential Compagnie des Quinze.

After 1928, Copeau's directing became international. He staged an English-language production of *The Brothers Karamazov* for the Theater Guild in New York (1928); several spectacular outdoor religious pageants in Italy, including the 15th-century *The Mystery of Saint Uliva* (1933), which used multiple locales in an actual monastery; a few productions for the Comédie Française and other Paris theaters; and a 1938 outdoor staging of Shakespeare's *As You Like It* in Florence's Boboli Gardens. He became the head of the Comédie Française in 1940, but resigned in 1941, presumably because of problems with the Nazis. His final production—after which he retired to the country—was a medieval play adapted as *The Miracle of the Golden Bread,* staged in a courtyard at the Hospices de Beaune.

Copeau was a fanatical idealist and purist whose aspirations and methods led others to call him a theatrical Jansenist, Jansenism being a puritanical religious sect. He sought an audience that cut across all class lines, but he attempted to regulate their behavior by banning tips to the ushers, insisting on punctuality, preventing spectators from entering after the play had begun, and from leaving before the final curtain.

His theater was stripped-down and functional so as to focus attention on the actor. In 1913, he removed the Vieux-Colombier's proscenium and gilt decor, tying auditorium and stage together in a single unit, making little use of mechanical devices. His designers (especially Jouvet) sought to capture the emotional essence of locales, so his sets used a minimum of place-establishing means. The effect was austere, but visually attractive.

Another architectural advance occurred in New York, but the most famous plan was created in Paris in 1919. A two-tiered forestage (that removed 140 seats in order to enhance the feeling of intimacy) with a trap system, an upstage balcony with a large archway beneath it at stage level, and steps leading down from either side of the balcony were added. With the addition of the proper scenic plugs, curtains, masking flats, and decorative adornments, an extremely wide range of locales could be suggested within the features of the permanent architecture. At stage left was a solid wall, preventing entrances there.

Copeau disliked anything that could get between the audience and the text, and became famous as one whose respect for the playwright and desire to serve him outweighed all other considerations. Actors were not permitted to perform in self-serving ways, and all performances were trimmed of distracting mannerisms. His productions were noted for their clean, uncluttered lines, their rhythmic perfection, their lyrical beauty, and the actors' physical and vocal command. The implicit theatricality of his work led others to think of it as nonillusionistic. Performances sometimes seemed self-consciously didactic, as if Copeau were using the occasion as a lesson for the audience.

Copeau loved improvisation as a training method, believing that it strengthened ensemble acting and aided the actor in reaching the role's inner nature. Eventually, improvisation became a production tool as well (during his Burgundy period), and he spent time trying to devise a modern equivalent of commedia, with character types drawn from the contemporary world.

Choreographic patterns played a big part in Copeau's stagings, and he diligently composed his actors' movements. Because of his simplified settings, movement took on an increased importance. His Molière productions were considered "balletic," although the movements were rooted in reality and never seemed artificial. He constantly sought to elicit truthful, organic performances, regardless of their external theatricality. Theater was never to abandon its humanizing function as a place for the community to share in mankind's foibles and achievements.

Copeau began his preparations by reading the script with all of the production elements in mind, from the casting to the design. Deeper reading colored these initial feelings, and he was soon able to determine the visualization precisely. Then followed preplanning of all movement and business, including the timing and pauses, along with consideration of the characterizations. Unity of style within the work's overriding idea remained primary. Despite his fondness for improvisation, he felt it necessary to have a well-thought-out plan before rehearsals began. Rehearsal discoveries were adapted to his preconceptions.

To Copeau each play was an independent artwork with its own inherent nature. He refused to think of plays in stylistic categories. He mined a play for its innate style and did not fit it into some more general pattern, thus making each of his productions unique and fully expressive of the play itself.

Copeau, a brilliant reader, recited the script to the actors at the first rehearsal. Although time was limited, a period was provided for discussion and analysis. "At table" rehearsals, deemed crucial for unifying the group's approach, went on as long as they could turn up fresh insights. Occasionally, these early sessions were abandoned in favor of improvisations, with the scriptless actors creating characters and situations like those in the play.

While blocking, Copeau moved the actors around but always justified his choices. These sessions, despite being prearranged, remained flexible. Once the actors were off book, they dug into their characters to seek truthful behavior. Copeau struggled to refrain from demonstrating moves, business, or readings, thinking it better to get the right effects through more psychologically sensitive measures, although he occasionally had to show what he wanted. The best way, he said, was halfway between total freedom and coercion. He moved about on stage with the company, whispering, joking, and criticizing.

Copeau was the first great French director of the New Stagecraft, moving theater away from stultifying realism into the realm of pure art, with an eclectic repertoire and method, simplified settings, a permanent architecture, ensemble-based presentational acting, and rigid moral and artistic standards.

Further reading:

Copeau, Jacques. *Copeau: Texts on Theatre.* Edited and translated by John Rudlin and Norman H. Paul. New York: Routledge, 1991.

Rudlin, John. *Jacques Copeau.* Cambridge, England: Cambridge University Press, 1986.

Also: Johnson, *Directing Methods;* Knapp, *The Reign of the Theatrical Director;* Leiter, *From Stanislavsky to Barrault;* Marshall, *The Producer and the Play;* Whitton, *Stage Directors in Modern France.*

NOEL COWARD (1899–1973)

NOEL COWARD was born in Teddington, Middlesex, England. His father worked for a music publisher and later as a piano salesman after the family moved to Surrey. Coward became a child performer, making his debut in 1910. A childhood friend in the profession was Gertrude Lawrence, who later figured importantly in his career.

In the 1920s, after a brief stint in the military, Coward began to gain acceptance as a song writer and playwright. The prodigy starred in many of his

Design for Living. *Directed by Noel Coward. (1933) L to r: Lynn Fontanne, Coward, and Alfred Lunt.* (Photo: Theater Collection, Museum of the City of New York)

own shows and, beginning with 1924's *The Vortex*, directed them as well. (His first professional directing experience, however, had been of Dot Temple's one-act, *The Daisy Chain* in 1912, performed for a special matinee.) After its success in London, *The Vortex*, a sensationalistic drama about a young opium addict (Coward) in conflict with his vain mother, took New York by storm. Although he usually staged the London premiere of his plays and musicals, Coward did not always direct the transatlantic version. The designer of *The Vortex* was G. E. [Gladys] Calthrop, who became his most frequent designer.

Coward's directorial and playwriting career encompasses emotional dramas, high comedies, sentimental operettas, and satirical musical revues. He was a versatile dramatic and musical performer, although best known for portraying flippant sophisticates. Coward became a universal symbol of jaded upper-class elegance, even though he hailed from humble middle-class origins. He gained a worldwide reputation as a stage, screen, and nightclub star in material written by himself and others.

Following *The Vortex*, his directorial contributions during the twenties were of his own plays, *Hay Fever* (London and New York, 1925) and *Bitter Sweet* (London and New York, 1929). The former, a comedy about a weekend at the home of a star actress (Marie Tempest), was not successful, but later became a popular standard. When Coward, still unsure of his abilities, was reticent about giving Tempest instructions, the feisty star demanded them, telling him to stop sitting there and to show her what he wanted. From then on, he grew stronger and more confident. *Bitter Sweet*, for which Coward provided the touching book, lushly melodic music, and sparkling lyrics—it had a score including such standards as "I'll See You Again"—was a hit operetta covering half a century of dramatic time.

Coward began the thirties with his still frequently performed high comedy, *Private Lives* (London, 1930; New York, 1931), in which he costarred with Lawrence as a pair of wittily quarrelsome but still-in-love divorcees who meet by accident and reconcile. The fight scene in which they go at each other with lamps and phonograph records is a classic of comic mayhem.

Cavalcade (London, 1931) revealed an unsuspected side of Coward, being a gigantic, patriotic spectacle with music celebrating British pluck and resilience from 1899 to 1930. This pageant was Coward's masterpiece of directorial organization and skill, requiring 22 elaborate scene changes and a huge company of actors and technicians. He devel-

oped an influential method of rehearsing the crowds. The actors were divided into groups of 20, each group identified by a color, and each actor by a number. A captain headed each group and all the actors wore numbered plaques in their group's color. Coward could then refer to each actor by calling out a color and a number instead of having to know everyone's name.

In 1932 came *Words and Music* (London), a revue that introduced the Coward classics, "Mad About the Boy" and "Mad Dogs and Englishmen"; *Design for Living* (New York, 1933), a hit high comedy about the romantic entanglements of a trio of very close friends, in which Coward costarred with the Lunts, the close friends for whom he had written it; *Conversation Piece* (London, 1934), a musical comedy in which he appeared with France's Yvonne Printemps, who overcame all resistance when she sang "I'll Follow My Secret Heart"; *Point Valaine* (New York, 1935), a sex drama that flopped, despite the Lunts; *Tonight at 8:30* (London and New York, 1936), an extraordinary undertaking in which he and Lawrence acted, sang, and danced in nine of his one-acts, given over three nights in successive triple bill performances; an operetta failure, *Operette* (London, 1938); and another revue, *Set to Music* (New York, 1939). His other thirties directing assignments included revivals of his earlier works and a few plays by others, none of them successful, including the London version of S. N. Behrman's *Biography* (London, 1934).

During the war Coward contributed in various significant ways to the uplifting of national morale, and also provided the public with a distraction from their worries via his hugely successful comedy, *Blithe Spirit* (London, 1941), a satire on spiritualism that forced audiences to laugh in the face of death. In 1943, he toured it around the provinces in a three-play repertory including the semiautobiographical *Present Laughter* (London) and the patriotic *This Happy Breed* (London). He offered London the smart revue *Sigh No More* (1945); the ill-received romantic musical *Pacific 1860* (1946), starring Mary Martin; and, on alternate nights, revivals of *Present Laughter* and *This Happy Breed* (1947).

Coward's gangster-musical, *Ace of Clubs* (London, 1950), fell flat at the onset of the fifties, but he did well with *Relative Values* (London, 1951), a high comedy starring Gladys Cooper. However, *Quadrille* (London, 1952), a lavishly decorated period piece codirected with the Lunts, who starred, pleased few. *After the Ball* (London, 1954), codirected with Robert Helpmann, who also choreographed, was Coward's charming musical adaptation of Oscar Wilde's *Lady Windermere's Fan*. His biggest moneymaker, though, *Nude with Violin* (London, 1956), was staged by star John Gielgud, with Coward "supervising" the production. *Look After Lulu* (New York, 1959), an adaptation of a Georges Feydeau farce, was codirected with Cyril Ritchard.

In the sixties, Coward directed his satirical musical *Sail Away* (New York and London, 1961) and *High Spirits* (New York, 1964), Hugh Martin and Timothy Gray's musicalization of *Blithe Spirit,* starring Bea Lillie. Finally, he staged a major revival of *Hay Fever* (1964) at Britain's new National Theater, a sign that Coward, the frequent butt of critical censure for his presumably shallow dramaturgy, had become a modern classic.

Multiply talented as he was, there are those who believed Coward's greatest gifts were as a director, especially because of his ability to coax splendid performances from actors. Laurence Olivier admitted that Coward rid him of a habit of giggling on stage, which the director (who appeared with Olivier in *Private Lives*) accomplished by making the actor laugh when they were on stage together, thereby forcing Olivier to keep a straight face.

Coward held that an actor should be more dependent on his technical abilities than on the need to fully feel the emotions of a role at every performance. He wanted actors to have complete control of all their resources, especially their thinking processes, and not allow them to get muddled by a sea of emotions. The actor must experience the character's feelings during the rehearsal process, but subsequently should be able to duplicate the physical reactions associated with the feelings without reexperiencing them. He must move the audience, not himself. In Coward's view, the art of comedy acting is vastly underrated, and deserves as much respect as the acting of serious roles. Comedy acting requires all the aspects of emotional and physical control that Coward held in high regard. It also requires perfect timing, one of Coward's hallmarks. But all acting must be honest; anything smacking of self-indulgence is the height of vulgarity.

As a director, Coward gave total focus to his actors, practically wearing blinders and tuning out everything that did not relate to the piece at hand. Although very definite about his goals, he allowed his casts considerable latitude to experiment before interrupting them to add something of his own. He believed in the process of rehearsals as a search for the final form of the script, which he considered little more than a sketch of the ultimate production. Rehearsing with everything worked out beforehand would have belied this belief.

Because he wished to save time, and because he believed it liberating, it was Coward's idiosyncratic practice to require that his actors know all their lines by the first rehearsal (some stars resisted). Coward felt the actor could not be thinking about his interpretation or his character's feelings if he had to worry about lines. He held a company reading, then had them return 10 days later with all their words memorized, even if they did not know all the meanings or motivations. He thought this to be especially valid with comedy, because so much of the actor's work concerns timing. The actor was not to have a polished performance ready at the commencement of rehearsals, merely the confidence in his words which would free him to engage wholeheartedly in a search for the truth of the character and for business that would fill the stage with interesting life.

Because he cast his actors meticulously and then trusted in their inventive instincts, Coward's productions seemed organic and natural. Many found that Coward's method was very helpful, and that it gave the director increased freedom in his capacity to see what areas needed development. Whereas Coward at first may have seemed manipulative, actors soon learned that he had great faith in their imaginative strength. This was seen in his failure to load his scripts with stage directions, which he felt hindered, and did not truly release, creativity.

Coward disliked presenting a company lecture on concept or interpretation, preferring to get them on their feet immediately. He considered such talks limiting, as he needed to give the actors the chance to invent the production under his guidance. He was reticent about providing blocking at the early rehearsals, allowing the actors to select their movements, with him interjecting whenever necessary. As the staging took shape, and the company became comfortable with blocking that they themselves largely had originated, details were increasingly added until a polished form emerged. This was set precisely, and Coward brooked little deviation, not even in the number of steps required to go from one place to another. He thought that such external perfection freed up the actor to provide deeper resonances to his performance; total ease with the externals allowed the actor to add "improvisational" touches that could only arise because of such familiarity with the form. To help bring performances to such a point, he insisted that, whenever possible, technical elements (costumes, sets, props) be ready from the start.

This consummate craftsman worked especially hard to refine rhythm and timing, but sought to create a sense of spontaneity rather than automatism. Still, he often insisted that certain effects could work only if the actor followed his strict count in the way a piece of business was done. It was not always easy to say why the business worked when so performed, but actors learned that, if they followed his directions precisely, laughs that otherwise were absent suddenly appeared. He only gave such specific advice after the actor had already done his analytical homework; the actor thus would have no difficulty realizing the motivation behind the business, although the reason for the results created by the timing may have remained a mystery.

He was loved for his patience and kindness, and he made actors feel comfortable and relaxed. When necessary, he could drill them endlessly, but his sense of humor always kept things pleasant. Much quoted is his response to Edith Evans's tendency (in the 1964 revival of *Hay Fever*) to say "On a *very* clear morning you can see Marlow," although "very" is not in the text. Unable to correct this interpolation by other means, Coward remarked, "Dear Edith. . . . The line is 'on a clear morning you can see Marlow.' On a very clear morning you can also see Beaumont and Fletcher."

He preferred to encourage an actor by helpful hints; only when all else failed did he demonstrate

himself. Rather than dictating, he was more likely to suggest, so that the actor felt as if the result was part of a shared experience. In his later years, however, Coward worked with many actors who were unhappy with his disciplined style, and thought his insistence on craftsmanlike precision bordered on cruelty.

Noel Coward's directing contributions, although not as widely publicized as his playwriting, short-story writing, screenwriting (*Brief Encounter,* among others), acting, singing, composing, and lyric writing—were largely responsible for the success of his plays and musicals, and deserve the recognition he achieved in other areas. Knighted in 1973, he was a unique figure in modern theater deserving his appelation of "the Master."

Further reading:

Coward, Noel. *Present Indicative.* Garden City, N.Y.: Doubleday, 1937.

————. *Future Indefinite.* Garden City, N.Y.: Doubleday, 1954.

Lesley, Cole. *Remembered Laughter.* New York: Alfred A. Knopf, 1976.

Mander, Raymond, and Joe Mitchenson. *Theatrical Companion to Coward.* New York: Macmillan, 1957.

Morley, Sheridan. *A Talent to Amuse.* Garden City, N.Y.: Doubleday, 1969.

GORDON CRAIG (1872–1966)

[EDWARD] GORDON CRAIG was born at Stevenage, Hertfordshire, England, the illegitimate son of actress Ellen Terry and architect Edward William Godwin. In 1889, after being educated at several private schools, Craig joined the Lyceum Theater company, where his mother was leading lady to actor-manager Henry Irving. From 1889 to 1897, Craig was a well-known actor of juveniles.

Craig's first practical experience as a director was in 1893, when, following two months of preparation, he staged Alfred de Musset's *No Trifling with Love* for his own company in Uxbridge. He designed the production and played the leading role. Between 1896 and 1897, he staged and starred in four works, including *Hamlet.* His revolutionary theories had not yet been formulated and these productions—which he later discounted—were imitative of conventional methods. He was, however, growing dissatisfied with

the theater of his day and was absorbing vital influences through his reading. In 1897, he stopped acting.

Unhappy with the scenography and acting of his day, Craig began to view theater in an almost mystic light, seeking to purify it of commercialism and crude realism and to place it on an idealistic pedestal where it could express spiritual values. He sought practical ways to embody his ideas. Meanwhile, his beautiful woodblock carvings, many published in a nontheatrical magazine he edited, became known. His drafting was also seen in his fanciful design projects for actual and nonexistent plays.

An opportunity to put his burgeoning notions into practice came with *Dido and Aeneas* (1900), an 18th-century operatic work by Henry Purcell offered for three showings by the newly founded Purcell Operatic Society. Between 1900 and 1903, Craig offered two more operatic works, plus four other pieces, this being the most intense period of directorial activity he would enjoy during his career. Most of these productions were short-lived and not widely noticed; his enormous impact derived eventually not so much from his practical work as from his prolific writings, lectures, and exhibitions, and from the reams published about him.

Dido and Aeneas was staged in a London concert hall on whose podium Craig constructed a temporary, wide, and low oblong-shaped proscenium. He illuminated the action entirely from overhead, using both a lighting bridge erected over the stage (before such bridges became widespread) and two projectors mounted at the auditorium's rear. For a period of six months, a cast of mostly untrained amateurs (except for the leads) allowed Craig to manipulate them just as he wished; he later resented professionals who resisted his demands. The movement was highly selective, chosen to express the aesthetic values of the music, which was also the rationale behind the remarkably unified costumes and setting (created largely by a novel arrangement of curtains). The mise-en-scène, perfectly harmonized in terms of color and the painterly use of light, was minimalist, atmospheric, and suggestive. Craig directed the actors and designed the sets, costumes, and lighting. He later claimed that the director could not have complete artistic control without mastery of each area of production.

Craig spent eight months preparing another amateur group for *The Masque of Love* (1901), adapted from Purcell's *Dioclesian*. Simplicity ruled, with an arrangement of neutrally colored curtains lit to manifest all the appropriate moods and emotions. The suggestive austerity reminded some of Japanese art. Another opera, Friedrich Handel's pastoral *Acis and Galatea* (1902), followed after another eight months of preparation.

Craig's last work with amateurs was Laurence Housman's nativity play *Bethlehem* (1902). Unimpressed by the writing or musical accompaniment, Craig exercised the extreme textual adaptation that he claimed to be the director's prerogative. He presented the piece in a large hall that he halved into stage and auditorium, providing another temporary oblong-shaped proscenium. Representative of his symbolic effects was the final scene, in which the stable was evoked by having the shepherds gather in a semicircle around Jesus's crib. As Mary withdrew the baby's blanket, a light beamed upward into the faces, suggesting the divine presence.

Craig first handled important professionals when he staged and designed Henrik Ibsen's romantic historical tragedy, *The Vikings of Helgeland* (1903), for his mother. This was intended as the first in a series of Craig-directed plays for Terry's company; lack of money ended the scheme. Craig arranged the music, designed every element, and employed unusually dark lighting to bring out the drama's primitive aura and pagan-versus-Christian symbolism. The nonspecific designs, employing carefully arranged cloth hangings, created an atmosphere in which actors and background could be aesthetically united. The minimal set pieces, such as a great round banquet table over which hung a large candelabrum, stood out against their neutral surroundings. Craig tried to get the company to follow precisely his directions for stylized movement, but they clung to their more familiar methods.

Their next effort was Shakespeare's *Much Ado About Nothing* (1903). The obstinate actors again criticized his abandonment of illusionistic scenery. Craig's approach created memorable effects, such as the church scene, which was merely an arrangement of curtains across which fell a stream of multicolored beams of light, suggesting the presence of a stained glass window.

Apart from the aborted and partly fulfilled projects that distressed Craig during the next few years, he was gaining international admiration via the exhibition of his models and pictures. They were intended to illustrate his ever-evolving ideas, also disseminated through his writing and editing.

Craig's projects were mostly aimed at discovering a theater of the future using a simplified method that allowed for ultimate flexibility in being able to represent any locale while being in itself nonspecific, like the architectural facades of the classic theater. One of his first conceptual breakthroughs came in the mid-1900s when he arrived at his "Scene" project, which represented his absorption in the nature of movement. It was a plan for a mobile stage in which square, vertical pillars of differing dimensions could be mechanically manipulated to rise from or sink into the floor, and move similarly overhead. Combined with lighting, this would provide a kaleidoscopic vision of scenic movement and variety for its own sake, and, if fully developed, be controlled by the artist at a console. The result would be a new art notable for the absence of the human form.

Craig became equally obsessed with his "screens," which grew out of Scene and was basically a geometric arrangement of nonrepresentational, neutrally colored, multipanelled, vertical screens of differing widths. These could be placed next to one another and, with the carefully selected addition of steps, windows, or other elements, be unfolded to evoke an infinite variety of locales. Primitive technology required that they be moved manually. With the addition of imaginative and frequently altered lighting, the effects made possible represented an exciting discovery, but few were ready to accept them on Craig's terms. Certain principles influenced various directors, however, especially Max Reinhardt. Ireland's Abbey Theater made good use of the screens for several plays directed by someone else in 1911.

Craig's first opportunity to put his screens to use himself came when he directed and designed *Hamlet* for the Moscow Art Theater (1912), collaborating with Stanislavsky, who was anxious to find a system that went beyond psychological realism. Because of unforeseen delays, the project took over three years to fructify, with Craig visiting Moscow periodically, describing his aims to Stanislavsky and Leopold Sulerjitzky, and allowing them to carry out the staging in his absence. Craig demonstrated his desires by using a large model—equipped with lighting—of the stage. He showed the blocking by manipulating small figures. Stanislavsky disagreed with a number of Craig's ideas, so the production fell short of the latter's aspirations. However, for all its imperfections, it became a landmark mounting.

Craig viewed the play as a symbolical monodrama in which the only real character was Hamlet, the others being unindividualized figures skewed by his vision of them. Hamlet, neither mad nor highstrung, is a superhuman representing truth and purity, the others falsehood and degradation. To suggest the widespread evil confronting Hamlet, an indelible image placed the king and queen on a level upstage, while before them were the court members massed in such a way as to seem as if they were merely a sea of heads poking through the king's vast golden cloak, covering the entire stage; Hamlet was sharply differentiated from them in the foreground. One Craigian idea that Stanislavsky rejected would have had Hamlet on stage all the time, even in scenes in which he had no part. In fact, many of Craig's wishes for a stylized performance were contravened. The acting was declamatory and Craig's desire to use no curtain was abandoned because the scene changes proved too clumsy to reveal to the audience.

Craig deemphasized the literary importance of drama and stressed that theater was an art made up of all its component elements. None was to be understood as a separate art as, say, painting or poetry might be; instead, Craig spoke of line, color, words, action, and rhythm as the arts of which theater is composed. As "artist of the theater," it is the director's job to join these elements into a unity that—in interpreting the work by discovering its central themes and images (a new concept when Craig discussed it)—represents the finished work of theater art.

Only after months of meticulous preparation were rehearsals to begin, and only after months of rehearsal would the final work be complete. Craig's ideal director was an individual who could control and design every aspect of the production, and a leader whose word could not be questioned. Craig, a consistent proponent of antirealistic methods, disliked the actor's subjective emotionality and wished to completely objectify acting. He was fascinated by the art of puppetry and wrote a controversial treatise in which he proposed replacing the actor with an *über-marionette* (literally, "super-puppet," intended to imply an actor with the self-mastery of a puppet).

Despite his rejection of acting as an art (he claimed that it lacks calculation and is interpretive, not creative), Craig's intention was not to discard the actor, but to establish a hieratic style wherein, like a well-articulated puppet, the actor could repress his unity-destroying ego and perform with total vocal and physical control. Irving was the only actor he felt had been capable of such performance. Closely related to Craig's entrancement with puppetlike acting was his great fondness for masked acting.

Craig established a unique experimental school in an outdoor theater in Florence, in 1913, but the war forced it to close. The work was a predecessor of the workshops popular later in the century, where the emphasis is primarily on research and discovery. Perhaps Craig's finest project was the creation of a 12-foot-high stage model for an unrealized production of Bach's *The St. Matthew Passion*. Its permanent arrangement of levels and steps influenced Jacques Copeau's postwar theater Vieux-Colombier.

Craig's later years were spent mainly in Italy and France. His most notable work was Ibsen's *The Crown Pretenders* (1928) for the Royal Theater in Copenhagen, where he collaborated on the staging with Johannes and Adam Poulsen.

Craig occasionally provided designs for other directors' productions, but usually found that his work was considered too advanced, and was adapted to suit more conventional tastes. Ultimately, he refused to work on any project over which he did not have complete control. This meant his withdrawal from the world of practical theater.

When he died, Craig was recognized as one of the theater's greatest visionaries. Criticized by those who believed, incorrectly, that he was a dreamer incapable of realizing his paper projects, Craig demonstrated in his actual productions his multitalented capabilities. He gave up hands-on work when he refused to compromise with the philistinism that would have diminished his dreams. Despite his small production output, he is remembered as a revolutionary and influential director.

Further reading:

Bablet, Denis. *The Theatre of Edward Gordon Craig.* Translated by Daphne Woodward. London: Eyre Methuen, 1981.

Craig, Edward. *Gordon Craig: The Story of His Life.* New York: Alfred A. Knopf, 1968.

Craig, Edward Gordon. *On the Art of the Theatre.* London: Heinemann, 1911.

———. *Index to the Story of My Days.* London: Hulton Press, 1957.

Innes, Christopher. *Edward Gordon Craig.* Cambridge, England: Cambridge University Press, 1983.

Also: Johnson, *Directing Methods*; Marshall, *The Producer and the Play.*

AUGUSTIN DALY (1838–1899)

[JOHN] AUGUSTIN DALY was born in Plymouth, North Carolina, where his father was a sea captain. Later, his widowed mother moved to Norfolk, Virginia, then New York. He left school at 16; by 1856, he was managing a troupe of Brooklyn thespians.

Daly began writing plays and, in the mid-1860s, his derivative melodramas and French and German adaptations began to find success. During his career, he produced 80 of his own adaptations from foreign sources, in addition to those adapted by others. A great number of the many plays for which he was credited were to a considerable extent the work of others, most notably his brother, a judge whose theatrical talents were kept secret. Among his early successful plays were the German-derived *Leah the Forsaken* (1862), the Charles Reade novel-inspired *Griffith Gaunt* (his first important directorial work; 1866), and the original *Under the Gaslight* (1867). In these and in later hits, such as the original frontier play *Horizon* (1871), the revuelike look at urban low-life *Round the Clock* (1873), the novel-based *Divorce* (1871) and *Pique* (1875), and his most popular French adaptation, *The Lottery of Love* (1888), he provided colorful, but often highly improbable, melodramatic and/or comic situations and characters dished up in a form that audiences relished. When adapting foreign material after 1880, he invariably Americanized it, using American locales and character types. Daly had a flair for the melodramatically spectacular, as witnessed by the heart-stopping scene in *Under the Gaslight* in which the heroine saves a man tied to the railroad tracks from an onrushing train.

Daly was active in the 1860s as a drama critic, at one point writing for five newspapers. Moreover, he gained recognition as a manager (something like today's producer) by handling the engagements of several touring stars performing his plays. In 1869, he undertook the management of his own Fifth Avenue Theater.

Daly's stock company management revealed him as zealously ambitious; within six months, he had produced 21 plays, his first hit being his own adapation, *Frou-Frou* (1870). The bills he produced were changed often. His fine company became one of New York's most successful and survived for six years, until the uninsured playhouse burned down in 1873. Daly turned his attention to renovating a Broadway theater, also called the Fifth Avenue when it soon opened. The same name was given to a newly built theater he opened at the end of the year on 28th Street. The Fifth Avenue succumbed to financial problems in 1877.

By 1877, Daly's achievements in molding a superb ensemble company were widely acknowledged. His actors were noted for the naturalness of their style, even though their repertory was an eclectic blend of modern European and American pieces, 18th-century English comedies, and Shakespeare. This was at a time when American audiences were used to a highly colorful, flamboyant style of acting, especially in melodramas. Daly's actors were restrained and soft-spoken, preferring subtly nuanced gestures and subdued vocal shadings to the declamatory flourishes of most contemporary acting. His company appealed to discerning audiences and would have bored spectators used to blood-and-thunder. The decorative—often sumptuous—elements of Daly's productions were on the same high level as the acting.

After the closing of the Fifth Avenue, Daly undertook various ventures, including a failed attempt to establish himself in London. In 1879, he renovated a theater at Broadway and 13th Street and called it Daly's. At this premiere playhouse, with leading players John Drew and Ada Rehan, his repertoire resembled that of previous years. From 1879 to 1881, musical comedy played a major role, especially following the vogue set by Gilbert and Sullivan. But after 1881, the emphasis was on straight comedy (including new American and English plays by Bronson Howard, Edgar Fawcett, James A. Herne, and Arthur Wing Pinero, and old English ones by Colley Cibber, Richard Brinsley Sheridan, and George Farquhar). Silly German farces were a regular part of his repertory as well. His French adaptations were dominated by the works of Victorien Sardou, but included pieces by Alexandre Dumas *fils*, Eugène Scribe, and many others. It was a Daly custom to employ new one-acts as curtain raisers.

Daly's most unusual offerings came in the nineties when he experimented with pantomimes in the European manner, using French sources; they did not go over. His repertoire was aimed strictly at the box office; apart from classical revivals, his productions were mainly potboilers. Their success stemmed from the delights of staging and acting and not their literary qualities. He rejected plays by George Bernard Shaw and Henrik Ibsen.

His Shakespearean productions gained attention because they were, for their time, among the most lavish produced in America and because of their radical editing. For his opulent sets, Daly was not averse to sending a scene painter overseas to copy the Ardennes Forest or to basing a background on a painting by Veronese. He demonstrated both in Shakespeare and in other plays a predilection for keeping the action moving by avoiding scene shift waits; this necessitated combining or reordering the multiple scenes into uninterrupted one-scene acts, and of removing chunks of the play that hindered the dramatic progress. The plays were reduced from five to three or four acts. In addition, they were cut to run three hours or less. Critic William Winter did most of the tailoring, although his connection was not publicly revealed. A principal object of most of Daly's Shakespeare staging was to provide vehicles for the redheaded Rehan, who was outstanding as Katharine in *The Taming of the Shrew* (1887), Rosalind in *As You Like It* (1889), and Viola in *Twelfth Night* (1893). The plays were rearranged to emphasize Rehan's roles by providing her with the closing lines of the acts in which she appeared, even when it meant giving her someone else's words.

Although Daly had staged Shakespeare earlier (including the first New York production of *Love's Labour's Lost* in 1874), his major Shakespearean period ranged from 1885 to 1899, during which he offered 11 plays, concentrating on the comedies, and doing nearly one a year, while reviving the more successful ones on later occasions. Only *Romeo and Juliet* (1895) and *The Tempest* (1897)—the latter done more as a spectacular musical than as a straight play—fall outside the comic canon. Among the important offerings were *The Merry Wives of Windsor* (1886), *Love's Labour's Lost* (1891), and *The Merchant of Venice* (1898). Both *The Taming of the Shrew* and *Twelfth Night* ran over 100 times. The *Shrew*, Daly's best work, was notable not merely for its rich scenery and costumes, but for its having restored the Induction scenes and the Bianca subplot. Despite its flaws, including textual mutilation (most painfully, the emasculation of the act two quarrel) and a too ornate decor, the production was truer to Shakespeare than any contemporary staging. Shakespeare's bawdry was refined (to "lie" with a woman became to "sup" with her) or eliminated (words like "lechery," "guts," and "fornication") in these shows; so were descriptions that could be replaced by scenery in the pictorial style then fashionable. These productions, for all their bowdlerizing and rearrangements, were instrumental in confirming Daly as America's foremost contemporary director.

Unlike typical practices, his theater carefully rehearsed each play and abandoned the traditional "lines of business," in which actors were hired to play specific character types acted according to established methods (thereby decreasing the need for extensive rehearsal). He favored ensemble over stars; the ambition of several fine players, such as Agnes Ethel and Clara Morris, led to defections. A few stars, including Edwin Booth and Adelaide Neilson, worked briefly for Daly after 1869.

Daly brought his troupe to London in 1884, and scored a remarkable success that led to their frequent return. They also played in France, Germany, and Ireland, and were recognized as the first complete American company to visit Europe. Daly was so gratified by his troupe's foreign reception that he opened Daly's, a London theater, in 1893. His company only played one other engagement there, its management being taken over by others in 1894. Their subsequent English engagements were at other

London theaters and at Stratford. Meanwhile, Daly's company made summer tours to various American locales, including California.

Daly was indefatigable, arriving at the theater at 7:30 A.M. and leaving at midnight or later. Technical rehearsals for a new production were likely to be held with the crew after the final curtain of the evening and sometimes lasted through the night. The sleepless Daly would begin the next day's business after breakfast. His duties extended from casting, rehearsing, and selection of the repertory to overseeing the theater's business aspects. He rarely missed a performance and his ability to memorize every line of a play led him to chastise careless actors. Despite his own tailoring, he was adamant about actors' respect for the final text and threatened a fine for unauthorized changes.

Few American theaters of the time had so authoritarian a director as Daly, whose martinetlike insistence on discipline led him to be labeled "the autocrat of the stage." He had a fiery temperament and frequently quarrelled with artists. Sometimes, he reduced an actor to tears before the company. Good Victorian that he was, he sought the same control over his actors' private lives as over their artistic ones, his goal being to keep everyone as respectable as possible. "Bohemianism" was strictly curtailed.

Daly completely controlled all aspects of production and quickly criticized or punished anyone who did not follow his requirements. A finable offense was to discuss the company or a work in progress with outsiders. The frequent notes and warnings he posted backstage were part of the Daly legend.

Daly was thoroughly prepared before rehearsals and knew his aims precisely. He rehearsed so incessantly that performances were like fine-tuned engines. Rehearsals often began at 10 or 11 A.M and ran until a 5 P.M. dinner break, followed by sessions that could last until 3 or 4 A.M. Despite his own lack of acting experience, he was a master acting teacher and instructed his casts in every detail, from inflections to movements to gestures to facial expressions. However, what began as a revelation of naturalness in acting—such as his demand for actors to keep active in scenes of lengthy dialogue—eventually tended to grow predictable and old-fashioned. His motto was "acting is action." Theater people even used the term, the "Daly cross," to refer to those moments in which actors, to keep the stage busy, motivated a move during an unbroken speech. Some claimed that Daly's control sometimes led to mechanical performances, as if the actors were his puppets. This could not be said of his famed central quartet, featuring Drew, Rehan, and character actors Mrs. G. H. Gilbert and James Lewis.

Daly's theater reflected the contemporary tastes of the educated, socially prominent citizens who frequented his productions. With a repertory ranging from American and European claptrap to gutted English classics, he managed to create one of the nation's best (and last) stock ensembles and helped to establish the new position of the nonperforming director.

Further reading:

Daly, Joseph Francis. *The Life of Augustin Daly.* New York: Macmillan, 1917.

Felheim, Marvin. *The Theater of Augustin Daly: An Account of the Late Nineteenth Century American Stage.* Cambridge, Mass.: Harvard University, 1956.

Odell, George, C. *Shakespeare from Betterton to Irving.* 2 vols. New York: Dover, 1966.

GORDON DAVIDSON (1933–   )

GORDON DAVIDSON was born in Brooklyn, New York, where his father taught theater at Brooklyn College. He studied electrical engineering at Cornell University before switching to theater. He acquired a master's degree from Case Western University.

In 1960, Davidson staged a season of stock with stars in Highland Park, Illinois, worked as a stage manager, and then met John Houseman, who hired him to assist on his 1964 production of *King Lear* for the Theater Group, the professional company Houseman ran at UCLA. Davidson, who became artistic director, produced eleven plays for the company. He also staged several operas in Texas around this time. His most successful play direction included Rolf Hochhuth's provocative *The Deputy* (1965), which suggested the pope's failure of responsibility during the Holocaust, and the Leonard Bernstein musical, *Candide* (1966), which benefitted from Davidson's revival of numbers cut during the original's tryouts and his paring down of the cumbersome book.

Gordon Davidson (l) directing John Rubinstein and Phyllis Frehlich in Medoff's Children of a Lesser God. *(1979)* (Photo: Mark Taper Forum/Jay Thompson)

In 1967, Davidson's Theater Group (renamed the Center Theater Group) took over Los Angeles's publicly owned, 742-seat, Mark Taper Forum, then considered experimental because of its pentagonal thrust stage and cyclorama projection wall. Davidson wanted the Taper to have an identity that made it distinctive among the nation's regional theaters. The Taper's annual five- or six-play season would be devoted to mainly new plays that, while they did not sacrifice entertainment values, were packed with thoughtful, but often uncomfortable or challenging, content. This sometimes set off sparks, which was in fact the reaction to Davidson's first production, John Whiting's *The Devils* (1967), based on a true story about the psycho-sexual fantasies of a hunchbacked, 17th-century mother superior and her nuns. Despite a public, clerical, and political outcry, influential persons rallied to defend Davidson's freedom of speech.

Davidson subsequently produced and directed many controversial works. Because of his extensive managerial reponsibilities, he directed one or two plays a season, with guests handling the remainder. His largely uncommercial repertory focused on social, political, and cultural issues. Some were redone in New York. His second (or third) productions of a play are important because he feels that with-

out them his work on the material is incomplete.

Davidson made a national splash with his second Taper play, Heinar Kipphardt's nearly three-hourlong *In the Matter of J. Robert Oppenheimer*, based on the 1954 security-clearance hearing of the eponymous scientist by the Atomic Energy Commission. The intellectually stimulating production, which moved to New York, was a docudrama using actual transcript material. Newsreels (with original narrations and music) of nuclear explosions were shown to heighten the visceral effect. The *New York Times* observed:

> Mr. Davidson has obviously been to pains to emphasize the play's common touch—he concentrates on the grandstand curtain line, the histrionic legal gestures of pointing fingers and pregnant pauses, the eccentricity of witnesses, and so wraps up the playwright's ideas as beguilingly as possible. This struck me as excellent.

Davidson was quickly identified with such "theatre of fact" plays although they form only a small portion of his oeuvre.

Davidson's premieres have included Harvey Perr's *Rosebloom* (1970) and Conor Cruse O'Brien's *Murderous Angels* (1970), about the suspicious death of Dag Hammarskjöld, which moved to Broadway (1971). More impressive was Saul Levitt's adaptation of radical priest-author Daniel Berrigan's *The Trial of the Catonsville Nine* (1971), also seen in New York (in a church). This morally intense antiwar docudrama dramatized the 1964 draft file-burning trial of nine "freedom fighters" by adapting the transcripts. During a workshop period, Davidson was heavily involved in evolving the final script. Berrigan, in hiding, was absent. Part of a tape recording he smuggled to the cast was used to open the show. During the preparations, Davidson's phone was tapped and the FBI's presence haunted the company.

John Simon praised Davidson's cinematic staging:

> Davidson has found a technique that lets testimonies blend aurally into one another even as the physical presence of one defendant on the . . . stand is suddenly, in mid- sentence, superseded by another's; the same effect is achieved by a lateral wipe in the movies. This rapidity and fluidity suggests the length and endlessness of the trial, as well as the seamless oneness of the eternal agon between the Soul of Man and the Law. . . .

At the end, Davidson showed an actual film of the "crime." Later, a reactionary Los Angeles group sued the Taper over the play.

British playwright Christopher Hampton's *Savages* (1974), given its American premiere at the Taper before Davidson staged it Off-Broadway, concerned colonial exploitation. Davidson, who had seen it in London, got Hampton to completely rewrite the play, changing its focus and structure; he also gave it a completely different, improved staging. The *Times* reported:

> Mr. Hampton has always had difficulty in play structure. . . . Davidson has helped him out in power and emphasis. More than that in the original London production he has provided the play with a sharper emphasis, and this moral tale of woe is handsomely staged and acted. . . . A most moving play that is staged with the fierceness of poetry.

Hampton's *Tales from Hollywood* (1982) was a world premiere, as was Jon Robin Baitz's *Dutch Landscapes* (1988) and three plays by Michael Cristofer. The first was the Pulitzer Prize-winning *The Shadow Box* (1977), which premiered in New Haven before becoming a Broadway hit. It dealt with terminally ill cancer patients, yet attracted audiences and won Davidson a Tony. Again his editorial input was extensive; he used his *Savages* experience in helping Cristofer develop a nonlinear form to change what were originally separate playlets about three individuals into a drama in which the stories develop simultaneously.

During the Los Angeles run of Cristofer's *Black Angel* (1978), the author was called a Nazi and the Jewish Davidson was accused of anti-Semitism. The drama—seen Off-Broadway in 1979—confronts the true story of how the people of a French town brutally murder an already punished Nazi war criminal discovered to be living in their midst. For a change of pace, Cristofer provided Davidson with *The Lady and the Clarinet* (1980), a lightweight sex comedy that played in New Haven (1983) before moving to Off-Broadway (1984). New York critics rejected both plays.

Davidson also has collaborated closely on Mark Medoff's *Children of a Lesser God* (1979), which became a major New York success (1980) and later became a successful film, and *The Hands of Its Enemy* (1984). The former dealt with the refusal of a young deaf woman (played—in a revolutionary piece of casting—by deaf actress Phyllis Frehlich) to speak or lip-read because she is happy in her world of silence. Staged on a practically bare platform with movable benches, it required that the hearing actors learn to sign. In the second play, also starring Frehlich, sign language was integrated into the story and used to interpret the action, about a deaf playwright's confrontation with her abused childhood.

William Merkin (l) and John Rubinstein in Children of a Lesser God. *Directed by Gordon Davidson. (1979)* (Photo: Martha Swope)

Other Davidson-directed American premieres include Joshua Sobol's *Ghetto* (1986), set in a German concentration camp, and Sybille Pearson's *Unfinished Stories* (1992). Because of "artistic differences" over revisions he demanded, he was fired from one of his rare comedies, Neil Simon's Broadway flop, *Fools* (1981).

Among Davidson's nonpremieres have been Tom Stoppard's comedy, *The Real Thing* (1986), Marsha Norman's *Traveler in the Dark* (1985), Ted Tally's *Terra Nova* (1979; in Japan, 1986), and Oliver Hailey's *And Where She Stops Nobody Knows* (1976). He also staged several television dramas and directed Bernstein's *Mass* (1971), subtitled "A Theater Piece," which opened the Kennedy Center in Washington, D.C. This was, wrote the *Times*,

> an eclectic, ecumenical, multiracial, multiethnic, multipurpose pageant. . . . Thanks to the ingenuity of Gordon Davidson . . . and Alvin Ailey, the choreographer, this is never a staged cantata. They both make adroit use of a limited space offered by Oliver Smith's sparsely effective setting—a row of pews . . . separated by a staircase.
>
> In front of this, Mr. Davidson and Mr. Ailey stage a celebration and a fiesta. . . . Mr. Davidson has combined all his disparate elements—such as a boy's choir, marching brass band and slouching jazz band—into an animated and often compelling stage picture.

The Taper has done many classics, because David-son believes it necessary for actors to stretch. He underlines the need for the classics to be related to present concerns, but he himself has directed only _Henry IV, Part 1_ (1972) and _Hamlet_ (1974). Regard-ing his selections, Oliver Hailey argued that David-son "settles for second-rate factual dramas sometimes at the expense of plays that explore the human condition—especially comedically" (quoted by Thomas Thompson).

Several important works were developed in Taper workshops, but although his influence was great, Davidson did not direct them. The most popular in Los Angeles (it bombed on Broadway) was Luis Valdez's _Zoot Suit_ (1979), based on an idea of David-son's, who commissioned the author to write it.

Davidson is a playwright's director who feels that the theater must serve the writer's needs before the spectator's, although the eventual merger of play and audience excites him most. Before he can work on a play, he told Mimi Leahey, "I have to find my way into it instinctively and intuitively. . . . It's how I find out where I stand with the material. I have to be drawn to it by something inexplicable which grabs me." A process of intellectualizing fol-lows as he plagues the playwright with questions, some of which are unanswerable. Bernstein told Thompson that "Gordie has a genius for digging into a play and locating those hidden truths that perhaps even the playwright overlooked." He appreciates writers who are receptive to his editing, yet he always respects the author's work. Cristofer told Don Shewey that his relationship with Davidson

> is like a marriage. . . . He does things that annoy me, and I'm sure that I do the same to him. But he takes care of the play. There's a huge misconception . . . about directors supposedly writing plays with play-wrights. A lot of plays have been ruined because not enough time is spent figuring out what the play is, before directors start trying to transform it into something they think it should be. Gordon treats the material for what it is instead of what he wants it to be.

Davidson is an even-tempered, affable, well-orga-nized individual. He sits on various important local and national arts committees and is considered one of American theater's most influential figures. His theater was one of the few to receive a special Tony honoring its contribution to the regional movement.

Since Los Angeles is the home of the television and movie industry, Davidson—who has no perma-nent company—is able to employ strong casts, often including major film stars, because of the local talent

Harry Groener (l), Andrea Marcovicci, and Alan Feinstein in Sobol's Ghetto. _Directed by Gordon David-son. (1986)_ (Photo: Mark Taper Forum/Jay Thompson)

pool. However, he has not succeeded in creating the kind of free interchange between theater and film acting he envies in London's situation; he says too many American stars return to the stage only when their sagging careers need a boost.

When he rehearses a politically sensitive script, he ties the cast together into a family of engaged participants through research, field trips, and invited speakers, enlarging their experiential scope and un-derstanding of the issues. Although he is not an actor, he is sensitive to the way actors think and work. He admitted to Thompson that in his earlier years he was more impatient and would shout, "Now! Do it!" to those under his command, "But as I have developed a greater sense of myself and my work, and I know more surely what I want, I'm satisfied to get it _then_, not now. I'm less in a rush. I'm more aware of process."

He has no specific theory and uses whatever suits a particular play, always in the interests of stylistic unity. An atmosphere of trust is established so the actor can take risks and fail. He informed Arthur Bartow: "My métier is related . . . to taking simple human truths that are inherent in an individual, marrying them to the style of material and letting the actor speak through that." One critic complained to Thompson that Davidson "sometimes functions more as an editor than as a director. . . . He'll tell an actor, 'Get out there and interpret the character the way you want.' Then he whittles the performance down to fit his specifications." During the Taper's generous preview period, which Davidson considers his favorite time, he shapes the finished performance. After the opening, he keeps the play on track by returning at regular intervals.

Davidson has been called Los Angeles's "true cultural czar" and "L.A.'s Mr. Theater" because of his impact in making the city a viable theater town. His obligation to a theater of ideas is not common in a culture where directors are usually concerned with creating hits or developing innovative new aesthetics. Few other American directors have so

often been at the center of controversy and have survived with as much respect.

Further reading:

Eder, Richard. "He Doesn't Merely Direct New Plays, He Nurtures Them." *New York Times,* March 27, 1977.

Leahey, Mimi. "Gordon Davidson: Directing a Disturbing Play." *Other Stages,* December 16, 1982.

Shewey, Don. "A Playwright Asks Thorny Questions." *New York Times,* December 12, 1982.

Thompson, Thomas. "A Dynamo Named Gordon Davidson." *New York Times Magazine,* March 11, 1979.

Also: Bartow, *Director's Voice;* Simon, *Uneasy Stages;* Zeigler, *Regional Theatre.*

GEORGE DEVINE (1910–1965)

GEORGE DEVINE was born in Hendon, England, and raised in Hampstead Garden Suburb, near London. His father was a bank clerk. At Oxford he headed the Oxford University Dramatic Society, but left school before graduating. His Oxford experience familiarized him with all aspects of backstage work—especially lighting—and he became an avid technician as well as an actor-director. He played mainly small roles on the West End; joined the Old Vic in the 1932–1933 season; and was business manager for the design firm of Motley (later marrying one of the designers).

An early influence was actor-director Michel Saint-Denis, who had recently moved to London. Devine considered starting a company under Saint-Denis's leadership, with actors prepared by the two of them. They opened the London Theater Studio (LTS) in 1936, and instituted an advanced and rigorous regimen, with then novel (for the English) classes in improvisation, mask work, and mime. Devine, a brilliant acting teacher, was happier in a group enterprise than in an independent venture; he remained committed to collective work in which each worker was equally respected.

He directed regularly at the LTS. Many of his productions, there and, later, professionally, benefitted from his creation of teeming life and vitality via the incorporation into rehearsals of his training exercises. Devine designed the lights and sound for most LTS productions. He became a leading West End lighting designer in the late thirties.

The school, which lasted four years, never created a professional company. Devine cofounded the Actors' Company, for whom he made his successful professional directing debut at Rudolf Steiner Hall with Alec Guinness's version of Charles Dickens's *Great Expectations* (1939), an episodic work tied together by narrators. Devine adapted the physically unsuitable theater for the presentation, the company's only one.

Devine's directorial freelancing began with a hit, Daphne du Maurier's *Rebecca* (1940). He codirected (with Marius Goring) *The Tempest* (1940) at the Old Vic, starring John Gielgud. The use of multiple speakers around the auditorium to encircle the audience with sound at selected moments was notably effective when Mozart's C Minor Piano Fantasy was played during the shipwreck scene, inspired by a medieval painting. George Bernard Shaw's *The Millionairess* (1940), starring Edith Evans, closed out of town.

During the war Devine fought in Southeast Asia. Meanwhile, his social and artistic beliefs underwent readjustment; he hoped to expand the range of English theater in the postwar years, to find and nurture a new generation of writers, and to bring plays to a wider and more diverse popular audience than before.

Back in London, Devine and Saint-Denis worked on an Old Vic Theater Centre, with himself in charge of a children's branch that became the Young Vic; the latter—associated with the Old Vic's new classical acting school, in which Devine was active—preoccupied him for a decade. He directed its first production, Carlo Gozzi's *King Stag* (1946), at the Lyric, Hammersmith. Intended for children, it was replete with magical effects, animal transformations, and broad comedy. Devine's organizational genius helped turn the Young Vic into a major national touring children's company. (The plays were of equal interest to adults.) His inventive Young Vic stagings were mostly of classical comedies, including works by Francis Beaumont and John Fletcher, Carlo Goldoni, Shakespeare, and others. Devine's *As You Like It* (1948) and *A Midsummer Night's Dream* (1949) were among the first works the troupe toured abroad. He wanted his actors to develop a strict performance score within which they would have the freedom to improvise. But he often grew so upset by their performances that he would storm backstage to reprimand the offenders.

The public presentations of the Vic's school were staged by its managing directors (Devine, Glen Byam Shaw, and Saint-Denis), each work running a week on the West End. He staged innovative school versions of Shakespeare, Arthur Wing Pinero, Anton Chekhov, Eugène Labiche, and others, concentrating on comedy. Meanwhile, internal crises at the Vic led to the release of the leadership in 1949. The Centre's leaders merged with the new artistic director, but this arrangement proved unworkable. Before it crumbled in 1951, Devine offered an effective revival of Ben Jonson's *Bartholomew Fair* (1950) on the clumsily redesigned Vic stage. Controversy erupted when the board, facing the transformation of the company into the National Theater, ended the school and the theater's association with Devine, Saint-Denis, and Shaw. Devine's last Centre production was a revival of John Vanbrugh's *The Provoked Wife* (1951), codirected with Frank Dunlop.

Devine prospered on the West End, beginning with Samuel Taylor's Broadway comedy, *The Happy Time* (1951). Between 1951 and 1955, he freelanced, including at least one classical play per season at the Stratford Memorial Theater, and found a new challenge in directing operas. At Stratford, he began with Ben Jonson's *Volpone* (1952), a rare divergence from the theater's usual diet of Shakespeare. It was a triumph of scene-shifting devices, including two side revolves and a 44-foot-wide sliding stage that parted in the middle to reveal a pair of huge elevators rising to fill the space vacated by the moving stage floor. His other Stratford entries (in several of which he also acted) included two

King Lears (1953), one with Michael Redgrave and the other, far more controversial, with John Gielgud (1955), who codirected; *The Taming of the Shrew* (1953); *A Midsummer Night's Dream*, with Anthony Quayle; and *Much Ado About Nothing* (1955), starring Gielgud, who again codirected. Devine also directed *King John* (1953) at the Old Vic, with Richard Burton. Each made an unusual contribution, but none more so than the second *Lear*, designed by avant-garde sculptor Isamu Noguchi. Its bizarre modernistic sets and costumes, using geometric patterns, were created to find a timeless environment for the play, and had the effect of making the actors, dressed in colors keyed to their personalities and made up with "neutral," nō-like faces, look like living sculptures. Among the strange symbols was a large, floating screen representing fate or time. Despite Devine's noble attempts at a magnified style, the conflict of traditional acting with the nontraditional decor created an uncomfortable disparity. More successful was *Hedda Gabler* (1954), costarring Devine and Peggy Ashcroft, its 19th-century look updated somewhat to make it more accessible to modern theatergoers.

The great project of Devine's final decade (1955–1965) was the English Stage Company at the out-of-the-way Royal Court Theater. (The renovated Royal Court employed innovative features, including an extended forestage and the undisguised display of the lighting instruments.) Devine, closely associated in the partly subsidized, nonprofit enterprise with director Tony Richardson, helped establish the company in order to produce the best foreign playwrights, but this was soon scrapped in favor of developing new, mainly native, playwrights, using a permanent acting company (ultimately replaced by *ad hoc* casting) with a training arm attached. The school never materialized, but under various auspices, Devine and others did teach Royal Court and National Theater actors. It was hoped that a distinctive style would emerge. Stars occasionally supplemented the company.

Outside of club theaters, challenging new work was scarcely seen in England. Devine's own early directing included Angus Wilson's *Mulberry Bush* (1956) and Arthur Miller's *The Crucible* (1956), in its English debut. The latter conveyed Devine's belief in "essentialism," a minimalist manner making the most of the fewest, but best-made, props and scenic elements. (Essentialism was eventually replaced by fuller visual approaches.) An unsuccessful double-bill of Ronald Duncan plays, *Don Juan* and

The Death of Satan (1956), was also directed by Devine.

It was Richardson's presentation of John Osborne's antiheroic *Look Back in Anger* (1956) that made the company famous. They changed the face of modern English drama, especially with works that mirrored the concerns of "angry young men," a committed antiestablishment generation reflective of the profound political, social, and economic changes in the postwar world.

Devine offered the unsuccessful British premiere of Bertolt Brecht's *The Good Woman of Setzuan* (1956). Seeking a money-maker, Devine turned to one of his fortes, Restoration comedy, and revived *The Country Wife* (1956) with Joan Plowright, who was brilliant as Margery Pinchwife (Devine himself was Pinchwife), and with a black-and-white scheme of lacy elegance using a sharply raked checkerboard floor. This was his only piece ever transferred to Broadway. (In 1960, he did a showcase staging for invited audiences of *The Way of the World* for New York's IASTA, an educational institution which specialized in importing international directors to work with professional actors.)

Devine stimulated considerable interest in the experimental plays of the absurdists, himself becoming expert at the staging of Samuel Beckett, including *Endgame* (1956); *Happy Days* (1962); and, for the National Theater, *Play* (1964). Devine was grateful to have Beckett himself participate in rehearsals. In the same vein were Eugène Ionesco's *The Chairs* (1956) and *Exit the King* (1963). The company offered encouragement to many of the important new British writers, although the only play of theirs that Devine himself directed was Nigel Dennis's *August for the People* (1961), a disaster starring Rex Harrison. After the opening season, in which he did five plays, he averaged only one a year, being occupied with other matters. His productions included Jean-Paul Sartre's political satire *Nekrassov* (1957), a dud; an ineffective *Major Barbara* (1958), by George Bernard Shaw; a powerfully underplayed, hit revival of Henrik Ibsen's *Rosmersholm* (1959), with Ashcroft; Sean O'Casey's *Cock-A-Doodle Dandy* (1959); Noel Coward's adaptation of Georges Feydeau's *Look After Lulu* (1959), with Vivien Leigh, a failure; and a successful version of Chekhov's *Platonov* (1960), with Harrison.

For *Platonov*, then rarely produced, the script was greatly edited to make it playable; the problem was made more complex because Devine restored the normally omitted first act, which he believed was important to underline Chekhov's commentary on

Endgame. Directed by George Devine. (1955) (Photo: Theater Collection, Brooklyn College)

the political irresponsibility of the play's young intellectuals. Vital was Devine's exploitation of the play's melodramatic devices, especially Sasha's escape from an onrushing train (a lighting effect).

In 1962, Devine offered *Twelfth Night*. Illness forced him to cut back drastically on his work from 1963 on. Among his final efforts was participation in Richardson's staging of Brecht's *Saint Joan of the Stockyards* (1964). He acted regularly and was in a play when he suffered a fatal stroke.

Devine carefully prepared an annotated promptbook, but he frequently abandoned it to work spontaneously when actors differed with his ideas. Some thought him uncomfortable when deviating from his plan, but others found him very free, allowing actors to try whatever they wished, and editing as needed.

While less dictatorial than many of his contemporaries, he was generally more rigid than the improvisationalists who flourished in the postwar years. Devine was apt, for example, to impose a character interpretation that he had carefully prepared, even to the extent of creating a metaphorical description, such as "a sweating bird of paradise" to describe a seductive Chekhov female.

A perfectionist, he worked at a scene over and over to get its timing, movement, and interpretation right, even if it was simply a matter of producing an effect for a single laugh. Devine had an unerring feel for rhythms and psychological nuances in dialogue. He was cautious about accepting rehearsal accidents that seemed to work, because he preferred effects that came from planning. Preparation was a safeguard against wasting time.

He usually began rehearsals with a lecture on the play. He said, "I like to get all that out of my system, and then be prepared to scrap the lot of it" (quoted in Irving Wardle). Actors trusted him because he had done his homework, but he often allowed stars to dominate the director-actor relationship and to make the productions more theirs than his. Harrison loved working with him on *Platonov*, remembering how witty he could be when directing and giving notes. But their mutual experience with *August for the People* was not of the same pleasant caliber.

Without Devine's support many vital playwrights might never have been produced, and the tenor of postwar British theater would have been different. (Devine also encouraged the development of an entire generation of new directors, such as John Dexter and William Gaskill.) He believed in the writer (but not literature) as the theater's seminal force, and his work at the English Stage Company, where he ardently opposed censorship, was devoted to this faith.

Further reading:

Wardle, Irving. *The Theatres of George Devine.* London: Eyre Methuen, 1979.

Also: Browne, *Playwrights' Theatre*; Findlater, *25 Years of the English Stage Company*; Leiter, *Shakespeare Around the Globe.*

JOHN DEXTER (1925–1990)

JOHN DEXTER, the son of a plumber, was born in Derby, England. He dropped out of school at 14 to take a factory job. During his World War II military service, he turned to acting. In the mid-1950s, he began directing amateur productions. Playwright John Osborne helped get him into George Devine's English Stage Company (ESC), where he concentrated on the work of the new school of British playwrights.

Following "productions without decor" of Michael Hastings's *Yes—and After* (1957) and Doris Lessing's *Each in His Own Wilderness* (1958), and of William Butler Yeats's *Purgatory* at the Devon Festival (1957), Dexter began a fruitful collaboration with Arnold Wesker, beginning with his trilogy about the East End's Anglo-Jewish working-class world (which matched Dexter's own background), *Chicken Soup with Barley* (1958), *Roots* (1959), and *I'm Talking About Jerusalem* (1960). He also staged *The Kitchen* (1959; revived in 1961) and *Chips with Everything* (1962). The latter transferred to Broadway, where Dexter's ability to recreate life in a boot camp was lauded. Dexter also worked on the West End, where his productions included Lillian Hellman's *Toys in the Attic* (1960). At the ESC, he offered Gwyn Thomas's *The Keep* (1961) and *Jackie the Jumper* (1963), and Osborne's *Plays for England* (1962). After staging David Heneker's hit musical, *Half a Sixpence* (1963), he joined Laurence Olivier's new National Theater in 1963 as an associate director. (His only subsequent ESC mounting was Wesker's *The Old Ones* in 1972.)

Among Dexter's best National productions were George Bernard Shaw's *St. Joan* (1963), which he already had staged at the Chichester and Edinburgh festivals (1962); Harold Brighouse's *Hobson's Choice* (1964); a renowned *Othello* (1964), starring Olivier as a blacked-up, West Indian-accented Moor; Peter Shaffer's epic-scaled *The Royal Hunt of the Sun* (1964); John Arden's *Armstrong's Last Goodnight* (1965); Shaffer's farcical one-act, *Black Comedy* (1965), shown first at Chichester; and Osborne's *A Bond Honored* (1966). A dispute concerning his wish to do an all-male, rock music *As You Like It* led to Dexter's resignation.

He freelanced on Broadway, offering Richard Rodgers and Stephen Sondheim's musical, *Do I Hear a Waltz?* (1965); Peter Ustinov's *The Unknown Soldier and His Wife* (1967); Simon Gray's *Wise Child* (1967); Wesker's Shylock play, *The Merchant*

John Lithgow (front) and B. D. Wong in M. Butterfly.
Directed by John Dexter. (1988)　(Photo: Martha Swope)

(1977), which bombed when star Zero Mostel died before the opening; Tennessee Williams's *The Glass Menagerie* (1983); David Henry Hwang's *M. Butterfly* (1988), a hit for which he won a Tony; and Bertolt Brecht's *The Threepenny Opera* (1989), a flop despite having Sting as Macheath. London saw Terrence Rattigan's *In Praise of Love* (1973) and Shaw's *Pygmalion* (1974), redone with Americans in Los Angeles (1979). In 1966, he began directing opera. He also made several films (including *I Want You,* 1972).

　Dexter returned to the National as associate director from 1971 to 1975, directing George Middleton's *A Woman Killed with Kindness* (1971); Adrian Mitchell's *Tyger,* "a celebration of William Blake," codirected with Michael Blakemore (1971); Oliver Goldsmith's *The Good-Natured Man* (1971); Molière's *The Misanthrope* (1973), controversially updated to 1960s Gaullist France; Peter Shaffer's *Equus* (1973), starring Alec McCowen and Peter Firth; Trevor Griffiths's *The Party* (1973), a political drama in which Olivier, playing a frail, old Trotskyite, made his farewell to the stage; and *Phaedra Britannica*

(1975), Harrison's adaptation of Jean Racine's tragedy, set in 19th-century India. Dexter also directed *Equus* (with Anthony Hopkins and Peter Firth, 1974) and the Gaullist *Misanthrope* (with McCowen and Diana Rigg, 1975) on Broadway. The former won him a Tony.

　For many, the highlight of Dexter's career was *Equus,* about a disturbed young stable worker who blinds six horses and undergoes a dramatic psychoanalysis. Despite using a proscenium stage, Dexter created an operating theater atmosphere with 60 spectators observing the action—lit with white light—from upstage bleachers. He also kept actors awaiting their entrances on benches surrounding the sparely furnished acting platform. The horses were portrayed by a mimed chorus of actors in dark slacks and turtlenecks shod with six-inch-high, cothurnoi-like wire hooves and wearing similarly constructed horse masks through which their faces could be clearly seen.

　Dexter's subsequent freelancing in England (where he had come to feel unappreciated) included such major productions as the National's *As You Like It* (1979) and Brecht's *Galileo* (1980), the latter—which made a star of Michael Gambon—being one of England's few successful Brecht productions; T. S. Eliot's *The Cocktail Party* (1986), at the Phoenix, a failure that prevented him from starting his own West End troupe; Christopher Hampton's *The Portage to San Christobel of AH* (1982); Shaw's *Heartbreak House* (1982); and Jean-Paul Sartre's *The Devil and the Good Lord* (1984).

　In 1980 Dexter was named artistic director of Ontario's Stratford Festival; he had to give up the job because of discord over his not being Canadian. Another job that ended in controversy was his leadership of New York's Metropolitan Opera House.

　Dexter was eclectic, capable of staging most modern and classic genres. He had his flops, but was generally as capable with Wesker's intimate, realism as with such spectacles as *Galileo* or *The Royal Hunt of the Sun,* about Pizarro among the Incas of Peru. (A stage direction, "They climb the Andes," inspired him to direct it.) Critics often noted how he could take a marginal drama—like *M. Butterfly,* about a French diplomat who believes the Chinese male transsexual spy he lives with for two decades is a woman—and turn it into theatrical gold.

　He was known for his visualizations, often displayed in realistic images placed on a minimally furnished open stage—even showing the real stage walls—that gave full play to the actors' movements. Such decors revealed the influence of *nō* and Brecht.

When preparing *As You Like It,* for instance, his inspiration came from the concept that "all the world's a stage." He thus demanded a bare platform with a white floorcloth for winter and a green one for summer. That, together with the actors, the elaborate props, costumes, and the architecture of the National's Olivier Theater was all the set he needed. For *M. Butterfly,* a sweeping floor-to-overhead-ramp dominated; Chinese theater conventions inspired much of the staging.

He was "enormously" influenced by his designers, he told Judith Cook, "because it's from the designer's response that you lay out certain guidelines and make concrete your own ideas, out of argument, out of discussion." Andy Phillips, whose use of a visible overhead lighting rig and sculptured white light was a Dexter commonplace, was his most frequently used lighting designer, while Jocelyn Herbert—from whom he even accepted movement notes—designed many of his sets. Herbert claimed in an obituary:

> he put enormous work into preparing a production. Once he had agreed to the model and discussed every scene and how it would work for the actors and how you would get from scene to scene with no hold-ups, he would want a replica of the model, to take home to work with, and reduced ground plans of every scene, to put into his script.

Dexter had no formula. "You read a play," he told Cook, "you like it, you decide to do it, and you find a way of doing it. . . . It's a private process." He knew that his instincts were working if a project stirred a visual response.

Before he began rehearsals, all moves were noted in his script, and he blocked (he called it "plumbing") early and rapidly, avoiding "at table" discussions. An act a day was not unusual, nor was a runthrough at the end of the first week. He remained open to change, however, when something better appeared. According to Jim Hiley, actor Simon Callow appreciated that "He comes with it all ready and gives it to you. He doesn't tell you what the scene's about, but has a marvelous sense of when the baton passes from one actor to another." Dexter's educational shortcomings led him to make intuition his guide; the intellectual reason for his choices was irrelevant, he declared, so long as those choices were fruitful. If he pleased himself, he had done his job. Dexter did not consider himself to be in a power struggle; he expected good actors to come up with improvements.

He needed precise preparation when he had to choreograph large crowds, one of his strongest talents. (Some thought him weak on handling intimacy and ideas.) Important examples are the sequences of Indian ritual in *Royal Hunt* and the complex yet formalistically theatrical behavior suggesting the activity in a large restaurant's kitchen in *The Kitchen.* He was also outstanding at using movement in smaller plays, such as *Black Comedy,* in which the actors employed extensive physicality to suggest (with the lights at full blast) that they were stumbling about in a pitch-black space. When necessary, a movement specialist assisted, as mime Claude Chagrin did for the horses in *Equus.*

Dexter's productions were often as noteworthy for great acting as for directorial ingenuity, but he could be rough with actors. He began rehearsals—from which smoking and newspapers were forbidden—with warmth but, as his insecurities increased, transformed into a martinet who would often wither coworkers with scathingly profane insults barked in his Midlands accent. Marian Seldes was hurt when he yelled out, "Watch those Jewish hands, Seldes" during an *Equus* rehearsal. He may even have bit an actor once. He was technique-oriented, drilling scenes and business repeatedly and running through as often as he could. Anything less than total commitment, no matter how small one's part, raised his ire. Detecting carelessness, he might shout, "Get on with it, you bastard!" Anthony Hopkins swore he would never work with Dexter again (but changed his mind). On the other hand, a number of actors were loyalists, claiming that he was only cruel in the interests of getting actors to be honest. They found him cooperative, helpful, decisive, and wickedly funny.

Although his methods often belied his philosophy, Dexter claimed that actors can only be creative if they are able to relax and have confidence in themselves. "I aim to create time and atmosphere in which this can happen," he informed Robert Rubens, "and in which I can be aware of the actor's needs before he is aware of them himself." Early blocking was one way he felt actors could be helped to relax. He was also likely to give the actors relaxation exercises, as Seldes says he did on *Equus,* where the actors also had to practice verbal dexterity by poetry readings. A script was like a score he had to conduct. For *Galileo* a voice coach gave the actors daily workouts and notes.

Dexter respected his texts, and declined to impose auteurist attitudes on them. He was, though, forceful with playwrights. He once threatened Terence Rattigan with "handbags at dawn" if the playwright's emendations were unsatisfactory. To Wesker, he is alleged to have declared: "If you don't shut up, Arnold, I'll direct this play as you've written it." His input into Wesker's plays was considerable. In *The Kitchen,* for example, Dexter got the writer to provide a quiet scene between the two main dynamic ones, so that a contrast could be established. In *The Old Ones,* Dexter inspired many revisions; one character's sex was changed to help balance the cast's vocal "music." Ronald Hayman adds:

> A revolving stage was used very cleverly to bring more characters into a scene than Wesker had envisaged, and a complex counterpoint was . . . evolved by using singing or dancing as a background to speech or by using a tape recorder to back speech or action.

Prior to a friendship-ending quarrel, Dexter's collaboration with Peter Shaffer was equally productive. A chief accomplishment was the rewriting of the psychiatrist in *Equus* into a central role from its much less significant one in the pre-Dexter draft. The action came to be shared by the problems of both doctor and patient.

His acerbic wit may have been a mask to disguise a sense of inferiority Dexter felt about his educational and class background. He was, however, an avid autodidact and possessed a passion for language and ideas. When working on a production he was able to refer coworkers to background research in numerous books, paintings, and other sources. During *The Merchant,* for instance, he told the company to study the Titians at the Metropolitan Museum and to find something of use in them for their characters. At *Galileo* rehearsals, Dexter passed around pictures by Breugel and asked the players to base their makeups on them.

Although he could be a tough taskmaster, Dexter remained faithful to actors he trusted, and often used the same people over and over. Dexter told Rubens

that he worked best when he knew his players well, "what they laugh at, if they don't laugh at all, where they come from, how they think politically." He was also encouraging to new artists. When working with actors, he disliked extensive discussions and sought emotional responses, not intellectual ones. He would often say, "Don't tell me: show me!" "And I," he told Gow, "make an emotional response to what is shown, in approval or disapproval, or questioning, or whatever."

John Dexter was one of the postwar British theater's most exciting directors, likened by some to Tyrone Guthrie for his imagination, flair, range, and ability to move readily from noncommercial to commercial fare.

Further reading:

Dexter, John. Interviewed by Robert Rubens in *Behind the Scenes: Theater and Film Interviews from the "Transatlantic Review."* Edited by Joseph F. McCrindle. New York: Holt, Rinehart and Winston, 1971.

Gow, Gordon. "The Struggle." Interview with John Dexter. *Plays and Players* 27 (Fall 1979).

Hayman, Ronald. *The Set-up: An Anatomy of the English Theatre Today.* London: Eyre Methuen, 1973.

Hiley, Jim. *Theatre at Work: The Story of the National Theatre's Production of Brecht's 'Galileo.'* London: Routledge and Kegan Paul, 1981.

Seldes, Marian. *The Bright Lights: A Theatre Life.* New York: Limelight, 1984.

Also: Cook, *Directors' Theatre*; Findlater, *25 Years of the English Stage Company*; Johnson, *Directing Methods.*

*Note: the following appeared too late to be used for this entry:

Dexter, John. *The Honourable Beast: A Posthumous Autobiography.* London: Nick Hern, 1993.

CHARLES DULLIN (1885–1949)

CHARLES DULLIN, the 18th and last child of a justice of the peace, was born and raised on a rural estate located near Yenne, in the Pre-Alp section of the Savoy, France. He was educated at a Catholic school. In 1902, he moved to Lyon, where he became enamored of the theater and took acting lessons.

Dullin moved to Paris in 1904 and endured considerable privation for a decade as he gradually became recognized as a cabaret poetry reciter and as an actor.

He played villains in melodrama theaters; acted for two years for André Antoine at the Odéon; acted in Jacques Rouché's avant-garde Théâtre des Arts; was a founding member of Jacques Copeau's Théâtre du Vieux-Colombier and—apart from three years in the army—remained there until 1919; and, under the management of Fermin Gémier, became known as a major acting teacher. In 1921, the impoverished 36-year-old began his own theater.

Dullin's earlier directorial experiences included an

abortive 1909 attempt at staging fairground productions in commedia style and the direction of three plays at the Théâtre des Arts (1911–1912). The first had some interest, being a restaging of the Chinese classic, *Sorrow in the Palace of Han* (1911). Dullin introduced the fruits of his research into Chinese art and demonstrated a talent for creating a stylized mise-en-scène, especially when compared to the company's earlier, more realistic, staging. During his military years he staged programs—often using improvisation—for the soldiers. Dullin loved improvisation, but more as a training and rehearsal tool than for production.

In 1921, Dullin, supported by a number of young actors he had trained under Gémier, created the Atelier (Workshop), a combined acting school and producing venture. To prepare for their Paris opening, he borrowed a leaf from Copeau and took them to the tiny village of Néronville, away from the city's distractions, for months of training and rehearsal, with the company—including his wife, actress Francine Mars—working cooperatively as actors and technicians. They showed three plays locally in various primitive settings and operated this way for two more summers.

The Atelier moved from one small venue to another, occasionally giving unpublicized performances. Finally, in 1922, they took over and renovated the Théâtre de Montmartre (renamed the Atelier), where they remained until the company ended in 1940. The small stage required designers to exercise the utmost ingenuity for the sometimes rather expansive productions. The company was rarely far from bankruptcy, which was temporarily staved off by an occasional hit. Effective sets were often constructed of found objects. During their first eight years, they offered a prolific repertory, but the last 11 years saw a decline as monetary problems intruded. (They totaled 69 plays.) Dullin was able, however, to spend more time polishing each play.

Dullin's first Atelier staging was an excellent revival of Pedro Calderón de la Barca's masterpiece, *Life Is a Dream* (1921), its costumes designed by Antonin Artaud. Dullin had a deep interest in the Spanish dramatists and, especially in the early years, directed a number of Spanish classics and moderns. Few were as successful as *Life Is a Dream,* to which he occasionally returned. Dullin frequently revived his successes—in new interpretations—to shore up his income. Programs often consisted of a full-length play and a curtain raiser, and the early years saw many one-acts. Dullin, a great character actor, usually played a leading role.

The critics eventually realized how fine the work was, and how expertly Dullin had created a unified ensemble to perform in his nonnaturalistic productions. Dullin was respected for giving many young, unknown playwrights an opportunity. The company's forte was comedy, especially satirical plays; these supplied the bulk of the programming, but eventually a number of tragedies also were produced. In the classics, Dullin aimed to avoid museum recreations and instead to revivify the play in modern terms, even if it meant, in comedies, introducing topical revisions. His comic touch was light-hearted and lacked Copeau's sobriety.

Dullin's productions were praised for their stylized movement, including dance and acrobatics; a unique reliance on music, often by the finest modern composers; imaginative decors by the cleverest young designers, including Dullin himself; and brilliant staging that tied all the components into a unified package. At times he was criticized for insisting on overly stylized performances and fanciful designs, which often employed architectural decor. Few other directors made as much use of music, for atmosphere, characters' leitmotifs, and the dances he often created. He argued for a theater of the imagination, where the visual impression was free of realistic dross.

Dullin railed against a reliance on modern technology, although he was sometimes guilty of using turntables and the like. His work was invariably on proscenium stages, but he expressed a longing for the audience-actor contact found in the Elizabethan and Japanese theaters, and even in theater-in-the-round. When possible, he allowed actors to use the aisles for exits and entrances. For all his emphasis on theatricality, however, much of his fame—like that of Copeau—came from his absolute devotion to the playwright. His conceptions were always intended to assist the text, not to glorify his own presence.

In the twenties, Dullin's most admired stagings of new works included Luigi Pirandello's *The Pleasure of Honesty* (1922), which introduced the Italian to France. Pirandello was present to assist Dullin (he would do two other Pirandellos, *Each to His Own* in 1924 and *All for the Best* in 1926); Alexandre Arnoux's prose and verse *Huon of Bordeaux* (1923); Marcel Achard's *Do You Want to Play with Me?* (1923), whose circus story allowed the actors to present clowning skills; Bernard Zimmer's *The Fatted Calf* (1924); Sholem Asch's *The God of Vengeance* (1925), given a nonrealistic staging despite its realistic text; and Nikolai Evreinov's *Comedy of Happiness* (1926), in which he created a bustling Watteauesque carnival. Two plays by controversial Stève Passeur (he later did a third) were among Dullin's other works of the period.

Dullin's adaptations of old plays sometimes amounted to nearly new works. The most exciting were Molière's *The Miser* (1922; he had played Harpagon for Copeau and would revive the play two more times); a fascinating, modernized version of Sophocles' *Antigone* (1923) by Jean Cocteau (his first play), with a blue-toned set by Pablo Picasso, abstract makeups, a crowd of masks hung on a backdrop to represent the chorus, and Cocteau's offstage voice as the chorus; Ben Jonson's *The Silent Woman* (1925), the first of several successful Elizabethan plays; an even more effective Jonson satire, *Volpone* (1928), based on Stefan Zweig's German version, and invested with a delightfully exaggerated satirical tone; and the first of three adaptations of Aristophanes, a brilliantly updated *The Birds* (1928). Bird masks and costumes were worn, and the music suggested specific character traits, such as blues for the nightingale.

Dullin's authoritative position was solidified in 1928 when he and idealistic directors Louis Jouvet, Gaston Baty, and Georges Pitoëff formed the mutual protection society they called the Cartel des Quatre. The Atelier's mature years were from 1928 to 1940, during part of which, in addition to producing plays, it published a review called *Correspondances* (1928–1932), in which Dullin and others expressed their thoughts. The most widely appealing of Dullin's new plays included Raymond Roleau's *The Wonderful Visit* (1928), in which Dullin created remarkable dream effects with sound and light; several plays by Dullin protégé Armand Salacrou, including *Atlas-Hôtel* (1930) and *The Earth Is Round* (1938); Romain Rolland's *Musse* (1930); and François Porché's epic-proportioned, *Tsar Lenin* (1931), about the Russian revolutionary, produced in a constructivist-influenced set.

Among Dullin's topflight revivals were George Farquhar's late Restoration romp, *The Beaux' Strategem* (1930), wherein the cast of 24 demonstrated Dullin's talent at handling large groups; Aristophanes' *Peace* (1932), which introduced audience participation when spectators were asked to pull a rope extending to the balcony to draw forth the half-nude figure of Peace from the bottom of a well; Dullin's first Shakespeare, a constructivist *Richard III* (1933), in André Obey's heavily adapted version; John Ford's Carolinean *Tis Pity She's a Whore* (1934); an outstanding adaptation of Honoré de Balzac's 19th-century *The Promoter* (1935), containing one

great scene in which a chorus of creditors bathed in eerie green light danced and chanted about the death of credit; and a choreographic *Julius Caesar* (1936).

Dullin staged plays by Pirandello, Molière, and Pierre de Beaumarchais at the Comédie Française, where his novelties—such as the use of a boy (instead of the traditional woman) to play Chérubin in *The Marriage of Figaro*—shocked conservatives.

Dullin's final decade was initially marred by artistic misfortune but he managed a comeback. His first assignment was a success, however, when he guest-directed Jean Sarment's *Mamouret* (1940) at the Théâtre de Paris. Tired of the Atelier's diminutive stage, he obtained a larger theater in 1941, when he took over the Théâtre Sarah-Bernhardt, its name changed (until 1944) by the Germans to the Théâtre de la Cité. Dullin found it difficult at first to use its vast stage, and his productions of modern plays by Simon Jollivet, Anatole France, Paul Morand, Zimmer, and Sartre, and classics by Lope de Vega, Molière, and Shakespeare (a *King Lear* [1945] that later was recognized as a work of genius) failed to win approval. Although it was initially rejected, the most important was Sartre's *The Flies* (1943), his first play, a retelling of the classical Orestes myth with an anti-Nazi subtext. Dullin sprang back with a series of successes: Salacrou's *The Soldier and the Sorcerer* (1945), Rolland's *The Year One Thousand* (1947), and, most notably, his first French classical tragedy, Pierre Corneille's *Cinna* (1947), which powerfully demonstrated the play's poetic and dramatic viability. However, the theater's debts forced Dullin to resign.

He did Salacrou's *Lenoir Archipelago* (1947) at Baty's Théâtre Montparnasse; it was a hit, even going on tour. Balzac's *The Step-Mother* (1949), which premiered in Lyon and then toured, was Dullin's last production. He acted in it until his death.

Like Copeau, Dullin was a theatricalist, but an eclectic one with no specific doctrine. He approached each play on its own terms and sought to discover its unique quality. David Whitton suggests that if any one thing marked his work, it was character, rather than language or visuals. Dullin's repertoire of close to 80 productions was broad, with a special talent for the Elizabethans, Calderón, and Aristophanes, but also a great interest in the development of young playwrights.

Dullin preferred rehearsing through trial and error, although he was thoroughly prepared with a mental plan. Only once did he begin a production with all the moves preblocked; they had been worked out on a checkerboard, each square of which had a specific number assigned to it, so that he could communicate moves by saying the number. He abandoned this in midrehearsal as being too constricting. Instinct was his guide, rather than academic cogitation. Dullin was known for his reliance on actors' imaginations and was less dictatorial than many of his colleagues, but he could drive a company to tears in his constant repetitions. The actors were not forced to mirror his wishes but to seek in themselves for the answers to their problems.

The roster of actors, playwrights, and future directors—among them Jean Vilar and Jean-Louis Bar-rault—who trained and worked under Dullin is impressive. His dedication to noncommercial theater was distinctive; he sometimes closed hits when their popularity interfered with his artistic development. The Atelier's location is now the Place Dancourt-Charles Dullin.

Further reading:

Bradby, *Modern French Drama*; Guicharnaud, *Modern French Theatre*; Hobson, *French Theatre Since 1830*; Knowles, *French Drama of the Inter-War Years*; Whitton, *Stage Directors in Modern France*.

NIKOLAI EVREINOV (1879–1953)

NIKOLAI NIKOLAYEVITCH EVREINOV, the son of a successful engineer, was born in Moscow, Russia, and grew up in a number of cities. He took an interest in puppets, wrote a parodistic play when he was seven, and displayed musical talent. He entered St. Petersburg's Imperial School of Jurisprudence at 13, and participated in school theatricals. He graduated in 1901, studied philosophy and music, and held a civil service job.

His philosophical studies influenced his theoretical writings on the nature of theater; his musical abilities were valuable in his practical theater work, for which he occasionally composed the scores (he also wrote operas and operettas); and his theatricalist, symbolist, antirealistic playwriting gained him a distinguished reputation. His multifaceted career also involved painting and historical writing. Some say his significant directorial inroads were overshadowed by his contributions to playwriting and theory (especially his ideas on "the theater in life" and a unique form of subjectivist play he called "monodrama").

In 1907, he and Baron Driezen cofounded St. Petersburg's controversial Ancient Theater. Influenced by tendencies then talked of in advanced circles, it sought to produce ancient plays in authentic reconstructions of their original presentations. Circumstances prevented the Ancient Theater from carrying out a series that planned programs ranging from the Greeks to Molière, but they did produce two cycles, from the medieval theater and Spain's Golden Age. Evreinov was fascinated by the nature of conventionalism or stylization, and wished to mine the old plays for their nonillusionistic methods and dependence on imagination. There is debate over whether he or Vsevolod Meyerhold should be credited with the introduction of "theatricalism" into Russian theater.

In preparation for the medieval cycle, the actors—forced to share the space—sometimes rehearsed from midnight to 8:00 A.M. and would then resume work at 1:00 P.M. Members of the creative staff traveled abroad to do research and collect materials. Specialists lectured on relevant medieval subjects. Authentic medieval musical instruments were located or recreated. Similar pains were taken with the costuming. The five-play cycle, containing works ranging from an 11th-century liturgical play to 16th-century farces, given over two evenings, ran for a month and toured to Moscow. Evreinov directed Adam de la Halle's 13th-century pastoral drama *The Play of Robin and Marion.*

Because Evreinov wished to recreate not only the semblance of the original staging, but the ostensible circumstances surrounding it, he directed the play as if it were being given at a banquet in a knight's castle. The rehearsed reactions of the costumed onstage spectators (a process Evreinov called "reconstruction of the spectator") were intended to break the fourth wall and draw contemporary audiences into participating in an overtly theatrical presentation. *The Play of Robin and Marion* seemed like a play-within-a-play. The stage was richly dressed to resemble a castle hall, and musician-minstrels mingled with the guests. After a master of ceremonies's introduction, the play's artless accoutrements—including toy sheep and a cardboard house—were set up as the audience watched. The self-consciously presentational show included the entrance of the Knight on a hobby horse. Evreinov's actors gave rhythmically precise performances employing song, dance, declamation, and mime.

The Spanish cycle, three years later (1911), again sent the staff abroad to do research. Evreinov went to Naples because of its lengthy occupation by Spain. The company spent two-and-a-half months imbibing Spanish culture and theatrical style, with extensive movement and dance work under the guidance of specialists. Audiences heard a background lecture before the plays began. The performance hall—both foyer and auditorium—was transformed into a stylized Golden Age environment. For Lope de Vega's *Fuente Ovejuna*, Evreinov paid close attention to rhythm, movement, and verse speaking. It was played on a footlight-less set resembling a town square in which a traveling troupe would arrive to perform on a platform stage resting on barrels, backed by traverse curtains, and occupied by a costumed onstage audience. Spanish conventions were followed. The acting—to critical dismay—mirrored the ostentatious manner that would have been necessary in an out-of-doors venue. Between the three acts were miscellaneous entertainments, including a period Spanish dance. Possibly because of censorship fears, though, Evreinov revised the text.

Despite the abundance of well-researched details and the archaeological intent of these reconstructions, they were appreciated for allowing the ancient material to be viewed through a prism that stylized the originals in terms of modern tastes. For most, however, the work was too academic and the actors not sufficiently talented. Various problems—including the outbreak of war—led to the closing of the theater.

Evreinov's direction, meanwhile, had brought him to the attention of St. Petersburg star Vera Komisarjevskaya, for whom he served as artistic director from 1908 to 1909, staging such plays as Gabriel D'Annunzio's *Francesca da Rimini* (1908) and Oscar Wilde's controversial *Salomé* (retitled *The Tsar's Daughter*; 1908). The latter was banned as blasphemous.

Longer lasting was Evreinov's directorship of the Crooked Mirror Theater, which had been founded in 1908 as an outgrowth of the current fashion for cabaretlike "theaters of small forms," usually specializing in parodies of theatrical genres. Some of the best young theater artists participated in the programs, which were attended primarily by the intelligentsia. In 1910, Evreinov's achievement at the Ancient Theater and at the Merry Theater for Grown-up Children—where he and Fyodor Komisarjevsky had produced a number of pieces, including

his harlequinade *A Merry Death* (1909) and his "monodrama" *The Presentation of Love* (1909)—convinced the producer, A. R. Kugel, to hire him as artistic director. Evreinov remained through 1917 although he was not active there in 1915–1916.

He changed the previously late-night performances to 8:30 P.M. and transferred to the larger, better-equipped Ekaterinski Theater, seating from 650 to 800. Because it catered to an elite crowd, the theater often played to empty seats. Evreinov was involved in about 100 presentations, writing, directing, translating, and advising. There were three or four short plays on each program and three or four programs each season; Evreinov directed about 80 pieces, 15 of them his own originals, adaptations, or collaborations; several were musical-dramatic works for which he composed the scores. He directed plays by Leonid Andreyev, Fyodor Sologub, Anatole France, Arthur Schnitzler, and others.

His professionalism was noted in all aspects of production, from makeup and staging to the excellence of the ensemble. The casual cabaret feeling was abandoned in favor of polished artistry, but the imaginative offerings always offered surprises. A panoply of parodistic pieces was seen, ranging from burlesques to monodramas to grotesques; usually, the satirical blows were against targets such as critics and the clichéd mannerisms of melodrama, operetta, opera, ballet, futurism, Henrik Ibsen, movies, and farce. There was much interest in subtly satirical material cleverly disguised to keep the censors at bay.

Of particular interest were the monodramas, which showed the world from the changing perspective of a single character whose psychological attributes were played by several actors. An example of this genre was Boris Gejer's *Aqua Vitae* (1911), which depicts how circumstances gradually alter the more the protagonist guzzles beer. Another genre sponsored by the Crooked Mirror was called "ceremonial conference," and constituted either an evening parodistically celebrating the writing of a favorite satirist or the satirical pursuit of a specific theme. Regular plays with travesty intentions were offered, such as Evreinov's *A Feast of Laughter* (1913), which presents a theater panel assigned to judge five comedies, Russian and foreign, by how well they demonstrate their native humor when dealing with an assigned story. Topics ranging from stereotypes of international dramaturgy to the differences among comedic modes were mocked.

One of Evreinov's most successful contributions was his coadaptation of Nikolai Gogol's *The Inspector General* (1912) in which five strikingly different condensations were shown in order to mock different directorial styles. A Gogolian clerklike narrator appeared before each one to explain in mockingly scholarly tones how it was a distortion of the author's original. One was in outdated 19th-century presentational style. Another, in the Stanislavskian mode (a frequent butt of Evreinov's satire), was pause-filled, hazily moody, and super-naturalistic. A third, Max Reinhardt-influenced, had a rhymed-verse text suggestive of Hugo von Hoffmansthal, Engelbert Humperdinck-like music, a circuslike performance with entrances through the auditorium, and allegorical dancing figures of "Laughter," "Satire," and "Humor." Next came a symbolist version à la Craig, set in "interplanetary space," employing masks for some characters, "mystical" line readings, an offstage choir singing the "Requiem," and the actors posing statuesquely. The final one spoofed the silent movies as directed by an acolyte of Max Linder, complete with comic chase. (Whether the last two sections were ever staged at the Crooked Mirror has been questioned.) A chief purpose of the piece was to demonstrate the director's right to be considered the author of the performance, just as the writer is considered author of the text.

From 1918 to 1922, the Crooked Mirror was closed because of Revolutionary conditions. In 1922, Evreinov attempted to resume similar work at a similar venue, the Crooked Jimmy, where he worked briefly and staged several of his plays. This led to the reopening the same year of the Crooked Mirror in a new space, where former works were revived. The company ended in 1931. Evreinov's Crooked Theater period was his most productive, and strengthened his theoretical perceptions about theatrical humor.

In 1920, Evreinov, although not a firm supporter of socialism, nevertheless employed his theater-in-life ideas by staging a remarkable post-Revolutionary pageant, *The Storming of the Winter Palace,* similar to the mass spectacles then being given under other Russian directors and whose aesthetic principles were a subject of debate. Ten thousand participants—including theater professionals and students, military personnel, and workers—reenacted the eponymous November 7, 1917, event in which the Soviets grasped power from the old regime. Many players had taken part in the actual storming on Uricky Square, the very place of the production. A simplified script, prepared by Evreinov in collaboration with nine others, clarified the issues.

Realizing that the piece represented an outstanding effort of organization and coordination, Evreinov

worked with collaborators. The large cast was broken down into smaller units, each led by its own "foreman." During the performance the directors coordinated their mass effects by using signal lights and field telephones. Evreinov conducted the entire spectacle from a position on a command bridge in the center of the square.

Evreinov's highly theatricalist presentation—another "artistic reconstruction" and not an attempt at literal recreation—employed two huge stages, a red one supportive of Lenin on the left and a white one supportive of Kerensky on the right (as viewed across the square from the palace), with an arched bridge connecting them for the struggle between the opposing forces. Broad expanses of steps led up to the stages. Important action—including the use of military vehicles—also took place in the square, where 100,000 standees were packed into two groupings separated by a wide central corridor. Scenic elements on the stages were expressionist and nonillusionistic; they jarred strangely with the surrounding architecture. Costuming satirized the wealthy bourgeoisie while the proletariat was dressed in straightforward clothing. Spotlights focused attention on the relevant action. Performers sang, danced, and spoke in unsubtle, highly expressive, and presentational fashion; much of the mass movement was rhythmically uniform. An orchestra of 500 provided musical support. At the end, as Kerensky faced his debacle, the masses cried Lenin's name in unison, 30 Lenins appeared and gave a speech, the Reds defeated the Whites on the bridge, the nearby cruiser *Aurora* fired off its cannons, the gigantic audience joined the victorious soldiers in singing the "Internationale," and the midnight sky blazed with fireworks.

From 1920 to 1925, Evreinov was preoccupied with scholarly research and writing; apart from his small forms work, his directing was confined to operas. Uncomfortable in post-Revolutionary Russia, where he felt unappreciated, and using the occasion of a Crooked Mirror tour to Poland, he emigrated to Paris in 1925. Working with emigrés, he directed Russian operas, ballets, and plays (mostly classical) until his death, but made no breakthroughs. He also lectured and wrote scholarly works and plays. In 1934, he was artistic director of the short-lived theater, the Wandering Comedians (1934), and in 1943 guided the Theater of Russian Drama (1943), operating under Nazi watchfulness.

One of the earliest theatricalists, Evreinov made worthy contributions as a historian, theorist, composer, playwright, and director. His pre-emigration career reveals bold advances in the theater of small forms, the "artistic reconstruction" of ancient styles, and the exploitation of the political mass genre.

Further reading:

Carnicke, Sharon Marie. *Nikolai Evreinov and the Russian Theatre of the Early Twentieth Century.* New York: Peter Lang, 1989.

Evreinoff, Nikolai. *The Theatre in Life.* Edited and translated by Alexandeer I. Nazaroff. New York: Benjamin Blom, 1970.

Golub, Spencer. *Evreinov: The Theatre of Paradox and Transformation.* Ann Arbor, Mich.: UMI Research Press, 1984.

Also: Rudnitsky, *Russian and Soviet Theater.*

RICHARD FOREMAN (1937–   )

RICHARD FOREMAN was born in Staten Island, New York, but raised in the suburb of Scarsdale where he was active in community and school productions. He attended Brown University from 1955 to 1959—graduating magna cum laude—received an MFA from Yale in 1962, and became a traditionally oriented playwright before exposure to experimental filmmakers caused a shift toward the avant-garde. In 1968, he founded the Ontological-Hysteric Theater (OHT) in New York's Soho area. Ontology refers to the science of being or reality, hysteria to the traditional theater's basis in conflict, which, writes Kate Davy, Foreman renders "phenomenologically—retarding and breaking up the hysterical situation or state, and focusing on the moment-to-moment reality of things-in-and-of-themselves."

Because no one else would direct his plays, Foreman did them himself, eventually staging 30 or so for the OHT. Some have straightforward titles such as *Angelface* (1968), *Total Recall* (1970), *Particle Theory* (1973), *Egyptology* (1983), *The Cure* (1986), *Symphony of Rats* (1987), *What Did He See?* (1988), *The Mind King* (1992) and *Samuel's Major Problems* (1993). Others bear enigmatic titles such as *HcOhTiEnLa or Hotel China: Part I and II* (1971); *Sophia = (Wisdom) Part 3: The Cliffs* (1972); *Vertical Mobility (Sophia = [Wisdom]): Part 4* (1974); *Pandering to the Masses: A Misrepresentation* (1974); *Rhoda in Potatoland (Her Fall-Starts)* (1975); *Book of Splendors: Part Two (Book of Levers): Action at a Distance* (1977); *Penguin Touquet* (1981); and *Film is Evil: Radio is Good* (1987). These premiered in New York, but Foreman also created new plays for Paris, Stockholm, Rome, and Seattle.

In addition, since 1968 Foreman has collaborated with composer Stanley Silverman on a series of offbeat musicals—including the Off-Broadway hit, *Dr. Selavy's Magic Theater* (1972)—most of which premiered at Massachusetts's Berkshire Music Festival. Foreman also branched out and directed established modern and classical works. His major New York offerings began with a highly successful *Three-penny Opera* (1976), by Bertolt Brecht, and went on to include Botho Strauss's *Three Acts of Recognition* (1982), Vaclav Havel's *Largo Desolato* (1986), and H. Leivick's *The Golem* (1984), all produced by Joseph Papp. He was also active at regional theaters, showing Molière's *Don Juan* (1981) at the Guthrie (also in Central Park); Arthur Kopit's *End of the World with Symposium to Follow* (1987) at the American Repertory Theater; and Georg Büchner's *Woyzeck* (1990) at the Hartford Stage Company. Foreman has directed operas, plays by Gertrude Stein and Kathy Acker in Paris, and films and videos.

Foreman is best known for his OHT work. Until

Kate Manheim in Penguin Touquet. *Directed by Richard Foreman. (1981)*   (Photo: Carol Rosegg)

he opened his loft theater on downtown Broadway in 1975 (he closed it in 1979), Foreman worked mainly in various Off-Off-Broadway venues. The 70-seat loft's auditorium was 16 feet deep, the spectators packed together on seven backless tiers to watch performances on a tunnellike, curtainless endstage 80 feet deep by 14 feet wide, built on a floor divided into multiple levels providing raked hills and valleys as it moved upstage. Technical appurtenances, walls, and ceiling remained undisguised.

Although he believes that his writing, which he likens to lyric poetry, is more important than his directing, Foreman is best known for his aural and visual images. Certain patterns became representative. Unsettling tableaux of actors and nonrepresentational scenery came eerily to life. Horizontally sliding screens and panels reshaped the scenic area into diverse spatial configurations in which tricks of perspective drew the eye toward seemingly distant objects. During the intermissionless proceedings, new visual patterns would emerge to startle and amuse; cubist effects were emphasized when actors assumed slanting postures and props, and furnishings were glued to allow for gravity-defying tilting.

The fundamental Foreman decor consisted (and, with a few changes, still does) of a few simple colors, such as blacks and browns; right angles, and a parallel placement of furniture and props; striped or checked wall patterns; environments that could suggest multiple locales; projected, handwritten, or other verbal commentary incorporated into the design; nongelled, unatmospheric, "primitive" lighting, some of it directed into the audience's eyes; white or dotted strings drawn tightly across the stage and to and from actors in various arrangements to break up the space in "force lines" creating geometric patterns; and an odd assortment of bizarre, varifunctioned (i.e., a couch-table), and crudely made (by Foreman himself) props ranging in size from miniature to very large (frequently providing multiple versions of the same object). Within this painterly world the actors moved like androids through a complex series of rigidly established, highly formalized, even grotesque movements, gestures, and tableaux composed down to the very direction in which their eyes were staring, with slight shifts in movement occurring on each new word or phrase. Generally, this stare was directed straight at the audience. Pointing was common; props that directed focus heightened the effect. The connection between physical behavior and text could be minimal or nonexistent, forcing the spectator to see unexpected relationships. Foreman wanted to engage attention

to the entire picture, each part of which in some way participated in the effect.

As the actors and sets moved into ever more eccentric pictures, Foreman's voice was heard over the speaker system, reciting commentary. Various methods of mingling tape with live performance were used; for example, a layered effect would be created by the actors' speaking slowly over their rapidly recorded voices, so that they never actually finished their words.

Throughout, Foreman remained visible, seated in a niche, surrounded by his equipment, running the sound and lights as a stage manager-conductor, creating pauses in the tapes, and interrupting and prodding the actors to make transitions by using loud sound and audience-awakening effects, including thuds, drums, a metronome, boings, bells, a buzzer, or even the word "cue." An eclectic arrangement of loudly amplified, fragmentary taped musical passages—their original tempo often distorted, and often heard in the form of overlapping loops from different recordings—has remained a vital constituent. Music is chosen to comment on the writing. Foreman sometimes creates choreographic dance interludes, although he interrupts when they threaten to become too enjoyable. These methods were modified as Foreman's style matured; he eventually abandoned his live presence on stage, although in one play he was visible on a TV monitor as a godlike robot figure, and he appeared on film in another.

Foreman's literary style has been strongly influenced by Gertrude Stein, while his thinking has been shaped by his vast reading in behavioral and natural sciences, mysticism (including the Jewish Kabbalah), aesthetic theory, and philosophy. Foreman's intricate, narratively incoherent plays are written in a state of meditative semiconsciousness. They are intended as "moment-by-moment" expressions of the artist's shifting states of consciousness and thought processes during their composition; as "diary plays," they are autobiographical. To retain their authenticity as self-expression, they used to be essentially undigested, unrevised, fragmentary collages taken in hour-and-a-half chunks from his extensive notebooks and directed as is. Over the past dozen years, however, he has preferred rearranging and rewriting the material before or during rehearsals. He also attempted to stage the numerous graphic elements (diagrams, sketches) accompanying his notes. (The more tricky the material, the more he appreciated it.) Wishing to alter their consciousness, he aims to challenge the audience to confront their passive thinking and perception.

After Foreman left his loft, his plays were produced in association with such companies as the Public Theater and the Wooster Group, although he finds a danger in the slick professionalism achieved when working at the former. Having begun with amateurs—preferably inexperienced ones with interesting qualities (like "found objects")—he now uses professionals, whom he has started to allow opportunities for creative participation; for years, the only consistently colorful presence in his casts was his voluptuous wife, Kate Manheim (now retired and suffering from an as yet undiagnosed illness), who often appeared nude. Foreman, a master of mind games, deliberately injected eroticism into his work as a way of both alienating the spectator's response while simultaneously capturing it.

Foreman allowed the actors in his early work to be their sometimes idiosyncratically awkward selves and denies having used them as puppets, although he demanded that they follow his orders precisely. His actors continually reappeared as the same characters from work to work, Manheim even becoming identified with the role of Rhoda. (Also, around a half-dozen anonymous personnages appeared in many early plays to perform as an onstage crew, arranging props and furniture as well as participating in scenes requiring additional numbers.) None were conventional, internally developed characters (although Foreman has begun to introduce psychological attributes); all had symbolic functions related to Foreman's mental attitudes. Precisely who spoke what lines was frequently not set until rehearsals. The abstract actions and meanings had to be accepted on subliminal levels.

Audiences often find Foreman's nonnarrative productions surrealistic, expressionistic, or dreamlike, but not threatening or nightmarish. Boredom is common; in the early days, many theatergoers left early. There is no sense of empathetic identification with the characters or action; Foreman, powerfully influenced by Brecht, deliberately embraces an array of estrangement devices for frustrating the tendency to become thus absorbed. Scenic elements, like a wall of glass at the front of the acting space, may create further distancing. When frustrated, the spectator is forced to think in unanticipated ways, to exercise his brain continuously in adapting to the shifting intellectual nuances served up in the densely allusive, yet monotonously intoned (more so in the past than at present), text. Most watch and listen without making an effort to puzzle out the slippery references and thematic purposes, although Foreman's recent writing, while remaining fragmentary, disassociative,

and abstract, has become not only richer linguistically but has increasingly tended to focus on more consistently expressed ideas—including politics and cultural concerns—and has even allowed emotion to intrude. Some consider this a betrayal of his standards.

The fundamental OHT methods sometimes appear in Foreman's staging of other writers' work. For example, his *Woyzeck*, writes Robert Brustein, was set in "an abstract gunmetal-gray hell, constructed of platforms and ramps and a wooden boardwalk along which Woyzeck runs like a rat in a maze." The actors wore expressionistic makeups of "white pasty faces with dark hollow eyes and black lips," and there were such "alienating techniques" as "suspended strings, groaning sound collage, harsh glaring lights, suspended skulls and chandeliers [to] create an atmosphere of searing intensity like a fevered dream."

This noncollaborative playwright-designer-theorist-performer's vision dominates his provocative productions. Almost everything seen and heard emerges from Foreman's imagination. The staging is merely the active phase of putting on the passively written play, all of it part of the same artist's expression.

Before the beginning of rehearsals, which last about eight weeks, he completes a tape of the music, sound, and dialogue, although all will undergo change. This tape—not the script—becomes the staging's foundation. The set, evolving from many sketches and models, is constructed and the actors work on it from day one. In the 1970s, the set might have been up even though the text to inhabit it had not yet been selected. The set contains movable sections that allow Foreman to improvise. When he directs someone else's script and uses a designer, he still prepares sketches and models. Until 1978, the costumes were determined by what the actors wore to the first rehearsal; they were asked to wear similar clothes to subsequent sessions because Foreman considered their appearance when devising the blocking.

Foreman's direction is largely intuitive; his rehearsals proceed in painfully slow increments as he creates and revises on the spot, and visitors have described them as chaotic, although the precision of the performances is noteworthy. Foreman's result-orientation focuses on staging, the actors—who never improvise themselves—being expected to carry out instructions exactly, to memorize every decision, and not to ask questions; recent productions, though, have seen more discussion. In *Film Is Evil*, for the first time, he even allowed Manheim to make suggestions that influenced the final nature of the piece and are considered responsible for its surprising coherence. His direction of conventional plays is as choreographed as when he does his own, but he says he will not ask actors to do anything they find uncomfortable. He told Barbara Confino: "I'm gentle, I'm nice, I'm not a sadist like some directors are, who are maybe more collaborative." He prefers to provide physical images, such as asking the actor to imagine how he would feel if fluids were streaming from all his orifices. He asks actors to do such things as maintain a hostile attitude toward the audience, to remain on the defensive against possible attack, to think of everything they say or do as a brilliant strategy, to imagine themselves linked to their fellows by taut rubberbands pinned to their chests, and to perform for only the most intelligent people in the audience.

In the early plays he tried to illustrate the text, but ultimately evolved a method of "productive counterpoint" whereby there may be no conscious relationship between the movements and the words; this is intended to allow the expression of hidden psychological undercurrents. Foreman fights any tendency toward specific expression or imitation of ideas; he will shift gears to avoid an "emotional flow." Within the work's overall complexity, he strives toward each moment's total intellectual and perceptual clarity; only thus can all ambiguities be realized.

Richard Foreman acknowledges the therapeutic function of his theater, both for himself and for his audiences. He has increasingly expressed disillusion, however, about the theater and even his own work, and talks of retiring. If he does, the theater will lose one of its most imaginatively subversive artists.

Further reading:

Confino, Barbara. "Theatrical Wavelengths: Richard Foreman." *TheaterWeek*, May 2–8, 1988.

Davy, Kate. *Richard Foreman and the Ontological-Hysteric Theatre.* Ann Arbor, Michigan: UMI Research Press, 1981.

Foreman, Richard. *Unbalancing Acts: Foundations for a Theater.* Edited by Ken Jordan. New York: Pantheon, 1992.

Also: Bartow, *Director's Voice*; Brustein, *Reimagining American Theatre*; Cole, *Directors in Rehearsal*; Savran, *In Their Own Words*; Shank, *American Alternative Theatre.*

BOB FOSSE (1927–1987)

ROBERT LOUIS FOSSE, whose father was a salesman, was born in Chicago. At age nine he began to study dance, concentrating on tap and jazz; later he regretted not having studied ballet. From his early teens, he danced in local nightclubs, strip joints, vaudeville, and burlesque shows. This background often cropped up in his stage and film work. He gained additional experience in the special services division of the postwar navy.

In 1946, Fosse settled in New York. His first Broadway appearance was in *Dance Me a Song* (1950). As his choreographic career skyrocketed, his dancing gradually wound down. Fosse made his Broadway choreographic bow with *The Pajama Game* (1954), which earned him a Tony. The three-dancer routine "Steam Heat" epitomized the eventual Fosse dance style: black suits, derbies, knee slides, tucked elbows, finger snapping, pushed-forward pelvises, complex steps, and angular arm, head, leg, and ankle movements—including pigeon-toed positions—performed to sharp percussive rhythms. He himself dressed mainly in black, some would say because he had a morbid death wish (expressed also through constant smoking, drinking, and drug use).

At the insistence of his second wife, dancer-actress Joan McCracken, he studied acting and dancing with respected teachers. Nevertheless, he attributed his technique mainly to his penchant for spending hours in studios teaching himself. When he discovered he could not master certain movements, he created compensatory ones or developed other idiosyncratic methods to mask his deficiencies. He thus evolved a manner based on his own small-framed, tight, and wiry physique. Fosse also overcame a musical illiteracy that prevented him from being able to count beats.

Fosse choreographed a series of important musicals, including the Tony-winning *Damn Yankees* (1955), score by Richard Adler and Jerry Ross; *Bells Are Ringing* (cochoreographed with Robbins, 1956), score by Jule Styne, Betty Comden, and Adolph Green; and *New Girl in Town* (1957), score by Bob Merrill. Each, apart from *Bells Are Ringing*, was staged by George Abbott. *Damn Yankees* and *New Girl in Town* also starred redheaded Gwen Verdon.

Fosse's relationships with the beautiful dancers

who worked for him formed an integral part of his persona, none more so than Verdon. She became his third wife in 1960 and—despite his philandering—remained married to him until he died. Verdon, who had been an acolyte of choreographer-dancer Jack Cole, became an essential part of Fosse's artistic life, and often assisted on major projects. Her sensual performance in *Damn Yankees,* abetted by Fosse's erotic numbers, led to controversy, which would accompany Fosse as he created ever more provocative numbers.

Verdon was the perfect Fosse dancer in other ways too. He acknowledged that his choreography was often fueled by creative contributions from his dancers, with whom he worked collaboratively. Verdon had an affinity for such cooperation. She also inspired him with her Cole background, already an influence on his style. He was happy to accommodate her qualities to his own brand of dancing, which led to an invincible combination.

The fifties saw Fosse become active as a film performer and choreographer, although he did not direct movies until *Cabaret* (1972). He moved into the Broadway directorial chair much earlier, with *Redhead* (1959), starring Verdon. As a still rare example of a director-choreographer, he was able to provide a complete unity to the movement aspects of the performance.

Redhead had a turn-of-the-century plot about the search for the perpetrator of a series of Jack the Ripper-type murders. The troubled show underwent numerous revisions but ran for 452 performances and won Fosse a choreography Tony. Outstanding dances included "Erbie Fitch's Twitch," which gave Verdon a shot at a Chaplin-inspired routine with baggy pants, bowler, and cane (which became a Fosse trademark, as did white gloves with splayed fingers); and "Pickpocket Tango," in which Verdon seductively danced with a jailer while attempting to snatch his keys. Fosse was especially apt at tying the songs to the libretto by having the music come in under the dialogue well before the song began, and then asking the actors to speak the first line of the song.

Fosse failed to conquer with his direction-choreography of *The Conquering Hero* (1961), score by Moose Charlip and Norman Gimbel, from which he was fired out-of-town. He had a major hit (1,417 performances) with Frank Loesser's *How to Succeed in Business Without Really Trying* (1961), directed by Abe Burrows and with choreography credited to Hugh Lambert. Fosse, who joined the project late, was credited for musical staging (he also had this

credit on *New Girl in Town*), which meant the direction of the song numbers, but also included his revision of most of the dances. His unified effects put the show on the road to success, especially in such bits as the riotously funny "Coffee Break," in which workers needing caffein behave like addicts needing a fix.

He did the musical staging for the flop, *Little Me* (1961), score by Cy Coleman and Carolyn Leigh, starring Sid Caesar. Another musical, *Pleasures and Palaces,* closed in Detroit.

In 1966, Fosse clicked with the 608-performance *Sweet Charity* (1966), score by Coleman and Dorothy Fields. It was sparked by Federico Fellini's film *Nights of Cabiria*; this musical adaptation provided Fosse an opportunity to explore his darkest and most challenging material yet. Cabiria, now called Charity, was converted from a prostitute into a taxi dancer (Verdon) by Fosse, who was responsible for the entire concept and the original book, the final version of which was credited to Neil Simon. Fosse determined to write his own material thereafter.

More than in any previous Fosse show, his dances cast off sexual inhibitions and were frankly libidinous. Fosse's heterosexuality-celebrating choreography commonly used tall and voluptuous women, accentuated the naughty parts of their anatomies, and elicited unabashed carnality from their movements and attitudes. Among the highlights was the musical staging for the sleazily seductive "Big Spender," with its line of mini-skirted dance hostesses displaying their long limbs in provocative, occasionally knock-kneed positions as they leaned against or straddled a vertical bar while staring with blank expressions.

Stephen Schwartz's *Pippin* (1972), Fosse's longest run (1,944 showings), had a thin Roger O. Hirson book based on the story of Charlemagne's confused son as filtered through a 1970s generation gap, anti-war perspective. It had sex (some typically raunchy Fosse staging), revolution, politics, and the like. The intermissionless show, representing Fosse's moving closer toward totally integrated staging and dance, owed its success to his control of all its elements. He even rewrote the book without credit. Most essential to his vision was the central image of Pippin's tale being told by the flashily diabolic Leading Player (Ben Vereen), a modern-day song-and-dance man dressed in Fosse black, and acknowledging the presence of the actual theater (the unadorned stage was exposed at the unsentimental ending). Accompanying him was a troupe of strolling comme-

John Rubinstein in Pippin. *Directed by Bob Fosse. (1972)*   (Photo: Martha Swope)

dia Players, in clownlike makeup, whose performances commented on the action.

Shows with such striking theatricalist cores came to be known as concept musicals because their form was more dynamic than their content. Fosse argued violently over the concept with Schwartz, but such conflicts were frequent between the director and his collaborators. One of the Players was Ann Reinking, with whom Fosse began a longtime personal and artistic relationship. With the two Tonys Fosse won for this show, the Oscar he snared for *Cabaret,* and the Emmy for *Liza with a Z,* Fosse was the first person to capture entertainment's triple crown in a single year.

Fred Ebb and John Kander's *Chicago* (1975), on which Fosse shared credit for the book, was based on a cynical 1926 drama about murderess Roxie Hart, whose notoriety makes her a celebrity. Fosse told this story of social corruption through the medium of archetypical vaudeville images (such as having the killer sit on her lawyer's lap like a ventriloquist's dummy in a courtroom scene). Verdon came out of retirement to play the tempestuous Roxie. The massively overhauled hit show shaped up as a spectacular, misanthropic, vaudevillesque distillation of the jazz age, as represented by such glitzy, decadence-reeking numbers as "Razzle Dazzle" and "All That Jazz."

Dance having become more and more the heartbeat of Fosse's work, and Michael Bennett's production of *A Chorus Line* (1975) having demonstrated the power of a practically all-dance show, it was not difficult to appreciate the impetus behind Fosse's 1978 hit, *Dancin'* (1,774 performances). Part of a trend toward bookless musicals, this was a plotless revue consisting—apart from some commentary on the dances—of 13 eye-catching routines both in the jazzy Fosse manner and in other modes and set to established tunes. Ann Reinking burned up the stage in the practically X-rated "Dream Barre" routine, in which brazen sexual positions were assumed with a male partner. Although reviewers were not unduly impressed, and there was carping over Fosse's failure to blend ballet and jazz, he won yet another Tony for choreography.

The last new Fosse show was *Big Deal* (1986), an enormously expensive flop adapted by Fosse from the Italian movie *Big Deal on Madonna Street*. The action was shifted to the world of black Chicago gangsters of the thirties. Now distrustful of collaborators, Fosse used a score composed of well-known standards. Two *Pippin*-like narrators linked the many scenes together. Every movement was choreographed, and all was tied together by a technically complex deployment of moving sets, cinematic lighting (200 cues), and 23 songs (many truncated), but the mix did not gel, the book was flimsy, and the performances belied the title. Yet again, however, the Tony for choreography was Fosse's.

Six days after *Big Deal* opened, Fosse's revival of *Sweet Charity* appeared. It was a success but closed soon after star Debbie Allen departed.

Fosse was a perfectionist who could not rest until fully satisfied and would drill his performers until they dropped. Every move had to be exactly as set, no matter how minute, or the effect would be ruined. His detailed choreography even focused on the movement of a finger. Although he allowed for collaboration, he always was extremely well prepared, having spent countless hours working out his routines beforehand with someone like Verdon. For *Sweet Charity* the pair made numerous incognito visits to actual New York dance halls. He also freed his dancer's imaginations by allowing them to play with props in his "Magic Trunk."

He could not resist demonstrating even when illness made it painful to do so. Fosse was able not only to pull memorable dance performances out of his players, but was also able to get solid dramatic interpretations, although his method was limited to a few well-chosen hints rather than verbose discussions. His aim was to evoke complete honesty, and he would often manipulate players psychologically to achieve results.

Most of his dancers claimed an undying admiration for him and a willingness to do anything he asked for. He used the same people frequently. Some remembered him as kind and understanding, but others recalled his cruelty when performers did not fulfill his demands. As he grew older and more self-destructive, his misanthropy increased and he often bullied coworkers.

Fosse generally kept his cool, but he did wear a whistle around his neck which he would blow to calm down noisy auditions and to otherwise keep his companies orderly. His auditions typically brought out hundreds of dancers (800 was not unusual). Job-seekers were put relentlessly through what had become the well-known Fosse Combinations. These, writes Martin Gottfried, were usually to the tune of "Tea for Two," and were "a set of moves and poses and gestures as well as dance setups. They ranged from finger snapping to sudden sidewise slides and undulating pelvic thrusts. As a concession to actual dance there were also elevations and jumps, a bit of ballet and jazz movement." He was remarkably unintimidating and would carefully thank each dancer for having tried out. When auditioning actors, he would give them helpful directions as a spur to getting creative responses, just as he would suggest emotional qualities for his dancers to invest in their auditions so that they acted as much as they danced.

Fosse was a brilliant choreographer who, despite the limitations of his dance vocabulary (he claimed to have only 10 steps), was astonishingly successful at creating and sustaining an immediately identifiable personal style. His shows were mature and unsentimental and usually had an antiheroic slant; many revealed a preoccupation with the seamier sides of his own profession. He was instrumental in establishing the role of the director-choreographer in the Broadway musical and demonstrated the potency of the concept musical.

Further reading:

Gottfried, Martin. *All His Jazz: The Life and Death of Bob Fosse*. New York: Bantam Books, 1990.

Grubb, Kevin Boyd. *Razzle Dazzle: The Life and Work of Bob Fosse*. New York: St. Martin's Press, 1989.

Also: Gottfried, *Broadway Musicals*; Kislan, *Hoofing*; Laufe, *Broadway's Greatest Musicals*; Mordden, *Broadway Babies*.

DAVID GARRICK (1717–1779)

DAVID GARRICK was born in Hereford, England, where his father was serving as a military recruiter. He was raised at Lichfield, and, as a teenager, took part in private theatricals. In 1734, he and his teacher, Samuel Johnson, set off together for London where he was a wine merchant. His professional debut came in 1741 at an unlicensed theater. Within months he was acclaimed for the revolutionary naturalness of his acting.

Soon Garrick was England's reigning star, most of his successes coming at Drury Lane Theatre. In 1747, he and James Lacy became comanagers there. Garrick—who ultimately became sole manager—remained until retiring in 1776, being gone for just two years (1763–1765) in order to sightsee in Europe. Under his management, the playhouse underwent several historic renovations, which improved not only its appearance but greatly enlarged its audience capacity. He also was responsible, in 1762, for ending the custom of permitting audience members to sit on the stage.

He turned the theater from failure to success, played 96 roles, wrote 21 plays and "entertainments," adapted many others, produced 85 new mainpieces, 150 new afterpieces, and revived 140 mainpieces and 59 afterpieces—more productive totals than that of his rival theater, Covent Garden. Garrick did, though, produce spectacles and pantomimes in order to compete with Covent Garden's John Rich, who specialized in such extravaganzas. In terms of longevity, the most significant new plays Garrick produced were George Colman's *The Jealous Wife* (1760), his and Colman's *The Clandestine Marriage* (1766), and Richard Cumberland's *The West Indian* (1770). Apart from pantomimes and afterpieces, usually delegated to someone else, Garrick (assisted by his prompter) directed almost every new play and oversaw rehearsals of most revivals. Infrequently, playwrights directed their own new plays.

Garrick was ever vigilant for worthy material, and—despite the patently commercial extravaganzas he had to produce—held high standards, but he was accused of suppressing plays by eager new dramatists, who thought him jealous of competitors. Yet he continually read new plays (or had them read) and gave the authors of those that interested him forthright critiques. When he began to stage a new play,

it was normal—despite possible objections from the playwright—for him to make considerable alterations, hoping to enhance to the fullest its theatrical possibilities. Offensive and outdated language was revised, performance time was shortened, dramatic action was clarified, and technically impractical requirements were overhauled.

Garrick invented considerable stage business to enliven static scenes. To avoid audience boredom, Garrick had otherwise silent characters interrupt another's speech with brief comments. He concentrated on the pacing, and often added entrances and exits to keep the characters moving. The use of standard flat wings and shutters helped him stage multiscened plays with rapidity and fluidity; Garrick employed this scenic tradition with imagination and originality. Of particular interest was the way he enjoyed ending a scene downstage and then withdrawing the shutters to discover the next scene's actors in position.

Shakespeare was high on the list of Garrick's accomplishments. The actor-manager's Drury Lane tenure witnessed 14 Shakespearean productions, ranging from such popular works as *Much Ado About Nothing* (1749), *Hamlet* (1742), *King Lear* (1742), *Romeo and Juliet* (1748), and *Macbeth* (1744), to the then infrequent *Cymbeline* (1761) and *Antony and Cleopatra* (1759) (dates are of Garrick's first productions, some predating his management). His most often shown non-Shakespearean plays were John Hoadly's *The Suspicious Husband* (1747), John Vanbrugh's *The Provoked Wife* (1744), George Farquhar's *The Beaux' Strategem* (1742), the duke of Buckingham's *The Rehearsal* (1741), Nicholas Rowe's *The Fair Penitent* (1741), and Ben Jonson's *Every Man in His Humour* (1751) and *The Alchemist* (1747). His most popular original contributions included the farces *Lethe* (1740), *The Lying Valet* (1741), the comedies *A Peep Behind the Curtain* (1767) and *The Irish Widow* (1772), and the pantomime, *Harlequin's Invasion* (1759).

A typical season saw about 80 different mainpieces given on 180 nights of playing, with from three to six shows a week, and with new mainpieces normally running no more than nine times. Bills changed frequently, often to the public's confusion. A typical bill presented a five-act mainpiece, a pantomime and/or three-act afterpiece, and a veritable variety show of *entr'actes*. Under this system, Garrick had major problems scheduling plays and casting; he worked out his tentative repertory in the summer and told his actors what parts to be up on for the fall.

Garrick's Shakespeare productions, while often praised for being more faithful than any of his immediate predecessors, were a product of 18th-century sentimentality. For *Macbeth*, he abandoned William Davenant's eviscerated Restoration period adaptation and attempted to create an authentic text, although his version removed 269 lines and even included his own expository dialogue to clarify obscure passages. Changes included the replacement of the coarsely drunken porter by a decorous servant and the removal of the murders of Lady Macduff and her son, while some of Davenant's musical interpolations for the witches (clownishly played, according to tradition, by men) were retained. Macbeth's head was not brought on, but his sword was, and before he expired, he spoke a speech of Garrick's own devising (Garrick loved grandiose death scenes). Garrick's direction included such touches as his use in IV. i. of a cave setting in which the witches' visions around the cauldron were fully enacted, with practical steps for Garrick's entrance into the cave, traps for the apparitions, and a transparency device upstage left through which the kings and Banquo could be seen moving in procession.

Also outstanding was *Romeo and Juliet*, although Garrick was less effective as Romeo than the romantic Spranger Barry. Garrick's 1750 version (also played by Barry), which remained popular into the 19th century, respected the original in many ways, but omitted Lady Montague and, to avoid a suggestion of Romeo's fickleness, any mention of Rosaline; Romeo was in love with Juliet from the start. An elaborate funeral procession for Juliet was interpolated, and following earlier adaptations, Juliet awakened to observe her dying lover and, with the aid of 65 Garrick lines, emerged with him to the graveyard, where, closer to the audience, they enacted their death scene.

For all his modifications, Garrick usually gave the most faithful renditions available of Shakespeare, but he was also guilty of selecting such mutilations as Nahum Tate's Fool-less, happy-ending *King Lear*. (A slightly more faithful version was offered in 1758, and a 1776 revival used "Old English" costumes.) Garrick's action-oriented *Hamlet* was, for all its emendations, a viable adaptation. He offered an aberrant version in 1772; among other questionable revisions, its last scene—written by Garrick—dis-

played Hamlet bursting in on the court; quarreling with Laertes; stabbing the king when the latter reprimands him; preventing Horatio's revenge; requesting his mother's repentance before she dies of madness; and binding Laertes and Horatio together with a vow "to calm the troubled land."

Because of the general use of stock scenery and costumes and the employment of lines of business, i.e., role-types in which actors specialized, rehearsals of revivals were normally not very demanding. Tradition often dictated the placement of the actors, which was normally well downstage, partly because of the lack (until later in the period) of sufficient upstage lighting. However, some rehearsal was required for even the most familiar plays, as circumstances altered their casts; also, the frequency of their performance was never enough to permanently imprint lines and business on the average memory.

Garrick began his managerial career with a brilliant company of 70; among the principals were such legendary figures as Peg Woffington, Charles Macklin, Spranger Barry, Mrs. Hannah Pritchard, Mrs. Susannah Cibber, and Mrs. Kitty Clive. Despite his own power and the awe in which his acting was held, he tried to create an ensemble company, although his enormous talent (as well as his vanity) enticed him to undertake the fattest parts and even to further thicken some of them. There were also occasions on which he allowed others to perform in roles he had made famous. Because of the "possession-of-parts" convention, however, only rarely did the casting of a stock play vary from traditional patterns, and actors often played youthful roles into old age. Garrick had more freedom casting new plays, although in deference to tradition, the playwright often had input. Garrick was an expert judge in fitting the actor to the role.

The art of directing was still in its infancy during Garrick's career, a time of highly conventionalized staging, but his practices as actor-manager display elements that legitimize him as one of the earliest directors in the modern sense. He used his authority to impose an atmosphere of discipline and decent behavior on his troupe and levied fines for infractions, such as lack of punctuality, absence from rehearsals, or failure to learn one's lines. If his actors displayed incompetence or foolishness, Garrick could become a mean-tempered martinet.

In contrast to former beliefs about the casualness and infrequency of 18th-century rehearsals, modern scholarship reveals that Garrick's company held comparatively careful rehearsals, even to the point of requiring attendance by important actors already familiar with their roles. Although the average number of rehearsals is not known, many works received only brief brushups, while those revived after a long layoff needed at least several, especially for a new cast. Premieres received the most attention, commonly being rehearsed sporadically over a three- to eight-week period, or longer. *Every Man in His Humour* was prepared for a year. Now and then, a play that had opened was further polished. Still, reports of opening night awkwardnesses demonstrate that plays were often not ready for an audience.

Garrick began by reading the script to the company in the greenroom, acting all the roles to demonstrate his goals. He also talked about the play, mingling humor with specific commentary. As the actors took on the roles, Garrick continually demonstrated how to achieve his interpretation, realistically assuming female as well as male behavior as appropriate. He wanted the actors to copy him precisely, but there is a story of how he once approved an alternative interpretation when it was demonstrated to the company by a rebellious player who did not know Garrick was nearby, spying. Garrick's auditions followed similar principles; actors who could take his direction were likely to be hired.

Despite the world of traditions to which he was heir, Garrick often invented business and byplay, which some observers occasionally thought distracting. He was a master at effecting striking pictures and at employing the visual effects of contrast among his characters in behavior and costuming. He instructed his actors to be as natural as contemporary tastes would bear, although pictures and descriptions of his own performances reveal a predilection for posing. It was primarily his "conversational" speech (he was notorious for breaking up his lines with pauses and sudden transitions), combined with a comparatively restrained and perfectly controlled use of gesture and movement, that set the realistic standard he sought to inspire.

Garrick followed standard scenic practices (wings, borders, and shutters) for most of his regular plays. Considerably more imagination was expended on pantomimes and spectacles. During Garrick's management, however, scenic practices in regular plays improved and growing sums were spent on bettering the backgrounds, including the expanding practice of using arches and practical doors between the wings and on the backscenes, and such experiments as

placing the normally parallel wings on an oblique angle. Noteworthy is the relative frequency with which new sets were prepared in lieu of using stock pieces; this practice became increasingly common from the late 1750s, and some productions were exceptionally set and costumed.

Garrick's major scenic contributions came when he hired Alsatian designer Philippe Jacques de Loutherbourg, in 1772. De Loutherbourg's main achievements were in the more spectacular presentations, but he also did important work in regular dramas. His achievements included a skillful use of machinery; the deployment of ramps, platforms, set-pieces, and profile-wings; and advances in colored lighting, all of which advanced the cause of romantic-realism. Garrick himself had introduced important lighting changes in 1765, when he eliminated the chandeliers over the stage and lit the actors by a French system of side-lighting from the wings. These and other improvements allowed the actors to move off the apron to upstage within the setting, a practice enhanced by the ever more popular use of an act-curtain to separate scenes. Just as he paid increasing attention to his sets and lighting, Garrick also insured that the costumes were theatrically attractive; on several occasions, he experimented with what was then perceived as authentic historical dress, which was not accepted until the following century. In general, contemporary clothes were worn for most plays, regardless of the period.

Garrick was not merely the greatest English actor of his century, dubbed "the age of Garrick." His enlightened 29-year management of Drury Lane saw scenic and lighting advances, dramaturgic improvements, the creation of a disciplined ensemble, a balanced repertory, careful rehearsals, and the progress of acting toward greater realism.

Further reading:

Barton, Margaret. *Garrick.* Westport, Conn.: Greenwood Press, 1978.

Burnim, Kalman. *David Garrick, Director.* Carbondale and Edwardsville: Southern Illinois University Press, 1973.

Stone, George Winchester, Jr., and George M. Kahrl. *David Garrick: A Critical Biography.* Carbondale and Edwardsville: Southern Illinois University Press, 1979.

WILLIAM GASKILL (1930–)

WILLIAM GASKILL was born in Shipley, Yorkshire, England, and took an interest in theater as a teenager. His first appreciation of directing came under the influence of Esmé Church, whose classes he attended in Bradford, and who would one day act for him. Gaskill also became involved in a local group founded by Tony Richardson. The group disbanded when Richardson and Gaskill left to attend Oxford, where both directed for the Oxford University Dramatic Society. Gaskill's best work included productions of Cyril Tourneur and Molière (including a modern dress *Georges Dandin* in French). He became committed to Samuel Beckett's advice, "A theater stage should have the maximum of verbal presence and the maximum of corporeal presence."

Gaskill, who held jobs as a nurse, baker, and factory hand, studied theater in Paris (including mime with Etienne Decroux). He then acted in weekly repertory in the provinces, acquiring his professional directing spurs with St. John Ervine's *The First Mrs. Fraser* (1954) in Redcar. He moved on to assist Richardson on *The Country Wife* (1955) at London's Stratford East, staged his first London play at the Q Theatre (1955), and directed for TV.

George Devine's English Stage Company (ESC) at the Royal Court Theatre recently had become an exciting venue known for new, often socially committed writing. The left-inclining Gaskill was invited to direct a sceneryless, single Sunday night performance of N. F. Simpson's absurdist *A Resounding Tinkle* (1957). Although Gaskill said, "I really didn't understand it," and its nonsensical style forced him to abandon normal Stanislavskian techniques, it proved so successful that Devine made him an assistant artistic director and allowed him to stage a one-act version for a regular run on a bill with Simpson's *A Hole* (1958).

Between 1958 and 1960, when he left the ESC, Gaskill directed six new plays there, among them John Osborne and Antony Creighton's *Epitaph for George Dillon* (1958), which moved to the West End and Broadway; Simpson's *One Way Pendulum* (1959), another transfer; and John Arden's *The Happy Haven* (1960). With such young, regionally accented actors as Frank Finlay and Colin Blakely, he sought to establish an ensemble capable of bringing a compelling realism to a wide range of plays.

Gaskill taught acting to a core of ESC playwrights

(the Writers Group) for about three years, sometimes influencing their writing in the process. His teaching included mask work, and several of his productions (such as *The Happy Haven*) employed masks, although he was dissatisfied with the disjunction he found between what the mask suggested and what the text demanded. Teaching remained an important adjunct to his directing.

During this first ESC period he also staged the Broadway version of Friedrich Dürenmatt's *The Deadly Game* (1960). After leaving the ESC, his freelancing included Fred Watson's provocative *Infanticide in the House of Fred Ginger* (1962) at the New Arts Theatre Club. Laurence Olivier named him an associate director of the new National Theatre (NT) at the Old Vic in 1963. By then he had been acclaimed as Britain's leading director of Bertolt Brecht (whose Berliner Ensemble's 1956 London visit had powerfully affected Gaskill) because of his successful Royal Shakespeare Company (RSC) production of *The Caucasian Chalk Circle* (1962), which used masks for the evil characters. (Gaskill thought artistic director Peter Hall's taking the show over just before it opened was "foolish," but Hall worked only on polishing and pacing.) Gaskill's other Brecht productions in the 1960s included an ineffective West End staging of *Baal* (1963) with Peter O'Toole and *Mother Courage* (1965) for the NT.

Many non-Brecht plays Gaskill directed—including Shakespeare's—employed epic theater methods, especially their scenic spareness and reliance on selective, well-used, realistic props. His most frequent ESC set designer was Jocelyn Herbert, while Andy Phillips provided sculptured white lighting that emulated the Brechtian aesthetic. Gaskill combined Stanislavskian subtext, objectives, and structural units with a Brechtian need to explore human encounters for social and economic meanings. The action necessary to communicate these meanings is obscured when surrounded with excessive decor. He said, "The human figure must exist in space with only such elements of architecture and physical properties as were absolutely necessary."

An early example of Brecht's influence was Shakespeare's *Richard III* (1961), starring Christopher Plummer and Edith Evans, given for the Shakespeare Memorial Theatre on a nearly empty stage save for a huge pillar and several shields flown in from overhead. Other Gaskill classics of the time were the anonymous *Arden of Faversham* (1961) at Cambridge; *Cymbeline* (1962) for the RSC; the York mystery cycle (1963) in York; and George Farquhar's *The Recruiting Officer* (1963), Sophocles' *Philoctetes* (1964), and John Marston's *The Dutch Courtesan* (1964) for the NT (which also produced his and John Dexter's coproduction of John Arden's *Armstrong's Last Goodnight* [1965] at Chichester).

Gaskill admits that living writers taught him how to stage the classics, while working with classical actors gave him insight into the speaking of all types of dialogue. He pays close attention to spoken inflections, and ignores punctuation when it interferes with meaning. One lesson he drives home is to stress the verb, especially in sentences with "I" in them: "I *love* you," not "*I* love you." He sometimes gives line readings.

The most renowned of his early classics was *The Recruiting Officer,* Farquhar's late Restoration comedy from which Gaskill, partly under the pull of Brecht's *Trumpets and Drums* adaptation, removed all the conventional foppish behavior and props associated with the period, used well-worn garments, and played it for its inner realism as a social document. René Allio's set used prismatic units (*periaktoi*) to change the locales and succeeded in creating the lifelike impression of a Queen Anne-style town. The revelatory production influenced Restoration productions for years; Gaskill himself made a specialty of such plays.

After two years, Gaskill left the NT, where he was disappointed by the failure to create a "socialist ensemble," and succeeded George Devine at the ESC in 1965, remaining for seven bumpy but vibrant years, his first production being one of the most controversial postwar plays, Edward Bond's *Saved* (1965), revived with some production differences in 1969. This scorchingly realistic play, which had to be produced under club auspices to avoid being banned, was about South London's societally oppressed working-class. The most disturbing scene pictured a group of thugs led by a psychopath assaulting a baby (not seen) in a carriage. The leader gently pulled its hair; one of them softly punched it; soon they were all battering it, rolling its face in its dirty diaper, and dancing around it. They picked up (imaginary) stones and showered them on the infant until, realizing it was dead, they ran off. The play became historically important when it instigated a legal battle against state censorship which ultimately—following additional difficulties with Bond's *Early Morning* (1968)—crushed England's

centuries-old tradition of banning controversial plays.

Gaskill's other ESC ventures included a few classics: Bond's adaptation of George Middleton's *A Chaste Maid in Cheapside* (1966); a critically blasted but unusual *Macbeth* (1966), with Alec Guinness and Simone Signoret acting in a golden boxlike setting glaringly lit, even for the night scenes (to allow for scientific observation of the action), and with black actors as the witches; Bond's version of Anton Chekhov's *The Three Sisters* (1967); and William Congreve's Restoration comedy, *The Double Dealer* (1969). Beckett and Brecht were also staged. Gaskill's new British plays included Arnold Wesker's *Their Very Own and Golden City* (1966), Charles Wood's *Fill the Stage with Happy Hours* (1967), Bond's *Early Morning* and *Lear* (1970), Howard Barker's *Cheek* (1970), and Howard Mueller's *Big Wolf* (1972).

Gaskill quit for several reasons, including a lack of public enthusiasm for his choices, the company's growing economic difficulties, and the failure to make the ESC conform to his dream of a writers' theater. His contributions included expanding the facilities by opening the workshop venue, Theatre Upstairs. He returned to direct such plays as Bond's *The Sea* (1973), Nicolas Wright's *The Gorky Brigade* (1979), Stephen Lowe's *Touched* (1981) and *Tibetan Inroads* (1981), and Middleton's Jacobean *Women Beware Women* (1986). His greatest collaboration was with Bond, although he parted with him because "the images in the plays had become icons of inhumanity and suffering that failed to touch me."

By 1969, Gaskill had begun to accept outside assignments, including Farquhar's *The Beaux' Stratagem* (1970; premiere in Los Angeles) for the NT and *Measure for Measure* (1972) in Exeter. He was in demand on the Continent, particularly in Germany, where he directed Brecht. He staged moderns and classics in Luxembourg, Australia, Scotland, Yugoslavia, Italy, and Norway. In America, Gaskill was represented Off-Broadway by two Shakespeares and a revival of Osborne's *The Entertainer* in 1983, by George Bernard Shaw (1985) and Pierre de Marivaux (1987) at Minneapolis's Guthrie, and by plays staged for the University of California at Davis. His London career continued unabated, both with independent productions and those for established institutions such as the NT (Barker's *The Madras House* in 1977, Middleton and William Rowley's *A Fair Quarrel* in 1979, Luigi Pirandello's *Man, Beast and Virtue* in

1989, and Mikhail Bulgakov's *Black Snow* in 1991); the Lyric, Hammersmith (*She Stoops to Conquer* in 1982, John Vanbrugh's *The Relapse* in 1983, and Michael Wilcox's *Rents* in 1984); and the Royal Academy of Dramatic Art.

Most important of his post-ESC work was his longstanding association with the Joint Stock Theatre Group, an alternative company founded in 1974. Among his Joint Stock stagings, which he believes realized his ensemble ideals, were his and Max Stafford-Clarke's adaptation of Heathcote Williams's *The Speakers* (1974); David Hare's *Fanshen* (1975); Barrie Keefe's *A Mad World, My Masters* (1977); Stephen Lowe's *The Ragged Trousered Philanthropists* (1978); the improvisationally devised *An Optimistic Thrust* (1980), in which Gaskill used masks again; and Wright's *The Crimes of Vautrin* (1983). The principle behind Joint Stock was the workshop creation of socially relevant plays by a democratically organized group, using research and improvisation, with a writer-in-residence who would go off to write his script before bringing it back to be rehearsed in conventional fashion. Despite the others' input, the writer retained script control, although the final product represented the ensemble's statement.

Gaskill was one of the first British directors to regularly employ rehearsal improvisations. The degree to which he uses them differs from play to play as do the exercises. Gaskill wants the actors to think about everything they do. He tries to begin rehearsals without specific staging ideas and to discover with the cast the author's intentions and how best to realize these. Blocking and business evolve organically. This sometimes includes omitting the traditional first read-through, because he does not want the actors to consider the words until character and situation are comprehended. He will do warm-ups with transformation exercises, such as seeing how many uses can be invented for a single prop; having the actors transform an imaginary object as it is handed around; or begin a two-person improvisation only to have someone else enter and change the action.

At an early rehearsal of *The Caucasian Chalk Circle*, he wanted to discover the social *gestus* (see *Bertolt* BRECHT) beneath the action of each scene, so he engaged the actors in a Socratic discussion of the reasons why an actress had given him a cigarette at his request. Both the social and economic reasons were elicited, leading to improvisations in which the characters' behavior was scrutinized for underlying factors. In one increasingly simplified exercise, actors narrated their actions before doing an improvisation, so the outcome was known in advance. An example was a bus driver who chose to remove a passenger who refused to pay. This allowed them to focus on the process by which the outcome was reached and how alternative decisions were possible. He wrote that "I began to understand that . . . it is the action itself that counts, that character is a secondary consideration. Theatre is about what happens, not what people are."

When he rehearsed *The Recruiting Officer*, he had the actors read each scene before repeating it improvisationally, an exercise aimed at seeing if the actor has understood the action of the play and to note what elements were emphasized and what omitted. Scenes outside or prior to the action were made up to help understand the milieu. Following an exercise, Gaskill would ask questions concerning motivations, social background, and economic status. Class and power relationships were explored. After this drilling, the actors returned to the scene with scripts. Gaskill also might have asked actors to switch roles, thereby forcing them to see their characters externally. Character understanding came naturally, not by directorial decision. Despite his improvisations, Gaskill orchestrates speech, movement, and timing.

Gaskill is text-oriented and deeply respects the writer's intentions. Still, he is not averse to occasional tampering to clarify a play. For *The Recruiting Officer*, in order to improve the narrative flow, he transposed the final act's fifth and sixth scenes and made minor cuts. He prefers to have an ongoing relationship with a writer such as he had with Bond but, apart from Stephen Lowe, has not found another author with whom to work. He expresses disrespect for conceptual directors who put themselves before the playwright, claiming that "the attempt to create images and concepts separately from the play makes for cumbersome and inelegant work." The director must serve the play by revealing its identity, not by trying to rival the playwright's imagination.

Gaskill has grown disillusioned with directing, because of its loneliness and frustrations. Still, this artist has assured his leadership role in postwar British theater by his achievements in establishing Brecht in Britain, by introducing improvisation to mainstream rehearsals, by renovating approaches to Restoration drama, and by developing new playwrights.

Further reading:

Gaskill, William. *A Sense of Direction: Life at The Royal Court Theatre.* New York: Limelight, 1990.

Tynan, Kenneth. *The Sound of Two Hands Clapping.* New York: Holt, Rinehart and Winston, 1975.

Also: Browne, *Playwrights' Theatre*; Findlater, *25 Years of the English Stage Company*; Johnson, *Directing Methods*; Marowitz and Trussler, *Theatre at Work.*

GEORG II, DUKE OF SAXE-MEININGEN (1826–1914)

GEORG II, duke of Saxe-Meiningen, was born in the Thuringian city of Meiningen, the son of Duke Bernhard of Saxe-Meiningen. He came to the throne in 1866. Georg, who excelled at art and music, attended university in Bonn and Leipzig, and spent time in Paris, London, and Berlin. As duke, he kept a firm hand on the duchy's political problems and took an active role in the court theater. Of enormous value was his third wife, actress Ellen Franz, whom he married morganatically in 1873. Equally important to the Meiningen Theatre was another actor, Ludwig Chronegk, who formed the third part of what was, in effect, a directorial collective.

As crown prince, Georg's activity in improving the court theater from 1860 to 1866 was hidden from public view. As duke, his participation became apparent. After opening his first season in 1866 with *Hamlet,* he offered a well-balanced mix of classical and popular modern plays, although his greatest efforts were expended on the former. Any aim less exalted than using art for mankind's benefit was frivolity. Among the classics and semiclassics shown were works by Shakespeare, Sophocles, Aeschylus, Johann Wolfgang von Goethe, Friedrich Schiller, Pedro Calderón de la Barca, Heinrich von Kleist, Pierre de Beaumarchais, Franz Grillparzer, and Molière. Until 1869, most plays were staged by Friedrich von Bodenstedt. When the duke began to direct regularly in 1869 he did so through an intermediary, Karl Grabowsky; this remained his method when Chronegk took over in 1873.

During these years, the rapid advances made by the Meiningen company brought it the respect of outside critics. One of the first productions to garner such acclaim was *Julius Caesar* (1867). Outsiders seeing it in 1870 were particularly impressed by its historical authenticity, which relied on advice from a costume historian who showed the cast precisely how to wear their garments. New actors joining the company were not permitted to wear their own costumes but had to dress in togas that ran to 30 ells (an old English measure, one ell equals 45

inches) in length. The performances were greatly enhanced by the stateliness imposed by the heavy robes.

In addition to its visual accuracy, the production gained credit for its unusually well-staged crowd scenes, which became a trademark; the simplification of the scenic plan to allow for a minimum of scene changes; and the acting's ensemble unity. A drawback, also noted in later productions, was the lack of artistry in major parts. (Nevertheless, such greats as Ludwig Barnay and Joseph Kainz were Meiningen products.)

The appreciation of respected outsiders—and the desire for additional revenue—convinced the triumvirate to tour, beginning with a season in Berlin in 1874. *Julius Caesar* was the opening salvo in an array of 13 attention-getting productions. The audience appreciated the scenic realism; the carefully drilled battles (aided by dim lighting); and the effect of Caesar's ghost—created by dressing Caesar in the same red color as the tent against which he appeared, and picking out his face with a well-focused spotlight.

Annual tours brought the Meininger (as they were popularly called) international acclaim and influenced European directors and writers. From 1874 to 1890, the troupe visited 36 cities in 14 countries. When not touring, they played at home, where only a small portion of the plays produced were chosen to tour. Gradually, the home seasons became little more than rehearsal and tryout periods for the tours.

Classics made up most of the schedule, although Georg's daring led him to produce, among his relatively few modern plays, two showings (there were censorship problems) of Henrik Ibsen's highly controversial *Ghosts* in its German premiere (1886). *Ghosts* exemplified the relationship between behavior and environment that underpinned Georg's romantic realism better than did the classics. A total of 43 works—a number of which became permanent parts of the repertoire—were ultimately toured. The most frequently shown (at least 150 performances) was *Julius Caesar*, followed by *The Winter's Tale*, four Schiller plays—*William Tell*, *The Maid of Orleans*, *Wallenstein's Camp*, *The Piccolomini*—and Heinrich von Kleist's *Kathy of Heilbronn*. Georg did not himself accompany the tours, leaving the troupe in the hands of Chronegk, who was responsible not only for maintaining the productions but for rehearsing the extras who had to form the crowds in each city visited. The very concept of touring was revolutionized by the Meiningen company. The tours came to an end because of Chronegk's failing health, the duke's belief that there was nothing more to gain from them, and escalating costs.

The Meiningen company continued to produce until 1914, but Chronegk passed away in 1891, others succeeded him, and the duke, growing deaf, curtailed his involvement. At 86, he directed George Bernard Shaw's *Caesar and Cleopatra* (1912).

Georg's artistry was thought revolutionary, although many of his ideas had been tried by predecessors in Germany and abroad. Presumably, it was his assimilation of the new currents, the totality of his approach, and its highly successful implementation, as well as its broad international exposure, that led him to be considered the first modern director.

Among the reforms he effected (or perfected) were the abandonment of the star system in favor of a harmonious ensemble; a concentration on true-to-life acting; the darkening of the house to put focus on the lighted stage; the extraordinary crowd scenes; the elimination of lines of business and using actors more expressively, even casting against type; the lengthy, meticulously detailed rehearsals, with actors giving their all, instead of following short-cut procedures; an improvement of the previously trivialized repertoire by emphasizing classics and important new plays; the elimination of calls for the actors after dramatic exits; the incorporation of imaginatively created—and dramatically justified—sound and music to enhance the realism; and, perhaps most noticeably, a remarkable—if distracting to some—attention to realistic details of costumes, props, and scenery, with new designs for each play produced.

The latter was an area of considerable concern to several directors. Such spectacular productions—set in the era provided by the playwright—particularized time and place in a way that contrasted radically with conventional, idealistic, and generalized contemporary techniques that resorted to ill-suited stock sets and actors' costume preferences. Nevertheless, because of his preoccupation with the visual side, Georg was accused of neglecting the literary and philosophical aspect. Proof exists, however, that he spent as much time working on a script's inner life as on its outer. He claimed his purpose was to bring out the drama's spirit; he believed this was served by the physical side of his productions, which created the mood appropriate for luring the spectator into the playwright's world.

Georg designed the costumes and provided his scene painters with preliminary studies for their designs. He also gave the painter-designers appropriate maps, documents, and books. (Some thought his zeal pedantic.) Doors and windows were practical and no furniture was painted on the walls. Various devices reduced the complexity of scene shifting. One was the so-called "Meininger room," wherein interiors were made shallow enough to fit inside more complex settings to ease their set-up and removal. Georg's aim, though, was to convey the artistic essence of the play, not merely to produce an externally accurate manifestation. His sketches showed the actors how their beards, makeup, and hair should be done. Fabrics approximated the originals and authentic props and furnishings were provided from the ducal possessions. Not only were the food and drink real, but one production even suggested the smell of "poisoned candles."

Sometimes Georg introduced debated interpretations of familiar works, such as his insistence that the title role in *William Tell* be played as an everyday man, not a near-mythical hero. He was quick to substitute more accurate translations of Shakespeare than those in use, and revised traditional conceptions of Shakespeare's work. Thus the conventional classic white costumes associated with *The Winter's Tale* were replaced by Botticelli-inspired creations, with Bohemia inspiring the clothing of the peasants as a way of bringing the locales of Sicilia and Bohemia to life. Often, he restored (and published) classic texts to a form much closer to their originals than was found elsewhere. Occasionally, his staging was bold, as when he simulated a steed killed in battle by using a stuffed horse in *The Maid of Orleans*, and had Talbot propped against it to give his dying speech.

Georg favored dynamic, asymmetrical stage pictures, with the focus anywhere but at stage center. Standing too near the perspective scenery was discouraged, to avoid scale discrepancies. Wherever possible, scenery was constructed three-dimensionally. This led to a combination of two- and three-dimensional scenery that had to be carefully planned to prevent a jarring contrast between their levels of illusion.

An advantage of acting for the duke of Saxe-Meiningen was his insistence on decor being used early in the rehearsals. When the actual sets, props, or costumes were not ready, close substitutes were used. By the time the play opened, the actor felt at home in his surroundings. Employing the props from the beginning aided the duke in varying their visual lines. He would remind the actors to hold their spears and halberds at different angles to give the picture a lifelike look. Numerous methods suggested a more pleasing and less obvious stage picture: curved movements were stressed over straight ones; actors were placed on multiple levels to vary the composition; one foot was placed higher than the other by using steps, and so on.

To produce his famous mobs, Georg broke the extras up into groups led by experienced actors who would captain their charges under his commands. Because the ensemble was a ruling factor, even principals could be asked to do crowd work or walk-ons. The captains were given dialogue written by the duke to replace ad-libbing. Each crowd member was individualized, and a variety of crowd types of varying ages and temperaments was created. They were told to keep their eyes on their fellows and be careful not to duplicate postures or attitudes. To make the group seem larger, it was usually extended into the wings.

Rehearsals were more extensive than elsewhere, up to 25 not being unusual. All actors, no matter how small their role, were asked to remain throughout. A single scene might be practiced for several days before the duke was satisfied. Sessions were notoriously long, a dress rehearsal of *The Maid of Orleans* once lasting 10 hours; the duke was present to the end.

There was no promptbook present; Georg's ideas were contained in his head. He explained his aims to Chronegk, who then instructed the actors himself. Chronegk, who called actors to order with a bell, was viewed by some as a dictator. Such autocracy was shown not at Meiningen, however, but on the road. A runner brought the duke's instructions to Chronegk from an auditorium seat, usually in the center of the first balcony, where the duke was accompanied by his wife. Only the duke could stop a rehearsal to fix something, which might be the tiniest error. The duke occasionally instructed an actor in his business although Chronegk was the acknowledged expert when it came to rehearsing actors; Stanislavsky thought him the ruling genius of the enterprise. During tours, Georg sent a steady supply of telegraphs.

Adding to the complex but apparently workable procedures was the contribution of Franz, who coached the actors in their interpretations and participated in their broader education as well. She also took part in the auditions, held before the triumvirate, and helped select the repertoire. There has been debate as to who did precisely what, but the consensus is that the work depended on the collective's combined input, with the duke at the apex.

Discipline was exacting. Actors could be fined for committing any of a detailed list of infractions, but the paternalistic duke generally treated his players with equanimity. For all his specificity, Georg was not a tyrant, and often accepted others' views.

Georg II may not actually have been the first true director, but that does not lessen the impact he had on modern theater. His contributions were so notable and were seen by so many, that he was certainly the most important director of his age.

Further reading:

DeHart, Steven. *The Meininger Theater 1776–1926.* Ann Arbor, Mich.: UMI Research Press, 1981.

Grube, Max. *The Story of the Meininger.* Translated by Ann Marie Koller. Edited by Wendell Coles. Coral Gables: University of Florida Press, 1963.

Koller, Ann Marie. *The Theater Duke: Georg II of Saxe-Meiningen and the German Stage.* Stanford, Calif.: Stanford University Press, 1984.

Osborne, John. *The Meiningen Court Theatre 1866–1890.* Cambridge, England: Cambridge University Press, 1988.

Also: Braun, *The Director and the Stage;* Brockett and Findlay, *Century of Innovation.*

JOHN GIELGUD (1904–   )

JOHN GIELGUD was born in London, son of actress Kate Terry-Lewis, through whom he related to a long line of famous players. He is one of England's finest classical actors on stage and in film, but also holds a high position as a leading stage director.

Gielgud made his professional acting debut in 1921 but did not begin directing until 1932, when he staged *Romeo and Juliet* for the Oxford University Dramatic Society, with Edith Evans and Peggy Ashcroft. The designers, the team known as Motley, were to do many other works for Gielgud. He mounted three other plays in 1932, his major breakthrough coming with Gordon Daviot's (Elizabeth Mackintosh) *Richard of Bordeaux,* in which he played the title role and established himself as a leading actor-director.

Gielgud directed over 50 plays, more than half being contemporary works, including Tennessee Williams's *The Glass Menagerie* (1948), in its British premiere, and Edward Albee's *All Over* (1971). Major new British plays included Christopher Fry's *The Lady's Not for Burning* (1949), Enid Bagnold's *The Chalk Garden* (1956), and Peter Shaffer's *Five Finger Exercise* (1958). He has a fundamentally conservative taste for plays that tell strong stories, have dramatic climaxes, and possess theatrically interesting and vital characters. Gielgud long held a desire to stage musicals, but when the opportunity came, with 1973's *Irene,* starring Debbie Reynolds, he was replaced out of town by Gower Champion.

His eight Shakespearean selections—some of them done several times—include: *Hamlet* (1934, 1935, 1939, 1946, 1964, the last with Richard Burton); *Romeo and Juliet* (1932, 1935, with Gielgud and Laurence Olivier alternating Mercutio and Romeo in the latter); *Much Ado About Nothing* (1949, 1950, 1952, 1955, 1959); *Richard II* (1936, 1937, 1953); *The Merchant of Venice* (1938); *Macbeth* (1942, 1952); *Twelfth Night* (1955); *King Lear* (codirected with George Devine, 1955); and Benjamin Britten's opera of *A Midsummer Night's Dream* (1961). Non-Shakespearean revivals included: Oscar Wilde's *The Importance of Being Earnest* (1939, 1946, 1947); William Congreve's *Love for Love* (1943, 1944, 1947); Robinson Jeffers's *Medea* (1947); Anton Chekhov's *The Cherry Orchard* (1954); and Richard Brinsley Sheridan's *The School for Scandal* (1962). Gielgud also directed major opera productions. His principal venues were on Broadway and in the West End, but he also directed at the Old Vic, at Elsinore Castle, and in Toronto and Stratford-upon-Avon.

Gielgud fit the mold of the imaginative but faithful interpreter of the classics. Norman Marshall said that he

[gives] *interpretations which are sincere rather than novel. . . . He has what so many Shakespeare produc-*

ers lack—*confidence in his author. The distinctive feature of his productions is an affectionate appreciation of all that is best in the plays, a belief that if these are given their full value there is no need to attempt to surprise and intrigue the audience by doing something nobody has never thought of doing before.*

Gielgud only rarely moved the setting of a classic from one period to another, and then only in subtle ways. His *The School for Scandal* pushed the play ahead 20 years into the 1790s and *The Importance of Being Earnest* moved from the Victorian to the Edwardian era, primarily because of decorative values, not thematic ones. In Gielgud's opinion, moving a play, especially a classic, from one epoch to another, produces a discordant note when the language comes in conflict with the period. He believes that cutting classics or transposing scenes is often necessary, although he made such changes as prudently as possible. His trimming was usually of parts that were verbose or obscure.

Despite his aversion for gimmicks, Gielgud was responsible for two noted experiments, his and George Devine's *King Lear* and his 1964 *Hamlet,* both of them generally considered interesting failures. (See *George* DEVINE for the former.) The latter's concept was to stage the play in modern dress as if it were a final run-through before costumes were added, an idea stemming from Gielgud's belief that such rehearsals often had a believability destroyed by the addition of decorative investiture.

Gielgud believes in repertory companies, especially because of the longer rehearsal time ideally permitted. Having to stage Shakespeare within the commercial system, with only a month or less for rehearsals, is exceedingly unhealthy, especially when it comes to verse speaking. Nothing in a Shakespeare play is as important as the words, which should be as carefully orchestrated by the director as the notes of a musical composition are by a conductor. He considers movement of secondary importance to the beauty of the language. Gielgud does not want empty beauty or hollow phrases and is concerned that the words be infused with the appropriate feelings and meanings. He always sought to strike a balance between an aurally appealing, poetically authentic performance and one that was fundamentally honest and real.

Gielgud's multiple talents included a sensitivity to music, which formed an important part of many of his productions, and an aptitude for drawing. He once thought of becoming a set designer and actually codesigned two of his productions. Gielgud collaborated closely with his designers, showing them his own rough sketches or providing an explicit description of what he wanted. Because of his sensitivity to color, composition, and harmony, his sets were eye-filling and dramatically appropriate. He advocates total unity of impression, with every visual and aural ingredient carefully selected for its part in the whole. His Shakespeare mountings were especially beautiful, being outgrowths of the influences Gielgud imbibed from Gordon Craig, Harley Granville-Barker, and William Poel. He favored unit sets that could, with the simplest means, provide the suggestion of a change of locale. In order to keep the action moving without delays he used minimal furniture, as in his 1948 *Much Ado About Nothing,* when the only pieces on stage for much of the action were a pair of angled benches, rearranged as necessary.

Gielgud's productions employed the finest actors available, such as Peggy Ashcroft, Edith Evans, Laurence Olivier, and Ralph Richardson. The ensemble counted above any star's performance, he felt, although this ideal was not always realized. Good actors were especially important when his own attentions were divided by the double task of starring and directing. The problems of this split task often disturbed his own performance, because of his need to watch and worry his fellows while concentrating on his own acting. Although he sometimes worked with a codirector, he knew that the best way to obviate some problems was to thoroughly prepare all the technical details in advance of the rehearsals so as to forestall obstacles. No matter how thoroughly he planned, however, he was aware that in rehearsals most of his ideas—at least those relating to the acting—would be abandoned or modified. Part of his preparations involved repeated reading of the play (and the relevant scholarship for classics), so that he began rehearsals with a clear idea of its meanings.

In general, he was uncomfortable with preplanned blocking, preferring to invent on the spot. Not everything was left to be discovered during the rehearsals; Gielgud had a mental picture of what he wanted to accomplish. Sometimes his staging was worked out with chesspieces on a model, on other occasions it was just a vague idea. His attitude was not to impose his plan but to allow for it to be a foundation on which the actors could grow. The cast was free to explore movements and characterizations.

At the first read-through, Gielgud—apart from

the showing of sketches and models—usually avoided a detailed lecture but plunged right into the text. The significance of first readings was to break the ice before putting the play on its feet.

Still, Gielgud occasionally provided an extensive talk at the first reading, as he did for the 1964 *Hamlet,* when he discussed his concept, what he sought from the actors, and the uses to which he wanted to put the set. His talk was practical and offered little of a thematic or philosophic nature.

During the reading itself Gielgud would interject brief comments on the characters or provide hints about the musical relation of one speech to the others. He might even have provided a line reading when an actor's version seemed erroneous.

On the second or third day the blocking commenced. Gielgud moved his actors about as he improvised the staging. He often manually placed the actor precisely where he wanted him. These sessions could be intense, with the dynamic director darting hither and thither. He strived to find a balance between being a puppet master and allowing creative freedom, realizing that the best ideas often come from unfettered players.

One of the most notable features of Gielgud in rehearsal was his unending inventiveness and the constant changing of his mind. "Johnny G. seems to have sixteen new ideas a minute. Write and erase, write and erase. Script covered with lunatic markings," wrote Hume Cronyn in his diary (quoted by Ronald Hayman) when acting in Hugh Wheeler's *Big Fish Little Fish* (1961). This continued throughout rehearsals and even after previews. The results could be inadvertently amusing, as when he asked actor Esmé Percy before a performance of *The Lady's Not for Burning* to change a chair in which he sat, but forgot to pass this information on to the actress previously told to sit there. In the course of the performance, the one-eyed thespian found himself sitting in the actress's lap.

Gielgud's blocking was interlarded with commentary on atmosphere and character. He would interrupt a speech to question a motivation and to suggest possible answers when needed. It was of the utmost importance that the actor have a precise picture of why he was saying these words. Just as he was prone to offer line readings at first read-throughs, Gielgud was as likely, if not more so, to give them during rehearsals proper. Still, he often told actors not to fix readings or business too soon.

Gielgud realized that each actor had to be handled according to his temperament and abilities. He might speak very tactfully to an actor of Richard Burton's caliber to get a specific response, but might be more severe with a lesser actor, even going so far as to cut his lines, cover his presence with distracting business, or dictate his entire performance (a procedure limited to stubborn or negligent actors).

Although most found him kind and considerate, Gielgud has a reputation for impatience that has claimed for him a string of anecdotes concerning his verbal gaffes. Alec Guinness remembered his first day of working under the frenetic Gielgud's baton:

> Gielgud's directions to the actors were interrupted frequently, in full flight, by his calling out to the designers. . . . "Motleys! Motleys! Would it be pretty to have it painted gold? Perhaps not. Oh, don't fidget, Frith Banbury! Alec Guinness, you are gabbling. Banbury, your spear is crooked. Now turn upstage. No, not you. You! Turn the other way. Oh, why can't you all act? Get someone to teach you how to act!"

Gielgud, while consistently charming, varied from aloofness to punning wittiness to warm emotionalism, being an easy weeper. He tried not to describe how some famous actor had played a certain moment but would likely describe that actor's general creative method as a spur to getting a proper response.

After the show opened, if he was not in it, he made return visits every six to eight weeks and gave notes or even called a polishing rehearsal, which actors resented. If he were in the play he could keep the company alert by his mere presence. Even then he occasionally provided them with notes or found time to rehearse scenes as needed. He devoted most of his energies during out-of-town tryouts to his players, slighting his own performance, and keeping his understudy up to the mark; this allowed him eventually to call a special rehearsal with his understudy playing the role so that Gielgud could observe how the role fit within the overall production before taking over himself.

Gielgud's directing career is important primarily because it was an adjunct to his career as one of the century's greatest actors. Had he not been a notable stage and film actor (among his many lauded screen performances: *Julius Caesar*, 1953 and 1970; *Becket*, 1964; *Portrait of the Artist as a Young Man*, 1977; *Arthur*, 1981), his direction would probably still have made a sharp impression. His productions were visually tasteful, excellently acted, textually faithful, unified, and directorially subtle.

Further reading:

Hayman, Ronald. *John Gielgud*. New York: Random House, 1971.

Leiter, Samuel L. "Get Someone to Teach You How to Act!: Sir John Gielgud Directs." *Theatre History Studies* 8 (1988).

Sterne, Richard. *John Gielgud Directs Richard Burton in "Hamlet": A Journal of Rehearsals*. New York: Random House, 1967.

Also: Gielgud, *Early Stages*; Gielgud, *Stage Directions*; Gielgud, *An Actor and His Time*; Marshall, *The Producer and the Play*.

JOHANN WOLFGANG VON GOETHE (1749–1832)

JOHANN WOLFGANG VON GOETHE was born in Frankfurt, Germany, to a well-off merchant family. He went to university in Leipzig and Strassburg, and received a law degree in 1771. While practicing law in Frankfurt he met privately with a group of young intellectuals involved in the "Storm and Stress" (*Sturm und Drang*) preromantic literary movement, which influenced his playwriting aspirations. In 1775, Karl August, duke of Saxe-Weimar, invited Goethe to Weimar. Here, while occupied in a remarkably diversified career involving affairs ranging from finances, highways, and forests to scientific research, and while continuing to write plays, he became the court theater's adminstrator.

When Goethe arrived, theatrical life was represented by court amateurs with whom he participated as actor and director, sometimes with his own plays, but his duties allowed only a passing interest in dramatics. His most important drama was the prose version of *Iphigenia* (1779; the verse version came later).

The productions were done in relatively makeshift circumstances, using the traditional wings, borders, and backdrop. A well-equipped, permanent theater, with five sets of mechanically shifted wings, was erected in 1780. Although productions were often beautiful, they could not rival big city opulence.

The last amateur performance was in 1783. A professional company played from 1784 to 1790, when the duke established a new theater under Goethe. Goethe organized a company and also created a summer theater at the spa town of Lauchstädt, to which the actors would repair annually at the close of the Weimar season. (In later years, other resort towns also were visited.) In 1791, the new theatrical regime debuted, giving three performances a week. Goethe was supervising director, with an actor as "régisseur," a role requiring responsibility for many of the actual directorial duties, although Goethe himself assumed these when it suited his interests. (In 1796 came a system of three régisseurs rotating the position, one a week; in 1799 there were two alternating régisseurs; after 1808 there was a single régisseur.)

Goethe sought constantly to improve the usually uninspired acting (low salaries did not attract top talent). He aimed to rid the actors of artificial habits and unpleasant dialects, and to encourage a unified ensemble. The early repertoire mingled revivals of popular comedies, serious dramas (including Friedrich Schiller's *Don Carlos* in 1791), and operas, as well as new works. Goethe hoped to gradually improve local tastes. He offered Shakespeare's *Henry IV* (1792) and *King John* (1793), but only the second succeeded. Of special noteworthiness was the acting of young Christiane Neumann (later, Becker-Neumann) as Arthur, Goethe—hoping to inspire the company to achieve her level—having accorded the actress special attention. To make her seem truly terrified at Arthur's danger, Goethe took the weapon and practically attacked her, causing her to faint.

Goethe had less success with a new, especially revised version of *Don Carlos* (1792), which failed because of inadequate verse speaking. The experience, though, was invaluable, and training his actors to speak verse rhythmically but naturally became a principal task. Schiller had taken up residence in nearby Jena several years earlier but had not had much to do with Goethe. Their artistic and personal relationship began to blossom in 1794; it was largely through Schiller's plays that Goethe got to test his evolving theatrical ideas.

In 1793, the company was reorganized under a constitution that established rules and regulations covering discipline and casting, as well as administrative matters. The major directorial responsibilities were placed in an actor's hands, with Goethe remaining the supervising director, although his participation was sporadic and even bothersome both because of the press of other business and because of his disillusionment with Weimar's actors. Only the duke's insistence kept Goethe from quitting. He increasingly concentrated his directing on celebratory presentations and an occasional new play. Often, his participation was limited to a single phase,

such as the dress rehearsal. The selection of the repertory was normally left to a subordinate.

One momentary spur to his eventually renewed activity was the 1796 guest appearance of the exceptionally versatile actor-playwright August Wilhelm Iffland. Another stimulus, which he would come to regret, was the engagement in 1797 of the gifted Karoline Jagemann, who became the leading actress-singer, assumed the position of the duke's mistress by 1799, behaved arrogantly, and figured in Goethe's retirement from the theater. His studies of Greek dramaturgy, his discussions with Schiller over the latter's imposing new historical trilogy, *Wallenstein*, the extensive 1797 renovation of the theater, and Goethe's growing respect for the formalism, compositional beauty, and musical verse-speaking of French tragedy were other influences at the time.

Wallenstein's Camp, the trilogy's first part, opened the rebuilt playhouse. The meticulously prepared production's visualization was based on research into the Thirty Years' War. Leading actors played minor parts (a new rule held that actors had to accept any role they were given), which greatly strengthened the performance. Part two, *The Piccolomini*, was directed by Goethe in 1799. His preserved stage directions display a pattern of alternating shallow scenes with deeper ones, revealed by the opening of the rear shutters, with upstage furnishings preset but with those needed for downstage areas brought on by actors dressed as servants. During the shifts, the downstage flats were changed to match those now revealed upstage. Goethe's blocking often employed symmetrical pictures, but never rigidly so; sometimes the groupings were distinctly original. The groupings were always precise, including the arrangement of heads, feet, and the positions of hands and fingers. He usually divided the stage on paper into squares and triangles on which he could plan out his movements (the stage itself bore a similar grid pattern).

Later in 1799, the trilogy was completed with *Wallenstein's Death*. Schiller moved to Weimar to focus on his writing and to work at the theater, where he often directed. This inaugurated the famed era known as "Weimar classicism."

Among Goethe's major directorial projects at this time were operas, his own *Tancred* (1801), and Schiller's poetic version of *Macbeth* (1800), with Schiller assisting at rehearsals. The presentation offered the tragedy in 15 scenes with eight or nine settings, in an interpretation that filtered the play through a unified and heightened "classical" style, employing considerable music, and eliminating all suggestions of grossness (the porter's indecorous comic speech was replaced with a prayerful song, and Macbeth's armor was substituted for his head). Macbeth was viewed as a noble victim of fate, the latter being personified by playing the witches as men dressed in classic robes. In an 1804 revival, Goethe's witches were three beautiful girls, to emphasize that evil may be more fascinating when internal reality contradicts outside appearance.

A substantial step forward came in 1801 when Goethe, desiring to develop a sophisticated audience appreciative of the great variety of world drama, codirected with Schiller a rare showing of Terence's Roman comedy, *The Brothers*. Its experimental staging employed commedia-like *lazzi* (comic business), Roman garments, and masks that had foreheads, noses, and chins but left the actors' eyes, cheeks, and mouths exposed.

Goethe staged Gotthold Lessing's *Nathan the Wise* (1801), slighting the visual to focus on the language, with the director making great demands on the delivery of the difficult text. Goethe directed August Schlegel's romantic drama *Ion* (1802) in which Goethe managed, despite rudimentary equipment, to create striking lighting effects. He also continued his experiments with classical costuming and masks (on selected characters). Goethe's control of the mise-en-scène resulted in a remarkably unified and subtly nuanced impression. Masks reappeared in Carlo Gozzi's *Turandot* (1802) for which Goethe again explored commedia acting, even demonstrating the character types to the actors himself.

Subsequently, Goethe's activity slackened but, because of the duke's unwillingness to allow him to resign, picked up again in 1803 when he produced a list of disciplinary rules designed to control his actors. An 1807 version fined actors for such infractions as missing entrances, refusing walk-on parts, rehearsing with a stick in one's hand, and joking during a performance.

Goethe's directing, apart from revivals, included Schiller's *The Bride of Messina* (1803); his own *The Illegitimate Daughter* (1803); Schiller's *The Maid of Orleans* (1803); and *Julius Caesar* (1803), exemplifying his interest in simplified Shakespearean staging, with only the most necessary accessories, but creating visual excitement through lictors (minor Roman officers) and flagbearers and a colorful use of a variegated crowd. Goethe took pride in the beauty of his actors' Shakespearean verse speaking, but he grew disillusioned about the contrast between his formal style and Shakespeare's external vitality. He came to doubt that his productions' cool, statuesque move-

ments and gestures, influenced by French performance, was appropriate for the English playwright.

Following *Julius Caesar* Goethe opened a school to train young actors and composed a now famous list of 91 acting rules, many of them amusingly narrow from a modern viewpoint. He was the chief instructor and, at his home, began to present performances that he had worked on with his students.

Schiller's expansive *William Tell* (1804) was staged by Goethe, with Schiller's assistance. The large company demanded expert compositional grouping and crowd direction. Goethe was inclined to arrange actors in a loose semicircle that allowed room for gestures but did not permit obvious gaps in the picture. Great attention was paid to the scenery, which Schiller insisted be based on actual landscapes and which Goethe once revised by taking a brush to the scene-painter's work.

After Schiller's death in 1805, Goethe continued to direct, although the theater was confronted by various political and economic problems. His productions included his own *Torquato Tasso* (1807); Heinrich von Kleist's *The Broken Jug* (1807); Sophocles' *Antigone* (1809); Zacharias Werner's *The Twenty-fourth of February* (1810), a somewhat sensationalistic success based on a recent crime, and staged with unusually natural performances; Pedro Calderón de la Barca's *The Constant Prince* (1811), produced after eight years of study with Goethe's trainees, and with the dialogue precisely orchestrated, down to the smallest pauses and punctuation marks, yet surprisingly effective; Vittorio Alfieri's *Saul* (1811); Goethe's much altered version of *Romeo and Juliet* (1812), with a Falstaffian Mercutio and a bowdlerlized Nurse, but granted a superb pictorialization using brilliant Italian costumes and sets designed by Goethe himself and indicating his recent preoccupation with visual effects; Calderón's *Cenobia the Great* (1815); Goethe's monodrama with music, *Proserpina* (1815); and his *Epimenides' Awakening* (1816).

In 1817, the duke overrode Goethe's decision not to permit a performance by a traveling troupe featuring a trained poodle. The duke, presumably under Jagemann's influence, relieved Goethe of his directorship, although inviting him to continue in an advisory capacity. Goethe did later participate in several theatrical events, but basically, his Weimar theater career had ended.

Weimar rehearsals were few, although *The Constant Prince*, which stemmed from his school, opened after years of work. Actors were encouraged to prepare thoroughly before rehearsals began. Goethe began rehearsals at the head of a long table with his régisseur at the other end. The actors sat according to rank. A rap on the table by Goethe's key signalled the rehearsal's commencement. Four scripts were passed from hand to hand as the company read the play aloud, reading whatever passage was before them, while Goethe maintained a rhythm by the tapping of his key. Individual parts were read at the second rehearsal, rhythm being the prime focus, while characterization appeared at the third reading rehearsal. Goethe considered these readings crucial because all errors and misinterpretations could be eliminated at them, while corrective measures could be introduced.

Once the words were memorized (Goethe demanded accuracy) blocking began, followed by several run-throughs and a dress rehearsal. Goethe paid attention to the tiniest details at the latter sessions and was prone to get up on stage and demonstrate.

Outside of rehearsals, he would instruct actors privately.

When Goethe worked, directing was a barely acknowledged art yet, in many ways, he displayed the signs of a director well ahead of his time. Marvin Carlson noted that Goethe "was the first example of the modern director as the creative artist ultimately responsible for every aspect of the production."

Further reading:

Bruford, W. H. *Theatre, Drama, and Audience in Goethe's Germany.* London: Routledge and Kegan Paul, 1950.

Carlson, Marvin. *Goethe and the Weimar Theatre.* Ithaca: Cornell University Press, 1978.

Williams, Simon. *German Actors of the Eighteenth and Nineteenth Centuries: Idealism, Romanticism, and Realism.* Westport, Conn.: Greenwood Press, 1985.

Also: Johnson, *Directing Methods.*

HARLEY GRANVILLE-BARKER (1877–1946)

HARLEY GRANVILLE-BARKER was born in England, the child of an architect and an actress. Originally an actor, he gained valuable experience working with William Poel and George Bernard Shaw. His first directing opportunity was a 1900 program of one-acts for the progressive, noncommercial London Stage Society. For several years, he continued to act and direct for them. He also began to gain recognition as a playwright.

Barker advocated a subsidized, subscription-based repertory company, with productions that expressed the most advanced theatrical ideas. The repertoire would consist of the best classics and contemporary plays, and would be in sharp contrast to the moribund commercial theater.

In 1904, he took over the management of the slightly off-the-beaten-path, 642-seat Court Theater, beginning with revivals of *The Two Gentlemen of Verona* and *Candida.* In partnership with J. E. Vedrenne, Barker ran the Court for three years, producing a succession of mountings, mainly of new works, the average run being two weeks. Of the 988 performances accumulated, 701 were of 11 Shaw plays. Shaw, credited with the direction of his own plays, may have been assisted considerably by the uncredited Barker. Shaw's plays shared Barker's attentions with those by such notable dramatists as Henrik

Ibsen, John Masefield, Gerhart Hauptmann, John Galsworthy, Arthur Schnitzler, Euripides, and Barker himself, making the Court repertory London's most advanced. The three Euripides productions (*Hippolytus* in 1904, *The Trojan Women* in 1905, and *Electra* in 1905) were largely responsible for reviving interest in Greek dramas. (Barker later staged two other Euripides plays.)

From 1907 to 1914, Barker directed at various theaters. In 1910, he established with American impresario Charles Frohman, The Repertory Theater, a London company at the Duke of York's that opened with Galsworthy's *Justice.* The company survived for only four months. Among Barker's other important activities was his producing partnership in 1911 with his actress wife, Lillah McCarthy. Their productions, offered at several theaters, included Euripides' *Iphigenia in Tauris* (1912) and a unique adaptation of Thomas Hardy's *The Dynasts* (1914). Three of the performances of *Iphigenia* were shown in an open-air Greek theater at Bradford College, with Barker ending his acting career as Orestes. Most memorable of the Barker-McCarthy productions were the three Shakespeare stagings at the Savoy, *The Winter's Tale* (1912), *Twelfth Night* (1912), and *A Midsummer Night's Dream* (1914).

Barker directed abroad in 1915 when he staged Shaw's *Androcles and the Lion,* Shakespeare's *A Midsummer Night's Dream,* Anatole France's *The Man Who Married a Dumb Wife* (which brought American designer Robert Edmond Jones to fame), and Shaw's *The Doctor's Dilemma* in New York. He also presented Euripides' *Iphigenia in Tauris* and *The Trojan Women* at college stadiums in New York and elsewhere. These marked the end of Barker's active directing career, for after divorcing McCarthy and marrying wealthy American writer Helen Huntington, his theatrical work practically ceased. He wrote and lectured, returning to practical theater work only rarely, mostly to work on plays his wife had translated from the Spanish or to help with a revival of one of his own plays. In 1940, he spent 10 days assisting on Lewis Casson's production of *King Lear,* starring John Gielgud.

Barker's directorial style was noted for its clarity, restraint, understatement, and psychologically detailed verisimilitude. This approach was perfect for naturalistic plays, but a more theatrical style was necessary for the productions of plays by writers such as Euripides and Shakespeare. Even when the overall impression of a Barker production was nonrealistic, the acting always stemmed from internal honesty and believability.

Barker thought that acting should be limited physically to only what was essential, and that a director should not fill his stage with business just for effect. He preferred minimal movement, except for scenes of dancing, acrobatics, and fencing; when these were called for, Barker's productions were exemplars of choreography, as in the choral movement and larger-than-life gestures used for the Greek plays.

Barker favored harmonious, nonstar ensembles. He wanted the focus to be on the play and not a specific player's performance. His respect for the text was paramount, and he made his decisions primarily on the basis of how they would enhance clarity and meaning. Thus he castigated directors who gained their reputations from the idiosyncracies of their choices, which may have been eye-catching but were often detrimental to the respective plays. His own imaginative conceptions of the Shakespeare plays he staged were never intended as external ideas forced upon an unwilling text, but were created from an inner necessity dictated by the world of the play itself.

Barker was gifted at expressing the fundamental musical values and rhythms of a work, despite what superficially seemed a random or haphazard flow of natural events. He resorted to a pianola in preparing for rehearsals, seeking to discover rhythms that he could translate into performance. Actors were often given specific musical terms as a stimulus.

Barker believed in the importance of comprehending the original conditions under which plays of specific periods were created so that a semblance of them could be employed in reviving such works. This did not mean antiquarian reconstructions, but implied the reestablishment of those essential features of a play's original staging that could be adapted within the framework of contemporary attitudes. He concluded that classical plays could best be recaptured on a thrust stage set within a horseshoe-shaped auditorium, both because of the actors' increased three-dimensionality and because of the warmth felt by spectators able to see others in the audience sharing the same experience.

Forced to work within proscenium theaters, Barker was able to come up with only compromise solutions, usually by building aprons out over the orchestra pit and front rows and by deploying curtains to alter stage space. He rejected such scene-changing devices as the revolving stage, wagons, and traps, preferring instead the challenges of the bare stage. Despite its importance, decor for a classic must not distract from the play or hinder the swift progression of the scenes. His Shakespearean settings were artistic masterpieces, combining extreme simplicity and flexibility with imaginatively nonillusionistic means for establishing locale. When one compares the spare and symbolic, yet striking and colorful, Shakespearean sets created for him by designers Albert Rutherston and Norman Wilkinson with the pictorially illusionistic ones still popular at the time, the magnitude of Barker's contributions can be appreciated.

Barker's Shakespeare productions employed a tripartite stage divided into fore, middle, and rear areas. The 12-foot forestage, sans footlights, was below the proscenium; above it, set within a false proscenium, came the middle stage; and above that was the rear stage, elevated on a four-step platform with curtains hung across it. An assortment of beautifully designed curtains were stretched across the middle stage and could be pulled aside as needed to vary the depth of the stage and to suggest changes of locale. The effect was formal and nonrepresentational, and fostered the acceptability of the actor's occasional stepping forth on the forestage for scenes of direct address. Action could progress from scene to scene without any time wasted on scenic changes, apart from the pulling on or off of a curtain traveling horizontally.

Barker's Shakespeare actors spoke crisply and quickly, which was in striking contrast to the period's more leisurely elocutionary methods and consequently annoyed those who could not adjust to the rapidity of the speech. It was Barker's mission to get audiences to learn to listen more attentively than they were used to; he claimed his actors spoke far more naturally and in keeping with Elizabethan usage than was customary. He barely cut the texts, removing only the more archaic or bawdy expressions, a revolutionary style at the time.

He made similar inroads in the staging of Greek tragedy, then rarely seen on Western European or American stages. The characters were always fundamentally believable; full choruses were retained with close attention to ritualistic choreographic patterns and unified, musical speech (the latter not always successful); there was a return to out-of-door equivalents of Greek theaters, while the indoor stagings made use of a forestage extension; and the sets, utilizing a three-door facade, were spare yet powerful.

Barker was meticulous, taking great pains to get inside the thought patterns of the characters. Unfortunately, circumstances normally forced him to open in three weeks or less. Although he expressed a casual attitude toward sets and costumes, he was responsible for inspiring designs that were extraordinarily influential.

He looked for versatile, easy-to-work-with actors. When possible, he employed the repertory concept whereby an actor who plays a lead in one play is likely to have only a bit in another. This provided even the smallest roles with a stability and talent that ordinary productions could not equal.

At the first rehearsal Barker normally read the play to the cast, giving an outline but not complete characterization of each role. A discussion followed. As much time as possible was used for such "at table" talks. He sought to get the actors to contrive clear character biographies, so that they could justify their behavior by reference to an actual past. He felt that each play required a different amount of discussion and that such sessions would lead to a comprehension of the play's form, which had to be grasped before blocking could begin.

Blocking was introduced slowly during the table sessions, a scene here or there, as a way of dealing with momentary obstacles in understanding the work or of adding life to tired conferences. During such preliminary blocking, actors were advised to concentrate on thoughts and feelings and not lines, which they were allowed to mumble. The characters' interior life was always given preeminence. Players were not permitted to "perform" until they first had mastered understanding of the text, blocking, and memorization of their lines. Barker's lack of preoccupation with "staging" was true primarily of the more realistic plays, whereas his productions of the classics would see him taking extreme pains with picturization, movement, and gesture. Still, to help the actors with their movements—even in less elaborate productions—he always kept a scale model of the set before them as they rehearsed.

One of Barker's idiosyncratic beliefs held that actors should do all their work on a role at rehearsal, not at home. Only the atmosphere of the ensemble, he felt, could inspire the actor's cooperation in the totality, a harmonious union that he thought would be disrupted by the actor's focus on his own performance apart from his fellows.

The degree of Barker's directorial autocracy has been debated. He has been described as extremely patient and gentle, but also as tyrannical, albeit operating more by implied threat than by actual screaming. Barker himself said that he preferred to give his actors great freedom, and to be an editor who advised on what did or did not work, rather than act as a drill master. He thought a musical conductor was able to exercise dictatorial control, but not a theatrical director, as the latter would be in danger of robbing an actor of spontaneity.

Despite his insistence that a director be a diplomat, Barker could not always live up to his ideals. One reason for the contradiction is the rapid timetable under which he worked. Thus, he was often forced to move actors about physically when blocking them, to offer notes that were predominantly critical rather than supportive, and to demonstrate—including giving line readings—when explanations proved insufficient. Some remembered him as a taskmaster who managed to exert his authority without losing respect. Others recalled him as being a despotic puppet-master. On balance, he seems to have been truly autocratic only in the final throes of rehearsal when pressured by the imminence of an opening.

Although there had been fine English directors before Barker, he was the first truly modern one, a man in tune with all of the finest ideas in theater evolving during his time. His thinking was instrumental in the eventual formation of Britain's National Theater; he reintroduced the importance of the thrust stage; he proved the value of ensemble companies; he revolutionized Shakespearean staging; and he made Greek drama integral to the classical repertory.

Further reading:

Dennis Kennedy. *Granville Barker and the Dream of Theater.* Cambridge, England: Cambridge University Press, 1985.

C. B. Purdom. *Harley Granville Barker.* London: Barrie and Rockliff, 1955.

Also: Leiter, *From Belasco to Brook;* Mazer, *Shakespeare Refashioned.*

JERZY GROTOWSKI (1933–   )

JERZY MARIAN GROTOWSKI was born in Rzeszow, Poland, where his father was a forest ranger and painter and his mother was a teacher. Grotowski studied at Krakow's Theatre School from 1951 to 1955, while also studying Eastern philosophy. In Moscow, he investigated the techniques of Russia's directorial masters and held Konstantin Stanislavsky in high regard.

In 1956, Grotowski entered the directing program at Krakow's Theatre School. Outside of school, with Mahatma Gandhi as his role model, he took part in the anti-Stalinist youth movement. He taught at the school from 1957 to 1959. He also published philosophically oriented articles on art and theater. His professional directing debut was the costaging of Eugène Ionesco's *The Chairs* (1957). His other stage projects of the period included Prosper Merimée's *The Woman Is a Devil* (1957), his master's degree project, and an unconventional staging (including masks) of *Gods of the Rain* (1958), based on a Jerzy Krzyszton play. It was the first Grotowski production to radically adapt a drama to suit his own purposes—in this case, to make a statement about the younger generation's search for the meaning of existence—by rearranging the text and interpolating material from others. He believed, controversially, that a script should be a stimulus for the creation of an independent work of theater art.

Anton Chekhov's *Uncle Vanya* (1959) eschewed naturalism in acting and design. A revolving stage was divided into two principal areas, placing in visual opposition what the director believed to be the play's conflicting "attitudes," one for those alienated from nature and another for those at one with it.

Grotowski was concerned with the possibilities of a theater in which there was a dynamic interaction or "dialogue" between the actors and the audience. This blossomed when he became director of the Theater of 13 Rows in Opole, with critic Ludwig Flaszen as his literary collaborator. The enterprise was intended as a subsidized, experimental theater, although Opole, a city of about 60,000, proved too small and provincial for Grotowski's revolutionary works. The bantam company opened with an adapta-tion of Jean Cocteau's surrealistic *Orpheus* (1959). As with its successors, it played locally and on tour to other Polish cities.

Many native critics denigrated Grotowski's early work. Only when—as the result of frequent foreign visits—the international theater community vener-ated him as one of the greatest modern artists did the tide, albeit reluctantly, begin to turn at home.

Byron's *Cain* (1960), in its first Polish staging, was presented as a "philosophical cabaret" because of its montagelike structure, ritualistic decor sugges-tive of Bosch, substitution of Alpha (the forces of nature) and Omega (the forces of reason) for God and Lucifer, blatant mockery of philistinism in Adam, Eve, and Abel (the latter resembled a Hitler youth), loud music, strange masks and costumes, and intermingling of the tragic and the grotesque. The audience was viewed as Cain's descendents.

In 1961, Grotowski used a neoconstructivist set to stage Johann Wolfgang von Goethe's *Faust* in Poznan, his only production away from his own troupe. One critic noted these "objective effects": "a radical unhistoricization of the costumes, intellectual brevity, loading the Goethe text with contemporary philosophical problems (Freud, existentialism), and the elimination of mythology from the heavens" (quoted in Zbigniew Osinski).

In Opole, Grotowski offered a jeering version of Vladimir Mayakovsky's *Mystery-Bouffe* (1960), in-tended, says Osinski, as a "scathing polemic on the meaning and form of art that occurs in conditions inundated by petty bourgeois tastes pretending to be official ones." It employed a few basic props to represent numerous objects and a half dozen actors who made rapid changes in order to play numerous characters.

In 1960, Grotowski began an important collabora-tion with designer Jerzy Gurawski. Their experimen-tation with environmental techniques, in which the audience-actor relationship varies according to the production's needs, began with Kálidása's Sanskrit classic, *Sákuntalá* (1960), in which the audience faced the stage area (occupied by a phallic construc-tion) on two sides, with a pair of yoga-commentators placed behind the seats. The script included segments from Indian ritual sources. Six actors played the multifarious roles, the gestures and movement were choreographically precise, and the actors not only incorporated liturgical sounds and comments in their speech but used their bodies to produce a variety of sounds. Grotowski, fascinated by the highly developed systems of signs and gestures in Eastern theater (especially India's *kathakali*), hoped to find his own equivalent so as to create a ritualized theater. Eventually, he evolved an organic acting system that would be among his most remarkable contributions.

Grotowski's first excursion into the Polish classics was 19th-century romantic playwright Adam Mickiewicz's *Forefather's Eve* (1961), conceived and adapted as a ritual drama, with fragments from Shakespeare, Jean-Paul Sartre, and the playwright's own preface. There was an acting space shared with the audience, the latter in chairs scattered about the space and encouraged to participate in the performance. Props were minimal but were all present from the start and capable of transformative uses. Period costuming was replaced by a grab bag of choices, such as a rug used as a cape. A few cylindrical spotlights were manipulated by the actors themselves. In typical Grotowskian fashion, the action continually undercut the play's mythic elements of tragedy and spirituality with ironic or blasphemous commentary. Gustav-Konrad, the Christ figure, bore a broom on his shoulders instead of a cross. Grotowski believed it necessary, in such works, to create a dialectic of "apotheosis and derision" to confront established Judeo-Christian myth with the reality he and his company experienced as witnesses to Poland's painful history.

For another much-altered 19th-century drama, Julius Slowacki's nationalistic *Kordian* (1962), Grotowski put his own grotesque spin on the original's romantic concern with self-sacrifice. The entire action was set within a mental institution, with the audience, seated on hospital bunk beds, treated—like the actors—as patients in the asylum. At times audience members were coerced into participating (Grotowski later abandoned such measures). The company was known now as the Laboratory Theatre of 13 Rows.

Grotowski's international reputation was beginning, via his appearances at foreign conferences and seminars, and publications about his work. He became even better known following Stanislaw Wyspianski's turn-of-the-century *Akropolis* (1962). In this expressionistically conceived montage adapta-

tion (on which Josef Szajna collaborated), the play symbolized the graveyard of humanist civilization, so its action was placed in a concentration camp (Opole is 80 miles from Auschwitz) and the action—the enactment of mythical scenes by Easter Sunday tapestry figures—was transmogrified into the activities of the camp's prisoners. The androgynous characters wore identical torn burlap sacks, berets, and heavy boots and repeatedly uttered incantory phrases such as "Our Akropolis" and "cemetery of the tribes." They used extraordinary muscular control to create facial masks. Lighting was primitive but nightmarishly powerful, and the actors suggested numerous objects (many resembling parts of a crematorium) through the creative deployment of a minimum of props; this usage was often ironic, as in the substitution of a stovepipe for a bride. At the pessimistic conclusion, the Christ-Apollo savior figure was a headless dummy carried into a box representing the crematorium. The stylized, rhythmic acting was the outgrowth of lengthy rehearsals incorporating improvisational techniques.

Akropolis epitomized Grotowski's "poor theater," in which the actors, aided only by the barest technical means, conveyed all the necessary elements of the mise-en-scène. The audience was part of the action as "witnesses," not participants. They were the living in the presence of the dreamlike dead.

Grotowski was deemed a messianic priest of what Peter Brook called "holy theater," and his actors were novitiates in his theater-temple. In daily two- to three-hour sessions (apart from rehearsals), the actors worked on difficult psycho-physical exercises designed by a process Grotowski called *via negativa* ("negative way") to rid them of emotional, muscular, and vocal blockages in order to reach the spontaneous, natural impulses leading to action. Exercises were tailored to suit individual needs. Grotowski deplored the practice of others borrowing the exercises but not their ethical basis. Many were based on Eastern disciplines, including hatha yoga, but the practices of Western predecessors like Stanislavsky, Vsevolod Meyerhold, Charles Dullin, and François Delsarte were also employed. Grotowski's tapping of the body's vocal "resonators" was considered revolutionary. Psychological researchers such as Jung and Pavlov provided further inspiration. Actors attained unusual technical perfection. Theater magic was created through seemingly impossible physical and vocal feats, and the actors seemed to approach spiritual transcendence. From among these dedicated actors emerged Ryszard Cieslak, who best represented Grotowski's ideals. By being exposed to such revealing actors, the audience was expected to engage in self-analysis as well. The ritual nature of the performing experience was intensified by the tiny theater, which seated only 50; Grotowski made a fetish of such intimate arrangements (100 was a large audience for him).

Grotowski directed Christopher Marlowe's *Tragical History of Doctor Faustus* (1963), a free adaptation (using all of Marlowe's words) in which the theater became a refectory dining hall and the spectators sat as guests at long tables on which the action—conceived as Faustus recounting moments from his life—transpired. Necessary props were suggested by the actors' bodies. Seen at an international theater festival in Poland, it was responsible for quickly spreading the director's name abroad. By 1966, the company made the first of numerous foreign tours, presenting their frequently revised plays to major capitals and gaining universal renown. Grotowski lectured widely, spreading his influence. Foreign students came to study at his feet.

The chief importance of *The Hamlet Study* (1965), based on texts by Shakespeare and Wyspianski, lay in Grotowski's shift from dictator—making all performative choices—to improvisational collaborator. Process began to take precedence over product.

Opole was not fertile enough, so the company moved in 1965 to the larger, more culturally endowed city of Wroclaw. Here they presented Slowacki's version of Calderón's *The Constant Prince* (1965), rehearsed for a year. The audience peered down on the action from above, as if watching an operation or a bull fight. There was only a small acting platform that could serve multiple purposes. The remarkable Cieslak, dressed in a loin cloth, enacted the prince who accepts torture with humility and love; he seemed engaged more in an act of sacral offering than a performance. Because there seemed no separation between the premeditation of acting and the spontaneity of being, Grotowski—who helped develop the performance through an intense improvisational process—eulogized it as "the total act." Such performing was considered an act of sacrifice.

In 1966, the company became the Laboratory Theatre Research Institute of Acting Method. Two years later, they presented Grotowski's masterwork *Apocalypsis Cum Figuris* (official premiere, 1969). It was created collaboratively from exercises and improvisations based on the Gospels and ideas relating to the Second Coming. Although selections from T. S. Eliot, Simone Weil, and Fyodor Dostoyevsky were used, it was the least literary of Grotowski's works. There was no separation of acting from audience space: in one version, spectators sat on benches against three walls; in another, they sat on the floor. They watched an apocalyptic drama about a small group of drunken revelers who role-play at biblical characters engaged in taunting a Christ-like Simpleton; the action leads to a dangerous absorption in the roles, which are viewed in blasphemous, contemporary terms. There were six symbol-laden props and all the lighting came from two spotlights. The entire performance represented a "total act."

With this work, Grotowski's directing career ended. Believing that he could go no further in the paths he had been researching, he abandoned new works, although *Apocalypse* continued to be shown until 1981. Even his appearance changed; following a 1970 trip to India, he cast off his business suit and dark glasses for sandals and beard, and lost over 80 pounds. Having gone as far as he could in altering—but not demolishing—the relationship between audiences and actors, he turned to what he called paratheatrical activities in which he explored the possibilities of nontheatrical interhuman relationships. Process preceded product. Those involved sought to achieve psychological and emotional wholeness, to enhance their creative possibilities, and to discover a higher plane of consciousness. In 1982, Grotowski moved to Southern California to continue these researches, in 1984 the Laboratory was dissolved, and in 1985 he moved to Italy. His posttheatrical work has gone through major developmental steps (best known as "Theater of Sources," "Objective Drama," and "Ritual Arts"); they bear a relation to theatrical art and are an outgrowth of his earlier directing work.

Interest in Jerzy Grotowski's ideas continues, even though he has abandoned theatrical production. It is, however, his 11 years of work as an innovative avant-garde director that established his revered place in the modern theater. Although his ideas are often misused and abused, he remains a dominant influence.

Further reading:

Grotowski, Jerzy. *Towards a Poor Theatre*. New York: Simon and Schuster, 1968.

Kumiega, Jennifer. *The Theatre of Grotowski*. London and New York: Methuen, 1985.

Osinski, Zbigniew. *Grotowski and His Laboratory*. Translated and abridged by Lillian Vallee and Robert Findlay. New York: PAJ Publications, 1986.

Temkine, Raymonde. *Grotowski*. Translated by Alex Szogyi. New York: Avon, 1972.

Also: Innes, *Holy Theatre*.

TYRONE GUTHRIE (1900–1971)

TYRONE GUTHRIE was born at Tunbridge Wells, England, to well-off parents. The six-foot-five-inch-tall Guthrie acted in school theatricals while attending Oxford University. In 1924, he performed professionally for James B. Fagan's London company, but soon switched to directing, staging Christopher Scaife's *The Triumph of Death* (1924), at the tiny Barn Theatre in Oxted.

After several years of directing radio plays and semiprofessional productions for the Scottish National Players, Guthrie, in 1929, began directing at the Festival Theatre, in Cambridge. He staged a play a week, ranging from the Greeks to the expressionists. In 1931, he made his London debut with James Bridie's *The Anatomist* at the Westminster Theatre. His West End career began with J. B. Priestley's *Dangerous Corner* (1932). After staging a series of Shakespeare productions at the Old Vic (OV), he was appointed its administrator in 1939, holding the post until the war ended, although he

Tyrone Guthrie directing Hamlet *at the Guthrie Theater. (1963) L is George Grizzard, lc is Lee Richardson (in same pose as Grizzard).* (Photo: Guthrie Theater)

George Grizzard in Henry V. *Directed by Tyrone Guthrie. (1964)*   (Photo: Guthrie Theater)

returned on a number of occasions. His New York debut was in 1936 with a pair of his West End productions.

Guthrie's OV work, to which he brought his unconventional ideas about the classics, was his major contribution during these years. He introduced star actors there and exchanged its tired pictorial illusionism in favor of simplified, Elizabethan-inspired staging. This required some never fully satisfactory modifications of the picture-frame stage, including the building of a thrust platform over the orchestra pit.

Among the offerings of Guthrie's inaugural 1933–1934 OV season was a *Macbeth* that eliminated the opening scene of the witches on the heath in the belief that it was not by Shakespeare. Instead of stressing the influence of supernatural forces, he made the play into a study in abnormal psychology by demonstrating the Macbeths' responsibility for their own fates. Subsequent seasons saw many more Shakespeares, as well as other classics. Some of Guthrie's work showed a clear Freudian influence.

Hamlet was played as the victim of an Oedipal conflict and Iago's treachery stemmed from repressed homosexuality.

Following the war, Guthrie worked internationally; he was busy not only in London and New York, but in Finland, Canada, Israel, Scotland, Ireland, Australia, and elsewhere. His eclecticism proved remarkable, with plays representing most periods in Western theater history, and with multiple revivals of such works as *Hamlet*, Sophocles' *Oedipus Rex*, Luigi Pirandello's *Six Characters in Search of an Author*, and Anton Chekhov's *The Cherry Orchard*. Guthrie was also in demand for operas and, on occasion, even staged his own plays. He worked in the popular theater as often as he worked in institutions, although he had true commercial success only with Thornton Wilder's *The Matchmaker* (1954) and Paddy Chayefsky's *The Tenth Man* (1959).

Guthrie founded two major institutional theaters, the Festival Theater at Stratford, Ontario (1953), and the Tyrone Guthrie Theater at Minneapolis

(1963). Both expressed his faith in repertory and the viability of the thrust or open stage. The Festival Theatre opened in a tent before a permanent structure was provided. Both it and the Guthrie had semi-Elizabethan stages designed by frequent collaborator Tanya Moiseiwitsch.

Guthrie's influential open stage productions were among his most important contributions. He had experimented with such stages ever since the late 1920s, seeking to create a unit set that could serve for any Shakespearean play, with the addition of specific decorative elements. On such a stage banners, props, easily shiftable units, and costumes were all that was needed to create spectacle and locale. In 1937, he experienced a breakthrough when he was forced to stage *Hamlet* in a hotel ballroom at Elsinore, Denmark, because rain cancelled the outdoor production at the castle. A more carefully planned opportunity came in 1948 when he directed David Lindsay's 1540 allegory, *Satire of the Three Estates*, at Assembly Hall of the Church of Scotland,

Edinburgh, with the audience seated around three sides of the stage. This production led to the creation of the Festival and Guthrie stages, with their large thrusts, vomitoria, and multiple-level, permanent facade settings against the rear stage wall.

Guthrie appreciated the intimacy such stages effected between audience and actors. Pace and rhythm could best be served when there were no undue waits for shifting. Equally important was the sense of ritual fostered by the spectator's awareness that he is not alone, but sharing an experience with others he can easily see. Guthrie acknowledged that the proscenium was more suitable for certain plays, yet he successfully directed proscenium-type plays like *The Cherry Orchard* on the open stage.

Guthrie, seeing theater as larger than life, was drawn to plays that allowed for directorial scope. Classical plays, especially, stimulated his theatrical imagination and allowed him to play with color and movement on a grand scale and to get actors to perform with an expressivity absent from contempo-

Lee Richardson (l) and Jessica Tandy (r) in The Cherry Orchard. *Directed by Tyrone Guthrie. (1965)* (Photo: Guthrie Theater)

rary realism. He felt a special affinity for Greek tragedies, not only because of their opportunities for spectacular staging, but because they are perfect exemplars of the relation between ritual and theater. He viewed the tragic hero as a symbolic priest who must suffer sacrificially for the good of the community. *The House of Atreus* and *Oedipus Rex* were outstanding examples of his views.

Guthrie was pragmatic. He did not care for anything mystical or excessively psychological in an actor's approach and felt that technical accomplishment was superior to methods that overstressed feelings. Of primary importance was the voice, which should have color, clarity of diction, and excellent breath control. He wanted actors who could bring a musical awareness to their lines; the values of pausing, rhythm, pitch, volume, and timbre were strongly emphasized. He even staged scenes as though he were a conductor working with singers.

Guthrie's often spectacular productions demonstrated his genius at moving actors about in interesting choreographic patterns and effective groupings. A small example of his masterful creation of business was when he had the ghost in *Hamlet* whisper his message into his son's ear as if poisoning him with ideas of revenge, just as Claudius had poisoned the ghost himself. Sometimes his choices were so novel and absorbing that they obscured the values of the play they were supposedly enhancing.

Despite his fondness for visual effects, Guthrie did not care much for color in his lights, preferring ungelled instruments that brought out the color in the costumes and decor. He was also unusual in his appreciation for footlights, which he thought could not be matched at lighting actors' faces.

Each character in a Guthrie work had three-dimensionality and individual business to perform. Realistic byplay among the spear-carriers was sometimes more interesting than the words of the leads. Whenever appropriate, Guthrie inserted pageantry into his classics, such as when a brief section in the text of *All's Well That Ends Well* inspired him to introduce a 10-minute segment showing the duke of Florence inspecting the troops.

Guthrie was well known for shifting the period in his Shakespeare revivals to make the themes contemporary. His self-conscious cleverness led to his becoming the epitome of the "wouldn't-it-be-fun" school of directing. Among his transpositions was a 1938 *Hamlet* set in the 1930s, with its funeral scene played under dripping black umbrellas, and with Fortinbras's army wearing gas masks and car-

rying carbines; a *The Taming of the Shrew* (1954) done as a Wild West, turn-of-the-century farce set in the Pacific Northwest; and an antiwar *Troilus and Cressida* (1956) set just before World War I to suggest the decadence of European society on the brink of its downfall. Guthrie argued that moving such plays to more recognizable periods made it easier for audiences to comprehend the differences in rank among the characters, their occupations, and even the time of day.

Guthrie held that there should be no restrictions—especially not traditional ones—in the staging of a classic. A script was raw material on which to exercise one's imagination; subjectivity entered into any interpretation, no matter how "faithful." To Guthrie, even a living author was not a valid interpreter of what he had written because so much creativity is subconscious. He thus avoided asking playwrights for their opinions.

Guthrie both cut and added material to suit his needs. Shakespeare was often not only sharply edited but his scenes were sometimes rearranged. Lines from one play might be inserted into another, to clarify plot concerns, and background characters were likely to have ad-libs written out for memorization.

Distrustful of conventional auditions and interviews, Guthrie liked to work with familiar actors. He hated typecasting and selected actors in terms of how they fit the total picture, especially in vocal terms. Whenever possible, he chose unknowns whom he could shape, rather than veterans set in their ways.

He prepared by reading the play numerous times, often reading aloud to test the quality of the lines. He had little use for scholarly interpretations because he found such writing too ignorant of theater values. When it came to preblocking, he differed according to the play. He liked having a loose idea of the blocking that could be changed at a moment's notice. Rehearsals were a congenial time for working out the details of movement and furniture placement. Only rarely did he consult a script in rehearsal, his method being to work as spontaneously as possible.

Guthrie conferred with his designers and his leads before rehearsals commenced so that all would be in harmony. During rehearsals he abhorred windy discussions as time-wasting and boring. His work with his designers was especially productive, although he was more of a guide than a dictator. He worked out a system of shorthand with Moiseiwitsch whereby the pair would draw rough sketches together, move on to rough models, and then finished ones, with a similar process followed for the costuming. Skilled at drawing, he did his own ground plans and made sketches of his important ideas before they were carried out.

Guthrie's rehearsals lasted a week to two months, varying according to the project. Each play had different requirements, and he said that if he and the leading actor agreed on the approach, even *Hamlet* needed only two weeks. His sessions were tightly organized to make the best use of the time alloted. As he grew more experienced he came to feel that first read-throughs were unnecessary and either abandoned them completely or had the actors read for 10 or 15 minutes before putting them on their feet. Rather than lecturing, he conveyed his desires in his unique, clipped manner of speech, which allowed him to communicate in a few carefully selected words. Nevertheless, Guthrie's rehearsals were considered great fun, largely because of his wit, offhand manner, surging energy, and good spirits.

He moved constantly, both on the stage and in the house, reacting dynamically to the players and sending out a barrage of eccentric vocal sound effects supplemented by handclaps and finger clicks. This normally gentle and slovenly giant sometimes wielded the mailed fist, and many actors felt the lash of his anger or sarcasm—couched in ripe profanity—when they offended him, although the storms quickly passed.

He blocked quickly, often moving the actors physically, asking them not to write their moves down, believing that good ones would be remembered and bad ones revised. He also wanted immediate memorization of lines. A firm foundation was quickly established, so the actors could feel comfortable with

improvements as the rehearsals progressed. Guthrie wanted full-out acting and meaningful readings as early as possible. He often gave line readings although he had a distaste for them. Once the actors responded appropriately, he allowed them time for experimentation and exploration in ensuing sessions. Guthrie wanted to evoke performances, not to demand them; his touch, however, was so sure that actors came to appreciate his specific assistance, although he normally coached in terms of pace, mood, business, and the like, not in analytical character concepts.

Sir Tyrone Guthrie staged over 400 productions, spreading his influence internationally. Among many other achievements, he set the Old Vic on a path of glory, popularized the idea of the open stage, gave a tremendous impetus to the regional theater movement, and stirred great interest in the theater as ritual.

Further reading:

Forsyth, James. *Tyrone Guthrie: A Biography.* London: Hamish Hamilton, 1976.

Guthrie, Tyrone. *A Life in the Theatre.* New York: McGraw-Hill, 1959.

———. *In Various Directions: A View of Theatre.* New York: Macmillan, 1965.

Rossi, Alfred. *Minneapolis Rehearsals: Tyrone Guthrie Direct "Hamlet."* Berkeley: University of California Press, 1970.

———. *Astonish Us in the Morning: Tyrone Guthrie Remembered.* London: Hutchinson, 1977.

Also: Johnson, *Directing Methods*; Leiter, *From Belasco to Brook*; Marshall, *The Producer and the Play.*

ADRIAN HALL (1927–   )

ADRIAN HALL was born in Van, Texas, and raised on his parents' ranch. He majored in speech at East Texas State Teachers College, studied at California's Pasadena Playhouse, taught junior high school, and received an M.F.A. from Pasadena in 1950. In 1950 and 1951, he led his own theater-in-the-round summer theater in Galveston. From 1951 to 1953, he served in the Army's Special Services, and created an ensemble that toured Europe in one-acts he directed; he also staged an original army musical. Meanwhile, he gained closeup views of Europe's major troupes.

Back in the States, Hall acted at Joanna Albus's Playhouse Theater in Houston, where, in 1954 and 1955, he directed five shows. One of his guiding lights was Albus's mentor, Dallas director Margo Jones, whose production of Jerome Lawrence and Robert E. Lee's *Inherit the Wind,* redirected by Herman Shumlin, brought Hall to New York as a member of the company.

Hall staged his first New York play, Lillian Hellman's *Another Part of the Forest* (1956), for the noncommercial Equity Library Theater, where, in addition to ventures at other small playhouses, he

Adrian Hall directing Warren's All the King's Men.
(1987)   (Photo: Trinity Repertory Company)

directed four more productions. One was a revival
of Tennessee Williams's *Orpheus Descending* (1959)
that warranted a commercial Off-Broadway move,
and gained acclaim for demonstrating the drama's
value. Most of Hall's selections were American,
although he offered the American premiere of
Agatha Christie's British mystery, *The Mousetrap*
(1960) at the Greenwich Mews, where a number of
his productions were seen.

From 1957 to 1959, Hall's summers were spent as
director and coproducer of the Phoenicia Playhouse,
in the Catskills, where he staged two dozen plays,
averaging one a week. Most were from the standard
Broadway repertory. Some of the same people—such
as actress Katherine Helmond and designer Robert
Soule—who worked with him here also joined his
Off-Broadway ventures, and would be with him
when he began his major work.

Hall continued to build up his résumé, staging
summertime musicals in North Carolina (1961);
summer-stock comedies in New Hampshire (1962
and 1963); the national tours of two Broadway hits;
John Jennings's hit Off-Broadway musical *Riverwind*
(1962); and productions in Omaha, Abingdon (Virginia), and Milwaukee, where he directed Brendan
Behan's *The Hostage* (1964) at the Milwaukee Repertory Theater; he later worked there frequently. His
watershed year was 1964, when he became artistic
director of Providence, Rhode Island's new Trinity
Repertory Company.

Trinity was one of the many theaters that sprang
up during the 1960s, when the American theater's
decentralization was being urged. Hall was able to
abandon the disillusioning hit-or-miss economics of
the commercial arena to build a permanent ensemble, and to explore his ideas on the nature and
purposes of theater. The company was housed in

the 300-seat, thrust-stage Trinity Square Playhouse,
formerly a church, where Hall opened with *Orpheus
Descending.* He remained for 25 years and achieved
remarkable results in a wide variety of productions,
from original scripts to classics to familiar contemporary works to lesser-known foreign and American
scripts. Hall developed as permanent an ensemble
as any regional theater in America has known; some
actors remained for over two decades.

In 1983, he assumed the artistic directorship of
the Dallas Theater Center while retaining his Providence post, thus making him the only director in
the American theater ever to hold two such positions
simultaneously. Some of the productions done with
one company were later redone with the other,
although a few works, such as Oliver Hailey's rowdy
Kith and Kin (1986), were specifically aimed at Texas
audiences. By 1989, the difficulties of the arrangement overwhelmed even the indefatigable Hall, who
also wished to pursue other interests, and he resigned
from Trinity to concentrate on Dallas (where he
worked in several venues, including a temporary
barnlike structure that provided total flexibility).
Hall was fired, however, partly because of his imperi-
ous ways and partly because his "in-your-face" productions offended too many subscribers. He
subsequently directed at other regionals, including
his first New York production in over a decade,
Shakespeare's *As You Like It* (1992), in Central Park
for the Public Theater. The chief innovation of this
anachronistic, backwoods-Americana interpretation
was to remove the theater's back wall and substitute
for conventional scenery the park's natural beauty,
although it confused the play's contrast between city
and forest; abetting what was more a rustic than a
pastoral approach was an array of antique cars and
tractors, and live chickens, sheep, and goats.

Hall aimed to make Trinity an integral part of its
community's life, appealing to all segments of the
population, especially those who normally would
not attend a play. His relentless efforts saw the
subscriptions grow from 800 to 20,000. Although
his controversial productions sometimes shocked and
discomfited people, those who refused to return were
replaced by others who welcomed the confrontational experience Hall provided. However, his provocative staging and repertory often got him into
trouble with the board of directors. Hall believes
that theater is basically a transaction between the
actor and the audience, and it is the director's job
to make that transaction as electric as possible, to
surprise, and even, when necessary, offend, in order
to provoke complete attention.

A crucial influence was the company's success, under the terms of a 1966 pilot program, in bringing theater to high school students. This led to a funded project designed to continue the program, for which a local 1,000-seat auditorium was employed. The opportunity to enlarge his audience base challenged Hall's ingenuity. When students reacted with destructive behavior, he was forced to discover ways to capture their attention. In *Julius Caesar* (1967), for instance, he made the events intersect with the students' lives through the insertion of "a contemporary figure" who commented on the action along with film clips, percussion, and slides of political figures. He also began to consider ways to reshape the theatrical space into a more dynamic entity to assist in making it a single place shared by actor and audience. Such methods were increasingly used in his nonproject stagings as well and developed into a signature approach.

Hall's post-1967 collaboration with designer Eugene Lee was very important. Lee typically avoids traditional, painted scenery in favor of densely atmospheric environments (Hall calls them "atmospheres") through a selective use of real objects, weathered surfaces, and striking audience-actor spatial formulations that change from show to show. Hall's notions of reconfiguring the space and of the possibilities inherent in suggestive environments—such as creating the effect that the entire theater is a ship—were inspired by Jerzy Grotowski's work. White light and only absolutely necessary scenic pieces became frequent elements in Hall's increasingly minimalist lexicon.

The actor is at the heart of Hall's direction; he eliminates props and decor if he can get the actors themselves to communicate time, place, and atmosphere. The confrontation between actor and spectator must force the latter to think, to use his imagination, or he will become lazy, complacent, and bored.

In 1973, the company moved into an oldtime vaudeville theater renamed the Lederer Theater. It was completely renovated and turned into two theaters, a variable, proscenium-less, 800-seat (later reduced to 550) upstairs space and a 297-seat, modified thrust, downstairs space for smaller productions.

Hall's list of mainstream authors includes Shakespeare, Jean Racine, Henrik Ibsen, Anton Chekhov, George Bernard Shaw, Tennessee Williams, Bertolt Brecht, Jean Genet, Harold Pinter (in 1982, Hall brought *The Hothouse* to Broadway), Sam Shepard, Franz Xaviar Kroetz, and so on, many represented by several plays.

Hall has directed various world premieres, including, among others, a new musical version of Truman Capote's *The Grass Harp* (1966), Roland Van Zandt's *Wilson in the Promise Land* (1970), Shepard's *Seduced* (1978), David Berry's *The Whales of August* (1981), and two unusual works by James Schevill, *Lovecraft's Follies* (1970) and *Cathedral of Ice* (1975). The latter, about Hitler's rise and fall, led to one of Hall's most notable environmental productions, in which much of the action involved the active participation of the audience, who wandered from area to area to view scenes played on different mobile stages.

Hall's honored works include a series of adaptations for which he himself (working with other writers) was responsible. A partial list includes *Brother to Dragons* (1968), based on Robert Penn Warren's poem about an 1811 atrocity committed by Thomas Jefferson's nephews; *Billy Budd* (1969), from Herman Melville's novel; *Son of Man and the Family* (1970), about murderer Charles Manson; *Feasting with Panthers* (1973), about Oscar Wilde's incarceration on charges of sodomy; *Eustace Chisholm and the Works* (1976), from James Purdy's homosexually oriented novel, and which graphically presented an abortion; *A Christmas Carol* (1977); *In the Belly of the Beast: Letters from Prison* (1983), based on killer Jack Abbott's book; and *All the King's Men* (1986), adapted from Warren's book about a southern demagogue. Most deal with dark themes and antiheroic outsiders, which Hall says derives from the alienation he has felt as a gay male.

These epic-scaled, strikingly episodic works usually use narrators, choruses, and prologues (even standard scripts may get a prologue); because of Hall's "process is more important than product" philosophy, they are meant to be developed collaboratively with the actors, who contribute many creative ideas and often play multiple roles. Hall's dependence on his ensemble leads him to prefer actors with physical, even athletic dexterity, and musical ability. He prefers live music over tape, although he has sometimes made imaginative use of taped music and sound. (Richard Cumming is his most frequent composer.) Often, actors are asked to mime horses, trees, and the like, and might even create such sounds as the hissing of a fire. Hall often employs both cross-racial and cross-gender casting.

A famous Hall moment was in *Brother to Dragons*, when the act of portraying the hacking-off of a slave's hands and feet was conveyed by hauling the actor playing the slave overhead by his ankles as a real side of beef was chopped at under the fluorescent light of a butcher store. In *Billy Budd*, it was startlingly effective when the title character was hung and plummeted 20 feet.

Hall may employ anachronisms, like the fluorescent light in *Brother to Dragons,* because he is more concerned with emotional truth than precise historical accuracy. Costuming too can cut across eras. In *Troilus and Cressida* (1971) the Greek and Trojan military gear was gleaned from many wars, including Vietnam.

Hall no longer does extensive formal preparation (promptbooks and notes) before rehearsals. Regardless of the script, even one he has done before, Hall begins with a ground-zero attitude. He reads extensively and likes to visit authentic locales, but waits until the process of rehearsing to discover what is in the text and how to "explode" it. He wants to know, What does this play mean at this particular time in history? The actors, encouraged to do their own research, bring in their discoveries; ultimately, they are told to personalize the material, to bring it "closer to themselves." Instead of imposing, Hall prefers to let the actor discover the performance via directorial quests and suggestions. In his performance-centered theater no text is inviolable, and Hall, despite occasional complaints, has no compunction about cutting and revising a work to suit his needs.

Hall avoids blocking for some time, electing to have the actors read and explore the text at table, sometimes for three weeks in a six-week rehearsal period. To deepen the sense of "family," the entire cast, no matter how small their parts, must always be present. When the actors finally get on their feet, most of their lines are memorized, and their emotional relationships are clear. They can now work intensely on developing their spatial and physical relationships without wasting time writing and rewriting blocking notes. Hall's method means that he does not know what the work will be like until it is revealed in the rehearsal process. He revises incessantly, even after a play has opened. His attention remains constantly on making the story-line—the "clothesline" of events—clear, especially in the

nonlinear plays of which he is very fond. Part of this orientation involves having the designers and composer create their designs and music in the crucible of rehearsal.

Hall amazes actors by his volubility, energy, and ability to stimulate imaginations. He refuses to accept artificiality and, though it can be painful, strips away defenses, preconceptions, and tricks. He searches for ways to make the script meaningful and alive, and, being extremely sensitive to potential reactions, strives to consider the role of the spectator. Actors are warned against illustrating; if a gesture duplicates a line, the gesture is removed. The actors are told not to "kiss and tell."

Hall's diversity makes it difficult to classify him. Perhaps the best summation is that of Don Shewey, who places him among those who "commute freely from classical to contemporary . . . , who don't recognize the distinction between mainstream and avant-garde . . . who see text-oriented naturalism and visual-oriented nonnaturalism as aesthetic choices rather than ideologies, who patch up the rift between Meyerhold and Stanislavsky, so to speak."

Further reading:

Block, Carolyn. "Adrian Hall." *Theatre* 15 (Spring 1984).

O'Quinn, Jim. "Company Man." *American Theatre* 1 (December 1984).

Schevill, James. *Breakout! In Search of New Theatrical Environments.* Chicago: Swallow Press, 1973.

Shewey, Don. "A Boot in Two Camps." *American Theatre* 3 (October 1986).

Woods, Jeannie Marlin. "Adrian Hall Explores the Poetry and Prose of Robert Penn Warren." *Theatre Topics* 1 (September 1991).

Also: Bartow, *Director's Voice.*

˙Note: The following appeared too late to be of use in this entry: Woods, Jeannie Marlin. *Theatre to Change Men's Souls: The Artistry of Adrian Hall.* Newark: University of Delaware Press, 1993.

PETER HALL (1930–   )

PETER REGINALD FREDERICK HALL was born at Bury St. Edmunds, Suffolk, England, the son of a stationmaster. In 1939, the family moved to Cambridge. After teaching in the RAF's Education Corps, he entered Cambridge University, where he

staged over 20 plays, one of which, Luigi Pirandello's *Henry IV* (1953), was transferred to London's Arts Theater. His professional career began with plays for the Theater Royal, Windsor; weekly rep at Worthing; the Elizabethan Theater Company; the Oxford Playhouse; the West End; and the Arts, where he became artistic director in 1955 and staged Federico Garcìa Lorca, André Gide, Eugène Ionesco, Eugene O'Neill, Jean Anouilh, and others. His fame spread after he staged the English-language debut of Samuel Beckett's *Waiting for Godot* (1955), which he said he did not understand.

Hall founded the International Playwrights' Theater, but lacking funds, it offered only Tennessee Williams's *Camino Real* (1957) and Anouilh's *Traveller without Luggage* (1959). His London freelance assignments included *Gigi* (1956) and the British premiere of Williams's *Cat on a Hot Tin Roof* (1958), performed in a club to avoid censorship. Hall debuted on Broadway with Morton Wishograd's *The Rope Dancers* (1957).

In 1956, Hall debuted at Stratford-upon-Avon's Shakespeare Memorial Theater with *Love's Labour's Lost,* which he followed with *Cymbeline* (1957), *Twelfth Night* (1958), *A Midsummer Night's Dream* (1959), and *Coriolanus* (1959), starring Laurence Olivier. During this "romantic" phase, Hall made use of gorgeous sets and costumes. His *Dream*—a repertory item for a decade—stressed the comedy and sensualized the fairies; it was set mainly in the oak-timbered great hall of an Elizabethan manor house, with decorative accessories added to suggest differing locales.

By 1960, Hall was Stratford's leader, retitling it the Royal Shakespeare Company (RSC) in 1961. He won a large government subsidy; updated its stage with a rake, a thrust, and a false proscenium; and, through a rare combination of artistic and administrative genius, transformed it from a regional festival into one of the world's foremost ensembles, with a reputation for innovation and for a revolutionary anti-Victorian, coolly analytical and intellectual approach to Shakespeare. Within a democratic ensemble deemphasizing stars, greats such as Peggy Ashcroft flourished alongside such newcomers as Glenda Jackson. For a time, Hall headed a directorial triumvirate including Peter Brook and Michel Saint Denis. He also helped develop a unique codirecting methodology for epic-scaled productions.

Hall established a London outlet at the Aldwych Theater to be used mainly for modern plays and non-Shakespearean classics, while Stratford concentrated on Shakespeare, thus giving his actors—hired, innovatively, on three-year contracts—an opportunity for cross-fertilization. This socialist director's Shakespeare work was further enhanced by his conviction (inspired by Cambridge Professor F. R. Leavis) that contemporary social perspectives should

be worked into the classics, an idea fortified by the actors' exposure to new works. Another influence was the selective naturalism of John Bury's austere, Brechtian sets, in which metaphorical, minimalist backgrounds built of wood and metal mingled with realistic costumes and props. Hall came to dislike placing Shakespeare in a precise period, preferring designs combining a Renaissance foundation with relevant historical elements.

Hall's celebrated RSC stagings included *The Two Gentlemen of Verona* (1960); *Twelfth Night* (1960); an antiheroic *Troilus and Cressida* (codirected with Barton; 1960), notable for its unusual setting of a large white sandbox backed by a "dried-blood" cyclorama, and for uncovering the play's modern relevance; *Romeo and Juliet* (1961); *Hamlet* (1965); and *Macbeth* (1967). Most remarkable, though, was *The Wars of the Roses* (1963) project. This comprised an award-winning trilogy (coadapted with Barton), *Henry VI, Edward IV,* and *Richard III,* constructed from *Henry VI*'s three parts and *Richard III.* In 1964, Hall added *Richard II, Henry IV, Parts 1 and 2,* and *Henry V,* thus offering the entire canon of Shakespeare's histories within two seasons.

The Wars of the Roses and *Hamlet* were benchmarks. To exemplify his preoccupation with the modernity of Shakespearean power politics, the plays constituting the *Wars* were greatly cut and rearranged; they even employed 1,400 new pseudo-Shakespearean lines by Barton. Hall's work on the verse and characterizations was acclaimed as was the visual imagery, notably a council table around which power waxed and waned. The Machiavellian slant was also instrumental in *Hamlet,* starring David Warner, whose nonromantic, hippielike appearance, speech, and behavior so closely resembled the disaffected anti-Establishment youth of the 1960s, that the play became a sellout among young audiences.

Before Hall resigned in 1968, he also directed various non-Shakespearean plays for the RSC. These included Jean Giraudoux's *Ondine* (1961), Anouilh's *Becket* (1961), Henry Livings's *Eh?* (1964), Nikolai Gogol's *The Government Inspector* (1966), and Charles Dyer's *Staircase* (1966). Simon Gray's *The Dutch Uncle* (1969) and the British premieres of Edward Albee's *A Delicate Balance* (1969) and *All Over* (1972) followed his resignation. His brilliant stagings of Harold Pinter included *The Collection* (codirected with Pinter in 1962); *The Homecoming* (1965), which won Hall a Tony on Broadway; *Landscape and Silence* (1969); and *Old Times* (1971), also staged in Vienna (in German).

His work with Pinter—whose dependence on "precise verbal form" Hall compares with Shakespeare—is enhanced by Hall's musical talents; he is a genius at digging out the writer's subtext and orchestrating the timing, indicated textually by three dots for a small pause, "pause" for a longer one, and "silence" for major ones. Hall even conducts dot-and-pause rehearsals. He wants the actor to express both Pinter's "architectural" as well as "emotional" linguistic values and to understand clearly all the motivations, regardless of their ambiguity. Hall, who finds Magritte an excellent visual inspiration for Pinter, and who keeps the movement in these works to a bare minimum, has been especially successful at conveying their enigmatic menace.

Hall's post-RSC freelancing included Peter Shaffer's *The Battle of Shrivings* (1970) and Galt McDermott's Broadway flop musical *Via Galactica* (1972). In 1973, he became head of the RSC's rival, the National Theater (NT), later renamed the Royal National Theater, shortly before its 1976 move—following numerous delays—from the Old Vic to a giant, $32-million South Bank complex. Its three theaters are the large, fan-shaped, thrust-stage Olivier; the middle-sized, proscenium Lyttleton; and the intimate, flexible Cottlesloe. Hall cherishes the Olivier because it allows actors—in Chekhov as well as in Shakespeare—to acknowledge the audience's presence while remaining in the world of the play.

In 1977, Hall was knighted. But the following decade was marked by controversy. His diaries, published in 1983, provoked a storm. He was sharply criticized for using the subsidized institution to stage works that would earn personal income. A workaholic, he was also castigated for doing operas that removed him from the NT.

Hall staged eight star-plus-ensemble Shakespearean revivals at the NT. *The Tempest* (1974), starring John Gielgud, suggested that Prospero's magic was Shakespeare's response to the theater's moving indoors. The baroque beauty of the masque was captured in Inigo Jones-like designs. Albert Finney headed the fast-paced, uncut *Hamlet* (1976) that opened the new complex. Unlike the 1965 production, it refused to impose an idiosyncratic interpretation. Finney starred in *Macbeth* (1978); Paul Scofield in *Othello* (1980); and Anthony Hopkins and Judi Dench as passionate, middle-aged lovers in *Antony and Cleopatra* (1987), Hall's NT Shakespeare pinnacle. Hall's final NT mountings were a 1988 trilogy of late works—*The Winter's Tale, The Tempest,* and *Cymbeline*—demonstrating the author's final creative gusto.

Kevin Anderson and Vanessa Redgrave in Orpheus Descending. *Directed by Peter Hall. (1988)* (Photo: Martha Swope)

Among Hall's other classics were Henrik Ibsen's *John Gabriel Borkman* (1974); Ben Jonson's *Volpone* (1977); Christopher Marlowe's *Tamburlaine* (1976); William Congreve's *The Country Wife* (1977); Anton Chekhov's *The Cherry Orchard* (1978); an all-male, masked *The Oresteia* (1981), by Aeschylus; and Oscar Wilde's *The Importance of Being Earnest* (1982). Hall's modern works—several transferred to Broadway—included Beckett's *Happy Days* (1974), with Beckett assisting in the rehearsals; Pinter's *No Man's Land* (1975), *Betrayal* (1978), *Family Voices* (1981), and *Other Places* (1982); Allan Ayckbourn's *Bedroom Farce* (1977), codirected with Ayckbourn; Shaffer's London and Broadway hit, *Amadeus* (1979) and *Yonadab* (1985); Marvin Hamlisch's flop musical *Jean Seberg* (1983); Hall's adaptation of George Orwell's *Animal Farm* (1984), banned from Baltimore's 1986 Theater of Nations because of communist objections to Hall's interpretation; Brian Clark's *The Petition* (1986); Stephen Poliakoff's *Coming in to Land* (1987); and David Edgar's *Entertaining Strangers* (1987), a "community play" based on research about their past done by Dorchester townsfolk and staged as a visually rich "promenade" piece in which the audience and 20 actors (playing 50 roles) mingled together in the Cottlesloe. The *New York Times* noted the "great bridges that carry actors in tableaux (a horse race, a circus parade) above the heads of the assembled spectators."

On resigning in 1987 from the NT, Hall formed the commercially based Peter Hall Company (PHC). The company provided London and New York mountings of *Orpheus Descending* (1988) starring Vanessa Redgrave in a hallucinatory staging, using electronic music and sound effects, with the prologue—cut from the 1957 original—restored; and *The Merchant of Venice* (1989), with Dustin Hoffman, cast specifically to exploit his Jewishness. There were London-only showings of Ibsen's *The Wild Duck* (1990), Ionesco's *Born Again* (1990), a reprise of *The Homecoming* (1991), *Twelfth Night* (1991), Williams's *The Rose Tattoo* (1991), Molière's *Tartuffe* (1991), and, for the RSC, a surprisingly funny *All's Well That Ends Well* (1992). Hall also mounted John Guare's *Four Baboons Adoring the Sun* (1992) at Lincoln Center, the leadership of which he once rejected. His final 1992 effort was Shaffer's *The Gift of the Gorgon* for the RSC. In 1993, the sixty-two-year-old Hall was unusually prolific, having five plays on in London: a revival of Rattigan's *Separate Tables*; Aristophanes' *Lysistrata* in a lauded staging; *All's Well That Ends Well* for the RSC; Oliver Goldsmith's 18th-century *She Stoops to Conquer*; and Pam Gems's biodrama, *Piaf,* a revival of her 1980 play.

Hall can only do a play if he believes that the moment is right for it. It must have something to say to an audience and even change their lives, if only temporarily. Moreover, the right collaborators must be available. Hall reads the play frequently to isolate its meaning, although this may not be expressed to the actors. Relevant academic criticism and historical works will also occupy him, but most important is his own scholarly examination of the text. With a living author, Hall listens to his tone of voice as an aid to performing his words. Referring to his self-styled "militant classicism," Hall objects when directorial ideas detract from the text.

Hall believes that the theater's principal element is "the word." Although some of his earlier work involved extensive revisions, at the NT he treated the text as sacrosanct, arguing that cutting, like rewriting, is a distortion. Excisions were minimal and made only when absolutely necessary. He notes, however, that his Shakespeare mountings are usually 20 minutes faster than those by others, due, in part, to his rapid linking of scenes, with one overlapping the other without pauses.

Despite being accused of having become too commercially oriented, Hall says he works "not for plays—not for money," but for a good rehearsal. He declares "the director's main function is to be the man who sits there and judges the quality of life, judges whether it is alive, particular, unique—or whether it is a cliché, tired, usual, that which is accepted." He makes the play live by revealing the characters' behavior in terms of their "signals" (speech, appearance, etc.). Classics make the job complex because they must, through extensive study of the social background, be appreciated in the author's terms; Shakespeare in modern dress is inappropriate because too many of his signals are lost.

Cambridge don George Rylands, a student of William Poel, influenced Hall's command of Shakespearean verse-speaking, which his actors deliver like "clear, tripping, focused speech" (quoted by Vera Lustig) and not prosaically. He told Gerard Raymond that the tradition "is based on common sense and being able to get through the text quickly and nimbly without being rhetorical and boring and pompous." He takes pride in having recovered a high standard of Shakespearean speaking and understanding at the RSC.

Hall, who says he is "totally instinctive," delivers a talk about his view of the play and its world before moving to multiple readings, with frequent discussions, as the company searches for every nuance of inflection and attitude. Tirzah Lowen called him "a generous father-figure," who provides "a net of security within which [the actors] have the freedom to explore." He denies being an "autocratic interpreter," preferring the image of "the trainer of a football team. The director trains and develops the group, but the group . . . has to do the play, or play the match." He avoids preset concepts so as to create a collaborative, give-and-take, trial-and-error workshop atmosphere where he can permit actors to make discoveries, experiment—even if they look foolish—and develop their own blocking. This often turns up things he did not know were in the material. When doing *Hamlet,* he encouraged breakthroughs by providing actors with punctuationless scripts so that they themselves might unravel the phrasing.

Intellectually gifted and emotionally calm, Hall respects his actors' minds and engages with them in text-based discussions in which the focus, wrote James Flannery, is on "the basic situation of the scene in question and its purpose in the play as a whole." Modern parallels are made to assist identification. Crowd scenes are conducted like musical pieces, with Hall shaping "them into rhythmic and sculptural patterns with sweeping gestures and grunts, punctuated with stabs from a cigar. . . ." Improvisation is used sparingly, but avoided on

plays—like Pinter's—with strict formal requirements. When rehearsals are well under way, ruthless
editorial choices are made. Often, this entails scenic
stripping down; he feels that the simpler the physical
arrangement, the more powerful the actors can be.

Sir Peter Hall has had a prolific and eclectic
career in theater, opera, film, and television, and
has branded with his mark each of the two greatest
postwar British companies. He reigns as one of the
directorial kings of the English stage.

Further reading:

Flannery, James W. "Portrait of a Theatre in Its Community: the Royal Shakespeare Company of London." *Educational Theatre Journal* 19 (October 1967).
Hall, Peter. "Is the Beginning the Word?" *Theatre
Quarterly* 2 (July–September 1972).

———. Interview by Catherine Itzin and Simon
Trussler. "Directing Pinter." *Theatre Quarterly* 5 (No-
vember 1975–January 1976).
———. *Peter Hall's Diaries: The Story of a Dramatic
Battle.* Edited by John Goodwin. London: Meth-
uen, 1983.
Lowen, Tirzah. *Peter Hall Directs "Antony and Cleo-
patra."* New York: Limelight, 1991.
Lustig, Vera. "Born Again?" *Plays and Players* No. 444
(November 1990).
Raymond, Gerard. "Peter Hall: As He Likes It." *The-
aterWeek,* October 17–23, 1988.
Also: Addenbrooke, *Royal Shakespeare Company*; Beau-
man, *Royal Shakespeare Company*; Berry, *On Directing
Shakespeare*; Cook, *Directors' Theatre*; Leiter, *Shake-
speare Around the Globe*; Marowitz and Trussler, *Theatre
at Work.*

JED HARRIS (1900–1979)

JED HARRIS (*né* Jacob Hirsch Horowitz) was born
in Lemburg, Austria, shortly after which his family
moved to Newark, New Jersey, where his father ran
a grocery store. After briefly attending Yale, he wrote
for a theatrical paper, did some press agenting, was
an uncredited associate producer on a 1922 play, and
changed his name on becoming a full-time producer.

From 1925 to 1929, he amazed Broadway by the
acumen represented in properties produced with "the
Harris touch." He began with Lynn Starling's flop,
Weak Sisters, but rebounded with four plays directed
by George Abbott, but practically codirected by
Harris: Abbott and John V. A. Weaver's *Love 'Em
and Leave 'Em* (1926), Abbott and Philip Dunning's
Broadway (1926), George S. Brooks and Walter B.
Lister's *Spread Eagle* (1927), and Abbott and Ann
Preston Bridgers's *Coquette* (1927). Then came
George S. Kaufman and Edna Ferber's *The Royal
Family* (1928) and Ben Hecht and Charles MacArthur's *The Front Page* (1928), which saw his income
zoom to over $40,000 a week. Only *Spread Eagle*
bombed. Harris, who later said he hated the theater,
began to express his iconoclastic views. He put on
plays to make money, not for some higher purpose.
He observed, however, "I had never regarded the
theater as a profession or even a business, but as
an adventure."

As a producer, he took an intense interest in
every detail of his productions. He annoyed directors
by interfering in their jobs, even giving acting notes.
Every script was subjected to incessant rewriting
aimed at stripping away all irrelevancies that detracted from the central action. Audiences had to
be shown, not told, what a play was about. Sometimes, he spent up to a year working with a writer
and usually considered himself as much the author
of a hit as the playwright himself.

Several times in the twenties, the director was
fired during the tryouts and Harris took over. Although David Burton was the credited director of
The Royal Family, Harris referred to him as his "stage
manager" in his memoirs. Self-glorification was a
major part of his persona, so he gave the impression
that he was the actual director. According to Maurice Zolotow, Harris's productions were distinguished
by "brilliant casting, suave direction, sets in perfect
taste and subtle lighting."

"Destiny's tot," as Noel Coward dubbed him, was
acknowledged as one of Broadway's most unconventional figures, an image he helped to sustain through
his typical three-day stubble, the rakish slant of
his fedora, his habitual lateness, cutting cynicism,
middle-of-the-night phone calls, and offbeat, but
strangely glamorous, demeanor as an egocentric genius with a talent for giving abuse. Harris's nastiness
was often responsible for his losing scripts that became hits in other hands. At least two novels were
based on him, and (though some idolized him) several stars based their characterizations of cads on
Harris.

Harris's credited directing debut was an unsuccessful tryout version of Edwin Justus Mayer's *The*

Gaoler's Wench, later shown on Broadway by another producer as *Children of Darkness.* Harris received no credit for staging S. N. Behrman's adaptation of Enid Bagnold's novel, *Serena Blandish* (1929), starring Ruth Gordon. When the play closed, Harris announced (a frequent ploy) that he was abandoning the theater, calling his achievements "a great hoax." The $3-million loss he suffered in the Wall Street crash, however, convinced him to return to the scene of the hoax.

Anton Chekhov's *Uncle Vanya* (1930) was his first actual Broadway directing credit (he continued to produce most of his choices). His gift for brilliant casting was acknowledged when he chose birdlike silent-screen star Lillian Gish to play Helena, conventionally viewed as a flirtatious tease but now unorthodoxly interpreted as a creature of great desirability and beauty. *Uncle Vanya,* with its Chekhovian indirectness, differed from Harris's usual rapidfire comedy and melodrama, but the ensemble, authentic Russian atmosphere, and sense of relaxed naturalness were lauded. Worthington Miner, then a fledgling director, later claimed responsibility for the staging, Harris having taken the reins during tryouts but without making substantive changes.

Harris followed with five consecutive flops: Frank B. Elser's *Mr. Gilhooley* (1930); Nikolai Gogol's *The Inspector General* (1930), one of only three revivals Harris ever staged; Sheridan Gibney's *The Wiser They Are* (1931); *Wonder Boy* (1931); and Michael Morton's *Fatal Alibi* (1932).

Harris came up with a *succès d'estime* in Mordaunt Shairp's *The Green Bay Tree* (1933), an exquisitely produced British drama about a beautiful young man—played by Laurence Olivier—kept by an elegant, older homosexual. Harris (*sans* Shairp's approval) diligently reduced all overt homosexual references, seeking thematic understatement. Harris usually picked on one actor in every show as a scapegoat. In this production, the victim was Olivier, which deeply embittered the great actor.

Two months later, with British writers Dorothy Massingham and Murray MacDonald's *The Lake* (1933), Harris failed again, despite the presence of Katharine Hepburn. Harris again usurped Miner as director, and Miner later insisted that Harris, who had a cruel inclination for damaging his stars' self-esteem, had sadistically destroyed Hepburn's performance.

He then added John Whedon and Arthur Caplan's *Life's Too Short* (1935) and Philip Barry's *Spring Dance* (1936) to his list of turkeys. A reprieve came with a revival of Henrik Ibsen's *A Doll's House*

(1937), starring Ruth Gordon (a frequent Harris star and the mother of his illegitimate son). Despite mixed reviews, the piece enjoyed a record-breaking (for Ibsen) 142 performances.

Thornton Wilder's *Our Town* (1938) was the highpoint of Harris's career. As usual, Harris devoted an inordinate amount of time to revising the script (Wilder refused his request for coauthor credit). It was Harris's suggestion that Wilder write the scene in which George and Emily first meet. The nonnaturalistic play, staged without scenery and a minimum of props on a bare stage, and using a folksy Stage Manager as a narrator to tell its microcosmic tale of birth, marriage, and death in a small New England town, became a modern classic (although the work had failed in Boston where Wilder blamed Harris for destroying it). Part of its artistic and emotional power was owing to Harris's accepting Wilder's advice to do it as dryly and unsentimentally as possible. Harris's contributions were vital, especially the cemetery scene in which the mourners all carried black umbrellas. When Rosamond Pinchot, a former actress in love with Harris and working backstage on the show, committed suicide during the tryouts, Harris forced the company to rehearse the third act (concerned with death) twice in a row and would have had them do it again had not Martha Scott, playing Emily, objected. Harris was possibly trying to motivate the actors to appreciate the theme of the need to value life before it is too late.

Surprisingly, few new, quality scripts were now submitted to Harris. After a five-year hiatus, he returned to Broadway with Elena Miramova and Eugenie Leontovich's hit comedy *Dark Eyes* (1943). Nunnally Johnson's *The World's Full of Girls* (1943) and Ruth and Augustus Goetz's *One-Man Show* (1943) failed, as did Kenyon Nicholson and Charles Robinson's *Apple of his Eye* (1946) and Dale Eunson and Katherine Albert's *Loco,* but these were forgotten in the wake of *The Heiress* (1947), adapted by the Goetzes from Henry James's novel *Washington Square.*

Initially, the authors were not pleased by Harris's rewrite demands, nor by his insistence on using then unavailable British star Wendy Hiller to play the plain heroine preyed on by a fortune hunter. The play was a calamity during its Boston tryout under another director. Harris surprised everyone by resuscitating it, but he convinced Hiller to costar with Basil Rathbone as her father, and, among other revisions, to change the unconvincing happy ending to one less sentimental but with Jamesian integrity. Masterfully directed, except for too much static pic-

Basil Rathbone and Wendy Hiller in The Heiress. *(1946) Directed by Jed Harris.* (Photo: Theater Collection, Museum of the City of New York)

turization, the play was a great success. Harris and the Goetzes disputed who was mainly responsible for the final version.

Harris's subsequent productions were commercial duds. They included Jean-Paul Sartre's *The Red Gloves* (1948); Herman Wouk's *The Traitor* (1949) (called Broadway's first anticommunist play); and Arthur Miller's *The Crucible* (1953), later recognized as an American classic, but given to Harris when his powers had flagged (although he helped cut the thick script down to manageable size). Despite Miller's desire for a lyrical use of light and space, Harris bogged the work down in realism, melodramatics, and picture-making. His rehearsals were marred by tantrums. Had he not been recalcitrant about his contract, he would have been fired. During the run, Miller restaged the play himself without seeking Harris's okay.

Harris's last production was of an inferior James adaptation, *Child of Fortune* (1956). The stage manager did more directing than he did. In 1970, he nearly returned with a play about the troubles in Northern Ireland, but circumstances—including his

own resistance to outside suggestions—prevented its realization. He remained Jed Harris to the end, even though it meant living on handouts and dying in poverty.

Despite his often bizarre behavior, Harris had an acute, mostly self-educated intellect and was capable of talking on almost any issue. A restless, high-strung insomniac, he was obsessive when staging a play, focusing on it to the exclusion even of food and sleep. He drove writers and actors to distraction. His irritating personality was exacerbated by his manner of whispering his comments. Zolotow tells of how he stopped a well-known actress who was having trouble with her lines to warn her never to drink before rehearsals. She nervously replied that she didn't drink. Harris snapped his fingers for a cigarette and snapped them again for a light. After this dramatic pause, he pounced: "My dear, the only excuse I can see for a performance like you have just been giving is that you are drunk!"

Although writers like Zolotow called him "the most superb director on Broadway," Harris claimed that he worked from instinct and never planned his staging. He said his talent came naturally, and that he was aware of it the moment he first told an actor what to do. Although he did not preblock, he studied a script zealously for as long as a year before rehearsals.

Harris strived to pare the action down to its fundamentals, eliminating all potential distractions of action and dialogue, and expressing in stage behavior only what emerged from the characters' inner reality. His brain was an encyclopedia of psychology, and he had an uncanny knack for knowing how different kinds of people behaved in specific situations. Although he never acted professionally, he had excellent acting skills, if only for those brief moments at rehearsal when he demonstrated how to do something. Actors were impressed by how skillfully he could show them some piece of business or provide a correct reading. Infinitely patient, he took hours to teach an actor to do something seemingly insignificant, as when he showed Patricia Collinge how to play with her knitting in *The Heiress*. Sooner or later, he acted out all the parts for his company; some stars declared that Harris understood their roles better than they did themselves.

Harris always began rehearsals "at table," and kept his actors seated, reading and analyzing, for as long as 10 days before blocking them. This allowed him to have full control of their thinking and reactions, which he felt he would lose when they were moving about. As they read, he constantly interrupted with questions about the purposes of a scene or feelings and thoughts. He insisted that the actors not learn their lines automatically, but study instead their characters' psychology, which would make them retain the words organically. His rehearsal behavior was—at least in his heyday—intensely concentrated; he paced alongside the actors, observing and empathizing like a devoted parent watching his children play.

Although he was a Broadway legend, Harris admitted that he directed only a half-dozen plays he considered important. Broadway may have brought out his most dazzling talents, but it also provoked him to behave in perverse ways that prevented him from making a more consistent contribution to the American stage.

Further reading:

Gottfried, Martin. *Jed Harris: The Curse of Genius.* Boston: Little, Brown, 1984.

Harris, Jed. *Watchman, What of the Night?.* Garden City, N.Y.: Doubleday, 1963.

————. *A Dance on the High Wire: A Unique Memoir of the Theatre.* New York: Crown, 1979.

Also: Zolotow, *No People Like Show People.*

ARTHUR HOPKINS (1878–1950)

ARTHUR MELANCTHON HOPKINS was born in the old Newburgh section of Cleveland, Ohio, where his father was a wire mill foreman. Following his education at Western Reserve Academy, he worked in the mills, wrote journalism, and booked vaudeville acts. He also wrote and staged vaudeville one-acts starring famous actors and, in 1912, had a play produced on Broadway. His switch to producing and directing was partially influenced by his exposure to Europe's New Stagecraft during a 1913 trip abroad.

In New York, Hopkins tried without luck to employ his ideas of unified production in Thomas Broadhurst's *Evangeline* (1913), in which he introduced an adjustable proscenium. In 1914, he staged Elmer Rice's *On Trial,* the first play to use a cinematic flashback; a jackknife stage changed scenes swiftly. It was not until Edith Ellis's *The Devil's Garden* (1915), however, when he teamed up with designer Robert Edmond Jones, that he found the right approach to introducing the New Stagecraft's simplified realism. Especially effective was a scene in a bureaucrat's office: a shallow, rectangular box set with a door at either side, three chairs and a desk at stage right, a chair at left, and a plain rear wall dressed only with a map above the desk.

One of Broadway's most prolific directors, Hopkins eventually mounted 82 productions. Forty eight were designed by Jones. During the teens and twenties Hopkins averaged four a year. His devotion to meaningful themes, excellent writing, and expert acting raised Broadway's commercial standards.

By 1920, he had become closely associated with the plays of Clare Kummer (including *Good Gracious Annabelle* in 1916, *A Successful Calamity* in 1917, and others); had staged a 1918 season of three Henrik Ibsen dramas starring Alla Nazimova, including the American premiere of *The Wild Duck;* and had begun a close collaboration on serious dramas with John Barrymore, then best known as a light comedian. Barrymore starred for Hopkins in Leo Tolstoy's *Redemption* (1918); Sem Benelli's Italian melodrama *The Jest* (1919), costarring Lionel Barrymore; and *Richard III* (1920), notable not only for Barrymore's cynically wicked king but for Jones's unit set—possibly Broadway's first—in which the Tower of London figured as the unifying motif. Hopkins was one of the few to bring important European drama to Broadway; his subsequent mountings included Henning Berger's *The Deluge* (1917, and several later revivals) and Maxim Gorky's *Night Lodging* (a.k.a. *The Lower Depths,* 1919).

In the fertile 1920s, when John, Lionel, and Ethel Barrymore each became Hopkins regulars, the director's highlights included such foreign works as Sven Lange's *Samson and Delilah* (1920); Henry Bernstein's *The Claw* (1921), with Lionel; Gerhart Hauptmann's *Rose Bernd* (1922), with Ethel; and Alfred Sutro's *The Laughing Lady* (1923), also with Ethel. American products included Zoe Akins's *Daddy's Gone A-Hunting* (1921); Eugene O'Neill's *Anna Christie* (1921), memorably acted by Pauline Lord; Don Marquis's *The Old Soak* (1922); Maxwell Anderson and Laurence Stallings's bawdy but powerful war play, *What Price Glory?* (1924), highly controversial because of its use of profanity (two later Hopkins-directed Anderson-Stallings works failed); several plays by Philip Barry, most notably *Paris Bound* (1927) and *Holiday* (1928), which made socialite Hope Williams a star; George Watters and Hopkins's *Burlesque* (1927), with the young Barbara

Stanwyck; Sophie Treadwell's expressionistic *Machinal* (1928), with Clark Gable; and Donald Ogden Stewart's *Rebound* (1930). Revivals included the famous John Barrymore *Hamlet* (1923) and a version of Arthur Wing Pinero's *The Second Mrs. Tanqueray* (1924) with Ethel. Major flops included *Macbeth* (1921), with Lionel, and *Romeo and Juliet* (1922), with Ethel, a performance outrivaled by Jane Cowl's Juliet during the same season.

Macbeth used a now famous, daringly abstract set of black drapes, expressionistic arches, and huge suspended masks that represented the Fates; all was strikingly illuminated with bold shafts of light. It also had a then idiosyncratic interpretation in which neither Macbeth nor his wife was responsible for their deeds, both of them being driven by forces beyond their control.

The thirties, despite contributions from such respected playwrights as Sidney Howard and Barry, saw a drastic decline in the acceptance of Hopkins's work. He refused to deal with the social problem plays that were attracting attention during the Depression. Many of the best actors had been lost to Hollywood. His sole success was Robert E. Sherwood's *The Petrified Forest* (1935), with Leslie Howard and Humphrey Bogart. Hopkins's output in the forties dropped off sharply, but he scored with *The Magnificent Yankee* (1946), Emmett Lavery's biodrama about Oliver Wendell Holmes, starring Louis Calhern and Dorothy Gish. His final production, a revival of *Burlesque* with Bert Lahr brilliant as a burlesque comedian, came the same year. Its 439 showings was a Hopkins record.

Although most of his work was in realistic American drama, Hopkins was one of the few Broadway directors of the day to delve—if only briefly—into the classics; his record also shows a noteworthy interest in foreign dramas. Hopkins surprised audiences by revealing how much humor there is in Ibsen. His modern selections ranged from farce to tragedy, and included many sophisticated comedies. He did only one musical, Frank Harling and Laurence Stallings's *Deep River* (1926), a controversial attempt at a "native opera" using a jazz score and with a miscegenation theme that foreshadowed 1927's landmark musical *Show Boat*.

Hopkins sought plays that promoted worthwhile values and that found affirmation in even the direst circumstances. He eschewed theater as simple entertainment. A religious man, he believed that it should serve a useful purpose by exposing universal spiritual and moral truths and bringing deeper understanding of the world. As his career progressed, however, he failed to appreciate the best efforts of American dramatists and, except for two plays and one revival, had a persistent string of flops during his last two decades. He was more interested in theater art than theater business. Most of his plays between 1917 and 1935 were at the Plymouth Theater, which he leased.

Hopkins's activities included several incursions into filmmaking. His books were considered among the first examples of a major American practitioner expressing a distinctive theory. He also produced a distinguished 1944 radio series, "Arthur Hopkins Presents," based on Broadway hits.

Probably the best-known production of Hopkins's career was *Hamlet*, which, in its initial engagement, broke by one the play's American record of 100 consecutive performances. Many consider Barrymore the century's best American Hamlet, largely because of his low-keyed believability unmarred by artificiality of tone, and his personal beauty and wit. In the Freudian production—four hours-plus despite cuts—Hamlet seemed to have an incestuous relationship with Gertrude. Jones's unit set allowed for rapid scene shifts but was criticized because its combination of a central arch and an impressive set of midstage stairs with an extended downstage apron made it seem that Ophelia's burial was taking place in a space previously used as an interior. The ghost was represented by a wavering light and an offstage voice.

Hopkins believed that the pillars of good theater are the script and the actors. Scenery should be evocative, suggestive, nonobtrusive, and supportive of the author. Hopkins's Shakespeare stagings established the unit set, with the same basic elements visible in all scenes but altered by lighting and decorative devices to create multiple locales. The more realistic the detail, the more artificial the effect, he believed.

Hopkins began rehearsals after all revisions were completed. He did not wish to be bothered with the annoyance of script changes during rehearsals. Those revisions he allowed were primarily to strengthen the author's intentions, because he feared changing a play into something that became more the director's vision than the writer's. He enjoyed having the latter present, presumably to remind the director to remain faithful to the play's purposes. He gave classical authors extreme respect. When he did his first Shakespeare, he conducted careful research, but then chose, questionably, to ignore previous interpretations in the belief that attention to the text would be sufficient. Despite his avowed respect for authors, Hopkins cut *Richard III* severely and combined it with material from *Henry VI* to present a more complete picture of Richard's downfall. This was his most overt example of textual meddling. His preparation was always so thorough that he seemed to know the lines by heart at the first rehearsal and to work without a promptbook.

Although he asserted that the director should clearly know his goals, Hopkins felt that the play needed only a minimum of directorial or scenic interference. Averse to imposing his ideas on others, he believed that, properly cast, it had only to be gently nurtured as it brought itself to fruition.

It was Hopkins's practice to cast via interviews rather than readings. He searched for what he called "radiance." Because he disliked typecasting, a number of actors, such as Barrymore and Bogart, enhanced their careers when he cast them against type.

His goal was a completely unified production that appealed hypnotically on an unconscious level (he called his idea "unconscious projection") and that deterred active participation by the conscious mind. He wanted the play performed so unobtrusively that it would be absorbed by everyone on a universal, prerational level. Thought was to emerge from emotion, not the other way around. Nothing was to detract from the process, so that all action appeared inevitable rather than planned. To this end, he kept his staging simple and natural, avoided clever or intrusive business, and restrained the actors from unnecessary moves and gestures. His insistence on natural speaking voices rather than theatrical projection sometimes led to inaudibility. The less theatrical the effect, the better Hopkins liked it.

To achieve these ends and to weld an unselfish ensemble, Hopkins barely seemed to direct at all. He sometimes skipped a few rehearsals to reduce his influence on the actors. He was famous for his laissez-faire methods, and most actors respected him for the great freedom he provided and for his ability to get them to behave honestly. (Critics sometimes thought the casual manner meant a need for more rehearsal.) Once Hopkins clarified his ideas about a character, the actor was pretty much allowed to work on the role himself.

The script became very familiar through the week to 10 days spent reading and rereading (with Hopkins often absent) before the blocking began. When he blocked, Hopkins verbally described a generalized pattern and then let the actors themselves work it out. This allowed him to block an act in only an hour or so. He let the actors run their scenes over and over without interruption until they felt comfortable. He considered blocking a minor function, and he often relied on the author's stage directions. Concepts such as picturization, composition, and rhythm did not much concern him. Nor did he have patience for lengthy disquisitions.

Hopkins disdained having actors build character biographies or become preoccupied with their characters' offstage lives; he was afraid that these practices might inspire ideas not in the author's mind. His note-giving was invariably in private and couched in a few pithy, stimulating words. He often asked provocative questions that led the actor to a deeper comprehension of his problem. Actors were told to bring the audience to the play, not the play to the audience. This implied a conception of the stage as a closed space; actors sometimes turned their backs to the "fourth wall" to increase the impression of a separate reality. He had faith that his casting was right (he rarely fired an actor) and that, given his editing, artistic censorship, and encouragement, they would discover their characters themselves.

While he was never an autocrat, it was always clear that Hopkins was in command. His methods worked because he had a unique sensitivity to which actors responded. Although he hardly ever lost his temper, few wanted to disappoint him. Once a production opened, he lost interest in it except for occasional checkups to keep the actors from embroidering.

Hopkins's many failures stemmed largely from inadequate scripts; with the right play, his methodology usually attained his aims. Walter Prichard Eaton described Hopkins's early work in words that can be applied to much of his later career as well:

> In productions so different in kind as Richard III *and* A Night Lodging . . . *or* . . . Redemption, *Hopkins reached the mass emotions and at the same time achieved a new and disturbing beauty even in brute realism, as if the soul of the play were somehow translated into an impression that was not vocal, not visual, not a thing of words or settings or lights and colors or actors' personalities, and yet was all these things.*

Further reading:

Eaton, Walter Prichard. "Arthur Hopkins." *Theater Arts* 5 (July 1921).

Hopkins, Arthur. *How's Your Second Act?* New York: Philip Goodman, 1918.

———. "Producer and Play." In *Our Theatre Today.* Edited by Herschel L. Bricker. New York: Samuel French, 1936.

———. *To a Lonely Boy.* New York: Country Life Press, 1937.

———. *Reference Point.* New York: Samuel French, 1948.

Also: Johnson, *Directing Methods.*

HENRY IRVING (1838–1905)

HENRY IRVING (*né* John Henry Brodribb) was born in Keinton Mandeville, Somerset, England, where his father was a traveling salesman. At 10, after being raised by an aunt, he moved in with his parents in London, where he left school at 13 to take a clerk's position. He became an actor at 18, gaining enormous experience in provincial stock companies, where he played hundreds of roles and gained acclaim. His London fame commenced in 1866 when *The Two Lives of Mary Leigh,* a provincial hit which Irving staged and in which he was a sensation, came to town. From 1864, Irving directed most of his plays.

In 1871, Hezekiah Bateman hired Irving as leading man at London's Lyceum Theater, where the company was headed by the manager's actress-daughter. Irving became the theater's *raison d'être* when he directed and starred as Mathias in *The Bells* (1871), Leopold Lewis's version of a French melodrama, and periodically repeated throughout Irving's career. To this tale of a respected Swiss burgomaster who is haunted by the guilt of having killed a Polish Jew years earlier, Irving brought the full force of his powers, especially in the dream scene in which the innkeeper dies of fright after imagining his murder trial. Irving's startlingly vivid interpretation viewed the burgomaster—previously played as an unrepentant villain—as a basically good man who committed a crime in a moment of dire need. He altered various lines to heighten their impact, an example being the change of "The Rope! The Rope! Cut the rope!" to "Take the rope from my neck, take the rope from my neck!" The production's mesmerizing effect, aided by Irving's dictating each actor's inflections and business, established him as an actor-director.

Irving gathered power in his Lyceum stagings of historical and romantic melodramas, such as G. W. Wills's *Charles I* (1872) and *Eugene Aram* (1872), and revivals of such works as Edward Bulwer-Lytton's *Richelieu* (1873), *The Lyons Mail* (1877), and *Louis XI* (1878).

He also showed his mettle with Shakespeare, beginning with *Hamlet* (1874). It revealed Irving as a brilliant if unconventional Shakespearean and had a previously unparalled run of 200 nights. One of its most exceptional features was Irving's disregard for the traditional "points" or actor's highlights. He provided an unorthodox approach in which the verse rhythm was sacrificed to the communication of meaning, a considerable amount of fresh business was created, and the prince was given a surprisingly realistic and human realization. Over the years he returned to the play often, and continued revising it in light of contemporary studies. He followed tradition in many of his cuts, including the omission of references to Fortinbras and the ending of the play just after "The rest is silence."

Other significant revivals included *Macbeth* (1875), *Othello* (1876), and *Richard III* (1877). *Macbeth* was played as the tragedy of a craven coward. The title role in *Othello* was adjusted from its traditional African aspect, the Moor's skin bronzed instead of blackened, and the familiar turbans and burnouses replaced by the clothes of a Venetian general. *Richard III* was revolutionary in abandoning Colley Cibber's rearranged and garnished version of the play for Shakespeare's original. Irving deserted the tradition of playing Richard as a crass villain, and brought out his historical qualities as a man of dignity and charm. For the tent scene, in lieu of the conventional use of two opposing tents for Richard and Richmond, Irving substituted Richard's tent alone, lit only by a small table lamp. After studying the plans of the coming battle, the ill-shaped king rose wearily, limped upstage, and opened the flap, revealing the starlit sky; the picture sharply underlined Richard's tragic position. Despite his many novel touches, Irving took a great interest in learning how earlier Shakespearean productions had been done.

In 1878, Irving took over the Lyceum management, ushering in a radiant era that would glow for over two decades. Throughout most of his management, Irving's leading lady was Ellen Terry, who helped form one of history's greatest acting partnerships. The Lyceum company became a model of discipline and decorum.

As the artistic leader of the Lyceum, where he would stage 37 new and old plays, Irving was quickly acknowledged as England's leading actor-manager. He remained locked in the embrace of 19th-century tastes, however, and was the frequent butt of George Bernard Shaw for not producing such advanced authors as Henrik Ibsen. The most respected author of Irving's new plays was the poet laureate, Alfred, Lord Tennyson. Irving's new plays were almost entirely costume melodramas or historical pseudo-tragedies with applause-gathering star parts and exciting *coups de théâtre*. These gave him an opportunity for displaying his idiosyncratic acting style and for producing lavish visual displays. Among them were Tennyson's *The Cup* (1881) and *Becket* (1893); Watts Phillips's *The Dead Heart* (1889); Comyns Carr's *King Arthur* (1895); Laurence Irving's *Peter the Great* (1898); and Victorien Sardou's *Robespierre* (1899) and *Dante* (1903). Several non-Shakespearean works, such as George Colman's *The Iron Chest* (1879), Bulwer-Lytton's *The Lady of Lyons* (1879), and Dion Boucicault's *The Corsican Brothers* (1880), figured among his revivals. His greatest moneymaker was Wills's spectacular and truncated adaptation of Johann Wolfgang von Goethe's *Faust* (1885), in which Irving was a sardonic Mephistopheles.

Irving staged 12 Shakespeares: *Hamlet* (1878), *The Merchant of Venice* (1879), *Othello* (with Irving and Edwin Booth alternating Iago and Othello in 1881), *Romeo and Juliet* (1882), *Much Ado About Nothing* (1882), *Twelfth Night* (1884), *Macbeth* (1888), *King Henry VIII* (1892), *King Lear* (1892), *Cymbeline* (1896), *Richard III* (1896), and *Coriolanus* (1901). These represented not only the standard works, but a few surprises as well, notably *Lear*, *Cymbeline*, and *Coriolanus*, each then rarely seen. The less successful shows were dropped after their initial run, but some plays remained in the repertory. The failures often stemmed from Irving's inappropriateness in the leading roles (Romeo and Lear are examples), but he provided revelatory, if controversial, presentations of certain plays.

Perhaps the most unorthodox was *The Merchant of Venice*, which had a record-breaking seven-month run, and in which he abandoned the tradition of depicting Shylock as a vindictive villain—although Edmund Kean had given him a touch of humanity—and made the moneylender a sympathetic and mor-

ally superior figure. The play's only major excision was the Prince of Arragon scene. Irving's most notable innovation occurred following Jessica's elopement. As the maskers swept across the stage near Shylock's home, the curtain fell slowly. A moment later, it rose on an empty stage. Shylock entered on an upstage bridge, crossed to his door, and knocked, the echo resounding. As the curtain fell again, Shylock's desolation, wordlessly expressed, was conveyed with heartrending pathos.

Many of Irving's productions were seen abroad; he took his company on eight profitable American tours. His earnings from foreign and provincial tours subsidized the London seasons, the costs of which became increasingly expensive. Managerial errors led to the Lyceum's loss in 1902; Irving died penniless.

An autocrat, Irving supervised every facet of production, inspiring those responsible and then seeing to it that their inspirations met with his well-researched requirements. The rough sketches of costumes and groupings he created revealed an artist's imagination. Even when the critics were negative about a play or its acting, they were normally ecstatic about its physical appointments. Since so many of his plays were set in the past, Irving studied the respective period's literature and art. Regardless of the artistic unity he achieved, however, his ultimate aim was to display his own starring performance.

An affirmed illusionist, he believed that theater must convince audiences of the reality it purveys, including historical accuracy in sets and costumes. His designers (most notably Hawes Craven) were the best of their day (famous "academic" painters were often employed), and made various technical advances, such as their increasing use of three-dimensional set pieces (the "free plantation" system) in combination with illusionistically painted two-dimensional elements. To cut down on scene-shift waits, Irving usually alternated heavily built-up scenes with simpler scenes played in front of a suitably painted drop, changing scenery while the actors played before the drop, which flew out when the scene ended. Despite their length, Irving's Shakespeare revivals were the fastest moving of the day.

Irving was a lighting master, but drew the line at accepting electric lamps, which he considered too harsh; he preferred the hazy glow of gaslight. Under his supervision, the Lyceum technicians made notable progress; his chiaroscuro effects were famous. A favorite device was to darken the stage and allow only a single source of onstage illumination—such as a fireplace or lamp—while a pinspot focused on his face, his fellow actors reduced to ghostly presences. He was one of the first to darken the house so that attention would be concentrated on the stage.

For all the research he and his scene painters did (including a trip to Germany in preparation for *Faust*), Irving readily sacrificed academic accuracy for theatrical effectiveness. When he slipped and allowed the spectacle of an overproduced *Henry VIII* to bury the play, he immediately made amends, and his subsequent Shakespeare stagings were considerably simplified.

Just as he bestowed great care on the visual side, so did he attend to the music, hiring top composers—such as Arthur Sullivan—to write incidental scores. Music underlined much of the action, as in movies. When trying to explain his requirements to a composer, Irving provided what Laurence Irving calls "a combination of rhythmic pantomime and suggestive hummings."

Irving carefully preplanned his ideas and began rehearsals with a fully edited text. Often, he devoted several months to studying the play's problems. At the first rehearsal, he read all of the roles. He also indicated crudely the general staging, describing groupings and movements. Rehearsals usually began on a Thursday. Friday was devoted to the actors checking their sides with the prompter for cues or errors. No rehearsals were called on the first Saturday and Sunday, the actors being expected to memorize their lines on those days. On Monday, they had to be perfect.

Rehearsals were held with rough approximations of the sets and with appropriate props. The company learned an act a day, going through it twice at each rehearsal, taking nourishment on the fly, as no lunch breaks were provided. Irving was the complete master. When his infinite patience was tried, he could be sarcastic, self-possessed, and discourteous. An iron-willed taskmaster, he made actors go over and over a move or line reading until he was completely satisfied, although the result commonly was simply a frail imitation of Irving himself. Rehearsals usually required only three weeks.

Only the most gifted and trusted actors were allowed some creative freedom. Principal players gave no thought to radical interpretations, being content with following the overall intentions sought by the actor-manager. Irving appreciated solid actors who could follow his commands and support him con-

vincingly but not draw focus by anything idiosyncratic. Such an approach does not require charismatic supporting actors. Although many leading players performed with Irving at one time or another, his companies were now and then accused of mediocrity. Because he expended so much energy in rehearsing the others, he himself would rarely be in top form until he had played several performances. He typically ignored his own part at rehearsals, preferring to work out his characterizations at home before a mirror.

Irving was primarily concerned with translating human behavior into effective action. A romanticist, he believed that the springboard for drama is character, and sought to discover those impulses that made each character three-dimensional. His values stressed ideal truth; anything suggesting vulgarity was pruned.

Irving was noted for his groupings and tableaux and his actors' detailed byplay. Having seen the Meiningen company, he sought to individualize each crowd member, and was expert at manipulating large groups. Because he was responsible for detailed, large-cast productions, however, he was forced to delegate authority to others, and the size of his staff was immense.

Irving was the most important Victorian actor-manager. The first actor ever to be knighted (in 1895), he was devoted to raising the profession to a position of eminent respectability. He brought the frayed conventions of his day to their ripest development, and set the stage for the reaction that followed.

Further reading:

Craig, Gordon. *Henry Irving.* London: J.M. Dent and Sons, 1930.

Hughes, Alan. *Henry Irving, Shakespearean.* Cambridge, England: Cambridge University Press, 1981.

Irving, Laurence. *Henry Irving: The Actor and His World.* New York: Macmillan, 1952.

Also: Brockett and Findlay, *Century of Innovation*; Johnson, *Directing Methods*; Marshall, *The Producer and the Play.*

'Note: The following appeared too late to be used for this essay: King, W.D. *Henry Irving's "Waterloo": Theatrical Engagements with Arthur Conan Doyle, George Bernard Shaw, Ellen Terry, Edward Gordon Craig, Late-Victorian Culture, Assorted Ghosts, Old Men, War, and History.* Berkeley: University of California Press, 1993.

LEOPOLD JESSNER (1878–1945)

LEOPOLD JESSNER was born in the East Prussian city of Königsberg. He worked in banking before becoming an actor and director. From 1905 to 1915, he headed Hamburg's Thalia Theater, where his outstanding production was Molière's *Tartuffe* (1911). From 1915 to 1919, he ran Königsberg's Neues Schauspielhaus, providing productions that revealed the expressionist methods he later exemplified. His greatest contributions, however, were at Berlin's Staatliches Schauspielhaus (or Staatstheater), formerly the court theater but a government-subsidized venue when he became artistic director in 1919. Jessner was promoted by the postwar Social Democratic government who hoped he would uphold republican principles. The Staatstheater had fallen into low esteem, but it was revived under Jessner's spell.

From 1919 to 1933, Jessner directed 44 plays in 47 productions; three were given a second, different interpretation, and a few were staged elsewhere in Berlin. His premodern choices were Friedrich Schiller's *William Tell* (1919; 1923), *Fiesco* (1921), *Don Carlos* (1922), *Wallenstein* (1924; 1931) *The Maid of Orleans* (1930), and *The Robbers* (1932); Shakespeare's *Richard III* (1920), *Othello* (1921; 1932), *Macbeth* (1922), *Hamlet* (1926), and *King John* (1929); Christian Dietrich Grabbe's *Napoleon* (1922) and *Hannibal* (1925); Johann Wolfgang von Goethe's *Faust* (1923) and *Egmont*; Friedrich Hebbel's *Maria Magdalena* (1924), for the Schiller Theater, and *Herod and Mariamne* (1926); Heinrich von Kleist's *Amphitryon* (1926); Sophocles' *Oedipus* (1929); and Gotthold Lessing's *Emilia Galotti* (1931). Well-known modern dramas included Henrik Ibsen's *Enemy of the People* (1923), for the Schiller; Frank Wedekind's *The Marquis of Keith* (1920) and *King Nicola* (1924); Brandon Thomas's *Charley's Aunt* (1924); Gerhart Hauptmann's *Florian Geyer* (1927), *The Weavers* (1928), and *Gabriel Schilling's Flight* (1932); August Strindberg's *Gustav Adolf* (1930); and George Bernard Shaw's *Heartbreak House* (1931). Indigenous moderns were represented by Ernst Barlach, Hermann Essig, Arnolt Bronnen, Fritz von Unruh, Georg Kaiser, Lion Feuchtwanger, Paul Kornfeld, and, among others, Richard Billinger, whose *Horses* (1933) was Jessner's final German production.

Jessner's great impact was between 1919 and 1926, when he overshadowed even Max Reinhardt. He was a target of right-wing factions, not only because of his radical stagecraft, but because of his Judaism, socialism, and republicanism. His classics—often incited by actual events—were usually played in timeless environments and infused with a contemporary political message. *Richard III,* intended to denounce political careerism, had behind it not only a recent abortive attempt to establish a German soviet republic but also the brief overthrow by an East Prussian politician of the Weimar Republic. *Macbeth* was inspired by the 1922 assassination of the foreign minister. Jessner's politics, expressed in a broad philosophical spirit, avoided the sociological overtones of Erwin Piscator and Bertolt Brecht.

Jessner opened with a bombshell that incited outraged opening-nighters to try stopping the performance. Into *William Tell,* usually staged with painted Alpine scenery, Jessner injected expressionist abstractionism. Previously confined to the specifically expressionist dramas of the 1910s, this style was used by Jessner for nonexpressionist plays, although Jessner—whose love of lucidity and order opposed the inchoate emotionalism of some expressionist works—resisted having the label applied to him. Jessner communicated "a cry for freedom" without specifically referring to time and locale. Interested in emotional intensification and keeping the action moving, he removed both inessential dialogue that introduced unwanted sentimentality and speeches that bore too patriotic a tone. He called his nondecorative, symbolic, sculptural, essentially bare-stage approach "theatre of motifs," and used it to focus on themes and not distracting externals. When he revived the play a few years later, he softened his earlier approach both aesthetically and politically.

Illuminated by an architectonic use of directional lighting, Schiller's classic—scenery by Emil Pirchan, Jessner's representative designer—disclosed gray-green decor composed primarily of a white cyclorama with a geometric mountain pattern fronted by wide steps used for all the scenes, with only a rearrangement of curtains and the addition of a few selective props to signify a change of locale. A door suggested Tell's house; a cross, the Rütlu meadow. Fritz Kortner, Germany's chief expressionist actor and Jessner's frequent leading man, played Gessler with a red face and black uniform loaded with medals, mocking Prussian militarism. This abstraction, inspired by Adolphe Appia and Gordon Craig, and intended to place the drama on a mythic level, would be repeated in various forms in other productions.

The director's name became irrevocably linked to the term *Jessnertreppen* ("Jessner-steps"), a method which became a critical albatross. The steps served many purposes. Macgowan and Jones wrote:

> They give the stage one general shape for each play. They establish a formal quality. They tend to banish representation in scenery, since only indications of settings harmonize with their frank artificiality. And— their main purpose—they provide the director with most interesting opportunities for manoeuvering his actors.

Actors were able to move in various directions, creating an impression of three dimensionality. Even in crowds, each actor could be seen clearly because of improved sight lines created by the levels. The steps were not used in all scenes, though, nor were they precisely duplicated from play to play. *Richard III* began with a gray-green wall about 10 feet high running across the stage before a much higher rear wall beyond which a red strip of sky was seen. From Richard's coronation on, blood-red steps rising in a pyramid were seen. Jessner used the scarlet-robed Richard's position at the top to convey the idea of his dominance over the red-gowned courtiers kneeling in descending order on both sides. As Richard's power crumbled, he took lower and lower positions. When Richmond entered, his and his army's white costumes made a startling contrast with the crimson steps. (Four actors represented each army, and they fought a dancelike, drum-accented battle, in which no actual contact occurred.)

For *Othello*, there was an oval platform backed by a cyclorama and reached by several wide, curved steps; at center was a smaller platform of similarly curved steps. Symbolic units were placed on it as needed. At the rear was a trap, so actors could emerge from upstage as if out of the depths.

The steps, combined with dramatically costumed actors, created unforgettable images. According to Macgowan and Jones, "In *Richard III*, when Gloucester appears as king in a red cloak upon the top of the red steps, his retainers, also in red, sink down in a heap below him like a pile of bloody skulls."

The main purpose of the steps was to heighten the meanings in the dialogue, which Jessner considered the most important element; he left them out where they were of no use. External means expressed interior content. According to Colby Lewis:

> the inner continuity and unity of the play is . . . presented through the spatial arrangement of the actors.

> The contour of the stage space signifies either the inner relation between characters or the inner life of an individual character. . . . The emotional or spiritual potentialities of the spatial arrangement . . . save it from the dangers of an empty formalism.

Light and color were of even greater significance than the steps, wrote David Thomas:

> The almost translucent, ethereal blue of the cyclorama . . . [in] the opening scene of Faust conveyed a sense of heavenly serenity. . . . And the cryptic conclusion of Part I, where a voice from Heaven . . . announces that Gretchen . . . is saved . . . was amplified in the most effective visual terms when Gretchen was seen standing transfigured against the same heavenly blue cyclorama, which had been kept pitch black throughout the earlier part of the dungeon scene.

In *Richard III*, Richard delivered the prologue dressed in black against a black curtain, his face pinspotted. The white-garbed Richmond closed the play with an epilogue against a white curtain, symbolizing the end of evil and the restoration of purity.

Jessner used light symbolically to underline dramatic values, making frequent shifts in its direction, color, and intensity. Looming shadows were a distinctive element, with lights placed in the prompter's box casting eerie figures on the scenery. At the end of *Othello*, Iago's shadow hovered on the cyclorama along with that of the canopied bed on which the dead Moor and Desdemona lay. Another example was the hunchbacked Richard's exit, for which a grotesque shadow was cast following his lines:

> Shine out, fair sun, till I have bought a glass
> That I may see my shadow as I pass.

Jessner's representative productions overlooked realism in favor of expressive presentationalism stressing universals. The actor's individuality was subjugated to the director's vision. Actors were rehearsed so that they repeated the precise rhythms, gestures, movements, and vocal tones imposed on them. No one was allowed to move—not even hands or fingers—while another was speaking. This freeze effect was even seen in a ballroom scene with the dancers immobile as the principals conversed. Only necessary movements were made. Thus all moves made twice their normal impression. In Shakespeare, actors strode straight toward the audience to be isolated in a shaft of light as they spoke monologues directly to the house. A famous example of Jessner's controversial acting touches followed Richard's offstage defeat in battle. He appeared atop the steps, his torso bare, offering his "kingdom for a horse," and then rode his sword like a hobby horse down the steps until he collapsed.

In some contemporary plays, the actors were driven along at a frenetic pace like haunted nightmare figures. In *The Marquis of Keith,* wearing stylized costumes and makeup, they behaved like frenzied marionettes, and were backed by such abstractions as empty frames to represent pictures, a pointed piece of wood for a glass of Champagne, and doors that opened and closed before being touched. Michael Patterson wrote, "The actors plunged on . . . as though thrown in from the wings. Instead of a bell, a drum-roll heralded their entrances, so that they appeared to be coming on as though, circus-like, to perform a turn." Some writers rebelled, including Ernst Barlach, who wanted realism, not puppet-like acting in *The Real Sedemunds* (1921).

Jessner's actors spoke with clear diction, intellectual grasp, and emotional control. They also had a tendency to shout that drove writer John Galsworthy from a performance. Not wishing a syllable to be missed, Jessner even had the choral song in *The Weavers* declaimed rather than sung, which gave the words surprising force. Another highly valued aural component was music, which was carefully integrated into the dramatic pattern and was used to represent offstage sounds—drums suggesting thunder, and violins rolling storm.

Jessner gradually reduced the more overtly subjective expressionist devices and shifted toward the cool approach associated with the period's "new objectivity" (*neue sachlichkeit*) movement. Thus he used relatively representational sets and props for plays such as *An Enemy of the People, The Weavers,* and even *Hamlet.* His famed tempo slowed down and critics even complained it was dragging. In *King John,* reported Lewis, "he made all the characters speak in a low and indolent tone, following the neonaturalistic doctrine that facts, not feelings, should be expressed, for facts are more important than sentiments." His later stagings may have been influenced by his fears about his fate. The *New York Times,* lamenting the ineffectiveness of *King John,* declared: "One prays fervently that he would for a moment forget his fear of the Reichstag and do something vital again."

Jessner found himself in increasing trouble. In 1927, he was charged with the bolshevization of the classical drama when his *Hamlet,* blaming the former

monarchy for current problems, was considered communistically inspired. Influenced in its direct reference to contemporary politics, according to Andreas Höfele, by Piscator's epic theater, it eschewed "timeless" costuming in favor of modern-dress consisting mainly of Wilhelminian court garments. Hamlet was a normal, slovenly young man adrift in a world of militaristic automatons. The icy Claudius, whose withered arm reminded audiences of Kaiser Wilhelm, spoke with "the machine-like precision of the Continental military officer," noted the *Times.* In the first court scene, instead of speaking extemporaneously, he read the eulogy on Hamlet's father from a prepared speech. Caspar Neher's scenically realistic highlight was the rococo setting for the play-within-a-play scene, denoting the court's degeneracy. The players looked upstage and Claudius and Gertrude faced the audience from a baroque balcony box, with Hamlet and Ophelia in the front row of the orchestra.

Jessner was forced to resign in 1930, but he directed until 1933, when Hitler's advent finished his German career and he left the country. His depressing post-German years included an abortive attempt to make films in England; a rejected opportunity to head Tel Aviv's Habimah Theatre, for whom he staged two plays by Schiller and Shakespeare; and employment in Hollywood as an MGM scriptreader, from which he resigned when they ignored his suggestions. When he died, he was under consideration to head the reorganizion of the postwar German stage.

Despite the weakness of his final productions, Jessner was called "the most important figure in the post-war German theatre" by the *Times* in 1933. Some have criticized him for having no poetic feeling and for being too crudely simplistic in his symbolic choices. Yet his antiillusionistic, expressionist experiments had a definite influence, including the better known productions of Brecht, whose "estrangement" ideas he prefigured.

Further reading:

Höfele, Andreas. "Leopold Jessner's Shakespearean Productions, 1920–1930." *Theatre History Studies* 12 (1992).

Kuhns, David F. "Expressionism, Monumentalism, Politics: Emblematic Acting in Jessner's *Wilhelm Tell* and *Richard III." New Theatre Quarterly* 25 (February 1991).

Lewis, Colby. "Leopold Jessner's Theories of Dramatic Production." *Quarterly Journal of Speech* 22 (Spring 1936).

Macgowan, Kenneth, and Robert Edmond Jones. *Continental Stagecraft*. New York: Benjamin Blom, 1964.

Thomas, David. "Leopold Jessner in Berlin." *New Theatre Magazine* 17 (Summer 1967).

Also: Dickinson, *The Theatre in a Changing Europe;* Patterson, *The Revolution in German Theatre;* Willet, *Theatre of the Weimar Republic.*

MARGO JONES (1911–1955)

MARGARET (MARGO) VIRGINIA JONES was born in the rural community of Livingston, Texas. Her father became a land attorney and her mother taught school. At 11, she staged plays with her siblings in a barn. While participating in theatricals at the Girls' Industrial College of Texas (later, Texas Woman's University), Jones commenced her lifelong practice of reading a play a day. She also was impressed by George Bernard Shaw's notes on directing. Jones received her B.A. in 1932 and her M.S. in 1933.

In 1933, Jones studied at Dallas's Southwestern School of the Theater. She enrolled at California's Pasadena Playhouse Summer School in 1934, where she codirected the Chinese play, *The Chalk Circle.* She also directed for the Ojai Community Theater.

Back in Texas, after an eye-opening round-the-world trip, Jones was an assistant director with Houston's Federal Theater Project. This planted in her a dream for a decentralized national theatre. Almost all noteworthy American theater was then in New York; the provinces had to rely on amateurs and Broadway tours. Her desires were further sparked by her 1936 visit to the Moscow Art Theater Festival, which inspired her to create a similarly exciting, noncommercial theater.

Jones convinced the powers-that-be to let her take over a disused building with a tiny stage and auditorium for her new Houston Community Players. These amateurs opened in 1936, with a fanciful black-and-white staging of Oscar Wilde's *The Importance of Being Earnest;* Jones cast all nine actors who auditioned. At the opening, the chicly dressed director greeted the audience personally, a practice she continued throughout her Texas career.

While occasionally directing for others, Jones concentrated on the Houston Community Players, for whom she staged over 60 plays, both classics—her biggest successes—and moderns. She did several new plays, the best being Edwin Justus Mayer's *Sunrise in My Pocket* (1940), which she subsequently failed to get produced in New York. A believer in total immersion in, and dedication to, her craft, Jones was involved in every facet of management and production. More than 600 Houstonites were in the membership pool when she left. Her company included future Texas theater founder Nina Vance and actor Ray Walston.

In 1939, Jones visited Washington, D.C., where, in a hotel ballroom, she saw a theater-in-the-round (or arena) presentation. That summer, she offered a theater-in-the-round series of six comedies in a Houston ballroom. This type of staging appealed to her because of its intimacy, its low cost, and its freeing up of Jones's blocking, which normally caused her agony, and which she preplanned in these days by moving small figurines on a ground plan.

By 1942, when she began teaching at the University of Texas, Jones was nationally known for her theater work and for her conference participation. She proselytized for decentralization as a means both to provide theater jobs for those outside of New York and to bring plays to the hinterlands. This was essential for the growth and development of native theater art. Her dream was to establish a network of nonprofit professional theaters. She also began to fight for the production of new scripts, instead of Broadway retreads, in the regional centers.

Between 1942 and 1944, Jones directed at the university level and elsewhere. She worked on revisions of Tennessee Williams's and Donald Windham's *You Touched Me,* the premiere of which she staged at the Cleveland Playhouse (1943), although company director Frederick McConnell, nervous about her blocking, hurt Jones's pride by taking over during the final week of rehearsals. Shortly afterwards, she did the piece in Pasadena. In 1944, she directed Williams's *The Purification* (and two other new plays) at Pasadena. She also received a Rockefeller Foundation grant to investigate the possibilities of her resident theater plans by studying the mostly amateur theaters already operating

Williams's The Glass Menagerie. *Directed by Margo Jones and Eddie Dowling. (1945) L to r: Anthony Ross, Laurette Taylor, Eddie Dowling, Julie Haydon.* (Photo: Theater Collection, Museum of the City of New York)

throughout the country. She hoped to create a prototype in Dallas.

Jones's first Broadway assignment was as codirector with Eddie Dowling (who played Tom) on Williams's "memory play," *The Glass Menagerie* (1945), which included an unforgettable performance by Laurette Taylor as Amanda. Jones's sole involvement in the casting was the choice of Anthony Ross to play the gentleman caller. Jones joined the handful of woman directors in the male-dominated commercial theater. The early rehearsals were shared between Jones and Dowling, the latter staging his own scenes and the former handling the gentleman-caller scene (it was her idea to have it played on the floor). As Dowling

became preoccupied with his role, he allowed Jones to take increasing responsibility. Taylor's performance was left largely up to the actress, but Jones contributed to her authentic Southern accent. She also aided designer Jo Mielziner with his 102-cue lighting plot.

While struggling to start her Dallas theater, Jones worked on Broadway, doing Maxine Woods's critically drubbed *On Whitman Avenue* (1946), about a black family's struggle against racial prejudice. (Jones was very sensitive to racism; among other signs of her progressive spirit, she was the first to hire black actors for a professional civic theater production in Dallas and also directed for Dallas's black amateurs, the Round-Up Theatre.) She also did Maxwell Anderson's play-within-a-play drama, *Joan of Lorraine* (1946), starring Ingrid Bergman, a crushing experience that saw Jones fired by Anderson during the tryouts when he considered her not tough enough. She shared directing credit with Sam Wanamaker, who played the young director.

The Dallas project got off the ground in 1947 when Jones decided it should be an arena theater. The owners (Gulf Oil) of a 1936 building constructed for the Texas Centennial allowed it to be used rent-free. It was renovated as a 198-seat, keystone-shaped auditorium with a 24-foot by 20-foot trapezoidal acting space. Aisle entrances were in three of the auditorium's four corners. A professional company of New York actors opened the subscription-supported theater for a five-play summer season under the name Theater '47; it was changed every New Year's Eve to mirror the new year. Theater '47, which prospered economically—despite low-priced tickets—under Jones's leadership, became the harbinger of the resident theater movement. It was the first professional arena theater in the country.

It was Jones's base until 1955, when, at 43, she died in a tragic household accident. (She had inhaled noxious fumes from a carpet cleaning solution.) Her policy was a judicious blend of new plays—made viable by the theater's nonprofit status and by grants for playwright development—and classics. Seventy percent of her offerings were premieres. An average season witnessed eight productions. Several new scripts moved to Broadway productions (usually under another director), although the shift to proscenium staging invariably proved damaging. The two she stayed with both failed. One was Owen Crump's *Southern Exposure* (1950); the other was Williams's *Summer and Smoke* (1947). Mielziner's overwhelming set for the latter, with its distractingly impressive stone angel, was a problem; a birdbath sculpture had served better in Dallas. The play had to wait for a 1952 Off-Broadway revival before its quality was acknowledged.

The biggest commercial hit originally staged by Jones was Jerome Lawrence and Robert E. Lee's *Inherit the Wind*, about the 1925 Scopes "monkey trial." It succeeded even in Bible Belt Dallas and went on, under Herman Shumlin's direction, to become an 806-performance Broadway bonanza. Jones's staging was a company landmark; the evangelical fervor of the prayer-meeting was noteworthy because the audience—so close to the actors—felt as if it was directly involved in the inspirational proceedings.

Over the years, there were occasional new plays by writers who would become well known; the company's initial production, for example, was the first play (*Farther Off from Heaven*) by the soon-to-be acclaimed William Inge. Most new writers produced by Jones remained unheralded, and she was sometimes faulted for her taste in plays. Many felt few of her choices were intellectually challenging, her preference frequently being for melodramas and comedies.

Whenever possible, Jones insisted on the presence of the writer, although the brief period of preparation (two weeks at first, eventually four) offered little time for extensive revisions. Jones preferred rewrites to be finished before rehearsals began. She was sometimes criticized for placing too much faith in her dramatists—her close friend Williams, in particular—and for not demanding crucial changes when necessary.

Jones's classics included five by Shakespeare: *The Taming of the Shrew* in 1947; *Twelfth Night* in 1948; *The Merchant of Venice* in 1950; *A Midsummer Night's Dream* (her only Shakespearean failure) in 1951; and *As You Like It* in 1954. Shakespeare adapted well to arena staging. Other classics were by Wilde, Richard Brinsley Sheridan, Molière, Henrik Ibsen, Anton Chekhov, Oliver Goldsmith, Ben Jonson, and George Bernard Shaw. She did the world premiere of Sean O'Casey's fantastical *Cock-a-Doodle Dandy* (1950), although the arena hampered its realization.

Jones directed most of the plays, although associates sometimes did plays under her management. One play was rehearsed during the day while another was running at night. They ran in modified repertory, each succeeded by the other for runs of several weeks (two at first, more later), with periods put aside for rotating all of the current plays. Her core company consisted of approximately eight players; additional actors came from the local populace. Company selection took great skill, as the balance had to be broad enough to play a wide variety of roles. Several actors became standbys and remained for a number of seasons. Jack Warden was her most successful find.

Jones's directing was based more on intuition than analysis. She preferred trial and error to methodical preplanning. Creative enthusiasm marked her personality and she could wheedle out good performances and technical results via a wide range of methods, using a blend of bewitching charm, impetuous dynamism, and nurturing cajolery. Still, she was surprisingly nonauthoritarian.

Her preference was to give actors great freedom, letting them worry about the details of characterization while she "edited" their choices and attended to larger matters of rhythm, scenic fluidity, and picturization. Some (like Ingrid Bergman) found this frustrating, as they depended on more specifics than she was able to provide. Instead of focusing on small details, she implored actors to seek truth and honesty in their feelings; they had to discover for themselves how to achieve sincerity. If an actor was properly cast, she thought, the problem would mostly solve itself. Only as a last resort did she think it proper to demonstrate or give an actor a line reading. Expending her warmth to create an atmosphere of maternal caring and concern, she habitually addressed everyone as "baby" or "honey." Normally able to hold her temper, she could, under pressure, explode in profanities at slow-to-respond performers. This chain-smoking, heavy-drinking "Texas tornado" let no obstacle stand in her way.

Arena staging proved a godsend to Jones's talents, which had trouble handling the requirements of proscenium theaters. She was an eclectic without a distinctly personal stamp, but her arena contributions guaranteed her a unique position. (She actually preferred a multipurpose theater that could accommodate a variety of arrangements.) The flexible demands of arena staging allowed her to block improvisationally; she constantly checked the results from every vantage point although admitting that, with experience, arena blocking became second-nature. She liked to imagine what the blocking would look like from the ceiling. She learned to keep her actors in frequent motion so that they could be seen multidimensionally all around the house, and reminded them to "make the rounds," meaning to find reasons to continually vary their positions. She might also tell them to "pull down the girdle," a hint to find a physical action that helped spectators behind them see something amusing when audiences on the opposite side were laughing at a facial expression.

Her ingenuity was sparked by the need to stringently minimalize all scenic requirements so that sightlines remained unimpeded and a host of locales could be conjured up suggestively, even when multiple settings were required. The conceptions she and her designers created ranged from the naturalistic to the fanciful, revealing that arena staging is highly variable.

She used the theater's aisles to expand a scene's dimensions; employed only the most authentic-seeming and attractive furniture (always low enough to see over) and costumes as well as the subtlest makeup; served real food; eliminated any prop that could be conjured up by the dialogue or an actor's expressiveness; arranged her furnishings to provide the greatest number of playing areas; and utilized highly flexible and imaginative lighting and sound design to evoke places and atmosphere. Everything was deployed to create a cinematical fluidity that often required actors to change (or cleverly disguise) sets in the dark with a minimum of waiting time. Jones insisted—questionably—that any play could be staged in arena fashion. She trusted in the audience's ability to imagine what was not there.

Jones made vividly apparent the workability of nonprofit resident professional theater. Her influence on decentralization was immeasurable. She pioneered the professional use of theater-in-the-round and fostered the idea that new plays should be the primary concern of regional companies.

Further reading:

Jones, Margo. *Theatre-in-the-Round.* New York: Rinehart and Company, 1951.

Sheehy, Helen. *Margo: The Life and Theatre of Margo Jones.* Dallas: Southern Methodist University Press, 1990.

LOUIS JOUVET (1887–1951)

LOUIS JOUVET was born at Crozon in the Finistère, France, where his father was a civil engineer. In 1902, Jouvet's family moved to Rethel in the Ardennes, where he was active in school theatricals. At 18, he studied pharmacy in Paris while training and working as an actor. After becoming involved with experimentalists calling themselves the Groupe d'Action d'Art, he founded the Théâtre d'Action d'Art (1909), offering plays and poetry at Paris locales frequented by popular audiences.

He was hired by Jacques Rouché's Théâtre des Arts where he was impressed by the almost religious devotion to theatrical art expressed by these progressives. Meanwhile, he studied every aspect of the theater, including directing, design, lighting, architecture, and history. He eventually gained acclaim as a lecturer, writer, and teacher.

In 1912, Jouvet and a friend rented the small Théâtre du Château d'Eau and began a series of low-budget productions that gained him experience. His next major step was to join Jacques Copeau's revolutionary company at the Théâtre du Vieux-Colombier where—for over a decade—he became a famous actor, created the theater's famous permanent set, designed the lights and decor for numerous productions, invented a lighting instrument called the Jouvet, and taught technical classes.

When Copeau left the Vieux-Colombier, he transferred his repertory and a number of actors to Jouvet's care. Before that occurred, though, Jouvet, in 1922, had been hired by Jacques Hébertot to become technical director of the Théâtre des Champs-Elysées, one of whose two playhouses was the fourth-floor Comédie des Champs-Elysées. Jouvet produced a dignified and thought-provoking yet commercially appealing repertory. His audience was from the well-to-do, well-educated elite. The first production (direction was credited to Hébertot) was Jules Romains's *Mr. Le Trouhadec Seized by Debauchery* (1923); it began a close relationship with Romains, nine of whose plays Jouvet premiered.

Jouvet played major roles in most of the plays he directed; he also was a movie star. At first, he was his own designer; he continued to be largely responsible for the lighting of his shows but, from 1925, gradually turned the other design functions over to various artists, in particular Christian Bérard. He wrote in 1936, "Such things as wood, paint, nails and light are not, as one might suppose, lifeless, inorganic things but formidable entities whose favor toward the play and its interpreters is to be won only by a secret and long-premeditated accord." Jouvet, influenced by the Vieux-Colombier, yet with his own individualized style, abandoned the fixed stage and worked within a proscenium. The audience was never to forget it was in a theater, but whenever possible, he preferred actual things to pasteboard substitutes, and also liked materials that glinted in the light. He was, however, fond of creating effects through clever technical devices. His set for *Mr. Le Trouhadec* depicted a Monte Carlo locale in which, to comment symbolically on the action, the placement of two palm trees was altered by bringing them together or separating them and having them bend toward or away from one another. In *Donogoo-Tonka* (1930), the idea of people in different cities reading about the newly founded Donogoo-Tonka was

evoked by placing the actors behind a series of scrims onto which an identifying locale in each city was painted, then moving them sideways as one tableau faded into the next.

Sound design was another Jouvet skill. He often employed effects as an orchestrated background against which the play was performed. Similarly, he elicited atmosphere by an extensive use of music. Background scores were written by such notables as Georges Auric and Francis Poulenc.

In 1923, Jouvet directed and starred in the hit that would be a career mealticket, Romains's satire on a country quack, *Doctor Knock*. Jouvet and Jeanne Dubouchet's famous cartoonish settings were long associated with the play. Jouvet presented the piece 1,298 times in Paris and 142 times on tour.

In 1924, Hébertot placed Jouvet in charge of the Comédie des Champs-Elysées. Together with other Copeau actors, Jouvet revived a handful of Vieux-Colombier pieces, but his repertoire was mostly devoted to contemporary French writers such as Marcel Achard (three plays), Romains, Charles Vildrac, Stève Passeur, the Belgian Fernand Crommelynck, and, among others, Jean Cocteau, including the latter's Freudian Oedipus play, *The Infernal Machine* (1934). There were several translations, notably Nikolai Gogol's *The Inspector General* (1927) and Sutton Vane's *Outward Bound* (1926). Even more noteworthy were the productions of four Jean Giraudoux plays (*Siegfried* in 1928, *Amphitryon 38* in 1929, *Judith* in 1931, and *Intermezzo* in 1933). *Judith* was premiered at the Théâtre Pigalle, where, from 1930 to 1932, Jouvet directed several plays, focusing on contemporary French works. Some pieces premiering during these years were later revived. Tours allowed non-Parisians and foreigners to enjoy Jouvet's work.

Giraudoux was already a respected writer, but his transition to one of France's most respected dramatists was largely owing to Jouvet. Giraudoux and the director had a deeply collaborative relationship that continued throughout the playwright's life. Giraudoux learned from Jouvet about things such as character enhancement, the creation of suspense, and the clarification of the story-line through the elimination of the extraneous. Giraudoux revised continually before satisfying his director. (It was Jouvet's practice to keep revising, even after the opening.)

To perform these verbally challenging, idea-oriented, character-rich works, Jouvet developed a slowed-down, muted, unelaborated, almost incantatory method of delivering the frequently rhetorical dialogue. He deemphasized emotionalism and sought a fluid delivery, musically expressive and precisely articulated yet careful to avoid undue stress on words or phrases; nuances of feeling and life emerged organically. "You're trying too hard," he once said to an actor. "Simply speak your lines, don't act them out." He required the actors to "breath the text," hoping that by capturing the dialogue's breathing patterns they would relive the author's experience in writing it. He carefully observed Giraudoux at rehearsal to note the playwright's own breathing as he reacted to the players. Lengthy hours went by as Jouvet orchestrated his rhythmic approach.

In 1927, Jouvet formed with Paris's three other leading director-producers, Gaston Baty, Georges Pitoëff, and Charles Dullin, the famed Cartel des Quatre ("Cartel of Four"), an association designed for mutual artistic and moral support.

By 1934, economic difficulties caused Jouvet to abandon the Comédie des Champs-Elysées and to take over and renovate what he called the Athénée Théâtre-Louis Jouvet. Giraudoux was installed as the house playwright, with productions of such works as *Tessa* (from Margaret Kennedy's novel, *The Constant Nymph*; 1934), *The Trojan War Will Not Take Place* (1935), *Electra* (1937), and *Ondine* (1939). Other works included Jouvet's first original staging of a classic, Molière's *The School for Wives* (1936), and works by Passeur and Achard. He also guest-directed at the Comédie Française, including a fantastical staging of Corneille's *The Comic Illusion* (1937). His *School for Wives*, staged after years of preparation, was renowned as a refreshingly new look at the oft-produced comedy. It rejected the well-worn Comédie convention of portraying Arnolphe (Jouvet) as a mean-spirited grouch in favor of a good-humored, younger-than-usual fellow with supreme but self-deceiving confidence in his ability to sustain the fidelity of his juvenile wife. The colorful production was scenically unconventional in its use of a single locale that was mechanically manipulated so that the walls before Agnès's house could be parted before the audience's eyes to reveal the garden they concealed. Overhead, despite the exterior setting, were four chandeliers.

Jouvet spent the early portion of the war in unoccupied France. Nazi prohibitions against his "anti-cultural" repertory prevented his playing in Paris. He toured to Switzerland and then, in 1942, took the troupe to South America, where they remained for four years. Their repertoire included established works as well as new plays by Passeur and Giraudoux and revivals of works by Alfred de Musset, Paul

Claudel, Molière, and others. After tours to Haiti and Mexico, the company went home in 1944.

Reinstalled at his theater in 1945, Jouvet drove himself to regain his old standing, working up to 18 hours a day, and displaying a lack of self-confidence that led to frequent changes of his mind. Nevertheless, he achieved his goal, especially with his premiere of Giraudoux's posthumous satire on the corrupt world of finance, *The Madwoman of Chaillot* (1945). He also confronted two of the leading postwar avant-garde, metaphysical authors, Jean Genet and Jean-Paul Sartre, introducing the former's examination of decadence, *The Maids* (1947), and the latter's existentialist *The Devil and the Good Lord* (1951). There were brilliant revivals of Claudel's *The Tidings Brought to Mary* (1946) and Molière's *Don Juan* (1947), *The Tricks of Scapin* (for Jean-Louis Barrault; 1949), and *Tartuffe* (1950).

His radical ideas—reflecting his own religious struggles—for *Don Juan* included a completely unromantic view of the leading character, played not as an atheist but as a man fleeing his own belief in God, perhaps to invite his own punishment. He shocked traditionalists when he justified Sganarelle's comic delivery of "Oh! My wages! My wages!" by bringing the curtain down after Juan's death, then bringing it up a minute and a half later with Sganarelle in front of Juan's tomb, speaking the words in a tone of comic irony as he placed a wreath at the tomb's base.

Tartuffe abandoned its usual comic style (one critic counted four laughs all evening) and presented its traditionally villainous title character as a charming and sincere skeptic. At the finale, Jouvet, seeking an ironical effect, replaced the officer's long speech by distributing the lines to a group of seven actors (the officer and six wigged judges), revealed in a law-court setting when the rear wall flew up.

Jouvet was an assiduous reader, completing a play a day. When he found one he liked, he let it ferment for months or even years until a complete mental picture of it formed. As soon as he felt ready, he spent months preparing its production. He lived a disciplined life, allowing him to divide his time as a director (sometimes directing at two theaters on alternate days), designer, theater manager, lecturer, and movie actor (*Carnival in Flanders*, *The Lower Depths*, *Volpone*, etc.) as efficiently as possible.

A night at a Jouvet production guaranteed sophistication, polish, and classical clarity. His choices reveal a taste for literary works—predominantly comic in tone—the textual integrity of which he respected, but whose aesthetic delights he did not ignore. His productions rarely employed spectacle for its own sake, but did so to enhance the writer's aims. He advocated "the theatre of dramatists and poets which makes of dramatic art a literary form of the highest order. Here the important thing is the text, and the spectacular elements are admitted only as side-issues and supplements." Good drama was good writing (writing that attends to rhythmic and emotional values, as well as intellectual ones, and employs expressive language). A dramatist must make his audience feel, even before making them understand. A play's purpose is to stimulate the imagination and sensory faculties through stylistic means. But good direction occurs when the director "makes his devices disappear into the text, so incorporating them that the play absorbs [the] directions without being deformed by them." When he died, Jouvet was working on a version of Graham Greene's *The Power and the Glory* that would have experimented with an objectified, Brecht-like method.

His goal was a complete integration of text and visuals. He was skilled at making talky plays viable through his manipulation of actors, lights, and decor. Although far from emulating Copeau's spareness, Jouvet's sets were simple and classical, making great use of the barest essentials; when appropriate, though, he could indulge in the fantastical and rococo. He trusted experience and intuition over aesthetic theories.

The theater is grateful to Jouvet for his enhancement of the modern French repertoire by his devotion to its outstanding native authors; his tradition-busting interpretations of Molière; and his demonstration of the integrity possible from a director possessing academic scholarship, literary-theatrical taste, technical and design ability, and acting genius.

Further reading:

Jouvet, Louis. "The Profession of the Producer, I." *Theatre Arts* 20 (December 1936).

———. "The Profession of the Producer, II." *Theatre Arts* 21 (January 1937).

Knapp, Bettina L. *Louis Jouvet, Man of the Theatre.* New York: Columbia University Press, 1957.

Also: Bradby, *Modern French Drama*; Johnson, *Directing Methods*; Knowles, *French Drama of the Inter-War Years*; Marshall, *The Producer and the Play*; Whitton, *Stage Directors in Modern France.*

TADEUSZ KANTOR (1915–1990)

TADEUSZ KANTOR was born in the Eastern Polish town of Wielopole, near Krakow, and not far from Auschwitz. His father, a teacher, was drafted into the army during World War I and died without Kantor knowing him. Kantor was raised by his grandmother's brother, who lived in a presbytery. A talented painter, he studied scene design before the war at Krakow's Academy of Fine Arts; around this time he founded a puppet theater.

During Poland's occupation by the Germans, Kantor was part of Krakow's Independent Theatre, an underground group of painters producing plays clandestinely in private residences. In these circumstances, he staged Julius Slowacki's *Balladyna* (1942), Jean Cocteau's *Orpheus* (1944), and Stanislaw Wyspianski's *The Return of Odysseus* (1944), the latter designed with found objects. Kantor noted how these objects could assume a separate reality from their utilitarian ones. It represented his idea of theater as an abstract, nonliterary, "autonomous art." Although bound by the text, each element (sound, lights, color, movement, actors, etc.) must be al-

lowed to speak with its own expressive capabilities. The stage experience must create its own reality.

After the war, Kantor painted and designed. A position as an art professor was revoked because of his formalistic tendencies. In 1956, under liberalized artistic policies, he directed and designed Federico García Lorca's *The Shoemaker's Prodigious Wife*, George Bernard Shaw's *St. Joan*, and Shakespeare's *Hamlet* and *Measure for Measure*. The same year, he founded Krakow's nonsubsized experimental theater, Cricot 2 (named for an avant-garde 1930s theater; *cricot* is an anagram for the Polish "this is the circus"). The mostly amateur actors were artists and poets (many remained for years), and their repertoire was for a long time based on the work of prewar surrealist painter-writer Stanislaw Ignacy Witkiewicz (or Witkacy). *The Cuttlefish* (1956) was the first postwar production of the previously prohibited playwright.

Kantor painted, designed, taught, directed operas, headed Cricot 2, and published manifestos describing, in often opaque prose and verse, the thinking

Tadeusz Kantor. (1980)   (Photo: Carol Rosegg)

1966 German tour, Kantor's international fame blossomed.

Later manifestos bore such titles as "Emballages Manifesto" (referring to his artistic experiments with wrapping people and objects as packages, sometimes employed in his theater images), "Theater Zero Manifesto," and "Manifesto 70." Theater Zero was represented by Witkiewicz's *The Madman and the Nun* (1963). Gerould says it displayed

> radical destruction of the dramatic text and the stage
> creates its own reality. The play itself is not performed,
> but the text is quoted, commented upon, and repeated.
> Actors and objects are equalized; an enormous pile of
> folding chairs . . . fills the . . . area, forcing the actors
> to struggle to stay on stage and to fight against the chairs.

The Polish government, assuming that the chairs were a symbol of itself, forced the play to close.

Kantor took part in activities that prefigured the "happenings" (a kind of semispontaneous, nonliterary event combining theatrical elements with visual arts) of the sixties; after 1965, he created many happenings in international locations.

A happenings-type production was Witkiewicz's *The Water Hen* (1968). According to Klossowicz, "Kantor gave his actors complete freedom of action, while rejecting audience participation. The central motif . . . was a journey. The actors were eternal wanderers, bums packing and unpacking, always on the move carrying all their earthly possessions." The characters were attached to things that tormented them, such as a woman who was chained to a bathtub in which she was repeatedly drowned.

In 1972, Kantor staged a French version of Witkiewicz's *The Shoemakers* (1972) in Paris. One year later, Cricot 2 toured Witkiewicz's *Dainty Shapes and Hairy Apes, or the Green Pill*, also called *Lovelies and Dowdies*, during a phase Kantor called Theater Impossible. He intended to produce a formless work without aesthetic qualities, meaning nothing but simply being. It took place in a cloakroom. Spectators close to the action were packaged together in wide aprons with neck loops. A selected number represented the 40 Mandelbaums, Hasidic Jews, who, at one point, were led out and whose amplified wailing suggested the sound of victims going to the gas chambers. Bizarre figures appeared, some as "emballages." A cleaning woman scrubbed a huge, wheeled rat trap (most characters had repetitive, set activities). A man bore a half dummy at his waist, giving him two more legs that he could manipulate. Denis Calandra observed, "Kantor isolates theatrical

behind his latest endeavors. His first was called "Manifesto of the Informel Theatre," using the French term *informe* (shapeless, imperfect) to suggest a method that would be "accidental, spontaneous, impetuous, incandescent, fluid, elemental, hallucinatory, spasmatic, obsessive, ecstatic, insane, profligate, exaggerated, unexpected, informal" (quoted by Daniel Gerould). His Informel Theatre period began with Witkiewicz's *In a Small Country House* (1961; later called *The Wardrobe*), in which random chance was allowed to explode the text. When an old wardrobe was opened, "an incredible number of big bags fall out. One could not clearly distinguish between the bags and the actors who also fell out. . . . From that moment on, the action . . . takes place in a space filled with bags, stools, and actors constituting together the 'matter' of the performance" (quoted by Jan Klossowicz). After this work's

Wielopole, Wielopole. *Directed by Tadeusz Kantor.*
(1980)   (Photo: Carol Rosegg)

ingredients, abstracts them and, in the post-Surrealist, post-Happening tradition, puts them into an unusual relationship to one another. Actors, text, director, physical objects, and performance space all have an equalized status."

The production began the gloomy-looking Kantor's idiosyncratic convention of appearing as the conductor of the performance, dressed in a black suit with an open-collared white shirt, and whispering to or wordlessly adjusting the actors (who sometimes showed annoyance), snapping his fingers to correct the pace, and giving signals to the technicians. He believed that he had to be present not only to guarantee the communication of his visions, but to destroy any sense of illusion. This "illegal" intrusion, as he called it, was very controversial.

Kantor's greatest period stemmed from 1975, when, in relation to his "Theater of Death Manifesto," he created *The Dead Class,* a masterwork he called a "dramatic séance," based on his own text plus works by Witkiewicz, Witold Gombrowicz, and Bruno Schulz. Like his subsequent work, it was a partly autobiographical, memory-driven dream play,

preoccupied with visions of death. A schoolroom setting revealed four, old-fashioned, long wooden desks and a number of aged people nearing death, their faces chalky white, each carrying a childhood version of himself in the form of a dummy, perhaps symbolic of wasted youth and vanished innocence. The "Waltz François" was played repeatedly and loudly. *The Dead Class* toured widely for many years.

Dummies—first used in *The Water Hen*—played a significant role in Kantor's work. He believed that they bore the aura of death and enhanced the actors' expression of life. Klossowicz thought that for Kantor, "the dummy is a symbol of artistic creation, of debased reality, of an awkward, cheap imitation of life." Often, they were stabbed by bayonets or torn to pieces.

A brilliant series of pieces followed, winning Kantor many international prizes. *Wielopole, Wielopole* (1980), first seen in Italy, has a title that echoes Kantor's fondness for using repetitive devices. Certain dream images were continually reenacted as if caught in a faulty memory track; an example was the repeated act of Jews being gunned down. Autobiographical tendencies were evident as Kantor observed nightmarish scenes from his World War I childhood. The work was inspired by a photo of Kantor's conscripted father in uniform. Although there was no story per se, all scenes were set in a single room of childhood with a ceiling that kept getting higher. The scenes were titled "Marriage," "Insults," "Crucifixion," "Adam Goes to the Front," and the "Last Supper" (in which dummies could hardly be differentiated from live actors). The characters were Kantor's deceased family—transmuted into religious figures—and seven dehumanized soldiers, dressed in decrepit uniforms, representative of death and Kantor's father. The latter was shown marching off to battle only for his bride to be raped by the others. Two family members were bowler-hatted, mustachioed twin uncles, a striking duo recurring in several Kantor works. After the Last Supper, the family was tossed in a group pit along with naked dummy doubles.

Let the Artists Die (1981) was created when Kantor overheard someone use the title phrase disparagingly. This grotesquely humorous "revue," premiered in an old factory in Nuremberg, focused on memories of death and militarism. Its politically motivated, Poland-related themes were based on the story of Veit Stoss, a medieval artist, symbolic of artists martyred by their society, and of a modern military hero-dictator, Jozef Pilsudski, seated astride a horse's skeleton. Kantor himself was represented threefold: by a child playing him at age six; by himself as the author (Prime Mover) of the drama; and by himself dying. The child, dreaming of toy soldiers, is confronted with the awkwardness of full-sized ones who cannot be controlled. A clownish doctor ran from one Kantor-persona to another, taking their pulses to determine which one was dying. Past, present, and future intermingled without chronological logic in this apocalyptic vision—replete with overtones of Auschwitz—that had such figures as a man repeatedly hanging himself in a lavatory.

The images in *Where Are the Snows of Yesteryear* (1982), premiered in Paris, included machinelike, white-overalled men and typically Kantorian Jewish and Catholic figures (including two tangoing bishops). Kantor's metaphorically dense *I Shall Never Return* (1988) surveyed his theatrical accomplishments with bits and pieces of former works going back to *The Return of Odysseus*. A lifesize Kantor-dummy played a crucial role.

Kantor's final work was 1991's posthumous, autobiographical *Today Is My Birthday*. His presence was signified by an empty chair and his prerecorded voice. Set in the "poor room of the imagination," most of the reminiscent action occurred behind three large picture frames. One showed an actor as a self-portrait of Kantor, another showed a dadaesque version of Velasquez's Infanta, and the central frame, set with a Last Supper-like table, reproduced images from a family photograph on a table by Kantor's chair. Character-emballages that came to life were arranged about the space. The personages represented friends, historical figures, allegorical characters, and so on, and the main action evoked the catastrophes wrought by World War I, the Nazis, and the Soviets, ending in a scene of chaos stopped short by a freeze frame using all 31 actors.

Kantor was a total director who controlled the entire mise-en-scène, from the actors to the smallest props, to create a completely unified art work. His career has been likened to a journey because of its constant progression through new and increasingly exceptional phases that expressed his interior processes. He was a creator of painterly surrealistic montages and tableaux, usually in muted shades of blacks and grays. The props and sets could be magically transformed so that a hurdy gurdy could become a child's coffin or a camera a machine gun. Some were pure inventions, such as a bed in *Wielopole, Wielopole* that was also a torture machine. A graveyard became a brothel. Kantor said the effect was like placing one photographic negative over another. The acting—which turned characters into arche-

types—was stylized, using controlled gestures, precisely timed movements, and masklike makeups.

Kantor's works, largely inspired by the tragic side of Polish history and culture, combined horrific images with darkly comic ones in an Eastern European tradition of grotesquerie. Many images criticized the decline of humanism, showing suffering and war. Heavily metaphoric, his multilayered, collagelike, nonlinear, memory-laden texts were like paintings and sculptures come to life, and were open to multiple interpretations, although it was less necessary to analyze them than to experience them emotionally; the predominantly nonverbal images were accessible on a prerational, associative level.

His final works began rehearsals without a text, often starting with notes or imagistic drawings that would eventually be realized by actors and props. Over what sometimes took five years, Kantor provided the company with themes and images in which they invested their own experiences and language. Using tape recordings, Kantor selected those contributions that reached the final production. He used his visual genius to shape the material, choreographing it and setting its rhythms against amplified music. Some of the finest moments were inspired by accidents, as when a broken gramophone provided a funereal pace for a lively piece of music. Five hours of material would be winnowed down to one and a half or less. When the editing process ended, the words—heightened and rearranged versions of improvisations—were added. Kantor categorically refused to consider his works collaborative, having little patience for works created under such methods. He was really a notorious disciplinarian who expressed himself in tirades when displeased with actors or technicians. Asked if the company feared the director, an actor replied, "A better word would be *terrified.*"

Some consider Kantor a greater artist than his more influential countryman Jerzy Grotowski, whose "poor theatre" Kantor claimed to have invented first. Regardless, he was one of the modern theater's most powerful artists, able to turn his national and personal agonies into art of universal proportions.

Further reading:

Calandra, Denis. "Experimental Performance at the Edinburgh Festival." *The Drama Review* 17 (December 1973).

Gerould, Daniel. "Tadeusz Kantor: A Visual Artist Works Magic on the Polish Stage." *Performing Arts Journal* 4, no. 3 (1980).

Jenkins, Ron. "Ringmaster in a Circus of Dreams." *American Theatre* 2 (March 1986).

Kantor, Tadeusz. "The Writings of Tadeusz Kantor." *The Drama Review* 30 (Fall 1986).

Klossowicz, Jan. "Tadeusz Kantor's Journey." *The Drama Review* 30 (Fall 1986).

˙Note: The following appeared too late to be used for this essay: Kantor, Tadeusz. *A Journey Through Other Spaces: Essays and Manifestos, 1944–1990.* Edited and translated by Michael Kobialka. Berkeley: University of California Press, 1993.

GEORGE S. KAUFMAN (1889–1961)

GEORGE S. KAUFMAN, whose father had an unsettled career in business, was born in Pittsburgh, Pennsylvania. The lanky and bespectacled young man entered Western University of Pennsylvania (now the University of Pittsburgh), but withdrew because of illness. He later took an acting class and a couple of Columbia University extension courses. He became a journalist and, in 1917, was made drama editor of the *New York Times*, a job he held until 1930, well after he gained success as a playwright.

During the 1920s, Kaufman struck it rich with a series of hit comedies, almost all written in collaboration with someone else; most frequently it was Marc Connelly. Of the dozen writers with whom he eventually collaborated, his most successful and frequent partnerships were with Connelly, Moss Hart, and Edna Ferber. He was a dependable "play doctor" who could be called in to minister to a troubled play. Kaufman was author or coauthor of 45 Broadway plays and musicals, most of them moneymakers.

Before 1928, Kaufman was uncredited as a director, although he had influence on a number of plays. On the few occasions when he started out as the credited director, he stepped down because he was too shy to assert the required authority. His breakthrough came with Ben Hecht and Charles MacArthur's *The Front Page* (a title conceived by Kaufman), the hit farce about cynical, pungently profane Chicago newspapermen covering an execution. Kaufman, thoroughly conversant with the background, provided a jet-propelled but physically realistic production. Its remarkable comic timing—Kaufman amazed the actors by his prediction of just where the laughs would come—and emotionally truthful acting became a paradigm of his style. When the prudish Dorothy Stickney balked at saying, "I've been looking for you bastards," he broke down her defenses by explaining that the words were written for the sole purpose of arousing sympathy for her prostitute character. The production also displayed his propensity for continual revisions to "take out the fat,"

i.e., eliminate all unneeded words and business. Kaufman knew that actors could be funnier by underplaying than pushing for laughs.

Kaufman received credit for 43 more works (24 from his own pen). Invariably, he invested in his own productions, partly to make money, and partly to gain more authority over them. A workaholic, he was generally involved with several projects simultaneously. Sometimes he leaped into the staging of a new work the day after a previous one opened. He wrote comic essays, became a broadcasting celebrity, and directed a movie.

Among Kaufman's long list of directorial accomplishments were his collaboratively written comedies, the most popular ones being *Once in a Lifetime* (1930; he acted in it too), *Dinner at Eight* (1932), *First Lady* (1935), *Stage Door* (1936), the Pulitzer-winning *You Can't Take It with You* (1936), *The Man Who Came to Dinner* (1939), *George Washington Slept Here* (1940), *The Late George Apley* (1944), and *The Solid Gold Cadillac* (1953). Top comedies by others included Joseph A. Fields and Jerome Chodorov's *My Sister Eileen* (1940), Ruth Gordon's *Over 21*, and Peter Ustinov's *Romanoff and Juliet* (1957), a British piece starring its author and restaged (and Americanized) by Kaufman. His musical comedies included the Marx Brothers' hit, *Animal Crackers* (1928), on whose book he collaborated; the Pulitzer-winning *Of Thee I Sing* (1931), book by Kaufman and Morrie Ryskind, score by George and Ira Gershwin, which he revived in 1952; *I'd Rather Be Right* (1937), book by Kaufman and Hart, score by Richard Rodgers and Lorenz Hart; and Cole Porter's *Silk Stockings* (1955), book by Kaufman, Leueen MacGrath, and Abe Burrows, from which he was fired for refusing to gag it up more than he already had done; those by others were *Face the Music* (codirected with Hassard Short, 1932), score by Irving Berlin, and Frank Loesser's *Guys and Dolls* (1950), for which he won a Tony. Interestingly, Kaufman had an inability to appreciate music and—to the consternation of his composers—often neglected the musical scenes in favor of working on the book.

His production of serious plays was rare, but he did a magnificent staging of John Steinbeck's powerful, socially conscious, *Of Mice and Men* (1937), and a less effective one of Jean Giraudoux's whimsical but unsuccessful *The Enchanted* (1950), which was simply not in Kaufman's line. Steinbeck was enormously grateful for Kaufman's dramaturgical suggestions, such as his advice on adding humor to the somber tale. Featured in *The Enchanted* was Kaufman's young, second wife, Leueen MacGrath, a British actress with whom he also collaborated on writing several shows. On occasion, he staged the London production of one of his New York hits.

A large number of these plays take pleasure in depicting—usually satirically, but sometimes sympathetically—politics, big business, and show business. Kaufman was a proponent of plays that were clear, tightly constructed, and consistently entertaining, especially when they had a storehouse of wisecracks. The worst thing that he could detect in a production was a dead spot, and he worked overtime to eliminate such shortcomings.

Several Kaufman shows were quite elaborate, such as the extravagant anti-Nazi drama, *The American Way* (1939) coauthored with Hart, and an expensive failure produced at the huge Center Theatre. Its 60-actor cast was supplemented by 200 extras. Another costly loser was his and Hart's *Merrily We Roll Along* (1934), employing 91 actors and 150 costumes. In Kaufman and Hart's *George Washington Slept Here* (1940), he staged a farcical scene in which the characters vandalize the interior of a country house. After 150 performances, wrote Malcolm Goldstein, the scene had gone through "1200 window panes, 550 light bulbs, 1500 banister spindles, 1200 plates, and 76 pairs of curtains," not to mention 150 bottles of seltzer used to spritz the scenery.

Kaufman's greatest directorial period was from 1928 to 1940, when he was also extremely consistent in his writing output. Between 1940's *My Sister Eileen* and 1950's *Guys and Dolls*, when he had 11 flops, only two hits surfaced, both in 1944. His failing health was damaged when he was fired from *Silk Stockings*, and he did only one more play, *Romanoff and Juliet*. It set him back even further, because Ustinov wanted him removed. Producer David Merrick saved his job, however.

Kaufman saw directing and playwriting as closely related skills. He took great pains with a script, demanding frequent revisions. Despite his improvements, he declined authorial credit in noncollabora-

tive scripts, claiming these were part of his responsibilities. When a significant problem arose, he left the actors in the hands of his stage manager, repaired to a nearby typewriter with his collaborator or the author, and redid the scene. As soon as he returned he immediately staged the new material. But he rarely brooked the actors' changing or adding lines, unless they first had permission. He was famous for his caustic cracks to actors who sought to embellish their parts, and once chastised William Gaxton by sending him a telegram saying, "Am in back of house. Wish you were here." Stage managers kept Kaufman fully informed of infractions, and he maintained a close watch on performances to guard against "improvements" or quality slippage. He often called for refresher rehearsals.

With characteristic modesty, Kaufman downgraded the director's role. While admitting that a "theatrical ignoramus" could ruin a good play, he insisted that "if a director has a competent sense of theatre and a bit of an ear he will turn out a success when the play is good and a failure when it isn't." The best direction was the least noticeable: "Once it begins to call attention to itself, something is wrong." Yet, few could match his skill at creating comic business or devising a score in which movement, gesture, and dialogue were so precisely timed that laughter was assured even in dull material. In the stately comedy *The Late George Apley*, cowritten with John P. Marquand, Kaufman created a hilarious scene in which a group of upper-class Bostonians walked, one by one, into a living room in a way that suggested how each, in his or her own way, was reacting to the effect of having eaten too much Thanksgiving dinner. Emotional scenes, however, made him itchy. During *My Sister Eileen* rehearsals, he surprised the up-until-then impressed authors when the play reached a sentimental passage. "All right," he said as he put down his script, "you two wrote it. Now you can direct it."

Kaufman began rehearsals with about four days of "at table" readings before rapidly blocking the action. He watched most rehearsals from the third or fourth row, or paced at the theater's rear, and concentrated intently, often with his eyes closed, on the lines and tempo. He often counted the beats to himself, perhaps clicking his fingers, to determine the relationship between a line and a movement before making the proper adjustment to bring them into harmony. Words would be cut or added to correct the imbalance. Ten minutes might be spent on finding the exactly right moment for a door slam. Once a scene was staged, the actors ran it without interruptions, and then he either conversed quietly with his cowriter or the author or took the actors aside individually and whispered to them. He hated to point up an actor's weaknesses in front of others. Often, despite his underlying firmness, his manner of addressing actors sounded almost contrite, because he did not wish to hurt feelings.

Kaufman retained his shyness. Rarely did he give in to tantrums, his demeanor—even at exasperating moments—remaining quiet and reserved. No one accused him of tyrannical behavior.

As rehearsals continued, his ideas took root, not by being imposed but because he gently insinuated them into the actors' consciousness. This laissez-faire approach actually inspired faster progress than was true of more authoritative directors. His pragmatism when it came to timing specific moments could be quite direct. According to Howard Teichmann, he once told an actress, "My dear young woman, you are playing the part of a maid. You have very little dialogue. You come on in two beats, you stand for four beats, and you exit on five." Kaufman tended to be more demanding of inexperienced actors; with those he trusted, especially improvisational geniuses like Groucho Marx, he would interfere as little as possible.

Normally, he refrained from socializing with his players, maintaining a reserve that increased his sense of authority. He even referred to his actors as Mr., Miss, and Mrs. This aloofness was heightened by his sparing use of compliments. His response to actress Ruth Gordon when she questioned this behavior was, "You're supposed to be good. I'll tell you when you're not."

While most directors have to wait until late in rehearsals to have a set to work in, Kaufman usually insisted that one be ready very early, sometimes a week after work began. This cost a great deal of money to accomplish. Another unusual Kaufman feature was his preference for rehearsing backwards. With a play that had been completely blocked, he was likely to begin rehearsals with the last act and

then proceed in reverse, with the first act last. He ran problem scenes over and over, focusing on the timing. But, if he was content with certain scenes, he might skip them and work only on those that were under par. He hardly ever looked at the script, concentrating constantly on the stage. Whenever a word or line sounded wrong, he revised it instantly.

Kaufman believed that good direction was a matter of common sense and did not require lengthy discussions and explorations of the playwright's intentions and ideas. He did not believe himself so brilliant an actor that he could demonstrate exactly what an actor should do, either physically or with a line reading. When necessary, he would correct a reading by pointing up the key words that the actor was misstressing. If his actors were well cast, they could figure out their characters for themselves. He honed his casting skills by attending every new show and remembering what made each actor unique. He had a special knack for finding amusing actors who could raise a chuckle by their mere presence.

George S. Kaufman today is best known as the coauthor of some of America's funniest plays. Had he not written them, however, he could as easily be remembered for his contributions to the business of directing fast-paced, perfectly timed, wisecracking Broadway comedies.

Further reading:

Eustis, Morton. *"The Man Who Came to Dinner* with George Kaufman Directing." *Theatre Arts* 22 (November 1939).

Goldstein, Malcolm. *George S. Kaufman.* New York: Oxford University Press, 1979.

Kaufman, George S. "What Is Directing, Anyhow?" In John Gassner, *Producing the Play.* Rev. ed. San Francisco: Rinehart, 1953.

Meredith, Scott. *George S. Kaufman and His Friends.* Garden City, N.Y.: Doubleday, 1974.

Teichmann, Howard. *George S. Kaufman: An Intimate Portrait.* New York: Atheneum, 1972.

ELIA KAZAN (1909–   )

ELIA KAZAN (*né* Kazanjioglou) was born in a small Turkish town to a family of Anatolian Greeks that later settled in New Rochelle, New York, where his father sold rugs. Kazan attended Williams College and did graduate theater work at Yale, where he

was dubbed "Gadget" or "Gadge" because of his nervous energy.

Kazan's first professional directing job was at Atlantic City's Toy Theatre, where he staged S. N. Behrman's *The Second Man* (1931). In 1932, he joined New York's Group Theatre, dedicated to the production of socially conscious plays with a Stanislavsky-oriented ensemble. Kazan was primarily active as an actor and stage manager, although, a brief member of the Communist Party, he wrote and directed for the left-wing Theatre of Action. His erstwhile connections became an issue in the 1950s when he appeared before the House Un-American Activities Committee and alienated former colleagues by providing the names of those he knew to have had party affiliations.

His first Group directing opportunity was Robert Ardrey's *Casey Jones* (1938), which failed. Before the Group's 1941 demise, He staged four other plays for them, the most successful being Ardrey's *Thunder Rock* (1939).

His first significant hit as a freelancer was Thornton Wilder's comedy-fantasy *The Skin of Our Teeth* (1942), about man's survival through the ages, which starred Fredric March and Tallulah Bankhead. A selection of his other 1940s successes might include Florence Ryerson and Colin Clements's *Harriet* (1943), starring Helen Hayes as Harriet Beecher Stowe; Kurt Weill's musical fantasy *One Touch of Venus* (1943), with Mary Martin; Franz Werfel's comedy *Jacobowsky and the Colonel* (1944), about a Jew fleeing the Nazis; Arnaud D'Usseau and James Gow's *Deep Are the Roots* (1945), about a black veteran who returns home to confront racial bias; Arthur Miller's *All My Sons* (1947), concerning a man who sold defective goods to the military; Tennessee Williams's sensual confrontation between flesh and spirit, *A Streetcar Named Desire* (1947), which catapulted Marlon Brando to fame as Stanley Kowalski; Weill's offbeat musical critique of American marriage, *Love Life* (1948); and Miller's towering *Death of a Salesman* (1949), about the failure of the American dream. Several became classics and owe part of their stature to Kazan's direction.

In the 1950s, Kazan's most interesting offerings included Williams's *Camino Real* (1953), *Cat on a Hot Tin Roof* (1955), and *Sweet Bird of Youth* (1959); Robert Anderson's *Tea and Sympathy* (1953); William Inge's *Dark at the Top of the Stairs* (1957); and Archibald MacLeish's *J. B.* (1958). These plays covered such topics as impotence, homosexuality, anti-Semitism, and the universe's injustice to man. The only commercial failure was *Camino Real*.

By the end of the decade, Kazan had grown weary of the Broadway rat race, with its financial pressures and lack of rehearsal time, and longed to do quality work in a subsidized theater. His dream was realized when he was appointed to co-run, with Robert Whitehead, the new, partly subsidized Lincoln Center Repertory Company. He staged his final three productions here, Miller's *After the Fall* (1964), Behrman's *But for Whom, Charlie?* (1964), and William Rowley and George Middleton's Elizabethan drama, *The Changeling* (1964), Kazan's only classic. His Lincoln Center experience turned out to be an artistic and bureaucratic disaster and both he and Whitehead quickly resigned. Apart from some workshop activity, Kazan—also one of America's finest film directors (*Gentleman's Agreement*, 1947; *Viva Zapata!*, 1952; *On the Waterfront*, 1954; *Splendor in the Grass*, 1961; and others)—devoted himself to movies and writing novels.

Many expressed their dissatisfaction with Kazan's regime, quarrelling with his repertoire, his acting company, and his directing. There were also mixed opinions of the large and hard-to-use stage—a combination proscenium and thrust—at Lincoln Center's Vivian Beaumont Theatre, designed under his influence.

In 1947, Kazan cofounded the Actors Studio, an environment in which professionals could work on their craft with teachers employing personalized variations of Stanislavsky's system, which, in the hands of Lee Strasberg, came to be called the Method. The Method was an internalized technique emphasizing psychological depth and spontaneous honesty, but its practitioners were often criticized for sloppy technical execution and poor speech. The plays Kazan staged and the actors he employed were frequently exemplars of the Method.

Kazan's productions were noted for their fast pace, dynamic energy, melodramatic touches, and gut-level emotionalism. They were also recognized for their probing psychological intensity and combination of acting realism with theatricalized sets and lighting. He believed in total emotional commitment. His intention was to affect the spectator by creating the impression that the action was actually happening, although Kazan's staging avoided conventional realism in favor of groupings and positions that were carefully composed for archetypal or symbolic effects. When possible, he used theatricalist devices, including direct address or the miming of imaginary props. As his adherence to the Method weakened, he leaned toward actors who could go beyond surface realism and provide larger-than-life performances.

The impressionistic sets designed for Kazan by Jo Mielziner suggested locales through skeletal structures and chiaroscuro lighting, often using scrims. For example, Williams calls for rather detailed scenery in *Cat on a Hot Tin Roof* but the Kazan-Mielziner solution was to provide little more than a large, square platform jutting into the audience at one of its corners, with only the barest minimum of props to create the impression of a bed-sitting room. Such sets were intended to express metaphorically the interior lives of the characters, especially under ever-shifting, complexly cued patterns of light. Kazan combined music and sound with staging and lighting to evoke atmospheric effects that expressed subtextual essences.

Kazan specialized in new American plays, often with socially significant or psychologically provocative themes. He only rarely did comedy and musicals. He liked plays of powerful feelings and sinewy but not obscure thought. His preparation involved examining the social milieu to see what lay behind the characters' behavior, and he often traveled to the play's locale to soak up the atmosphere. He was known for the efforts he expended in getting to know his playwrights, because he felt that such knowledge would lead to insights into the play. He saw his own role as that of a creative servant in the dramatist's service. In this capacity, he often felt it necessary to request—usually in the form of lengthy letters followed by face-to-face discussions—extensive revisions. Kazan did not make such revisions himself. If the principal changes were not made before rehearsals began, he might have refused the project. His most famous revision was the third act of *Cat on a Hot Tin Roof*, published with both versions so the disgruntled Williams could let the reader judge between his original and the one he wrote under Kazan's prodding.

Kazan kept a working diary of his thoughts, an idea he picked up from Harold Clurman. He expressed his ideas in bold statements, but he used these for his own mental refreshment and did not rely literally on them during rehearsals. Their style is fragmented and nondiscursive, and ideas do not necessarily flow coherently. Comments on theme, characters, style, and the like fill the pages. Remarks on sets, costumes, and lights are often set down as an aid to working with the designers. (Elsewhere he prepared precise groundplans, including measurements, because of his belief that designers need all the help they can get.)

Thematic concerns were his chief focus, even when commenting on technical matters. Despite this emphasis, he believed it necessary to leave the theme ambiguous rather than to make it crystal clear, as the audience would otherwise have little to ponder when the curtain fell. His words were also often about the "spine" of the play and of each character. The play's spine was a psychological or emotional kernel that tied all its parts together into a whole. Characters' spines were phrased in terms of active verbs leading to an objective.

Kazan also liked to prepare annotated promptbooks, placing his notes on the blank pages facing the script. The pages were divided into three columns, one to describe the general situation, one to write detailed analytical notes, and one to note business, with comments for the actors couched in terms of actions that reflect emotional states. Kazan's purpose was constantly to find a physical correlative to internal feelings.

Kazan distrusted auditions, except for minor roles where an actor's appearance was sometimes more important than his talent. When he wanted his coproducers or the playwright to agree to a choice he already had made, he was likely to privately prepare the actor to help make the best impression. He preferred actors he knew. When seriously considering an unfamiliar actor, he did what he could to gain some insight into the actor's character. He sought those whose inner lives were likely to bear fruit, not actors who simply looked right, and many of his casting choices were against type. In fact, the most famous performance ever inspired by Kazan, Brando's Stanley in *A Streetcar Named Desire*, was considered by many to be at odds with Williams's character, who demanded a far more brutish quality than the handsome, sensitive-looking Brando could provide. Anthony Quinn, who replaced Brando and toured in the play, under Harold Clurman's direction, was considered by some to be a more suitable choice. Kazan also liked nonstars because they are more willing to take risks than established players.

Kazan joined those who read the script—in its entirety or in part—to their casts at the first rehearsal. He read to communicate meaning but not to stress readings. When the actors read, he constantly interrupted with interpretive comments. On at least one occasion, the first rehearsal for *J. B.*, he had the author himself read; Kazan believed MacLeish could invest the play's verse with the poetic feeling he had when he wrote it.

After the first reading came several days of "at table" rehearsals, with the script being read and analyzed. Only when a solid understanding was shared did the blocking commence. Not a moment was wasted, as Kazan knew that the three weeks of rehearsal were vastly insufficient.

His preference was for keeping playwrights away, although he changed his procedure when the circumstances warranted it. Williams invariably was permitted to attend, although he once so offended Kazan by making comments to an actress that the director banned him from rehearsals thereafter.

True to his nickname, Kazan actively moved about with the actors as he blocked them based on his preplanning, which he revised when necessary and which he continued to develop. He occasionally gave broad-outlined demonstrations, allowing the actor to fill in the gaps. The script's directions were regarded as intrusive "chicken shit."

He insisted on immediate line memorization and would not stand for paraphrasing. A firm believer in external as well as internal technique, Kazan wanted the words to be spoken clearly and accurately, regardless of emotional honesty.

By week three the play was in uninterrupted run-throughs. When it was set, he disapproved of any change that he had not approved. Once it opened, he turned his back on it, leaving the job of keeping it fresh to the stage manager. He even avoided the road and London stagings of his productions.

Kazan was enthusiastic and friendly at rehearsals, with the director assuming the role of father to the company-family. He swore freely, dressed casually, and behaved unconventionally but with charm. When wrong or confused, he admitted it, believing it harmful to shield his fallibility. But he was so overflowing with ideas that he could be distressingly changeable.

The fundamental lesson drawn by Kazan from Konstantin Stanislavsky was that everything on stage had to be motivated, and that actors always had to know what their given circumstances were, what they wanted, and why they wanted it. The director must make sure each actor understands his character's objective and finds actions expressive of the need to satisfy that objective. The director turns psychology into behavior. In Kazan's terms, this can be accomplished through Stanislavsky's "method of physical actions," in which the actor concentrates on the object or action itself and not on an imaginary substitute. Kazan sought to find actions that presented the subtextual strata of the play.

He used his "Anatolian cunning" to inspire actors, to play on their fears, or to provoke their emotions to get the truest responses. Each actor represented a different problem that required a special solution. He was undogmatic, giving actors freedom when he thought they could handle it, and being autocratic where that was required. He listened to intelligent questions and arguments and rarely insisted that his was the only way.

One frequent method—except when the actors were unresponsive—was improvisation. A Kazan improvisation set up a situation related to the action of the play, with the characters playing strong objectives while unaware of those being acted by the others. It was especially important that a character not enter until fully aware of where he had come from and what he had just done. As the exercise was played, Kazan kept changing the circumstances and forcing the actors to adjust.

For all his flaws, especially his narrow range, Kazan was clearly the greatest mid-century American director. He established a style of "poetic realism" that typified the best theater of his day and that occupied the stage for many years afterward.

Further reading:

Kazan, Elia. "Look, There's the American Theatre." Interview by Richard Schechner and Theodore Hoffman. *Tulane Drama Review* 8 (Winter 1964).

———. *On What Makes a Director.* Los Angeles and New York: Directors Guild of America, 1973. (pamphlet)

———. *Elia Kazan, A Life.* New York: Alfred A. Knopf, 1988.

Stevens, Virginia. "Elia Kazan, Actor and Director of Stage and Screen." *Theatre Arts* 31 (December 1947).

Also: Johnson, *Directing Methods;* Jones, *Great Directors at Work;* Leiter, *From Belasco to Brook.*

THEODORE KOMISARJEVSKY (1882–1954)

THEODORE KOMISARJEVSKY was born in Venice, Italy, the son of a princess and a Russian opera singer. He studied at the School of Architecture at St. Petersburg University while taking summer classes in Germany. In 1907, he worked for his actress-manager sister, Vera Komisarjevskaya, overseeing her scenery before taking over as director when Vsevolod Meyerhold was fired. He next ran a Moscow theater school until 1919.

Komisarjevsky gained renown as a theatricalist genius while serving as resident director at the Gay Theater (1909–1910); the Moscow Nezlobin Dramatic Theater (1910–1913); the Imperial theaters, the Maly and the Bolshoi Opera (1913–1914); the expansive Private Moscow Opera House (1913–1917); the intimate Vera Komisarjevskaya Memorial Theater (1914–1918); and the Sovietized Bolshoi Opera and Ballet (1918). Among his finest productions was Carlo Gozzi's *Turandot* (1912), staged in a seemingly improvisatory commedia style that predated by a decade Evgeny Vakhtangov's better-known revival. He could also give an unconventional antirealistic mounting to a realistic play like Alexander Ostrovsky's *Not a Sixpence and Suddenly a Farthing* (1910).

Komisarjevsky was recognized as a master designer of sets, lights, and costumes. He also possessed considerable architectural and musical skills. His very busy schedule during the revolutionary period led to a breakdown in 1919, and he moved to England. He lived there until 1939, when he moved to New York and opened an acting school. During these years, he directed mainly in England, but—a polyglot—also staged plays, ballets, and operas in France, Germany, Scotland, Austria, America, and Italy. Trained in Russia's highly subsidized theater, and more concerned with art than money, he was often at loggerheads with the philistinism of the commercial theater. Although he staged West End plays, he was also happy directing amateurs and noncommercial enterprises, which saw some of his most acclaimed productions.

Komisarjevsky's British career began with a successful West End revival of Nikolai Gogol's *The Government Inspector* (1920), the first of many Russian plays he would direct in the West. Maurice Maeterlinck's *Sister Beatrice* (1920) was done at a curtainless concert hall that he decorated to give the unified impression of a church. In 1921–1922, working under severe budgetary limitations, he did four plays for the Stage Society, including *Uncle Vanya* (1921), London's most successful Anton Chekhov production yet, and the English premiere of Luigi Pirandello's *Six Characters in Search of an Author* (1922).

With Lee Simonson collaborating on the designs, Komisarjevsky directed three plays for New York's Theater Guild in 1922–1923, including Paul Claudel's *The Tidings Brought to Mary* (1922) and Henrik Ibsen's *Peer Gynt* (1923), given an expressionistic staging and using Edvard Grieg's music. Claudel's mystical play benefitted from powerful yet surprisingly simple sets and lighting. From New York the director went to Paris where, despite an abortive attempt to found his own theater, he offered a 1923–1924 season at the Théâtre des Champs-Elysées.

In London he worked for the Stage Society and on the West End before being employed to direct the 1925–1926 season at the small, poorly equipped Barnes in Hammersmith, where he enjoyed a company of excellent young actors, most notably John Gielgud, on whose career he had a powerful influence. Komisarjevsky—who designed as well—directed *The Government Inspector* again, Leonid Andreyev's *Katarina*, and four Chekhov plays (*Ivanov*, *Uncle Vanya*, *The Three Sisters*, and *The Cherry Orchard*). His work—particularly with *The Three Sisters*—was so distinguished that it made the season at the out-of-the-way venue one of the British theater's highlights in the twenties. Norman Marshall, admiring the actors' inner reality, recalls: "There were no obvious showy effects but a wonderful sense of atmosphere which was due to Komisarjevsky's ability to make his actors absorb not only the characteristics of their own part but also the mood and background of the play." Gielgud observed that Komisarjevsky was the first to teach him how to avoid acting for outside effects while working "from within to present a character." In Chekhov, he learned that one acts with "the fourth wall down," and therefore focuses completely on the internal action without cognizance of the audience.

Komisarjevsky gave *The Three Sisters* a romantic interpretation set in the 1880s. Controversially, he eliminated mention of Tusenbach's (Gielgud) homeliness and made him a handsome juvenile, presumably to provide a love interest. Gielgud remembers:

> The whole setting . . . , a permanent arrangement of flats, brilliantly rearranged for each of the four acts, evoked a simple yet convincing atmosphere of different times of year, and also managed to convey, on the very shallow stage, a remarkable effect of depth, and of different rooms opening one out of another into a garden.

From 1926 to 1937 Komisarjevsky, apart from his international work, directed three dozen English productions, including six at Stratford-upon-Avon. Most of his assignments were freelance, his 1927 attempt at founding his own theater at the Royal Court failing after two productions. He also organized a private theater club at the Kingsway in 1932 to provide plays banned by the censor, but again gave only two productions, one of them starring Peggy Ashcroft, whom he married. His biggest hit was an all-star revival of his own translation of Chekhov's *The Sea Gull* (1936), with Gielgud as Trigorin, Ashcroft as Nina, and Edith Evans as Arkadina. With a lavish production completely designed by Komisarjevsky, *The Sea Gull* demonstrated a harmonious interpretation that brought great acting and direction together in the service of Chekhov's masterpiece. Gielgud was again the medium of a quirky innovation, in that Trigorin was viewed not as a shabbily dressed writer but as a dashingly garbed roué.

Komisarjevsky's eccentric West End production of Shakespeare's *Antony and Cleopatra* (1936) had a laughably incomprehensible Queen of the Nile in Russian actress Eugenie Leontovich. Apart from his uninspired *The Taming of the Shrew* (1939), Komisarjevsky—the theater's first guest director in its history—provided a series of unusual and highly provocative Stratford productions from 1932 to 1939. These included *The Merchant of Venice* (1932), *Macbeth* (1933), *The Merry Wives of Windsor* (1935), *King Lear* (1936), and *The Comedy of Errors* (1938), all provided with ahead-of-their-times designs that startled Stratford regulars. His sets made remarkable use of Stratford's technical equipment, especially a pair of sliding stages. Even the week-long rehearsal limits provided proved no obstacle. He gave the actors considerable interpretive freedom so that he could attend to the detailed choreographic and orchestrational aspects of his job.

Hired as a *machine de guerre*, he presented tradition-smashing, emphatically influential stagings that were attacked by conservatives, but considered revolutionary by others. Because he believed it was his function to express what he thought to be the author's ideas, Komisarjevsky felt it appropriate to employ textual adaptation, even redistributing certain lines.

As an example of his radical concepts, which always were arrived at with a view to reflecting up-to-date attitudes, he viewed Shylock, not as the sympathetic, wronged Jew of sentimental tradition, but as a vengeful villain. Komisarjevsky's fondness for commedia dominated the visual approach (as it did in several of his other Shakespearean comedies), and Launcelot was played like Harlequin. Morocco was a minstrel-show blackamoor, and Portia wore spectacles and a beard during the trial.

Komisarjevsky's most controversial mounting was an expressionistic *Macbeth*, its action backed by his own curving staircases and aluminum scroll-like screens. He abandoned the supernatural motif and told of Macbeth's descent into madness (Lady Macbeth's role was sharply trimmed). The witches were ragged, all-too-human fortune-tellers, busily stripping dead bodies on the battlefield. The cauldron scene was Macbeth's nightmare and Banquo's ghost was Macbeth's enlarged shadow. Germanic-looking helmets were worn by the soldiers along with military gear from other eras. (The overall effect, though, was of World War I.)

The Merry Wives resembled a Viennese operetta, and the acclaimed *Lear* abandoned conventional trappings and was backed by stark steps and platforms against a sky drop. Combined with a complex, unusually evocative lighting scheme, it conjured up all the locales. Rhythmic tensions contrasted one scene with another. Apart from selected pieces of furniture, the stage remained bare.

Komisarjevsky emigrated to America in 1937. He taught, coauthored and directed two Broadway flops, and worked in opera. His final theater assignment was the unsuccessful version of Rodney Ackland's hit London adaptation of Dostoyevsky's *Crime and Punishment* (1947), with Gielgud as Raskolnikoff. Komisarjevsky had grown increasingly embittered and expressed his distaste for the adaptation and decor, which he was not permitted to redo.

A noted theorist, he advocated "internal eclecticism," in which he felt it appropriate to mingle periods in the same work, regardless of anachronisms, provided the choices (most notable in costuming) expressed some fundamental point. "Internal eclecticism" was markedly apparent in Komisarjevsky's period revivals, especially Shakespeare. Elizabethan ruffs were likely to sit atop Victorian silhouettes. Costuming was used to comment on the action, even through topical referents. Theatrical styles also could be mixed, so that Ibsen's *Peer Gynt* could have sets ranging from realism to cubism. Despite the dangers, he often succeeded in unifying the mixed ingredients. The production was deemed its own excuse, and there was no need to satisfy pedantic concerns.

Komisarjevsky viewed theater as a synthetic art in which dance, music, and drama were mutually supportive and should be conjoined in a complete representation. His ideal actor was multitalented; he had more access to such actors in Russia, which made his early work more theatrical than in his émigré years. His musicianship aided him immensely, and the rhythmic bases of performance (established as much in the lighting and other external means as in the acting) and the utilization of extensive accompaniment remained fundamental to his technique. As he directed, he frequently called out the word "pause" ("powse," he pronounced it), as he imposed a rhythm on the actors. Such pauses would be rigorously rehearsed as he orchestrated the staging. But he sometimes inspired the actors to sense this rhythm for themselves. According to Gielgud, when Komisarjevsky directed Chekhov at the Barnes,

> He allowed the actors to feel instinctively that the pauses and business spring naturally out of the dialogue and processes of the action. The result is a closely patterned rhythm flowing backwards and forwards between the characters covering any weakness in individual performances, and shifting the focus of attention continually without breaking the illusion of continuous life and movement. . . .

Komisarjevsky placed great emphasis on the visual side, and carefully preplanned all moves. Gielgud was surprised by the detailed chalk patterns drawn by the director on the floor prior to the cast's moving to the tiny Barnes stage. When they reached the stage and put the blocking into practice, they realized how significant this meticulous planning was for the proper effect. His visual acuity led him to design multileveled sets, thereby permitting great variety in groupings as well as offering many opportunities for his extraordinarily expressive use of light.

When time allowed, Komisarjevsky's actors sat around a table reading the script for days before blocking commenced. Regardless of his preblocking,

he rarely imposed readings and gestures, preferring to allow the actor to devise his own interpretation, which he would then help perfect. So inconspicuous was his method that some actors felt he wasn't directing them at all. When he did demonstrate, vocally or physically, he did it to stimulate the actor, not to induce a copy. Most actors liked Komisarjevsky (fondly called "Komis") because of his respect for their inner workings and his ability to suggest in a few, perfectly chosen words how they might improve their performances. However, if Komisarjevsky disliked an actor, he could be cold and nasty, offering little help and even undermining his performances by cuts or weak stage positions.

Many of the greatest actors first found success in plays directed by Theodore Komisarjevsky, an amazingly versatile director. Any one of his abilities was sufficient for a successful career. He was one of a rare breed breaking from the traditions of realistic staging and bringing to the English stage the best ideas in formalistic theater.

Further reading:

Komisarjevsky, Theodore. *Myself and the Theatre.* New York: E. P. Dutton, 1930.

————, and Lee Simonson. *Settings and Costumes on the Modern Stage.* London: The Studio Limited, 1933.

Also: Beauman, *Royal Shakespeare Company;* Gielgud, *Early Stages;* Gielgud, *Stage Directions;* Gielgud, *An Actor and His Time;* Marshall, *The Producer and the Play;* Sayler, *Russian Theatre;* Slonim, *Russian Theater.*

MARK LAMOS (1946–   )

MARK LAMOS was born and raised in Chicago. He entered Northwestern University intent on a career as a concert violinist but switched midway to theater. During the seventies, the handsome Lamos enjoyed a busy acting career in regional theaters as well as on Broadway. He later sometimes acted in plays he staged.

His first directing was in 1976, at Minneapolis's Guthrie II, where he staged Jerome Kilty's adaptation of the George Bernard Shaw-Mrs. Patrick Campbell letters, *Dear Liar,* and Athol Fugard's *Hello and Goodbye;* this was followed by Shaw's *Too True to Be Good* (1977) and Shakespeare's *Hamlet* (1977) at San Diego's Old Globe. He staged plays in 1978

and 1979 for the Arizona Theatre Company and Connecticut's Hartford Stage Company before becoming Michael Langham's associate at the California Shakespeare Festival in Visalia, California (1979). Circumstances led to Lamos's assuming Langham's job and to critically lauded stagings of *Romeo and Juliet* and *The Taming of the Shrew.* He did the *Shrew* as a sexual battle between a 1934 Paduan woman and Fascist machismo.

From 1979 to 1980, Lamos headed the Arizona Theatre Company, staging three plays, including *Twelfth Night,* before returning to Visalia to mount *Hamlet* (1980) and *A Midsummer Night's Dream* (1980). *Shakespeare Quarterly* commented that each

Mark Lamos (r) directing Janet Zarish and Bradley Whitford in A Midsummer Night's Dream. *(1988)* (Photo: Hartford Stage/T. Charles Erickson)

theater, where he remains today. He developed here one of the nation's most respected companies. Despite a need for frugality, "his most impressive work has been plays on an epic scale . . . ," wrote Mel Gussow. Belt-tightening is antithetical to his aesthetic values, but it has resulted in a method praised for an imaginative spareness that he attributes to a sort of "erase" effect. At one point he became disillusioned with the thrust's limitations, but, he told Gerard Raymond, an outside job in a proscenium house made him realize "how distant and separate and *anti-sculptural* the proscenium was"; he returned to Hartford recharged about its space.

Over the years, he evolved seasons that mingled the challenging with the widely popular. And he has prevented the Hartford from becoming a Broadway tryout house, although several works—mainly by others—did move on to commercial productions. He appreciates being able to call all the shots and to build up a "body of work," and says he would not be happy freelancing.

By 1992, doing approximately three works a year, he had directed approximately 30 plays at Hartford; a partly recast version of one, Timberlake Wertenbaker's *Our Country's Good* (1990), provided him with his Tony-nominated Broadway debut (1991). He guest-directed operas and plays elsewhere, the latter at such venues as the Shakespeare Festival in Stratford, Ontario (1984), California's La Jolla Playhouse, and New York's Lincoln Center (*Measure for Measure*, 1988), as well as in Sweden (1986) and the USSR (Eugene O'Neill's *Desire Under the Elms*, 1988), where he was the first American invited to direct a play with Russians.

His Hartford Shakespeare repertory includes *Cymbeline* (1981), *Antony and Cleopatra* (1981), *As You Like It* (1983), *The Tempest* (1985), *Twelfth Night* (1985), *Pericles* (1987), *Hamlet* (1987), *Julius Caesar* (1991), and *The Merchant of Venice* (1993). He has presented innovative as well as conservative interpretations of antique and modern classics such as George Farquhar's *The Beaux' Strategm* (1980); Arthur Schnitzler's *Undiscovered Country* (1981) and *Anatol* (starring Lamos; 1984); Molière's *The Misanthrope* (1983), *The School for Wives* (1987), *The Miser* (1990), and *Tartuffe* (1992); Anton Chekhov's *The Three Sisters* (1984); Henrik Ibsen's *Hedda Gabler* (1988), *Peer Gynt* (1990), and *The Master Builder* (1991); Pierre Corneille's *The Illusion* (1989); Oscar Wilde's *The Importance of Being Earnest* (starring Lamos, 1989); and the ambitious, nine-play, seven-hour, 27-actor John Barton-Kenneth Cavander con-

was "informed by an intelligent, carefully-conceived concept, [and], to a greater degree than is usual for most directors, [he] involved himself actively in every aspect of production."

Lamos's fondness for shifting Shakespeare's periods was seen in *Hamlet*'s being set in a fin de siècle Hapsburg background, suggesting the era's opulence and decadence. Hamlet's mind had to examine every side of a question before acting. "Metamorphosis" was the ruling idea of the *Dream*, played before a giant moon that showed the fairies in silhouette. Most of the fairies were nonhuman, the minor ones made amorphous and insectlike by stockings over their faces. They sometimes carried the stretched-out Oberon and Titania to make them fly.

Lamos became artistic director of the Hartford Stage Company, home of a 489-seat, thrust-stage

Wertenbaker's Our Country's Good. *Directed by Mark Lamos. (1990)*   (Photo: Martha Swope)

flation of ancient tragedy, *The Greeks* (codirected with Mary B. Robinson, 1982). Among other revivals have been Ben Hecht's *The Great Magoo* (1982) and Jean-Paul Sartre's *Kean* (1981).

Lamos told Raymond, "I never feel as *exercised* by a new play, as I do by a classic. I don't know why, but I don't feel quite so spiritually agonized." Still, his new-play record is admirable and includes several American and world premieres. Among them are Jaston Williams, Joe Sears, and Ed Howard's *Greater Tuna* (codirected with Howard in 1982); Christopher Hampton's adaptation of George Steiner's *The Portage to San Christobal of AH* (1983); Peter Nichols's *Passion Play* (1985); Kevin Heelan's *Distant Fires* (1986); Eric Overmyer's *On the Verge or the Geography of Dreaming* (1986); Constance Congdon's version of Mark Twain and Charles Warner's *The Gilded Age* (1986); Allan Havis's *Morocco* (1987);

Our Country's Good (1990); and Simon Gray's *Hidden Laughter* (1992). Many are nonrealistic and require theatrical flourishes. Lamos prefers to challenge rather than to coddle audiences, although his choices can occasionally stir a hornet's nest, as when he staged *The Portage*, which humanizes Hitler.

Although Lamos has added dazzlingly original touches to most of his classic conceptualizations, and has given straightforward ones as well, he is best known for his interpretations of Shakespeare's comedies and romances. To date, the only major tragedy he has done is *Hamlet* and the only histories he has done are two Roman ones. Most productions blend periods and styles to create an ambiguous, anachronistic mix. Lamos wishes audiences would appreciate that Shakespeare's ambiguity is part of his greatness, and would not require having everything painstakingly clarified.

His productions have mostly been set by John Conklin or Michael Yeargan, lighted by Pat Collins, costumed by Dunya Ramicova, and set to music by Mel Marvin. (Fond of the collaborative process, he loves to work consistently with the same artists.) The togaed *Julius Caesar* and his pre-Hartford work aside, Lamos likes environments that he does not fully understand, spaces "in which the play can discover itself," as he informed Kim Powers.

His research is assisted by a dramaturge who gathers and annotates articles and reviews (of past productions), which Lamos studies along with pictorial and musical sources. In fact, the *Times* reviewer covering his recent *Merchant of Venice* pointed out that the production "often seems to be the work of a director who has studiously read a lot of scholarly criticism of the play and assembled the elements that would be most palatable to a contemporary audience." Although not overtly political, he enjoys political plays. He staged *Antony and Cleopatra* not to emphasize the romantic leads but to reveal them as irrelevant in the new world order. He chose to do *Julius Caesar* immediately after the assassination of Romanian leader Ceaucescu; the staging underscored the gruesome contrast between political talk and bloody revolution. His frequent use of multiethnic casts sometimes bears a political hue; in *Our Country's Good*, black actors played both nonwhites and bigoted whites.

Lamos's successful *Cymbeline* was viewed, said the *New York Post*, as "a fairy story for adults of the most exquisite sensibility," stressing its "mythic and poetic elements." Set in "a brilliant abstraction suggesting a pastoral world," it resulted in "a pure flight of fancy . . . that sees the play as a metaphor for divine justice." Mary Layne, Lamos's most regular leading lady, was a memorable Imogen. His *Measure for Measure*—evoking claustrophobia via a minimalist set backed by a wall bearing lines of Bible-quoting graffiti—turned the problem play into a modern-dress love story about Duke Vincentio and Isabella.

As You Like It was set in a painterly world in which pastoral values had transformational powers over the city-bred characters. "The Forest of Arden," wrote the *New York Times*, "moves the play into a field of French Impressionism, an autumnal environment where men wear shapely straw hats while they picnic on the grass." *Hamlet* had costumes ranging "from European court garb to contemporary casual," wrote the *New York Daily News*.

The Tempest viewed the island as a laboratory for social experimentation; when Prospero eventually abjures his magic, "one is left with an image not of fulfillment but of forbearance. He has made his treaty with the real world and has decided to terminate a noble experiment," reported the *Times*. After the flying Ariel was given his freedom, his wings formed the final stage picture. In the *Dream*, one of Lamos's most iconoclastic notions was to contrast the idlike dream-cosmos of the forest with a "Pyramus and Thisbe" scene enacted in a soberly conventional manner behind a proscenium arch and footlights; this suggested, said the *Times*, "that art, like life, often fails to match the truer, uninhibited passions lurking beneath its surface."

The festive modern dress world of *Twelfth Night*, conceived to suggest the end of youthful innocence, came alive amidst a 1930s, sophisticated, confetti-adorned party accompanied by Porter and Gershwin tunes. *Pericles* (titled *The Painful Adventures of Pericles, Prince of Tyre* after an Elizabethan novel) was set in a surrealistic, Magritte-inspired universe inhabited by men in tails and bowlers, a rocking chair floating over a cloud-painted floor, and the broken head of a goddess's statue brooding over the action. The *Times* wrote that Lamos underlined his conception of the play as a dream in which sudden metamorphoses transpire by having "various fathers, mothers and daughters . . . played by the same quick-changing actors. This family motif is carried out even in the brothel scene, where the pander and the bawd are made to seem like a working-class domestic couple."

Budget constraints often force Lamos to create economical but potently ambient conceptions, as when *Undiscovered Country*, staged previously in a lavish British version, was given a highly simplified yet expertly panoramic realization by eliminating extraneous detail (including the action-impeding *entr'acts*, material performed between the acts). According to the *Times*, *The Greeks* contained an image of "the captive Trojan women huddled behind barbed wire awaiting slavery; the chorus lurking in deep shade . . . like watchful figures in a Kazantzakis novel; a bright white beam of light leaping out of an open door and impaling an act of matricide."

Many consider the five-hour *Peer Gynt* his crowning non-Shakespearean glory. Richard Thomas (a frequent Lamos star) remained buoyantly youthful through Peer's half-century of experiences, making no attempt to age physically. In an example of Lamos's benefitting from frugality, Peer's childhood props, seen at the beginning, figured symbolically throughout his many vicissitudes; thus, Asa died in Peer's crib. Peer was thus, states Robert Brustein, "a perpetual adolescent imprisoned in an eternal nursery." To suggest the many locales, different colored clothes were employed (yellow silk equalled the desert, a black oilcloth the storm at sea). The king of the snout-nosed trolls, asserts Brustein, was "a sweating, slavering, pork-bellied Stanley Kowalski with horns—who garrots Peer with his tail, farts over his prone body, and forces him to drink his daughter's urine."

Lamos stages a play based on what he wants the audience to feel, combining his preconceptions with rehearsal discoveries. His method changes from play to play. He is now less "rigid" with actors than formerly; after acting again himself, he began to sympathize more with the actor's problems.

Some directors, he feels, let the actors flounder too long before making clear their objectives. He seeks results sooner than others but strives to let the actor believe the discoveries are theirs so that they can experience them organically. Although he wants rehearsals to be fun and to allow everyone to feel free to fail, Lamos has a reputation for tantrums. Thomas told John Istel, "Mark screams and carries on but he's never vicious or personal." An instinctive director who appreciates the surprises revealed by rehearsal, he may get carried away, demonstrate, and give line readings. Sometimes he inspires actors with musical metaphors or has them listen to carefully selected music. Disciplined actors who think for themselves, come well prepared, provide ideas, and ask penetrating questions are warmly welcomed.

Lamos believes Americans are better suited to playing Shakespeare than the British, not only because the former are more willing to expose themselves emotionally, but because they do not have the baggage of a rich tradition and can approach the roles with greater openness. Having been trained by Langham and Charlotte Lee, he pays great attention to the verse and—not always successfully—cautions actors to respect the language's literary values. He tries to get the Shakespearean actor to trust the words, to let them do the work, and to make them personal. Nevertheless, he is likely to cut or change obscure words, rewrite lines, or rearrange scenes to clarify language and action.

Lamos told Arthur Bartow that it is the artist's "social responsibility" to reveal "Dreams. Coherencies." "He has an ethical responsibility to organize responses to the current world, feelings and visions through artifice—to attest to mysteries, hear oracles, present possibilities, unearth treasures."

Further reading:

Gussow, Mel. "Director Uses Hartford Stage as a Blank Canvas." *New York Times,* June 23, 1985.

Istel, John. "Shakespeare U.S.A." *Village Voice,* March 14, 1989.

Lamos, Mark. "Mark Lamos." Interview by Kim Powers. *Theatre* 15 (Spring 1984).

Raymond, Gerard. "Mark Lamos Conquers the Classics." *TheaterWeek,* December 10–16, 1986.

Also: Bartow, *Director's Voice;* Brustein, *Reimagining American Theatre.*

ELIZABETH LECOMPTE (1944–   )

ELIZABETH ALICE LECOMPTE, daughter of an engineer, was born in New Jersey, majored in art at Skidmore College, and acted Off Off-Broadway. In 1970, she and Spalding Gray joined the Performance Group (PG), an avant-garde, Soho-district collective situated in the Performing Garage on Wooster Street. The company was headed by Richard Schechner, guru of communally created, environmental theater. LeCompte assisted Schechner on *Commune* (1971) and acted in it. Several plays later, she abandoned acting.

In 1975, she and Gray formed what was later called the Wooster Group (WG), to create improvisationally developed pieces inspired by his autobio-

graphical reminiscences. These enigmatic works made great demands on audiences. Some considered the WG elitist because the company resisted interpretation. LeCompte focused on structuring Gray's experiences through space and form without worrying about meaning.

LeCompte and Gray composed and directed *Sakonnet Point* (1975), a largely nonverbal, hour-long, dimly lit, dreamlike series of activities evocative of Gray's boyhood summers in Maine; any thematic coherence was presumably accidental. Gray—in bathing suit and hiking shoes—appeared with three actresses and a boy. Numerous nonlinearly related aural and visual images—many maternal—were revealed. "Characters" were replaced by "energies," although the performers' personal qualities were exploited.

LeCompte appreciates each actor's unique style and needs: "I use their work in terms of the frame/context of the piece, which I set," she informed Leonora Champagne. Some refer to the "defictionalization" of WG acting, in which the self is more theatricalized than the "character."

Rehearsals employed activity-oriented improvisations (walking in a pattern, whittling, etc.) founded on free associations sparked by objects introduced by Gray, who considered the work as abstract dance. He promoted the exercises and LeCompte noted the results in a book, choosing and refining what pleased her. LeCompte thinks of herself as a painter, choreographer, or architect who makes what she interprets; her sets and costumes privilege images over text and narrative expression.

Sakonnet Point became part of an autobiographical trilogy containing *Rumstick Road* (1977) and *Nayatt School* (1978). The entire trilogy, *Three Places in Rhode Island,* was performed as a unit in 1978. In 1980, *Point Judith,* an epilogue, was added. The quartet established the WG as America's leading experimental collective. They later toured nationally and internationally.

Rumstick Road, LeCompte's first true collage, was a confessional exercise concerned with Gray's coming to terms with the 1967 suicide of his mother. The piece was "part dream, part nonliteral imagery, and part factual documentary," wrote LeCompte, with each element intermingling with the others so that the factual became indistinguishable from the imaginary. Documentary material was present in slides, letters, and tape recordings around which improvisationally created material was added. Le Compte's preoccupations were, typically, with physical and emotional resonances, not intellectual ones. The production became as much about the group's individuals as about Gray.

In keeping with the WG's evolving style, actions frequently were not literally comprehensible although their ironic tone was implicit. Many critical explanations of the WG's pieces have been published, but the group intends its works to assume whatever associations spectators project onto them.

The use of taped material became a trademark, as did a tendency to raise questions of ethics. For example, controversy surrounded two taped conversations—one of them taken from a phone call with Gray's mother's psychiatrist (whose name was changed). He had not known he was being recorded and had not given permission to use the call. The doctor was heard on tape; Gray spoke his own words live (recreating his original behavior during the call), enabling it to seem as if the call was actually occurring during the show.

Props, actions, colors, and scenic elements from earlier work were incorporated, but in new and unusual configurations. "I circle around ideas," she told Champagne, "rotate the viewpoint. I see what I do as creating a body of work, a continuum." *Rumstick*'s set was a triptych consisting of two rooms at either side depicted in forced perspective and with an upstage picture window in one; they were separated at center by a control booth area from which lights and sound were operated in view of the audience. An examination table was in front of the control booth.

Nayatt School, wrote Theodore Shank, "grew out of Gray's interest in social themes relating to madness, anarchy, and the loss of innocence." Performed by the WG's core actors (Willem Dafoe, Ron Vawter, Libby Howes, and Gray) and four children, it connected images from Gray's life with scenes from T. S. Eliot's *The Cocktail Party,* becoming the first of the WG's ongoing deconstructions of an established text placed within the framework of personal preoccupations. Gray saw in the martyred Celia Coplestone similarities to his mother.

The audience sat in steep bleachers, at the base of which was a long table from which Gray spoke about Eliot's play and played moments from the Alec Guinness recording of it. Scenic elements included a roofless room from *Rumstick Road,* placed upright, seen in reverse perspective, and viewed from above and through a window facing the audience. The room revealed scenes involving a dentist, a doctor performing a breast exam, and a chicken heart growing uncontrollably. Another segment involved a cocktail party acted by the children, dressed as grownups. At the end, madness exploded as the adults partly disrobed and destroyed the records in an outburst of sexual frenzy.

Point Judith, written by Jim Strahs after observing improvisations, was built around an iconoclastic approach to Eugene O'Neill's *Long Day's Journey into Night,* made to intersect with Gray's biography. A sequence on an oil rig, exploring ugly machismo attitudes, was set against a film about a group of nuns. Film, usually created by Ken Kobland, became a vital WG feature. Shank notes:

A house, which can be identified with the earlier plays, floats above the floor. Its inhabitants are engaged in repetitive actions of chaotic madness. There is no dialogue . . . , but many surreal visual images, including film projections, which create a metaphor for the destruction of the American family.

The first piece created after Gray left for an outside career was *Route 1 & 9 (The Last Act)* (1981), dealing with thoughts of death as revealed through a deconstruction of Thornton Wilder's *Our Town,* which the WG believes treats the subject sentimentally. Part one included a video on four suspended monitors replicating an old film in which a professor delivers a lifeless lecture on Wilder's humanism. Part two contrasted with the inhibitions of Wilder's world by showing a raucous, scatological Pigmeat Markham sketch about a party, performed by the white cast in blackface with stereotyped black accents/behavior and—with amplification allowing both parties to be heard—actual phone calls for deliveries of fried chicken; simultaneously, a video send-up of soap-opera acting in *Our Town* was shown. Part three revealed *Our Town*'s cemetery scene in video closeup as the blacks partied and danced anarchically. In part four, as the actors sat about quietly, video images of a van leaving New York were seen simultaneously with a video of two actors copulating. The production forced us, said *Other Stages,* "to look at our own attitudes towards life's essence and values." The Markham bit led to charges of racism and the cutting of the troupe's NEA grant; defenders insisted on the irony intended in the caricatures and Le Compte called the blackface a distancing technique.

Questioned about her use of technological mediation, LeCompte told Roger Copeland, "I'm excited about the amount of information coming in from various media and I want my work . . . to reflect and make use of that data. . . . I love and honor the old realist tradition, but I also subvert it." She thinks the theater must use any means available to tell a story, regardless of those who consider high-tech devices as "cheating."

A second trilogy evolved, *The Road to Immortality,* comprising *Route 1 & 9, L.S.D.: Just the High Points* (1984), and *Frank Dell's The Temptation of Saint Antony* (1987). Gray returned for the briefly shown *North Atlantic* (1984), set on a naval carrier, dealing with sexual divisiveness in the military, and conceived as part of *L.S.D* before being made a separate piece.

The iconoclastic *L.S.D* underwent various manifestations, largely because it attempted to turn to its own account Arthur Miller's *The Crucible,* which comments on the anticommunist hearings of the

1950s via a story about colonial witchcraft trials. The four-part work, investigating images of religious rapture, madness, and repression, originally placed a 50-minute version of Miller's play within a House Un-American Activities-like hearing (complete with long table, bright spotlight, audio-video equipment, and microphones), with the females dressed in period clothes—Tituba also wore blackface—and the male inquisitors in business suits. There was little realism and some speeches were spoken at an unintelligible rate. Interlocking with *The Crucible* were scenes connecting contemporary conservativism with the drug culture of the fifties and sixties as led by Timothy Leary; the words of Leary's onetime babysitter framed the action. Among the distinctive segments was a precise reenactment—based on a study of videotapes—of a *Crucible* rehearsal done while stoned on acid. Among other notable features was a scene showing Leary being confronted by a man crippled by a drug user; meanwhile, a tacky Latin dance act in Miami was performed with an actress straddling a seated male actor whose stamping, sneakered feet—projecting through her skirts—were multiplied by six sneakers manipulated at her sides by two bare-chested men in a trough.

Miller fought to close the work, despite its criticism of thought control. When a drastic reduction of his writing failed to satisfy him, *L.S.D.* was cancelled. A version called (. . . *Just the High Points* . . .) arrived as part two of *The Road to Immortality* in 1987. *The Crucible* was replaced by a related text, *The Hearing,* by Michael Kirby.

Frank Dell's The Temptation of Saint Antony, which employed some ideas contributed by Peter Sellars, who was involved in the early stages, went through four incarnations. Although its narrative was clearer than earlier WG works, it pushed the envelope with its use of company nudity (in a video originated on a cable TV show) within a structure collating such things as the decadent eroticism in *The Temptation of Saint Antony,* Gustave Flaubert's treatment of a fourth-century Egyptian saint's desert visions; a plot derived from Ingmar Bergman's film *The Magician;* the life of comic Lenny Bruce, likened to Flaubert's martyr; 19th-century French puppet shows; and Geraldine Cummins's 1932 book about the afterlife, *The Road to Immortality.*

Various familiar devices were employed in this work concerning the rehearsal of a magic show in a fleabag hotel room by a fugitive troupe of mediocre magicians—who must prove that they are not mountebanks—led by the dope-zonked Frank Dell (a name once used by Bruce). The *Village Voice* noted the production's theatricalism: "Walls rise and descend, doors with actors strapped to them fly dangerously open and slam shut. There are also trashy costumes, wigs, beards, sensational lighting . . . ," and music drawn from Art Tatum, Brahms, Civil War ballads, and so on.

"Lust and death—they are the themes I come back to again and again," LeCompte informed Stephen Holden. "Clarity doesn't suit my esthetic temperament. I seem to go from mess to mess." A *Village Voice* critic noted the self-referential focus on "a theatre troupe on the lam performing mystery plays about temptation."

The group turned in 1991 to Chekhov for *Brace Up!*, an outgrowth of *The Three Sisters*, a play Le-Compte had never seen. It utilized a mike-holding, vaudeville MC to introduce the characters, comment on the action, shift its pace, answer a phone, and so on. The disillusioned young Irina was played dispassionately—with a touching effect—by an elderly actress. Contemporary allusions were tossed in. In addition, writes Charles Marowitz, it used "video images, snippets of Japanese action films, American commercials, and close-ups of 'characters' interacting with live action."

LeCompte spends lengthy periods, often years, in creation, painstakingly constructing text and staging communally with her actors, concentrating mainly on the actions performed. Casting is often not completed until late in the process. Although she reads and ruminates extensively, she is unable to preplan her staging; she works by trial and error, watching numerous approaches to each problem before making her decisions. The actors view rehearsal tapes to enhance their sense of the process. Blockages are often solved by returning to rejected material or performing the opposite of the matter in question. Despite her commitment to improvisation, she will, when necessary, impose an idea authoritatively. Productions are shown as works-in-progress to gauge audience reactions; this often leads to nightly changes.

LeCompte's nonimitative, dialectically composed, collectively created, postmodernist mosaics challenge traditional conceptions of theater. She combines the deconstruction of pirated dramas and nondramatic texts, autobiography, blackface, nudity, pornography, music, films, recordings, electronic media, and dance to make politically aggressive but ambiguous, nondogmatic statements about modern culture. In early 1993, she was working on a version of Eugene O'Neill's *The Emperor Jones*, which was shown in New York as a work-in-progress under that name. After presenting the work under its new title, *Fish Story/diverse parts*, at festivals and theaters in Denmark, Stockholm, and Frankfurt, the company was preparing to open it in New York in December, following which tours to Hong Kong and Berlin were scheduled. The advertising brochure said part I, with Dafoe and Kate Valk, was based on *The Emperor Jones*; part II "is the flash forward of *Brace Up!* Composed of 5 'dances,' it features the dramatic conclusion of Chekhov's *Three Sisters.*" Audiences await the aesthetic, social, and ethical explosions it is likely to set off.

Further reading:

Champagne, Leonora. "Always Starting New: Elizabeth LeCompte." *The Drama Review* 3 (Fall 1981).

Copeland, Roger. "Avant-Garde Stage: From Primal Dreams to Split Images." *New York Times*, January 11, 1987.

Holden, Stephen. "Wooster Group on Love, Lust and Lenny Bruce in *St. Antony.*" *New York Times*, April 3, 1987.

LeCompte, Elizabeth. "The Making of a Trilogy: an Introduction." *Performing Arts Journal* 3 (Fall 1978).

Marowitz, Charles. "Letter from Minneapolis." *TheaterWeek*, May 27–June 2, 1991.

Savran, David. *Breaking the Rules: The Wooster Group.* New York: Theatre Communications Group, 1986.

Also: Cole, *Directors in Rehearsal*; Greene in King, *Contemporary American Theatre*; Shank, *American Alternative Theatre.*

EVA LE GALLIENNE (1899–1991)

EVA LE GALLIENNE was born in London. Her father, a well-known writer, and her mother, a Danish journalist, divorced and she was raised by the latter, receiving a cultivated education in Paris and London. In 1914, Le Gallienne made her prof-essional acting debut in London. She studied at Herbert Beerbohm Tree's Academy for Actors, but left to try her luck in America, where she was a tremendous success in Ferenc Molnár's *Liliom* (1921).

Le Gallienne was preparing for special matinees of Gerhart Hauptmann's *The Assumption of Hannele* (1924) when the director fell ill, forcing her to take over and make her directing debut. In 1925, she worked at the Hedgerow Theatre in Pennsylvania, performing her first Henrik Ibsen heroines in *The Master Builder* and *John Gabriel Borkman*, directing the plays as well. Ibsen, most of whose dramas she translated, would play a dominant role in Le Gallienne's career. Back in New York, she redirected Ibsen's plays for special matinees, and then toured the minirepertory.

These works became the genesis of the Civic Repertory Theatre (CRT), a European-style repertory company charging low prices that Le Gallienne—backed by millionaire Otto Kahn—initiated at the Fourteenth Street Theatre in 1926 with Jacinto Benavente's *Saturday Night*. For six years, she put on three to five plays a week, playing to a more working-class audience than attended Broadway, and providing 34 plays (directing most of them) in 1,581 performances. Many remained in the repertory for years; tours took them to places starved for theater.

Le Gallienne's eclecticism emphasized old and new plays of literary value and included a number barely known in America. Shakespeare was represented by *Twelfth Night* (1926) and *Romeo and Juliet* (1930), with the director playing, respectively, Viola and Juliet. *Twelfth Night* had a fantastical setting—by resident designer Aline Bernstein—accompanied by imaginative puppetlike wigs and makeups, and stressed the comedy more than the romance. The dynamically paced *Romeo* had a musical background by Peter Tchaikovsky, used entrances from the orchestra pit, and employed a forestage to enable scenes upstage to be shifted behind a curtain. The *New York Times* reported:

> One expansive device of several flights of stairs climbing into a blue background introduces the tragedy with three major acting levels. For the rest, a triangular structure, easily turned about, serves to suggest beautifully the balcony, the interior of Juliet's chamber and Friar Laurence's cell. . . . These units . . . make an ingenious compromise between concrete representation and conventional background.

Other antiques were Molière's *The Would-Be Gentleman* (1928) and Carlo Goldoni's *La Locandiera* (1926). The less old included Ibsen's *Hedda Gabler* (1928), which received a controversial updating in a simplified setting composed of artfully composed gray draperies, with Le Gallienne's chain-smoking Hedda dressed in short skirts and bobbed hair.

Anton Chekhov was represented by *The Three Sisters* (1926), with Le Gallienne as Masha; *The Sea Gull* (1929), with Le Gallienne as Masha; and *The Cherry Orchard* (1928), with Le Gallienne as Varya. For the first, she sought to create an ensemble by having the company rehearse outdoors in the country. They worked in the fields and woods and called each other by their characters' names. The actors discussed things improvisationally and then shifted into Chekhov's dialogue. The *Times* said: "The organization has caught splendidly the atmosphere. It is a *genre* picture of fine artistic sensibility and compares favorably with the production the Russians did some time ago."

Susan Glaspell's *Inheritors* (1927); Herman Heijerman's *The Good Hope* (1927); Gregorio Martinez-Sierra's *The Cradle Song* (1927); James M. Barrie's *Peter Pan* (1928); Leonid Andreyev's *Katerina* (1929); Leo Tolstoy's *The Living Corpse* (1929); Alexandre Dumas *fils*'s *Camille* (1931); and *Liliom* (1932) were the other revivals. Most memorable were *The Cradle Song*, of which a critic wrote, "The whole movement and flow . . . is faultless, replete with humor and tenderness"; the captivating *Peter Pan*, in which a flying Le Gallienne (as Peter) soared to the balcony during the curtain calls; and a brisk showing of *Camille*, starring Le Gallienne as Marguerite in a production moved forward to 1875 and backed by Giuseppe Verdi's *La Traviata* score.

Le Gallienne's emphasis on rotating repertory, in which the profits were less promising than open runs, discouraged Americans from sending her their plays, although she did stage four new native works, Walter Ferris's *First Stone* (1928); Glaspell's Pulitzer Prize-winning *Alison's House* (1931), inspired by Emily Dickinson; Eleanor Hinkley's *Dear Jane* (1932); and Le Gallienne and Florida Friebus's adaptation, *Alice in Wonderland* (1932). American premieres of European works were Jean-Jacques Bernard's *L'Invitation au Voyage* (1928); Max Mohr's *Improvisations in June* (1928); Serafín and Joaquín Quintero's *The Lady from Alfáqueque* (1929) and *The Women Have Their Way* (1930); Claude Anet's *Mademoiselle Bourrat* (1929); and Jean Giraudoux's *Siegfried* (1930).

The schedule was grueling, the company sometimes rehearsing one play in the morning, acting another in the afternoon, and a third at night. There were 18 productions during the 1930–1931 season alone. Le Gallienne was often criticized for acting in the plays that she directed, thereby being prevented from total concentration on either task. Her

CRT responsibilities were further increased by her managerial chores. She was called "the General" or "the Colonel" or "the Abbess of Fourteenth Street."

A solid but unspectacular troupe, occasionally supplemented by such luminaries as Jacob Ben-Ami and Alla Nazimova, was developed, and a number of later well-known players were nurtured at the company's free training school Le Gallienne established.

The CRT was damaged by the Depression, and was forced to try its luck uptown in 1932 with an open run of the popular *Alice in Wonderland* in repertory with *The Cherry Orchard*. The experiment failed and the CRT ended in 1933. *Alice,* aimed at adults as well as children—and in which Le Gallienne played the White Queen—employed puppets made by Remo Bufano, trick effects (props grew or shrank), an original musical score, scenery that rolled in on tracks, and a decor based (except for the addition of color) on John Tenniel's original illustrations. Much of Le Gallienne's inventiveness derived from a period she had spent under the tutelage of the European clowns, the Fratellinis.

One reason for the demise of her CRT idea, it has been argued, is that Le Gallienne's attempt at a populist theater emphasizing the classics and modern works of literary value ignored the era's social consciousness. This argument is faulty, as many politically oriented companies failed as well.

In 1934, Le Gallienne tried to revive her repertory idea with a four-play Broadway season composed of Edmond Rostand's *L'Aiglon,* costarring Le Gallienne and Ethel Barrymore, and three of her former productions. It bore the CRT's name as coproducer, but despite good reviews and energetic attempts to find some form of subsidy, the venture sank.

Henceforth, Le Gallienne mainly acted for others; directing assignments were sporadic. One was *Hamlet* (1937), at Cape Cod, with herself in the lead, but she declined to face New York with it. She viewed Hamlet as a 19-year-old adolescent but came off like a weak-kneed 14.

From 1940 on, Le Gallienne acted on stage, films, and TV, translated plays and stories (she commanded eight languages), wrote, lectured, gave recitals, recorded plays, taught, and directed. All her subsequent directing consisted of revivals, mostly of plays she had already done. She returned to Broadway with a decent revival of Eugene O'Neill's *Ah, Wilderness!* (1941) for the Theater Guild, although it was too leisurely and needed cutting. Richard Brinsley Sheridan's *The Rivals* (1941) was also sponsored by the Guild. Bob Acres was played hilariously by comedian Bobby Clark. The production used a new prologue, several new songs, and lots of inventive comic business, but some thought it too farcical. In 1944, Le Gallienne, who played Ranevskaya, returned to *The Cherry Orchard,* codirected with Margaret Webster. Joseph Schildkraut, Le Gallienne's favorite costar, played Gaev. Some of the more negative reviews pointed to its excessive use of broad humor. Still, it toured for five months and its 96 Broadway showings were a record.

Le Gallienne, Webster, and Cheryl Crawford were partners in another abortive stab at a quality rep company, the American Repertory Theatre, which lasted from 1946 to 1947. The plays lacked wide appeal, the 1,100-seat International Theatre was on out-of-the-way Columbus Circle, prices were too high, the unions were stifling, and the lack of subsidy fatal. Le Gallienne staged *John Gabriel Borkman* (1946) and *Alice in Wonderland* (1947).

After reviving *Hedda Gabler* (1948) in New York, Le Gallienne did not direct for over a decade. She continued to champion the popular-price repertory concept, both for its educational and cultural importance and for its value in developing actors' versatility. She called for endowments and declaimed against the commercial theater of "best sellers." In 1961, she was instrumental in the founding of another company, the National Repertory Theatre (NRT), which normally played on tours. For it, she staged *The Sea Gull* (1964), popular enough to be brought to Broadway, with Le Gallienne as Arkadina. She also did NRT tours of *Liliom* (1965) and *Hedda Gabler* (1965).

Her *The Cherry Orchard* (1968) was for the Association of Performing Artists, while *A Doll's House* (1975) was for the Seattle Repertory Theatre. Her final directing project was another *Alice in Wonderland* (1982), in which, aged 83, she played the White Queen and even did some flying. Unfortunately, *Alice,* codirected with John Strasberg, and attempting to replicate the earlier versions, was visually outstanding but tedious.

Le Gallienne insisted directors should be well educated and technically skilled. She once said the director should be "an actor, scholar, persuader, teacher—he must be . . . everything." Talking to Harold Schonberg about her CRT days, she stated,

We couldn't afford a good director, so I did it myself. I did the castings, lighted my own shows, laid out the playing spaces. A director has to have a vision . . . and then try to fulfill that vision. I firmly believe that a director should always be or have been an actor. . . .

A good director has to be a psychologist. Some actors have to be told everything and others resent being told a single thing. Some you can yell at. Others you have to . . . explain things.

There are two kinds of actors, she found, those who develop their roles from the inside and those who work from external ideas before they achieve the proper inner state. The director should leave the former alone until they have found a footing for themselves, and then "help them mostly through suggestion, seldom through meticulous detailed direction," because of the danger of blurring "the clarity of their own conception," thereby making "their performance lifeless." External actors, however, welcome detailed specifics and "feel lost without it." She disdained as an error the widespread practice of treating all actors alike.

Le Gallienne was exceedingly well prepared, having read the play many times and worked everything out—from physical activity to emotional values—in detail. She even prepared a model that the designer was expected to use to design the set. The actors were required to familiarize themselves thoroughly with the script before rehearsals commenced. Following a first rehearsal at which Le Gallienne read the script, with all inflections and nuances (at least for plays she had done before), the company engaged in several days of "at table" readings and discussion.

While stressing the importance of a single, unifying concept, Le Gallienne worked collaboratively, seeking a cohesive ensemble. Her role, wrote David Carb, was "more that of an elected leader than that of a dictator. . . . Every command carries its reason with it. And, as a result, the actors play for the whole, instead of . . . against each other for individual advantage."

Le Gallienne rehearsed with deep concentration, demonstrating self-control and imposing an air of formality only rarely lightened by humor. She demanded high standards of professional discipline; when necessary she reprimanded an actor with force. When she had to interrupt, she often took an actor aside and whispered privately. But she also gave notes publicly. She was most open to suggestions when it came to blocking and often revised when an actor had a better idea; the actor had to feel his moves were "right." Colleagues' comments on her own performance were duly considered and tried out.

To many, Eva Le Gallienne was the First Lady of the American Stage. Producer, director, star, scholar, translator, writer, and adaptor were titles she bore with distinction, but it was her dogged commitment to repertory that made her contribution unique.

Further reading:

Carb, David. "Eva Le Gallienne." *Theatre Guild Magazine* 8 (February 1931).

Le Gallienne, Eva. *At 33.* New York: Longmans and Green, 1934.

———. *With a Quiet Heart.* New York: Viking, 1953.

Schanke, Robert. *Eva Le Gallienne: A Bio-Bibliography.* Westport, Conn.: Greenwood, 1989.

———. *Shattered Applause: The Lives of Eva Le Gallienne.* Carbondale: Southern Illinois University Press, 1992.

Schonberg, Harold C. "Eva Le Gallienne: 'If I Only Played Myself That Would Be a Bore.'" *New York Times,* January 11, 1981.

Also: Johnson, *Directing Methods.*

ROBERT LEWIS (1909–)

ROBERT LEWIS, son of a jeweler and a musically talented mother, was born in Brooklyn, New York. He attended City College and studied the cello at the Institute of Musical Art. After working briefly with Sue Hastings's Marionette Company, he took small parts in Eva Le Gallienne's Civic Repertory Theatre. His first directing experience was with the Civic Rep when he staged a training production for them.

Lewis became the youngest original member of the socially oriented Group Theatre, founded in 1931. He remained through most of their history,

gaining some distinction for his eccentric character parts. Like all Group actors, he was deeply affected by cofounder Lee Strasberg's idiosyncratic interpretation (the Method) of Konstantin Stanislavsky's acting system, but shifted allegiance to the Russian's later ideas as imbibed in 1934 during a personal visit with the master by actress Stella Adler. Although Lewis never completely abandoned Strasberg's "affective" or emotional memory techniques, he was more inspired by Stanislavsky's ideas about emotion being stimulated by belief in the given circumstances and the playing of specific intentions. Lewis eventually became one of America's leading acting teachers, propagating a nondogmatic, common-sense approach that allowed an actor to use whatever worked best for him. Unlike Strasberg, he always stressed the need for the actor to play the character and not himself. Supported by his background in music and dance, he devoted much of his career to attempts to introduce into actor-training what he called a "third force," i.e., a method that, in seeking to produce a truthful emotional response, paid equal attention to both the external means and the internal ones. Many of the productions Lewis directed exemplified his personalized, "poetic realism" style in contrast to the more prosaic realism with which Group adherents were often labeled. His variation from the company's line led him to be branded a "theatrical Trotskyite."

In addition to his Group acting, Lewis occasionally acted in outside productions and taught under various auspices. Along with Group stalwarts Elia Kazan and Cheryl Crawford, he founded the Actors Studio in 1947. He also wrote two important books on acting.

The Group taught Lewis to analyze a script in terms of its theme or "spine" and the overall and individual character intentions that motivate the action. Everything was broken down moment by moment for each role to weld the whole into a unified artistic expression. If actors wrote down the intentions of each line, they would have insurance against losing focus during a run.

Lewis did not have much opportunity to direct with the Group; when given his chance, he made a marked impression. His first endeavor was a 1934 summer workshop staging of an unfinished piece about a strike and presented in a stylized fashion reminiscent of Evgeny's Vakhtangov's "fantastic realism"; the sounds of the hills or a train passing were created vocally.

Lewis's first fully realized production was for the Federal Theater Project in Los Angeles, where he staged Maxwell Anderson and Harold Hickerson's *The Gods of the Lightning* (1937). He then directed the touring version of Clifford Odets's *Golden Boy* (1938). His subsequent assignment, William Saroyan's unusual *My Heart's in the Highlands* (1939), was the turning point in his career.

Billed as an experimental offering for only five performances (it was actually given 44), this was a sentimental, whimsically poetic, loosely constructed, 90-minute one-acter set in 1914 San Francisco, concerned with the artist's need to be connected to his society. Saroyan, believing the play was "virile realism," was dissatisfied with Lewis's stylization, but the novice turned it into a *succès d'estime*. He was commended for his use of symbolic settings, expressive lighting, engaging music, and imaginative staging that went beyond behavioral psychology to create physical images that communicated the subtext. Most notable was a climactic scene in which the cast was grouped in such a way as to suggest the image of a blossoming tree. Nervous at his big chance, Lewis prepared so carefully (a trait he would retain) that the play was staged in a week and a half; to keep the cast occupied, he had to find ways of filling out the remaining weeks.

In Lewis's published notes on the play, he declared:

> The Spine *is to create nature in a world that is not natural. This gypsy living of the artist, however, is a worrisome thing. These artists . . . have to deal with the world whether they want to or not. . . . They lose themselves with the people who displace them. The progression must be the realization that they cannot stand alone, just the poets together. They need and are needed by the people.*

Another Group technique was extensive "at table" readings. He believed blocking comes much easier after the actors have a full comprehension of their characters' workings. He did not want actors to force feelings or develop characterizations until they came to a point where they were fully ready to do so. If they rushed, they were likely to perform clichés. Once the blocking was completed, another round of sit-down rehearsals was held to guarantee retention of the internal discoveries.

Lewis's success at poetic staging gave him a reputation as a specialist in this vein, but he did not impose such methods on plays that did not require them. There was no contradiction between realism and poeticism, he argued, the latter being only one of many styles—high comedy, tragedy, melodrama, etc.—in which a "realistic" play could be produced. Stanislavsky, if fully understood, could bring reality to any play in any style.

Lewis was really an eclectic and had a number of Broadway successes ranging from musicals to courtroom thrillers. However, his many failures reveal an inability to detect seriously flawed scripts. A weak literary background hindered his skill at working closely with playwrights to strengthen unsound plays. Also, his noncontemporary works were extremely rare. Moreover, inexperience with the classics hampered his various educational efforts in developing fully trained actors.

Lewis proceeded to stage the Theater Guild's production of Saroyan's *The Time of Your Life* (1939). Interpretive conflicts, however, led to his leaving and to Saroyan codirecting with star Eddie Dowling. Lewis declared that, while the director must be as faithful as possible to a play's meaning, the playwright must respect the vision of the director and actors as well.

Lewis directed a pair of flops, Albert Bein's *Heavenly Express* (1940), starring John Garfield, and Lucille Prumbs's *Five Alarm Waltz* (1941), with Elia Kazan as a Saroyanesque writer. His infusion of movement into an otherwise static script was becoming a trademark. He would often be accused of overproducing plays in order to disguise their otherwise too-apparent blemishes.

Lewis went Off-Broadway to direct Ramon Naya's short-lived *Mexican Mural* (1942), with Montgomery Clift, who liked Lewis's use of improvisations for loosening the actors up physically. Then, from mid-1942 to 1946, Lewis acted in Hollywood "B" films, directed a movie sequence (without credit), and staged some plays in Los Angeles, including André Obey's *Noah* with Lee J. Cobb. He returned to Broadway with Thomas Job's failure, *Land's End* (1946). In 1947, he struck gold with Alan Jay Lerner and Frederick Loewe's fanciful musical set in Scotland, *Brigadoon*. In a rare instance of a writer's acknowledging Lewis's assistance, Lerner revealed that he had been having trouble completing the script; Lewis explained it to him so brilliantly that he was finally able to finish it. After listening to Lerner's explanation, Lewis had contradicted him:

> *"That's not what you have written at all. What you have written is the story of a romantic who is searching, and a cynic who has given up. The cynic talks him out of his romantic notions and forces him to leave Brigadoon. In the end, cynicism is proven wrong."*

By closely watching choreographer Agnes de Mille's rehearsals, Lewis was able to seamlessly blend his dramatic scenes with the dances. He also succeeded in making the transitions between song and dialogue more natural by having the first words of the song half-spoken and then finding a way of eliding the moment between the end of the song and the beginning of speech; one thus flowed unobtrusively from the other. Regardless of the formal requirements of a musical, everything was "justified." These methods would be repeated in later musical productions.

At his newly cofounded Actors Studio (1947), Lewis staged a workshop version of Anton Chekhov's *The Sea Gull* (1948). On Broadway, he did Marc Blitzstein's respected, unconventional, but commercially unsuccessful operatic version of Lillian Hellman's *The Little Foxes*, *Regina* (1949), and later revived it for the City Center Opera company (1953). He had a hit with Samuel Taylor's comedy *The Happy Time* (1950), the follow-up to which was Arthur Miller's anti-McCarthyite version of Henrik Ibsen's *An Enemy of the People* (1950), one of several politically inclined, commercially unsuccessful dramas Lewis staged. Also unsuccessful, partly because of the author's resistance to changes, was Truman Capote's Southern whimsy, *The Grass Harp* (1952), but the 1,027-performance triumph of John Patrick's *The Teahouse of the August Moon* (1953) made everything look rosy. Lewis conceived the comedy as being about the clash that occurs when one culture (the American Occupation) forces its ideas on another (the Okinawans) but winds up being "occupied" itself. Another hit arrived in Agatha Christie's courtroom melodrama, *Witness for the Prosecution* (1953).

Thereafter, Lewis had a hard time staying on track. Several shows closed out of town. Among those that reached Broadway but did poorly were Norman Rosten's drama about colonial Africa, *Mister Johnson* (1956); Ruth and Augustus Goetz's *The Hidden River*, critically respected but commercially unattractive (1957); N. Richard Nash's self-consciously arty *Handful of Rain* (1958); the London production of the Hellman-Leonard Bernstein musical *Candide*; Anita Loos's Colette adaptation, *Cheri* (1958); a musical about miscegenation in Africa, *Kwamina* (1961); Robert Emmett Dolan's *Foxy* (Dawson City Festival, 1962; Broadway, 1964), a musical updating to Yukon days of Ben Jonson's *Volpone*, with Bert Lahr; and Jean Anouilh's *Traveller Without Luggage* (1964). The only plums in the pie were the black musical *Jamaica* (1957), starring Lena Horne, and the Alan Jay Lerner-Burton Lane musical, *On a Clear Day You Can See Forever* (1965), just shy of a hit.

Between 1970 and 1971, Lewis directed some regional theater, including August Strindberg's *Crimes and Crimes* at the Yale Repertory Theater; two Harold Pinter one-acts and *The Sea Gull* in Baltimore (1971); and a musical revue in Washington, D.C. (1971). In the late seventies, he formed the Robert Lewis Acting Company in Westchester, New York, in connection with a training program he operated. He directed two of its three plays, John Ford Noonan's *The Club Champion's Widow* (1978) and Albert Camus's *Caligula* (1978), but various problems doomed the company. Among Lewis's final projects were Eugene O'Neill's *Long Day's Journey into Night* (1979) in Australia and Colin Higgins's flop, *Harold and Maude* (1980), in which aging movie star Janet Gaynor made her Broadway debut. Lewis moved to Los Angeles to teach.

Lewis was generally more result- than process-oriented, and did whatever was practical to get his effects, giving readings and demonstrating when necessary. Visually oriented, he paid close attention to groupings and movements. If he asked for something for a purely technical reason, and the actor deemed the request arbitrary, Lewis provided a justification—even if it were a complete fabrication—to make the actor feel believable. In *Teahouse*, he lied by telling an actor that his character, presumably an Okinawan scribe, was, like all Oriental scribes, a dancer, and that the physical position demanded was that of a dancer. This gave the actor something real to play, and he was happy to act the direction. But Lewis could be demanding; because of his concern with formal perfection, he would express himself openly when confronted with lazy or undisciplined performers.

"Bobby" Lewis had an up-and-down career, marked by significant productions but marred by many ineffective ones. He was the only Group alumnus who dreamed of combining Stanislavskian realism with theatrical poetry, but he was never able to fully explore his potential. He may be better remembered as a teacher, but the theatrical beauty he brought to the predominantly realistic Broadway stage deserves recognition.

Further reading:

Chinoy, Helen Krich, ed. "Reunion, A Self-Portrait of the Group Theatre." *Educational Theatre Journal* 28 (December 1976).

Lewis, Robert. *Method—or Madness?* New York: Samuel French, 1958.

———. *Advice to the Players.* New York: Harper and Row, 1980.

———. *Slings and Arrows: Theater in My Life.* New York: Stein and Day, 1984.

Marowitz, Charles. *Prospero's Staff: Acting and Directing in the Contemporary Theatre.* Bloomington and Indianapolis: Indiana University Press, 1986.

Also: Gassner, *Producing the Play.*

JOAN LITTLEWOOD (1915–   )

JOAN LITTLEWOOD was born in Stockwell, South London, England, the illegitimate daughter of working-class parents (who later married). At 17, she won a scholarship to the Royal Academy of Dramatic Arts but, turned off by its conservativism, dropped out. Littlewood worked in radio and acted in Manchester before joining forces with Ewen MacColl, a politically active writer and folk-singer whom she married in 1935.

Littlewood and MacColl wanted to create left-wing agit-prop plays confronting timely social issues. In 1934, they helped found Theater of Action, where they borrowed advanced methods from Vsevolod Meyerhold, Erwin Piscator, and Rudolf Laban, all of whom were seeking unconventional ways of using the human body's expressiveness. Constructivist and epic techniques frequently appeared in Theater of Action's work, which used unpolished actors and played in makeshift spaces for the working-classes.

In 1936, MacColl and Littlewood cofounded Manchester's Theater Union, hoping to bring activist theater to the non-theater-going public. Offering mainly one- and two-night stands, they codirected Hans Chlumberg's antiwar *Miracle at Verdun* (1936), Lope de Vega's *The Sheepwell* (1936), Bertolt Brecht's *The Good Soldier Schweik* (1938), and Aristophanes' *Lysistrata* (1941), among other works. MacColl's anticapitalist Living Newspaper, *Last Edition* (1940), eventually banned, was constantly revised to keep it current. As music became more important to the troupe, new actors had to demonstrate musical talents. Meanwhile, Konstantin Stanislavsky's ideas became influential with the troupe.

The war forced a breakup in 1942. Those determined to regroup later studied specific aspects of theater history so they could pool their knowledge. They reformed near Manchester in 1945 as Theater Workshop. Littlewood hoped to create a noncommercial "British People's Theater," although money was a problem. The troupe, organized on a sharing basis, aimed to provide a radical alternative to the "posh" theater of the time, with actors who seemed like everyday folk and with methods exploring a wide range of physical, musical, and verbal techniques. They often played under trying conditions. In reality, they appealed more to middle-class than working-class audiences, and did not succeed in capturing the kind of spectators they sought.

Eight years of struggle, occupied principally in touring Britain and Europe, ensued. From 1949 to 1953, they were regulars at the Edinburgh Festival. An interesting work was MacColl's *The Travellers* (1952), staged in a set resembling the interior of a train that was placed down the auditorium's center aisle, with the audience facing the aisle. Lighting and sound created the impression of movement. MacColl contributed a series of topical, formally experimental works. There were also classics, old ones like Molière's *The Flying Doctor* (1945) and Shakespeare's *Henry IV, Part I* (1951), and modern ones by Federico García Lorca and Anton Chekhov. Each was the excuse for new experiments.

A major turn occurred in 1953, when they leased East London's Theater Royal (popularly known as Stratford East), a 512-seat Victorian playhouse half-an-hour away from the West End and situated in a working-class neighborhood. The move to a permanent base alienated MacColl, who resigned. At Stratford East, which opened with *Twelfth Night,* Littlewood began a true ensemble company with no stars, no long runs, and low prices. Financial survival was difficult although, beginning in 1958, a string of successes temporarily relieved matters.

Littlewood's repertoire was eclectic. It included Aristophanes, Shakespeare, Ben Jonson, John Marston, MacColl, and Brecht; there were also adaptations by Littlewood herself of work by writers such as Charles Dickens and Honoré de Balzac. Her classics were novel, as when she staged Jonson's *Volpone* (1955) in modern-day Italian terms. It and Littlewood's staging of the anonymous *Arden of Faversham* were hits of the Paris International Theatre Festival; the acclaim brought greater attention at home.

Perhaps the two most outstanding Littlewood classical revivals were *Richard II* (1954) and *Edward II* (1956). The first rivalled the Old Vic's more conservatively poetic version, and thus gained it publicity for its Marxist slant, rapid pace, spare scenery, imaginative lighting, and realistic earthiness.

In 1956, Littlewood's revival of *Schweik* was transferred to the West End. This procedure was followed by a number of Littlewood productions because of the need to capitalize on successful offerings. Major national recognition, however, did not happen until Littlewood discovered Irish working-class dramatist Brendan Behan's *The Quare Fellow* (1956), set in a prison. Littlewood made many script revisions and several playwrights cried foul; but such adaptation of new works became Littlewood's trademark.

The company began to have difficulty holding on to actors who left for more lucrative and less demanding pastures. Littlewood's troupe worked hard for minimal salaries, doing 36 plays, for example, between February 1953 and April 1955. Actors were expected to pitch in and help maintain the theater. Arts council subsidies were rarely large enough to pay a living wage.

Among the most significant Littlewood productions through 1961 were *Macbeth* (1957); 19-year-old Shelagh Delaney's *A Taste of Honey* (1958), an international hit; Behan's *The Hostage* (1958), another smash and an excellent example of the director's addition of music-hall antics; Frank Norman's *Fings Ain't Wot They Used T'Be* (1959), worked up through improvisations from a 48-page script into a full-length production that changed the play into a musical; Wolf Mankowitz's musical, *Make Me an Offer* (1959), which enraged the author because of the director's liberties; and Stephen Lewis's *Sparrers Can't Sing* (1960).

Disillusioned by various experiences, Littlewood took a two-year leave from 1961 to 1963. She worked in Nigeria and formed plans for an amusement and cultural complex called the Fun Palace, which never got off the ground. A 1969 idea for Bubble City, a multimedia theatrical park, also failed to float.

Littlewood's return was marked by her brilliant *Oh, What a Lovely War!* (1963), an antiwar musical collage based on familiar World War I songs, created communally with the company through research and improvisations. Performed within a commedia context of Pierrot costumes, it recreated through music, slides, newsreels, a running electric sign, choreography, and pantomime the war's searing impact on Britain. This hit moved to the West End and to Broadway, and was shown in Paris and both East and West Berlin.

Littlewood's most noted later work included her controversial modern-dress conflation of both parts of *Henry IV* (1964) into one play at the Edinburgh Festival; her activity in Tunisia, where she staged

Who Is Repito?, a play seeking multinational understanding (1966); her hit staging of the musical political satire *Mrs. Wilson's Diary* (1967), which moved to the West End; and a darkly realistic revival of *The Hostage*, sharply different in tone from the farcical nature of the original. Several freelance productions occupied her as well. In 1973, she moved to France.

Littlewood was a populist, trying to bring theater to the common man in a robust, vibrant, and fun way. She employed music-hall techniques, often introducing songs and gags, and allowing her actors to address the spectators directly. Music to which her audiences could relate, such as jazz, rock, and pop, was crucial, but nostalgic tunes also had an important place. Some dramas were so infused with music that they literally became musical comedies. Her subject matter, even in classical plays, was always topical, and she revised many works to make their messages pertinent. Sometimes, as in the first *Hostage*, she allowed the actors to revise nightly to bring the day's news on stage with them.

She had no pretensions about "art," considering her work to be a matter of opening doors to an understanding of pain and joy. Littlewood rebelled at theater as a museum, and wanted it to be alive in the present. Her productions often had a good share of vulgarity because people responded to it. She played comedy at bullet speed and in the custard-pie tradition. Her ideas were borrowed from everywhere, including Brecht and Stanislavsky, commedia, music hall, and the Elizabethans.

Despite Littlewood's fondness for stylization, her characters were rooted in reality to express their social relationships from the moment they appeared. Some scenes were naturalistic, especially in the documentary works exposing local conditions.

Stratford East's acting was new for English theater. Whereas most previous examples of acting had a certain polish, with refined accents, Littlewood's performers were rough-edged and colloquial, their speech emphasizing regionalisms, even in Shakespeare. They seemed real and their playing put them on intimate terms with the spectators, especially when they broke the fourth wall. They seemed the same in classics as in moderns, a subject of contention. Honesty was cultivated by improvisation, which forced the actors to behave organically. Also significant was the uninhibited ease and naturalness that emerged from working closely in an ensemble. Littlewood preferred to get her actors at their formative stage and to train them herself. She liked those who lacked theatrical sophistication but were flexible and uninhibited.

Littlewood was collaborative rather than authoritarian (although the autocrat—amplified by a megaphone—sometimes took over). She felt that only a cohesive company working under a sympathetic director could supply all the necessary input required to realize so complex a thing as a play. Evolutionary, process-oriented rehearsals were employed for binding the production into a unity. She despised fixed rehearsal periods, and even the eight weeks given to many of her works were deemed insufficient. Despite time limits, she kept improvising until the last day, and even into the run, to keep the actors fresh.

Improvisations (which she called "games" or "parallels") answered many purposes for Littlewood, who even used them for auditions. They often inspired props and costumes. However, she employed any and all methods to get a response. She veered from Stanislavsky's "method of physical actions" to "emotion memory," although she preferred the former for stimulating a truthful performance.

Littlewood broke the action down into units or beats, each with a clear objective. The objectives were usually the basis for improvisations, with imaginative twists. A situation in a period play, for example, was done in modern terms. Unwritten scenes happening before the performed action were created. Each play's requirements led to new exercises. To get the actors in *The Quare Fellow* to feel like convicts, they were taken to the roof and marched about endlessly, taking rest breaks as if they were prisoners. In this case, the actual casting was not done until well into the largely improvisatory rehearsal period, during which the play had only been introduced piecemeal. At other times, Littlewood had the actors play one another's roles. When appropriate, Littlewood, like more conventional directors, could assist by providing actors with vivid verbal images to play, especially ones connected to a dynamic objective. As a last resort, this gifted actress would demonstrate.

She could be nasty, and her comments were often couched in snide invective because she liked to keep her actors off balance when she sensed that they might become complacent. Still, her love for her "nuts" and "tosspots" was strong, and most actors would do whatever she asked, no matter how foolish.

Careful research into period, philosophy, art, and so forth preceded any Littlewood show, and she had the actors themselves do extensive research, especially for older plays. The research was often used in improvisations. On occasion, the actors explored the subtext extensively before acting the text. Once the play's heartbeat had been grasped through physicalization exercises, the words were added; this gave the speeches an unexpected depth. Littlewood's productions had a spoken and visual integrity and truth. Business and blocking seemed honest and attractive because founded on organic processes and inner justifications.

Joan Littlewood failed to find the audience of commoners she sought, but her ideas were absorbed by the mainstream theatrical community and her achievements made her the foremost female British director. She made political theater fun, broke down class-consciousness in acting, thumbed her nose at the Establishment, and advanced the cause of improvisation and collaboration.

Further reading:

Ansorge, Peter. "Lots of Lovely Human Contact! An Inside Look at Joan Littlewood." *Plays and Players* 19 (1972).

Bailey, Anthony. "Would Little Joan Littlewood Were Here!" *Esquire* 64 (January 1964).

Goorney, Howard. *The Theatre Workshop Story.* London: Eyre Methuen, 1981.

MacColl, Ewen. "Grass Roots of Theatre Workshop." *Theatre Quarterly* 3 (January–March 1973).

Tynan, Kenneth. "Joan of Cockaigne." *Holiday* 26 (November 1964).

Also: Bradby and Williams, *Directors' Theatre*; Johnson, *Directing Methods*; Leiter, *From Belasco to Brook*; Marshall, *The Producer and the Play*.

JOSHUA LOGAN (1908–1988)

JOSHUA LOCKWOOD LOGAN III was born in Texarkana, Texas, but was raised in rural South Mansfield, Louisiana, where his father—who died when Logan was three—was a wealthy lumberman. He enrolled at the Culver Military Academy in Indiana. Logan's childhood delight in amateur theatricals was continued at Princeton University, where he acted, wrote, and directed for the all-male Triangle Club musical comedies, and was a leader in the student-founded company, the University Players (UP).

The UP produced some of America's most distinguished theater artists (including Henry Fonda, Norris Houghton, and James Stewart). Beginning in 1928 as an amateurish Cape Cod summer stock company, they established themselves in 1931–1932 in Baltimore, Maryland, where they were the University Repertory Theatre. Logan's various duties included directing revivals of recent Broadway shows. In 1932, during their fifth Cape Cod season, the company produced Frank McGrath's *Carry Nation*, which moved unsuccessfully to Broadway, providing Logan, who assisted in the staging, with his New York acting debut.

Meanwhile, he spent six months (1930–1931) on a scholarship studying in Moscow with Konstantin Stanislavsky. Because the trip was made during Logan's final university semester, he never received his degree; Princeton later granted him an honorary one.

Logan's post-UP directing career began in London with Elsie Shauffler's bomb, *The Day I Forgot* (1933), but he managed a successful Boston revival of Alexandre Dumas *fils*'s *Camille* (1933), starring Jane Cowl.

At 27, Logan codirected (with Forest Haring) two Broadway flops, Maurice Braddell's *It's You I Want* (1935), and E. M. Delafield's *To See Ourselves*, which he also coproduced. The same year, he and former UP colleague Bretaigne Windust directed summer stock near Suffern, New York. Back in New York, he directed John Patrick's loser, *Hell Freezes Over* (1935), while simultaneously staging a Triangle show. Logan then spent some time in Hollywood, and codirected a movie.

His first Broadway hit came with Paul Osborn's *On Borrowed Time* (1938), a fantasy about death being trapped in a tree. Logan, who possessed dramaturgical skill, helped revise the play for production, a procedure he invariably followed on all new plays he staged. He kept the playwright on hand to make changes and to discuss the work in progress. Logan never staged a classic, preferring the give and take of collaboration with living writers. His most frequent relationship was with Osborn.

Logan's fame doing musical comedy began with Richard Rodgers and Lorenz Hart's popular fantasy, *I Married an Angel* (1938), with Vera Zorina. It was the first of several times when he had multiple hits (at one point there were four) running simultaneously.

Other important prewar productions were Osborn's Chekhovian comedy-drama *Morning's at Seven* (1939), respected but unprofitable; and a hilarious, enormously inventive version of Brandon Thomas's *Charley's Aunt* (1940), Logan's only Broadway revival, starring José Ferrer. Following a war stint in intelligence, he picked up with Anita Loos's *Happy Birthday* (1946), a hit romantic comedy with Helen Hayes; Norman Krasna's ticket-selling comedy of postwar romantic complications, *John Loves Mary* (1947); *Mister Roberts* (1948), coauthored with Thomas Heggen, and set on a cargo ship in the wartime Pacific, with Fonda as the idealistic title character; Logan's only effort at solo playwriting, *The Wisteria Trees* (1950), his flawed transposition of Anton Chekhov's *The Cherry Orchard* to a postbellum Louisiana plantation (one critic called it "Southern Fried Chekhov"), starring Hayes; *Picnic* (1953), William Inge's sensitive depiction of sexual frustration in a small midwestern town; Krasna's *Kind Sir* (1953), a trivial high comedy with Mary Martin (in her first nonmusical role) and Charles Boyer; *Middle of the Night* (1956), Paddy Chayefsky's realistic drama about a May-December love affair, starring Edward G. Robinson; James Leo Herlihy and William Noble's *Blue Denim* (1958), an unprofitable treatment of the generation gap and abortion; and Osborn's money-making *The World of Suzie Wong* (1958), about a romance between a Hong Kong hooker and an artist.

Logan's contribution to musicals was outstanding. He mounted the Kurt Weill-Maxwell Anderson *Knickerbocker Holiday* (1938), a political satire on New Dealism set in Nieuw Amsterdam; *Stars in Your Eyes* (1939), score by Arthur Schwartz and Dorothy Fields, a flop Hollywood satire starring Ethel Merman and Jimmy Durante; Nancy Hamilton's *Two for the Show* (1940), a revue whose sketches he staged; the Rodgers-Hart-Gladys Hurlbut turkey, *Higher and Higher* (1940), which he also coauthored; Rodgers and Hart's *By Jupiter* (1942), with Ray Bolger, about an Amazon society whose menfolk are sissies; codirection of the sketches in the hugely successful Irving Berlin wartime revue, *This Is the Army* (1942), which Logan joined shortly before it opened but on which he performed major surgery; Berlin's blockbuster, *Annie Get Your Gun* (1946), with Merman as sharpshooter Annie Oakley; Rodgers and Oscar Hammerstein II's unconventional, now classic, Pulitzer Prizewinning "musical play" about war and romance in the tropics, *South Pacific* (1949), with Logan collaborating on the book and with Mary Martin and Ezio Pinza enjoying career highs; Arthur Kober and Harold Rome's *Wish You Were Here* (1952), a long-run boy-meets-girl musical set at a Catskill mountain resort and using an actual swimming pool; and the

Horowitz and Mrs. Washington. *Directed by Joshua Logan. (1980) L to r: Patricia Roe, Sam Levene, Esther Rolle.* (Photo: Martha Swope)

charming S. N. Behrman and Rome *Fanny* (1954), an 888-performance achievement that Logan helped to adapt from a trilogy of French plays by Marcel Pagnol. *Mister Roberts* and the musicals *Annie Get Your Gun* and *South Pacific* each ran well over 1,000 performances, making Logan one of the only directors to have staged three such smashes. He was also rare in having won Tonys for both straight plays and musicals.

After 1960, starting with *There Was a Little Girl* (with Jane Fonda in her Broadway bow), Logan directed some 10 or so plays and musicals, but could no longer press the button of success. His failures included two 1962 debacles, Charles Strouse and Lee Adams's college football musical *All American* and Berlin's tiresome *Mr. President*. Several shows died out of town, most notably *Miss Moffat* (1974), a musicalization of *The Corn Is Green* starring Bette Davis. Logan's choices had become old-fashioned. His last work was Henry Denker's frail *Horowitz and Mrs. Washington* (1980). His movie-directing career, which had enjoyed such successes as *Picnic* (1955) and *Sayonara* (1957), also saw an increasing number of failures.

Logan was a victim of manic depression, and twice had to commit himself to institutions. Interestingly, despite the anguish caused by his condition, he found himself at his creative best during his psychological bouts. He even attributed many of the uproarious hijinks in *Charley's Aunt* to the manic phase of his illness. (Logan also noted that many of his funniest ideas were cribbed from an old silent film of the play.) He believed that his encounters with psychiatric treatment were of tremendous value in his helping actors to overcome their fears.

Logan took pride in his ability to assist playwrights and was considered expert at dramatic construction. Shows underwent extensive revision, and he cut wordy scripts ruthlessly. He was in demand as a play doctor on others' projects.

Being unabashedly commercial, Logan was a complete pragmatist. He believed in collaboration and compromise rather than egotistic autocracy although, when at his best, his energy and imagination were so abundant he was virtually a one-man production team. The audience was his main target, and he frequently revised his choices if new ones gained more approval. He was preoccupied with the audience, and continued to revise even during a run. A good example followed *Wish You Were Here*'s tepid reviews. Unwilling to abandon the show, Logan so thoroughly revamped it that the critics returned and made it a hit.

The same tendency to captivate with show-biz proficiency frequently led to charges that his shows were overproduced, relying on ingenious and eye-catching decor and business, when simpler methods might have been appropriate. He also felt it his duty to remove anything that might trouble or confuse an audience. He noted, though, that the best way to guarantee success is not to play it safe but to take chances and give the audience something new and original instead of the tried and true. Logan sought total emotional involvement, and considered that audiences should be so entranced that the "fourth wall" could be viewed as existing behind, not before them. Despite his theatrical tendencies, he thought his directorial presence should be invisible.

Among notable elements in Logan's productions were their lavish, colorful designs (Jo Mielziner was his most frequent designer); elaborate machinery, including mobile platform stages, treadmills, turntables, etc., often to "lap dissolve" from scene to scene by a complex combination of lights and moving sets;

unusual effects, such as realistic rain storms or an onstage pool; muscular male seminudity; an expert sense of timing (which he discounted as a conscious technique); dazzling comic business; creative movement (he sometimes choreographed), including moving large groups as a unit; a fondness for acrobatics in musicals; the individualization of extras in crowds; actors directed as much as possible to face out to the house for clarity of diction and expression; an inclination to employ musical interscoring in straight plays; meticulous typecasting despite occasional surprises, such as opera singer Pinza in *South Pacific* or the nonsinging Walter Huston in *Knickerbocker Holiday*; and the avoidance of musical encores to prevent disruption of the illusion.

The productions reveal an affection for fantasy; emotional—often sentimental—qualities (happy endings abound and were sometimes forced on the playwright, as in *Picnic*); solid construction and easy-to-follow stories; "integrated" musicals with organically related songs and dances (although some of the musicals offered surprisingly little dance); apoliticism (*Knickerbocker Holiday* was an exception), although generally expressing American idealism; a tendency toward sexual sensationalism; and themes of love and harmony, especially in interracial romances. Logan sought not to preach, however, but to entertain.

Logan came to rehearsals with his direction clear in his head, but not in a notebook. He said he did not impose moves and gestures before allowing the actors to try their own, but most accounts claim that, to save time, he liked to work quickly and was prone to demonstrating, albeit in an exaggerated way and mainly for novices. His ability to act out direction and move from one role to another with complete concentration, despite his height and heft, was marked and provided a show in itself. Even stars were interrupted and moved about or asked to try something new, no matter how deeply involved they were in a scene. But Logan insisted that a director should admit when he did not know a problem's solution, for if the actor found him out it could damage their working relationship. Logan remained open to spontaneity and gave imaginative veterans improvisational freedom.

He had a prodigious memory for dialogue and moves and could prompt even at the first rehearsal. Logan also was adept at the technical aspects and knew precisely the lighting, sound, and scenic effects he would be using before rehearsals commenced.

Logan usually had a first reading before beginning

the blocking, but occasionally skipped the reading to get the actors up and about at once. Regardless of Stanislavsky's influence, he was afraid of the actors getting bored, and believed that blocking kept their interest more than "at table" rehearsals. Above all, analytical sessions were taboo, although Logan used them early in his career. To increase a sense of everyone's involvement, advice was spoken for all to hear, and private conversations were avoided. The blocking began loosely so that he could gradually refine it by adding more details, the main focus being to insure that the story was being told clearly. Within a couple of days, this speed demon could roughly stage an entire play or musical. Two-thirds of *South Pacific* was completed in two days.

Joshua Logan was one of the most financially successful directors in Broadway history. He had a two-decade period of hits before encountering a precipitous decline. American theater owes to him some of the most entertaining midcentury plays and musicals, shows that combined commercial acuity with artistic integrity and often appealed to intellectuals as well as casual theatergoers.

Further reading:

Logan, Joshua. *Josh: My Up and Down, In and Out Life.* New York: Delacorte Press, 1976.

———. *Movie Stars, Real People, and Me.* New York: Delacorte Press, 1978.

Talese, Gay. "The Soft Psyche of Joshua Logan." *Esquire* 59 (April 1963).

Zolotow, Maurice. "Josh-of-All-Theatre-Trades." *Theatre Arts* 38 (October 1954).

Also: Cole and Chinoy, *Directing the Play*; Houghton, "B. Windust and J. Logan."

AURÉLIEN LUGNÉ-POE (1869–1940)

AURÉLIEN-MARIE LUGNÉ (he later changed his name to Lugné-Poe in honor of Edgar Allan Poe) was born in Paris, France, where his father was a banker and private teacher of English. While attending a lycée, he took an interest in the rising symbolist movement. Symbolism was quickly gaining new adherents to its search for means of expression presenting images of inner rather than external reality, then popular with the realists and naturalists. In 1888, a year after Lugné-Poe began acting professionally, he was accepted into the famed Conservatoire acting academy. He also acted at André Antoine's Théâtre Libre.

After leaving Antoine in 1890, Lugné-Poe acted in a variety of circumstances. Crucial was his tie-up in 1890 with Paul Fort, who had just founded his Théâtre Mixte (soon changed to Théâtre d'Art), devoted to symbolist and other imaginative, poetic, and nonrealistic modes. Fort introduced radical new plays and methods, but poor administration and often amateurish performances finished the theater by 1892. Lugné-Poe made the close acquaintance of Paris's most advanced painters, many of whom designed sets, posters, and programs for Fort and would do so for Lugné-Poe when he began his own company.

Between the closing of Fort's theater and the opening of his own, Lugné-Poe worked with an amateur group he had cofounded at the lycée, the Cercle des Escholiers, for whom he directed Henrik Ibsen's *The Lady From the Sea* (1892). He staged an independent production of Maurice Maeterlinck's symbolist masterpiece, *Pelleas and Melisande* (1893), whose success led to the cofounding with critic Camille Mauclair of the Théâtre de l'Oeuvre (TDL). Created as a symbolist bastion designed to counter Antoine's naturalism, it was noncommercial and depended on subscriptions. Lugné-Poe sought to incorporate all the arts of theater, including puppetry, mime, music, and dance.

Pelleas and Melisande, a portentous medieval romance written in heightened prose, was representative of the director's symbolist staging. The scenic backdrops of castle and forest (designed by Paul Voegler) evoked the Middle Ages, with subtly blended hues of blue, green, mauve, violet, and lavender. Costuming was influenced by 15th-century painter Hans Memling and contemporary illustrator Walter Crane. Dim, diffused lighting, a scrim through which the action was viewed, the removal of footlights, and a minimal number of props and furnishings evoked a dream world. A childlike simplicity marked the acting, which used slow, angular movements and ritualistically intoned speeches. The production was acclaimed for its expression of subconscious, archetypal images. Many of the same symbolist methods were employed in subsequent stagings, sometimes jarring with the texts enacted.

In *Pelleas and Melisande*, Lugné-Poe played the important role of Golaud. He would continue to act in most of his productions, and was one of Paris's most original actors. Also acclaimed was his wife and frequent leading lady, Suzanne Desprès.

From 1893 to 1899, during which it offered 51 programs, the TDL remained Paris's preeminent experimental, nonrealistic theater. Each production was preceded by a lecture. Occasionally, Lugné-Poe was assisted by the Danish director, Herman Bang. Although symbolism was the predominant style at first, the company's repertoire eventually became eclectic. French playwrights included Henri Bataille, Maurice Beaubourg, Tristan Bernard, Alfred de Musset, Romain Rolland, Denis Diderot, and Alfred Jarry. Two plays and one translation by Maeterlinck were given. There were English classics by John Ford, Thomas Otway, and Shakespeare, whose *Measure for Measure* (1898) was staged at a circus arena in the Elizabethan manner pioneered by William Poel. Modern British drama was represented by the premiere of Oscar Wilde's *Salomé* (1896), written in French. As further examples of Lugné-Poe's range, there were offerings from other international traditions, including two ancient Indian plays, and one from the Chinese. The Continent provided Gerhart Hauptmann, José Echegaray, and Nikolai Gogol. Perhaps the most significant offerings were the Scandinavians, Björnstjerne Björnson, August Strindberg, and Henrik Ibsen. Between 1893 and 1899—his most influential period—Lugné-Poe directed nine Ibsen plays, some of them twice. The foreign works offered by Lugné-Poe and Antoine helped make Parisian theater truly cosmopolitan.

Unfortunately, the company lacked a permanent home and had to play wherever a theater could be afforded. Productions were given only a couple of showings (one an open dress rehearsal) although some received up to 20 over a season. A few multiple bills were tried, but full-length plays were generally the rule. Additional performances were given on influential foreign tours.

Despite a number of failures, Lugné-Poe was not afraid of plays that showed little dramatic promise, especially if they expanded the theater's range. Some were little more than poems with dialogue, with Lugné-Poe striving to plumb them for dreamlike feelings and images. An unsuccessful but persuasive example was Henri de Regnier's poem *The Guardian* (1894), in which the director employed greenish lighting and a green scrim together with an unortho-

dox painted backdrop of blue trees and a violet palace to suggest an ominous mood. Also striking was the placement of the poem's reciters in the orchestra pit while the silent actors, slowly acting in dumbshow, were behind the scrim.

Of all the authors he staged in the 1890s, Lugné-Poe's favorite was Ibsen. In *The Lady From the Sea*, the mysterious Ellida was dressed like a spirit in a long white robe, and even the more concrete characters were given a ghostly air. Ritualistically intoned, musically modulated speech demonstrated what would become Lugné-Poe's signature approach to the Norwegian's dramas, which he originally viewed as symbolistic, ambiguous, and nonrealistic, requiring special techniques to bring out their hidden, transcendental qualities. Ibsen was not especially pleased with what he heard about Lugné-Poe's first productions of his plays; many critics were similarly annoyed. Some objected to a disparity between actors who exhibited the mysterious side of their characters and those who played matter of factly. The company had to recruit as needed, even mingling amateurs with professionals, and was unable to maintain a stable ensemble.

Before he modified his approach, Lugné-Poe sought a visionary manner; some detractors said the actors seemed to be experiencing hallucinations. Lugné-Poe began to alter his hieratic Ibsen style in the direction of greater naturalness and three-dimensionality when he played Allmers in *Little Eyolf* (1895); his staging began to seem increasingly straightforward. This reflected his growing realization that Ibsen was neither determinedly realistic, as Antoine had viewed him, nor as consistently mystical as he had first seemed, but that both aspects were present and that a balance had to be discovered. In 1897, Lugné-Poe—disappointed at the lack of good symbolist plays—announced that he wanted to be considered aesthetically independent.

His most ambitious Ibsen production was *Peer Gynt* (1896), which—with an orchestra of 60—used Edvard Grieg's suite for background and employed the designs of modernist painter Edvard Munch. Two Norwegians assisted Lugné-Poe in understanding the work. Because of economic considerations, the sparse decor employed realism for the realistically written scenes and a variable unit setting for the philosophical ones. The lengthy play had to be cut, including the fourth act's trip to Egypt. A major criticism was the lack of a clear line between the modes of dream and reality. Despite the four hours-plus performance, others regretted such omissions as the Button Molder's advice on the meaning of being oneself. Several scenes were exceptional, especially the one in which Peer comforts the dying Åsa, but some thought the rest too foggily symbolic, particularly the encounter with the Boyg. The director's decision to insert a fourth-act dream scene was upsetting to George Bernard Shaw. In the scene, Solveig in the North patiently awaited Peer's return, which Shaw said was a misinterpretation, as Peer never gives a thought to her. Shaw approved of how much better Lugné-Poe produced the play with his rough-hewn scenery than could London's big-budgeted managers.

The most notorious event in the TDL's early years was Jarry's *King Ubu* or *Ubu Roi* (1896). The eccentric Jarry had acted at the theater and was its secretary-general when his work—widely considered a harbinger of dada, surrealism, and absurdism—premiered. With this aggressively antirealistic, excoriating satirical attack on the cruelty, greed, and fatuousness of the bourgeoisie, he intended to shock the spectators out of their narrowminded complacency and to strip them of all the conventions that made the theater a safe harbor. He may also have hoped that by destroying their preconceptions of the real world, bombarding them with nonrational images and characters, and opening to them the secrets of the inner world, their psyches would be freed from constraints and their perceptions of reality enhanced.

Lugné-Poe was persuaded against his will to stage this provocative play, which had two showings. The author called for sets that bizarrely mingled the natural with the artificial, creating an atmosphere of grotesquerie. The cartoony characters wore masks that signalled the wearer's nature. They used stylized, puppetlike gestures to express their universality, and spoke in artifical tones. Placards indicated place, the set itself being a single backdrop for all scenes. On opening night, Jarry introduced the play in a 10-minute speech, revealing that the company had been up all night painting the cardboard steeds that represented real horses. Then was revealed the extraordinary setting of Poland (meaning "nowhere") designed by Paul Sérusier, and painted by such artists as Edouard Vuillard and Toulouse-Lautrec. A black marble fireplace that divided in half to serve as doors was accompanied by a painted bed with palm trees at its feet and—under blue skies—landscapes of the sea, the forest, and the snow-covered mountains, showing three different climatic zones. A skeleton hung from the gallows. Battles were shown by two soldiers, one for each army. The gluttonous Ubu—suggesting man's worst aspects—

was acted by Firmin Gémier in Jarry's idiosyncratic inflectionless speech patterns. He wore a huge, pear-shaped costume and carried a toilet brush as a scepter, but Gémier rejected Ubu's fantastic mask incorporating an elephant's trunk. When he spoke his opening word, "*Merdre*" (shit-e), he threw the place into an uproar, as no such word ever had been spoken on the stage. There was an eruption at each succeeding "*merdre.*" During the outbursts, the audience viewed fascinating *coups de théâtre*, such as Ubu slaughtering 800 persons, represented by decapitating 40 life-sized wicker dummies who were abruptly tumbled through a trap door into the basement.

By 1899, Lugné-Poe had grown weary of the enterprise. His theater often had to make do with shabby backgrounds minimally lit to hide their defects. To save money, a standard setting, slightly modified, was used for most of the Ibsen productions. The actors even economized on costume changes by wearing their coats inside out.

After a brief lapse, during which he closed the company, Lugné-Poe regained his impetus and operated the TDL irregularly at various playhouses through 1919 (except during the war), when a permanent, 350-seat venue was established. Among his most important 20th-century productions—many representing his dedication to uncovering the best work by France's young playwrights—were plays by André Gide, Gabriel D'Annunzio, Maxim Gorky, Paul Claudel (whose first productions were under Lugné-Poe), Shakespeare, Fernand Crommelynck, Salacrou, Stève Passeur, and Jean Anouilh. (Several were for other managements.)

For Claudel's *The Tidings Brought to Mary* (1912), an arrangement like that of the Munich Art Theatre was used. An inner-proscenium created a stylized background, and there were a series of nonrealistic drops, combined with minimalist props and furniture. *Hamlet* (1913) employed the latest Shakespeare concepts, with a neutral downstage wall decorated with simple heraldic designs and opened at the center by a large arch, with doorways to either side. The arched wall remained as new backdrops came in upstage, and suggestive props suggested new locales.

Picking up where Fort left off, Lugné-Poe became the first important director to successfully provoke an effective reaction to the narrowness of realism/naturalism. Although he later opted for eclecticism, his methods demonstrated the possibilities of a poetic, imaginative, and otherworldly theater of the imagination, and revealed the suggestive theatrical values of symbolism.

Further reading:

Jasper, Gertrude B. *Adventure in the Theatre: Lugné-Poe and the Théâtre de l'Oeuvre to 1899.* New Brunswick, N.J.: Rutgers University Press, 1947.

Also: Braun, *The Director and the Stage*; Knapp, *The Reign of the Theatrical Director*; Whitton, *Stage Directors in Modern France.*

YURI LYUBIMOV (1917–   )

YURI PETROVICH LYUBIMOV was born in Yaroslavl, Russia. At 17, he studied Stanislavskian methods at the Second Studio of the Moscow Art Theatre, entered the Vakhtangov School in 1936, and joined the Vakhtangov Theatre, where he became a leading actor. During the war he was master of ceremonies for a group that entertained soldiers and politicians. Despite being a communist, he grew disillusioned with the regime's hypocrisy.

While never completely abandoning Stanislavsky, Lyubimov became increasingly excited by Bertolt Brecht's use of theater to provoke social change. He took up teaching and, in 1963, at age 47, staged Brecht's *The Good Woman of Setzuan* as his students' graduation exercise. It led to his being made head of Moscow's Taganka Theatre.

Lyubimov turned the Taganka into an artistic mouthpiece for those discontented with the government, but this led to the outright banning or partial censoring of plays. Because of his manipulations, however, the Taganka survived. His productions submerged their anti-Soviet messages in difficult-to-censor ways; often the objectionable material was subtly couched in the staging and design. It was harder to justify the removal of a visual metaphor than it was of dialogue references. An example was Anton Chekhov's *The Three Sisters* (1981), in which the acting area's rear wall opened; as cold air and even snow blew in, the spectators could see Moscow—to which the yearning sisters always refer—spread out below them (the theater is on a hill). Then, a military band entered to block the view. (The arrogance of the military was continually underlined.) The effect contrasted the characters' romantic illusions with the harsh reality of Moscow under a repressive administration. In Lyubimov and Yuri Trifonov's version of the latter's novel, *The House on the Embankment* (1980), about Stalinist control of the arts, when ordered to remove a Stalinist's name from a poem, he had his actors clap their hands over their mouths when they came to the name.

Audiences queued up to see Lyubimov's productions. The more critical the press, the more popular the productions. Audiences usually avoided overt responses for fear that their reaction to double meanings might elicit censorship. Surprisingly, Lyubimov was appreciated by various bigwigs, especially KGB head Yuri Andropov, whose children—to Andropov's relief—Lyubimov persuaded against theatrical careers. Still, getting permission to put on a play was debilitating; ultimately, he found it easy to get the permission, the drawback being that works were banned just as they were to open. Nevertheless, the Taganka was allowed to exist as a half-hearted token of freedom of expression.

Yuri Lyubimov directing Crime and Punishment *in Washington, D.C. (1986)* (Photo: Arena Stage/Joan Marcus)

Lyubimov's first controversial use of the Taganka was for *Ten Days That Shook the World* (1965), John Reed's account of the Russian Revolution, banned under Stalin. Despite some censorship, it was a brilliant multimedia (dance, music, film) mounting.

Lyubimov offered over 50 major works (more "prose pieces" than plays, according to Peter Sellars) that revealed him as a master of stylized, politically confrontational theater. Many were adaptations by Lyubimov and other writers of the latters' novels, poetry, and songs. Each commented caustically on Soviet life. Many remained for years. Over 400 performances a year were seen, meaning that over 10 million theatergoers viewed Lyubimov's work during a two-decade period. A partial list would include his and Andrey Voznesensky's adaptation of the latter's poetry, *Anti-Worlds* (1965); *Listen!* (1967), based on Vladimir Mayakovsky's antibureaucratic poems; Voznesensky's *Watch Your Faces* (given two dress rehearsals before being banned, 1968); Sergey Esenin's poem *Pugachev* (1967); Molière's *Tartuffe* (1968); Boris Vassilyev's anti-Nazi *The Dawns Are Quiet Here* (1971); *Hamlet* (1971), with Elsinore a thinly disguised Kremlin, and a guitar-playing prince acted by popular balladeer Vladimir Vysotsky, who sang a selection from Boris Pasternak's censored *Dr. Zhivago*; Eugenie Yevtushenko's *Under the Skin of the Statue of Liberty* (1972), assumed to be anti-American, but meant to be anti-Soviet; Lyubimov and Fedor Abramov's adaptation of the latter's *Wooden Horses* (1974); a four-hour version of *The Master and Margarita* (1977), adapted by Lyubimov from Mikhail Bulgakov's satirical, fantastical novel (the book, which attacks censorship, was itself censored); his adaptation of Fyodor Dostoyevsky's *Crime and Punishment* (1979), originally shown in Hungary (1978) because of censorship problems; Brecht's *Turandot, or the Congress of Whitewashers* (1979); the banned production of *Vladimir Vysotsky* (1980), based on the beloved artist, who died at 40; Chekhov's *The Three Sisters* (1981); and Alexander Pushkin's *Boris Godunov* (1983), banned because the last line, spoken to the audience, criticized their inability to alleviate their misery.

Lyubimov was given permission to stage *Crime and Punishment* in London (1983), where, in the wake of the Soviet downing of a Korean airliner, he publicly criticized the government. He was stripped of his theater, his citizenship, and his party membership. (Andropov's recent death had removed his protector.) Various foreign assignments were undertaken, including *Crime and Punishment* at Washington, D.C.'s Arena Stage (1986). A year later, he

Randle Mell in Crime and Punishment. *Directed by Yuri Lyubimov. (1986)* (Photo: Arena Stage/Joan Marcus)

had begun rehearsals of *The Master and Margarita* at Robert Brustein's American Repertory Theatre when his dissatisfaction with the production arrangements led to its cancellation. In 1987, Sweden's Royal Dramatic Theatre premiered *A Feast in the Plague-Time*, his collage of three short Pushkin plays and other writings and a work by 19th-century Scottish writer John Wilson. This cautionary tale about people's behavior during a pestilence raging outside a room in which they are banqueting was also seen in Purchase, New York. When Mikhail Gorbachev's *perestroika* reintroduced intellectual freedom to the Soviet Union, Lyubimov returned to stage *Boris Godunov* (1988).

The next year, traveling on an Israeli passport (he staged a number of works in Israel, where he was lionized by the Russian emigrés), he was given a visa to return to Moscow for several months, and presented *Living*, which had been banned in 1968 and which he had repeatedly been unable to produce. Government officials and cultural celebrities jammed the opening. The work, which Alma Law calls a satire on "the obtuse management of collective farms," began with a monologue in which the hero told of how Leonid Brezhnev's minister of culture had told Lyubimov in 1968 that the play was "disgusting," and that he should be put on trial for it. Things had changed so radically that senior bureaucrats now laughed at lines like, "Did we really have a revolution?" Lyubimov wished to remain, and by mid-1989 was fully restored to citizenship and began work on Bulgakov's satire, *Black Snow,* about Stanislavsky's censorship of his work. He continued to live in Israel and to work abroad. However, one of his most recent premieres was his adaptation of Dostoyevsky's *A Raw Youth* (1990), in Finland, after which he turned his attention to an *Electra* for Greece and a version of *Dr. Zhivago* for Germany.

Lyubimov's theater is an antirealistic synthesis, making impressive use of unusual lighting, music, and heightened acting. He breaks the "fourth wall" to make theater a people-oriented, carnivalesque experience, with elements of the grotesque. To differentiate his style from officially approved theater, he calls it "theater of buffoonery." Realistic behavior and artifacts are combined with imaginative abstraction, establishing a dialectic that results in a unique vision of reality designed to make a statement on contemporary themes; it is especially important that the audience be startled from its apathy so that it will improve conditions. Lyubimov's work always deals with Russian life and culture. He was moved to do *Crime and Punishment* in order to counteract the official interpretation that makes Raskolnikov a czarist victim whose murders are a blow against capitalism. Lyubimov revealed him as a cold killer, emphasizing that no political philosophy should require a human death.

His scripts are usually nonlinear, nonchronological, and episodic, and are likely to be considerably rearranged from the originals on which they are based. Ideas emerge through the principle of montage. An excellent example is the script for *The Master and Margarita,* which interweaves the novel's three narrative lines, two set in 1930s Moscow and another in the biblical era, but with the three not only seeming to occur at the same time but also to reflect life in contemporary Moscow.

One reason for Lyubimov's bad boy image was his abandonment of the approved style of socialist realism in favor of a "formalistic" methodology. The productions are conceptualized around a strong thematic problem to which each actor and other contributor is required to have a personal commitment.

At the heart of a Lyubimov production is a visual metaphor that suggests his thematic ideas but is—through association—open to multiple interpretations. In *Hamlet,* an attack on bureaucratic lies and corruption, the primary metaphor was an overwhelming wool or hemp curtain that could move about in almost any direction. Margaret Croyden wrote that it

> moves like a great monster, dominating the action and containing within its folds the symbols of power and

> oppression: swords, goblets and thrones edged with knives. The curtain envelops all the characters . . . [,] sweeps the stage clean and moves menacingly toward the audience.

In *The Master and Margarita* he employed a selection of set pieces from earlier productions, each of which, because of its previous meanings, had strong associative values. (Only the knowledgeable Taganka spectator could catch all of the references.) One of these borrowed props, symbolic of time, was a huge pendulum clock, hung from the ceiling and swung to either side and from front to rear; characters could ride on it as when Margarita flies over Moscow as a witch. The *Hamlet* curtain, representing malevolent forces, was also present. The concept of borrowing earlier props served both to celebrate a decade of Lyubimov's work and to emphasize Bulgakov's ideas about artistic freedom.

Crime and Punishment, staged in black and white with splashes of red, contained two blood-spattered, white-painted doors that could be used vertically or horizontally and moved about as a central image. (Dostoyevsky's novel uses the word "door" over 200 times.) They served multiple purposes, in addition to functioning as a passage from one place (or dimension) to another. They could be a coffin, a bed, a witness to murder, and so on. Sellars understood them as "emblems of witness, emblems of concealment, and . . . emblems of violation when they were opened, thrown open, and forced open."

A man of sometimes fiery temper, Lyubimov is uncompromising, and some think him dictatorial. He never rehearses until all aspects of the physical production are clear in his mind, although he will make adjustments according to need. The designers and composers work with him throughout the rehearsals, providing an approximation of his requirements.

Whereas he begins rehearsals by discussing the work and displaying a model, he keeps this period to a functional minimum, having little use for "at table" sessions and preferring to concentrate on staging. He believes it better not to speak at length about his conception too early, because to do so before the actor is emotionally involved produces an overly rationalistic effect. Abroad, however, it is necessary to spend several days at table because of translation-related problems. Instead of psychological analysis he provides historical, political commentary. He seeks acting that is highly physical, and his own contributions, related to his obsession with tempo and rhythm, border on the choreographic.

The Taganka actors are singers, musicians, acrobats, and mimes, making his demands possible. They are also masters of direct address, always found in his presentations.

Lyubimov gives exuberant, skillful demonstrations; some resent this although he always provides "a subtle psychological motivation," according to Solomon Volkov. He desires the unconventional solution to a problem; when a Taganka actress playing a nurse had to inject her patient, Lyubimov had her do it in reverse, inserting the needle and then squirting the liquid, thereby suggesting the incompetency of Soviet medicine. The label of puppet-master offends him, as he wants actors to reveal their personalities as much as possible. Ensemble concerns, however, outweigh individualism. He might even observe actors offstage and then borrow characteristic but offbeat behavior. Often, rehearsal accidents become part of the score. Actors are told to show, not talk about, their ideas. Before his exile, he used a three-flashlight code to communicate during runthroughs; red meant he was displeased; green meant he was pleased; white signalled that something needed improvement.

Despite sometimes having to resort to primitive measures, he creates unconventional lighting effects. Flickering candles are a trademark. Much noted is Lyubimov's tendency to create looming shadows and chiaroscuro, often through the use of footlights or lights hidden beneath the floor. The shadows themselves might engage in interactive relationships reflective of the attitudes of those who cause them. Lighting constantly changes; Volkov noted of the light in *Crime and Punishment*, which had 250 cues:

It lives an independent life, as one of the cast of characters. The light sometimes enters into a confronta-tion with the actors, making them squint, contort, twist; at other times, characters use it in their struggle with one another or else in attacking the audience, as Raskol-nikov does in his opening monologue. Here he grasps a hand-held light and directs it at us, blinding and humiliating us; yes, that's us, we're trash; he torments us in our helplessness.

Lyubimov's renowned, highly selective sets possess metaphysical resonances. Music—both classical and popular—is vital, and continuous, taped sound tracks often accompany the action.

Lyubimov is important not only for his untraditional productions, but for his subversive use of art to confront the evils of tyranny. When the ax inevitably fell, the theater allowed his portrait to remain over his desk. Under it were the prophetic words, "No matter how paradoxical it may seem, I believe in my own return. It is not possible that my exile will continue forever."

Further reading:

Bly, Mark. "Lyubimov and the End of an Era: An Interview with Peter Sellars." *Theatre* 16 (Spring 1985).

Croyden, Margaret. "A Drama of Age and Exile." *New York Times Magazine*, December 21, 1986.

Gershkovich, Alexander. *The Theater of Yuri Lyubimov: Art and Politics at the Taganka Theater in Moscow.* Translated by Michael Yurieff. New York: Paragon House, 1989.

Law, Alma. "The Trouble with Lyubimov." *American Theatre* 2 (April 1985).

Volkov, Solomon. "At the Scene of Lyubimov's Crime." *American Theatre* 4 (April 1987).

GUTHRIE MCCLINTIC (1893–1961)

GUTHRIE MCCLINTIC was born in Seattle, Washington. In 1910, he traveled to New York to study acting at the American Academy of Dramatic Art. Three years later, starting as an assistant stage manager, McClintic began a nine-year relationship with producer-director Winthrop Ames, eventually became his casting director, and did some uncredited direction under Ames's aegis. He also worked temporarily for producer William A. Brady and his wife, star Grace George.

McClintic's first regular directing job closed out of town in 1918. He directed for a season with Jessie Bonstelle's Detroit stock company in 1920, doing a play a week for 17 weeks. In 1921, he married company member Katharine Cornell.

McClintic's Broadway break came with A. A. Milne's hit British comedy, *The Dover Road* (1921). McClintic soon became one of the busiest American directors, staging 26 more plays (two in London) by 1930, and producing many of them as well. Most were forgettable, but a few struck paydirt and several were significant. The first to star Cornell was Clemence Dane's *The Way Things Happen* (1924), a flop, but the debacle was overcome when he starred her in

Michael Arlen's controversial *The Green Hat* (1925). Cornell also headed McClintic's productions of Somerset Maugham's *The Letter* (1927); Margaret Ayer Barnes's *The Age of Innocence* (1928); and Barnes and Edward Sheldon's *Dishonored Lady* (1930). Among his successful non-Cornell productions were John Colton's *The Shanghai Gesture* (1926), Maxwell Anderson's *Saturday's Children* (1927), and Eugene Walters's *Jealousy* (1928). He staged the New York premiere of Noel Coward's *Fallen Angels* (1927). These works were often sensationalistic, and it was not until the thirties that McClintic's choices rose to a higher level. Many great stars appeared, a number of them reappearing with some frequency in later McClintic works, forming a sort of small-scale "McClintic stock company."

In the 1930s, McClintic reached his peak, beginning with the staging for Cornell of Rudolf Besier's *The Barretts of Wimpole Street* (1931), a frequently repeated item in the partnership's repertory. Cornell herself produced it as the first project under a scheme by which all profits were reinvested for future Cornell productions. McClintic directed Cornell's productions, but also produced and directed independently.

McClintic and Cornell's shared offerings in the thirties included André Obey's *Lucrece* (1932), Sidney Howard's *Alien Corn* (1933), Shakespeare's *Romeo and Juliet* (1934), and George Bernard Shaw's *St. Joan* (1936) and *Candida* (1937, and several revivals). Of the 26 other McClintic stagings of the decade, the most significant were S. N. Behrman's *Brief Moment* (1931) and *No Time for Comedy* (1939); Edgar Wallace's *Criminal at Large* (1932); Sidney Howard and Paul de Kruif's *Yellow Jack* (1934); Zoe Akins's *The Old Maid* (1935); Elsie Schauffler's *Parnell* (1935); Owen and Donald Davis's *Ethan Frome*; (1936); *Hamlet* (with John Gielgud, 1936); four Anderson plays, including *Winterset* (1935) and *High Tor* (1937); and Dorothy and DuBose Heywards' *Mamba's Daughters* (1939). These respected dramas demonstrate McClintic's commitment to a blend of middle- and highbrow selections.

In the 1940s, McClintic's totals declined, but the titles represent a continuation of his ability at selecting and staging noteworthy plays. His 19 offerings between 1941 and 1950 include six with Cornell: Shaw's *The Doctor's Dilemma* (1941), Henry Bernstein's *Rose Burke* (closed out of town, 1942), Anton Chekhov's *The Three Sisters* (1942), Jean Anouilh's *Antigone* (1946), Shakespeare's *Antony and Cleopatra* (1947), and Kate O'Brien's *That Lady* (1949). Among his other memorable productions were Howard Richardson and William Berney's *Dark*

of the Moon (McClintic received no credit, 1945), Tennessee Williams and Donald Wyndham's *You Touched Me* (1945), Howard Lindsay and Russel Crouse's *Life with Mother* (1948), Robinson Jeffers's *Medea* (1949), and Rosemary Casey's *The Velvet Glove* (1950).

In the 1950s, he directed about a dozen productions, the few of note being Mary Coyle Chase's *Bernardine* (1952) and two productions starring Cornell: a revival of Maugham's *The Constant Wife* (1952); and Christopher Fry's verse play *The Dark Is Light Enough* (1955). But by 1957, this prolific director's work was over.

Only George Abbott has staged more Broadway shows than McClintic. Although he had many modest hits, he never staged a 500-plus performance blockbuster; *The Barretts*, however, totaled more than 800 showings because of its frequent revivals. He respected commercial values, but was more apt to choose a work because of its emotional and aesthetic appeal. This did not prevent him from making many questionable selections.

Although always in favor of truthfulness, McClintic did not promote deep, internal analysis; he preferred actors who were technically skilled at voice and movement. His productions were noted for their polish and technique, not for their psychological realism. He wished to elevate the stage to a place of imagination and idealism, rather than to use it to confront people with a reflection of their own neuroses.

McClintic was a pragmatist, with no theory or methodology. His working methods remained fairly consistent. An eclectic range was needed, one that confronted each play on its own territory rather than made it conform to an alien perspective. His most important goal was to provide for the audience a feeling as close as possible to that which he himself had experienced when he first read the play. As soon as he read it, he had a good idea of what a play should look and sound like, and he devoted himself to realizing this impression. More than specifics, however, he sought to capture what he called the drama's "higher value," i.e., the playwright's ultimate intention.

An admittedly instinctive director, he could not explain many of his decisions other than by believing in their rightness. He infrequently talked or wrote about directing because he wanted to avoid overintellectualizing the process. Part of his success was owed to his casting skills. While not discounting physical appropriateness, he often chose actors more for their ability to act a part than to look it. Audiences viewing his productions knew that the best actors available had been employed.

Although not a playwright, McClintic—a respected play doctor—possessed fine editorial skills and knew how to cut and shape a manuscript to make it stageworthy. Months were spent with a dramatist before rehearsals began. Later, after noting an audience's responses, he rewrote scenes or had the author do so. It was his policy to forbid playwrights from attending rehearsals, because he felt they distracted the actors.

With revivals, his methods varied. His two Shakespeares showed great respect for the author (*Romeo and Juliet* was very faithful), but he blue-penciled Chekhov and Shaw (despite the latter's dislike of cuts). He worked closely with the translator of *The Three Sisters* for six months, going over each word, until the result was an extremely speakable version. His respect for Shakespeare was evident in the three years of prerehearsal work he did on *Romeo and Juliet* and the year and a half on *Antony and Cleopatra*. To restrict the number of cuts, the staging was swift and cinematic, making good use of rapid shifts that allowed one scene to begin almost before the previous one concluded.

McClintic normally held his first rehearsal (often at his apartment) by reading the script himself. Then, using a method borrowed from Ames, he would hold "at table" readings for a week or more before blocking (actors could move about during the readings). At first, he did not interrupt, but as the readings progressed he stopped to discuss and explain passages or to comment on timing and mood. He made clear precisely what the given circumstances were; if it took place in the past, he told period stories. Sets and costumes were carefully described to let the actors familiarize themselves with the show's look.

McClintic provided as much creative freedom as possible and was loath to offer readings, although he might have paraphrased. He listened to an actor's disagreements and argued over details, but was considered open to other points of view. Only when the actors fully comprehended their roles would he allow them to develop the blocking. They did not have to memorize their lines until they were blocked, as McClintic felt the process of learning movement and speech should be organically related.

Actors are not puppets, so he resisted imposing his ideas on them, yet he attended to the minutest parts of their performances. Prior to rehearsals, he prepared more in his head than on paper, although he highlighted key lines and stage directions in the text. He learned the entire play by heart so that he could discard the book while working with the actors. If required, he could instantly take over for any missing actor.

It was rare for him to demonstrate; more commonly, he asked the actor why his character did something or what the character might do in such and such circumstances, allowing the blocking to emerge through a collaborative approach. His demonstrations were exaggerated, even comical. Scenes being run were rarely interrupted; only at the end did he offer his advice.

Instead of castigating a slow learner, McClintic took him aside to speak to or work with privately. Actors who disagreed could show their own method. In general, Cornell received no special privileges, although she was given freedom to devise most of her business, with McClintic as her editor. He was respected for his ability to instill confidence, and for avoiding denigratory remarks. Still, when provoked, usually by a technician, he could demonstrate a furious, out-of-control temperament, followed by profuse apologies a day later. The flamboyant director in Moss Hart's play *Light Up the Sky*, is said to have been inspired by him.

In the thirties, McClintic gained a reputation as a director of verse dramas, and he even wrote an essay on staging such plays. His chief emphasis was on the rapidity of speech demanded. A quick tempo is especially important in the longer speeches, because it will force the audience to listen more closely and concentrate on the rhythms. In doing a verse play, he avoided any suggestion of "colloquial business," to avoid the disparity between excessive realism and idealized speech.

Because of the time required by reading rehearsals, McClintic demanded five, or even six, weeks of rehearsal, when most plays received four. This raised the costs considerably. Also adding to the expense was his demand for sets and props to be ready at the first blocking rehearsals. This was too impractical to be done regularly, but at the very least, McClintic made sure to have rehearsal costumes and props available from the start. He often used the same furnishings; the best pieces were stored for reuse, and he even borrowed pieces from his homes.

A gifted design collaborator, his knowledge of periods and styles made his input invaluable. His suggestions for the way the Brooklyn Bridge should tower over the set in *Winterset* gave Jo Mielziner the inspiration for one of the great Broadway sets of the thirties. In another Mielziner-designed show, *Romeo and Juliet*, his choice of 13th-century painter Giotto as the stylistic spark led to a set that immediately conjured up a believable, yet beautiful, background to the action. Designers appreciated the intense scrutiny he gave to every visual detail, yet he declined to allow sets and costumes to be distracting. He felt that design did its job best when it drew least attention to itself. He preferred selective realism for most of his plays, but on rare occasions, as in the constructivism of J. P. McEvoy's *God Loves Us* (1926), could branch into a more experimental mode.

McClintic was an expert lighting artist. His approach was to worry about atmosphere only after the actors were visible from the furthest part of the theater. He had no compunctions about lighting actors from unnatural positions, as effect and visibility counted more than the factuality of light sources.

McClintic's prolific record includes some of the finest classical and semiclassical revivals of his day as well as an exceptional lineup of major new plays. His intimate association with Katharine Cornell not only helped him direct many important works, it also had an indelible effect on her illustrious career.

Further reading:

Eustis, Morton. "The Director Takes Command." *Theatre Arts Magazine* 20 (February 1936).

McClintic, Guthrie. *Me and Kit.* Boston: Little, Brown, 1955.

———. "Directing Chekhov." *Theatre Arts Magazine* 27 (April 1943).

Mosel, Tad, with Gertrude Macy. *Leading Lady: The World and Theatre of Katharine Cornell.* Boston: Little, Brown, 1978.

Also: Gassner, *Producing the Play.*

ROUBEN MAMOULIAN (1898–1987)

ROUBEN MAMOULIAN was born in Tiflis, Georgia, in southern Russia, to a wealthy banker and a talented amateur actress. He was educated in Paris, and eventually mastered eight languages. In 1916, while studying law at the University of Moscow, he enrolled in Evgeny Vakhtangov's Third Studio of the Moscow Art Theater. His studies disrupted by the Russian Revolution, Mamoulian returned to Tiflis, where he cofounded a studio theater and wrote criticism before emigrating to Western Europe in 1921.

In London, Mamoulian directed émigré Russian theater artists in native plays at their Macaroff Theater. His first West End play was Austin Page's *The Beating on the Door* (1922), which he gave a realistic treatment, although he soon realized that he was more at home with theatricalist methods.

From 1923 to 1925, the musically literate Mamoulian became head of an opera theater program at the Eastman School of Music in Rochester, New York, where he staged 12 operas as well as teaching acting for the operatic stage. To take the job he had to reject a simultaneous offer to become—with Louis Jouvet and Theodore Komisarjevsky—part of a directorial triumvirate at Paris's Théâtre des Champs Elysées.

At Eastman, Mamoulian developed his unique ability to integrate all the elements of a musical production, from design to acting to singing. He exploited his strong belief in the values of rhythm in theatrical performance, and his stagings commonly employed unconventional interpretations. His final production was a memorable drama-ballet version of Maurice Maeterlinck's *Sister Beatrice* (1925), with a new score and with choreography by Martha Graham.

In 1926, Mamoulian assumed the directorship of the Theater Guild's acting school. At Scarborough, New York, he directed the students in Booth Tarkington's *Clarence*, Gilda Varesi and Dolly Byrne's *Enter Madame*, and Leonid Andreyev's *He Who Gets Slapped*. When the Guild told him that it would only consider European plays for him in their regular series, he put on a special matinee of George M. Cohan's *Seven Keys to Baldpate*, an American piece, in which he demonstrated his command of pictorial and rhythmic tools. Consequently, the Guild asked him to do a play in which no leading director was interested, Dorothy and Dubose Heyward's folk drama, *Porgy* (1927), about life in Catfish Row, a Charleston, South Carolina, black fishing tenement.

Mamoulian, who always prepared with extreme thoroughness, went to Charleston to absorb its atmosphere before beginning rehearsals. Barely familiar with blacks, he cast a large company (many of them inexperienced) at a time when serious Broadway plays with black characters were rare and even used whites in blackface (Al Jolson wanted to play Porgy). He helped the authors tighten their sprawling script, and was responsible for major revisions. Perhaps his greatest was the ending, which he altered from having the crippled Porgy accept his abandonment by Bess to having Porgy leave in his cart, resolving to win her back.

Mamoulian created a vivid panorama of the teeming tenement's life, mingled with spirituals, crap games, violence, and sensuality. The critics praised the emotional and atmospheric effects, the groupings, the vibrant use of light and shadow, and the unusual rhythmic style, much of it optimized by an inventive use of background sounds used in counterpoint to the action. This was a signature technique, used to disclose the interior nature of the characters. Mamoulian designed the lighting, as he would do on all his productions, gaining fame for his use of shadows.

Mamoulian sat at the rear of the house, shouting through a megaphone, controlling the tempo with a metronome, ending chaos with a whistle, and conducting the actors with a baton. The cast was drilled relentlessly to make their rhythms second nature. Only rigorous rehearsals could give him the air of spontaneity he sought. One scene, "The Symphony of Noises," was practically a musical composition made up of all the sounds associated with the activities of the denizens of Catfish Row.

Mamoulian directed eight more Guild presentations. Eugene O'Neill's epic-scaled satire on modern materialism, *Marco Millions* (1928), starred Alfred Lunt as the Babbitt-like Marco Polo. This opulent production used an ensemble of 15, which doubled and tripled to suggest a huge cast. Mamoulian was a master at making casts seem larger than they were. (He used offstage noise to increase his effects.) Robert Nichols and Martin E. Browne's *Wings Over Europe* (1928), which prophesied the atomic bomb, included an example of Mamoulian's rhythmic genius when the British cabinet was given 15 minutes to make a decision on which the world depended. A clock's ticking was counterpointed against the silent pacing of the actors, until the prime minister ended the deliberations by loudly closing his cigarette case.

Mamoulian staged Romain Rolland's *The Game of Love and Death* (1929), a didactic drama about the French Revolution, and a revival of Karel Capek's play about robots, *R.U.R.* (1930), in a version that, because of its sharpened satire, was superior to the Guild's 1922 original. There was a frightening moment when, just before a blackout, the menacing

robots seemed to be marching straight into the audience. Mamoulian staged the first American showing of Ivan Turgenev's 80-year-old romantic comedy, *A Month in the Country* (1930), with Alla Nazimova, and with sets and costumes based on the 1910 Moscow Art Theater mounting. It was the closest he would come to directing a classic.

The Guild produced Mamoulian's stagings of three landmark American musicals: *Porgy and Bess* (1935), George and Ira Gershwin's famed operatization of *Porgy*; Richard Rodgers and Oscar Hammerstein II's *Oklahoma!* (1943), based on Lynn Riggs's play *Green Grow the Lilacs*, about romance in the Southwest; and the same team's *Carousel* (1945), derived from Ferenc Molnár's romantic fantasy *Liliom*, but moved from Hungary to Maine. Mamoulian also staged the London versions of the latter shows.

Each of these shows benefitted vastly from Mamoulian's conceptions. *Oklahoma!*, one of Broadway's longest-running hits, is a prime example of the seamlessly "integrated" musical blending songs, music, dialogue, story, dance, and decor into an organic whole. Its emphasis on dramatic and psychological conflict was unusual for a musical. Even the acting of the nonmusical passages was informed by a rhythmic foundation that helped tie the package together. It included many novel features, including the replacement of a conventional big opening number with a simple scene of a woman churning butter as the offstage strains of "Oh, What a Beautiful Morning" began to fill the air. The use of dramatic instead of conventional musical comedy lighting, meaning the use of a larger-than-usual number of instruments, was another innovation. Mamoulian resented the inference sometimes made by Rodgers and others that the composer was actually responsible for many of the show's breakthroughs; he declared that Rodgers originally objected to many of his successful ideas.

Mamoulian began *Carousel* with a musical prologue that introduced the major characters and gave an idea of what was to transpire in an ingenious pantomimic sequence. Mamoulian also revised Hammerstein's libretto so that Billy's somber confrontation at the end with Mr. and Mrs. God became a charmingly fanciful one with a crusty, star-polishing janitor called the Starkeeper.

In 1928, outside the Guild, Mamoulian offered two out-of-town flops and two that made Broadway, a weak satire on feminism, *These Modern Women*, by Lawrence Langner, and Harry Hervey and Carleton Hindreth's *Congai*, a melodrama of racial and sexual oppression in French Indochina. In 1930, he did

Laurence Stallings's *A Farewell to Arms*, an adaptation of Hemingway's novel, and Lawton Campbell's *Solid South*, a satire on the unreconstructed South with Richard Bennett and Bette Davis. Thereafter, in addition to an opera at the Metropolitan Opera House, he staged three commercially unsuccessful Broadway musicals. *Sadie Thompson* (1944), by Vernon Duke, Howard Dietz, and Mamoulian himself, and based on Somerset Maugham's story, employed spectacular staging, including up- and downstage "water curtains" to imitate rain. *St. Louis Woman* (1946), by Harold Arlen, Johnny Mercer, Arna Bontemps, and Countee Cullen, was a black musical in which Pearl Bailey stole the show in her Broadway debut. Morton Gould, Mamoulian, and Dorothy and Herbert Fields's *Arms and the Girl* (1950), based on a play by Langner, was a catastrophe. There was also the mildly successful but artistically and socially provocative Kurt Weill-Maxwell Anderson musical about South Africa, *Lost in the Stars* (1949), which managed 281 performances. Mamoulian's only straight play of the period was Joseph Hayes's flop *Leaf and Bough* (1949). Meanwhile, Mamoulian gained renown as a film director. Although he later staged two non-Broadway revivals of *Oklahoma!* and one of *Carousel*, his Broadway career was over by 1950.

Most of these productions had large casts and spectacular designs. Mamoulian was renowned for crowd scenes in which even the most insignificant character was three-dimensional. Chorus characters were similarly individualized. He believed in the ensemble, and opposed any actor or production element from dominating. He did not hesitate to demonstrate for actors, using his considerable mimic talent. Actors were implored to consider the given circumstances of their roles so they would behave with motivated conviction. Mamoulian encouraged them to use their own imaginations before he applied his editorial brush. But nothing seen on his stage lacked his ultimate control. When absolutely necessary, he used cruelty to coerce a performance. He liked to challenge actors in hopes that they would retaliate with a good performance. His formal European manner, excellent grooming, and ever-present cigar made him intimidating for some, and he was considered an autocrat, but some claim he was a kindly figure dedicated to getting actors to hold nothing back in serving their art.

Knowledgeable in all the visual arts, he had a gift for picturization, and his tendency to rely on the visual—down to the remotest gesture—was often utilized to shore up weak dramaturgy. At a time when most Broadway directors were preoccupied with verisimilitude, Mamoulian's ability to integrate all the physical elements of a production in sensitive relationship to psychologically believable yet artistically heightened performances led to his reputation for theatricalist prowess. He worked very slowly and continually revised until satisfied. He was known for his ability to remain calm no matter how chaotic the circumstances.

Mamoulian insisted that writers listen to his suggestions openly. He was so persuasive and insightful that even O'Neill, known for his resistance to rewrites, made many cuts in *Marco Millions*. Rodgers lost a battle to retain a song in *Oklahoma!* that Mamoulian loved but considered extraneous. He contended that in an integrated musical there should be absolutely nothing—no matter how well done—not organically related to the material. Anderson also proved hard to convince, but a contractual agreement persuaded the author to make Stephen Kumalo in *Lost in the Stars* into a Gandhi-like rebel rather than the angry agitator Anderson preferred. Fearful of authorial or producer interference, Mamoulian insisted on a contractual clause guaranteeing him the power to make final decisions. Considerable rancor could attend the writer-director relationship, an egregious case being the one involving the production of *Leaf and Bough*. In that production, the author, anxious to get the play on, agreed to Mamoulian's many changes under duress. When he saw how his play was distorted from his original, he tried to have it closed out of town. The experience created bad blood between the playwright and the director.

Mamoulian's musicianship allowed him to work as closely with composers as with dramatists. Thus, he was responsible for having Gershwin make considerable cuts, including a series of pace-retarding recitatives, in *Porgy and Bess*. When Mamoulian staged a musical, he kept close tabs on the musical and choreographic components, even when they were rehearsed in separate places.

Many of Mamoulian's projects reveal liberally oriented social themes, but he always put artistic and entertainment considerations first and rarely chose tendentious works. His various assignments in which black characters figure demonstrate his progressive tendencies, and he is historically important for having directed important works bringing blacks to prominence.

Only 18 Broadway shows bore Mamoulian's directorial byline, but within that total were some of the century's most dazzling. He brought to the commercial stage a European aesthetic sensibility in his uncompromising integrity and ability to create cohesive, unified productions employing dynamic lighting, rhythmic behavior, pictorial genius, psychologically sound acting, meaningful scripts, and innovative musical-theater practices.

Further reading:

Eaton, Walter Prichard. *The Theatre Guild: the First Ten Years*. New York: Brentano's, 1929.

Horgan, Paul. "Rouben Mamoulian: The Start of a Career." *Films in Review* 24 (August–September, 1973).

Milne, Tom. *Mamoulian*. London: Thames and Hudson, Cinema One Series, 1969.

Silke, James R. *Rouben Mamoulian: Style Is the Man*. No. 2. Beverly Hills: The American Film Institute, 1971.

Waldau, Roy. *The Theatre Guild: The Vintage Years 1929–1939*. Cleveland: Case Western Reserve University, 1972.

Also: Gottfried, *Broadway Musicals*.

VSEVOLOD MEYERHOLD (1873–1940)

VSEVOLOD EMILOVICH MEYERHOLD (*né* Karl Theodore Kazimir Meyergold) was born in Penza, Russia, where his father owned a vodka distillery. An abortive stint as a law student was followed by his enrollment in the Moscow Philharmonic Society's theater school. In 1898, he became a charter member of the Moscow Art Theater's acting company, but left in 1902 to codirect a troupe in Kherson (1902–1903) and Tiflis (1903–1904), where he usually directed in the Moscow Art Theater's realistic style.

In 1905, Meyerhold was put in charge of Moscow's Theater-Studio by Konstantin Stanislavsky to explore symbolist methods. Despite Meyerhold's interesting experiments, his productions never formally opened. A combination of circumstances—including the revolution of 1905 and Stanislavsky's displeasure with the robotic nature of the acting—killed the studio.

Meyerhold directed the St. Petersburg company of Vera Komisarjevskaya, who was interested in exploring advanced methods. Their most renowned productions included Henrik Ibsen's *Hedda Gabler* (1906), done in the bas-relief style founded by Georg Fuchs; Maurice Maeterlinck's *Sister Beatrice* (1906), also in the bas-relief manner, with only seven feet between the spectators and the neutral background, and employing hieroglyphic, sculptural acting designed to express the psychological subtext; Alexander Blok's *The Fairground Booth* (1906), produced as a grotesque tragic farce in commedia style; and 10 other important works. Feeling overshadowed by him, Komisarjevskaya dismissed Meyerhold.

His work was increasingly non-realistic, creating its effects through allusive means, including nonrep-resentational sets and acting. He sought ways of increasing the intimacy between audience and actor. Like Bertolt Brecht, he emphasized the fact that the performance was a self-conscious event in which the audience played an active part.

From 1908 to 1917, Meyerhold directed the Imperial Theaters of St. Petersburg, staging plays at the Alexandrinsky and operas at the Marinsky. His most radical experiments—credited to the pseudonymous "Doctor Dapertutto"—took place at cabarets and private residences. The 14 plays he staged at the Alexandrinsky—always in elaborate mise-en-scènes usually designed by Alexander Golovin—included infrequently revived works by Knut Hamsun, Nikolai Gogol, Molière, Arthur Wing Pinero, Pedro Calderón de la Barca, George Bernard Shaw, Alexander Ostrovsky, Mikhail Lermontov, and Ibsen. Renowned was Molière's *Don Juan* (1910), which recreated the luxury of an 18th-century staging at Versailles and provided an apron extension over the orchestra pit; a stylized, curtainless set suggestive of Gobelin tapestries; wigged prompters, visible behind apertured screens; and two boys dressed as liveried blackamoors to set the props and furnishings, an idea inspired by the *kabuki*. Such "proscenium servants" appeared in several other stagings. The actors, who could see the spectators because the house lights remained on, came downstage to address them—including some improvisational banter—directly.

An example of Meyerhold's work in unofficial venues was Arthur Schnitzler's musical pantomime, *Columbine's Scarf* (1910). Commedia techniques helped create a mystico-symbolist style with overtones of the jarring, exaggerated, ironic manner called "grotesque." Actors mingled with spectators.

Meyerhold longed for a revival of the strolling player spirit, in which versatile actors (*"cabotins"*) had multiple talents. He favored "mask-like" acting according to conventions of fixed role-types.

In the post-Revolution period Meyerhold's leftist political beliefs were employed theatrically to help bolster the Bolsheviks. He joined the Communist Party and was made a theatrical commissar. He discovered, however, that his methods for using the theater politically did not jibe with those of the government. At first, though, the latter was too busy elsewhere to interfere.

The first post-Revolutionary Soviet play was Vladimir Mayakovsky's *Mystery-Bouffe* (1918), an anticapitalist farce directed by Meyerhold in Petrograd. The proletarians were dressed identically in factory uniforms, and the production employed acrobatic acting within abstract sets designed in suprematist style.

Meyerhold, who almost lost his life when captured by White Russians in 1919, directed Ibsen's *A Doll's House* (renamed *Nora*, 1920) at Novorossik before beginning his great Moscow period at the New Theater RSFSR 1 with a propagandistically revised version of Emile Verhaeren's 1898 symbolist drama, *The Dawns* (1920), about war between capitalists and proletarians. Every night there were inserted into the play reports from the Crimean civil war. Despite the theater's rundown condition, Meyerhold remained for years, eventually fixing it up; it underwent many name changes.

Meyerhold only occasionally worked elsewhere, as when he did plays by Alexey Faiko and Alexander Ostrovsky for the Theater of Revolution in 1923. He was promised an innovative new playhouse, but politics killed the dream. A selective list of his greatest productions at his own playhouse might include the updated version of *Mystery-Bouffe* (1921), starring Igor Ilinsky, Meyerhold's leading actor; Fernand Crommelynck's *The Magnificent Cuckold* (1922); Alexander Sukhovo-Kobylin's 1869 *The Death of Tarelkin* (1922); Marcel Martinet's *Night* (renamed *Earth Rampant* in Sergei Tretyakov's adaptation; 1923), in which real army vehicles moved between the stage and auditorium; a radical staging of Ostrovsky's *The Forest* (1924), its five acts rearranged into 33 montagelike scenes, a common Meyerhold technique; the agit-prop revue, *D. E. (Give Us Europe!)* (1924); Faiko's *Bubus the Teacher* (1925), which tried the device of "pre-acting," in which the actor demonstrated his transitional attitude toward an event in a pantomimic manner that preceded his actual response; Nikolai

Erdman's *The Warrant* (1925); Gogol's *The Inspector General* (1926), Meyerhold's most famous mounting; Alexander Griboyedov's classic *Woe from Wit* (retitled *Woe to Wit*, 1928); Mayakovsky's *The Bedbug* (1929), which boldly satirized the current government and helped to stir up anti-Meyerhold feeling by Stalinists; Mayakovsky's *The Bathhouse* (1930), another satire on the Soviets, soon after which the author killed himself; Alexander Sukhovo-Kobylin's *Krechinsky's Wedding* (1933); Alexander Dumas *fils*'s *Camille* (1934), important as a return to pre-Revolutionary aesthetics, possibly to quiet Meyerhold's antiformalist critics; and an evening of Anton Chekhov one-acters, *Thirty-three Fainting Fits* (1935). Several productions were banned before opening.

Meyerhold's company was liquidated in 1938 and he worked for Stanislavsky, who died later that year. After publicly rebuking the official artistic policy of socialist realism in 1939, Meyerhold was placed in a concentration camp and executed.

The Inspector General was Meyerhold's representative work. The script was a collation of all of Gogol's many drafts as well as of other Gogol writings. The five acts were edited into 15 titled scenes, each with its own musical motif, with everything conspiring to bitterly attack the bureaucratic mentality. An important nonspeaking character was introduced as an ironically detached shadow for Khlestakov. This tampering indicated Meyerhold's belief that a script was raw material in a director's hands. Such "distortions" eventually got him into trouble.

The acting area was restricted in many scenes to small, movable platforms that rolled on tracks with the cast frozen in crowded tableaux until hit by the lights. Silent-movie acting inspired the performances. The familiar characters were given startling new interpretations, most especially Khlestakov, who assumed a different "social mask" for each situation, thus requiring many costume and makeup changes. In the "Bribes" scene, 11 officials entered simultaneously through the 11 upstage doors in the semicircular backing wall, with Khlestakov viewing them while facing upstage; like a robot, he went to each in turn and snatched their offerings. At the play's conclusion, when Khlestakov's ruse has been uncovered, the three dozen characters began to wail and cry; joining hands, they snaked off through the audience and silence fell. A white curtain rose announcing the arrival of the true inspector general. When it disappeared overhead, an array of mannequins suggesting the petrification of all those now departed was exposed.

Of great importance to Meyerhold was an acrobatic acting method called "biomechanics." It turned actors into efficient acting machines, in keeping with the spirit of modern technology. Movement was pared of superfluities; rhythm was the basis of all activity; the actor moved from his center of gravity; and communication of emotional effects became possible through physiological rather than psychological means. (Actually, Meyerhold never abandoned psychological techniques for justifying onstage behavior.) Biomechanics was theatricalized but not abstract and always based on decipherable foundations. Moreover, the Meyerholdian actor (like the Brechtian), remained distinct from—and even commented on—his character through his performance.

A crucial adjunct to Meyerhold's twenties style was the functionalist mode called constructivism, in which scenery was an abstract but utilitarian image of the locales depicted; decoration *per se* was abandoned, and the physical components supporting the set were skeletally exposed. A classic case was *The Magnificent Cuckold,* which used a multilevelled combination of ramps, slides, and platforms designed to exploit biomechanical acting. A simplified windmill wheel turned at different speeds according to the emotional moods expressed, and actors made surprising entrances, as when a man showed his affection for a girl by plunging down a slide and knocking her off her feet.

Even when sets were not constructivist, they were distinctly original. Front curtains were rare; furnishings tended toward minimalism; expansive bridges, balconies, and sweeping staircases capable of suggesting multiple locales were incorporated; projected or painted titles were seen; neutral scenic pieces served diverse functions; costumes, wigs, and make-ups ranged from the exaggerated to the realistic; and a part of the theater's walls or equipment usually remained visible. From *The Forest* on, Meyerhold either designed or codesigned his productions.

Music was crucial to support rhythmic and emotional factors (Meyerhold occasionally composed his own scores), and some of the best Russian composers wrote for him. Even jazz was heard, and his production of *D.E.* (in which American musician Sidney Bechet performed) inspired a jazz craze in the USSR.

Meyerhold prepared with zeal, often spending several years considering a play and doing research on it, including its historical and social world. The results of his study were slowly funneled into a key idea or unifying concept. He normally kept his preparation in his head and conveyed it at rehearsals in a seemingly improvisational fashion. Promptbooks were abandoned in favor of spontaneity. Because of his restlessness, this often led to seemingly chaotic rehearsals, forcing everyone to be alert for fear of becoming confused amid his nonstop ideas.

Rehearsals began with a session devoted to discussing everything concerning the play in detail. The company reading came at the next session, with the director correcting interpretations and giving his own. He analyzed the lines in detail, gave line readings, and even demonstrated facial expressions.

Blocking began early, with most props and furnishings present. Even a rough version of the lighting—which Meyerhold created himself—was likely to be ready from the start. He sat in the house at a special table with a high stool but frequently ran to the stage along a special ramp. His directions were noted by many assistants who prepared a detailed record for reference.

Meyerhold's method was dictatorial, every move and gesture being shown, although accompanied by an explanation. He was wise enough to incorporate those occasional accidents that prove better than any preconception. He advocated collaboration, but many reports declare he treated actors as automatons. Others say this occurred only with uncreative actors and that working for him could be stimulating. He did not seek precise duplication, but a transformation in the actor's own terms. Those who infused their responses with appropriate inner life pleased him. Actors who could only ape him were ridiculed.

Rehearsals lasted for months, sometimes over half a year, because of Meyerhold's passion for polishing. He allowed small groups of visitors to observe, often asking for their opinions. From the 1920s on, he began to allow the playwrights to participate as well. Mayakovsky actually codirected his plays.

Meyerhold combined the skills of a designer, editor, composer, and theatricalist régisseur. His style has had enormous influence on today's auteur-conceptualists as well as on those of his time (including Brecht).

Further reading:

Hoover, Marjorie L. *Meyerhold: The Art of Conscious Theater.* Amherst: University of Massachusetts Press, 1974.

Leach, Robert. *Vsevolod Meyerhold.* Cambridge, England: Cambridge University Press, 1989.

Meyerhold, Vsevolod. *Meyerhold on Theatre.* Translated and edited by Edward Braun. New York: Hill and Wang, 1969.

Schmidt, Paul, ed. *Meyerhold at Work.* Austin: University of Texas Press, 1980.

Symons, James M. *Meyerhold's Theatre of the Grotesque: Post-Revolutionary Productions, 1920–1932.* Coral Gables: University of Miami Press, 1971.

Also: Braun, *The Director and the Stage*; Leiter, *From Stanislavsky to Barrault.*

JONATHAN MILLER (1934–   )

JONATHAN MILLER was born in London, England, where his father was a highly reputed neurologist and psychiatrist and his mother a respected writer. He studied at St. John's College, Cambridge, and University College, London, gaining a degree in medicine in 1959. At Cambridge, he and Dudley Moore, Alan Bennett, and Peter Cook wrote and performed the satirical revue *Beyond the Fringe,* which succeeded on the West End and Broadway. It diverted Miller from a career in medicine to one in theater.

The lanky Miller gave up acting when he directed John Osborne's *Under Plain Cover* (1962) at the Royal Court. More impressive was his New York

Jonathan Miller (seated r) with cast of Long Day's Journey into Night. *L to r: Jodie Lynne McClintock, Kevin Spacey, Bethel Leslie, Peter Gallagher, Jack Lemmon.* (Photo: Martha Swope)

directing debut: Robert Lowell's *The Old Glory* (1964), a two-part program composed of plays based on stories by Herman Melville *(Benito Cereno)* and Nathaniel Hawthorne *(My Kinsman, Major Molyneux)*. A forgettable new play staged in Connecticut preceded Lowell's adaptation of *Prometheus Bound* (1967) at the Yale Rep, followed by Miller's first Shakespeare, *Richard II* (1967), in Los Angeles. *Prometheus,* produced in London in 1971, was set in what he called "some sort of decaying seventeenth-century culture that has gone bad." Instead of chaining the title character to a rock, Robert Brustein told Michael Romani, "He . . . created an atmosphere of repression, in which Prometheus was imprisoned on a level of this massive structure that looked like a Pharos lighthouse—it went up as far as the eye could see, and equally as far down." Prometheus was an angry young man raging against tyranny (the production alluded vaguely to Vietnam), yet it preserved historical distance.

In 1968, he directed *Benito Cereno* at London's Mermaid. He took up a residency at the Nottingham Playhouse, where he provided unconventional stagings of Richard Brinsley Sheridan's *The School for Scandal* (1968), Anton Chekhov's *The Sea Gull* (1969), and Shakespeare's *King Lear* (1969). Each was one of several classics to which he kept returning; he redid *School for Scandal* at London's National Theater (1972) and at the American Repertory Theater (1982). Sheridan's comedy shed its traditional artificiality to pass through a Hogarthian sieve from which it emerged as a Rake's Progress of 18th-century decadence; the aristocrats had body odor, Lady Sneerwell was bald beneath her lice-ridden wig, and a maid was pregnant. Chekhov's play was revived for Chichester (1973) and the Greenwich Theater (1974), and *Lear* reappeared at the National Theater (1970) and the Old Vic (1989). In *Lear,* Edgar and Edmund were in a Lucifer-Christ relationship, and Miller called the wicked sisters "women exasperated by the demands of a silly old man" (quoted in Romani).

Twelfth Night (1970), *Julius Caesar* (1970), and *Hamlet* (1970; revived in 1982), were seen at the Arts Theater, Cambridge. In *Hamlet,* Claudius was surprisingly sympathetic. *The Tempest* was at the Mermaid (1970); he later did it in 1989 with Max von Sydow. To Miller, the play concerned issues of mastery and subordination. He replaced Ariel and Caliban's supernaturalism with African colonial images, casting the roles with black actors. Ariel was a competent, white-educated servant, ready to assume power from his master, Caliban a "demoralised,

detribalised, dispossessed, shuffling field hand" (quoted in Ralph Berry).

At the National, where he was an associate director, he provided *The Merchant of Venice* (1970) and *Measure for Measure* (1974). The former was set in late 19th-century Venice, with Shylock (Laurence Olivier) a morning-coated banker. It also drew a parallel between the friendship of Antonio and Bassanio and the love affair of Oscar Wilde and Lord Alfred Douglas. *Measure for Measure,* mounted on a Kafkaesque set whose walls were lined with doors of various sorts, each one evoking a new location by its usage, took place in a Freudian Vienna of the 1920s. It had two later productions (1975 and 1987).

These revivals exemplify Miller's desire to renovate (he uses the Renaissance term "renovatio") a classic by locating it in an unfamiliar period. He chooses this procedure sparingly and always with a careful logic. Much of his work has been preoccupied with exploring the 17th and 18th centuries, for which he has an affinity. He believes that the unusual background can bring out moral values otherwise overlooked, and can move it closer to our times. His ideas sometimes appear accidentally; for *The Merchant of Venice,* he happened to hear in his "mind's ear" Portia delivering her courtroom speech in an informal manner that suggested it was being done in a judge's chambers, not a courtroom; this implied a 19th-century setting which, he told Berry, "brought out and emphasised interesting features of the status of the intelligent woman, the woman stultified by the domination of men, the domination of fathers and suitors."

Miller deplores setting old plays in the contemporary world, and thinks the mediating factor (the "historical parallax") of a past period is necessary. He can draw lines between the period of composition, that of the background, that of the relocated period, and that of today. The point is not to establish "relevancy," but to draw attention to things that might not have been visible if more conventionally presented. When appropriate, as in his Tudor *King Lear* and *Twelfth Night,* the period of the writing or that in which it is set will be employed, and Miller will express what he terms the *mentalité* of the age. Nor does he seek oversimplification of a play's ideas, but prefers "to create as much complexity and indeed . . . strategic ambiguity as I can. . . . I choose a cluster of meanings which are centred around the salient issue, but which are not just simply that issue alone." Miller feels no guilt about removing jarring lines if efforts to make them congruent fail. He told Judith Cook, "I don't believe one has any duty or obligation to an author, once he's dead. . . . The only rules . . . are those of aesthetic consistency, formal elegance and accuracy and artistic finesse, and need have no bearing on what the author actually meant."

Often, Miller's concepts stem from something discovered during his study of literature, science, philosophy, sociology, history, aesthetics, music, photography, art, and architecture. He spends 80 to 90 percent of his spare time reading, but never for entertainment. His sets and lighting are frequently influenced by paintings or photos. He keeps extensive files and uses these and his personal collection of art books to spark his designers' imaginations or to inspire actors regarding period and mood. He has had long-standing relationships with several designers at different points in his career, and many of his productions have featured sets and costumes equivalent to the most imaginative in the European theater.

The National also produced his stagings of Georg Büchner's *Danton's Death* (1971) and Pierre de Beaumarchais's *The Marriage of Figaro* (1974), as well as one of Miller's rare contemporary dramas, Peter Nichols's *The Freeway* (1974). A conflict with the National's Peter Hall led to Miller's departure.

One of his finest contributions was a 1974 three-play series at the Greenwich, *The Sea Gull, Hamlet,* and Ibsen's *Ghosts* tied together by their similarity of "deep structure" and subsumed by Miller under the title, "Family Romances." The same actors played corresponding roles in each play. Miller was often present at the Greenwich during the 1970s, where he showed Oscar Wilde's *The Importance of Being Earnest* (1975), with Lady Bracknell—viewed as an ex-Gaiety girl—played with a German accent; *All's Well that Ends Well* (1975); and George Etherege's *She Would If She Could* (1979). Other revivals of the decade included *The Taming of the Shrew* (1972) at Chichester (in 1987, it would be his first production for the Royal Shakespeare Company); John Marston's *The Malcontent* (1973), at Nottingham, turned into a nightmarishly surrealistic comedy in which the insectlike characters wore white faces and black lipstick; and a Breugel- and Bosch-inspired *A Midsummer Night's Dream* (1970) in Vienna.

Miller ignored a topical, women's-lib approach to *The Taming of the Shrew.* He stressed what he felt was Shakespeare's 17th-century, Puritan-based view, in which order had to be preserved by the male head of a family; Petruchio's actions were tutorial and therapeutic. Perhaps his most memorable staging of

this lot was the award-winning version of Chekhov's *The Three Sisters* (1976), transferred to the West End from Guildford, and revealing a refreshingly deromanticized view of the title characters (a critic called Irena "a dogmatic adolescent," who reacted to the baron's death "as though a picnic had been rained off"). The work even managed to gain some sympathy for Natasha.

In 1974, Miller expanded into opera, which eventually took up the majority of his directing time. He also became active in film and television, especially the latter; from 1979 to 1981, he served as executive director of the BBC series that televised all of Shakespeare's plays. Moreover, Miller wrote, produced, and narrated a number of acclaimed documentary programs. His scientific bent led him to undertake a three-year position as a research fellow, from 1970 to 1973, and to occasionally lecture and teach in his field of neuropsychology. In 1984, in fact, having felt that he could be making more of a contribution to medicine than to theater, with which he had become disillusioned, he retired from directing. He soon realized that his age prevented him from making any medical breakthroughs and he returned to the stage. Among his other outside activities was the writing and editing of challenging, nontheatrical books, although *Subsequent Performances* concerned his ideas on "the afterlife of a play."

Miller's theater work in the 1980s not already noted included Gilbert and Sullivan's *The Mikado* (1986) for the English National Opera, later revived in America. This iconoclastic version set the action in an upper-class, English seaside hotel of the 1920s, removed all physical references to Japan (except for a vague view of Mount Fuji)—thus making the piece a satire on English foolishness—and based its comedy on the Marx Brothers. There was an excellent Broadway and West End staging of Eugene O'Neill's *Long Day's Journey into Night* (1986), starring Jack Lemmon, and exemplifying Miller's obsession with "speech act theory," whereby he seeks—regardless of the play—to capture psychologically authentic speech patterns, including much overlapping. Having described the drama to Ross Wetzsteon as "a fairly fast-moving, rattling, conversational piece," he knocked over an hour off its playing time. Also acclaimed was an adaptation of Ryszard Kapuscinski's *The Emperor* (1987), an all-black piece about Ethiopa, performed in Kafkaesque style in a Royal Court studio; Bertolt Brecht and Kurt Weill's *Mahagonny* (1989), set in early Hollywood, and shown in Los Angeles; and seven plays for the Old Vic, of which

Jack Lemmon and Bethel Leslie in Long Day's Journey into Night. *Directed by Jonathan Miller. (1986)* (Photo: Martha Swope)

he was artistic director from 1988 to 1990. Those he had not staged before were Jean Racine's *Andromache* (1988); N. F. Simpson's *One Way Pendulum* (1988); George Chapman's *Bussy D'Ambois* (1988), not seen since 1604; the Leonard Bernstein musical *Candide* (1988); and Pierre Corneille's *The Liar* (1989). This was the kind of challenging repertoire familiar on the Continent, but rarely seen in a major English company.

Among the reasons for Miller's preference for older plays are his wish not to have to confront a playwright with an idiosyncratic approach, his never having found a writer with whom he would like an ongoing relationship, and his belief that new plays direct themselves while old ones demand to be interpreted.

Miller commences rehearsals by creating an intellectual attitude in the "collective imagination of all those involved" (quoted in Berry) so that the play will reap unanticipated insights during the process. He concentrates on every role, seeking an ensemble. Many actors appear frequently in Miller's produc-

tions. Initial read-throughs are rare; Miller prefers to start by delivering a lecture on the play, and then rehearsing in an unprogramatic way. He is nondictatorial and collaborative. An open attitude allows him to discover from the actors how the lines should be spoken, and not to depend on preconceived ideas. Both he and his actors affirm that the best results come out of informal talks during the frequent tea breaks. Method acting annoys him. "I only want an actor to be an accomplished technician, who gives me the sense that I have seen something real," he told Wetzsteon.

Actors love his rehearsals because of his witty comments. His temperament and sense of timing make him a good comedy director, but he has injected unexpected bursts of comedy even into serious dramas by Ibsen and Racine. He is admired for his ability to elicit a performance by offering stimulating suggestions couched in concrete terms to which actors can relate. Miller can draw on knowledge from many disciplines to clarify his points. One of his strong interests is the nature of interpersonal relationships, especially as described by sociologists such as Erving Goffman, who is concerned with "the structure of conversation." This was particularly noticeable in Miller's productions of Chekhov and O'Neill. His medical training taught him to be a remarkable observer of behavior, so he is excellent at prompting natural performances, and he is of especial value to actors who must portray physical or mental pain. Miller's Ophelias have been almost uncomfortably accurate in their madness. The acting in his plays is rooted in detailed realism, although he employs stylized behavior as well, provided it is suitable to the play.

Because of his erudition, Jonathan Miller has been called a renaissance man, although he prefers to be called "a boundary figure," one who can do multiple tasks simultaneously and be able to make connections among them.

Further reading:

Miller, Jonathan. *Subsequent Performances.* New York: Elizabeth Sifton Book/Viking, 1986.

Romani, Michael. *A Profile of Jonathan Miller.* Cambridge, England: Cambridge University Press, 1992.

Wetzsteon, Ross. "The Director in Spite of Himself: An Interview with Jonathan Miller." *American Theatre 2* (November 1985).

Also: Berry, *On Directing Shakespeare;* Cook, *Directors' Theatre.*

ARIANE MNOUCHKINE (1939–   )

ARIANE MNOUCHKINE, daughter of Russian immigrants (her father was a filmmaker), was born in Paris, France. She was theatrically active at Oxford University before returning to Paris, where she directed Henri Bauchau's *Genghis Khan* (1961), given outdoors by a student group she founded. She then traveled extensively, especially in the Orient.

In 1964, she and her former colleagues founded the Théâtre du Soleil, incorporated as a workers' cooperative. All had to be familiar with theater's technical aspects. A naturalistic version of Maxim Gorky's *Smug Citizens* (1964) was followed by *Captain Fracasse* (1965), adapted from a Théophile Gauthier novel. After a year and a half of rehearsal, they opened Arnold Wesker's *The Kitchen* (1967) at the Medrano Circus. Rehearsals for the play, about the activities of a restaurant's kitchen staff, involved observation in kitchens, coaching from restaurant workers, and mastery of kitchen tasks to be transformed precisely into mime.

Shakespeare's *A Midsummer Night's Dream,* in a dark interpretation influenced by critic Jan Kott, with animalistically sensual sprites and a diabolical Puck, was also in the Circus. Titania and Oberon's sexuality was palpable in the performances of Béjart Ballet dancers. After France's political upheaval in May 1968, the company played for striking workers in factories. *The Clowns* (1969) was evolved collaboratively. The subtext examined each artist's position toward society.

International recognition arrived with *1789, The Revolution Must Stop When Complete Happiness Is Achieved* (1970), a collective work based on a Marxist interpretation of the French Revolution, and premiered in a Milanese sports arena. The piece was performed within an 18th-century fairground ambiance. A Brechtian technique was developed so that the actors—suggesting strolling players—could comment on their multiple roles. The episodic, frequently parodistic, four-hour production, which made much use of epic narration, was worked out improvisationally. It involved a great deal of physicalized, sometimes acrobatic acting, marionettes and giant puppets, music and singing, and performers mingling with the audience. Some spectators moved among five trestle stages, and some observed from bleachers.

Paris provided the subsidized company with the Cartoucherie, a huge munitions warehouse in the suburb of Vincennes. The place became a perfect environment for *1789.* This production began a policy of producing long runs before moving on to a new presentation.

Four hours of material excised from *1789* were employed in *1793, The Revolutionary State Is of This World* (1972), a more linearly structured docudrama. Each actor's single role was founded on his own politics. The context was the meeting of the *sans culottes* in the difficult days of 1793, the space made to resemble the interior of a large assembly hall. The audience gathered in an adjoining shed and was led into the main space, where the play was performed on three large tables with benches. Spectators watched from a two-story balcony along two sides. The multiple scenes showed in close detail the many crises through which the people had to pass in the post-Revolutionary period.

The Golden Age, The First Draft (1975) was another company-developed, antibourgeois work. It was a spectacularly produced, complexly lit piece employing narration, acrobats, masked commedia characters, circus and Chinese theater techniques, and improvisation. Many elements were inspired by discussions with laborers and school children. A 120-by-150-foot area of the Cartoucherie floor was reshaped with earth and concrete to create four thickly carpeted, pitlike amphitheaters, separated from one another by ridges on which the audience sat. Thousands of light bulbs were attached to the copper ceiling. Wraparound sound was created by 72 speakers. Few localizing props were used, the actors relying on mime to suggest places and furnishings. The action was preceded by a preliminary entertainment in another shed before the audience entered the main space, where an Arab woman storyteller led them to the appropriate sites. As the actors shifted from one pit to the other, so did the spectators.

Two stories were mingled, one about a 1720 Neapolitan plague for which the greedy mayor and the capitalist Pantalone are responsible, the other concerning the problems of an exploited Algerian Harlequin in modern France. At the end, the theater rocked with a storm during which the worker, employed on a construction project of the wicked Pantalone, climbed a dangerous scaffolding, lost his footing, and, as Giuseppe Verdi's "Requiem" played, fell in rhythmic progression to his death, followed by the revolt of the workers against the corrupt Establishment.

Mnouchkine confronted the conflict between an artist and his government in her adaptation of Klaus Mann's *à clef* novel, *Mephisto*, about a famous German actor who disclaims moral responsibility while siding with the Nazis. The audience sat on reversible benches and was surrounded on four sides with activity, with two stages at either end of the space. One recreated the leftist cabaret theater of the collaborationist's pre-Nazi period; the other was the ornate proscenium stage of his sell-out days. At the end, a projection over the barbed wire down one side of the space showed the names of artists killed by the Nazis.

Mnouchkine returned to Shakespeare, doing—largely in her own adaptations—*Richard II* (1981), *Twelfth Night* (1981), and *Henry IV* (1984). She used the plays to comment on the current world, but ideas took a back seat to the way they were expressed. Most notable was her employment of Asian-influenced methods. *Richard II*, for example, was strongly influenced by *kabuki*. The actors wore costumes combining Elizabethan elements, such as ruffs, with silhouettes reminiscent of Japanese garb. Their faces were white—some wore masks—and accented with stylized lines. They moved and spoke rhythmically, held poses, and spoke directly to the audience. Supporting them was a decidedly Oriental onstage musical accompaniment. A background of colorful draperies set off the stark hempen flooring with front to rear tatami-like striping. Leading to the stage from four silk-curtained areas were *hanamichi*-like horizontal runways. (Mnouchkine believes that an actor's entrance is one of the most important things in staging a play and that it should provide as much information about the character as possible.) The same setting—apart from the backdrops—was used in *Henry IV* and in *Twelfth Night*, although the latter's turbans, veils, harem pants, and caste marks conjured up an Indian atmosphere. The investigation of themes of love and power led to the treatment of contemporary materials in the next two productions, both by Hélène Cixous.

The Terrible but Unfinished History of Norodom Sihanouk, King of Cambodia (1985), again reflected a fascination with the East. With King Sihanouk's figure at its heart, this epic, two-part, 50-scene work, 11 hours long, confronted the horribly bloody events suffered during Cambodia's political upheavals. Props were typically minimal. The set resembled a Buddhist temple, and tiny brick tiling was laid over the entire theater floor. A slightly raised stage area

backed by a saffron drop and covered with walnut planking exemplified Mnouchkine's taste for elegant, as opposed to austere, simplicity. Surrounding the space were 700 haunting figures representing the Cambodian dead.

The five-hour *Indiad or India of Their Dreams* (1987) was about the partition of India, with Gandhi, Nehru, and Mohammed Ali Jinnah (Pakistan's founder) leading an array of characters. An Indian ambiance pervaded the space, from the food served to the audience to the music. A white marble stage, at the rear of which was a huge gold, red, and blue map of India, Pakistan, and Bangladesh, acted as the main focus of the performance and sets were transformed before the audience's eyes.

Instead of developing a planned work with Cixous based on Vichy France, which Mnouchkine decided was a topic too close in time and with too many personal associations, she staged *Les Atrides* or *The House of Atreus* (1991), a spectacular tetralogy in which Euripides' *Iphigenia in Aulis* preceded Aeschylus' *Oresteia: Agamemnon, The Libation Bearers,* and *The Eumenides*. The production toured to England, Canada, and America.

Near, Middle, Far, and South Eastern (mostly Indian) influences were prominent in movement, makeups, and costumes. Before each play, the audience watched the company dressing in a colorful, bazaarlike area. The actors employed athletic skills on a vast stage suggestive of a rectangular, wooden bull ring at the rear of which were two huge doors that opened periodically to allow a large, variously decorated rolling platform to roll in and serve different purposes. The leading players assumed multiple roles. Remarkable entrances and exits were made on a ramp that rapidly slid up to and away from stage center, with the actors frozen in positions of "tragedy, pathos, defiance, innocence or confusion," as *Plays and Players* put it. The chorus—whose casting was gender-neutral—wore *kathakali*-like makeup and costumes, portraying harmless women in *Iphigenia*, fierce warriors in *Agamemnon*, old men in *The Libation Bearers*, and a frightening cross between apes and dogs in *The Eumenides*. The interpretation stressed a feminist approach, setting the powerful female figures against the asininity of the men.

Viewers were impressed by the vibrant choral dancing, accompanied by music played in a large pavilion at stage left, where Mnouchkine's composer for many years, Jean-Jacques Lemêtre, assisted by acolytes, played 60 exotic instruments, providing a practically nonstop accompaniment that was a show in itself.

Mnouchkine, whose company aimed to eradicate the director, insists that she is little more than the master editor of her actors' collective creations. At one point in their growth the actors were able to expertly criticize one another's improvisations—in artistic and social terms—as well as their own. Nevertheless, her presence gradually became essential to the process although her precise input is hard to pin down. Instead of giving blocking conventionally, she offers images and then provides accurate insights on how effectively her suggestions have been realized. Her radarlike sense of the artificial refuses to accept what is not true. Eschewing preconceptions, she allows the play to develop "from ground zero" during rehearsals. At the start, there are "just some fragments, some desires. Perhaps the conviction that this path, unknown, must lead there—but how? So the actor or I discover a tiny part of the path." Pictures and books are present to stimulate the company during rehearsals.

Few dispute the importance of Mnouchkine's visions in shaping the company's work. Despite the commitment to collectivity and the equality of salaries and voting rights, many accept Mnouchkine's opinions as holy writ; some claim, however, that *de facto* assumption of power has betrayed her utopian mission.

In this troupe containing 50 to 60 people of over 20 nationalities, everyone, including Mnouchkine, serves in various nonacting, sometimes menial, capacities. A typical day is divided into technical or administrative work in the mornings (from 9:00 A.M.) and rehearsals in the afternoon (until 6:00 P.M. or later). Putting on makeup and costumes in front of the audience is a part of all productions.

Mnouchkine, who trains her company to think of the stage as a sacred space, has explored many world theater styles, Eastern and Western. Some productions have used several, without regard for consistency, provided they served the needs of character or situation. The same actor may vary his methods in the course of a single performance. Theatrical effect predominates over naturalistic illusion. Mnouchkine provides exceptional sets, lighting, costumes, makeups, and masks; sound and music are equally crucial. The Cartoucherie's interior is rebuilt from one show to another (the company even owns a

bulldozer). Seating arrangements—which are usually uncomfortable—differ from play to play and may involve physical participation on the spectator's part.

Casting follows the collective theme, with improvisational sessions—even using makeup and costumes—over a period of weeks or even months to determine who will play which role. Mnouchkine has evolved a working philosophy that seeks in every actor what she calls "the state," a central feeling that dominates him, physically and emotionally, at a particular moment. There is the basic state of the character, and then the secondary states that depict specific responses to the circumstances. At rehearsals, which normally last six months, Mnouchkine seeks to elicit these states, resulting in deeply felt but overtly physicalized performances; the term "silhouette" is often used to refer to the external realization of a character. She frowns on "psychological" acting and prefers emblematic characters, provided they convey strong emotions and images.

Mnouchkine's theater has taken on cult status in the French popular theater movement. She creates nonmilitant, socially and politically relevant works, and employs the widest possible assortment of theatrical techniques. Her company demonstrates an alternative power structure in which collaboration is as essential as directorial autocracy.

Further reading:

Cohn, Ruby. "Ariane Mnouchkine: Twenty-One Years of Théâtre du Soleil." *Theater* 17 (Winter 1985).

Feral, Josette. "Building Up the Muscle: An Interview With Ariane Mnouchkine" *The Drama Review* 33 (August 1989).

Kiernander, Adrian. "The Role of Ariane Mnouchkine at the Théâtre du Soleil" *Modern Drama* 32 (March 1989).

Kirkland, Christopher. "*The Golden Age, First Draft.*" *The Drama Review* 19 (June 1975).

Mnouchkine, Ariane. "*L'Age d'Or:* The Long Journey from 1793 to 1975." Edited and translated by Christophe Campos. *Theatre Quarterly* 5 (June–August 1975).

Also: Bradby and Williams, *Directors' Theatre;* Whitton, *Stage Directors in Modern France.*

PHILIP MOELLER (1880–1959)

PHILIP MOELLER was born in Manhattan, where his father, a successful businessman, had married

into a distinguished family. Talented at music, painting, and poetry, Philip participated in childhood theatricals. He matriculated at Columbia University, gaining his bachelor's degree in 1904 and a master's in 1905. Throughout his life, he made nearly annual trips to Europe. He was very familiar with Europe's advanced New Theater trends and would be significantly responsible for bringing them to New York.

Moeller began to engage in New York's amateur theater in 1912, when he and Edward Goodman organized play readings at the Ethical Culture Society. They also presented one-acts for the progressive Socialist Press Club, where Moeller directed one of his own plays, the melodramatic one-act, *Charity* (1914).

Moeller moved to Greenwich Village, where he became involved with that bohemian neighborhood's writers and artists and took an active part in MacDougal Street's Liberal Club. From this activity emerged, in 1914, the Washington Square Players, a semiprofessional group founded by Moeller, Goodman, Helen Westley, and Lawrence Langner. The Players were part of the Little Theater movement, which arose to reform a theatrical culture excessively devoted to commercialism. Instead of the traditional emphasis on dramaturgy, they focused intensely on stagecraft.

In 1915, the Players—a nonprofit group organized on the then still radical basis of a subscription plan— began producing at the 290-seat Bandbox Theater on East 57th Street, and then at the 700-seat Comedy on West 51st Street. A slight majority of their works were American plays. One-acts predominated, but several full-lengths were staged as well. Moeller wrote plays, adapted a few foreign ones, served as prop master, acted, did some designing, and directed 14 productions.

His first directorial effort was Langner's *Licenced* (1915), dealing with the controversial subject of birth control. One of his own better comedies was *Helena's Husband* (1915), a brief spoof of the *Iliad*. Light comedy remained his directorial forte. His first full-length production was a successful rendering of Maurice Maeterlinck's exercise in mystical symbolism, *Aglavaine and Selysette* (1916). Among other unconventional foreign writers he directed (and sometimes adapted himself) were Frank Wedekind, Nikolai Evreinov, and Leonid Andreyev (in whose *The Life of Man* Katharine Cornell made her Broadway bow in 1917). The locales were varied innovatively by lighting changes on a set of gray-green curtains. The troupe disbanded in 1918.

Between 1917 and 1920, Moeller wrote three plays about historical figures; the first two were directed on Broadway by others, but he staged *Sophie* (1920),

his last produced play, on what was not yet called Off-Broadway. He found his directorial niche when he and other leaders of the Players recombined in 1919 to create the influential Theater Guild. Led by six diverse personalities, the Guild competed with Broadway by doing the most advanced plays of the time, concentrating at first on European work but gradually becoming a home for major American playwrights as well. Eventually, the commercial managements weakened the Guild by producing work of a similar caliber.

Their brilliant epoch began at the 532-seat Garrick Theater. They leased and rented other theaters as well in order to keep profitable plays running while new productions were mounted for their expanding list of subscribers, both in New York and in the cities to which they toured. In 1925, they built the 914-seat Guild Theater (its too-small capacity proved disastrous), but continued to spread their repertory among other venues.

From 1919 to 1939, Moeller remained a member of the Guild's board of managers and directed only under their auspices, despite outside offers. (He also supervised other Guild productions and directed two films.) He attributed his greatest inspiration to Emmanuel Reicher, a German who was one of the Guild's first directors. Many Moeller productions were moneymakers that kept the company alive. His range of over 60 productions (about half of all contemporary Guild presentations) ran from their opening play, Jacinto Benavente's *The Bonds of Interest* to many other Continental dramas, including plays by Georges Courteline, Wilhelm Von Scholz, Bruno Frank, Marcel Pagnol and Paul Nivoux, and Franz Werfel. Truly memorable were Karel Capek's *R.U.R.* (1922), Ernest Vajda's *Fata Morgana* (1924), Ferenc Molnár's *The Guardsman* (1924), Evreinov's *The Chief Thing* (1926; Evreinov helped direct it), Luigi Pirandello's *Right You Are, If You Think You Are* (1927), Sil-Vara's *Caprice* (1928), and Frantisek Langer's *The Camel Through the Needle's Eye* (1929). His English and Irish repertory included A. A. Milne's *Mr. Pim Passes By* (1921)—Moeller's first hit—and *Ariadne* (1925), C. K. Munro's *At Mrs. Beam's* (1926), Denis Johnston's *The Moon in the Yellow River* (1932), James Bridie's *A Sleeping Clergyman* (1934), and, most significantly, 10 plays of George Bernard Shaw, including the world premieres of *Back to Methuselah* (1922) and *Saint Joan* (1923); the American premiere of *The Apple Cart* (1930); revivals of *The Devil's Disciple* (1923), *Caesar and Cleopatra* (1925), *Arms and the Man* (1925); a double bill of *The Man of Destiny* and *Androcles and the Lion*

(1925); *Major Barbara* (1928); and *Getting Married* (1931). Moeller staged a single classic, Ben Jonson's *Volpone* (1928), as adapted by Stefan Zweig.

Moeller's staging of important native playwrights did not accelerate until 1923, when he mounted Elmer Rice's *The Adding Machine*, followed by such representative works as Sidney Howard's Pulitzer Prize-winning *They Knew What They Wanted* (1924) and *Ned McCobb's Daughter* (1926); John Howard Lawson's *Processional* (1925); six S. N. Behrman comedies of manners, *The Second Man* (1927), *Meteor* (1929), *Biography* (1932), *Rain from Heaven* (1934), *End of Summer* (1936), and—Moeller's last production—*Wine of Choice* (1939), which was taken over by Herman Shumlin; Philip Barry's *Hotel Universe* (1930); Maxwell Anderson's *Elizabeth the Queen* (1930) and *The Masque of Kings* (1937); John Wexley's *They Shall Not Die* (1934); and works by various lesser dramatists. Towering above them all, however, are five plays by Eugene O'Neill. Moeller staged the first productions of the successful *Strange Interlude* (1928), *Mourning Becomes Electra* (1931), and *Ah, Wilderness!* (1933), as well as the flops, *Dynamo* (1929) and *Days Without End* (1934).

This striking sampling demonstrates that, despite his reputation for light comedy, he was an eclectic able to handle some of the darkest materials then being written; he had his share of failures with both comic and tragic material. Moeller succeeded with straightforward realism as well as with such expressionistic materials as *The Adding Machine* and *Processional*, and made a major stylistic breakthrough in his handling of *Strange Interlude*. This nine-act play required the actors to perform their inner thoughts as asides, and Moeller tried various devices to make the transition from dialogue to aside seem convincing. Finally, he had the nonspeaking actors freeze in natural positions as the speaker shifted tone slightly to convey his spoken thoughts. The technique came to be called "interludism," and was tried in *Dynamo* as well, but came to seem like a mannerism.

Another much discussed theatricalist staging was *The Adding Machine*, particularly the scene in which Mr. Zero is fired. "The desks and the actors whirl about against a wall on which battalions of figures dance," wrote *Theatre Arts*. "Suddenly in a great tumult everything is blotted out with two bloody splashes. Mr. Zero has 'seen red' and committed murder." (The phantasmagoric effect was created via a turntable and projections.)

The four-hour *Strange Interlude*—part one from 5:15 to 7:40 P.M., a dinner break, and part two from 9:00 to 11:00 P.M.—was not Moeller's only excursion into unusually lengthy scripts, although these were shortened from their even longer originals. (Ten thousand words were removed from *Strange Interlude*.) He and several other directors were responsible for the endless *Back to Methuselah*, a courageous five-part failure (Moeller staged Part 5) given over three nights, and Moeller was the sole director of the trilogic *Mourning Becomes Electra*. These productions had to request additional rehearsal time from the actors' union.

Although the Guild strived to emphasize ensemble over stars, Moeller's actors were Broadway's best during the twenties and thirties, most especially America's leading acting couple, Alfred Lunt and Lynn Fontanne, who appeared in seven Moeller-directed efforts. The designer most closely associated with Moeller was Lee Simonson, but he also employed such leading artists as Jo Mielziner, Aline Bernstein, and Robert Edmond Jones, among others. Generally, Moeller played down the importance of scenery, preferring sparsely furnished settings, and appreciating, above all, the atmospheric values of good lighting.

By the mid-thirties, Moeller, who at one time staged seven plays in a single season (1924–1925), declined in activity and seemed to grow bored and disillusioned. His failures increased dramatically, actors like Eva Le Gallienne (herself a director) found him incompetent, and he left the theater at the age of 59.

Moeller rarely flinched at the board's "death-watch" practice of visiting run-throughs a week or two before openings to offer criticism or cancel the production. That he managed to accept their criticisms graciously and still maintain his control is a mark of self-confidence and open-mindedness.

He also had to work within a system that not only selected his plays and designers, but took additional firepower out of the director's hands by allowing the casting to be done by a casting director (Theresa Helburn), with the final decisions made by the entire board. This occasionally led to egregious miscasting; Helen Hayes as the female lead in Shaw's *Caesar and Cleopatra* is a famous example. Moeller's ideal actor was technically proficient, intelligent, imaginative, and hard working. He preferred actors who resembled their roles. Many actors appeared frequently in Guild shows, and a loose company of Guild actors was created. At one point in the twenties, the Guild attempted to develop a repertory system by utilizing multiple theaters, but the plan proved too cumbersome.

Moeller represented the so-called "inspirational" directing school. He cultivated a legend that he barely prepared for a production, reading a play once or twice, if that, and then waiting for the inspiration of rehearsals to make his discoveries. He felt that years of technical preparation had honed his spontaneity. Overly conscientious planning, he felt, led to a lack of freshness. He thought the director brought a "mystical" understanding to the rhythmic and visual aspects of a drama. It was necessary to subdue choices that pointed to the director's presence. For the most part, his method was to simplify and pare away, although he sometimes devised excessive comic business.

Following up to eight days of "at table" readings, he allowed the actors to find their own blocking in a more or less improvisational framework; Moeller clarified and heightened their decisions. He knew when to take an actor's invention and build on it, but he rarely demonstrated or gave a reading and, in general, was not considered an actor's director.

Even in stylized plays, the acting in Moeller's work was essentially realistic. With the right actors, his method achieved insights into character psychology and emotional honesty, just as it brought out a playwright's comedy and wit. As in *St. Joan,* he made strenuous efforts to plan crowds but such scenes were among his weakest. Movement in many of his plays (notably in *Strange Interlude*) was minimal, and the emphasis was on dialogue. Yet he was praised for his attention to details of blocking and business. He was fond of pretty, if static, pictures.

Considered a playwright's director, he spent most of his rehearsal creativity on script revisions. This could be painful for writers. Despite Shaw's repulsion concerning cuts in his scripts, it seems that Moeller—aware that Shaw would not leave England—made them anyway, even in *Saint Joan.* Moeller's aim was always to serve the play; he conceived of directing as more of an interpretive than a creative art. When his interpretation jarred with the playwright's, he followed the latter's wishes.

Moeller held to no specific theory and treated each play on its own terms. In his mind, a production represented a confluence of elements that created "an accumulation of interacting psychological stimuli" that came together when imaginatively received by the audience. Among these elements was music; often he used musical terminology, such as counterpoint and harmony, to stimulate his casts. Dialogue was a musical component, he stressed, especially in O'Neill. Sound effects too played a vital role.

Philip Moeller was a colorful eccentric, noted for his sophistication, temperament, and flamboyance (he affected a long cigarette holder, dangling cashmere scarf, and black cape, and watched rehearsals from a deck chair). But he was responsible for introducing to America many of the finest dramas of his age.

Further reading:

Helburn, Theresa. "Staged by Philip Moeller." *Theatre Guild Magazine* 6 (May 1929).

Langner, Lawrence. *The Magic Curtain: The Story of a Life in Two Fields, Theatre and Invention.* New York: E. P. Dutton, 1951.

Wainscott, Ronald H. *Staging O'Neill: The Experimental Years, 1920–1934.* New Haven, Conn.: Yale University Press, 1988.

Also: Eaton, *The Theatre Guild;* Waldau, *Vintage Years of the Theatre Guild.*

MIKE NICHOLS (1931–   )

MIKE NICHOLS (*né* Michael Igor Peschkowsky) was born in Berlin, Germany, to a Russian émigré physician and his German wife. The family emigrated to the United States in 1938. Nichols entered the University of Chicago, intending to study medicine, but was diverted by theater. He studied acting in New York with Lee Strasberg, returning to Chicago to work in improvisational cabarets. He teamed up with fellow improvisationalist (and later film director) Elaine May to become one of the most popular comedy acts of the time.

After the act dissolved, he acted in a play of May's and then was asked to direct Neil Simon's *Barefoot in the Park* (1963), a comedy about the travails of newlyweds in a fifth-floor walkup, with Elizabeth Ashley and Robert Redford. Unsure of his ability, he agreed to stage a summer theater version and do it on Broadway only if it worked. It was staged in only one week, which Nichols later felt was a blessing because the time constraints forced him to eliminate discussions and to just "do it." The Broadway staging earned him a Tony. Because of the play's locale, Nichols had the actors practice running up five flights to give the impression of being out of breath when they entered; this proved one of the funniest things in the performance.

His gift for complex comic business and split-second timing made Nichols a great comedy director. (He is also an important producer and, since 1965, film director. His screen works include: *The Graduate*, 1967; *Carnal Knowledge*, 1971; and *Working Girl*, 1988.) After *Barefoot*, he did three other Simon blockbusters, all of them leading to directing Tonys (he eventually won six). *The Odd Couple* (1965) starred Art Carney and Walter Matthau as two mismatched, maritally separated roommates. *Plaza Suite* (1968) consisted of three one-acts set in the same hotel room, with George C. Scott and Maureen Stapleton. *The Prisoner of Second Avenue* (1971), starring Peter Falk and Lee Grant, was about the malaise of New York life. When Gordon Davidson was fired from *Fools* (1981), a farcical fantasy set in old Russia, Nichols took over but failed to save it.

Nichols's reputation for bringing out the human element in Simon's wisecracking plays was scarcely tarnished, though. Most of his other comedies had decent runs. One was Off-Broadway's *The Knack* (1964), Ann Jellicoe's British farce about youthful hijinks in London. Murray Schisgal's *Luv* (1964), starring Anne Jackson, Eli Wallach, and Alan Arkin, was a three-character existential farce concerned with marital angst. Jean Kerr's *Lunch Hour* (1980), starring Gilda Radner and Sam Waterston, was an old-fashioned comedy of adultery. Tom Stoppard's *The Real Thing* (1984), a witty yet moving British comedy of adultery, starred Jeremy Irons and Glenn Close. Andrew Bergman's sex farce, *Social Security* (1986), told, in part, of a geriatric sexual attraction between a Jewish mother and a nonogenarian painter. Olympia Dukakis, Marlo Thomas, and Ron Silver starred.

A shorter run accrued to Trevor Griffiths's *Comedians* (1976), a provocative British comedy, starring Jonathan Pryce in a socialist-oriented examination of the meaning of comedy as seen through standup comics. Another politically oriented mounting was E. L. Doctorow's intellectual black comedy, *Drinks Before Dinner* (1978). Both it and the equally unfruitful *Elliot Loves* (1990) by Jules Feiffer were Off-Broadway.

The only full-scale musical Nichols staged was Sheldon Harnick and Jerry Bock's *The Apple Tree* (1966), a hit in which Alan Alda and Barbara Harris cavorted through three separate pieces inspired by various famous writers. The Off-Broadway revue, *Standup Shakespeare* (1987), which set Shakespeare's words to music, had only two showings. An intimate musical (choreographed by Tommy Tune) called *Double Feature* was seen only in New Haven, and

Nichols quit work on the Latino *Sancocho* (1979) because he was uncomfortable with its cultural background.

Despite his comedy reputation, Nichols has provided compelling productions of serious, sometimes controversial, dramas. David Rabe's powerful *Streamers* (1976), moved to Off-Broadway from New Haven, dealt with irrational violence, racism, and homosexuality in a Vietnam-era army barracks. In D. L. Coburn's slight but touching *The Gin Game* (1977), Nichols surmounted the difficulty of staging a play that was little more than a series of card games played by two psychologically scarred nursing home residents, played by Hume Cronyn and Jessica Tandy. Rabe's *Hurlyburly*, a bleak tragicomedy with Sigourney Weaver and William Hurt, examined drug use, drinking, and misogyny among Hollywood's tawdry film community subculture. Chilean playwright Ariel Dorfman's three-character political melodrama, *Death and the Maiden* (1992), revealed how a woman who has been raped and tortured under a totalitarian regime behaves when she has the man she believes responsible in her power. It starred Glenn Close, Gene Hackman, and Richard Dreyfuss.

Nichols has staged only three revivals. Many lauded his coadaptation of Anton Chekhov's *Uncle Vanya* (1973), starring George C. Scott, Nicol Williamson, and Julie Christie. Also effective was Lillian Hellman's *The Little Foxes* (1967), starring Scott and Anne Bancroft. The *New York Times* declared, "The staging is severe, disciplined, brooding with intimation." Least admired was an Off-Broadway version of Samuel Beckett's *Waiting for Godot* (1988), with Robin Williams, Steve Martin, and F. Murray Abraham, unconventionally set in a rubble-littered dirt circle suggesting an American desert. Nichols emphasized vaudevillesque shtick and missed the necessary pathos.

Nichols, a realistic director with an eye to the tiniest details of human behavior, brings a well-thought-out vision to his productions, but serving the playwright is his prime objective. He chooses only plays he likes or finds important and that he believes will prove similarly appealing to an audience. He told Roy Newquist, "It's up to you, as the director, to try to achieve the play . . . in the way that the playwright has suggested both openly, in his words, and in the more subtle and mysterious things contained in the play."

He appreciates collaboration, especially when working with artists who attempt to clarify and improve their own contributions and are open to admitting their problems. The playwright is normally present at rehearsal, but the lines of demarcation are clearly drawn. Most disasters, he told Newquist, stemmed from situations in which "You had people saying 'You must do this' and the writer saying 'No, if it were performed properly it would work' and the director saying 'But if you change it will work' and the actor saying 'You must give me other material.' " When the "atmosphere is right," though, you can tell a collaborator where his flaws are or vice-versa, and "you're very apt to say, 'Yes, I see where I did it wrong; thank you.' "

In comedy, Nichols believes it necessary to remove small, extraneous laughs that dissipate the big ones. "Laughter is energy. You can interrupt the flow, the arc, of a large laugh by getting these little piddly ones on the way. The energy builds up if you take out the little ones" (quoted in Otis Guernsey). He has an inborn "ear for comedy," but he does not direct to get laughs; a good play will work even if there is no laughter. Simon notes (in Guernsey),

> He never treats the play like a comedy. The first day [of Barefoot rehearsals] we were sitting around and he said, "We have to treat this play as though we're doing King Lear. You must have that kind of conviction. This is life and death to you people."

"The audience is meant to laugh," he informed Barbara Gelb, "but not to see the director's efforts." A Nichols trademark is the seriousness with which his actors leap through their hilarious hoops. The *New York Daily News* noted of *Luv* that the actors play "as solemnly as if it were some Russian folk tragedy."

Nichols is a perfectionist with a short fuse. He will spend high sums to make sure the ingredients are correct. Distinguished stars are hired not only for their draw, but because their talent is required by his ultrahigh standards. The smallest deviance from his goals may raise his temperature. A barely noticeable flicker of light in a blackout might be greeted with, "What in God's name is that *searchlight* doing onstage?"

When staging plays originally done in London, he alters their casting, design, and even their basic concept to suit his own interpretation and make it acceptable to Americans. In the case of *Death and the Maiden*, some critics disapproved of his having domesticized and comically lightened a drama that had been far more chilling in its London version.

Plays that appeal to him contain a premise or situation immediately establishing tension and conflict so that something can "happen." "You can

have the greatest lines, the greatest gags, the most beautiful language . . . it makes no difference if it isn't set up" (in Guernsey). Gelb says he stages only works about man's everpresent tendency to self-delude. In his own words, "Life is hopeless—but it isn't; love is fleeting—but eternal; our personal lives are important—but we are unimportant." Above all, he wants to feel that he is the best possible director for a play because he is in touch with its secrets.

Neil Simon, wishing to direct, tried to study Nichols but concluded, "I never saw what he did. It was so mysterious" (in Guernsey). He spends much time reading the text and discussing the characters. Exploratory questions are asked about every phase of the work. The actors often do improvisations. His technique is basically intuitive and open to discovery, each rehearsal evolving in its own trial-and-error way.

There is much laughter at rehearsals because of his comedic bent, although things become more tense as the opening nears. Nichols's comments are couched in self-effacing remarks, such as "Here's what I *think*" or "Why don't we try this?" followed by "Does it seem right to you?" Rabe claims that Nichols's advice, wrong or right, is invariably *clear*. His assistance to actors usually stems from his own personal experiences, which he has no qualms about revealing if it will help overcome obstacles. "Partly, I do this," he told Gelb,

> because it's all I know, and partly because I very much want to encourage them to pour their lives into what they're doing. I believe that the process can illuminate a scene and it also lets us learn a little more about each other, so that we can work together a little better.

When, in staging *Hurlyburly*, Weaver had trouble reacting to Hurt's character's irrational jealousy, Nichols remembered a similar incident in his own past and asked, "Have you ever been with an insanely jealous person?" and described the experience. He then provided the vivid image: "Being with an insanely jealous person is like being in a room with a dead *mammoth*."

Nichols relaxes his casts for openings by having them run their lines while lying on mattresses. Actors appreciate how he inspires their trust. Jeremy Irons told Gelb, "He's like the best of lovers; he makes you feel he's only for you."

Nichols searches for what he terms the play's "event." Gelb says this is "the truthful moment or series of moments—that will illuminate the author's meaning, that will reveal 'real people living their lives.' " The "event's" importance stems from his

Gene Hackman (l), Richard Dreyfuss, and Glenn Close in Dorfman's Death and the Maiden. *Directed by Mike Nichols. (1992)*   (Photo: Martha Swope)

experience of it in plays he saw in his youth directed by Elia Kazan and from his improvisational work with May. The actor must bring to authentic physical life what is only hinted at in the script, to get at "what is really going on."

In a play with few stage directions, such as *Hurly-burly*, he uses rehearsals to discover how to express the subtext physically. In that play there is a scene between a man and a woman in which they bandy about romantic clichés; it could have been done by having them talk across a table. Nichols, however, staged it by taking a hint from the man's suggestion that the two have sex; he had them play the scene by undressing each other preparatory to making love. This led to a highly comic scene in which the characters' behavior pointedly countered the emptiness of their phrases and revealed their underlying feelings. Still, author David Rabe later complained that Nichols's approach had distorted his intentions, which led the playwright to begin directing his own plays.

An uproarious example of his sight-gag genius occurred in *Plaza Suite*. In the scene, Scott's daughter has locked herself in the bathroom on her wedding day and he must get her out. According to the *Times*, the moment when

> Scott picks up a chair, darts across the bed, aims the chair at the door, thinks better of it, and subsides to the other side of the room, is masterly. And best of all the whole sequence is conceived and executed in one arc of movement.

The *New Yorker* reported, "Nobody takes bigger chances with sight gags than Mr. Nichols; part of the enjoyment they give us springs from our sense of his having pushed them to the limit and then, cooly and outrageously, a tiny fraction past the limit."

Nichols works his way bit by bit through the play, recalling a valuable lesson he learned from Strasberg when a vague actress, asked to describe how to make a fruit salad, detailed the process item by item. Nichols related this to directing, telling Gelb, "You do the first job as neatly as you can: *She comes in.* Then you do the next job: *He sees her.* And so on."

Few directors have had so high a percentage of successful commercial productions as Mike Nichols. Some of his choices have been primarily for entertainment value, but he has also made serious offerings with plays by Rabe, Griffiths, Stoppard, and Dorfman.

Further reading:

Berkvist, Robert. "How Nichols and Rabe Shaped Streamers." *New York Times*, April 25, 1976.

Gelb, Barbara. "Mike Nichols: The Special Risks and Rewards of the Director's Art." *New York Times Magazine*, May 27, 1984.

Newquist, Roy. *Showcase*. New York: William Morrow, 1966.

Probst, Leonard. *Off Camera*. New York: Stein and Day, 1978.

Also: Guernsey, *Broadway Song and Story*.

TREVOR NUNN (1940–   )

TREVOR ROBERT NUNN, the son of a cabinet-maker, was born in Ipswich, Suffolk, England. At 16, he established the Ipswich Youth Drama Group. In 1962, he graduated from Cambridge University, where he was involved in 32 productions and was deeply influenced by literary scholar F. R. Leavis, who taught him to seek the moral dimension in every work of literature.

In 1962, he directed at the Belgrade Theatre, Coventry, where he staged such authors as John

Arden, Arthur Miller, Henrik Ibsen, and Bertolt Brecht. This led to his joining Stratford-upon-Avon's Royal Shakespeare Company (RSC) where his early assignments included the codirection of *Henry V* (1965) and solo jobs on Robert Bolt's children's play, *The Thwarting of Baron Bolligrew* (1965), and Slawomir Mrozek's *Tango* (1966). None of his work was especially impressive until his Fellini-esque, black comedy staging of Cyril Tourneur's rarely seen Jacobean melodrama, *The Revenger's Tragedy* (1966). Tourneur's decadence was made relevant through a theatricalized presentation employing a bright silver circle painted on the stage floor, monochromatic black and silver costumes, and the gravitation of the power-hungry characters toward the circle's bright center. It concluded with a phantasmagoric, skull-masked dance of death during which 12 characters were murdered.

In 1967, Nunn provided excellent versions of *The Taming of the Shrew* (starring Nunn's first wife, Janet Suzman), later taken to Los Angeles, and John Vanbrugh's *The Relapse*. When Peter Hall resigned his RSC directorship in 1968, he appointed the 28-year-old Nunn to succeed him. In 1978, Nunn appointed Terry Hands as his joint director, but continued as chief executive.

Nunn's subsequent RSC productions, some of which opened at Stratford before moving to London, others of which premiered in London, were mainly classics. Early examples included a ritualistic *King Lear* (1968), staged in an empty gray box; *Much Ado About Nothing* (1968), enacted in Elizabethan garb in a bare Elizabethan chamber; *The Winter's Tale* (1969), memorable for using a lighting effect to solve the problem of Leontes' sudden jealousy and for borrowing Carnaby Street fashions for the court and hippie gear for the rustics; *Henry VIII* (1969), in which projected headlines clarified the historical and political context, processions wound through the audience, and Henry opened the play standing triumphantly as a Sun King and closed the action standing apprehensively with his infant daughter in his arms as the company chanted "peace, truth, plenty"; and *Hamlet* (1970), in which Alan Howard's prince—a neurotic on the brink of madness— wore black in contrast to the court's white fur representing celebration, not mourning. Christian symbolism abounded, Hamlet even visiting Gertrude in a cowl.

Nunn and his then main designer Christopher Morley broke away from the Brecht-influenced methods fostered under Hall. Believing that the central component of Shakespeare's plays is language and not pictures, they created a "chamber" aesthetic that placed the action in an austere, nonnaturalistic, boxlike setting lit from above like a pool table and dressed with only essential, carefully chosen, props. With a hydraulically equipped new stage, they could "make something which could be a chamber, walled, roofed and enclosed, and which could be a totally open platform or anything between those two extremes," Nunn told Judith Cook. Nunn has expressed more interest in the domestic, private side of Shakespeare than the political one. This slant was greatly aided by the chamber's bareness, in which the actor and his feelings stood out in sharp relief. The approach—abandoned after it became predictable and the machinery proved cumbersome—encouraged several outstanding mountings.

Nunn demonstrated a taste for a schematic, even allegorical use of color to assist the audience in assessing a character's nature. He told Peter Ansorge that he hoped this would "crystallise appearances so that what people represent is at least part of what they look like." Some thought this an oversimplification.

In 1972 came Nunn's controversial "Roman Season," featuring *Coriolanus, Julius Caesar, Antony and Cleopatra,* and *Titus Andronicus,* the staging of which—despite codirectors—was so exhausting that Nunn was hospitalized. It was argued that the plays were not closely enough related to warrant such a cycle, although the sequential London presentation (1973) weakened this judgment. The series, demonstrating the decline and fall of Roman civilization, employed a steeply raked thrust—varied by hydraulic platforms—within a white box. *Coriolanus,* to cite just one production, was placed in a vaguely Central American environment and used strobes to heighten slow-motion battles. It emphasized the anthropological differences between Romans and Volscians to the detriment of the human element, but it was vastly improved when Nicol Williamson assumed the lead for the London transfer.

A sampling of Nunn's remaining work during the decade might include *Macbeth* (1974), starring Williamson and Helen Mirren, reconceived for London (1975); Nunn's "black comedy" adaptation of Ibsen's *Hedda Gabler* (1975), with Glenda Jackson, which played in Australia and North America before opening in London; *Romeo and Juliet* (1976) with Ian McKellan and Francesca Annis in a design that attempted to recreate the Swan Theatre as drawn by Johannes DeWitt; *The Comedy of Errors* (1976), staged ingeniously as a modern-dress musical set in a flea-bitten Mediterranean town, with lyrics by Nunn himself; a second *Macbeth* (1976), starring

Nicholas Nickleby. *Directed by Trevor Nunn. (1980)*   (Photo: Martha Swope)

McKellan and Judi Dench; codirection of new versions of *The Winter's Tale* and *King Lear* (1976); *As You Like It* (1977), staged as a "baroque pastoral opera" into which songs and dances intruded distractingly; Ben Jonson's *The Alchemist* (1977); Tom Stoppard's *Every Good Boy Deserves Favour* (1977); "a spare, witty and primal" *(Time) Three Sisters* (1978) by Anton Chekhov; and a codirected *The Merry Wives of Windsor* (1979).

Especially distinguished was the 1976 *Macbeth,* staged at Stratford's new, small The Other Place. Returning to an idea exploited in *The Revenger's Tragedy,* the simple set consisted of a large circle, implying magical forces, painted on the floor and surrounded by boxes on which the black-dressed cast, when not directly involved, sat watching. Only by entering the circle did they exist, a convention that created fascinating reverberations, as when Macduff witnessed the slaying of his family. The witches "disappeared" simply by stepping out of the circle. Macbeth was like a participant in a black mass and the circle, wrote Hersh Zeifman, was "the

battleground for a *psychomachia:* a struggle between good and evil for the possession of a man's soul."

Nunn's masterpiece was not by Shakespeare but was a faithful adaptation commissioned from David Edgar of Charles Dickens's *Nicholas Nickleby* (1980). Over a lengthy collaborative period, the actors contributed significantly to the show. "Two actors presented a slide-show about the early Victorian theater. Others did research projects on the class system, education, medicine, hygiene, anything that might prove relevant," wrote Benedict Nightingale. Casting was not completed until the actors had played many roles—even those of the opposite sex— in rehearsal.

Nunn and codirector John Caird turned Dickens's novel—contrasting idealism with cynicism in 1830s England—into an 8 ½-hour, two-part commingling of realism, melodrama, and farce. A company of 42 participated in an exceptional staging that reproduced the novel's many scenes with a minimum of scenery (designed by John Napier). A few actors, boxes, and planks created a crowded stagecoach.

Apart from several principals, most played multiple parts, often changing costumes as the audience watched. The ensemble watched and reacted as a chorus from an overhead ramp; they also provided sounds and shifted props. When it came to New York, where Nunn and John Caird shared a directing Tony, *Nicholas* sold out despite tickets costing $100 each. Nunn revived it in 1986.

During the 1980s and early 1990s, Nunn collaborated with composer Andrew Lloyd Webber on *Cats* (1981); *Starlight Express* (1984), a pop-rock extravaganza originally conceived for children and employing actors as anthropomorphized trains who roller skated—at speeds up to 40 mph—on computerized ramps around the theater (the show was reconceived for New York in 1987); *Aspects of Love* (1990), based on a 1955 novel about complex romantic relationships among a group of postwar French sophisticates; and *Sunset Boulevard* (1993), a musicalization of the famous Billy Wilder film about a fading screen star and a struggling screenwriter. The latter, starring Patti LuPone, opened in London to mixed reviews but was a major hit nonetheless; a Los Angeles production, starring Glenn Close, opened later in the year, and a New York version was scheduled for 1994. The $6 million *Cats*, an independent show, made Nunn a millionaire. Despite tepid reviews, *Cats*, based on T. S. Eliot material and using Nunn's lyrics for the hit song "Memories," remains a worldwide megahit. Set on a giant, unearthly garbage dump, its characters are stray cats performed by specially made-up actors.

Nunn directed several operas and two major non-Webber musicals. Tim Rice, Benny Andersson, and Bjorn Ulvaeus's *Chess* (1986) was about the politics surrounding an American-Russian chess competition. He replaced Michael Bennett on the high-tech London production and reconceived the show for New York (1988).

Much more profitable was Alain Boublil and Claude-Michel Schönberg's ambitious 3½-hour *Les Misérables* (1985; New York, 1987), based on Victor Hugo's novel about revolutionary France and using a revolve to effect the theatrical equivalent of filmic wipes and tracking shots. While most scenes were relatively simple, the erection of a huge barricade was unforgettabe. Following an earlier French staging, the English version was originated at the RSC where Nunn—doing his first original RSC production in four years—codirected it with Caird.

Although the RSC survived largely because of the profits earned by this international success, Nunn was castigated for profiting from the use of a subsi-

dized institution. As his outside interests grew, Nunn was also knocked for ignoring the RSC.

Early in the eighties, he directed such RSC revivals as *Henry IV, Parts 1 and 2* (1982), done outstandingly in a single eight-hour staging to open the RSC's new London theater, the Barbican; an Edwardian-era *All's Well That Ends Well* (1981) that emphasized class and gender distinctions and was warmly approved in New York (1983) as well; and a lovely, codirected *Peter Pan* (1984) by James M. Barrie. Having turned the RSC over to Hands, Nunn returned as "Director Emeritus" to stage such works as Thomas Heywood's Elizabethan comedy, *The Fair Maid of the West* (1987), given a lauded *Nicholas Nickleby*-like production at RSC's new Swan Theatre; a moving *Othello* (1989) starring McKellan and black opera singer Willard White, done in costumes suggestive of characters in a Thomas Mann novel, within an intimate staging at The Other Place that intensified Iago's as well as Othello's tragedy; and Pam Gems's adaptation from the German, *The Blue Angel* (1991). For the Young Vic, Nunn offered a modern dress *Timon of Athens* (1991) stressing the recession, and *Measure for Measure* (1992). He also provided George Bernard Shaw's *Heartbreak House* (1992) on the West End and Tom Stoppard's *Arcadia* (1993) at the Royal National Theater.

Nunn's theater is a combination of striking imagination and textual insight. He is as adept at eye-boggling spectacle as at bare-stage intimacy. His classics underscore their relation to contemporary concerns. Taking a cue from Peter Hall, he treats each Shakespearean play as if it were a new drama just dropped through the letterbox. Cutting is often necessary: "What you decide to leave in is your version of the play," he told Ralph Berry. Nunn may add his own words or those of other Elizabethan writers.

Although his procedures vary, Nunn—who keeps his rehearsals private—rehearses with a variety of improvisational techniques, games, and exercises. Some of the greatest moments in his Shakespeare productions stem from situational improvisations that return to the most naturalistic premises. To break down inhibitions, the cast of the *Shrew* kicked a fluffy ball about, happily making themselves look silly in the process. When the court in *The Revenger's Tragedy* had to search for the duke, whose corpse they eventually locate, Nunn and the actor playing the duke hid from the company, who had to find them. They then had to improvise the thrill of discovery and their disgust at the corpse's smell.

Nunn is as much concerned with creating an ensemble as with exploring the material at hand. He allows actors to take risks and to demonstrate their own ideas. Time is found for exercises on voice, verse speaking, imagination, emotions, relationships, and so forth. Actors appreciate his warmth (he is famous for his bear hugs), humor, openness, calmness, and comprehension. Peggy Ashcroft told Steve Lawson, "What a nose for the text! *Enormously* exact! Yet he stays open to your ideas, your contributions." Still, he has a steel spine. Someone informed the *Observer* that his gentleness is "genuine . . . though the gentleness always has a purpose, and is accompanied by a powerful force."

Nunn's manner varies with the project. On *Starlight Express* he was an athletic coach, giving pep talks. On *Les Misérables,* he treated the cast like Chekhovians or Shakespeareans, focusing on psychology. "You don't react to something simply because of what the music or lyrics say," he told Stephen Silverman. "You do it because it is real and part of human behavior."

The *Observer* characterized Nunn as "a sort of cultural Superman, an alchemist of the theatre whose gentle touch rarely fails to produce pure gold." He is among the finest and most influential directors of classical drama; he is also the most financially successful director of musical theater ever. He told Michael Owens, "Working in classical theatre my instinct is to want to popularise and make it accessible socially, emotionally and intellectually while in popular theatre my instinct is to make it intellectually sound and of some moral value."

Further Reading:

Ansorge, Peter. "Director in Inverview." *Plays and Players* 17 (September 1970).

Lawson, Steve. "Trevor Nunn Reshapes *Cats* for Broadway." *New York Times,* October 3, 1982.

Nightingale, Benedict. "How 42 Actors and 2 Directors Assembled *Nicholas Nickleby.*" *New York Times,* October 4, 1981.

Owens, Michael. "Trevor's Back." *Evening Standard,* July 21, 1989.

Silverman, Stephen M. "Two-fisted Attempt to Save Broadway." *New York Post,* February 17, 1987.

Zeifman, Hersh. "*Macbeth.*" *Theatre Research International* 4 (October 1978).

"The Magician Theatre Angels Love." *Observer,* October 13, 1985.

Also: Addenbrooke, *Royal Shakespeare Company;* Beauman, *Royal Shakespeare Company;* Berry, *On Directing Shakespeare;* Cook, *Directors' Theatre;* Leiter, *Shakespeare Around the Globe.*

NIKOLAI OKHLOPKOV (1900–1967)

NIKOLAI PAVLOVICH OKHLOPKOV was born in Irkutsk, Siberia, the son of a military officer. He studied art, learned the violin, and designed and acted at a local theater. He demonstrated remarkable powers in his very first production, *The Struggle between Labor and Capital* (1921), a successful "mass-action" which he wrote and acted in and presented in Irkutsk's central square on May Day. It deployed 30,000 local citizens and militia in a celebration of the Bolshevik victory. The following year, he offered at the Youth Theatre a praiseworthy version of *Mystery-Bouffe,* by Vladimir Mayakovsky. He won a scholarship to the State Institute of Theatrical Arts (GITIS) in Moscow.

From 1922 to 1926, he played mainly minor roles for Vsevolod Meyerhold, being introduced to Greek theater, *commedia dell'arte, kabuki,* and biomechanics. Okhlopkov went on to act in and direct movies. The techniques of film montage he learned were useful in his stage directing. His ardent belief in doing plays to further the revolution led, in 1931, to his appointment as head of the slightly over 300-seat Realistic Theatre. He would have preferred a socialist mass theater of epic proportions, like the Greeks.

Okhlopkov ignored the rectangular house's architecture and dismantled the stage and proscenium, creating flexible platforming for the acting, and putting the seats on movable sections. He rearranged performance-audience relationships for each production. Arena staging, end staging, sandwich staging, L-shaped staging, and so on were used in his 1930s work.

He was unlike those theatricalists who underlined the theater's artificiality. Doing away with conventional realism, Okhlopkov's scenically spare productions evoked a compelling illusionism through realistic props, costumes, and acting.

Having once witnessed two soldiers embracing on a station platform before reboarding their trains, he sought to establish a similar fusion between audience and artist. "On my stage, when the mother cries, a dozen in the audience must be ready to spring forward to dry her tears," he told Norris Houghton. His actors treated the spectator as a partner, acting with, not for him. Houghton thought—partly because of the fervency of the themes the director employed, partly because of the way in which the actors physically resembled the members of the audience, and partly because of the naturalistic acting—that no other director in his experience had succeeded so well in uniting the stage and spectator while increasing, instead of breaking, the illusion. Okhlopkov's experimental productions fused Meyerhold's and Konstantin Stanislavsky's styles.

Four of the seven productions he directed at the Realistic were adaptations of ideological prose writings, beginning with Vladimir Stavsky's *The Start* (1931), about a village's collectivization, and played on a central acting platform, with the spectators seated arena-fashion. Overhead was a circular bridge ending in ramps like highway cloverleafs that extended down to auditorium level on two sides and continued down part of each side wall; the action occurred in montage on multiple levels simultaneously or in lightning-fast transitions from area to area. The ramps were robbed of their functional characteristics by disguising them with greenery. In one scene, two fishermen lowered their net practically onto the spectators' heads.

Also idiosyncratic was Maxim Gorky's *The Mother* (1932), about how a simple woman is radicalized. It was coadapted (from the novel) and codirected with Pavel Tsetnerevich (to whom many of the best ideas belonged). The auditorium was surrounded by a walkway with two short, stepped platforms in the middle of the rectangle's longer walls facing each other across the space and one longer one (somewhat like a *kabuki* runway) projecting into the center from a short wall. These projections divided the audience into three sections facing a round, stepped platform in the middle. Actors entered the central section via the side projections or through two aisles. The action took place around and in front of the audience. Actors and audience were blended, as when a spectator was handed a loaf of bread and a knife to hold. The production imaginatively opened up the space via a minimal use of props and a maximum use of light to define locales.

Guerrilla warfare during the 1918 Civil War was evoked in an episodic adaptation of Alexander Serafimovich's novel, *The Iron Flood* (1933). Its seating, facing one of the rectangle's longer walls, was divided

into three sections by lavalike peninsulas separating one from the other, with the peninsulas connected as part of a rocky embankment, backed by the blue sky, along the wall. "An avalanche of people moved incessantly throughout the auditorium and across the stage, making noise, bawling songs, being tormented by hunger and the burning sun, carrying wounded and children . . . , lugging cannons . . . , dragging their pathetic belongings on creaking carts," wrote Konstantin Rudnitsky. Exiting actors shook hands with spectators or patted them on the shoulder. Comedy and tragedy mingled indiscriminately and each character was strikingly individualized. In darkened scenes, a spotlight picked out individuals or small groups, but the focus was on the iron flood of the drama's participants.

For Nikolai Pogodin's *Aristocrats* (1934), a popular, romanticized picture of Stalin's gulag, Okhlopkov situated two bare, oblong platforms, connected at a single point, in opposite corners of the rectangle, with most of the audience occupying the other corners. Adapting Asian conventions, he brought on masked stage assistants in full view of the audience to assist the actors or to place and remove props; they suggested a snowstorm by tossing white flakes or created the impression of a woman skiing by running past her with branches. (Such a Japanese-like use of stage assistants would also figure in several later Okhlopkov works.) Scenery was restricted to Eastern-style side panels depicting the seasons.

With *Othello* (1935) and Romain Rolland's *Colas Breugnon* (1936), Okhlopkov increasingly introduced carnivalesque features, such as impressed him in his study of Renaissance street theatricals. His fullest expression of this tendency was in Edmond Rostand's *Cyrano de Bergerac* (1942) at the Vakhtangov Theatre, where he had begun to direct in 1940. (He had been removed from his theater in 1937 and was forced to merge with Alexander Tairov's Kamerny Theatre, an unholy alliance that lasted 13 months.) The audience was cast in the role of the swirling Paris crowds, while the scenery for each act incorporated mute, gigantic effigies, meant to reflect the audience's feelings toward the action. The scene in which Cyrano woos Roxane on behalf of Christian revealed a huge figure resembling Roxane holding a guitar. In its sounding board was a circular balcony and the actress spoke through the strings. Eventually, the production was forced by government pressure to resort to more traditional means.

From the Vakhtangov, Okhlopkov moved to the Theatre of Drama in 1943 (he later renamed it the Mayakovsky Theatre), where many of his productions were of epic scale (such as Victor Gusev's posterlike, allegorical *Sons of Three Rivers* in 1943, or Pyotr Vilyams's *The Ferry Girl* in 1944, which used a stage reservoir for water scenes and employed a ferry). One of his most outstanding productions was an adaptation of Konstantin Fadeyev's propagandistic novel, *The Young Guard* (1947), in which a large red flag was brilliantly manipulated to evoke atmospheric shifts in mood. Another was an unusual revival of Alexander Ostrovsky's *The Storm* (1953), codirected with A. V. Kashkin, seen as a mystery play at whose heart is the redeeming symbol of the storm, meant to suggest Katerina's revolt against suffocating provincialism. A "stormy" atmosphere was created by a mountain on the edge of a ravine, bursts of lightning, the sounds of an offstage chorus, and actors moving in circular patterns on a revolving stage. During Katerina's confession, the mountains commenced to move, suggesting the awakening of dormant natural forces.

In 1954, after nine years of study, Okhlopkov offered *Hamlet*, one of his most acclaimed productions. Nick Worrall wrote:

> He saw Hamlet as a humanist who takes up arms against despotism, rebels against Denmark as a prison and recognises that a tragic fate awaits those prisoners who keep aloof from the struggle and bide their time while an army of murderers is growing.

Hamlet's remark that "Denmark's a prison" led Okhlopkov to stress the prisonlike world of Elsinore. The actors played in front—and when it parted, upstage—of a huge, metal gate set across the stage. Sections could be removed to reveal multileveled, cell-like rooms. Gail Lenhoff noted that the disposition allowed many locales to be suggested: "one room, a graveyard, the sea, an enormous cage, or the twelve cells of a sumptuous dungeon. The space marked by these gates (or walls) expanded, contracted, multiplied, receded and advanced with each successive event." When the Danes attempted to revolt against the king, a portcullis dropped in between the gates; the mob upstage of it glared and shouted in frustration toward the audience (where Claudius and his court were seemingly located), safely separated from them. Okhlopkov also alternated two actors in the title role, using a veteran one night and a newcomer the next.

Alexander Shtein's *Hotel Astoria* (1956), a psychological drama based on the bombardment of Leningrad and the false accusations made against a pilot during Stalin's purges, made use of a *kabuki*-like bridgeway running from the stage to the far end of the auditorium. Symbolic of the city's many bridges and important in bringing the audience into proximity to the hero's anguish, the bridgeway was used by him only during moments of spiritual duress. To present it as a "production concert," Okhlopkov introduced a symphony orchestra placed on either side of the forestage. All of the action was accompanied by the music of Franz Liszt and Eugene Scriabin and the sounds of warfare.

In Alexei Arbuzov's *Irkutsk Story* (1960), actors entered on another bridge, as well as from the orchestra pit, the proscenium boxes, and on a revolve. In an attempt to achieve universality, Okhlopkov replaced Arbuzov's narrator with a chorus of 20 who seemed randomly selected from the spectators themselves. "At the finale they became a musical choir that, with the assistance of two thundering pianos and heavy drum rolls, did much to contribute to the epic quality of the production," wrote Houghton.

Okhlopkov's last important production was Euripides' *Medea* (1967), at the Tchaikovsky Concert Hall. Some viewed its title character as a barbarian destroyed by social forces in her new land, an interpretation related to contemporary political grievances in the treatment by the U.S.S.R. of various nationalities within its borders. Others saw in the ruthless Medea a reflection of Stalin, who hailed from the same region (Colchis, now Georgia). The hall was made to resemble an ancient amphitheatre, with the audience surrounding the action on three sides. A giant statue of Euripides oversaw the action. A symphony orchestra accompanied the action and there was both a vocal choir (singing music from A. S. Taneyev's opera, *The Oresteia*) and a masked pantomime chorus of Corinthean women. Oversized masks with faces torn by terror were brought on by actor-stagehands who held them before the faces of the principals at climactic moments. Medea's blood was a lengthy strip of red ribbon trailing behind her.

Okhlopkov conceived a picture of the entire production in his head, basing his interpretation on a careful analysis of the play's class consciousness, and predetermining all its details, particularly the choreographic blocking. Working with a company of supple actors, he focused on movement and gestures, with psychological elements incorporated only after the visual part began to coalesce. Impatient and capable of blowing up when dissatisfied, he dictatorially demonstrated for the actors every aspect of the external work, some of it borrowed from Meyerhold's biomechanics. He did, however, appreciate the values of improvisation to help blocked actors achieve physical and emotional freedom. Okhlopkov's variations on theater in the round necessitated a strict directorial hand in setting the moves and gestures, so they would look acceptable from many angles. His settings also required constant movement, and his productions were noted for their dynamism.

Okhlopkov did not want mechanical repetition of his directions. When the physical business was set, he asked his actors to think about the meaning of their movements and what they were feeling when they did them. Occasionally, he had them write character sketches to present to their fellow actors. Houghton believed, however, that it was in the psychological area that Okhlopkov's actors were weakest, largely because the director did not grant them sufficient creative freedom.

Underlining the movement was music, available in its completed form from the beginning of rehearsals. A piano accompanist was present at all regular rehearsals and a full orchestra at all run-throughs. Music, drawn mainly, but not entirely, from classical composers, played a vital part in all of Okhlopkov's work.

Because the official Soviet style was socialist realism, Okhlopkov's apparently formalistic methods were often criticized, although his politically correct repertoire and audience popularity kept Stalin at bay. After he died, though, the criticism became sharper. In the West, his reputation glows because of his achievements as a forerunner of environmental theater and for employing theatricalist conventions while simultaneously establishing emotional communion between artists and audiences.

Further reading:

Lenhoff, Gail. "The Theatre of Okhlopkov." *The Drama Review* 17 (March 1973).

Also: Cole and Chinoy, *Directors on Directing;* Houghton, *Moscow Rehearsals;* Rudnitsky, *Russian and Soviet Theater;* Slonim, *Russian Theatre;* Van Gysegham, *Theatre in Soviet Russia;* Worrall, *Modernism to Realism on the Soviet Stage.*

ERWIN PISCATOR (1893–1966)

ERWIN FRIEDRICH MAX PISCATOR was born in Ulm, Germany, where his father was a clothing and fabric merchant. While attending Munich University, he interned without pay at the Munich Court Theater, but was drafted in 1915, an experience that taught him the insignificance of a politically uncommitted theater.

Piscator acted in a theater unit for the troops during the war. Shortly before the armistice, he worked at a theater in Courtrai. In 1918, traumatized by the war and by the murders of activists Karl Liebknecht and Rosa Luxemburg, he joined Berlin's Communist Party, in which he became an active participant.

From 1919 to 1920, with the Weimar Republic struggling for stability, Piscator directed expressionist plays in the Königsberg town hall. Soon after, he began Berlin's Proletarian Theater, directing amateurs in political works under primitive conditions. A singular production there was Lajos Barta's one-act agit-prop, *Russia's Day* (1920). It stirred emotions through posterlike techniques; at the end, everyone sang the Internationale.

Dissatisfied with the Berlin Volksbühne's failure to present proletarian theater, Piscator and Hans Rehfisch founded the Central-Theater. Piscator staged Maxim Gorky, Romain Rolland, and Leo Tolstoy. In 1923, he joined the Volksbühne itself, opening with Alfons Paquet's *Flags* (1924), an episodic Marxist piece about the events leading up to Chicago's Haymarket Affair. Elements that would be essential to his hallmark epic-theater style, made even more famous by Bertolt Brecht, included a political subject; an episodic script; a revolving set; projections of documentary materials and commentary; and a narrator.

Piscator continued these techniques in two party-sponsored agit-prop revues. The athletically performed *The Red Revue* (1924), with music by frequent collaborator Edmund Meisel (Kurt Weill and Hanns Eisler were later musical collaborators), contained a dozen anticapitalist sketches and songs and culminated in the singing of the Internationale. All was united by the commentary of two proletarian "spectators," and scenes were highlighted by tendentious projections. *Despite All!* (1925), seen at the Grosses Schauspielhaus, depicted communist events of 1914–1919 in 24 scenes aided by Piscator's innovative idea of archival war footage projected behind the live action.

Piscator's didactic productions were noted for their use of slides and films (often using multiple surfaces and projectors) mixed with large acting companies; complex scenery using extensive—but sometimes clumsy or noisy—machinery; and unconventionally plotted texts (both revered classics and new works) freely rewritten and reconstructed—to some authors' dismay—as montages to express a Marxist historical/social analysis. The films expanded the scenic vista and illustrated or commented on the action—sometimes ironically contradicting the actors' lines—by using either documentary footage or specially produced materials (including animation). They showed everything from floods to crowds to battles to unusual locales. Piscator coined the phrase "political theater" in 1928 to describe his approach, aimed at educating the proletariat; his critics pointed out that his lifestyle and audiences were more bourgeois than not. His methods were also accused of not following the party line. Many of his devices were adapted by other groups, both in agit-prop formats and the familiar guise of the Living Newspapers of the 1930s.

At the Volksbühne, his landmarks included Paquet's *Tidal Wave* (1926), about the Bolshevik revolution; Paul Zech's *The Drunken Ship* (1926), a tangentially political play about Arthur Rimbaud; and, among half-a-dozen others, Ehm Welk's *Storm over Gottland* (1927), about a 14th-century conflict between early capitalists and communists, made contemporaneous through film sequences. One showed the characters marching forward through history, their costumes changing until the ancient hero was transformed into Lenin. Such radicalism offended the theater's leaders and led to Piscator's ouster.

Meanwhile, Piscator was staging plays elsewhere in Berlin and Munich. The most controversial was Schiller's *The Robbers* (1926), moved out of the 18th-century into more or less contemporary dress and cut and reshaped to conform to an interpretation inspired by recent events (Spiegelberg resembled Leon Trotsky and the Internationale played at his death).

Piscator created the Piscator-Bühne at the Theater am Nollendorfplatz, where he also founded a training studio. He formed a dramaturgical collective (including Brecht) to develop scripts. A Total-Theater capable of being used in proscenium, arena, and thrust configurations was designed by Walter Gropius, but never realized. In order to suggest that art could flourish only in a Marxist society, where politics would be inconsequential, it was proclaimed that "This theater has been founded not in order to make politics but in order to free art from politics."

Piscator directed four milestones before the theater went bankrupt. The first was Ernst Toller's *Hoppla!*

We Live! (1927), Piscator's revisions of the original included the transformation of the hero from a bourgeois into a proletarian. The action took place both on the full stage and in a number of rooms placed on a four-level constructivist set, while films and slides were viewed on a tall central screen. A technically impressive scene showed prisoners tapping out messages to one another as the words flickered between the cells like the moving headlines in Times Square.

Alexei Tolstoy and Pavel Shchegolev's anti-czarist *Rasputin* (1927) was adapted to allow for documentary information to be included. A hemispherical construction, symbolic of the world, sat on the revolve, with sections that could be lifted to show various rooms. Films were projected on its rounded surface and on an overhead screen. So nasty was the political attack that living figures represented (including the Kaiser) sued for defamation.

Most popular was Jaroslav Hasek's *Adventures of the Good Soldier Schweik* (1928), starring Max Pallenberg as a comically antiheroic soldier whose wartime escapades ridicule the powers that be. It introduced a new technique, two treadmills set on the revolve and used to bring actors and scenery on and off. Scenic elements—including Georg Grosz's caricature cutouts of pompous personages—going in one direction while the actors went in the other or remained in place were used in conjunction with films, slides, and cartoons. Leo Lania's *Boom!* (1928), a satire on the international oil trade, was less successful.

Piscator rebounded elsewhere with Maxwell Anderson and Laurence Stallings's antiwar *What Price Glory?* (1929), then headed a second Piscator-Bühne to do Walter Mehring's *The Merchant of Berlin* (1929), a four hours-plus work on the sensitive subject of a Jewish immigrant's accumulation of wealth during 1923's inflation. It had a complex scenic scheme (designed by the Bauhaus's Laszlo Moholy-Nagy), employing the revolve, two treadmills whose positions could be altered, mechanically operated bridges that could be raised or lowered, four projection screens, and so on. Numerous rearrangements of the mise-en-scène were possible. A bit in which a soldier's corpse was maltreated caused condemnation from nationalists and led to the theater's demise.

Some actors formed their own Piscator Collective and toured his staging of Karl Credé's polemic against the criminal code on abortion, *§ 218*; actors planted in the audience discussed the issues with those on stage. The spectators voted on their beliefs at the end. The group took it back to Berlin and started yet another Piscator theater. Working under difficult conditions, they also presented his production of Theodore Plivier's *The Kaiser's Coolies* (1930), an antiwar drama about a mutiny, employing films, a text expanded to cover events from 1919 to 1930, and again including the Internationale as a finale; and Friedrich Wolf's *Tai Yang Awakes* (1931), shorter and less complex than most Piscator productions, making minimal use of film, and telling of an actual Chinese laborer who helped organize a strike. The actors dressed and made up on stage; several lectured to the spectators at certain points. It used a set composed of cloth banners with informative comments on one side and nothing on the other, which served as a projection screen when turned around.

Around this time, Piscator was briefly imprisoned on a questionable charge of tax-evasion. In 1931, he went into exile in the U.S.S.R. where he directed a film, was politically active, and was involved in inconclusive theatrical projects. The only play he directed was closed at the dress rehearsal. He eluded Stalin's purges, was mainly in Paris from 1936 to 1938, and emigrated to America.

In Washington, D.C., he completed his first production in nine years, George Bernard Shaw's *Saint Joan* (1940), with Luise Rainer and a cast of amateurs. He was centered, however, in New York at the Dramatic Workshop, which he founded in 1940 at the New School for Social Research (the alliance dissolved in 1949). There he produced and directed plays with mixed student and professional casts in an intimate playhouse. Many of his actors—Marlon Brando among them—later became stars. He produced several plays staged by others, and himself directed *King Lear* (1940), set on a wedding cake-like, four-tiered revolving set, with stagehands holding written banners to note locales, and Lear (Sam Jaffe) a fascistic dictator; his and Alfred Neumann's adaptation of Leo Tolstoy's *War and Peace* (1942), which had gone through several versions and which had been considered for Broadway; and Eugene O'Neill's *Mourning Becomes Electra* (1943). Union problems forced the semiprofessional company to cease activities.

Piscator offered student productions at Off-Broadway's Rooftop Theater of Heinz Herald and Geza Herczeg's *The Burning Bush* in 1949 and uptown at the President Theater of his and Robert Penn Warren's *All the King's Men* (1948), based on the latter's novel about a Southern demagogue; Wolfgang Borchert's *Outside the Door* (1949); John F. Mathews's *The Scapegoat* (1950), an adaptation of Franz Kafka's *The Trial*; and *Macbeth* (1951). He did some summer stock, but his one commercial Broadway try flopped. Several productions were abandoned in midrehearsal.

Few New York critics were impressed by Piscator, whose work—sensitive to the conservative climate—eschewed excessive controversy while nevertheless introducing, in limited circumstances, some of his epic techniques, such as the revolve, projections, and actors mingling with spectators. He produced several German plays that New York might never otherwise have seen.

In 1951, the aging director, who had never attained American citizenship, returned to Germany (thus avoiding a summons from the House Un-American Activities Committee), remaining in the Western sector despite his communist past and invitations from the East. He offered a prolific assortment of freelance productions in Germany's midlevel provincial theaters and elsewhere in Europe. After a decade, he was reestablished at the better venues, especially in Berlin. His repertoire—often not of his own choosing—included operas and an eclectic range of dramas by German-language and foreign (mainly English, French, and American) authors. He became head of the Freie Volksbühne in 1962.

A new *War and Peace* (1955), produced in Berlin, was especially noteworthy, and was shown at Paris's Théâtre des Nations (1956), as was William Faulkner's *Requiem for a Nun* (1957), albeit without his permission. Both employed a translucent stage floor lit from beneath, a method he introduced in a Frankfurt production of Jean-Paul Sartre's *Iron in the Soul* (1953). In *War and Peace,* the acting area was divided into a raked, upstage "destiny-stage" (lit from below), a circular downstage "action-stage," and three pulpitlike "reflection-stages" practically in the auditorium at down center and either side. A narrator stood near a desk below the "destiny-stage." The battle was enacted by toy soldiers moving about on the underlit platform.

Piscator made his greatest postwar contribution with three documentary plays reminiscent of his 1920s dramaturgy and inspired by West German guilt over World War II and Nazism. Rolf Hochhuth's provocative *The Deputy* (1963) told how the Vatican had ignored the Jews during the Holocaust; Heinar Kipphardt's *In the Matter of J. Robert Oppenheimer* (1964) was a courtroom drama based on the 1954 Atomic Energy Commission hearings; and Peter Weiss's *The Investigation* (1965) concerned the extermination camp horrors described at the Frankfurt war crimes trial of 1963–65. The latter two used texts based on transcripts.

Piscator rarely used stars, preferring a politically dedicated collective trained in his methods. He required an objectified, non-Stanislavskian acting style that paid more attention to the message than the messenger, although he recognized the value of emotion in acting. John Willett notes, "He never worked out a new approach to acting to match his approach to dramaturgy and stage technology," nor did he adopt Brechtian estrangement.

Erwin Piscator was not the first to employ many of the specific techniques for which he became renowned, but he was the first to consistently put them to use in an organic, politically oriented framework, thereby establishing a new form of theater committed to contemporary relevance.

Further reading:

Innes, C. D. *Erwin Piscator's Political Theatre: The Development of Modern German Drama.* Cambridge, England: Cambridge University Press, 1973.

Ley-Piscator, Maria. *The Piscator Experiment: The Political Theatre.* Carbondale and Edwardsville, Ill.: Southern Illinois University Press, 1967.

Piscator, Erwin. *The Political Theatre: A History 1914–1929.* Translated with notes by Hugh Rorrison. New York: Avon, 1978.

Willett, John. *The Theatre of Erwin Piscator.* New York: Holmes and Meier, 1979.

Also: Willet, *Theatre of the Weimar Republic;* Patterson, *The Revolution in German Theatre.*

GEORGES PITOËFF (1884–1939)

GEORGES PITOËFF was born in Tiflis, Georgia, Russia, where his father directed the state theater. Between 1902 and 1905, Pitoëff lived in Paris, took part in amateur theater, and obtained a law degree, before returning to Russia, where he joined Vera Komisarjevskaya's company, working under Vsevolod Meyerhold.

When Komisarjevskaya died, he toured Russia as far as Siberia with her sister's company. He moved to St. Petersburg and, between 1912 and 1914, ran the amateur Our Theater. In his excellent version of Anton Chekhov's *The Three Sisters* (1912), the actors carried most of the burden as the minimalist set, backed by a velvet curtain, consisted of little more than screens, lamps, and chairs. By 1911, Georges had come under the influence of Emile Jacques Dalcroze, proponent of eurhythmics. Subsequently, rhythm would play a dominant role for him in harmonizing script, performance, and decor. Every aural and visual moment of a Pitoëff production was informed by rhythmic concerns. He was also influenced by Swiss designer-theorist Adolphe Appia.

He established himself in neutral Switzerland from 1915 to 1921, playing in Russian at first at Geneva's Plainpalais. He next developed the Théâtre Pitoëff, a mixed amateur-professional French-language troupe with an international repertory. With him now was his recent bride Ludmilla, another Tiflis native, who, in plays Pitoëff staged, became one of Europe's greatest actresses.

Geneva saw Leo Tolstoy's *The Power of Darkness*

(1917) and Paul Claudel's *The Exchange* (1917), as well as plays by Henri-René Lenormand, dramatist of "the unconscious," including *Time Is a Dream* (1919) and *The Failures.* Lenormand became Pitoëff's most frequently produced French playwright. The company saw its reputation grow as its attendance declined. After the war, the Théâtre Pitoëff gained further attention during its tours to Paris.

In 1922, the Pitoëffs settled in Paris; during the next two decades he became one of France's outstanding actor-directors. An apostolic reformer with idealistic aspirations, he wished to restore a sense of greatness to a theatrical tradition he considered no longer relevant or creative. In 1927, he cofounded the Cartel of Four ("Cartel des Quatre") with Charles Dullin, Gaston Baty, and Louis Jouvet; it was a loose confederation created to provide mutual support among Paris's leading studio theater directors. He was an *homme de théâtre,* able to act, direct, design, translate, adapt, and produce plays. As an actor he was highly regarded, despite a heavy Russian accent. Because the Pitoëffs were so accomplished, their star qualities detracted from any intended ensemble effect.

Unlike his Cartel associates, he was not long connected with a specific playhouse. His major work was at the Comédie des Champs-Elysées, the Théâtre des Arts, the Théâtre des Mathurins, the Théâtre de l'Avenue, and the Théâtre du Vieux-Colombier. From 1934 to 1939, he remained at the Mathurins. The scenic resources at these small, unprofitable venues could not match his imagination.

Pitoëff's large repertoire (204 plays by 114 dramatists) was remarkable for a director lacking the wherewithal or imprimatur of a subsidized theater. He was best known for non-French plays but did strongly support native writers. The authors of his 75 French plays included Jean Anouilh (including the early *Traveller without Luggage* in 1937 and *The Savage* in 1938); Jean Cocteau (including his first important drama, *Orpheus*, in 1926); Roger Vitrac; Georges Duhamel; Jean-Jacques Bernard; Jules Romains; Stève Passeur; Roger Martin du Gard; Jules Supervielle; André Gide (including his first major drama, *Oedipus*, in 1930); and Claudel. His classics were limited to Alfred de Musset, Pierre de Beaumarchais, and Alexander Dumas *fils*. His new plays usually were poetic or romantic. David Whitton declared, "With Pitoëff the Idealist reaction that generated the French Symbolist theatre at the end of the nineteenth century enjoyed a final fling."

Chekhov, Luigi Pirandello, George Bernard Shaw, Henrik Ibsen, and Shakespeare were the great foreigners highest on Pitoëff's list. Others (many of them Russian) included Nikolai Gogol, Leonid Andreyev, Alexander Pushkin, Leo Tolstoy, Gerhart Hauptmann, Ferdinand Bruckner, Seneca, Arthur Schnitzler, Eugene O'Neill, Ferenc Molnár, J. M. Synge, Oscar Wilde, August Strindberg, Rabindranath Tagore, and Carlo Goldoni. His company was referred to as a theatrical League of Nations.

Uncle Vanya (1921), *The Sea Gull* (1922), and *The Three Sisters* (1929) remain highwater marks of French Chekhov. Benefitting from the director's roots, they were atmospherically Slavic but avoided Stanislavskian realism. He repeated his St. Petersburg minimalism, removing all but the essential furnishings in order to focus on inner lives.

Although it was Dullin who introduced Pirandello to Paris, it was Pitoëff's production of *Six Characters in Search of an Author* (1923) that made the Italian a French household name and added enormous stature to Pitoëff. He had had to convince the fearful author to allow him interpretive freedom; only Pirandello's incognito viewing of a rehearsal won him over. The director brought a nightmarish quality to the play; its tragic nature dominated all other moods. The "characters" were funereal, their faces ghostly white. Instead of following Pirandello's direction to have them enter from the world of the spectators, Pitoëff had them appear, lit eerily in green, on the scenery elevator, to suggest their existence in the world of the theater. His Pirandello plays included *Henry IV* (1925), *Right You Are, If You Think You Are* (1926), and *Tonight We Improvise* (1935).

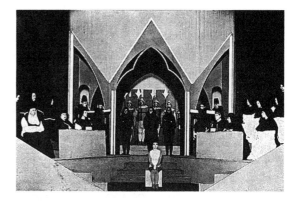

Shaw's Saint Joan, *with Ludmilla Pitoëff. Directed by Georges Pitoëff. (1925)* (Photo: Collection Rondel, Bibliothèque de l'Arsenal)

Shaw was introduced in a memorable *Saint Joan* (1925), with Ludmilla a moving Joan, but there were fine productions of eight other Shaws as well. (Ludmilla also played Joan in René Arnaud and Pitoëff's docudrama, *The True Trial of Joan of Arc* in 1929.) Pitoëff revived such great Ibsen dramas as *A Doll's House* (1930), *The Wild Duck* (1934), and *An Enemy of the People* (1939), eliminating both André Antoine's naturalism and Aurelien Lugné-Poe's symbolism, and revealing the plays in an entirely new light.

Pitoëff was a great pioneer of contemporary French Shakespeare. He produced some of the most stylistically diverse revivals, demonstrating the importance of the dramatist's poetic vision in a culture that tended to force him into a rational straitjacket. Pitoëff's Geneva repertoire had included *Macbeth* (1921) and *Hamlet* (1919), but only the latter was repeated in Paris (1926), which also saw a fast-moving farce interpretation of *Measure for Measure* (1922)—with the characters as commedia types—and *Romeo and Juliet* (1937). The decor ranged from the relative literalness of *Measure for Measure* and *Romeo and Juliet* to the metaphysical abstraction of *Hamlet*, but each had unit sets allowing full expression to Shakespeare's use of time and place. Linguistically, they hewed closely to the originals' nuances.

The barely cut, five-hour *Hamlet* was Pitoëff's masterpiece. To suggest the prince's groping for the truth, all its scenes took place at night (and all the characters—except Fortinbras, his men, and the mad Ophelia—wore dark costumes); day broke only during the final entrance of Fortinbras. Hamlet ran frantically after a ghost that was merely a growing and shrinking shadow. "To be or not to be" was an objectified, gestureless discourse spoken from the back of the stage by a lonely man "deliberating and weighing up the odds of life," wrote Rudolph Weiss.

The nonlocalized setting employed four black pillars at each stage corner to which were attached an arrangement of black-and-silver screens that could be moved into 224 varying positions. When, after 100 performances, their shifting seemed distracting, Pitoëff discarded all positions except one.

In *Romeo and Juliet*, planned for 20 years, Pitoëff designed a more localized unit setting, with the Capulet and Montague houses facing each other at either side of the stage, and with Friar Laurence's cell placed before a black curtain down right. Tension was evoked by the sharp angles of the platforms suggesting the town square between the houses. For the tomb, a black curtain obscured the houses, a trap opened down center, a simple white cross hung over the grave, and the families were grouped at the rear. The performances—starring the middle-aged Pitoëffs as the star-crossed lovers—stressed the forward rush of the plot; all inessential details were omitted.

Working under adverse economic conditions, Pitoëff survived by hook or crook, creating ingeniously simplified creations that resulted from both an aesthetic vision and empty pockets. "Pitoëff has produced more plays for less money than any manager who ever lived," commented John Palmer, "and he has produced them without giving any impression of meanness or conceptions thwarted by a lack of capital." His realistic work did not overlook realistic attributes; they merely eliminated nonessentials, until only what was required to evince the play's essence remained. This jibed with his tendency toward "simplicity and abstraction," as Palmer notes, although he never lost touch with a play's humanity. Always, the actor was the dominant force, not the decor. "Reality was transposed," wrote Dorothy Knowles, "idealized, to the point of making the real more intensely real."

Usually, Pitoëff's productions combined a small number of furniture pieces within a geometrically conceived setting. Jacques Guicharnaud said that he created

> three-dimensional structures on several levels, tinged with expressionism or cubism, with special emphasis on color and the succession of planes in depth. His objective was to reach a strange and inner poetry that would touch the modern soul, and he tried to bring out 'a

> reflection of our thinking' and 'the stirring questions of our times.'

Pitoëff's effects were often enhanced through the clever use of lighting on blue, black, or gray velvet fabrics. The decor of Lenormand's *The Eater of Dreams*, for example, was able to suggest a room or even the Mediterranean with long strips of colored ribbon draped before a black velvet background. But the lighting was fairly uncomplicated, using a minimum of well-placed instruments.

Despite his antinaturalistic proclivities, Pitoëff was nondogmatic and declared that his prime objective was to be faithful to the text. The director was an independent artist, an autocrat responsible for drawing on many arts—including playwriting—to compose a stage production. Although he demanded from dramatists complete autonomy in interpreting their work, he had total respect for the text and employed his staging and designs to express every aspect of it. Theatrical means, including expressive groupings, conveyed what the script could not. He searched for the "secret forces" that had driven the author to create the work and—unlike most of his great contemporaries—followed no idiosyncratic system other than what the play itself dictated. His productions differed radically from one to the other.

Once Pitoëff discovered the play's internal, poetic truth he realized it through his metaphorically apt—but sometimes controversially idiosyncratic—direction and designs. Bettina L. Knapp declared, "The mise-en-scène emerged directly from the text and was designed to point up its greatness and concretise its verbal images and rhythms, thus filling the proscenium with electric charges." To Pitoëff, the central idea of *Saint Joan* is "saintliness," and it must make miracles seem possible. Thus he unified the sprawling play by employing a religion-inspired setting that was, according to Knowles, "reminiscent of an altarpiece, a triptych formed of an arch in the centre and a half-arch on either side." To convey the miraculous nature of Joan's being able to select the Dauphin, whom she has never seen, from a crowd, Pitoëff had the tiny, mystically possessed Ludmilla enter the strange place and stand there baffled by the light and noise. Palmer, remembering Pitoëff's indelible tableaux, observed:

> For a breathless instant she pauses like a child, sensitive to mockery, bewildered. Then, suddenly uplifted by her inspiration and purpose, she braves them all, and, led by the intuition with which she is suddenly illumined,

goes straight to her goal. We do not see the Dauphin ourselves. She suddenly dives into the midst of them and brings him forth. Then for just an instant the whole stage is immobile, as though time stood still . . . making a picture that remains in the eye after . . . the action [has] resumed.

Pitoëff's conceptions often surprised the playwrights themselves. An example was his staging the end of Pirandello's *Henry IV,* in which the title character's self-created world comes crashing around him, by having a clearly artificial wall begin to topple so that Henry could rush to keep it in its place. Pirandello said this was so fine he should have indicated it in his own text.

The Pitoëffs brought their work all over Europe; often, they were more appreciated abroad than at home. Georges was acknowledged for his ability to blend the ideas of the greatest directors of the day, both conservative and revolutionary, into a uniquely harmonious style that could not easily be defined.

Further reading:

Knapp, Bettina L. *French Theatre 1918–1939.* New York: Grove Press, 1985.

Marx, Magdalene. "The Pitoëffs." *Theatre Guild Magazine* 7 (May 1930).

Palmer, John. *Studies in the Contemporary Theatre.* London: Martin Secker, 1927.

Weiss, Rudolph. "Georges Pitoëff—His Shakespeare Productions in France." Translated by Brian Keith-Smith. *Theatre Research* 5, no. 2 (1963).

Also: Guicharnaud, *Modern French Theatre;* Knowles, *French Drama during the Inter-war Years;* Marshall, *The Producer and the Play;* Whitton, *Stage Directors in Modern France.*

ROGER PLANCHON (1931–   )

ROGER PLANCHON was born in Saint-Chamond, France, and grew up in his peasant family's region of the Ardèche and Lyon. After a year of absorbing art and culture in Paris, he took a theater course in Lyon, where he established a group of artists (including actor Jean Bouise). Planchon's directorial debut was with a play by the company's Claude Lochy. In 1950, Planchon directed *Ankle-Boots and Starched Collars,* a prize-winning cabaret farce drawn from Georges Courteline and Eugène Labiche.

A year later, Planchon staged *Twelfth Night* and *The Merry Wives of Windsor.* Shakespeare became a Planchon favorite; he staged *Henry IV* (1957), *Troilus and Cressida* (1964), *Richard III* (1967), and on alternate nights in 1978, *Antony and Cleopatra, Love's Labour's Lost,* and *Pericles.*

In 1952, the young company created the tiny Théâtre de la Comédie in an abandoned printer's shop. Audiences were drawn by their topically funny, *Hellzapoppin'*-like burlesque-farces, such as *Cartouche* (1953). In addition, plays by Michel de Ghelderode, Arthur Adamov (two premieres), Ferenc Molnár, Heinrich von Kleist, Christopher Marlowe (three different versions of *Edward II* in 1954, 1960, and 1961), and Bertolt Brecht were on the bills in 1953–1954, making the company well-respected for its larger-than-life acrobatic style, surrealist and absurdist-influenced avant-gardism, and commitment to an unfamiliar repertory of modern plays and foreign classics. The troupe's mission was the creation of theater for a single provincial community.

Brecht's *The Good Woman of Setzuan* (1954, 1955, and 1958) was given three strikingly different pro-

Roger Planchon. (Photo: Théâtre National Populaire/ Brigitte Enguerand)

ductions. These ranged from a fanciful but unsuccessful version staged on the tables of a gambling casino, with *kabuki*-like runways extending table to table, to one directly influenced by Planchon's 1955 conversation with Brecht and employing the Berliner Ensemble's music but avoiding their masks because of the actors' inexperience. Other Brecht plays included *Fear and Misery of the Third Reich* (1956) and an occasionally expressionistic *Schweik in the Second World War* (1961), played on a revolving stage.

Meanwhile, works by Pedro Calderón de la Barca, Eugène Ionesco, J. M. Synge, Jacques Prévert, Roger Vitrac, Jacob Lenz, and Michael Vinaver saw the company through 1956. Vinaver's *Today, or the Koreans* (1956), was politically controversial because— at the cold war's apex—it dealt with an American soldier being rescued and taken care of by a village of North Koreans, with whom he comes to sympathize. In 1956, the actors debuted in Paris.

The next year, Planchon's troupe took over the 1,300-seat municipal theater of Villeurbanne, a working-class suburb of Lyon. The leftist director, an advocate of theater's social value, created an audience of 20,000 by reaching out through reduced prices, group bookings, seminars, a redecorated theater, school visits, public opinion surveys, a free newspaper, and so on.

Planchon opened with Adamov's scathing Brechtian "chronicle play" attack on *belle époque* capitalism, *Paolo Paoli*, which began Planchon's close collaboration with designer René Allio, whose set incorporated projections of period clippings and photos. The relationship of Adamov and Planchon was later commemorated in *A. A. Plays of Arthur Adamov* (1975), a surrealistic collage.

The company changed their name to Théâtre de la Cité de Villeurbanne, offering Shakespeare's *Henry IV* (1957) and a new adaptation of Alexandre Dumas's *The Three Musketeers* (1958) as their premiere productions, both hits. The satirically slanted, hilariously antiromantic, antimilitaristic, dance- and slapstick-oriented *Three Musketeers* was produced with conscious naivete to create a childlike vision of the musketeers' world. The gag-filled piece exposed Dumas's misogyny and debunked the characters (Richelieu fried eggs while plotting with Lady de Winter).

The nearly uncut, technically complex, six-hour Shakespeare was broken into two parts (*Henry V* and *Falstaff*). It used epic theater techniques and Marxian ideas to emphasize the decline of feudalism and the rise of materialism within the context of a political power struggle. A raked stage was backed by large medieval maps, and projected slogans prefaced each scene. Locales were suggested by models at the sides. Scenic abstraction was coupled with realistic props, and the emblematic costumes mingled the contemporary with the historical. Mimed interpolations pointed out the common man's sufferings and the rulers' cruelty. Similar social approaches underlined later Shakespeares as well.

Molière's *The Tricks of Scapin* and *Georges Dandin* joined the repertoire in 1958. *Georges Dandin* (revised in 1986) viewed the commedia-like farce in class-critical terms. In 1959, the company became France's first permanent, subsidized provincial theater. Planchon remained at Villeurbanne, although frequent tours in France and abroad occupied the troupe after 1960.

Following France's May 1968 political disruptions, which strongly affected theater, Planchon realized that while it was impossible to attract the working classes in large numbers, he had to demonstrate to them not only the existence but the privilege of culture. Anything less, he said, would be demagogy. He aimed at a wider clientele, middle as well as working class.

Planchon added playwriting to his work with *The Return* (1962), about a youth who returns to his ancestral village following his grandfather's murder. Although he has declared that—because of his lack of objectivity—an author is the last person who should direct his own plays, Planchon directed most of those he wrote. Representative examples—all naturalistically inclined—are *Blues, Whites, and Reds, or the Libertines* (1967); *The Infamous* (1970); *The Black Pig* (1974); *Gilles de Rais* (1976); and *Alice, By the Dark Roads* (1983). These works, written for his Villeurbanne audience, are set in the provinces (Planchon revels in their "provincialism"), based on real (often bloody) incidents, and have complex plots and strong local interest.

Meanwhile, he staged foreign authors such as Shakespeare, Sean O'Casey, John Arden, Harold Pinter, and Ionesco, and natives such as Jean Racine (including an unorthodox *Bérénice* in 1966, in which Titus does not love Bérénice, and three others in the eighties), Molière, Pierre de Marivaux, Roland Dubillard, and Vinaver. The latter's 1974 *Overboard*, a satirical attack on ruthless American business practices, was whittled down from a potential 10-hour script and staged like an American musical comedy.

In 1991, Planchon directed two of his own plays, *Old Winter* and *Fragile Forest*, which were still being

Roger Planchon (l) and Guy Tréjean in Tartuffe. *Directed by Roger Planchon. (1973)* (Photo: Théâtre National Populaire/Rajak Ohanian)

presented in rotating repertory two years later. These works, telling of a historical confrontation between Catholic and Huguenot military forces on opposite sides of a river, with the former set in the Catholic camp and the latter in the Protestant, remained on the boards through 1993, playing at Villeurbanne and other French cities. Early in 1994, Planchon was scheduled to stage his period comedy of the French Revolution, *The Libertines,* a revision of a work originally staged by Jean Vilar at Avignon in 1967, and never done at Villeurbanne.

Sometimes, Planchon restaged plays he already had done, but with a new interpretation. Molière's *Tartuffe* (1962, 1973) typified Planchon's belief that a classic's stage language must be constantly reinvented in the light of contemporary socio-historical perceptions. His most controversial idea for the comedy was that Orgon, not Tartuffe, is the active agent and that his behavior is motivated by an unconscious homosexual attraction for the hypocrite. This infatuation, to Planchon, stems from a diminution of the power of Orgon's class following the Fronde and the character's sublimation of his need to exercise

political power via a resort to immersion in religious beliefs.

In 1962, the box set's walls revealed period paintings combining images of religiosity with sexuality. The costumes conveyed a sense of both the 17th-century and the present day, and the actors suggested everyday life in a typical bourgeois household. The conclusion communicated Louis XIV's power, with the implication that Orgon's salvation stemmed from the king's awareness that the man might be of future use to him.

Certain elements of the 1962 decor reappeared in 1973's highly physicalized version, but the religious paintings were partly hidden by tarpaulins and the set filled with scaffolding. Orgon's home—in the midst of renovation—reflected a society in transition. The characters went about their business with myriad everyday details, and except for certain moments, dressed informally to imply family intimacy. Orgon's homoerotic infatuation was accentuated more than before; Tartuffe was young, handsome, and charming, to make Orgon's feelings for him immediately obvious. The unconventional ending further established the unforgiving absolutism of the monarchy when the king's armed men burst in, the floor beneath the family became a pit into which they stood waist-deep with muskets trained on them, Tartuffe and his servant (shown as the king's spy) were manhandled, and the walls were stripped away to reveal a dungeonlike environment.

In 1969, while the company toured, the Villeurbanne theater was closed for several years of renovations that reduced the seating to 800. When it reopened in 1973, it was designated the new Théâtre National Populaire (TNP) and Patrice Chéreau became codirector. The government wanted the well-subsidized TNP to remain in Paris, but Planchon resisted. They toured regularly, paying month-long visits to various cities.

Planchon's early work often copied directly from Brecht. Brecht's influence could be found in, among other things: Planchon's early favoring of a play's action and story over its characters' psychology and dialogue (psychology later became important to him) to reveal the bases of human behavior; his faith in the ability of performance language ("scenic writing," a concept further influenced by Robert Wilson's productions) to communicate as much or more than the text, with interpretation necessary in every detail of the mise-en-scène; and his combination of distancing effects, such as nonillusionistic sets, scene shifts seen by the audience, multicued light plots suggestive of cinematic techniques, printed slogans, filmed sequences, and slide projections. The latter all comment on the play, while representational props, costumes, and acting allow for emotional involvement with characters and story. Like Brecht, Planchon prefers episodic plays whose scenes are linked cinematically yet require only minimal settings. Thus his fondness for Shakespeare.

Planchon believes that each play represents a specific social milieu that must be explored and communicated. He seeks a critical evaluation of society but has moved away from problem-solving. An opponent of militant theater, he holds that the answers to social dilemmas are the audience's responsibility. Planchon avoids excessively intellectual plays or ideas, keeping his work accessible while not lowering his artistic standards.

Planchon distrusts overly emotional acting; he eschews pathos and concentrates on the events enacted. The more relaxed the performance the better. He wants his highly intelligent actors to be fully conscious of the social reality of their roles and to place them carefully within the historical time and place represented. He gets the actors to be concerned not merely with their particular role but with the play as a whole. Planchon gives the actors considerable freedom, but subtly guides them to fit into and agree with his vision. If he is not satisfied he may require an actor to repeat something 20 times until he gets the desired result. A superb actor himself, and a man of excitable temperament, he often physically demonstrates.

Casting is not preestablished but evolves as the company begins to work on a play. After readings and discussions, the actors privately show Planchon their characterizations until the casting is finalized, which takes about two weeks. This works within the community-oriented world of the TNP, in which each artist is free to offer suggestions or to argue an interpretive point. Group work is favored over autocracy or "stars," although the director (sometimes working with a codirector) has the final word. Planchon originally dismissed lengthy "at table" sessions, but for recent productions he began with three painstakingly detailed weeks of readings (supplemented by behavior-based commentary) before the blocking. Once the scenery is in place, he blocks rapidly, taking three to seven days, although he

makes many revisions, with the actors's input essential to his final choices. He permits considerable improvisational freedom until a blending of his and the actors' aims takes place. Reading and blocking sessions are followed by three weeks of detailed work and 10 days of synthesizing, a total of about eight weeks.

Planchon's presence is as crucial to conventional productions as in the TNP's dazzling, company-created satires resembling musical spectacles, such as *The Three Musketeers*. Others include *O M'man Chicago* (1963), spoofing the legend of Al Capone; *The Tearing to Pieces of "The Cid"* (1969), inspired by the events of 1968 and using Pierre Corneille's classic as a springboard for parodying the theater ideas of leading practitioners; and *The Cat's Tale* (1972), set in 2000 and poking fun at such preoccupations as war, pollution, and overpopulation. These multidimensional works made social comments via extravagant sets and costumes, great dollops of music and dancing, surrealistic dream sequences, and slapstick and vaudeville.

Planchon is a unique figure who has succeeded in disturbing French culture's overcentralization by creating a large provincial and "popular" audience for world-class theater. He has demonstrated his commitment to the investigation of social concerns through theater; has explored a wide range of classical materials with iconoclastically contemporary, sociohistorically motivated interpretations; and has written a series of respected plays.

Further reading:

Daoust, Yvette. *Roger Planchon: Director and Playwright.* Cambridge, England: Cambridge University Press, 1981.

Kustow, Michael. "Life and Work of an Illuminated Man." *Theatre Quarterly* 2 (January–March 1972).

Planchon, Roger. "Creating a Theatre of Real Life." Interview by Michael Kustow. *Theatre Quarterly* 2 (January–March 1972).

———. "Taking on the TNP: Theatre as Social and Artistic Adventure." *Theatre Quarterly* 7 (Spring 1977).

Also: Bradby and Williams, *Directors' Theatre*; Knapp, *Off-Stage Voices*; Whitton, *Stage Directors in Modern France.*

WILLIAM POEL (1852–1934)

WILLIAM POEL (*né* Pole), the son of a distinguished civil engineer, was born in the London borough of Westminster, England. Physical problems kept Poel from attending a university; at 17, he joined a company of building contractors. He first visited a play at 20, but quickly became an ardent theatergoer.

In 1876, the tall, impressive-looking Poel began acting and working backstage for provincial companies. Two years later, he began offering recitals of classical drama. He believed that Shakespeare was hampered by the constraints of the proscenium stage and that scene shifting should not impede the action's progress and rhythm. It was necessary to return to the principles of Elizabethan staging, with its reliance on imagination to envision time and place. Poel studied Elizabethan practices; he attempted, through his publications, lectures, and productions, to convince his contemporaries of the validity of his controversial and oft-disputed findings. Despite his excesses and wrong-headedness, he had an enormous impact on Shakespearean staging.

In 1879, Poel formed a tiny touring company to perform staged and costumed readings of Shakespearean and other scenes. He discovered that the acting editions of Shakespeare were mutilated compared to the originals. The editorial practice of indicating act and scene divisions where Shakespeare used none irked him.

It was with excitement that Poel read the newly published (1880) first and second quarto editions of *Hamlet*. The idea that the first was likely to have been an actual acting script, shortened and otherwise adapted for stage use, was appealing. This led to his directorial debut in 1881 when he staged an intermissionless version of the first quarto at St. George's Hall on a stage dressed only with draperies. Poel played the prince, a boy played the Player Queen, the usually cut dumb show was reinstated, and Ophelia carried a lute rather than flowers in her mad scene. Instead of the typical Nordic costumes, the innovative concept of Elizabethan clothes was used. Poel wished to emphasize that Shakespeare's plays were about his own time and place, despite their commonly being set in foreign locales and earlier periods.

The work demonstrated Poel's preference for arriving at fresh solutions to staging problems instead of relying on tradition. He did not, though, seek to be distractingly clever. His basic approach was to read the play meticulously and to seek the most logical way of revealing behavior. Although he demanded textual authenticity, he often blue-penciled freely, claiming that his cuts were in the interest of continuity and speed, and that—unlike others—he never removed entire scenes. Nevertheless, his cuts could be damaging. Rehearsals commenced with the full text, but when structural weaknesses appeared, Poel began making adaptations. He was sometimes guilty of revising because of offenses to his Victorian sensibilities. He altered *Measure for Measure*'s "He got a wench with child" to "He will shortly be a father." Poel argued that he sometimes had to reconstruct old plays because he found the playwrights weak in plot architecture.

Like almost all of Poel's later productions, *Hamlet* was acted by amateurs in an out-of-the-way, nontheatrical location. (On several occasions, though, he produced Shakespeare in authentic Elizabethan spaces, such as Gray's Inn or the Middle Temple.) His audiences were small and confined to enthusiasts, and he did not have a commercial career. In fact, theater's commercialization was one of his bugbears. Some of his amateurs went on to illustrious stage careers, among them Lillah McCarthy and Edith Evans. His most eccentric casting habit was a tendency to use women in leading male roles (Dionysus, Everyman, and others).

Poel produced two other versions of *Hamlet*, one in 1900 (first quarto) and one in 1914 (second quarto). He also staged a hilarious, early 17th-century burlesque of *Hamlet*, the anonymous *Fratricide Punished* (1924). Plays he had staged earlier were often revived, with deeper insights. His productions had limited runs, but usually toured several locations.

Between 1881 and 1885, Poel managed the theater that later became the Old Vic, wrote plays, and stage-managed for actor-manager Frank Benson. He taught for the Shakespeare Reading Society in 1887, and directed staged readings—several costumed—of 15 Shakespearean plays for them through 1897. In 1893, he did a fully produced *Measure for Measure* for which the stage of the Royalty Theater was made to resemble an Elizabethan playhouse, the Fortune. For the Independent Stage Society, he offered a traditionally scenic version of *The Duchess of Malfi* (1892).

Poel's Shakespeare readings helped confirm his ideas concerning the need for an Elizabethan-type stage that would bring out the implicit dramatic values trampled on by traditional scenic staging. He dismissed the notion, popular among some Elizabethanists, of indicating locale by placards, but believed it crucial that locale somehow be made clear. The Elizabethan stage (the first picture of which became available in 1888), dressed up with a few easily moved pieces, could satisfy all the scenic requirements of the old plays, he insisted.

Poel never recreated an Elizabethan stage; what he did was to set up on a proscenium stage the architectural elements (painted on two-dimensional flats) of one—a balcony (or raised platform), a recessed inner stage, two doors, front pillars, and a semblance of a thrust. His 19th-century prejudices victimized him, though; most productions used a historically indefensible traverse curtain strung between the two front pillars to allow for establishing multiple locales by a process of alternating the action up- and downstage of the curtain. Only rarely was he able to build his platform out over the orchestra seats in order to evoke Shakespearean closeness. Moreover, the placement of much of the acting area upstage of the proscenium arch meant that—apart from the costumed spectators he sometimes placed on stage—Poel's actors were never surrounded by the audience.

Poel occasionally added pictorial elements to his stagings, such as the hellmouth he employed in Christopher Marlowe's *Dr. Faustus* (1896). He was a master of composition and grouping, and his pictures were reminiscent of Italian Renaissance paintings. He kept scrapbooks filled with articles on painting and reproductions of classical pictures. And he preceded Max Reinhardt by frequently having actors enter and exit through the audience; this was not Elizabethan but it was theatrically effective, which was always Poel's primary aim. Poel did not cling tenaciously to scenic Elizabethanism, and his 1914 *Hamlet* was closer to Gordon Craig than to the Globe. By then he could absorb the Elizabethan stage's principles and deploy them in a contemporary mode.

Poel pioneered in the use of Elizabethan stage clothes, his expensively made costumes (often paid for from his own wallet) normally being colorful and attractive. It was difficult for some to accept many of his advances, especially in the Roman plays,

from which Poel banned togas. However, Poel often modified his earlier approach and even sometimes mixed periods, seeking artistic effect over antiquarianism. In his later career, his costuming occasionally bordered on the bizarre, especially in *Coriolanus* (1931), wherein the hero first appeared in a leopard skin, then in the full-dress uniform of a Hussar colonel, and, finally, in breastplate and helmet. Poel showed actors at the start of rehearsals what their costumes would look like as a way of inspiring them to feel themselves into their roles.

Poel's major directorial work began in 1895, a year after the Elizabethan Stage Society was formed. From 1895—when he opened with *Twelfth Night*—to 1905, Poel staged for the Society an extremely wide range of classics, many not seen since their original presentations. These included nine Shakespeares and such authors as Marlowe (including a thoroughly rearranged *Dr. Faustus* in 1896), Francis Beaumont and John Fletcher, Thomas Middleton and William Rowley, John Ford, Ben Jonson (including one of his masques), and the anonymous *Arden of Faversham* (1897). The group's name apart, there were also such unusual foreign classics as Pedro Calderón de la Barca's *Life Is a Dream* (retitled *Such Stuff as Dreams Are Made Of*, 1899), Molière's *Don Juan* (its first English production, 1899), and even Kálidása's *Sákuntalá* (1899). Poel tried his hand at staging dramatic poems not originally intended for the theater, such as John Milton's *Samson Agonistes* (1900) and Walter Scott's *Marmion,* and he also tackled a shortened version of Friedrich Schiller's *Wallenstein* plays. His first production of a living poet was of Charles Swinburne's *Locrine* (1899). His only money-maker was the medieval morality play, *Everyman* (1901), which he rediscovered and praised as art while disputing its theology. Poel did not shy from applying Elizabethan principles to the realization of non-Elizabethan plays.

After financial problems led to the company's dissolution, Poel redirected many of his earlier productions. He added new Shakespeares, including the rarely produced *Troilus and Cressida* (1912), as well as classical writers such as Oliver Goldsmith, George Chapman, and Euripides. There were unusual attempts to theatricalize nondramatic materials, like Edward Arnold's poem, *The Light of Asia* (retitled *Buddha* in 1912), and *The Book of Job* (1912). In 1916–1917 he staged American college productions of Jonson's *The Poetaster*. His last production, done at 80, was of George Peele's Elizabethan *David and Bethsabe* (1932). Few directors have ever matched so diverse and off-the-beaten-path a record of classical revivals. Most of Poel's productions benefitted from the excellent musical accompaniments provided for them by Arnold Dolmetsch.

Often Poel interpreted familiar plays in ways at variance with existing attitudes. His decisions could be controversial, as when he produced *The Merchant of Venice* (1898) with Shylock (which he played) as a caricaturish, avaricious, red-wigged villain, in contrast to Henry Irving's more sympathetic approach. More appropriate was his reinsertion of all the casket scenes. Another distinctive interpretation was of Euripides' *The Bacchae* (1908), which Poel claimed was meant as a religious satire. In 1905, he cast real teenagers for *Romeo and Juliet,* and in 1909 offered an untraditionally sexy Lady Macbeth. The production also provoked debate by making the second apparition Duncan instead of Banquo.

Poel's premier concern in Elizabethan plays was how to speak them as they originally sounded. He sought a rapid, believable, and intelligible speech, which he hoped to obtain by two principal concepts, "exaggerated naturalness" and "tuned tones." A hard, if usually kind, taskmaster, he was indefatigable in providing actors with "key words." (He once locked his actors in a room of his house overnight, refusing to release them until they had learned his emphases.) Similarly, he drilled the "tune" into their heads by underlining the natural intonation the words would have in modern English. He did not want a mere imitation of reality, however, but a reasonably heightened impression of natural speech. For all his close study of the original texts, including paying great attention to their punctuation, he was often not able to demonstrate precisely the effect desired, and his unpaid amateurs were generally incapable of assimilating—as opposed to copying—his intentions. Many Poel productions were slighted for bad acting, which was exacerbated by the lack of rehearsal time.

As he rehearsed, he was likely to have his eyes closed to help him focus on the speech; meanwhile, he would coach incessantly. Once, when the duchess of Gloucester pleaded for her son's life in a rehearsal of *Richard II,* he kept saying, "More hysteria, more hysteria," and when he finally got it, declared, "That's the tone, keep it up." He had to be gently informed that the reason for the actress's success was that she had broken down hysterically from his ceaseless demands.

Poel rehearsed compulsively, ignoring the needs of actors for breaks and meals, and himself eating sparely if at all. Although usually mild, he once slapped an actress when he learned that, on a doctor's orders, she had drunk a glass of wine before rehearsal. His graceful apologies for such lapses were cherished. Frequently, he worked privately with actors, before the regular rehearsals began. This might take six weeks before the company rehearsals began. The time on stage was strictly limited.

Poel was the chief contributor to what is known as the Elizabethan Revival period. His work was not especially well recognized in his day, but he had a tremendous influence on future leaders who worked with him, such as Harley Granville-Barker, Nugent Monck, Elsie Fogarty (Laurence Olivier's speech teacher), and Lewis Casson.

Further reading:

Lundstrom, Rinda F. *Willam Poel's "Hamlets": The Director as Critic.* Ann Arbor, Mich.: UMI Research Press, 1984.

Speaight, Robert. *William Poel and the Elizabethan Revival.* London: William Heinemann, 1954.

Also: Brockett and Findlay, *Century of Innovation;* Mazer, *Shakespeare Refashioned.*

HAROLD PRINCE (1928–   )

HAROLD SMITH PRINCE was born in New York, where his stepfather was a well-to-do stockbroker. He attended the University of Pennsylvania, participated in campus theatricals, and graduated at 19. Producer-director George Abbott, his greatest influence, hired Prince as an assistant stage manager. After a stint in the army, Prince became Broadway's "wunderkind" when he coproduced five musical hits in a row (most directed by Abbott).

Prince first directed when he replaced Word Baker on James Goldman, John Kander, and Fred Ebb's musical, A *Family Affair* (1962). He continued to produce (and, usually, direct) Broadway musicals, but abandoned producing in the 1980s when the

Harold Prince (r) directing Pacific Overtures. *(1976)*
(Photo: Martha Swope)

costs went sky high. From 1976, Prince, who does not read music, staged various operas. In 1962, he directed a touring production of Thornton Wilder's *The Matchmaker,* and in the early 1970s, he staged several revivals for the Phoenix Theater. All his new commercial dramas (Stanley Hart's *Some of My Best Friends* in 1977, Joanna M. Glass's *Play Memory* in 1984, and Arthur Kopit's *End of the World* in 1984) failed.

After *A Family Affair,* Prince directed three more flops. The small-scaled, romantic *She Loves Me* (1963), its score by Sheldon Harnick and Jerry Bock, was a critically esteemed but commercially feeble show derived from Ernst Lubitsch's film *The Little Shop Around the Corner,* set in the environs of a Budapest-like perfume and cosmetics shop. It was followed by Marion Grudeff and Raymond Jessell's Sherlock Holmes musical, *Baker Street* (1965). In 1966, Prince directed Charles Strouse and Lee Adams's *It's a Bird . . . It's a Plane . . . It's Superman,* which used pop art techniques to bring the comic-book hero to campy life. The lack of dance in these works differentiated Prince from some of his famed director-choreographer contemporaries, such as Bob Fosse and Gower Champion.

Prince believed that his shows should combine serious issues with entertainment. *Cabaret* (1966), with a score by Kander and Ebb, demonstrated the effectiveness of this concept. Based on Christopher Isherwood stories, and set in prewar Berlin, the show explored the decadence surrounding the rise to power of the Nazis and confronted the problem of anti-

Semitism. Prince found the show's relevance heightened by the era's civil rights struggles. Its realistic story was highlighted by the expressionistic depiction of a metaphorically intended "Limbo" space presided over by a leering, androgynous, heavily made-up MC (Joel Gray). Dance was employed only as a natural aspect of the cabaret scenes. The fleshily vulgar chorus girls were also used as silent—implicitly commenting—observers, a technique Prince later employed with ever new permutations. In 1987, Prince directed an improved version of *Cabaret* that reinstated the homosexual theme, cut in 1966.

Because of its use of the cabaret as a mirror of society, and its deemphasis on conventional plotting, *Cabaret* is considered one of the earliest "concept musicals," a term that defines Prince's subsequent musicals in which the book was increasingly integrated into a revue-style structure that itself became the prime focus. Prince discovered the key to his method when he visited Moscow's theatricalist mecca, the Taganka Theater, which continues the traditions of Vsevolod Meyerhold, a vital influence on Prince. (Jerome Robbins and Joan Littlewood are others.) At the Taganka, Prince learned, among other things, of the effectiveness of stylized lighting devices (especially a curtain of light) as well as of the impression that could be made by combining scenic elements with a background of black velours.

Cabaret took several years to gestate, the first work on it having begun three years earlier. It underwent numerous revisions before being ready; Prince typically spends hundreds of hours deliberating with his collaborators on each major project. Although never credited as a writer, his shows could not have been produced without his authorial suggestions. A major advantage he holds over director-choreographers is his canny handling of writing problems. It is his practice to hold readings at various stages in a work's prerehearsal development. This helps him uncover undetected weaknesses.

His chief visual collaborator on this and many later shows was Boris Aronson. Like all of Prince's designers, Aronson provided excellent scale models, which allowed Prince (who cannot read plans) to make changes as the show evolved. A small number of designers, choreographers, composers, lyricists, librettists, and musical directors are closely associated with him.

Zorba (1968), adapted from a popular film and Greek novel, had a score by Kander and Ebb. The somber show's conceptual focus allowed the action to be performed by a company of bouzouki musicians who donned the appropriate costumes to become the characters, while the others observed like a Greek chorus.

Prince's first Stephen Sondheim musical, *Company* (1970), was far more revolutionary. A cool, plotless, chorusless show manifesting a sense of urban alienation, it employed projections and a brilliant set of metal and glass scaffolding (including two elevators) that represented the boxlike apartments of five New York couples, whose marital conditions were examined. It had only one dance number, choreographed by Michael Bennett.

More innovation followed with Sondheim's *Follies* (1971), a commercial failure but artistic success. Prince conceived it as a surrealistic, Proustian confrontation between aging former showgirls, now facing troubled marriages, and their own youthful selves, seen as ghostlike figures in black and white. Because movement was an invaluable aspect of the staging, Bennett codirected. Prince's filmlike approach blended scene into scene.

Inspired by Ingmar Bergman's film *Smiles of a Summer Night,* Sondheim wrote the score for *A Little Night Music* (1973). This hit romantic operetta was a bittersweet exercise about the "follies of love." Most of the music was in waltz-time, five choral characters acted as an observing frame, and the visual scheme was reminiscent of René Magritte.

Candide (Off-Broadway, 1973; Broadway, 1974) was a rewritten hit revival of a 1956 show based on Voltaire's story, its score by Leonard Bernstein. Its prankishly cartoonish, intermissionless production was given in Eugene Lee's environmentally designed space in which the acting areas were dispersed around the theater, with actors and audience forced into close proximity. Originally shown at a tiny Brooklyn space, it moved to Broadway, where a theater's interior was especially rebuilt for it. (Prince revived it for a New York City Opera proscenium staging in 1982.)

Pacific Overtures (1976), another Sondheim show, took the Japanese viewpoint to tell of the opening of Japan to the West, and of the fateful consequences of that event. Prince traveled to Japan to prime himself on *kabuki,* and borrowed many conventions, including an audience runway. He used an all-Asian, nearly all-male cast, employing female impersonation for the women's roles. For all its stylistic audacity, it proved too alien for most audiences. They thronged, however, to *On the Twentieth Century* (1978), a show whose only message was to have a good time. With words by Betty Comden and Adolph Green and music by Cy Coleman, it was an adaptation of a 1932 farce set entirely aboard a coast-

Soon-Teck Oh in Pacific Overtures. *Directed by Harold Prince. (1976)* (Photo: Martha Swope)

to-coast streamliner. The dazzling art deco train was designed in sections that enabled it to carry out Prince's wish for it to move electronically as part of the choreography. Dance figured mainly in the interpolations of the choruslike redcaps.

Evita (London, 1978; New York, 1979) marked the beginning of Prince's association with England's Andrew Lloyd Webber. Webber and Tim Rice had produced a successful rock-influenced album concerning Eva Peron, the B-actress who married Argentina's dictator Juan Péron. The bookless show, Prince's first to open in London, was a sort of documentary opera. Prince believes that a fully sung musical is less artificial and more organic than one in which speaking characters break into song. It represented a theatrical tour de force by Prince, who conceived striking dramatic contexts and conflicts for the presentation of the songs, and presented the revolutionary figure of Che Guevera as a passionately sardonic commentator on the action. Controversy was aroused as to the ambivalence of Evita's character, who many thought was romanticized. Tying the scenes together was the thematic concept—sparked by the film *Citizen Kane*—of the way in which the media creates public idols. Much of the action took place on a constructivist scaffolding, backed by black velours. Gigantic murals painted on the auditorium walls suggested Evita's people.

Sondheim's chilling *Sweeney Todd* (1979) was derived from a gruesome 19th-century revenge melodrama about a serial-killer barber whose corpses are ground into profitable meat pies. This "musical thriller" was performed in a remarkable set constructed of elements taken from an iron foundry. Prince saw this blackly humorous work as reflective of the destructive tendencies on the human spirit of the Industrial Revolution. Again, the idea of chorus as metaphoric commentator was employed. Its heavy reliance on music at the expense of dialogue moved it in the direction of opera. Prince restaged it for the New York City Opera in 1984.

Prince encountered six years of commercial failure after *Sweeney Todd*, his debacles including Sondheim's *Merrily We Roll Along* (1981), Larry Grossman and Comden and Green's *A Doll's Life* (1982), Grossman and Ellen Fitzhugh's *Diamonds* (an Off-Broadway revue, 1984), Grossman and Fitzhugh's *Grind* (1985), and Gilbert Bécaud and Julian More's *Roza* (Baltimore, 1986; New York, 1987). Prince rebounded stronger than ever with Webber's *The Phantom of the Opera* (London, 1986; New York, 1988), based on the Gaston Leroux romance about the malformed, love-obsessed composer who lurks in the bowels of the Paris Opera (which Prince visited when preparing the show). This lavish, nearly operatic musical became the biggest moneymaker in Broadway history. It recreated the mechanics of Victorian theatrics, employed notable special effects (some radio-controlled) and mysteriously shadowy lighting, and heightened audience interest through an erotic atmosphere designed to express the Phantom's psychological dilemma. Much discussed was a computer-operated chandelier above the audience that gave the impression of crashing to the stage. Prince subsequently worked on many international versions of the show.

Prince returned to straight drama with *Grandchild of Kings* (1992), his own adaptation of the first two of Sean O'Casey's six volumes of autobiography, done for Off-Broadway's Irish Repertory Theater, and intended as the first in an O'Casey-based trilogy. The large-scaled show, with 19 Irish actors playing 80 roles, and a quartet that accompanied with familiar tunes, received mixed notices, but its limited run had to be extended because of demand. Eugene Lee's environmental set—built before rehearsals started—placed the audience in the midst of Dublin pubs, theaters, shops, homes, and public conveyances. The script lacked weight, but Prince's imaginative staging was extolled.

Prince's most recent Broadway success is Kander and Ebb's *Kiss of the Spiderwoman* (book by Terrence McNally), which premiered to very sour notices in Purchase, New York (1990), but was vastly revised for Toronto and London (1992), winning the Evening Standard Award for Best Musical in the latter city. In 1993, it opened on the Great White Way, where it won the Tony for Best Musical. The show is based on Manuel Puig's novel (and the subsequent film version) about two convicts in a Latin American prison. Molina is a gay window dresser imprisoned for corrupting a minor, Valentin is serving time for political crimes. Aurora (dazzlingly played by Chita Rivera) is the film star whose role as the Spider Woman haunts Molina during the show's fantasy sequences. *TheaterWeek*'s reviewer noted, *Kiss of the Spider Woman* "not only ranks as one of the finer salvage jobs in musical theater history, but it qualifies as a complete rethinking. . . . We welcome back Harold Prince as the master director of musicals, the most daring and uncompromising of musical theater visionaries, still able to create miracles on stage." This observer pointed to the "gloriously theatrical" finale,

> from the moment the stage opens up to become a movie palace and Molina's mother, once an usherette, leads all the people in Molina's life into the rows of an upstage movie house, straight through to the end, with its vivid dance of doom and final love/death embrace.

Prince went straight from *Spider Woman* into another major effort, a revival of Jerome Kern and Oscar Hammerstein II's 1927 musical classic, *Show Boat*, premiered in late 1993 as the opening presentation of the new North York Performing Arts Center in Toronto, with New York the ultimate destination. The show was rattled by African-Canadian protests that it was racist, but most critics dismissed these complaints as revisionist nonsense, several writers observing that Prince's production had an emphatically antiracist edge and that the show was a historically valid, humanistic triumph. Prince did, however, alter the script (to some reviewers' dismay) by changing "niggers" to "colored folk," dropping the song, "In Dahomey," and making other cuts as a concession to political correctness. Among nonpolitical omissions were "At the Fair" and "Nobody Else but Me," while other material was added, such as "Till Good Luck Comes My Way." A not widely liked revision was taking the romantic duet "Why Do I Love You?" from Ravenal and Magnolia and giving it to Parthy as a lullaby to a baby granddaughter. The reviews, while less than happy with the acting, appreciated Prince's exceptionally powerful new staging from which most of the familiar saccharine had been removed. The staging, using a highly flexible design by Eugene Lee, had a lauded cinematic flow: "The entire stage becomes a levee that can accommodate everything that glides in, from the show boat's interior auditorium . . . to the Chicago Loop's Palmer House," noted the *Times*.

Most actors have found working with Prince intensely rewarding. He directs rapidly, concentrating on pictorial qualities and assuming that, if well cast, the actors can find their own way into their roles. Although big names have worked for him, he refuses to direct star vehicles and prefers, often at risk, to cast young, lesser known performers. Talented players appreciate his allowing them to provide collaborative input. With such players, Prince will simply edit, displaying an excellent sense of what works. He is result-oriented and hates to waste time; when necessary, he demonstrates or gives readings. The precision of his ideas usually allows actors to provide him with what he seeks in only a few minutes.

"Method" actors have to adjust to his external view. Still, he is devoted to honesty and believability. He does not hesitate to stop and repeat something until he gets it right. He prefers fixing on the spot to waiting until a complete scene is run and then offering notes. When an actor is having a serious problem, however, Prince is likely to take him aside for a private talk. Although he does not take the time to be polite (he yells more at tech people than at actors), his attitude is usually so boyishly enthusiastic, energetic, and positive that few take offense. Many have commented on the sense of family he creates.

Because of his strong visual orientation, Prince cannot work until he has an image of what the project will look like. This is what he calls finding the "motor." He brings to the first rehearsal costume sketches and a set model, whose workings he and the designer explain. After describing the show's look, he talks at length about its meaning and purpose.

His research is prodigious, especially as a show has usually been in the works for several years. He has a mental picture of what the staging should look like, and when he begins on the second day to block, he focuses on the images in his mind. However, he frequently makes adjustments and even gives the impression of improvising. Tabs are kept on his shows during their runs and he calls refresher rehearsals when he thinks they are slipping.

Hal Prince—winner of seven directing Tonys—sits in the pantheon of those conceptual directors responsible for the vast changes wrought in the Broadway musical since the 1960s.

Further reading:

Hirsch, Foster. *Harold Prince and the American Theatre.* Cambridge, England: Cambridge University Press, 1989.

Ilson, Carol. *Harold Prince: From "Pajama Game" to "Phantom of the Opera."* Ann Arbor: UMI Press, 1989.

Prince, Harold. *Contradictions: Notes on Twenty-Six Years in the Theatre.* New York: Dodd, Mead, 1974.

Also: Gottfried, *Broadway Musicals*; Gottfried, *More Broadway Musicals*.

JOSÉ QUINTERO (1924–   )

JOSÉ BENJAMIN QUINTERO, whose father was a successful businessman and onetime governor of Panama, was born in Panama City. He studied medicine at the University of California but transferred to Los Angeles City College, where he participated in theater, not having seen a play until he was 18. After graduating in 1945, he studied at Chicago's Goodman Theater. In 1949, he cofounded a summer theater in Woodstock, New York.

In 1950, his group—the Loft Players—produced a program of Quintero-directed one-acts Off-Broadway. That summer, he directed seven Woodstock productions.

In New York, the company turned a former Greenwich Village nightclub into a three-quarters-round theater, although Quintero had never worked in such a space. They called the 270-seat playhouse the Circle-in-the-Square (CIS). (In 1960 they moved to another Village location and in 1973 to Broadway.) The three pillars obstructing the acting space were integrated into each decor. Quintero made outstanding use of the semi-arena format, which allowed for inexpensive, imagination-stimulating settings, spectator-actor intimacy, and three-dimensionality enhanced via S-shaped movements. When he moved to proscenium stages, he frequently employed minimal furnishings and blocking (often showing actors' backs, for instance) reminiscent of his arena work.

The company opened successfully with Quintero's award-winning revival of Howard Richardson and William Berney's *Dark of the Moon* (1951). He left in 1963, after his relationship with his partner, Ted Mann, crumbled. Many feel those years—he staged all but two of the company's plays—were the CIS's finest.

His revivals included Jean Anouilh's *Antigone* (1951); Jean Giraudoux's *The Enchanted* (1951); John Steinbeck's *Burning Bright* (1951); Federico García Lorca's *Yerma* (1952), introducing Geraldine Page; Tennessee Williams's *Summer and Smoke* (1952), with Page as Alma, the role that made her a star; Truman Capote's *The Grass Harp* (1953), an improvement on the 1952 Broadway original; Arthur Schnitzler's *La Ronde* (1955); Gregorio Martinez-Sierra's *Cradle Song* (1955); a landmark revival of Eugene O'Neill's *The Iceman Cometh* (1956), with Jason Robards Jr. in the star-making role of Hickey; Edwin Justus Mayer's period comedy, *Children of Darkness* (1958), a hit revival that brought George C. Scott and Colleen Dewhurst to prominence; an acclaimed version of Thornton Wilder's *Our Town* (1959), which flourished in arena staging; Wilder's *Pullman Car Hiawatha* (1962); and— Quintero's final CIS production—a hit revival of O'Neill's *Desire Under the Elms* (1963), with Scott and Dewhurst.

Quintero became renowned for his ability to breathe new life into previously unfulfilled material. Sharing this acclaim was the intimate CIS, which demonstrated an ability to realize dramatic values lost on large proscenium stages.

The best new works staged by Quintero were Alfred Hayes's *The Girl on the Via Flaminia* (1954), which moved to Broadway, and Wilder's one-act program, collectively titled *Plays for Bleecker Street* (1962). American premieres of unconventional foreign dramas were Brendan Behan's *The Quare Fellow* (1958) and Jean Genet's ritualistic, nonlinear, sexually and politically provocative *The Balcony* (1960), a 672-performance success. Because *The Balcony* was

occupying the CIS stage, Quintero staged Williams's *Camino Real* (1960) at another venue.

Quintero—while still with the CIS—offered freelance Broadway productions of plays by Jane Bowles, William Archibald, Theodore Apstein, Eugene O'Neill, Hugh Wheeler, and Alice Cannon. Only O'Neill's *Long Day's Journey into Night* (1956)— repeated in London (1958)—succeeded.

In addition, he staged a trio of plays for a 1951 Catskill Mountain tour; was replaced on a Carson McCullers play (1957); offered Dewhurst in O'Neill's hitherto neglected *Moon for the Misbegotten* (1958) at Italy's Spoleto Festival; directed Robards in a melodramatic *Macbeth* (1959), in a Boston tent theater, with such novel features as having Macbeth bring on his wife's corpse in his arms; worked in film and TV; and mounted several operas.

The play that made Quintero and the CIS famous was *Summer and Smoke*, moderately appreciated in its 1948 Broadway bow, but revealed as a minor masterpiece by Quintero and the then unknown Page. It was a milestone in drawing increased uptown attention to Off-Broadway. The closeness and allusive power of the CIS's sparsely nonrealistically designed open space was instrumental in evoking the drama's poetic qualities. Two of the three pillars represented trees, the third the symbolic stone fountain.

In post-CIS years, Quintero staged the Broadway premieres of Williams's *The Seven Descents of Myrtle* (1968) and *Clothes for a Summer Hotel* (1980), which reunited him with Page, and a revival of *Cat on a Hot Tin Roof* (1983).

Quintero's reputation as America's foremost director of O'Neill—with whose life he feels deep affinities—commenced with the award-winning, uncut, 4 1/2-hour *The Iceman Cometh*, in which Quintero and designer David Hays (a favorite collaborator) turned the CIS into an environmental simulation of Harry Hope's squalid saloon, with the spectators like flies on the wall. Quintero—who had never read an O'Neill play before—refused to take the detailed stage directions literally, seeking the reasons behind them, not their mechanical replication. Among Quintero's accomplishments was his realization of the play's musical structure, enhanced by frequent repetitions of dialogic and thematic motifs. Musical orchestration of a text remained a Quintero preoccupation. Quintero later presented a middling revival of *Iceman* (1988) on Broadway, with Robards recreating Hickey.

Considered much better than the 1946 Broadway original, the passionate, 565-performance 1956 production reconfirmed O'Neill's reputation and so impressed his widow—who became a close friend—that she granted Quintero the rights to the American premiere (the world premiere was in Sweden) of the autobiographical *Long Day's Journey*, which O'Neill had asked not to be produced until 25 years after his death.

This lengthy tragedy, modified by Irish-American family humor that Quintero fully appreciated, starred Fredric March, Florence Eldridge, and Robards (as Tyrone Jr.); it was an American theater benchmark. Hays's set, using minimal furniture to allow for character isolation, was filled with windows that allowed the thematic substance of the title to take full effect. External sound, such as a foghorn and harbor bells, aided both mood and thematic coherence. At Mrs. O'Neill's insistence, it was uncut. The *New York Journal-American* wrote:

> *Quintero has directed . . . with great fidelity, resisting the getting of a dramatic impact at the expense of . . . total truthfulness. He begins the long day with the family normal and jovial. Indeed, one might assume that this was going to be a comedy. . . . Quintero makes no attempt to rush a grim tone into the proceedings. He allows the mutual recriminations to develop slowly and naturally. Thus, everything that ensues seems a part of life in the Tyrone summer-house rather than scenes from a play.*

Quintero experienced a year-long depression and alcoholism arising from fears of being unable to equal its success; he later underwent a cure. In 1988, Quintero revived *Long Day's Journey* at Yale and on Broadway—in repertory with Arvin Brown's version of *Ah! Wilderness*—with Robards (as Tyrone Sr.) and Dewhurst.

His other Broadway O'Neills include *Strange Interlude* (1963), for the Actors Studio, starring Page, with the asides done unobtrusively as the still speaker faced front and the others moved naturally but minimally; the American premiere of *Hughie* (1964), with Robards, also staged elsewhere; a colorful staging of *Marco Millions* (1964) for the new Lincoln Center troupe in their temporary downtown theater; the posthumous world premiere of *More Stately Mansions* (1967), starring Page and Ingrid Bergman; a Chicago-originated, Tony-winning revival of *A Moon for the Misbegotten* (1973), with Robards and Dewhurst (she had already done it for him in Buffalo in 1968); an unsuccessful *Anna Christie* (1977), starring Liv Ullmann, whom he had just directed in *A Moon for the Misbegotten* (1976) in Norway; and an appreciated *A Touch of the Poet* (1977), with Ro-

bards. At Columbia University he staged a professionally acted *Welded* (1981).

Apart from the O'Neill productions, Quintero's post-CIS career has been undistinguished. In addition to works already mentioned, his later Broadway stagings included flops by Jerome Lawrence and Robert E. Lee, Duke Ellington (a musical), Gurney Campbell, Thornton Wilder, Jules Feiffer, and Brian Friel. Off-Broadway losers included works by Herbert Lieberman and Kurt Weill. Elsewhere, his offerings included material by Mart Crowley (Los Angeles), a musical of his own composition (Washington, D.C.), and Per Olovquist (New Haven). A throat-cancer operation in the mid-1980s saw him fitted with a voice box. Much of his time recently has been spent in university work, although he did return to directing with *Our Town* at Houston's Alley Theater in 1993.

Quintero, proud never to have taken a lesson in directing, prepares by frequent rereadings, examination of historical and pictorial sources, and conferences with his designers (who receive considerable leeway). Rehearsals are usually in five-hour segments (he believes actors cannot concentrate for much longer). His skill at eliciting rich performances is related to his preference for working privately with actors apart from the rest of the company. Although many love him for his kindness, his vulnerability (he often cries at rehearsal), and the trust he fosters, he has been known to scream when frustrated.

Quintero increasingly employed a noncollaborative, result-oriented approach that some thought stifling, but he is best known for the days when he allowed actors to do most of the exploring themselves. When confident that they were demonstrating creative security, Quintero would provide feedback, develop discoveries, ask probing questions, and suggest ideas of his own, often couched in stimulating metaphors.

He prefers to avoid lengthy analyses and to work moment by moment on peeling away a text's layers; everything must be concretely motivated. Actors are encouraged to avoid "acting," even in period plays demanding formal behavior. He communicates by verbal shorthand with those on his wavelength; observers are often baffled by their interchanges.

Quintero commences by seating the actors in a circle—which he believes fosters trust—for readthroughs, during which he will interpolate commentary on the characters and—assisted by a model—describe his concept. He is gifted at expressing character traits, psychological complexities, and relationships, a knack fostered by his experience in the close confines of the old CIS, which required attention to truth, nuance, and atmosphere. His employment of pregnant silences, the commingling—where appropriate—of poetic fantasy with external reality, and the use of dancelike gestures and movement to express profound feelings are components of a style that seeks to represent an idealized realism.

Many of his successes have been with plays in which character dominates plot. A key factor in uncovering subtextual levels is his fondness for narrating analogous situations in his own life, even when they require personal or painful revelations. These are conveyed in character, as if Quintero were himself a person in the play. At times he will sidecoach, roaming from actor to actor and whispering motivations or asking questions before they speak or move; sometimes, this is done as the actors mix dialogue with improvisational paraphrasing. Partly rehearsed sections from later in the play may be improvisationally introduced to underscore earlier character-related problems. He prowls the auditorium, observing from different vantage points and, when necessary, jumps onto the stage to broadly demonstrate something. Most agree that he does not expect a direct imitation, but there are those who find he demonstrates too much. Many consider his communication of love for a play and its characters inspirational.

Quintero's intuitive process is related to his neglect of preplanned blocking; his working scripts have no marginal notations. He may come to blocking rehearsals early to walk through the scenes himself and imagine the potential movements, but the actors are usually permitted to work out their own staging, with Quintero refining and developing their discoveries, but not setting anything until shortly before the opening.

Intuition has played a large part in Quintero's casting; for years, his method was personal interviews, with readings given only when he was unfamiliar with an actor's work or when requested. Later, he made extensive use of readings, with Quintero reading opposite the actor and offering advice.

Many Quintero scripts, especially O'Neill's, were very long and required extensive—and controversial—cutting. The degree of his preediting varied, but he often began with an uncut script and even allowed actors to suggest omissions.

José Quintero's contributions to the development of Off-Broadway were of historical importance. He demonstrated the viability of arena staging in New York; was instrumental in the establishment of the acting careers of Page, Robards, Scott, and Dewhurst; and restored O'Neill to deserved respect.

Further reading:

Barry, Jackson G. "José Quintero: The Director as Image Maker." *Educational Theatre Journal* 14 (March 1962).

Little, Stuart. *Off-Broadway: The Prophetic Theatre*. New York: Dell, 1972.

McDonough, Edwin J. *Quintero Directs O'Neill*. San Francisco: a cappela press, 1991.

Paller, Michael. "Finding the Quintessential O'Neill: Jose Quintero." *TheaterWeek*, June 27–July 3, 1988.

Quintero, José. *If You Don't Dance They Beat You*. Boston: Little, Brown, 1974.

MAX REINHARDT (1873–1943)

MAX REINHARDT (*né* Goldmann), was born in Baden, Austria, to an affluent merchant family. He began to act professionally in 1892. By 1894, he had joined Otto Brahm's Deutsches Theater in Berlin, and in 1900, he made his formal directorial bow at the Deutsches with Henrik Ibsen's *Love's Comedy*. His multifarious interests blossomed in 1901 when he directed sketches at a Berlin cabaret, Die Brille. This was reorganized on a weekly basis at a midnight cabaret, Schall and Rauch. Success allowed him to establish the intimate Kleines Theater with a policy of challenging straight plays, including works by August Strindberg, Oscar Wilde, Frank Wedekind, and Maxim Gorky.

He obtained the larger Neues Theater in 1903 so that he could have two theaters of differing sizes to meet his repertory's disparate demands. Among his early productions was Hugo von Hoffmansthal's *Elektra*. Reinhardt demonstrated his eclectic ability to bring a different approach to each play, depending on its needs, without adhering to any particular theory.

At the Neues, Reinhardt did the first of many stagings of *A Midsummer Night's Dream* (1905); in each mounting he took a new approach. This illusionistic production, for which a three-dimensional forest (replete with tiny lake) was constructed, typified his expansive use of the theater's resources with its sumptuous employment of scenic contrivances, especially the revolving stage. The revolve became a favorite device—especially when Ernst Stern was the designer—because of its scene-shifting speed. Reinhardt eventually staged 22 Shakespeare plays.

Some of his influential stagings were faithfully Elizabethan and others realistic. In several cases he used natural settings, such as parks and gardens, or even a Venetian canal. The texts were cut minimally and the action moved swiftly.

The Deutsches replaced the Neues in 1906, and became Reinhardt's chief venue for a quarter of a century. He established an acting school with an advanced curriculum and developed a no-star ensemble in which famous actors often played tiny roles. Meanwhile, the Kleines was replaced by the 292-seat Kammerspiele, next door to the Deutsches, which opened with Henrik Ibsen's *Ghosts* (1906) in a striking production designed by modernist painter Edvard Munch. Plays requiring spectacular resources were done at the Deutsches, and intimate, conversational pieces were staged at the Kammerspiele. A controversial piece at the latter was Wedekind's previously banned *Spring's Awakening* (1906).

Reinhardt's theaters provided up to 10 plays a week, ranging from the classics to the avant-garde. One of his most important classics was Johann Wolfgang von Goethe's *Faust I* (1908), thought unproducible, and staged on several later occasions. (He eventually did *Faust II* in 1911 as well as the *Urfaust* in 1920.)

In 1909, Reinhardt turned international, touring abroad with his best works. He later worked independently in foreign theaters while maintaining his home bases. He also served briefly in other German cities. London and New York saw his work several times.

In 1912, he began his connection with Berlin's large Volksbühne and in 1918 added the intimate Kleines Schauspielhaus. More momentous was the 3,300-seat Grosses Schauspielhaus, obtained in 1919, where, until it failed in 1922, he experimented with grandiose classical productions (he opened with Euripides' *The Oresteia*) and modern plays according to his mass-theater idea, the Theater of the 5,000. The cavernous playhouse mixed a wide, curtainless proscenium stage with a revolve and a grand U-shaped thrust surrounded by spectators on three sides. Advanced technical equipment could create difficult effects, including projections of moving clouds on the plaster cyclorama. Reinhardt tried to create a hypnotic environment in which the audience would be enmeshed in a play's world. Actors, as in the courtroom scene in *Danton* (1920), sometimes mingled with audience members to tie the realms together; hundreds of extras furthered the connection.

Reinhardt ran Berlin's Komödie Theater from 1924. By 1932, the Jewish director was forced by the Nazis to relinquish his German theaters, and he thereafter worked elsewhere in Europe, especially Salzburg and Vienna, before emigrating to America in 1937. From 1920 on he staged, on the steps of the Salzburg Cathedral, annual outdoor productions of Hofmannsthal's version of the medieval morality, *Everyman* (still being shown), as well as other works in unusual locales, including the city's equestrian Riding Schools. In 1922, he converted a Viennese baroque court ballroom into the exquisite Theater in der Redoutensaal, retaining the original court decor and architectural features as part of each play's environment and using a proscenium-less stage set up at one end for nonillusionistic productions (even the house lights were kept on). He shifted in 1924 to the same city's elegant Theater in der Josefstadt (built in 1822).

It was his firm belief that each play required an architectural environment best suited to its needs. Therefore, he constantly acquired new playhouses, each designed to serve a particular range of drama. Circus arenas, ballrooms, church plazas, conventional proscenium houses, and forest parks were appropriate performance spaces in Reinhardt's hands.

In America he freelanced in proscenium theaters. Because of the different conditions, he failed to maintain a high level of achievement. Broadway saw his productions of Franz Werfel's biblical *The Eternal Road* (1937), a stunningly spectacular staging but a commercial flop, and Thornton Wilder's *The Merchant of Yonkers* (1938), the unsuccessful early version of *The Matchmaker*.

Certain plays became associated with him and continued to be revived, usually in new conceptions. Among those which reappeared most often were Shakespeare's *A Midsummer Night's Dream, Hamlet, The Winter's Tale, Twelfth Night, King Lear, Othello, The Merchant of Venice, Romeo and Juliet*, and *Much Ado About Nothing*; Sophocles' *Oedipus Rex*, Karl Vollmoeller's *The Miracle*, Gotthold Lessing's *Minna von Barnhelm, Everyman*, Friedrich Hebbel's *Judith*,

Werfel's The Eternal Road. *Directed by Max Reinhardt. (1937)*   (Photo: Theater Collection, Museum of the City of New York)

Spring's Awakening, Goethe's *Clavigo,* Friedrich Schiller's *Love and Intrigue,* and Molière's *The Imaginary Invalid.*

One of the many brilliant productions indelibly linked to Reinhardt was Vollmoeller's fantastical musical pantomime, *Sumurun* (1910), an international success based on *The Tales of the Arabian Nights.* Movement, music, lighting, and beautifully simplified scenery and costumes were exquisitely blended in a presentation that wove a hypnotic web convincing the audience of the reality of this fairytale romance. A runway through the audience, borrowed from *kabuki,* was used to memorable effect.

Another Reinhardt highlight was his first *Oedipus Rex* (1910), a production that furthered the régisseur's developing wish to increase the intimacy of contact between stage and auditorium. The Munich premiere was followed by presentations in circus arenas in other cities. In his passionately emotional presentation, he used vast, carefully choreographed crowd scenes (with hundreds of extras), a chorus of 20, statuesque acting, and a formidable palace set, with the audience on three sides.

In 1911 came the first of many stagings (through 1932) of Vollmoeller's spectacular pantomime, *The Miracle,* with music by Engelbert Humperdinck. Premiered at London's large Olympia Hall, and playing to audiences of up to 30,000 seated on three sides of a space that designer Stern had virtually transformed into the interior of a Gothic cathedral, it deployed 1,800 performers to enact the miraculous experiences encountered by a medieval nun. The remarkable production, staged even more impressively at New York's Century Theater in 1924 with designs by Norman Bel Geddes, combined ritualistic staging, choral singing, moving organ music, unforgettable lighting, stirring choreographic arrangements of immense crowds, exquisite costumes, and silent, formalized acting to convey a spiritually and artistically overwhelming experience.

Although a master director, Reinhardt preferred to be thought of as a collaborator who blended the best contributions of a team into a finished work of art. He considered the actor the theater's primary artist. Many of his visual conceptions combined an impressionistic disposition of form with light, mood, and color as well as with highly selective compositions devoid of unnecessary detail. A bush suggested a garden, two columns a church. Most contemporary "isms" were reflected in his work.

While remaining faithful to the text, he sought the total work of theater art—Richard Wagner's *gesamtkunstwerk*—in which each element contributed to the brilliance of the whole. Conventions from East and West were exploited to fulfill his needs. Reinhardt was a visionary who broke away from standard realism. Manner came before matter in turning the theater into a temple of beauty, one in which the audience would be absorbed into the illusionary world of the play.

One feature that aided in the illusionary feeling was Reinhardt's brilliant crowd scenes, in which hundreds might be marshalled to create truthful mob activity to which the audience would feel drawn. Each extra was drilled and given specific behavior to make him seem lifelike and individual. Nothing was left to improvisation, including sounds, byplay, and spoken comments, and all was timed for rhythmic effects.

Music (Einar Nilson and Humperdinck were his favorite collaborators) and sound were vital features of Reinhardt's productions, which were built on strong rhythmical foundations, suggested by movements even when no audible music was heard.

Reinhardt was among the most thoroughly prepared directors; his massive promptbooks *(regiebuch)* are famous for their meticulous detail. He anticipated each move, gesture, vocal tone, characterization, emotional transition, costume, makeup, scenic device, and musical, sound, and lighting effect. Numerous sketches and diagrams accompanied the notes. An elaborate production might require a year to have its promptbook completed. Still, he revised when something better was presented, and his promptbooks underwent considerable revision during rehearsals.

In working with his designers, he could be quite liberal, discussing his ideas and then allowing the designer to work independently before showing him sketches and models. The more he trusted the designer, the less he interfered. But with some designers, he provided detailed sketches, down to the furniture itself. Normally, to guarantee visual unity, the same designer did the sets, lights, and costumes.

Reinhardt opposed typecasting. His actors were cast according to the appropriateness of their personalities, rather than their physical qualities. His choices were often surprising. He also liked to give promising young actors important roles as a method of teaching them to run before they could walk.

Versatility was important and he tried to get his actors to play all kinds of roles, regardless of their physical type.

Despite the detail of Reinhardt's promptbooks, actors enjoyed working with him because of his ability to mold companies into familial ensembles. He was uncommonly mild and patient; eruptions were rare. He preferred to draw actors aside and whisper to them privately, saying just the right few words or offering the precise gesture to inspire their imaginations. Demonstrations ranked higher than verbal explanation and were couched in terms of the actor's own mannerisms and personality.

If an actor had a suggestion, Reinhardt listened with deep attentiveness. His attitude was fair and sensitive. He could be autocratic, but usually with lesser actors and not with true talents. His most dictatorial rehearsals were the early ones, in which his notes played a vital role. As the actors became accustomed to their roles, he allowed them greater freedom.

Reinhardt worked with a team of assistants without whom he could never have been as active. Often they shared his duties, directing the crowds or minor characters according to his demands, and drilling the company in his absence. When a production was being revived, a trusted assistant could stage it from Reinhardt's notes. He frequently turned the morning rehearsals over to an aide and appeared only in the afternoon.

Max Reinhardt—the quintessential eclectic—epitomizes the European régisseur of the first half of this century. He was an extraordinarily prolific artist whose works were more often seen because of his staging than the material being played.

Further reading:

Carter, Huntley. *The Theatre of Max Reinhardt.* New York: Benjamin Blom, 1964.

Reinhardt, Gottfried. *The Genius: A Memoir of Max Reinhardt by His Son.* New York: Alfred A. Knopf, 1979.

Sayler, Oliver M., ed. *Max Reinhardt and His Theatre.* New York and London: Benjamin Blom, 1968.

Styan, J. L. *Max Reinhardt.* Cambridge, England: Cambridge University Press, 1982.

Wellwarth, George E., and Alfred G. Brooks, eds. *Max Reinhardt 1873–1973: A Centennial Festschrift.* Binghamton, N.Y.: Max Reinhardt Archives, 1973.

Also: Johnson, *Directing Methods*; Leiter, *From Stanislavsky to Barrault*; Marshall, *The Producer and the Play.*

LLOYD RICHARDS (1923–   )

LLOYD GEORGE RICHARDS was born in Toronto, Ontario, where his father was a master carpenter, but he grew up in Detroit, Michigan. He entered Wayne University for prelaw but—after leaving to become one of the air force's first black fliers—returned to study in Wayne's theater program and to work as a disk jockey. Richards became a New York actor, taught at Paul Mann's studio, and was a founding member of acting companies in Detroit and Greenwich Village.

When he made his breakthrough by directing the Broadway premiere of Lorraine Hansberry's *A Raisin in the Sun* (1959), Richards was waiting on tables at Paramount Pictures' executive dining room

Lloyd Richards directing Wilson's Joe Turner's Come and Gone. *(1985)*   (Photo: Yale Repertory Theater/Paul J. Penders)

in Manhattan. This memorable, 530-performance, award-winning domestic drama—about a Chicago black family seeking to purchase a home in a white community—was a pathbreaker, being the first Broadway play directed by a black person and written by a black woman. It starred Sidney Poitier, Diana Sands, and Claudia McNeill, and established Richards as a leading figure in the emerging African-American theater. The work was in development for a year and underwent major revisions. Richards was praised for his excellent ensemble and his directorial sensitivity.

Richards abandoned acting in favor of directing. His next three productions, though, were Broadway flops. Ketti Frings's adaptation of Richard Wright's novel, *The Long Dream* (1960), was about a black undertaker who becomes enmeshed in corruption through his association with a crooked, white police chief. Seyril Schochen's *The Moon Besieged* (1962), was a biodrama-with-music about abolitionist John Brown. Richards's first actual musical was *I Had a Ball* (1964), by Jerome Chodorov, Jack Lawrence, and Stan Freeman. It was also the director's first non-race-related mounting. Buddy Hackett, Karen Morrow, and Richard Kiley starred. It was Hackett's largely improvised performance as a would-be Coney Island clairvoyant that drew audiences. Despite receiving credit, Richards left the show because of difficulties with the producers and several actors.

Following James Baldwin's *The Amen Corner* (1965), staged for a European tour, Richards turned to *The Yearling* (1965), a flop musical version by Herbert Martin, Lore Noto, and Michael Leonard of Marjorie Rawlings's backwoods story of a boy and a fawn. Again, production problems forced Richards to leave before the opening.

Richards spent the next decade Off-Broadway; his direction was superior to his scripts. Ron Milner's *Who's Got His Own* (1966) told of a black family's memories of their just departed father. *The Ox Cart* (1966) was Rene Margues's domestic drama about a Puerto Rican family's migration to the Bronx. Philip Hayes Dean's *Freeman* (1973) was about the way in which two young black men in a small Michigan town deal with their lives. A Brooklyn theater was the venue for Richard Wesley's one-acts, *The Past Is the Past* and *Goin' Thru Changes* (1974), domestic pieces focusing on the problems of young black men.

Richards returned to Broadway with Dean's one-actor, one-pianist biodrama *Paul Robeson* (1978), starring James Earl Jones as the African-American actor-lawyer-athlete-singer-activist. Some blacks thought its treatment of Robeson inaccurate and oversentimental.

In the 1950s, Richards held leadership posts at the Great Lakes Festival (1954) and the Northland Playhouse (1955–1957). He guest-directed at a number of professional theaters and frequently staged university productions. His active career encompassed such important positions as head of the acting program at New York University from 1966 to 1972, a professorship at Hunter College, the presidency of Theater Communications Group, and selection (by President Reagan) as the first regional theater artist appointed to the National Council for the Arts.

Throughout his career Richards has demonstrated profound interest in the promotion of new American plays. His most notable contribution came through his position (from 1969 to the present) as artistic director of the National Playwrights Conference at the Eugene O'Neill Theater Center in Waterford, Connecticut, an important nonprofit institution devoted to developing plays and playwrights through annual summer seasons at which readings and workshop productions are given. Many of the most significant actors and directors work here under Richards and numerous new and established playwrights are assisted.

His O'Neill activity was partly responsible for Richards being chosen in 1979 to succeed Robert Brustein as dean of the Yale Drama School and artistic director of the Yale Repertory Theater, one of America's premier regional companies. His academic administration was criticized because of frequent absences stemming from a perceived preoccupation with the theater at the school's expense; still, his efforts were responsible for furthering Yale's reputation as America's foremost training program. He shifted the Rep's focus from director-oriented stagings to an emphasis on socially committed new plays (American and otherwise, particularly the works of South Africa's Athol Fugard). A firm believer in nontraditional casting, he advocated using actors of color in roles normally given to whites. Because many works moved to Broadway, Richards came under fire by Brustein for using Yale as a "launching pad" for commercial success. He defended his activities as necessary for the American theater's evolution.

At Yale, Richards tackled such classics as Shakespeare's *Timon of Athens* (1980) with James Earl Jones; Henrik Ibsen's *Hedda Gabler* (1981) with Jones and Dianne Wiest, and *A Doll House*, with Wiest and Earle Hyman; Anton Chekhov's *Uncle Vanya* (1981) with Glenn Close; George Bernard Shaw's *Major Barbara* (1983); and Eugene O'Neill's *A Touch of the Poet* (1983) with George Grizzard.

His directorial involvement in new plays at Yale began in 1982, when Richards commenced an association with playwright August Wilson that he would call the "culmination" of his career. The first Wilson script he discovered was *Ma Rainey's Black Bottom* (1984), dealing with a famous black jazz singer at a 1927 recording session. It was the opening gambit in a major cycle of Richards-directed, Wilson-written realistic plays about post-Civil War black America. As with each of the subsequent Wilson dramas, it was first done at Yale and then moved to Broadway, where it had a healthy run and established Wilson as the most respected black dramatist of the day.

All of Wilson's plays were given preliminary hearings at the O'Neill; after their Yale showings, they were seen—and further polished—at other regionals before arriving in New York. The director desired to enhance the possibility of a national theater composed of regional companies that are not completely "bound" to their local constituencies. In this process, which may last four years, plays undergo continual rewriting and revision before being considered finished. The Wilson-Richards collaboration is one of American theater's greatest author-director partnerships.

Wilson fit the description of what Richards, in 1981, told Eric Pace he sought in a new dramatist: "I am looking for someone who sees an event in a particularly original way, has something that is important and distinctive to say about that event, and can evolve that into a dramatic form." When Wilson, a poet without a strong drama background, displayed problems in developing his works, Richards—not wishing to hinder the author's emotional fullness—declined to teach him the craft and persuaded him to learn it by experience. Thus Wilson's plays are often criticized for structural flaws, static moments, or verbosity, while also lauded for their theatrical power.

Other Wilson-Richards works (Broadway dates are given) include the Pulitzer- and Tony-winning (for direction as well as writing) *Fences* (1987), a powerful domestic drama set in the late fifties and starring Jones as a one-time Negro League baseball player bitter about never having been allowed to play in the majors; *Joe Turner's Come and Gone* (1988), set in 1911 Pittsburgh and concerned with following up the lives of those freed from slavery and their search for those who were separated from them; *The Piano Lesson* (1989), about a Pittsburgh family's conflict over the sale of an heirloom piano whose intricate carvings of the family history were done by a slave ancestor; and *Two Trains Running* (1992), set in a 1968 Pittsburgh luncheonette, near the locale of *The Piano Lesson,* and across the street from a funeral parlor where thousands of people seeking good fortune have come to rub the head of the deceased Prophet Samuel.

The only other plays directed by Richards during this period were an Atlanta staging of Lee Blessing's *Cobb* (1989), about baseball great Ty Cobb, and a Yale revival of O'Neill's *A Moon for the Misbegotten* (1991). In 1991, after a 12-year tenure, he was forced by school policy to retire from Yale.

Richards told Renfreu Neff that he is committed to "Plays that make audiences think, a work with some meat on its bones—that's the only thing worth your life, because you bet your life with every one of them." He wants dramas that relate to people's lives and are involving to a diverse audience. According to Lee Alan Morrow and Frank Pike, he asks himself:

> *Am I engaged by the play? Do I care about the play? Do I care about what the playwright cares about? Is his way of revealing what we both care about unique? Is his voice a valid one? Is the structure . . . essentially dramatic? . . . Is the playwright someone I want to work with? Can we emerge with something better than either of us can articulate alone?*

Richards collaborates by sensing in the dramatist materials that still need to be expressed and provoking him to put as much of them as possible in the play. He will incessantly study a piece he is going to stage, seeking to comprehend everything about it, including its characters' offstage lives. At his first rehearsal for *A Raisin in the Sun,* he followed the cast's reading by providing a complete history of every character in the play. Hansberry was so impressed, she said, "I hadn't thought of it that way, but it's true." The point was not how different the conceptions of director and author were, but that the director's comments were helpful to the actors. As a director, he puts the author's needs before his own; his work at the O'Neill makes a fetish of this respect for the writer, both famous and unknown. Playwrights are surprised by his ability to get to the heart of their work and by his complete accessibility.

Richards will not begin rehearsals until he is certain of a work's central theme or "spine" (a term he borrows from Harold Clurman, one of his great influences). He will reread it if he is unsure, because to begin rehearsals unprepared is too costly a proposition. "Rehearsals are like a toboggan slide," he advised Morrow and Pike. "You pass a certain point and you are going all the way; there's no getting off."

He seeks to stimulate his company to realize his view of the characters, but in a way that allows the players to feel that they themselves are the creative force. Line readings are distasteful because he believes they impede discovery. He prefers to suggest possibilities for exploration. "You can call it subtle imposition," he informed Irene Backalenick. Not given to effusive talk, he has a way of saying in a few words things that help actors open up. "What he does is offer these little gems, these *bonbons* of intuition," actress Frances McDormand informed Patti Hartigan. He welcomes actors who extend his vision because of his delight in having them surprise him with their findings.

Actors are asked to provide their ideas and opinions, instead of being required to follow his. His advice is offered within a conception of the total work, its meaning, look, and sound. He must understand not only the play's ideas, but whatever it was that inspired its writing. His conception extends to the metaphorical significance of the setting. Richards viewed the outside porch area in *Fences* as an extension of the classical Greek theater because, he told Arthur Bartow, "the nature of the play is classical and we had to connect with the totality of theater history as well as the history of the people involved." *Joe Turner*'s interior was conceived as a "way station," "the inn where Christ was born, the inn that exists historically in so many cultures and places that dealt with 'wanderers.' . . . "

Richards prefers that, at the point where the actors are uncertain about their lines and business, the writer not be present so as to avoid communicating his nervousness about their problems. The playwright's presence can also impede the director's necessary growth from a position of subjectivity to one of objectivity in judging the work. When the playwright returns, he too will be better able to view the piece objectively. The director must regulate the degree to which the author can address the actors, because, he informed Morrow and Pike, he is more valuable used "as a resource and not as a codirector."

Richards, a stocky, bearded man with glasses, is soft-spoken and fatherly. He is known for his self-effacing, serene but firm personality, and integrity. Playwright Wendy Wasserstein once called him "the black Santa Claus." This educator, administrator, and director is widely acknowledged to be one of the most influential forces of modern American theater.

Further reading:

Backalenick, Irene. "A Lesson from Lloyd Richards: Subtle Imposition Over Auteurist Vision." *TheaterWeek*, April 16–22, 1990.

De Vries, Hilary. "Theater's Godfather Reaches Entr'acte." *New York Times*, June 30, 1991.

Hartigan, Patti. "The Richards Mystique." *American Theatre* 8 (July–August 1991).

Neff, Renfreu. "A Talk with Lloyd Richards." *TheaterWeek*, April 18–25, 1988.

Pace, Eric. "Lloyd Richards Is Launching New Playwrights with a Winterfest at Yale." *New York Times*, January 11, 1981.

Also: Bartow, *Director's Voice*; Brustein, *Reimagining American Theatre*; Morrow and Pike, *Creating Theater*.

JEROME ROBBINS (1918–   )

JEROME ROBBINS (*né* Rabinowitz) was born in New York City but raised in Weehawken, New Jersey, where his parents shifted from the delicatessen to the corset business. Robbins dropped out of New York University because of money difficulties. At 18, he took up dance, studying with many masters while dancing on Broadway and in ballet. *Fancy Free* (1944), a ballet he conceived and choreographed with music by Leonard Bernstein, became the inspiration for *On the Town* (1945), a dance-oriented, George Abbott-directed show he choreographed to Bernstein's music.

Robbins's ascent in ballet was mirrored by his remarkable Broadway accomplishments. He made memorable choreographic contributions to a string of hit shows and began his uncredited practice of "show doctoring," bringing ailing shows to robust life.

Meanwhile, he codirected (with George Abbott) Hugh Martin's *Look Ma, I'm Dancin'* (1948). He was also the conceiver, colibrettist, and choreographer. Although there had been several earlier director-choreographers, none were more responsible than Robbins for demonstrating the value of combining these functions in one individual. *Look Ma,* a spoof on ballet with an arrogant Robbins-like choreographer hero, gave Robbins room to display his comic genius, especially in "The Pajama Dance," about insomniacs pretending to sleepwalk in a Pullman car aisle.

Robbins and Abbott codirected Richard Adler and Jerry Ross's *The Pajama Game* (1954); novice Bob Fosse choreographed. His first solo director-choreographer credit was for the musical adaptation of James M. Barrie's *Peter Pan* (1954), starring Mary Martin. Robbins's dances took place on the ground and in the air.

Robbins directed and, with Fosse, cochoreographed Jule Styne, Betty Comden, and Adolph Green's *Bells Are Ringing* (1956), a 924-performance hit starring Judy Holliday as an answering-service operator who falls in love with a client. Robbins built the show around her unique comic talents. The widely varied dances ranged from waltz parodies to Latin numbers.

Completely unconventional was *West Side Story* (1957), score by Bernstein and Stephen Sondheim; conception, direction, and choreography (with Peter Gennaro) by Robbins. The pathbreaking show, employing lyrically heightened realism, told a *Romeo and Juliet* story in terms of a New York slum rivalry between Puerto Rican and American street gangs: the Sharks and the Jets. It was surprising in its use of mostly unknown faces, which strengthened the ensemble feeling; its sharply individualized chorus; its focus on sordid actions and characters; and its tragic outcome. Nothing was as unusual as the way in which Robbins welded all the ingredients together into an entity depending more for storytelling power

Jerome Robbins directing Jerome Robbins' Broadway. *(1989)*   (Photo: Martha Swope)

on dance and movement—each character being sharply delineated—than on dialogue.

"The ingredients are all of a piece," wrote *Theatre Arts*. "Nearly everything is economical, streamlined and vital. And this not only results in a sense of immediacy but actually pushes the American musical theater several steps closer to that ultimate goal of integration of component parts. . . . "

The opening—originally conceived for singing—was novel. "For about five galvanic minutes all we see are male dancers leaping about in various menacing formations; and in that sequence . . . Robbins . . . has not only set the mood of the piece but foreshadowed much of the action," noted *Theatre Arts*. Robbins's dances ranged from the opening's threatening rumble to the pyrotechnics of "The Dance at the Gym" to the struggle for self-control of "Cool" to the lyricism of the "Somewhere" dream ballet to the humor of "America" and the comical masterpiece, "Gee, Officer Krupke!" in which the juvenile delinquents mocked society's efforts to control them. In the ballet's calm-before-the-storm romanticism, the surrounding tenement houses receded to reveal a cloud bank of fire escapes; then reality intervened and the prisonlike neighborhood returned. Every dance progressed the plot or explained the characters. "The finger-snapping, crouching, lurching, and leaping . . . movements not only epitomized perfectly the tensions, the brutality, bravado, and venomous hatred of the gang warriors but also had sufficient variety in themselves to hold audiences spellbound," wrote Abe Laufe.

The 720-performance *Gypsy* (1959), score by Jule Styne and Sondheim, was about the tribulations of the young Gypsy Rose Lee and her sister June as commandeered by their larger-than-life stage mother, Rose. Robbins wanted to do it in a dance-oriented framework redolent of vaudeville and burlesque, but his collaborators restrained him because the show had a powerful Arthur Laurents book and a star, Ethel Merman, whose main talent was singing, not dancing. Dance became subordinate to dialogue and songs.

Robbins—who originally wanted the number done as a ballet—displayed Merman's renowned talents to the full in her emotional roller coaster climax, "Rose's Turn," in which, playing to a presumably empty house, she demonstrated not only her singing strength but her command of her daughter's routines, including bumps and grinds. Despite its success, Robbins felt that *Gypsy* did not truly represent his type of staging.

Robbins directed two straight plays, beginning with Arthur Kopit's Off-Broadway absurdist farce, *Oh, Dad, Poor Dad, Mama's Hung You in the Closet and I'm Feeling So Sad* (1962). The piece was a comic hit, but when, after a successful national tour, it came to Broadway in 1963 with a partially changed cast and with Robbins broadening its humor, it faltered. The *New York Post* declared that the best scene:

> was the one in which the girl's plans to seduce the artless youth kept being interrupted because dad's embalmed body would tumble out of the closet and down on top of her. Now the body has been given a few pieces of stage business, and the effect is much less comic.

Robbins directed the New York premiere of Bertolt Brecht's epic drama with songs, *Mother Courage* (1963), starring a miscast Anne Bancroft, who, among other things, was far too young for the title role. The *Times*'s positive commentary noted, "Mr. Robbins has staged each scene incisively, and they build powerfully. He knows how to merge song into spoken dialogue and how to return to speech without fussy self-consciousness." It left a "bad taste" in John Simon's mouth, though, and was widely rejected. Despite having studied Brecht's own version, Robbins's produced a Broadwayized compromise. It had a non-Brechtian aesthetic that hid the light and sound sources, cut out several songs (possibly to prevent its being classed as a musical), intrusively editorialized via slides of warfare, had no revolve, and allowed actors to speak what Brecht projected on a screen.

Robbins's last original musical (it brought him two Tonys) was Joseph Stein, Sheldon Harnick, and Jerry Bock's *Fiddler on the Roof* (1964), starring Zero Mostel and based on Sholem Aleichem's stories about Jewish life in a turn-of-the-century Eastern European *shtetl*. Robbins used a metaphor suggesting the end of a way of life, symbolized by the Jews being forced from their village. He captured this in the rousing opening, "Tradition," which evolved out of the image of a fiddler seated on the roof of Tevye's home. Tevye entered, began to dance and chant ritualistically, and soon the stage was filled with the entire community—each person clearly identified—dancing and singing. Robbins wanted the metaphor present everywhere. According to Harnick (quoted by Richard Altman and Mervyn Kaufman), he would say,

> Well, if that's what the show is about, why isn't it in this scene? Why isn't it in that scene? Why don't we

The Fiddler on the Roof *sequence from* Jerome Robbins' Broadway. *Directed by Jerome Robbins. (1989) Jason Alexander is 2d from l.*   (Photo: Martha Swope)

see it in this character or that character? . . . He drove everybody crazy because he had a vision that extended down to the littlest brushstroke in the scenery and the triangle part in the orchestra.

Movement, musical values, and dramatic action were interwoven throughout, and one number blended into the next. An extended, 20-minute sequence tied three scenes together to present Tzeitel's wedding. For the heart-rending conclusion, Tevye and his family moved in one direction as the revolve moved in the other. According to Ken Mandelbaum:

Their house disappears, and other villagers appear, all walking against the direction of the . . . platform. The turntable halts, the villagers bow to each other and disappear, and only Tevye and his family remain. The fiddler emerges . . . and fiddles as they move away. Tevye stops, motions for the fiddler to join them, and

the curtain falls on the family beginning to walk off, the fiddler behind.

Martin Gottfried's review was typical:

What . . . Robbins has done is to create a time, a feeling, a warmth, and an enormous excitement. . . . He has done it with time, with swirling color, with rhythm, with rushing sweeps of changing moods. He has done it with movement that for sheer beauty and relevance is paralleled only by his own West Side Story.

Fiddler ran a record-breaking 3,242 performances.

Robbins, unhappy with Broadway's compromises and with the dearth of material, devoted his post-*Fiddler* career to the ballet. He returned to restage *West Side Story* in 1980, followed by a revival of *Fiddler* (1981). Nearly a decade later, he won a Tony for his direction of *Jerome Robbins' Broadway* (1989), an anthology of 15 of his greatest dance numbers

The King and I *("Uncle Tom's Cabin") sequence from* Jerome Robbins' Broadway. *Directed by Jerome Robbins.
(1989)*   (Photo: Martha Swope)

from 11 of his shows (1944–1964). Several were adapted to the format, but most attempted to be precise recreations of the originals, which meant an enormous amount of research, including the participation of those who had first danced them. An unprecedented 22-week rehearsal period and nine weeks of previews preceded the opening. The $8.5-million show, then the most expensive in Broadway's history, was lauded but, because of high costs, closed in the red after two years, hoping to recoup on the road.

Robbins is famed for using dance to express content through character-based dance. Every dancer has a specific character, no matter how uniform the steps. Moira Hodgson wrote:

> The choreographer does not have a characteristic style . . . but his works all have a polish (some critics consider him too controlled, even, at times, contrived) and a clarity and simplicity in the movement. His

musicality is subtle. He gives largesse to the smallest everyday gesture. His dancers, although their steps may be choreographed down to the little finger, always look vulnerable and human.

His storytelling methods are enhanced by his background in Stanislavskian techniques learned at the Actors Studio and with Stella Adler. Dancers as well as actors must bring inner justification to their behavior. They have to understand the given circumstances and the reasons for everything they do. Robbins's scrupulous research assists the players, as when he could speak from his personal experience of local gangs he had observed while preparing for *West Side Story*. Only the most thorough study could have produced the authenticity of *Fiddler*'s old-world society.

Robbins's creative techniques included having *West Side Story*'s actors increase their role identification by relating closely with their specific gangs and maintaining their relationships with fellow gang members outside of the theater. Each gang had a pep rally in the wings before entering, thereby bringing the tension on with them. Newspaper clippings about gangs were collected and pasted backstage. *Fiddler* exercises involved such things as having actors become sensitive to discrimination by improvising as blacks trying to buy books in a white-owned Southern bookstore or by acting out concentration camp situations.

Despite his interest in emotional truth, Robbins stages book scenes much like he does musical numbers, looking at them primarily from a visual angle. Actors are asked to try numerous physical approaches before the right one appears. Robbins once had his *Fiddler* cast play the same scene 15 different ways.

Robbins is a demanding martinet-perfectionist whose actors must swallow their egos and become putty in his hands. While he has a kind and caring side, he is better known for a fiery temperament that has reduced many to tears. Once, a cast was sufficiently alienated so that during a tirade they did not prevent him from falling into the orchestra pit as he backed away from them. Yet many agree that whatever his attitude, it is always in the interests of the show and that their performances—if not their psyches—do benefit. He told Emily Coleman:

I ask for a great deal, but no more than I give myself. I am extremely self-demanding. I do ask people to extend themselves as far as they can.

One thing I have absolutely no patience with in the theatre is anyone who works in it without being a completely dedicated artist and professional in all senses of the word.

No other artist has been as creatively successful both on Broadway and in ballet. Despite Robbins's acknowledged influence on the course of musical direction and choreography and on the rise of the director-choreographer, his other commitments have led him to direct a relatively small number of works, although his impact has been enormous.

Further Reading:

Altman, Richard, and Mervyn Kaufman. *The Making of a Musical.* New York: Crown, 1971.

Coleman, Emily. "From Tutus to T-Shirts." *New York Times Magazine,* October 9, 1961.

Hodgson, Moira. "Robbins Leaps from Ballet to Broadway." *New York Times,* February 10, 1980.

Mandelbaum, Ken. "Jerome Robbins: A Life in the Theater." *TheaterWeek,* February 27–March 5, 1989.

"On Broadway: Jerome Robbins Director." *Dance Magazine* 30 (December 1956).

Also: Gottfried, *Opening Nights;* Gottfried, *Broadway Musicals;* Guernsey, *Broadway Song and Story;* Laufe, *Broadway's Greatest Musicals;* Simon, *Uneasy Stages.*

ALAN SCHNEIDER (1917–1984)

ALAN (ABRAM LEOPOLDOVITCH) SCHNEIDER was born in Kharkov, Russia, where his parents were physicians. The family moved to America in 1923 and Schneider was raised mainly in Maryland. He attended Johns Hopkins University briefly, but obtained his B.A. from the University of Wisconsin, where he was active in theater. He apprenticed in summer stock; acted in and directed amateur plays; worked as a radio announcer-writer; and wrote political speeches. In 1941, he received his M.A. from Cornell University.

Draft-deferred for physical reasons, he spent much of World War II at Catholic University, where he taught theater off and on for a dozen years and eventually staged 21 plays, some with guest artists. Schneider frequently returned to university positions at such schools as the University of California at San Diego and the Juilliard Theater Center.

Schneider, who had acted in a Broadway flop in 1944, began directing professionally in 1947 when he presented George S. Kaufman and Moss Hart's *You Can't Take It with You* and Walter Kerr's musical *Sing Out, Sweet Land* at an outdoor Cleveland theater, doing three more shows there in 1948. He also spent six months in 1949 directing at a cultural complex in England called Dartington Hall. One play, Thornton Wilder's *Pullman Car Hiawatha,* became an often-revived Schneider favorite. His New York directing work began in 1947 with a showcase of Tennessee Williams's *The Long Goodbye* in a workshop he created. He gained attention with a noncommercial showing of Randolph Goodman's *A*

Long Way from Home (1948), an updated, black version of Maxim Gorky's *The Lower Depths*, its setting a flophouse in the deep South.

In the fifties, following summer stock on Cape Cod, Schneider came into prominence via work in Washington, D.C., and on Broadway. In the former, he formed a close relationship with Zelda Fichhandler, cofounder of Arena Stage. Schneider's inaugural staging in this new theater-in-the-round was of Williams's *The Glass Menagerie* (1951); he subsequently offered close to 40 plays there. Apart from a few by Shakespeare and Anton Chekhov (he staged *The Cherry Orchard* five times), these mountings concentrated on the modern repertoire represented by Wilder, Williams, John Patrick, Eugene O'Neill, Maxwell Anderson, Clifford Odets, William Saroyan, Arthur Miller, Ray Lawler, Samuel Beckett, Bertolt Brecht, Tad Mosel, and Michael Weller. He also did a number of premieres, several of which moved to New York (not always successfully), most importantly Lawler's Australian *Summer of the Seventeenth Doll* (1959), which ran a year Off-Broadway; two Weller plays, *Moonchildren* (1971) and *Loose Ends* (1979); and Preston Jones's *The Last Meeting of the Knights of the White Magnolia* (1975), the first play in *A Texas Trilogy*. Schneider staged the entire trilogy at the Kennedy Center in 1976.

Schneider mastered arena staging, enjoying its three-dimensionality. His *Glass Menagerie* showed his imaginative use of the form when, instead of hanging pictures of Tom's father about the space, he had an actor in the aisle hold an empty frame before his face, which was lit on cue.

Schneider's distinguished Broadway career began with William O'Brien's *The Remarkable Mr. Pennypacker* (1953), a hit comedy that did not have a third act when rehearsals began. Schneider and the producer improvised one as the dramatist took down their words; none of the critics was the wiser. Schneider's next outing flopped, but he soared with Guy Bolton's popular *Anastasia* (1954). Of his remaining 27 Broadway shows, his more memorable—if not always profitable—choices included a special all-star version (including Helen Hayes and Mary Martin) of Thornton Wilder's *The Skin of Our Teeth* (1955) designed for Paris's Théâtre des Nations festival, but also given a limited New York engagement; Shimon Wincelberg's *Kataki* (1959), about a Japanese and an American soldier stranded in the Pacific; Edward Albee's surgical exploration of marital agony, *Who's Afraid of Virginia Woolf?* (1964), Schneider's Broadway pinnacle (he won a Tony for it); Albee's murky *Tiny Alice* (1964); Joe Orton's *Entertaining*

Billie Whitelaw in Beckett's Rockaby. *Directed by Alan Schneider. (1981)*   (Photo: Martha Swope)

Mr. Sloane (1965); Williams's one-act program, *Slapstick Tragedy* (1966); Albee's sensitive *A Delicate Balance* (1966); Robert Anderson's one-acts, *You Know I Can't Hear You When the Water's Running* (1967), whose 775 performances were a Schneider record; Harold Pinter's enigmatic *The Birthday Party* (1967); and Anderson's touching *I Never Sang for My Father* (1968).

Ever since his 1958 staging of Beckett's *Endgame* at the Cherry Lane, he had found Off-Broadway more congenial to his tastes than Broadway. This idealist put artistry before money. He was active in the regional theaters as well. Those (other than the Arena) housing his work included Houston's Alley, San Francisco's Actors' Workshop, Chicago's Goodman, Princeton's McCarter, Minneapolis's Guthrie, Brooklyn's Chelsea (where he did the American premiere of Edward Bond's controversial *Saved* [1970]), and Kansas City's Missouri Rep. He directed in London and Tel Aviv, and took an Arena revival of *Our Town* on a celebrated tour of the U.S.S.R.

Those contemporary playwrights with whom Schneider was most intimately associated were Beckett, Albee, and Pinter. He directed the original American version of Beckett's masterpiece, *Waiting for Godot* (1956), starring Bert Lahr, but painful circumstances, including its premiere at a totally inappropriate Miami playhouse, led to his replacement by another director in New York. Still, he and Beckett formed an indissoluble relationship and he controlled the American rights to the Irishman's increasingly minimalist works, many of which he staged in multiple productions (including four more *Godots*). Most were Off-Broadway or in the subsidized theater. The Beckett list (some of them sharing a bill with others) includes *Krapp's Last Tape* (1960), *Happy Days* (1961), *Play* (1964), *Breath* (1971), *Come and Go* (1971), *Not I* (1972), *Act Without Words II* (1972), *Footfalls* (1976), *That Time* (1976), *Rockaby* (1981), *Ohio Impromptu* (1983), *Catastrophe* (1983), *What Where* (1983), and *Enough* (1984). *Film*, Schneider's only movie, was also by Beckett.

Schneider's first Albee was Off-Broadway's *The American Dream* (1960). In addition to plays already mentioned, Schneider went on to do *The Zoo Story* (1962), *The Ballad of the Sad Café* (1963), *Malcolm* (1966), *Box Mao Box* (1968), *The Lady from Dubuque* (1980), and *The Sandbox* (1983). The Pinter connection began in 1962 with *The Dumbwaiter*; later plays not mentioned above included *The Collection* (1962), *The Lover* (1964), *The Black and the White* (1983), *Victoria Station* (1984), *One for the Road* (1984), and *A Kind of Alaska* (1984).

Pinter, Albee, and Beckett are among the most oblique yet respected mainstream dramatists of the past 30 years, and Schneider's productions have been heavily responsible for their importance in the American theater. He told *Newsday*, "I like elusive material. . . . Material that isn't immediately accessible. I like poetic truth rather than factual truth." His staging of these authors symbolizes his credo of giving prime importance to the play and the search for a precise rendering of the author's intentions. He had little respect for showing off (the "colored lights" school of directing, he called it) and preferred trying "to do the play as though I weren't there. . . . I really try to do it as if there were no director."

In his early work he had every move down on paper before rehearsals commenced, and created beautiful groupings and movement while manipulating the actors like puppets. Later, having joined the Actors Studio, he came to believe that no matter how abstract the play, he had to bring inner truth to its performance in order to evoke its humanity. This meant abandoning his earlier emphasis on pictorial values. He sought to combine motivated reality

with an attention to formal staging concerns, rhythm (a preoccupation), and design. He wanted actors fully alive to the sensory world surrounding them, and used a variety of means to achieve his aims. From Lee Strasberg he learned that "the director's primary job and responsibility is to stimulate the sensitivity of the actor, not simply to steer him" about the stage. Subtextual questioning was thus crucial, although he realized that this can only go so far when dealing with certain nonrealistic materials. Once he began to work this way, he wrote, "I . . . tended more to consider what a character wants or needs, what he or she is doing, thinking, sensing, rather than what he or she happens to be saying or where he or she has to move."

He often cast Actors Studio members because he felt they knew how to fill even a superficial text with subtextual life. Schneider placed great faith in casting: "If you have a good script and you cast it well, it'll be good on stage. If you don't it won't. You're a director and not a magician."

Schneider was vibrantly youthful, even into his sixties, known for wearing a baseball or Greek fisherman's cap to rehearsals. A perfectionist, he grew furious when things went awry and had a reputation for firing actors who proved inappropriate.

Schneider studied the text extensively. He drilled the playwright with questions, in person, on the phone, or by mail. Nor was he shy about studying other productions of a play before he staged it, possibly returning night after night, and even seeking out the director for advice. For *Mother Courage* he carefully perused Brecht's modelbooks. And he had no ego problems accepting suggestions from playwrights who understood direction, such as Beckett and Pinter (Albee's ideas were less respected).

To keep rehearsals a time of discovery, actors were given freedom to find answers for themselves, with Schneider editing their choices. Only in a bind would he give readings or tell an actor to do something on a specific cue. He liked to provide actors with actable images, as when he told Frances Sternhagen to play her opening monologue in *The Skin of Our Teeth* as if she were going down a hill with no hands on a brakeless bicycle.

Because of his attention to subtext, Schneider took many notes during his preparations, writing down a "spine," breaking the play into beats, and conceptualizing it in terms of its thematic meanings. He considered this his most important task but was more likely than not to keep his notes to himself than to share them with the cast. He has described some of these notes:

Albee's AMERICAN DREAM . . . , was a 'cartoon sketch dealing with the hollowness of our current existence'. . . . VIRGINIA WOOLF was 'a dark legend of truth and illusion, musical in its structure and style.' . . . THE BALLAD OF THE SAD CAFE was a prose-poem about the search for love in a world which denies it.

He admitted, though, to being more intuitive than analytical and to making decisions based on an emotional sense of what was right rather than on an intellectual assurance.

After opening rehearsals by delivering a brief talk, he spent several days "at table" as the actors read and probed. When this ended, he blocked swiftly, often an act a session. He occasionally used improvisations, but thought them risky. An antidogmatic pragmatist, his feeling was that any rehearsal technique could be used, from games to stimulating music, so long as it produced results. He once injected life into a scene by having the actors shout their lines as they ran up and down the aisles. Flexibility was important, as the same production might include stars who required strikingly different treatment. When appropriate, he would take two or three actors aside and work with them privately to help break down their emotional blocks.

He disliked discussing the philosophical implications of a play, choosing to focus on what could be acted. He thus rooted the rehearsals, no matter how abstract the situation, in "the local situation," concentrating on the "human situation" of the given circumstances and character intentions. "Most importantly, what is their physical, their sensory reality?" By acting the characters and relationships, the meaning would emerge by itself. Beckett insisted that his plays be accepted at face value and not as metaphysical tracts. "It's just about two people who are like that," he said of *Godot*. When asked who

Godot was, the author answered that if he had known he would have said so in the play.

In directing Beckett, Schneider was careful to do precisely what the author indicated in his meticulous notes and textual indications (some criticized this). He felt that a living author must be fully respected. With an author like Beckett, the slightest deviation or interpolation might prove harmful; when Schneider added a billiard-table lamp over the desk in *Krapp's Last Tape*, he would have removed it if Beckett had not approved. But Beckett trusted him and always ended their talks with, "Do it a-h-ny way you like, Alan, a-h-ny way you like."

Alan Schneider hated to be pigeon-holed as a director of Albee, Beckett, and Pinter. His stagings of these dramatists were sufficient to guarantee him his niche, but he was widely eclectic. Peter Zeisler said of Schneider, who was killed by a motorcycle while in London to do a new play, "He has left behind a legacy that will carry forward into the future of our art form. What he cared about most was the American theater, and there is virtually no one in the theater today who has not been touched in some way by his work."

Further reading:

"Critics' Roundtable: A Director's Responsibility to the Play." *New York Theatre Review* 2 (November 1978).

Schneider, Alan. "Director as Dogsbody." *Theatre Quarterly* 3 (April–June 1973).

———. "What Does a Director Do?" *New York Theatre Review* 1 (Spring/Summer 1977).

———. *Entrances: An American Director's Journey.* New York: Viking, 1986.

Zeisler, Peter, "A Man of the Theatre" *American Theatre* 1 (July/August 1984).

Also: Guernsey, *Broadway Song and Story.*

PETER SELLARS (1957–   )

PETER SELLARS was born in Pittsburgh, Pennsylvania, where his mother was an elementary school teacher and his father worked for a radio station. At 10, Sellars joined Pittsburgh's Margo Lovelace Puppet Theater, which did both conventional children's plays and work by important avant-garde dramatists. Sellars and his sister created their own puppet company and produced puppet plays in Denver during the summers. At Phillips Academy in Massachusetts, he directed classmates in about 40 plays by writers

such as Harold Pinter, Jean Anouilh, and Fernando Arrabal.

From 1973 to 1974, Sellars lived in Paris, where he was impressed by directors Giorgio Strehler, Andrei Serban, and Peter Schumann (of the Bread and Puppet Theater). He entered Harvard in 1974. Despite its lack of a theater program (he was allowed to create his own curriculum), he staged over 40 productions. Shakespeare's *Coriolanus*, performed to Beethoven's music and staged in the Loeb Drama

Center's experimental playhouse, led to a disastrous mainstage production of Edith Sitwell's *Façade*, set in a seedy Edwardian hotel lobby, and employing actors who mimed as Sellars read Sitwell's nonsense verse to the accompaniment of William Walton's music. Sellars thereafter directed in a dormitory basement with a group he called Explosives B Cabaret. Their repertory included modern works by Samuel Beckett, Slawomir Mrozek, Gertrude Stein, Alexander Sukhovo-Koblyin, Pinter, Bertolt Brecht, Woody Allen, and Peter Handke. The classics included Aristophanes, Euripides, Henrik Ibsen (*When We Dead Awaken* with the protagonist played by a pile of newspapers), Anton Chekhov, Johann Wolfgang von Goethe, and Shakespeare. *Antony and Cleopatra* was done in a swimming pool and *King Lear* took apart a Lincoln Continental to symbolize Lear's declining power.

Just before Robert Brustein took over the Loeb with his American Repertory Theater (ART), Sellars used its stage for a four-show summer season, including Vladimir Mayakovsky's *The Bedbug* (1979), a reflection of his fascination with 1920s theatricalism, especially the work of Vsevolod Meyerhold. His four-hour version of Wagner's *Ring* cycle led to Brustein's inviting the well-read, musically knowledgeable, 23-year-old "wunderkind" to make his professional debut with the ART.

Sellars, still an undergraduate, provided Nikolai Gogol's *The Inspector General* (1980), played on a white set with actors entering and leaving by trap doors; adorned with surrealistic intrusions such as a giant pineapple and a huge, hanging fish; and ending with Khlestakov flying off in his nightshirt. It used powerful imagery to underscore Gogol's bitterness toward an unfeeling bureaucracy. (Sellars believes theater should be socially committed.) He insisted that the seemingly irrelevant references were tied to the text. To explain the pineapple, he noted, among other reasons, that being a fruit known only to the bourgeoisie, its presence suggested a class criticism. He wanted to avoid mirroring the text in favor of inserting oblique, counterpoint images that force the audience to think about them.

After graduating (in 1980), and traveling through Russia and the Orient, the puckish-looking *enfant terrible* divided his career between plays and operas, bringing his ideas ("gimmicks" to some) to both mediums.

Sellars's theater work was rarely seen in New York, although he offered Frank O'Hara and V. R. Lang's *A Day in the Life of the Czar, or I Too Have Lived in Arcadia* (1980) Off-Off-Broadway. This was a program of six eccentric verse-dramas (five by O'Hara) by two modernist poets. In Lang's *Arcadia*, in which young lovers viewed as pastoral shepherds find their utopian world destroyed by a temptress's arrival, the action, viewed by spectators seated on a wide staircase, took place on a white sheet beneath wispy canvas clouds. The *New York Times* praised Sellars for capturing O'Hara's wit and Lang's passions, but hoped he would return with "a postcollegiate play." Later that year, he directed *Kabuki Western* (no author given) for the National Theater of the Deaf. Sellars creatively adapts many Asian techniques in his work.

Following several impressive operas, Sellars began to develop *My One and Only,* a Broadway musical starring Tommy Tune and based on George and Ira Gershwin's 1927 *Funny Face.* He believes the American musical—along with the Greek and Elizabethan theaters—one of the greatest forms in Western history. After more than a year of work, Sellars was replaced by Tune before the Boston previews because the four hours-plus show—Sellers refused to cut—was suffering. (The 1983 work, from which Sellars's novelties—including its Meyerholdian constructivist settings—were removed or modified, became a hit.) Ironically, in the same week, he was awarded a MacArthur "genius" award.

Sellars moved on to W. S. Gilbert and Arthur Sullivan's *The Mikado* (1983), given an outlandishly comic interpretation for the Lyric Opera of Chicago in which the Mikado entered in a Datsun, the effects on Japan of Westernization were satirized, the setting displayed ads for cars, Minolta, and Coca-Cola, Nanki-Poo was a Presley-like rock star, Yum-Yum wore a miniskirt and carried a hotcomb, and the "gentlemen of Japan" wore identical blue business suits and fanned themselves with legal pads. The action was placed in the context of a roundtrip flight to Japan by Chicago politicians, some of whom were named.

In 1982, Sellars began to direct at the Boston Shakespeare Company, offering *Ping* (no author given, 1982) and a one-act, three-character version of *Macbeth* called *Play/Macbeth* (1982), before being named the financially shaky troupe's artistic director in 1983. When he left after a year, the company was even more unstable. His stagings included *Pericles* (1983) and an opera. *Pericles*—both hated and admired—used masks and exemplified Sellars's controversial method of combining anachronistic references. The distraught Pericles grew dreadlocks and slept in a refrigerator carton, while Marina's brothel was straight out of the inner city. Music was drawn from Beethoven, Claude Debussy, and Elmore Jones. Some appreciated how the staging reinforced emotional content through musical means; at moments, the piece recalled the ritualistic sobriety of nō theater.

During the same year, Sellars directed a spectacular, modernized version of Brecht's *The Visions of Simone Machard* in La Jolla, California. In 1983, after staging a 14th-century Chinese play at Harvard, he gained national attention for his four-hour-long hybrid, *Hang On to Me* (1984), at Minneapolis's Guthrie. Gershwin again inspired Sellars, who, using twin centerstage pianos, combined 16 songs taken mainly from *Treasure Girl* and *Lady Be Good* with a 1904 Maxim Gorky play, *Summerfolk,* which evokes a pre-Bolshevik world of alienation ripe for political upheaval. Believing the play had a contemporaneity that connected it to the American political situation, Sellars updated it with American names and props, such as *Hustler* magazine and KISS THE CHEF barbecue aprons. The auditorium—which remained brightly lit and shared the action with the stage—was dressed with posters of Lenin, Jesse Jackson, Ronald Reagan, Mao Zedong, and so on. At the rear of the set loomed—instead of birch trees—a row of huge cutouts of peasants. Despite the musical felicities and a distinctive cast, the work was considered better in conception than in execution. *Time* announced, "Gorky and Gershwin have nothing in common except Sellars himself."

In 1985, Sellars was appointed to head the new American National Theater (ANT) at Washington, D.C.'s Kennedy Center, where he staged his own productions and oversaw those of others. He announced that the American theater was "dead as a doornail" and that he was going to create an intellectually stimulating "theater of ideas" on a level comparable to the world's best. Many of his comments were sparked by his 1983 confrontation with Yuri Lyubimov's Moscow theater, the Taganka. The ANT was a debacle.

Its catastrophic opening production was by another director. Sellars followed by demonstrating his publicized commitment to 19th-century melodrama as a foundation for his repertory by directing a 3½-hour adaptation of Alexandre Dumas's *The Count of Monte Cristo* (1985), into which selections from Byron and the Bible were interpolated. With the onstage musical background provided by Beethoven and Kurt Schnittke, and the stripped-down set employing a few high-tech devices, Sellars, according to the *Times,* presented the script in a succession of modern and postmodern styles from expressionism

to epic theater to Wooster Group deconstructionism. A duel was played in darkness, the actors' words heard in whispers, in order to "deprive" the audience of their visual crutch and create an "authentic" response. Hidden political or social themes were highlighted via references to racial divisiveness and Napoleonic fascism. Sellars's postmodernist penchant for layering opaque anachronisms annoyed those hoping for swashbuckling melodrama, but others considered the peculiarities brilliant. Audiences avoided it.

During his ANT tenure, Sellars also staged Chekhov's *The Sea Gull* (renamed *A Seagull* in 1985), employing direct address, replacing the sound effects with Eugene Scriabin's music played by an onstage pianist, and with a new translation hewing closely— if clumsily—to the Russian syntax (Robert Coe called it "an incoherent mishmash"); a campy, flop revival of Robert E. Sherwood's *Idiot's Delight* (1986); and, most effective, a new adaptation of Sophocles' *Ajax* (1986), set on the loading dock of the Pentagon and intended as a criticism of President Reagan's militaristic foreign policy in Libya and Central America. As General Ajax, deaf actor Howie Seago—who signed his lines as they were spoken by a five-actor chorus—entered in a Plexiglas enclosure, his feet immersed in bubbling blood, his mouth uttering incoherent sounds recounting his murderous deeds. The action's frame was an inquest presided over by Athena. Many thought the production remarkable, but it was panned and did poor business, although it was an international success in Europe a year later. Sellars, realizing his inability to build an institutional company, left.

Sellars, named head of the biennial Los Angeles Festival in 1987, did only two plays between then and 1993. The first was Russian futurist Velimir Khlebnikov's linguistically and thematically obscure, three-actor, 1923 play, *Zangezi: A Supersaga in 20 Planes* in Los Angeles (1986), and Brooklyn (1987). At the time, Sellars said he was abandoning theater for opera, complaining that theater no longer served a valid purpose in our culture, that commercialism prevented a director from exploring a play's "secret world," and that theater should disappear. Nevertheless, after focusing on opera for half a decade, he returned to drama in 1993 with Aeschylus' *The Persians,* given in English at Austria's German-language Salzburg Festival. Its unique take on the Greek classic was to interpret the Persians as modern Iraqis suffering the effects of America's Gulf War invasion. Plans were for it to play in Paris, Berlin, Edinburgh, and Los Angeles.

Sellars, who aims for metaphoric rather than literal scenery, prefers to work with designers, such as Adrianne Lobel, who are also visual artists. Most of his productions have been of classics or older 20th-century plays in which he searches for ideas that can be translated into contemporary visual analogues. Images from multiple sources, both high- and low-brow, are poured into the mix, although audiences are often frustrated at not catching the allusions. Despite the frequent beauty of his sets, referential value always takes precedence over decorative. Sellars often changes his ideas, which can be trying to designers. He prefers side lighting to frontal lighting, and goes from very bright effects to deep shadows.

Sellars's style stems from his placing of ideas above plot. He thrives on chance taking and wants to disturb, even at the expense of being boring (which may happen when he slows the action down in Robert Wilson fashion). He appreciates the flaws in plays ("art exists to be chewy," he informed Arthur Bartow) and dislikes attempts to smooth over them in the name of perfectionism. "Few people realize that my work is painful, irritating and misshapen," he told Coe. "I'm stubborn that way. Because unless you get people to the point were something *snaps*, nothing happens." He acknowledges having "vandalized" the classics.

Sellars is committed to nontraditional casting, and often casts across ethnic (or even gender) lines. Declaring that he holds actors in awe, he says his basic rehearsal method is the Socratic one, continually asking questions, especially the obvious ones because those are the ones least likely to be asked. A good actor will use such queries to uncover a subterranean flow; "it suddenly starts to bloom and is given a mystery and a quality that is truly ineffable," he told Bartow. He likes to joke and create a sense of fun, but his presence is generally unobtrusive and carefully observant, waiting for the actors to do something that he can build on or relate to the ideas of other collaborators. "To him, this is the key to his directing," noted Richard Trousdell. "He does not invent, he gathers." His acting comments are offered more like off-the-cuff remarks than commands, so, even when he is being specific, there is no resistance to trying them out. Sellars avoids telling actors how to react, preferring their natural responses to preordained ones. But he does occasionally demonstrate improvisationally, not to elicit a copycat version but to help himself uncover an elusive emotional structure in a scene. Rehearsals rarely stay on one level, and constantly go deeper into the material, discovering new meanings, and often changing the staging radically in the process.

Peter Sellars's professional career in the theater was only seven years old when he left it for opera, yet he was already internationally renowned for the controversial audaciousness of his theatrical imagination. His recent return to drama will undoubtedly be welcomed by many theater lovers, while others are perhaps quaking at the thought of what conceptual mayhem he may yet wreak on the world's dramatic literature.

Further reading:

Coe, Robert. "What Makes Sellars Run?" *American Theatre* 4 (December 1987).

Jenkins, Ron. "Peter Sellars." *Theatre* 15 (Spring 1984).

Mikotowicz, Tom. "Director Peter Sellars: Bridging the Modern and Postmodern." *Theatre Topics* 1 (March 1991).

Trousdell, Richard. "Peter Sellars Rehearses *Figaro.*" *The Drama Review* 35 (Spring 1991).

Also: Bartow, *Director's Voice*; Shewey in King, *Contemporary American Theatre.*

ANDREI SERBAN (1943–   )

ANDREI SERBAN was born in Bucharest, Rumania, where his father was a sculptor and photographer and his mother a schoolteacher. He specialized in directing at the Film and Theater Institute. In 1965, he directed *Julius Caesar,* using Japanese conventions, and combined grotesque realism with choreographic abstraction in the anonymous Elizabethan play *Arden of Faversham.*

Ellen Stewart, doyenne of Off-Off-Broadway's La Mama E.T.C., brought him to America where he debuted at her theater in 1970 with *Arden* and Alfred Jarry's *Ubu Roi.* He provided a new version of *Arden* that pressed the work into 50 minutes, retaining only key words and phrases. Serban focused on melodramatically expressive action, such as a ritual murder in which a husband was castrated by his wife and her lover with a giant saw and—using eggs—his face rubbed with his severed genitals.

Serban assisted Peter Brook on *Orghast* (1971), a ritualistic work staged in Iran using ancient languages to express preverbal emotionalism. The experience revitalized Serban's perception of theater's purpose and prompted his convention-breaking Greek tragedies, beginning at La Mama with *Medea* (1972), a conflation of Euripides and Seneca, presented by his own company. *Electra* (premiered in France) was added in 1973, and *The Trojan Women* was born a year later. Ancient Greek and Latin were combined with other arcane languages, substituting emotional dynamics for intellectual comprehension. The plays were produced as *Fragments of a Trilogy* (1974); they played worldwide, sometimes for 3,500 people. They returned to the 300-seat La Mama in 1987.

Each play employed a different audience-actor configuration. *The Trojan Women* began with the audience herded together in the lobby and then pressed together in the open spaces of the darkened theater. Richard Eder wrote:

> *Cassandra, stripped to the waist, does a dance of rage on a high scaffolding, waving two torches. The rage turns to despair; she mews like a seagull. Greek soldiers burst through the audience—still in overcoats, and clutching purses and programs—put a halter around her neck and drag her away.*
>
> *Andromache holds up her child, keening and gently bathing the upturned face with water. Each drop, trickling down the bare arm, is like a word of lamentation. The child is torn away; Andromache plunges from a parapet, the spotlight snaps out and she and her anguish are extinguished.*

Bizarre wailing, barking, whispering, chanting, and moaning was heard, the actors using the words as springboards for emotional pyrotechnics. Frequent collaborator Elizabeth Swados wrote the unusual music. Serban forced the audience to experience the ritualistic underpinnings by becoming connected to the primal sources that had led to the creation of now forgotten tongues.

A meditative peace replaced disorder at the end, with the audience seated in side galleries in the now well-lit theater as the singing, captive women— seated in a row within a proscenium at one end— worked their spars, creating the image of a ship.

Serban's theatricalism eschewed literary significance for visual conceptions that culled effects from commedia, circus, and pantomime. Eder noted of Serban's early offerings:

> *They use radical images and sounds; they rely heavily on gesture and movement; they make an emotional calligraphy of space; they call for a deep involvement by highly trained performers; and they achieve stunning and unexpected effects from what had seemed to be familiar texts.*

Serban's theatricalist reputation expanded with Bertolt Brecht's *The Threepenny Opera* (1975) in San Francisco and *The Good Woman of Setzuan* (1975) at La Mama (and on a European tour), as well as Shakespeare's *As You Like It* (1976). *The Good Woman* received a children's story-style presentation replete with pantomimic chinoiserie that some felt failed to get beneath the play's dramatic skin. Six-foot rods were periodically laid on the stage floor to form a pattern. Eventually a maze was created through which the actors had to move. Finally, Shen Te (Priscilla Smith) collected the rods, "thus symbolically clearing away the ethical maze that the people have created," wrote the *New Republic,* "and shouldering those burdens herself."

Shakespeare's play was developed over several months in France. Staged outdoors in the Ardennes Forest, it asked the audience to walk from a village about a mile into the woods during the show. The *Soho Weekly News* called it "a Renaissance Fair, a countrylife celebration complete with technicolor costumes, live farm animals, music and mime." (*The Good Woman* was revived for the American Repertory Theater [ART] in 1987 and *As You Like It* went indoors at La Mama in 1980.)

Serban's fame leaped with Anton Chekhov's *The Cherry Orchard* (1977) at Lincoln Center (later in Tokyo), with a cast composed principally of non-Serban actors. Many considered it a historic breakthrough, but others attacked it. Arguing for a scenic environment that provoked emotions instead of providing information, Serban stripped away Chekhov's walls and placed the action on a practically bare, white-carpeted thrust stage adorned with a highly selective use of furniture and props and backed by an orchard of cherry trees. He believed the scenic sparseness would allow the human relationships to become more sharply focused, thus allowing him to capture Chekhov's reality, not his realism.

Serban—remembering Chekhov's calling the play a comedy—emphasized its farcical aspects. He also suggested the coming revolution by showing distant smokestacks and interpolating serfs laboriously pushing a plough across the backdrop.

Serban evoked archetypal images from the text and created atmospheric sensations rarely experienced in conventional Chekhov. Widely commented on was the climactic departure—developed from an improvisation—of Irene Worth's Madame Ranevskaya from her ancestral home. Wearing a long coat and with her hands in a muff, she swooped and circled, her speed accelerating and her moods shifting, as if simultaneously recalling the sensations

Gozzi's King Stag. *Directed by Andrei Serban. (1984)*   (Photo: American Repertory Theatre/Richard Feldman)

of childhood and bidding farewell to the beloved walls forever.

Subsequently, Serban did most of Chekhov's plays, including *The Sea Gull* (1980), first in Tokyo (in Japanese), then in a different interpretation in New York, where there was a definite Japanese influence, including the frequent use of a footbridge; an outstanding *The Three Sisters* (1982) at the ART, evoking a Beckett-like existential atmosphere of waiting on a minimally furnished stage using a backdrop of imaginatively varied red velvet curtains, with banks of footlights at the sides of the mirrored floor; and, at La Mama, a 90-minute *Uncle Vanya* (1983) with Joseph Chaikin. It was played for farce and melodrama on a huge, wooden, mazelike setting of rampways and levels requiring actors to walk and run to get from place to place, and with the audience watching from above.

Serban's only other work at Lincoln Center was Aeschylus' *Agamemnon* (1977) in which he used impressive masks, created—with Swados—a musically scored text using English and Greek, had the

principals play multiple roles, and, in some opinions, buried the play beneath flamboyant ceremonialism. The theater was transformed into an arena by onstage bleachers; when necessary, they separated to provide a dramatic passageway up center.

Serban has also been preoccupied with Carlo Gozzi, whose *The King Stag* (1985) and *The Serpent Woman* (1988) he has directed for the ART. The former was blessed with the masks, puppets, and theatrical constructions of Julie Taymor, and used Asian acting methods to bring Gozzi's fantastical world to life. The *Village Voice* loved "the fanciful birds and turtles materializing in sheer light, or a king in a silken stag's body and a giant, pale-blue fabric floating across the stage through a forest." Serban also has directed opera versions of other Gozzi plays.

Most of Serban's work has been seen at American resident theaters, although he also has been active in opera. From 1977 to 1978, he was associate artistic director of the Yale Repertory Theater, for whom he did a nightmarish *Ghost Sonata* (1977),

Stefanianne Christopherson and Dean Pitchford in The Umbrellas of Cherbourg. *Directed by Andrei Serban. (1979)* (Photo: Martha Swope)

filled with silences and slow-motion speech and movement; Sam Shepard's *Mad Dog Blues* (1978), staged on a beach; and Molière's *Sganarelle: An Evening of Moliere Farces* (1978, subsequently played in several cities), four slapstick playlets visually inspired by Jacques Callot's commedia etchings.

Many pieces originated at New York's Public Theater, among them his adaptation of Mikhail Bulgakov's satirico-political Russian novel *The Master and Margarita* (1978; Paris, 1983), produced in an environmental, sports arena-like setting; a lovingly Beckettian *Happy Days* (1979), with Worth; a stage adaptation of the French romantic musical movie, *The Umbrellas of Cherbourg* (1979; London and Los Angeles, 1980), with music by Michel Legrand; and George Walker's *Zastrozzi* (1982), a spoof of Italian revenge melodrama. *Cherbourg*, a lushly sentimental, bookless soap operetta, revealed a world of first love viewed through movable, mist-covered, Lucite window panels behind which loomed a giant mural of Cherbourg. Serban's manipulation of pastel-colored umbrellas and balloons suggested Magritte.

The Guthrie sponsored Serban's production of Pierre de Beaumarchais's *The Marriage of Figaro* (1982), later redone at New York's Circle in the Square (1985), while the ART produced the world premiere of Ronald Ribman's *Sweet Table at the Richelieu* (1986). *Figaro* employed white contemporary clothing in the first half and black 18th-century costumes in the second, but was chiefly memorable

for placing most of the action on wheels, with actors using roller skates, bicycles, skateboards, grocery carts, wheelbarrows, and wheelchairs. Figaro's famous monologue was performed from a swing. Serban explained that the physicality was meant to replace Mozart's music.

Following the 1990 downfall of Rumania's dictatorship, Serban returned as general director of Bucharest's National Theater, where he restaged his *Trilogy*, but he left to work elsewhere, including London, where he did Euripides' *Hippolytus* (1991) in a lauded expressionistic staging. In 1992, he became head of Columbia University's acting program.

Serban's initial encounter with American actors, whom he found excessively casual, was traumatic, but he instilled a sense of discipline and artistic respect in his troupe, using exercises in kung fu, tai ch'i, acrobatics, deaf signing, and elocution. Because his images are so specific, Serban has been considered autocratic, but he is actually collaborative, developing his ideas from improvisations. Although he rarely gets them, he likes lengthy rehearsal periods during which he can search with his actors for a production's form. Nothing is prepared beforehand, the entire production being realized in rehearsal. Numerous solutions to a problem are tried before an answer—usually a surprisingly novel one—is found. Serban says that he does not understand a play when rehearsals commence and that, even though actors find it disconcerting, he is constantly changing things and even making discoveries after the opening. Some argue that his nonintellectual innocence is a ruse to make the actors feel that they have created the production themselves. A Rumanian familiar with Serban told Mike Steele, " 'It . . . suits . . . American actors . . . but I don't believe for a minute that he doesn't know exactly what he wants, even from the beginning.' "

The Cherry Orchard rehearsals represent Serban's approach. There were improvisations based on extra-textual situations, such as the reunions at the station and who each person sat with on the carriage trip home. Some exercises concerned emotional and sensory reactions to seeing the orchard. For the first week, Serban rehearsed the cast physically while others read their words at the side. The actors also did demanding animal exercises; Worth's choice of a swan had a great impact on her performance. There were even improvisations based on things that happened after the play had ended (Varya became a nun, Trofimov a Leninist, and Yasha a Stalinist).

Even the scenery may be developed improvisationally and not be set until late, an approach he has fostered with design collaborator Michael Yeargan.

Serban's eye for actors' choices allows him to select, heighten, and refine ideas that will best express the material. He believes that emotion stems from behavioral choices, not from premeditative attempts to internalize it. He might spark an actor's imagination with a word picture, as when he told an actor in *Medea* to play his role "like a Japanese messenger announcing Hiroshima" (quoted in Eder). Similarly, when working with a composer, he draws on striking concepts, asking for music that sounds like fire or for an effect that sounds like "a huge chorus of centaurs running downhill screaming brutally!" (in Eder).

Because Serban brings a uniquely original perspective to his productions, his work often stirs violent controversy; some accuse him of self-indulgent experimentalism at the expense of the author, others applaud his adventurousness. He himself denies being an avant-gardist. "I want to go back to the origins of theater," he told Leo Seligsohn, "to the kind of mystery that takes place between an audience and live actors. I am trying to make theater that is unique, essential and alive."

Further reading:

Eder, Richard. "Andrei Serban's Theater of Terror and Beauty." *New York Times Magazine*, February 13, 1977.

Seligsohn, Leo. "Andrei Serban's Overhaul of *Figaro*." *Newsday*, October 6, 1985.

Shyer, Lawrence. "Andrei Serban Directs Chekhov: *The Sea Gull* in New York and Japan." *Theatre* 13 (Winter 1981–82).

Steele, Mike. "The Romanian Connection." *American Theatre* 2 (August 1985).

Also: Bartow, *Director's Voice*.

GEORGE BERNARD SHAW (1856–1950)

GEORGE BERNARD SHAW was born in Dublin, Ireland. He gained much of his artistic education from his musically talented mother (and her intimate friend, conductor John Vandeleur Lee), but his formal education was cursory. As a youth, he acted in amateur theatricals. At 20, he moved to London, wrote a series of novels, and became a respected critic, favoring the controversial plays of Henrik Ibsen and castigating the fashionable theater. He actively espoused Fabian socialism. Shaw's progressive ideas were developed in the antiestablishment comedies he started writing in the 1890s, beginning with *Widowers' Houses* (1892).

When productions of Shaw's early plays did not succeed with the general public, he published them in readable form, eliminating the standard acting-edition abbreviations, and writing stage directions and character descriptions in detail. To prepare for their publication, Shaw worked out all of the blocking on a chessboard with chess pieces. He used this system of preblocking even when aimed mainly as a rehearsal guide for his own use.

Beginning with *Widowers' Houses*, Shaw always took an active interest in the first productions of his plays in London (or its environs), and in most important revivals. When not working as the director, he attended rehearsals and offered advice. At first, the demands of his plays were beyond the comprehension of most actors, and he often failed to get desired results.

In his early years, he usually took no credit for staging his plays, although his participation may have been more significant than that of the credited director; this makes it difficult to determine those plays for which he was the chief directorial influence. Shaw's first known directing was on the 1894 premiere of *Arms and the Man*. Subsequently he directed, or participated in the direction of, nearly 30 of his plays, including several of their revivals. In some cases, he codirected, as he did with Johnston Forbes-Robertson on *Caesar and Cleopatra* (New York, 1906; London, 1907), J. B. Fagan on *Heartbreak House* (1921), or Lewis Casson on *Saint Joan* (1924), although—as in Casson's case—only Shaw might have been credited. When Harley Granville-Barker and J. E. Vedrenne ran the Court Theater from 1904 to 1907, where 11 Shaw plays were shown, Barker was frequently credited, although he himself pointed to Shaw's contribution. (Dennis Kennedy argues that Barker participated more than hitherto acknowledged in staging Shaw's Court productions.) Shaw's plays gained their first popular acclaim during the Court seasons. An enormous share in their success belonged to their unity as regulated under Shaw's baton. Shaw was the actual or codirector only on plays of his own authorship, but his written and spoken advice to actors and directors of plays by others was treasured.

Sometimes, Shaw's direction of one of his plays was not of the premiere, there having been one or more earlier showings, occasionally abroad. In addition to titles already cited, Shaw directed important London productions of *Mrs. Warren's Profession* (1902); *Major Barbara* (1905); *The Doctor's Dilemma* (1906); *The Devil's Disciple* (1907); *Man and Superman* (1907); *Getting Married* (1908); *Misalliance* (1910); *Fanny's First Play* (1911); and *Pygmalion* (1914). After *Saint Joan,* his credited work ceased, although he is listed as the director of 1934's *The Village Wooing.* In 1937, at 80, he oversaw a TV staging of one of his plays.

Whatever Shaw's precise credits are, it is clear that his staging was of extreme value in gaining for his plays the great popularity and admiration they came to claim as—in many cases—modern masterpieces. Shaw's primary interest was in conveying as clearly as he could the ideational foundations of his plays. To Shaw, the most fitting director was the playwright (the worst was the actor-manager), because no one else could have so comprehensive an understanding of a play's meaning. (Nor could anyone else be trusted to cut them.) Shaw considered his directing a natural adjunct to his playwriting, and prided himself so much on his ability that he left two instructive essays on the craft. Although involved in all areas of production, he was principally interested in the actors. When he began to direct, playwright-directors were fairly uncommon and theater was dominated by the actor-manager system. Shaw's methodical approach helped create a solid base on which the profession could develop.

Shaw sought to make the acting completely believable, seeking to eliminate the employment of self-centered staginess that drew more attention to the player than to the character. He advocated ensemble, and favored the idea of a company (such as at the Court) in which the same actors played leads and walk-ons.

His approach was pragmatic and he rejected the need to provide literary explanations. A director should be more concerned with the colors of his actors' makeup, for example, than with whether they understand a play's philosophy. His guiding principle was to make "the audience believe that real things are happening to real people." To this end he sought to provide an illusion that would make the play completely real in terms of the world presented by the author. Although he sought illusionistic acting, he paradoxically required a larger-than-life energy and theatrical feeling such as he remembered from the barnstorming performers of his youth, Barry Sullivan in particular. One of his most frequently used pejorative terms for actors in his plays was "underdone." The author's desires were to be trusted and the director was not to exceed those desires, either in the amount of furniture and props used or the length and structure of the text.

He deplored dictatorial methods, but required those he directed to use his instructions as their guide. The degree of independence he allowed depended on the actors involved. Gifted players were given leeway, but unimaginative ones were spoonfed.

To make the process easier, he gave considerable attention to the casting of his plays, knowing how crucial it was that an actor have the right looks and temperament, even if his intellectual comprehension of the role was inadequate. (He often wrote with specific actors in mind.) A primary requisite was the voice, because Shaw's highly developed ear led him to seek musical variety and balance in those he selected. Musical terms were often used in his direction. Shaw's plays, with their frequent resort to complex rhetorical speeches (which he compared to operatic arias), required virtuosity, and he demanded well-trained voices and perfect diction, as well as physical expressivity. A good Shaw actor was a good Shaw speaker.

Shaw believed firmly in extensive preparation, as indicated by the technically exact advice—down to the most minute business—he presented in his printed stage directions. Blocking and business were refined and elaborated during the rehearsals, which he attended with a meticulously worked-out promptbook, including floor plans of his own devising. He bemoaned directors who wasted time by trial and error. His rigorous preparation was particularly valuable in arranging crowds; in *Caesar and Cleopatra,* he even wrote numerous "ad-libs" for the extras—each of whom he individualized—in order to induce a feeling of authenticity.

His range of advice to actors was wide, and often helped with pertinent historical, psychological, and physical information. Both in his notes and in his practice, Shaw was helpful in offering detailed behavioral motivations. Subtextual concerns were a major source of his success at achieving stage truth. No matter how long a play ran, it was imperative that characters seemed to be experiencing their situations for the first time. Shaw also inspired actors by providing compelling images. A danger he watched for was a tendency to "take the tone," i.e., a mechanical habit of speaking in a tone influenced by that of the actor to whom one was speaking. He demanded that the actors ignore the audience, live their characters at every moment, and be fully immersed in the situations. For all his insistence on internal reality, however, Shaw was not averse to telling the actor precisely the pace at which to perform or how to speak a line; he often fixed misreadings by saying the lines himself, both with the incorrect stresses and his own correct ones.

Himself a talented reader, Shaw thought it best for the playwright or a proxy to read the play to the actors at the first rehearsal. Many marveled at how much insight they gained for their subsequent performances by the excellence of his reading, which clearly delineated all the characters. Because of time constraints, he got the actors on their feet right away, moving them around himself, and taking care of all the blocking, entrances, and exits with dispatch, while ignoring the line deliveries. As soon as an act was blocked, the actors ran it again to set it. An act a day was thus completed and, within a few days, the entire play was blocked. To accelerate the actors' focus on the staging, they were cautioned not to worry about learning their lines. Uncomfortable staging choices were revised.

During the second week, Shaw sat in the house as the actors ran the play, polished the blocking, and memorized their lines. He refused to take notes, interrupt, and work on problems, feeling it was better at this stage for the actor himself to correct the difficulties than for the director to interfere. When memorization was accomplished, Shaw took notes (sometimes hundreds), often observing the need to rehearse specific moments separately; these rehearsals followed the conclusion of the act in question. Memorization rehearsals took two weeks, and the final week (the fourth) was for dress rehearsals, with Shaw attending to numerous details. Three hours was the maximum needed for a good rehearsal.

Shaw refused to mention certain problems until he knew he had a solution for them. Because he feared overburdening the actors, he gave only a few notes at a time. Often, notes he resisted giving were obviated by the actors' own adjustments. When necessary, he demonstrated his objectives by broadly acting out a passage in a way that showed what he wanted but did not invite direct imitation. He knew that there were numerous ways of achieving a result, and that the actor should be trusted to find that best suited to his own nature.

Shaw rejected the dominating "schoolmaster" approach, instead dispensing advice in an exceedingly courteous manner, although he was sometimes cuttingly direct. Displays of temper were rare. When dealing with a powerful but obstinate actor, however, such as Herbert Beerbohm Tree, Shaw could be intransigent; rehearsals for *Pygmalion* were marred by disagreements. He praised so sparingly that his few compliments were more than ordinarily appreciated. The famous Shavian wit usually allowed him to couch his criticisms in humorous terms. Thus Shaw, directing Lillah McCarthy as Raina in *Arms and the Man*, sent her a note after a rehearsal, observing that what the character "wants . . . is the extremity of style—style *comédie Française,* Queen of Spain style. Do you hear, worthless wretch that you are? STYLE." (Quoted in Bernard Dukore.) Rather than shout out his requirements before the entire company, he spoke quietly and individually to the actors in question. Often, he supplemented his personal comments at rehearsal with detailed written notes sent to the actors.

Shaw took considerable pains with the physical side of production, spending many hours supervising sets, lights, props, costumes, makeup, sound, and music. He sometimes prepared costume sketches and scenic plans for development by the designers. As witnessed by his minute directions, his scenic awareness was acute. Although for the most part offended by techniques that detracted from the text, when one of his plays required special effects, he was insistent that the right ones be employed. He was also alert to the value of the pictures he created, rejecting those that seemed obviously posed and artificial in favor of those evocative of lifelike naturalness. Business that enhanced the dramatic meaning was used but that which drew attention to itself was eliminated. Pace and timing were major concerns, which is natural considering comedy's demands. Shaw, hating pauses and requiring the immediate picking up of cues, claimed that the only time there should be silence was when it was used as a special effect. But he was wise enough in his understanding of pace to know that the answer to preventing boredom was not mere speed but a well-calculated contrast among different tempi, and that sometimes the audience could best be held by slowing things down.

Shaw disliked painted 19th-century scenery and favored illusionism. Eventually, he concurred with Gordon Craig concerning unity of effect and the possibility of creating a deeper illusion through suggestion than through detailed representationalism.

Many of his own plays, he admitted, were too dependent on old-fashioned theater architecture to profit much from the new ideas. Only some of his later fantasies were capable of borrowing simplified modern practices. He was well informed about lighting and was an early proponent of removing the footlights. In costuming, he sought character appropriateness over fashionableness, and demanded a unity of impression rather than the confusion created by each player selecting his own wardrobe.

Shaw was not only a great playwright, but a historically significant stage director as well. His plays are enjoyable not only for their humor, characters, situations, and ideas, but for their stage directions, which reveal his brilliant perception of how they might best be realized in performance.

Further reading:

Armstrong, William A. "George Bernard Shaw: The Playwright as Producer." *Modern Drama* 8 (February 1966).

Dukore, Bernard F. *Bernard Shaw, Director*. Seattle: University of Washington Press, 1971.

Mander, Raymond, and Joe Mitchenson. *Theatrical Companion to Shaw*. London: Rockliff, 1954.

Shaw, George Bernard. "The Art of Rehearsal" and "Rules for Directors." In *Shaw on Theatre*. Edited by E. J. West. New York: Hill and Wang, 1959.

Also: Kennedy, *Granville Barker*.

HASSARD SHORT (1877–1956)

HUBERT EDWARD HASSARD-SHORT was born on an estate in Lincolnshire, England, to a family of distinguished landowners. He was educated at Charterhouse, but ran away at 15 to become an actor. His career began in London in 1895. He remained in New York following his 1901 debut there and gradually gained a reputation for playing "silly-ass" British juveniles (which even came to be called "Hassard Short parts"), but also began to explore direction and lighting design. In 1906, after being billed under various forms of his name, he settled on Hassard Short.

In 1907, he received his first professional directing credit, for Booth Tarkington's *The Man from Home* (1908), in which he also acted. Although he may actually have directed even earlier plays and sketches without credit, Short's abilities were not recognized until he began staging sketches in the annual Lambs Club benefit revues, called *Gambols* (1911–1913).

In 1919, Short made a strong impact with a series of all-star vaudeville shows produced as fund-raising efforts for Actors Equity, which was in the midst of a historic strike. Short subsequently staged three more Equity shows, done to enhance the union's public image. These demonstrated his mastership of theatricality and lighting effects, a notable instance being his staging of 200 actors for a satirical, pro-Equity peroration parodying Marc Antony's "Friends, Romans, countrymen" speech, strikingly lit on a stage backed only by an exposed brick wall. Although he later used lavish decors, he was always capable of indelible lighting effects with a bare stage and a few curtains.

Short's direction of Broadway book musicals began with 1920's *Honeydew*, music by Efrem Zimbalist. Invariably, programs credited him for conceiving, staging, and lighting, a combination rarely seen in the highly specialized Broadway world. Programs also informed that costumes and sets had been "devised and carried out under the personal supervision of Hassard Short." His book musicals of the twenties included Seymour Simons's *Her Family Tree* (1920); William Cary Duncan and Anselm Goetzl's *The Rose Girl* (1921); *Peg o' My Dreams* (1924), score by Hugo Felix and Anne Caldwell; Caldwell and Harold Levey's *The Magnolia Lady* (1924); Otto Harbach, Oscar Hammerstein II, and Jerome Kern's *Sunny* (1925); Caldwell, Harbach, and Vincent Youmans's *Oh, Please* (1926); Harbach, Bert Kalmar, Harry Ruby, and Kern's *Lucky* (1927); and Duncan, William Grey, and Jean Schwartz's *Sunny Days* (1928). The biggest hit (517 performances) was *Sunny*, an extravagant, circus-themed show starring Marilyn Miller.

Short also directed four straight plays, among them Russell Medcraft and Norma Mitchell's 478-performance hit, *Cradle Snatchers* (1925); two closed out of town. His genius, however, was best expressed in revues, his twenties examples including a marvelous series of *Music Box Revues* (1921, 1922, and 1923), all with music by Irving Berlin, whose new Music Box Theater they were created to occupy. These sophisticated, frequently satirical shows emphasized the theater's intimate proportions, and were intended to contrast with the more spectacular presentations of showmen like Florenz Ziegfeld. There

The Band Wagon. *Directed by Hassard Short. (1931) Adele Astaire and Fred Astaire on the l.*   (Photo: Theater Collection, Museum of the City of New York)

also were his own *Hassard Short's Ritz Revue* (1924) and the seventh *Greenwich Village Follies* (1925).

The 1930s saw even more laurels awarded to the revue-master with his stagings of such momentous offerings as the multi-authored *Three's a Crowd* (1930), with Libby Holman and Clifton Webb, and which began a long association with producer Max Gordon; *The Band Wagon* (1931), score by Arthur Schwartz and Howard Dietz, and starring Fred and Adele Astaire; and *As Thousands Cheer* (1933), score by Berlin. These successful shows exemplified the trend toward intimate revues and away from the decorative excesses of the twenties. The latter ran the longest—some 400 performances. There were also such book musicals as *Face the Music* (1932), score by Berlin; *Roberta* (1933), with a Kern score that included "Smoke Gets in Your Eyes"; *The Great Waltz* (1934), music by Johann Strauss, staged at

the huge Center Theater; *Jubilee* (1935), score by Cole Porter, including "Begin the Beguine"; *The Hot Mikado* (1939), which adapted W. S. Gilbert and Arthur Sullivan's operetta for an all-black company; and several others. *Roberta* (295 performances) ran the longest. Short staged a few other shows in London. His straight repertoire for the decade included the gargantuan anti-Nazi play at the Center Theater, *The American Way* (1939), by George S. Kaufman and Moss Hart.

Short remained active in the forties, providing several abbreviated productions for the World's Fair, backed by producer Michael Todd; the burlesque revue, *Star and Garter* (no authors credited, 1942); producer Billy Rose's inordinately expensive *Seven Lively Arts* (1944), score by Porter; and *Make Mine Manhattan* (1948), music by Richard Lewine. *Star and Garter* ran 609 times. Short made a considerable

Lady in the Dark. *Musical staging by Hassard Short. (1941) Gertrude Lawrence and Victor Mature at l, Danny Kaye (standing) at r.*   (Photo: Theater Collection, Museum of the City of New York)

impact via his book musicals. These included the brilliant Kurt Weill-Moss Hart *Lady in the Dark* (1941), a 467-performance hit starring Gertrude Lawrence and Danny Kaye; *Banjo Eyes* (1941), with Eddie Cantor, score by Vernon Duke, John Latouche, and Harold Adamson; *Something for the Boys* (1943), a 422-performance effort with a Porter score and starring Ethel Merman; *Carmen Jones* (1943), Oscar Hammerstein II's exceptional, updated, 503-performance adaptation of Bizet's opera for an all-black cast; Porter's *Mexican Hayride* (1944), a lark for Bobby Clark (481 performances); *Marinka* (1945), music by Emmerich Kalman; a revival of Kern and Hammerstein's *Show Boat* (1946); and *Music in My Heart* (1947), music by Peter Tchaikovsky.

Short provided only three more shows before his death, a 1950 revue with Clark and two book musicals, *Seventeen* (1951), score by Walter Kent and

Kim Gannon, and *My Darlin' Aida* (1952), a popularization of Giuseppe Verdi's *Aïda*.

His reputation was primarily as a stager of costly shows, with exceptional costumes and decor, performed with clockwork precision. Short's specialty was the fantastic, and he had little taste for realism. Despite the large sums of money involved, he was respected for rarely spending more than was actually needed. An efficiency expert, he oversaw all technical preparations, even observing costume fittings to guarantee against inaccuracy. Actually, he held a unique position on many of these assignments. Although he was the sole director on a few shows, when doing musicals and revues he was more likely to be in charge of the staging of the big production numbers and musical scenes, with another director handling the book or dialogue scenes. (Thus Moss Hart was the credited "director" on *Lady in the Dark,* with Short doing the musical staging.) Short also routined his revues, that is, decided which scenes went where, in order to coordinate all technical logistics as well as insuring that the show was most effectively structured. This was a complex task requiring the use of a special board with rearrangeable slots for placing all the scene titles. He worked closely with his collaborators (especially his designers). Despite his design skills, he could not draw.

His job demanded that Short be extremely well prepared at rehearsals. By the end of week one of a book musical's rehearsals, he ran through the first half of the show, with a complete run-through by the end of week two. Polishing occupied week three, and dress rehearsals week four. Revues required yet another week. Short—combining the roles of artistic and technical director—oversaw not only the performances, but the technical crew, and, being a perfectionist, insisted on the highest standards. His most often used stars were Charlotte Greenwood, Mary Boland, and Helen Broderick.

In spite of the demands on him, he was not a dictator, but a diplomatic artist, usually taking an actor aside to give him notes. The immaculately dressed, physically diminutive director, known as "Bobby," was kind and patient; he rarely displayed anger and believed that "Temperament is a poor excuse for incompetency." He held that happy companies gave their best.

In revues, he decided how to dramatize musical numbers, conceiving the physical look, the characters, backgrounds, costumes, atmosphere, and so on. Although not a choreographer, he staged much nondance movement in musical numbers. His ideas were prepared on a fully equipped miniature stage, including small lights for experimenting with lighting effects.

Lighting remained his preeminent tool. Short was responsible for a number of advances in lighting, including the elimination of footlights—which he hated—for musicals (starting from *Three's a Crowd*), replacing them with lights affixed to the balcony. Preeminent was his use of one or more steel scaffolding bridges behind the proscenium from which manned instruments could be manipulated—and their colors changed—for overhead effects and the illumination of otherwise impossible-to-hit areas.

His magnificent lighting often was seen in conjunction with cleverly manipulated curtains and scrims. Sometimes, up to six scrims were utilized in a single scene to create magic, such as underwater effects or miraculous transformations. He was fond of staging a number by having the star appear down-

stage before a scrim backed by a taffeta curtain. After a few bars, the taffeta curtain vanished and backlighting revealed the set and a company tableau hidden upstage of it. The scrim was then removed and the actors began moving. At the end of the scene, the scrim reappeared, another tableau was formed, and the taffeta was closed.

Among Short's most unforgettable combinations of staging and lighting were "Body and Soul" in *Three's a Crowd* and "Dancing in the Dark" in *The Band Wagon*. In the first, Libby Holman, lit by a pin spot, and dressed in a long black gown, walked slowly and sensually across the stage before black drapes, singing Johnny Green's song as Webb and Tamara Geva danced, with the perfectly aimed, moving spotlights (from the bridge) now showing only their heads and shoulders, now only their legs and feet. For "Dancing in the Dark," John Barker, in tails, sang the great song as, upstage, Tillie Losch danced with her reflections on a moodily lit, raked and mirrored floor, splashed with shifting colors and patterns. Lying on the raked platform and continually varying their gestures was a bevy of lovely chorus girls.

Another technical feature notable in Short's work was his extensive use of elevators, on which actors, singly or in groups, and scenic units, could be raised and lowered, usually in full audience view to achieve impressive effects. One example, used in several permutations, was to have a female performer rise on an elevator as the skirt or train of her dress expanded to cover the entire stage beneath and around her, with the chorus posed in a pretty tableau. He also made exceptional use of revolves, often using several (four in *Lady in the Dark*), including large ones with separate turntables at their center that could be moved in the opposite direction. A famous example was the revolve used for a carousel in *The Band Wagon*'s "I Love Louisa."

When Short staged his massive productions at the 3,822-seat Center Theater, he provided a number of extraordinary feats. For *The Great Waltz*, for instance, he was responsible for installing a mechanical device that allowed the lifting of the entire orchestra from the pit and, as the audience watched, moving it all the way upstage as a ballroom filled with swirling waltzers formed downstage in front of it.

Short's work was also renowned for his individualistic use of color. Most marked was his occasional tendency to give a scene a monochromatic effect, although subtly alleviated by other hues. For "Easter Parade" in *As Thousands Cheer*, the scene was done entirely in rotogravure brown to suggest an oldfashioned newspaper layout. In *Carmen Jones,* each of the four acts had its own dominant color, yellow, purple, blue, and red. On the other hand, his mingling of many differing colors in the finale of *The Great Waltz* was noteworthy for its surprising vibrancy.

Many of Short's ideas were borrowed by others, among them his frequent use of dazzling jewelry as a revue motif. The process began with a pearl-encrusted number in a *Music Box Revue.* Once the technique became passé, it ended with Short spoofing himself in *Face the Music,* which had a number literally drenched in diamonds. More novel was a mirror effect in a *Music Box Revue,* in which a dancer dressed as a Siamese jade figurine moved before a gauze-covered, mirrorlike frame; simultaneously, a similarly costumed dancer, backlit behind the gauze, did the exact opposite movements. Since so many movements were done with the dancers' backs to one another, spectators believed that a real mirror was being used. This concept grew considerably more complex in later shows, with multiple mirrors, dancers, and scenic elements.

Hassard Short directed over 50 shows, most of them musicals and revues, but it was in the latter genre that he was most distinguished. His masterful lighting and use of color, spectacle, and stage machinery put him in a special niche.

Further reading:

"Mr. Short's Long Career: Being an Account of the Doings of Broadway's Master Magician." *New York Times,* January 10, 1943.

Phillips, Henry Albert. "Hassard Short Banishes Realism When He Turns on the Lights." *New York Herald Tribune,* March 27, 1932.

Sederholm, Jack P. "The Musical Directing Career and Stagecraft Contributions of Hassard Short, 1919–1952." Unpublished Ph.D. diss. Detroit, Wayne State University, 1974.

Short, Hassard. "Staging a Spectacular Revue." *Theatre Magazine* 39 (February 1924).

Vandamm. "Hassard Short—Who Is Master of the Revue: Although He Was Never Much at Song and Dance." *Theatre Magazine* 52 (January 1931).

HERMAN SHUMLIN (1898–1979)

HERMAN SHUMLIN was born in Atwood, Colorado, where his Russian immigrant parents attempted to be ranchers. This failing, they moved frequently until settling in Newark, New Jersey. Shumlin dropped out of high school, wrote vaudeville and film reviews, became a Broadway publicist, worked for producer Jed Harris, and became a producer in 1927. After four flops he landed a hit with John Wexley's *The Last Mile* (1930).

When Shumlin found it difficult to hire a director for German author Vicki Baum's *Grand Hotel* (1930), he assumed the task himself, basing his approach on directors he had observed. Subsequently, Shumlin produced most of his own directing projects, but sometimes he worked for others. Now and then, he produced a play directed by someone else.

Grand Hotel, the first of a number of Shumlin-mounted plays with international origins, was set in Weimar Germany and interwove four subplots in a panoramic view of life in a swank hotel. Its 17-scene structure made it a paradigm for similar dramas in which a cross-section of humanity is concentrated in a single locale. An offstage jazz orchestra accentuated the changing moods. To assist the movement

among interiors (12 in all), a jackknife stage was employed, giving the production a cinematographic fluency with only the briefest waits as the sets shifted before the audience's eyes. When the overloaded lighting switchboard blew during a rehearsal, he improvised the montagelike opening "telephone" scene, in which the focus goes from one character to another, by having each actor carry a battery operated light that they could individually turn on and off.

Grand Hotel was followed by Samuel and Bella Spewack's political satire about foreign correspondents in Moscow, *Clear All Wires!* (1932), in which a large contingent of authentic Russians were hired to play the natives. Neither it nor the two flops that followed, Anthony Armstrong's *Ten Minute Alibi* (1933), a British psychological murder mystery, and Otto Indig's *The Bride of Torozko* (1934), a Hungarian comedy with Jean Arthur, made money. Then came Lillian Hellman's first play, the explosively controversial, 691-performance *The Children's Hour* (1934), concerning mendacity in a situation concerning the alleged lesbianism of two New England schoolteachers. It was the first of five Hellman plays Shumlin would stage before the pair quarreled and

Henry Hull and Eugenie Leontovich in Grand Hotel. *Directed by Herman Shumlin. (1930)* (Photo: Theater Collection, Museum of the City of New York)

parted. The play was brilliantly acted by a cast of relative unknowns (many famous actors had turned it down because of the homosexuality theme).

Richard Maibaum, Michael Wallach, and George Haight's flop farce, *Sweet Mystery of Life* (1935), used three revolves to speed its 54 scenes along. Hellman's garrulous *Days to Come* (1936), about a labor-management conflict, lasted a week. And S. N. Behrman's *Wine of Choice* (1938), one of the most trouble-riddled productions in Theater Guild annals, was an intellectual comedy of manners that had Shumlin taking over from Philip Moeller, after play doctoring had been administered by others. Shumlin found paydirt in Hellman's *The Little Foxes* (1938), a psychologically penetrating, melodramatic depiction of capitalistic greed in the postbellum South, starring Tallulah Bankhead. During the run, there was considerable acrimony between the politically conservative Bankhead and the liberal playwright and director, whom she considered "dirty Communists."

Another liberalist hit, James Thurber and Elliott Nugent's *The Male Animal* (1940), a domestic comedy about a professor's academic freedom, followed. *A Passenger to Bali* (1940), a feeble political allegory about a fugitive dictator with Walter Huston, codirected (without credit) with the star's son John, was succeeded by Emlyn Williams's semiautobiographical account of a schoolteacher's tribulations in a Welsh coal-mining village, *The Corn Is Green* (1940). It

restored the sagging career of Ethel Barrymore. Shumlin was replaced by Elmer Rice during rehearsals of Behrman's *The Talley Method* (1941) but rebounded with Hellman's *Watch on the Rhine* (1941), one of the best antifascist dramas of the day, with Paul Lukas in a major role. Shumlin also directed the film, one of only two movies he made. Frances Goodrich and Albert Hackett's southern folk comedy *The Great Big Doorstep* (1942) failed, but another Hellman hit, *The Searching Wind* (1944), about a diplomat's lack of antifascist commitment, helped make the 1938–1944 period Shumlin's most impressive.

From mid-1944 he encountered a decade-long slide, with often promising but always unfulfilled dramas. Desiring to stay in the race, Shumlin compromised on the quality of his selections. The decade was completed with Kenneth White's *The Visitor* (1944), a psychological melodrama; Luther Davis's *Kiss Them for Me* (1945), a comedy about servicemen on leave that provided Judy Holliday's outstanding debut; Robert Ardrey's *Jeb* (1946), starring Ossie Davis as a black serviceman confronted by postwar racism; and Dalton Trumbo's *The Biggest Thief in Town* (1949), transformed from a message play to a farce during its pre-Broadway tryout.

The fifties began with five unsuccessful plays, the first from Scotland and the others from England. These were James Bridie's *Daphne Laureola* (1950), with Edith Evans; Charlotte Hastings's *The High Ground* (1951); Aimee Stuart's *Lace on Her Petticoat* (1951); Roger MacDougall and Otis Bigelow's *To Dorothy, a Son* (1951), with Glynis Johns; and Enid Bagnold's *Gertie* (1952). Shumlin then directed Olivia de Havilland in a revival of George Bernard Shaw's *Candida* (1952); Alfred Drake in Drake and Edward Eager's *The Gambler* (1952); and Lee Grant in Theodore Reeves's *Wedding Breakfast* (1954).

Shumlin climbed back with Jerome Lawrence and Robert E. Lee's large-cast courtroom drama about the Scopes "monkey trial," *Inherit the Wind* (1955), a saga that reclaimed Paul Muni for Broadway in a role based on lawyer Clarence Darrow. The play, intended as a defense of freedom of thought at a time when McCarthy's communist witchhunts were still fresh in people's minds, originally had been staged by Margo Jones in Dallas.

Shumlin's subsequent efforts included a limited-engagement revival of Marc Blitzstein's opera version of *The Little Foxes*, *Regina* (1958); Howard Lindsay and Russel Crouse's basketball comedy, *Tall Story* (1959); Lawrence and Lee's *Only in America* (1959), based on Harry Golden's book; James Costigan's

Little Moon of Alban (1960), with Julie Harris; Leonard Spigelglass's *Dear Me, the Sky Is Falling* (1963) with Gertrude Berg as a Jewish matriarch who wields Freud as a weapon; Robert Thom's *Bicycle Ride to Nevada* (1963), starring Franchot Tone as Sinclair Lewis; *The Deputy* (1964), Rolf Hochhuth's sharply debated German docudrama condemning Pope Pius XII (Emlyn Williams) for failing to save the Jews during World War II; Shumlin's own play, *Spofford* (1967), with Melvyn Douglas as a retired chicken farmer confronting a nouveau riche family; another Hochhuth docudrama, *Soldiers* (1968), which accused Winston Churchill of political misdeeds during World War II, and which was banned in England; and Off-Broadway's *Transfers* (1970). Of these, the most successful were the artistically questionable but politically sensationalistic *The Deputy* (316 performances) and *Spofford* (202).

Shumlin staged more comedies than dramas, but his renown stems from the latter, especially those with melodramatic tendencies. Many productions had progressive or antireactionary themes; finding such plays in the postwar years became increasingly difficult because of conservative pressures. *The Deputy* attracted hate mail and aroused opponents—many shouting anti-Semitic remarks—to picket outside the theater, as they had in European productions. The choice to stage this play was an act of bravery.

He worked closely with authors in order to clarify and unify themes and structures. A Shumlin script was usually heavily edited; his dramaturgical suggestions were often responsible for crucial improvements. Sometimes he was accused of going too far, as when he pared Hochhuth's lengthy *The Deputy* down to Broadway proportions, lopping off important scenes and speeches. He had to work with Hochhuth by mail, and was upset by the latter's diffident responses. But his ideas on how to provide Henry Drummond (the Darrow character) in *Inherit the Wind* with thematically meaningful last-act material after he no longer had any important function to fulfill resolved the play's ambiguous conclusion and helped forge its success. He cut the opening scene as being simplistic, but the authors restored it to the published version.

Shumlin believed firmly in "invisible" direction. His primary purpose was to serve the play and to prevent any single performance or his own contribution from inserting anything distracting. He was a slow and meticulous craftsman, taking enormous pains, especially with his casting. When he read a play, he formed a mental image of all the roles and

then sought to find precisely those who fit the image, making adjustments as he encountered actor after actor. Whenever possible, he had the playwright at his side throughout, from casting through rehearsals, to see if his opinions and the writer's matched. When he was interested in a famous actor with whose work he was familiar, he would insist on an audition; lesser actors with whom he had worked were often cast without a reading.

A major weakness was Shumlin's frail visual imagination and inability to communicate with designers. He often found himself with problems related to his poor understanding of models and plans. His usual preference was for single-interior sets, and he generally used conventional realistic scenery. *The Deputy*'s non-realistic, open stage setting, capable of imaginatively conjuring up multiple locales, was a notable exception. His lighting frequently suffered from an overriding desire for shadowless illumination. But he showed an inordinate interest in the exact size of scenic elements, and even had Barrymore's backside measured to provide her with a correctly proportioned chair.

He knew precisely what he wanted in terms of physical props and had his staff scour the city to find what he was after. In one instance, he required a particular type of bowl. When a large number of possibilities were collected, they were lined up on the stage for him to ponder, just as if he were casting an actor. In *Inherit the Wind* he actually borrowed an ancient rock specimen from a museum for use in the trial scene.

Several Shumlin productions used crowds of extras. He made it his business to give all crowd members actual dialogue rather than have them make "crowd noises." For *Inherit the Wind* he had the authors give each extra a name as well as words to say.

He typically commenced by having the cast read the play through for two days, at least twice each day. These were his major opportunities to discuss the drama and to ask questions of the actors. Normally, he did not lecture, but when he came to direct such historically based plays as *Inherit the Wind* and *The Deputy*, he provided lengthy, erudite discussions of the background, although the play itself was discussed peripherally, if at all. As rehearsals progressed, he continued to edit and revise, although Hellman made it a practice to provide a script that required very little further alteration.

Shumlin's methodical technique meant a very slow progress as he liked to go over and over each step before moving along. He was amazed when it took him nine days to do the basic staging of *The Little Foxes* because this process usually lasted several weeks.

The acting in Shumlin's productions was known for its high quality. He took great pains with his actors, but he leaned increasingly toward being an autocratic pedagogue. At his best, during his early years, he worked by suggestion, giving enough general background for the actor to provide the details. But he grew increasingly mechanical. He was prone to demonstrating blocking, gestures, and readings. Once he had achieved a goal, he would freeze it. Many of his actors resented being treated as robots or chess pieces. A perfectionist, he could be belligerently dictatorial, unable to accept any other point of view than his own. Yet, he could also be appealingly kind and pleasant.

When dealing with difficult stars, he insisted on a 100 percent rehearsal contribution. He knew just what to say to reach such players. According to Maurice Zolotow, when Bankhead was holding back in *The Little Foxes,* he said to her,

Listen, Tallulah, . . . when you're out on the stage and a certain power comes out of you, you hypnotize people. If I don't criticize you any more, I know that on opening night you'll do it on instinct and nerve. I want you to bury Tallulah in Regina Giddens. Then you'll know why you do the things you do and you'll be sensational on opening night and every other night.

Bankhead agreed that was a habitual problem and that post-opening performances were always painful.

"From then on during rehearsal, she would point at Shumlin and say: 'There sits teacher.' "

Shumlin discovered on reading Konstantin Stanislavsky's *My Life in Art* that the Russian expressed ideas in which he already believed. Yet, after World War II, when the Americanized version of Stanislavsky (the Method) was de rigueur, Shumlin disparaged it for its inartistic tendencies, at least as misused by many actors.

For 40 years, Herman Shumlin was one of Broadway's key figures. With two exceptions, he did only new works, but his selections represented some of the most significant works of the day. *Grand Hotel, The Children's Hour, The Little Foxes, Watch on the Rhine, The Male Animal, The Corn Is Green, Inherit the Wind,* and *The Deputy* remain viable theater pieces. He was bold enough to use mainstream theater to advance his liberalism, demonstrating that social concerns and entertainment are not incompatible.

Further reading:

Bagnold, Enid. "The Flop." *Atlantic Monthly* (October 1952).

Goldsmith, Ted. "The Man Behind *Grand Hotel*— Herman Shumlin." *Theatre Magazine* 52 (March 1931).

Schumach, Murray. "Monkey Trial Staged." *New York Times,* April 17, 1955.

Also: Zolotow, *No People Like Show People.*

KONSTANTIN STANISLAVSKY (1863–1938)

KONSTANTIN STANISLAVSKY (*né* Konstantin Sergeyevich Alexeyev), whose father was a wealthy manufacturer and mother the daughter of a French actress, was born near Moscow, to which the family soon moved. He acted with his siblings and acquaintances—the Alexeyev Circle—in amateur theatricals staged in well-equipped small theaters at the family's homes. He began directing them at 18, playing the leading roles himself. Although his well-rehearsed shows were mainly vaudevilles and operettas, he began trying to make his actors as lifelike as possible.

The tall and handsome Stanislavsky acted in other amateur companies too. Four years later, he co-founded the Society of Art and Literature, where plays were produced on a high artistic level. One

of his triumphs was Alexey Tolstoy's *The Fruits of Enlightenment* (1891) in which he handled large groups and created a clear picture of class distinctions, which he accomplished by casting according to actors' actual class backgrounds. By this time, he had fallen heavily under the influence of the duke of Saxe-Meiningen's company. Stanislavsky emulated their disciplined rehearsals, treating his amateurs as professionals, and insisting on artistic dedication and ethical behavior. Among other major successes were Karl Gutzkow's *Uriel Acosta* (1895); Emile Erckmann and Pierre Alexander Chatrian's *The Polish Jew* (1896); Shakespeare's *Othello* (1896), *Much Ado About Nothing* (1897) and *Twelfth Night* (1897); and Gerhart Hauptmann's *The Sunken Bell* (1898). Each revealed an important development in his art, from

Konstantin Stanislavsky. (Photo: Theater Collection, Brooklyn College)

the use of crowds to the then unusual employment of three-dimensional scenery.

In 1898, Stanislavsky and Vladimir Nemirovich-Danchenko cofounded the Moscow Art Theater (MAT), created as an object lesson in high artistic standards. Their original agreement that Nemirovich-Danchenko would see to business and literary matters and Stanislavsky to those of production and direction lasted for years despite some overlapping. Nemirovich-Danchenko staged many plays, a considerable number (until 1907) in collaboration with Stanislavsky, with whom a system of sharing responsibility was worked out. Relations between them later became strained but they made their theater one of the world's best.

The MAT used the repertory system, changing bills often, and emphasized ensemble over stars. Devotion to art came before devotion to self. Many of the better productions survived for years, often with the original actors. The first company was composed of Nemirovich-Danchenko's best former

students and a corps of older provincial veterans. Several future greats were included, among them Olga Knipper (later, Anton Chekhov's wife) and Ivan Moskvin, with Vasily Kachalov joining in 1901.

To prepare for their first season, the company rehearsed on a farm near Moscow. All of the actors participated in nonperformance chores, such as sewing and cleaning, and strict decorum was maintained. Daily rehearsals were from 11:00 A.M. to 5:00 P.M. and 8:00 to 11:00 P.M. When Stanislavsky's insistence on stripping away artificiality irked those who were not prepared to give up their old methods, he resorted to dictatorial measures.

Decor was exhaustively researched, especially for Tolstoy's *Tsar Fyodor Ivanovich,* and special trips were made to purchase authentic materials and props. Scenery was solidly built and three-dimensional wherever possible. Offstage rooms—seen through windows and doors—were constructed so that life beyond the set could be suggested, and the illusion of real life was furthered by such devices as occasionally facing a chair upstage.

The MAT was first housed in the Hermitage Theater, but in 1902 they moved to the renovated, excellently equipped Omon Theater. They opened in 1898, with *Tsar Fyodor,* making the company an instant sensation because of its painstaking realism, honesty, and ensemble in which even walk-ons were individualized. The actors' adherence to Stanislavsky's belief that they must visualize an imaginary fourth wall between the stage and auditorium made them seem to be living the lives of their characters.

The plays that followed were not able to sustain enthusiasm, and business did not revive until Chekhov's *The Sea Gull,* which had failed in its 1896 St. Petersburg premiere but whose present success helped make the MAT famous, and led it to employ a sea gull as its symbol. Stanislavsky doubted the play's quality at first because it seemed untheatrical, but he soon became convinced of its greatness. He prepared a promptbook in which—in addition to detailed drawings—every move and vocal inflection was described. For most of the 26 rehearsals (many, by period standards), Nemirovich-Danchenko directed the actors according to Stanislavsky's notes. The result was a lyrically sensitive, yet often funny production filled with lifelike performances. Chekhov was not comfortable with the meticulous naturalism, including numerous sound effects to evoke the world offstage. In his subsequent Chekhov stagings (*Uncle Vanya* in 1899; *The Three Sisters* in 1901; and *The Cherry Orchard* in 1904), Stanislavsky toned down the naturalism and developed a more discriminating technique termed "selective" or "spiritual realism," focusing on the orchestration of moods, rhythm, sounds, and relationships so as to place internal over external values. He later claimed that his early naturalism was a mask to cover the actors' failings. Another source of irritation was his insistence that the plays were tragic and Chekhov's that they were comedies, although Stanislavsky eventually modified his approach. To a great extent, it was through his work on Chekhov's characters that Stanislavsky developed his famous acting system.

In addition to the epochal Chekhov work, Stanislavsky worked with Nemirovich-Danchenko' on Carlo Goldoni and various Russians, including Maxim Gorky, but the greatest frequency was accorded the plays of Ibsen and Hauptmann. Gorky's greatest contribution was *The Lower Depths* (1902), given a famous production whose naturalism was partly inspired by a company trip to a flop house. First-hand study of the ragged denizens led Stanislavsky to write a "biography" of each of the characters.

He tried to break away from realism with stylized productions of such symbolic works as Knut Hamsun's *The Drama of Life* (1907), Leonid Andreyev's *The Life of Man*, and Maurice Maeterlinck's *The Blue Bird* (1908, codirected with Leopold Sulerjitsky). In these he introduced many novel and interesting staging ideas. No matter how abstract the characters, he sought to conceive them psychologically in terms of an inner life. However, he did not find a fruitful blend of carefully motivated acting and theatricalist staging until he did *The Blue Bird*, which revealed Maeterlinck's fantasy world as seen through a child's eyes.

Stanislavsky returned to realism with Ivan Turgenev's *A Month in the Country* (1909), in which the psychological nuances were perfectly conveyed, helped partly by a scheme that pared down the number of available props so that communication could stem from facial and vocal suggestions. Stanislavsky got his cast to play the subtext with excellent results. For the first time he broke a script into segments called units or beats; he also abandoned his preplanned promptbook.

Since 1906, Stanislavsky had been preoccupied with discovering a systematic approach to helping the actor achieve the "creative state." This would allow him to focus totally on being so internally and externally in character, with each action triggered by a specific motivation, that he practically lived his role. Stanislavsky had to overcome considerable

Gorky's The Lower Depths. *Directed by Konstantin Stanislavsky and Vladimir Nemirovich-Danchenko. (1902) Stanislavsky is reclining on the table.* (Photo: Theater Collection, Brooklyn College)

resistance before his system was accepted by the MAT. Each play he directed between 1906 and 1917 was a test of some aspect of his ideas. These included works by Alexander Griboyedov, Leo Tolstoy, Molière, and others, including the famous collaboration with Gordon Craig on *Hamlet* (1911; see the Craig entry). In 1912, Stanislavsky founded the First Studio of the MAT to teach his system to younger actors. Other studios were later founded.

After the Russian Revolution, the MAT survived, although it was criticized by some as reactionary. It was forced to introduce a correct political line into its work, such as when Stanislavsky staged Lord Byron's *Cain* (1923) with Lucifer as a radical, God a conservative, and Cain a Bolshevik, or when he directed Vsevelod Ivanov's propagandistic Soviet drama, *Armored Train 14-69* (1927). During these years, the MAT and Stanislavsky toured America, leaving an especially indelible mark on the New York theater. Stanislavsky's postrevolutionary activity included Shakespeare, Nikolai Gogol, Alexander Ostrovsky, Marcel Pagnol, Mikhail Bulgakov, Pierre de Beaumarchais, Adolph d'Ennery and Eugène Cormon, L. M. Leonov, Moliére (*Tartuffe* was the last play he worked on), and others, and there were also various operas. After 1928, when he suffered a heart attack and had to stop acting, his ideas were often carried out by associates, with his duties being supervisory. He appeared sporadically at rehearsals, often shredding what he saw. Sometimes, the actors accommodated his frailty by working with him at his home.

Stanislavsky's work frequently revealed deep insights. He made striking advances in rhythmical acting in *Cain,* explored the exaggerated "grotesque" style in Gogol's *The Inspector-General* (1921), and offered a spectacular revival of Beaumarchais's *The Marriage of Figaro* (1927). The latter marked a major advance in his theoretical thinking in its emphasis on creating true emotion out of playing the "given circumstances" rather than concentrating on feelings as per his earlier "emotion memory" method.

Although usually considered naturalistic, Stanislavsky was eclectic and ranged from archaeologically accurate history plays to lyrical, psychologically subtle tragicomedies to rollicking satire to phantasmagoric symbolism, with excursions into other styles, including leftwing propaganda (which he disliked). He preferred plays with humanistic concerns and was more attuned to character perception than to intellectual content.

His rehearsal techniques continued to develop, especially with the lengthy periods the MAT increasingly allowed (300 rehearsals for *The Marriage of Figaro*). He refused to open unless satisfied. He demanded absolute cleanliness in the rehearsal room, with nothing permitted to distract him. Rehearsals were carefully planned to waste as little time as possible. When visiting a subordinate's rehearsals, Stanislavsky would spend hours working with an actor to achieve a result that he considered sincere. He worked closely with his designers, having sketches and models frequently redone until they were acceptable. He made his own preliminary sketches of costumes and sets before having them formally designed.

Throughout most of his career (until 1934), he began with analytical "at table" rehearsals, but he harbored doubts about the method, which was actually much more appreciated by his literary-minded partner. Whereas Stanislavsky's original approach had been autocratic, with unified productions achieved by imposing specific conceptions on every actor and even demonstrating results (which he never completely abandoned), he ultimately came to trust the actor's creativity, abandoned preplanning, and employed scene-related improvisation. He

sought to stimulate truthful behavior by, for example, having an actress playing a blind girl search for him in the dark. Or he might have the actors try to communicate using only their eyes until it became impossible not to use words expressively.

Other techniques were designed to discover the subtext or "inner monologue," as when the actors would speak both the text and the subtext, followed by the mere whispering of the subtext, and then no subtextual speech at all. Once the subtext was grasped the actor had to consider it in terms of specific objectives, with the smaller objectives linked to a "superobjective."

Actors had to know their characters' biographies so they could place their choices in the right context. Stanislavsky interrogated the actor to insure an appropriate response in terms of what the actor would do if he was the character in the play's circumstances. If the actor could not satisfy this search for truth, the director would declare, "I don't believe it."

Visitors were permitted only when the actors felt secure; otherwise, extreme privacy was maintained. Every effort was made to create harmony, and egotistical outbursts were frowned on. But Stanislavsky had a terrific temper. Nor was he averse to using his anger to provoke an appropriate emotional response. His standards often made players uncomfortable in his presence.

Although he was a great director, Stanislavsky is best known for his acting system, which was an organic outgrowth of his practical work. It would be difficult to find a major actor or director who has not, in some way, been affected by Stanislavsky's theories, even if only to rebel against them. He was never complacent about his ideas and always sought to improve them by moving in new directions, which is partly responsible for his having been misunderstood by those familiar with only one facet of his thinking.

Further reading:

Benedetti, Jean. *Stanislavsky: A Biography.* London: Routledge, 1988.

Gorchakov, Nikolai M. *Stanislavsky Directs.* Translated by Miriam Goldina. New York: Grosset and Dunlap, 1954.

Magarshack, David. *Stanislavsky, A Life.* New York: Chanticleer Press, 1951.

Stanislavski, Constantin. *My Life in Art.* Translated by J. J. Robbins. Boston: Little, Brown, 1924.

Toporkov, Vasily Osopivich. *Stanislavski in Rehearsal,*

The Final Years. Translated by Christine Edwards. New York: Theatre Arts Books, 1979.
Also: Braun, *The Director and the Stage;* Jones, *Great Directors at Work;* Leiter, *From Stanislavsky to Barrault.*

`Note: Routledge is presently preparing the publication of The Collected Works of Stanislavsky, a multivolume series that will appear between 1994 and 1998.

PETER STEIN (1937–   )

PETER STEIN was born in Berlin, Germany, the son of a senior industrial scientist. After studying art and literature at Munich University, he began his career as a dramaturge and then "assistant director" at the Munich Kammerspiele. His directorial debut was Edward Bond's controversial *Saved* (1967).

Stein's first classic was Friedrich Schiller's *Love and Intrigue* (1967), in Bremen. It began his practice of appropriating the classics for their contemporary relevance while respecting their original world. Stein returned to the Kammerspiele for Bertolt Brecht's *In the Jungle of Cities* (1968), given a stripped-down

Peter Stein directing Jutta Lampe (r) in Phaedra. *(1987)*
(Photo: Ruth Walz)

look by Karl-Ernest Hermann, Stein's most frequent designer.

The Kammerspiele also housed Stein's coproduction (with Wolfgang Schwiedrzik) of Peter Weiss's anti-American agitprop, *Vietnam-Discourse* (1968), closed quickly because of a dispute over the cast's requesting audience contributions for the Vietcong. This activism contrasted with the parodistic production, intended to satirize the uselessness of such political theater. The resistence it met after moving to the socialist-slanted Schaubühne am Halleschen Ufer led to its cancellation.

Stein's aesthetic basis, which depends on combining psychologically realistic acting with what he calls "*plakativ*" (posterlike) acting because of its expressive clarity, was formed by the late sixties. He aims for emotional involvement as well as a larger-than-life, critical style suggestive of Brechtian performance, including—when appropriate—"quoting" the characters to make their social position apparent. The relative proportions of one or the other types of acting vary according to the piece and what he and the actors deem suitable to express content. Music often heightens the acting, and crowd scenes may be choreographic.

In Bremen, Stein did a controversial version of Johann Wolfgang von Goethe's *Torquato Tasso* (1969), developed in collaborative rehearsals. Its relevance stemmed from its concern with the artist's place in society. Among Stein's "improvements" was the creation of a prologue and "interludes" in which, through the collagelike presentation of textual passages, the characters were introduced. Stein broke the linear progression of the plot into an episodic, epic-theater montage designed to invite critical thinking about Tasso's treatment. Each scene had a Brechtian title. The period was shifted from Renaissance Italy to Goethe's Weimar to underline the play's concern with the personal situation of Goethe himself. On the open setting's grass-colored carpet, only two or three pieces of furniture were placed; transparent screens surrounded the action, lit by undimmed white light. Goethe's poetically elevated lines were said conversationally, forcing the audience to recognize the dissonance between content and form. The actors conveyed a critical awareness of their roles' social dimensions. In the intermissions they read their own comments relating to the artist's alienation in society.

Stein's next three stagings were at the Zurich Schauspielhaus, where he offered works by Edward Bond, Sean O'Casey (codirected), and Thomas Middleton and William Rowley. By now he had his own ensemble, a group including Jutta Lampe, Bruno Ganz, Edith Clever, and Michael König. Most remained for his great productions at Berlin's Schaubühne, which he joined in 1970. He sought to put his Marxist beliefs to work in the creation of a communal company. A workable system was slowly developed in which participation in major decisions, including play choice, casting, concept, and design, was shared by the ensemble. The theater eventually achieved a high level of subsidy. Despite his strong antibourgeois politics, Stein accepted a subvention that allowed him to produce sumptuous productions. Better such money should be spent on theater, he reasoned, than on jet fighters. At the Schaubühne Stein produced only four plays a year (most rivals did 12).

Stein's first new production with his troupe was Brecht's "teaching drama" of the pre-Russian Revolution days, *The Mother* (1970), codirected with two others. It began Stein's practice of rearranging the architectural plan of the proscenium-style Schaubühne to satisfy his requirements. The audience sat around three sides of a thrust to enhance their dispassionate assessment of the work, a goal fostered by uniform white lighting.

Among the most important of Stein's other seventies stagings was Henrik Ibsen's *Peer Gynt* (1971). It represented his decision to stage plays for a bourgeois public after failing to attract a proletarian audience via political plays. He felt he could better serve his antibourgeois ideas by expressing them through Marxist views of traditional drama, a belief that upset left-wing critics who desired a more activist stance.

Peer Gynt's staging lasted six and a half hours over two evenings. The interpretation was an attack on bourgeois individualism, but the play retained a story-book quality. The grotesquely masked trolls, symbolic of the *petite bourgeoisie*, wore ill-fitting Victorian garments. Props, such as a stuffed horse on wheels, were theatrical quotations of what they represented. A similar effect was created by the acting, which, apart from a portion played as theater of cruelty, embodied the characters and commented on them. Titles and events were announced over a

loudspeaker. Peer was played consecutively by six actors, each taking over from his predecessor by simply assuming the position of the actor being replaced. Michael Patterson wrote that this was intended to "reinforce the critique of the individual and demonstrate how the central figure was conditioned by the circumstances of his life." A spectacular environment of multiple locales—some of which hid further locales revealed as needed—occupied the main stage and the rectangular orchestra area, with the audience seated on raised benches along the two side walls.

Each of Stein's impressive 1970s productions expanded his eclecticism, as in Vsevolod Vishnevsky's *The Optimistic Tragedy* (1972); Heinrich von Kleist's *The Prince of Homburg* (1972); Eugène Labiche's *The Piggy Bank* (1973); *Antiquity Project I* (1974), a company-developed presentation of ritualistic exercises inspired by ancient Greek theater, done as preparation for Klaus-Michael Grüber's staging of Euripides' *The Bacchae;* a two-evening, museumlike collage inspired by Shakespeare and his times, *Shakespeare's Memory* (1976), done as preparation for *As You Like It* (1977); a considerably adapted version of Gorky's *Summerfolk* (1974), acted in the mode of psychological realism, with cinematic touches, a prisonlike environment of real trees, and all the characters onstage throughout to emphasize the class criticism; and innovative versions of contemporary plays by Botho Strauss (1978) and Peter Handke (1974).

Stein's inventiveness continued in the 1980s, although some of his interpretations revealed cynicism regarding social change. In 1985, he resigned as Schaubühne head, but returned periodically while freelancing elsewhere. The decade began with a nine-hour, masked production of Aeschylus' *The Oresteia* (1980), given in a space recreating Greek architectural conditions, but with the audience on the floor. Jean Genet's *The Blacks* (1984) was staged—apart from the use of blackfaced white actors—in accordance with most of the playwright's requirements but also with outstanding new ideas—including an ending in which a giant map of Africa appeared with the independent nations shown in red as ecstatic African dancing replaced Genet's call for Mozart. In addition to recent plays by writers such as Strauss and Nigel Williams, he staged more Shakespeare, outstandingly realistic versions of three major Chekhovs, a physically arresting, thematically problematic version of Eugene O'Neill's *The Hairy Ape* (1986), and a bold realization of Jean Racine's *Phaedra* (1987).

Most recently, Stein has been preoccupied with operas at home and abroad. Theaterwise, his major work has been in Salzburg, where he is now director of theater for the annual month-long festival, whose theater component he has been working to restore to the level enjoyed there by opera; he hopes to make Salzburg the European center for the finest German-language productions. (From 1990 to 1993, largely because of Stein's efforts, the number of nonmusical theater seats rose from 34,000 to 80,000.) Employing the city's historical Riding School, made famous by Reinhardt's outdoor stagings of *Faust,* he staged a monumental *Julius Caesar* (1992), in which the massive crowd scenes made the strongest impression. It was followed in 1993 by his staging of the world premiere of Botho Strauss's *Equilibrium,* starring Jutta Lampe, with a revival of *Antony and Cleopatra* scheduled for 1994. Stein has been trying to mount an immense production of Goethe's *Faust* at the Schaubühne, but costs have prevented its full realization. Instead, he provided a five-evenings' long staged reading of the play's entire second half at Salzburg in 1993.

The prodigious, four-and-a-half-hour *As You Like It* was representative. Like several other Stein works, it was staged outside the Schaubühne, in this case a huge film studio in Spandau. (In 1981, a modernistic and remarkably adaptable Schaubühne on Berlin's Lehniner Platz replaced the original). Parts of the script were edited to suggest filmic cross-cutting, as actors in one scene froze after speaking a few lines and actors in another began. The court scenes were in a high-ceilinged room, painted a glacial blue-white with the Elizabethan-garbed performers mostly on high platforms that forced the crowded, standing audience to look up at them and move to where the focus was. A unique passageway with walls dripping water and filled with Elizabethan images led from the icy court to a vast studio in which a monumental forest, replete with real trees, a pond, a farmstead, bird song, and floral scent had been constructed; Robinson Crusoe and Robin Hood were introduced as characters. Bleacher-seated spectators surrounded it on three sides and the performers, dressed in costumes of no particular period, acted before, behind, amid, and above them. This pastoral Utopia—pervaded by a liberating aura of eroticism—was disturbed by the violent, extratextual arrival of the usurping duke's court, who immediately fell under the forest's spell. However, the bucolic world was an illusory retreat from reality and the characters eventually returned to civilization's harshness, which they would strive to reform.

Stein approaches a play with laser precision, mining every word for its significance. In his search for a Marxist perspective he reshapes the work to meet his needs. There is no predetermined concept, the approach growing from discussions and experiments with his actors. He chooses mainly established plays, only rarely doing a premiere. His choices are often dictated by a desire to confront problems encountered on a previous work.

Stein's actors do extensive research and read relevant literature; at one point they even prepared papers on specific topics for group discussion. Much of the research is reflected in the lavish programs. For *The Optimistic Tragedy,* preparation included watching Soviet movies about the historical circumstances of the Revolution as well as a TV version of the play, examining period illustrations (some of them reflected in the production), and plowing through a reading list totalling 63 titles. For some productions the ensemble visited foreign sites related to the action. The amount of research decreased, however, after dissatisfaction with such academic labors arose.

Before the 1980s, Stein usually made extensive revisions to make classics conform with his Marxist interpretations. As much as 25% might be eliminated (as in *Torquato Tasso*), characters cut, and material rearranged. Stein was noted for his changes in the endings, designed to emphasize themes through ironic twists, as when the prince of Homburg was borne off by fellow officers in the form of a life-sized puppet that suggested his subordination to the state. In the 1980s, Stein displayed greater fidelity to antique texts. His approach to new plays has been more respectful because he thinks that there will be few opportunities for audiences to become familiar with them in other productions.

Casting at the Schaubühne was a company concern, but believing that casting cannot be completely democratic, Stein intervened when choices disturbed him. Actors love the fastidiousness with which he observes and comments on their work. He believes in the actor's primacy. Despite the attention he gives to technical effects and decor, these are of secondary importance. His rehearsal attitude is vivacious; he can be both obscene and gentle from one moment to the other, and is admired for his modesty. He allows actors to show him what they can do, followed by his observations on their work. A man of great patience, Stein never bullies and only gets irritable when an actor is inept or not serious. He ignores improvisations and games; when a difficulty arises, he may suggest an external approach to finding an internal response or even give a rough demonstration. Normally, blocking is the actor's responsibility, with Stein making suggestions to enhance the actor's choices. An impressive diagnostician, he can quickly discern the minutest problem before collaborating on a solution. The reasons for everything performed, he insists, must be perfectly clear.

Stein eschews run-throughs until late in the schedule, just before the opening, beginning them only when every detail has been polished. For the actor, the effect is more like that of making a movie in fragments than putting on a continuous drama.

In a nation recognized for the high standards of its theatrical art and the genius of its régisseurs, Stein stands at the top. He brings a beacon of aesthetic and intellectual clarity to all he does and demonstrates the virtues of a collaborative methodology with an ensemble of dedicated artists.

Further reading:

Bradby, David. "Blacking Up—Three Productions by Peter Stein." In *A Radical Stage: Theatre in Germany in the 1970s and 1980s.* Edited by W. G. Sebald. Oxford, England: Berg, 1988.

Lackner, Peter. "Peter Stein." *The Drama Review* 21 (June 1977).

Patterson, Michael. *Peter Stein, Germany's Leading Theatre Director.* Cambridge, England: Cambridge University Press, 1981.

Zipes, Jack. "The Irresistible Rise of the Schaubühne am Halleschen Ufer: A Retrospective of the West Berlin Theatre Collective." *Theatre* 9 (Fall 1977).

Also: Bradby and Williams, *Directors' Theater.*

GIORGIO STREHLER (1921–   )

GIORGIO STREHLER was born in Barcola, near Trieste, Italy. His Austrian father died when he was three and he was raised by his Franco-Slovenian mother, a violinist. He studied acting at Milan's Accademia dei Filodrammatici; acted with a traveling company; entered law school; was drafted; made his directorial bow with Luigi Pirandello one-acts for a Milanese group in 1943; worked for the Italian Resistance; and founded an antifascist group in Switzerland, directing them in plays by T. S. Eliot and Albert Camus. When peace came, he wrote drama criticism and staged 10 productions in Milan in two years.

In 1947, he and Paolo Grassi cofounded Milan's 523-seat (later, 650) "people's theater," the Piccolo Teatro, which revolutionized the moribund native stage. It opened with Strehler's production of Maxim Gorky's *The Lower Depths.* Italy's first subsidized, permanent theater, it hoped to attract those who never previously attended plays. Strehler's challenging productions, however, appeal to what he calls a "popular elite."

Following conflicts with Milan's bureaucracy, he left the Piccolo to run Italy's first professional theater collective, the Gruppo Teatro e Azione, from 1968 to 1972, before returning, as the Piccolo's sole leader. From 1983 to 1989, Strehler ran the Théâtre de l'Europe at Paris's Odéon Théâtre, where—attempting to promote European cultural unity—he showcased the best Continental productions along with his own work. He remained active in Milan,

where he has been striving to overcome bureaucratic roadblocks to build a European theater center, the Città del Teatro. The construction of what is now called the "Gran Piccolo" began in 1982, but the money appropriated by the Socialist city government dried up and in 1993 the theater sat incomplete, wrapped in loose green netting and scaffolding, its architect recently dismissed.

Strehler's half-century of directing encompasses over 250 plays and operas, several of them done more than once, always freshly. During his early years he was prolific, but since the sixties he has generally concentrated on one new production each season. Despite his eclecticism, his major focuses have been Bertolt Brecht, Shakespeare, and Carlo Goldoni. Indigenous works—including premieres—also have played a part. He has been instrumental in demonstrating the forgotten values in 19th-century, bourgeois Italian theater works; has fostered the staging of native dialect dramas; and has done memorable Pirandello productions, notably *Giants in the Mountain* (1948, 1966).

Strehler has been most active with the international repertory. Representative authors include Eliot, Thornton Wilder, Samuel Beckett, and Tennessee Williams from the English-speaking theater; Gorky, Anton Chekhov, and Nikolai Gogol from the Russian; Armand Salacrou, Henri Becque, Alfred de Musset, Jean Giraudoux, Jean Genet, and Pierre Corneille from the French; Georg Büchner, Ernst Toller, Ferdinand Bruckner, Peter Weiss,

Friedrich Dürenmatt, Gotthold Lessing, and Johann Wolfgang von Goethe from the German-speaking; Henrik Ibsen and August Strindberg from the Scandinavian; Pedro Calderón de la Barca and Federico García Lorca from the Spanish; and Sophocles from the Greek. One of the most remarked-on works of the past two decades was his white-on-white, nonnaturalistic *The Cherry Orchard* (1974), staged under what one critic (quoted by Maria Nadotti) called "an immense white veil—a lyrical image of the foliage of the flowering cherry trees, and an aerial gloss for the action on stage."

In 1987, Strehler began developing a massive, several-year, multimedia project to produce his own abridged version of Goethe's *Faust*, with himself in the title role and sets by Josef Svoboda. This grand summation of the Faustian director's career was being staged, according to the *Observer*, "as a profound, metaphysical and theatrical treatise on the interconnecting natures of sensuality, magic and mortality." Strehler told Ron Jenkins, "It is a project on the rights of man." It began with the spectacular *Fragments of Part One* (1989) in the Piccolo's new 420-seat Teatro Studio and continued with *Fragments of Part Two* (1991). *Part One*—requiring two nights or one long day—revealed Mephistopheles, Faust, and Wagner dressed in black while reading their debates from lecterns. Nadotti noted its baroque theatricalism:

Mephistopheles emerges nude and spectral from a self-propelled pool hidden by a trapdoor . . . ; the witch's kitchen is a punk discotheque, where Faust is engulfed in an orgy of leather-clad or narcissistic and provocative nude bodies; God speaks through thunder, through lightning, and through [an] offstage voice . . . in an apocalyptic, tempestuous scene rent by luminous rays, fog, fumes of incense, and reverberations of sound.

For the 1992–1993 season, Strehler offered a Goldoni festival, with three productions available, to celebrate the 200th anniversary of the playwright's death. One was a seventh version of Strehler's much-vaunted staging of *Arlecchino, The Servant of Two Masters*, which he first directed in 1947. Strehler's initial fame derived from his reinvigoration of Goldoni, nine of whose plays he directed, all of them revealing the 18th-century dramatist as more complex than had been traditionally believed. The 1947 *Arlecchino* was produced with a sparkling combination of acrobatic commedia bits and human insight into the social underbelly of Goldoni's satire. The play became the centerpiece of Strehler's repertory and was shown worldwide in its various manifesta-

tions. The staging benefitted from extensive research and experimentation designed to rediscover commedia's traditions. Jenkins noted,

Its powerless hero is indefatigable in his efforts to overcome the obstacles society sets in his way. When his masters threateningly close in on him from opposite sides of the stage, it seems that nothing can save Harlequin from being beaten . . . but Strehler rescues the servant at the last moment by directing him to leap off the stage into the audience. . . . The laughing spectators are given the opportunity to participate in Harlequin's salvation by offering him refuge in their laps.

The completely new 1993 staging starred Ferrucio Soleri, who has played the title role since 1956. In it, each character apart from Arlecchino was played by from three to six actors (mainly students of Strehler's training school), thus compounding the hero's confusion as his several "masters" made demands on him. Rosette Lamont observed: "In the course of the performance, any given interpreter may be chased off the stage, pushed or pulled, and replaced by a classmate who has been studying the same role." "At the end," wrote the *New York Times*, "with the multiple characters chattering rapid-fire text in absolute synchronicity, the effect is like that of a Rossini opera finale."

Stanislavsky and Copeau were powerful, but indirect, influences on Strehler, while he actually studied under the mime Etienne Decroux; Louis Jouvet (whose 1940 theater lessons Strehler staged—with himself as Jouvet—in 1985); and Brecht, who, he told Rosette Lamont, provided him with a critical attitude by teaching him "the value of clarity and doubt." Brecht was impressed by Strehler's version of his *The Threepenny Opera* (1956 and 1973), but Strehler was no slavish Brechtolator. The first *Threepenny* moved the action from Victorian London to a mythical America—the world's new power center—in 1919, the second to a sinister pre-Depression America of the roaring twenties, with the streetsinger a top-hatted, white-faced *Cabaret*-like compère. A choice that Brecht loved because of its anticonsumerist thrust was making the stable into an abandoned garage.

Like Brecht, Strehler, a socialist trained in Marxian dialectic, approaches plays from a morally responsible, politically engaged perspective that aims to demonstrate a work's relevance to contemporary problems. Some declare that he is not so much concerned with estrangement effects as in exploring the theater's act of balancing illusion and reality, observable in his above-mentioned trilogy and his

Giulia Lazzerini (left) and Tino Carroro in The Tempest. *Directed by Giorgio Strehler. (1978)*   (Photo: Luigi Cimi-naghi)

fascination with Pirandello. His Brecht repertoire includes *The Good Woman of Setzuan* (1958 and 1981), *Schweik in the Second World War* (1961), *The Life of Galileo* (1963), and *Saint Joan of the Stockyards* (1970).

One of the first of Strehler's dozen Shakespeares was *The Tempest* (1948, 1978), first done outdoors at Florence's Boboli Gardens, where, according to Strehler (in Lamont), the effect was

> *more magical than philosophical. . . . We erected Prospero's isle in the center of a large fountain dominated by a statue of Neptune. Three meters of water separated the public from the stage. We floated a real boat upon the pool. At the end of the play, the whole island seemed to explode, as though a volcano had erupted.*

Strehler is fond of plays about magic and illusion, and even staged a so-called trilogy on the subject

including his second *Tempest*; Corneille's *The Illusion* (1985); and Eduardo de Filippo's *The Great Magic Act* (1986), a resuscitation of a little-known work about a magician. Although not about a magician, Strindberg's *The Storm* (1980) is also preoccupied with illusion.

In its emphasis on the theme of the Renaissance's failed Utopian dream—"We killed and spoiled the Calibans of America" (in Lamont)—the 1978 *Tempest* was preoccupied with metaphysical and political issues, but was also very theatrical.

The storm scene was magical, as was a tragicomic, Pierrot-like, white-veiled Ariel, who swam balletically through the air via a visible rope and pulley device, could perch on Prospero's hand or shoulder (their relationship was like that of actor and director), and, when given his freedom, lost his ability to fly and ran off through the audience. Prospero was a cross between Shakespeare and Strehler, manipulating the spectacle until the conclusion, when the obviously theatrical set was taken down to expose the brick walls of the theater, and Prospero, no longer a wizard but just another human, descended to the audience level to become one with them as he spoke his farewell.

Strehler's other Shakespeare stagings, mostly of plays rarely done in Italy, include *Richard II* (1947), *The Taming of the Shrew* (1949), *Richard III* (1950), *Henry IV* (1951), *Twelfth Night* (1951), *Macbeth* (1952), *Julius Caesar* (1953), *Coriolanus* (1957), a spectacular two-night adaptation of the three parts of *Henry VI* (1965), called *The Game of the Powerful* (which Strehler considers his greatest directorial contribution), and *King Lear* (1972). The Brechtian *Lear* was set in the abstraction of a circus ring–like set filled with a rubbery material that forced the actors to walk as if in quicksand. A half-curtain had a map on it used to divide the kingdom. Cordelia and the Fool were played by the same actress, which led to fascinating correspondences in the characters' relationships with Lear.

Strehler, who often designs his own lighting, is a master imagist whose sets—frequently designed by Luciano Damiani—are typically metaphoric. He will work on lighting a show for weeks before being happy with the atmospheric and thematic significance of his effects. Thus, wrote Odette Aslan of a Goldoni production, "With a ray of light shining directly in her eyes as she played cards, he could single out a woman whom he had placed in the least favourable position because she came from the lowest order of the social hierarchy." Each movement and grouping—even the folds of the costumes—is composed with the same painstaking care; often, images are based on paintings or photographs.

Strehler's rehearsals, open to the public, are at times that suit him; he may keep actors until late at night and go for hours without a break. Although he does extensive research, analysis, and preparation, productions remain in flux, with designers present to make changes. Design elements are employed as early as possible, so regular sessions often resemble dress rehearsals.

The handsome, white-haired Strehler, who usually dresses in black turtlenecks, is famed for his unstoppable energy; scathing, multilingual tantrums; and an authoritarianism that demands the highest standards from contributors, on- and offstage. Despite his fearsome presence and sparing use of praise, many find that working with him is liberating because of their faith in his ability to draw the best

from them. His productions are celebrated for the deep honesty and emotional power of their acting, which demonstrates a blend of Brecht and Stanislavsky.

Strehler is a detail- and perfection-obsessed director in complete command of every element, although he welcomes intelligent suggestions. He runs back and forth between auditorium and stage to move actors about, stand beside or improvise with them, perform each role, and explain or demonstrate business or line interpretations. His comments, frequently based on personal anecdotes, may be peppered with hilarious ribaldry. He might make an actor repeat a line 50 times; hollow imitation is rejected. Stagehands and technicians are shown exactly what is required of them, and a curtain might be raised and lowered endlessly to get its timing right. Because of the fundamental musicality of his work, he conducts a precisely composed performance score, using musical terms. Music is interpolated into the productions to heighten mood and guide the performances. Nothing is arbitrary and a careful explanation is offered whenever necessary.

Richard Trousdell wrote, "Consciously, he makes his listening and responding active by playing many roles, often simultaneously: teacher, genial host, clown, victim, mocker, social conscience, great man, blind idiot." An actor told Jenkins,

> Your mind is divided into three parts—concentrating on the role . . . at the same time you concentrate on him acting behind you. He is performing and penetrating you with the rhythm of his performance. It is like being possessed by his vision of the character.

Many contend that Strehler is today's most influential European director. His exceptional career has even included two stints as a political office holder. Unfortunately, despite his own anticorruption position, in 1993 he became a victim of the "clean hands" campaign to wipe out corruption in Italy. Along with associates and assorted Socialist politicians, Strehler was facing trial in Milan at the end of the year on charges that he had misappropriated $500,000 of European Community grants. The money was apparently used to rehearse his *Faust* project rather than to pay for actor training, which—claiming absolute innocence—he declared was an invaluable side product of the rehearsal process. The ruckus, which he blames on a hostile cabal, convinced him to take up temporary residence in Switzerland and to postpone plans to stage and star in his own script based on Goldoni's memoirs. Time will tell what the outcome of the scandal will be (some predict the demise of Strehler's theater), but it can by no means diminish the accomplishments of this theatrical giant.

Further reading:

Aslan, Odette. "From Giorgio Strehler to Victor Garcia." Translated by Fiona Strachan. *Modern Drama* 25 (March 1982).

Jenkins, Ron. "Master of Two Servants." *American Theatre* 5 (February 1989).

Lamont, Rosette. "Shakespeare with a Touch of Commedia dell'Arte." *New York Times*, July 22, 1984.

———. "Letter from Milano" *TheaterWeek*, April 19, 1993.

Nadotti, Maria. "Stages of Strehler." Translated by Marguerite Shore. *Artforum* 27 (September 1989–January 1990).

Sachs, Henry. "Profiles: The Storyteller." *New Yorker*, May 4, 1992.

Trousdell, Richard. "Giorgio Strehler in Rehearsal." *The Drama Review* 30 (Winter 1986).

·Note: The following appeared too late to be used for this essay: Hirst, David L. *Giorgio Strehler*. Cambridge, England: Cambridge University Press, 1993.

TADASHI SUZUKI (1939–　　)

TADASHI SUZUKI was born in the port city of Shimizu, Shizuoka Prefecture, Japan, where his father owned a lumber business. He was raised in a home in which classical Western music was as likely to be heard as traditional puppet theater chanting. At 19, planning to study political science and economics, he entered Tokyo's Waseda University, but became involved with an influential theater club, the Waseda Free Stage (WSF), which studied Konstantin Stanislavsky's methods and often staged leftist interpretations of Russian playwrights. The apolitical Suzuki, who graduated in 1964, frequently argued with fellow members.

As WSF chairman, from 1960 to 1961, he stressed artistic concerns over political ones, and staged five plays, three by Westerners Arthur Miller, Anton Chekhov, and Jean-Paul Sartre and two by WFS member, Minoru Betsuyaku, whose absurdist plays used experimental spatio-temporal techniques Suzuki appreciated.

Suzuki formed his own troupe, the Free Stage, in 1961, with Betsuyaku as resident playwright. They were part of the period's burgeoning "underground" theater movement. Suzuki sought to break away from the stultifying realism of *shingeki*, the modern, Western-influenced Japanese theater, and develop a more imaginative, nonrealistic approach. Betsuyaku's allusive, linguistically innovative plays and Suzuki's physically energetic mise-en-scène combined to create an influential blend that gained attention between 1962 and 1967, during which Suzuki staged five Betsuyaku plays, beginning with *The Elephant* (1962). Suzuki also did revivals of earlier productions and new ones, including Tennessee Williams's *A Streetcar Named Desire* (1963). In 1966, he renamed the company the Waseda Little

Theater (WLT), their first production being Betsuyaku's *Gate*. Beginning with Betsuyaku's *The Little Match Girl* (1966), the principal Suzuki-Betsuyaku success, the WLT settled down in their own 120-seat studio theater above a Tokyo coffee shop. The

Tadashi Suzuki. (Photo: SCOT)

postage stamp–size, curtainless, wingless, proscenium-style stage used entrances down a central aisle. Suzuki, avoiding most scenic devices, made the actors as physically and vocally expressive as possible. His early style was likened to the "poor theater" of Jerzy Grotowski.

Suzuki began to focus on the evolution of a groundbreaking acting method. He staged studio versions of several of his own adaptations of Japanese fables and seminal new plays by leading avant-gardists Makoto Satō and Jurō Kara.

Suzuki wanted to replace the text-based *shingeki* with an actor-centered theater. A well-published theorist whose ideas have undergone various modifications, Suzuki came to believe in the late sixties that acting signified the actor's subjective encounter with and expression of his own self, not the interpretation of another's text. The actor finds his focus in the objectification of his own emotional and physical being, not an outside role. Under the influence of existential philosophy, Suzuki explained the actor's behavior as an affirmation of self via the performer's encounter with the spectator or "other." Both the spectator and the actor discover their shared humanity—a humanity burdened by desolation and misery—through this confrontation.

The first major example of his evolving style was his own *And Then, and Then, What Then* (1968), a satire of a popular *kabuki* play, designed to explore non-Stanislavskian methods, including the use of explanatory placards. *Kabuki*, a powerful influence, played a crucial role in his next seven works.

At the time, Suzuki's company did a considerable amount of experimentation with improvisation, often using materials derived from classical and modern Western plays and from *kabuki*, as well as from nondramatic literature. The improvisations aimed to express not what the writers intended in their dialogue, but what the actors themselves—on a prelogical, subconscious level—connected to in the words. Thus the words—and the ways the actors physicalized them—took on new and unexpected meanings in the process. Suzuki, who believed that directing was the act of aiding actors to express a personal relationship to their roles by finding ways to tap their creative souls, took the results of these exercises and, using a method borrowed from the surrealists called *dépaysement* (dislocation), composed them into performable dramatic collages. The first was *The Folkloric Analysis of the Lower Depths* (1968), in which the denizens of Maxim Gorky's *The Lower Depths* were asylum inmates acting out dramatic scenes for their own amusement. The actor

took precedence over the script, so multiple acting approaches were on view.

More impressive was *On the Dramatic Passions I* (1969), a collage of famous scenes taken from both Western and *kabuki* sources. The scenes were organized in a surrealistic, nonlinear fashion that nevertheless retained coherence by being linked to a central situation, and the scenes were transposed from their original contexts to new ones created under Suzuki's guidance. Dialogue often conflicted with behavior, creating a sense of dislocation and illogic, but also producing new insights. The production was the first to make significant use of actress Kayoko Shiraishi, who exemplified the possibilities of Suzuki's methods, and whose physical, emotional, and vocal powers were so potent that international critics acclaimed her as one of the world's greatest actresses. She was the centerpiece in most of Suzuki's work through 1990, when she left to follow other goals.

Suzuki followed with the company's first major success, a collage titled *On the Dramatic Passions II* (1970), in which Shiraishi played a madwoman who fantasized herself into various dramatic situations from *kabuki* plays. (Reappearing in many Suzuki works are mad characters whose proclivity for role-playing offers a rationale for mingling diverse dramatic scenes.) Then came the collages *On the Dramatic Passions III* (1972) and *Re-dyed and Later Appearance* (1971). Suzuki's dissatisfaction with his work was compounded by company friction resulting from his decision to collaborate with another troupe on the *kabuki*-based collage *Summer Drama White Comedy* (1970). A number of WLT actors walked out in 1971, causing Suzuki to cease activity for a year.

In 1972, the WLT was invited to the Théâtre des Nations festival in Paris. Ultimately, Suzuki's actors would gain worldwide renown. In Paris, Suzuki was so taken by the fact that festival head Jean-Louis Barrault's temporary theater was situated in a place in which people had lived that he resolved to find a similar artistic home in Japan. In 1976, he located such a place in a thatched-roof farmhouse in the tiny, remote, mountain village of Toga, in Toyama prefecture, and set up his headquarters there, 400 miles from Tokyo. This demonstrated that Japanese theater need not be centralized in the capital city, although the troupe reestablished a Tokyo base in 1980. The 40-member company now spends the summer in Toga. In 1982, Suzuki set up the Toga International Theater Festival, bringing the world's finest avant-garde artists there annually, and playing to sell-out houses, despite the distant location. The farmhouse was converted in 1980 by a noted architect into a beautiful 200-seat wooden theater called Toga Sanbō that incorporated its natural features and employed a 20-foot-square thrust stage that, with its pillars, two upstage rampways, and neutral rear wall, superficially resembled that of the nō. An 800-seat lakeside amphitheater was constructed in 1982. These are "sacred places" to Suzuki, who thrives on Toga's natural surroundings.

For five years, until 1980, Suzuki's actors engaged at Toga in intensive practice in the "Suzuki method," adapted largely from classical nō and *kabuki* techniques as well as the martial arts and requiring rigorous discipline to carry out its demanding physical and vocal exercises. Suzuki has taught these exercises widely, and has trained a number of disciples. Maria Myerscough said that he is "a tough taskmaster and disciplinarian, at times almost tyrannical, [but] he can also be affable and relaxed, with a subtle and mischievous sense of humor." He drills his actors while holding a bamboo sword, which he raps loudly on the floor. He is extremely critical of the minutest acting flaws, may even insult an actor personally, and can shout ferociously.

His exercises were incorporated into a series of lauded productions, many derived from Western classics and thus revealing a fusion of Eastern theatrics with Western drama. The stress moved from a discovery of self to mastery of movement and vocalization. The words, he said, have to emerge from the actor's physicalization, not from an intellectual process: body and voice must be one. If possible, he wants his actors to become possessed, like shamans. His system's movements require extensive footwork, with the body employing a low center of gravity, and considerable use made of a variety of stamps, squats, shuffles, slides, and kicks. Suzuki originally claimed the exercises to be founded on a specifically Japanese form of movement; he now says more universal principles are involved. In performance, the movements are combined with minimalist decor; front-facing performances; rhythmic dancing; taped music, often at deafening levels; and a considerable amount of narrative speech delivered in long monologues using a wide range of heightened expression.

The first farmhouse production was the collage *Night and Feast I* (1976), which combined material from Chekhov, Samuel Beckett, and Euripides, among others. By 1980, three sequels had been produced. The major impact of the Suzuki style,

Dionysus. *Directed by Tadashi Suzuki.* (Photo: SCOT)

however, derived from several Greek tragedies on whose texts Suzuki practiced deconstructive rearrangements designed to express allusively communicated themes of social relevance. While being relatively true to the originals, these works sounded reverberations for contemporary Japan and for the world at large.

His innovative Greek productions, most of them revived and revised in the years following their premieres, were Euripides' *The Trojan Women* (1974), *The Bacchae* (1978), *Clytemnestra* (a collation of five tragedies, 1980), and *Dionysus* (1990), a new approach to *The Bacchae*. A spectacular (70 performers), but unsuccessful, revision of *Clytemnestra* called *The Tragedy: The Fall of the House of Atreus* played at Tokyo's 1,900-seat Imperial Theater (1983). *The Bacchae* and *Clytemnestra* also saw bilingual productions with Suzuki-trained American actors speaking English and their Japanese coplayers performing in Japanese; many found the effect both fascinating and strangely meaningful.

The most admired of his Greek works is his antinationalist *The Trojan Women*, conceived as a play-within-a-play (as was *The Bacchae*). In the revised and best-known version (1977), Shiraishi was a homeless old woman in bombed-out, postwar Japan who becomes possessed by the spirits of Hecuba and Cassandra, thereby conveying Suzuki's concern with the universal plight of women in male-initiated conflicts. An indelible image was the rape of Andromache by three ragged samurai and the dismemberment of her child (a large rag doll). Meanwhile, the god of children sat motionless upstage. The work was at once about ancient Greece, postwar Japan, and any war-ravaged nation. The original productions of *The Trojan Women* and *The Bacchae* (viewed as a conflict between freedom and totalitarianism as dreamed by political prisoners) employed a famous *nō* actor as well as Shiraishi (Agave and Bacchus). The collaboration was of importance in Suzuki's attempt to synthesize Japanese and Western theater. These mountings typically concluded with the playing of a familiar pop song whose lyrics in the unusual context created cynical, ironic resonances.

Suzuki's repertoire expanded from the mid-1970s on. His own collage dramas included, among others, *Don Hamlet* (1973), combining parts of *Hamlet*, Chekhov's *The Three Sisters,* and Japanese descriptions of World War II. *Night and Clock* (1975) combined parts of *Macbeth* and a *kabuki* drama and showed the patients in an insane asylum imagining themselves to be Macbeth. His deconstructed Western dramas included Oscar Wilde's *Salomé* (1978) and plays by Shakespeare and Chekhov. For his radically cut, all-male *The Tale of Lear* (1984), in which the daughters wore beards and Lear was an old man in a nursing home being read King Lear's story by a nurse (also the fool), he staged both

American and bilingual productions. Perhaps his most innovative Chekhov was the farcical, Beckettlike conflation of *The Three Sisters, The Cherry Orchard,* and *Uncle Vanya* (each had been given earlier Suzuki productions) titled *The Chekhov* (1989). In *The Three Sisters* portion, quarrelsome male characters—representing memory figures—sat in wicker baskets, only their comical heads visible. The three sisters, holding open umbrellas, faced the audience in armchairs, staring off toward Moscow.

In 1984, the WLT became SCOT (the Suzuki Company of Toga). In 1988, Suzuki was named director of Tokyo's Mitsui Festival and, in 1989, artistic director of the Acting Company Mito in Mito City. Future honors will undoubtedly accrue to Suzuki, an autocrat who brings social idealism and the highest standards to the task of creating a form of Japanese theater he hopes will endure.

Further reading:

Brandon, James R. "Training at the Waseda Little Theatre: the Suzuki Method." *The Drama Review* 22 (December 1978).

Goto, Yukihiro. "The Theatrical Fusion of Suzuki Tadashi." *Asian Theatre Journal* 6 (Fall 1989).

Myerscough, Marie. "East Meets West in the Art of Tadashi Suzuki." *American Theatre* 2 (January 1986).

SCOT: Suzuki Company of Toga. Tokyo: The Japan Performing Arts Center, 1991.

Suzuki, Tadashi. *The Way of Acting: The Theatre Writings of Tadashi Suzuki.* Translated by J. Thomas Rimer. New York: Theater Communications Group, 1986.

ALEXANDER TAIROV (1885–1950)

ALEXANDER YAKOVLEVICH TAIROV (*né* Kornblit) was born in the Ukrainian town of Romna, province of Poltava, where his father was a teacher. In 1904, he studied at the Law Faculty of the University of Kiev while acting for Vera Komisarjevskaya's company and Pavel Gaideburov's Mobile Theatre, where he debuted as a director with *Hamlet* (1907). Works by Yuri Zhulavsky and Anton Chekhov followed, each demonstrating Tairov's belief in music to create a unifying mood and an emotional stimulant for the actors. He directed actors in Riga and Simbirsk,

acting in all of his own stagings, and mounted Jacinto Benavente's *The Seamy Side of Life* (1912) in St. Petersburg, where he completed his studies in 1913.

After briefly trying a law career, he joined Konstantin Mardzhanov's Free Theater, staging George C. Hazleton and J. Harry Benrimo's Chinese parody, *The Yellow Jacket* (1913), and *The Veil of Pierrette* (1913), a musical mime based on an Arthur Schnitzler text (*Columbine's Scarf* in Vsevolod Meyerhold's version). Tairov's three commedia figures avoided

Alexander Tairov. (Photo: Theater Collection, Brooklyn College)

purely aesthetic movement in favor of combining choreographic expressiveness with tragic feeling provoked by the music. His production revealed his then belief in the purity of genre, avoiding the infusion of comedy into the tragic tone. Pierrette was acted by Alisa Koonen, who married Tairov and became his leading player.

In 1914, Tairov founded Moscow's intimate Kamerny (Chamber) Theater, geared for an elite clientele. He opened with Kàlidàsa's Sanskrit classic *Sakuntalá* and followed with innovative productions of plays by Carlo Goldoni, Mikhail Kuzmin, and Pierre de Beaumarchais. Most renowned was *Sakuntalá*, for which Tairov—as was typical—spent many hours in the British Museum studying the Indian background. The Russian futurist setting included four huge statues of horses on large pedestals, rearing on their hind legs, and framing the almost balletlike

stage. The dancerlike actors wore scanty costumes and body paint.

Tairov was a virulent antinaturalist and proponent of the "theatricalization of the theater" under a rubric he called "synthetic theater," a highly aestheticized, rhythmically unified form nurtured in the spirit of commedia and the Roman mimes, employing music, singing, acrobatics, dance, acting, clowning, juggling, and archetypal, heroic figures. He denied the separation of theater into separate genres of spoken drama, operetta, ballet, circus, and pantomime, and yearned for a method in which the distinguishing elements of all were merged. Tairov placed the actor at the theater's heart. The text was a pretext for performance that could be edited at will. He intended to make theater as technically exact as dance and music by requiring "master" performers in total physical and emotional control of themselves. Inner truth, springing spontaneously (improvisation was valued) from images formed by the actor's fine-tuned creative will, was as important as external skill. The actor was not to confuse his personality with that of his character, but to remain conscious that he was acting. Still, Tairov never eliminated the aesthetic distance separating actors from spectators.

Tairov's eclectic repertoire embraced many forms. No other contemporary theater possessed such versatile actors. During the 1919–1920 season, he started a training school to develop multiskilled actors and to provide what he termed a *corps de drame*, like a *corps de ballet*. His concern for an aesthetic theater led to criticism in a postrevolutionary state demanding that art serve political interests through government-dictated policies. The Kamerny's having been named a subsidized "academic" theater helped to protect it from charges of being counterrevolutionary.

By the end of the first season, Tairov's important collaboration with composer Henri Forterre had begun (he also worked with other avant-garde musicians). Another advance was in the setting for Beaumarchais's *The Marriage of Figaro* (1915). Tairov created for it a pathbreaking multileveled stage floor with vertical units designed to break up the monotony of the flat stage, improve sight lines, and offer a staging "keyboard," especially with regard to the rhythmic variations demanded by the differences among the steps and platforms. Three-dimensional elements accorded with the actor's corporeality.

This was stunningly seen in Isidore Annensky's pseudo-Greek tragedy *Thamira, the Cither Player*

(1916), designed by Alexandra Exter, representative of the advanced artists (and architects) used by Tairov. She combined cubism and constructivism in its sharply angled platforms. Such geometrical, abstract sets reappeared often; costuming was similarly abstracted. Sometimes there was a clash between actors' bodies and theatricalized decor.

Rhythm dictated movements from level to level, whose varying heights allowed for numerous transitions. Tairov, as concerned with speech as he was with movement, had some verses spoken and others half-sung to a musical accompaniment.

Numerous plays in a grab bag of genres were added during the Kamerny's 35-year history. Representative productions included Oscar Wilde's previously banned *Salomé* (1917), in its first Russian performance, with brilliantly colored, structural costumes designed almost like body masks; Claude Debussy's *The Toybox* (1917), a musical piece with a libretto by Tairov, employing the actors as marionettes; Paul Claudel's *The Exchange* (1918) and *The Tidings Brought to Mary* (1920), the former a collaboration with Meyerhold that demonstrated the directors' artistic disparity (they later had a long-running feud), the latter a good example of a play whose timeless qualities were suited to Tairov's style; Eugène Scribe's *Adrienne Lecouvreur* (1919), 19th-century romantic hackwork transmogrified into heartfelt theater, using varicolored and shaped moving screens to rearrange the decor; E. T. A. Hoffman's *Princess Brambilla* (1920), a fantastical, carnival-spirited harlequinade played on a spiral-filled set in tarantella rhythm and incorporating drama, ballet, pantomime, circus, and operetta; a strikingly cubist *Romeo and Juliet* (1921); a tragically austere *Phaedra* (1921), which, to stress Jean Racine's theme of consuming passion, allowed greater reign than before to emotional expression, but continued Tairov's employment of cubist-based decoration, with a steeply raked abstract set suggesting both a ship's deck and an ancient palace; and Alexander Lecocq's operetta *Giroflé-Girofla* (1922), provided with a new libretto, and realized as a joyously high-spirited theatrical piece inspired by the escapism of the New Economic Policy years. Eight months in rehearsal, it was replete with dancelike acting, cabaret-type staging, and properties accentuating the actors' physicality. A lighting effect showed kaleidoscopic transformations in the costumes created by the flames in a bowl of burning punch.

Because of its three far-reaching European tours, the Kamerny was better known abroad than other

Alice Koonen in Phaedra. *Directed by Alexander Tairov. (1921)* (Photo: Theater Collection, Brooklyn College)

Russian companies. Foreign critics were delighted at how effectively the remarkable acting transcended the barriers of language because of the complete command of expression. Following the first tour (1923), Tairov added Soviet premieres, although he now and then produced revivals. The latter included the Kamerny's first play about Russian life, Alexander Ostrovsky's *The Storm* (1924), odd for being acted realistically on a constructivist set, and such operettas as Lecocq's *Day and Night* (1926) and Alexander Borodin's "opera farce" *The Epic Heroes* (1936); the latter was politically offensive because it satirized national history. Unusual was *Egyptian Nights* (1934), Tairov's epic-scaled, Marxist-slanted, anti-imperialistic conflation of Antony and Cleopatra material from Alexander Pushkin, Shakespeare, and George Bernard Shaw.

Because of a dearth of suitable Soviet plays, Tairov staged many foreign works (sometimes retitled), making the Kamerny a leader in the international repertoire. Eugene O'Neill proved especially congenial to the Tairov touch. Tairov was criticized for his lack of Soviet choices, although there was a shift from the mid-1930s on. His staging gradually moved away from cubist abstractions toward a style called either "neorealism," "concrete realism," or "structural realism," which allowed for some mingling of genres, and which attempted to harmonize formalistic elements with naturalistic ones. Most of Tairov's sets were now designed by the Stenberg brothers, whose constructivism "combined a rather austere geometric outline . . . with fearlessly concrete detail of object and contemporary accuracy of costumes," according to Konstantin Rudnitsky. Whereas his early work was more concerned with beauty than with politics, from the early 1920s on Tairov increasingly, if with difficulty, selected anticapitalist works (part of O'Neill's attractiveness); nevertheless, his rationalizations concerning proletarian content sometimes smacked of expediency. This became more pronounced in the more severe climate of the late 1920s and early 1930s. Despite Tairov's assertion that he was attempting to convey the social content of his productions through new theatrical means, the Kamerny rarely succeeded in being politically mainstream.

Among his best-known premieres were G. K. Chesterton's detective story, *The Man Who Was Thursday* (1923), its robotlike characters inhabiting a skeletal constructivist setting with mechanically moving parts designed to suggest a threatening capitalist cityscape; an eccentric political revue (the first Russian example of the kind) called *Kukirol* (1925), satirizing American, French, and British capitalism; Walter Hasenclever's adaptation of Sophocles' *Antigone* (1927), emphasizing antifascism, dressed with futuristic costumes, and evoking the rag-garbed proletariat so successfully that, as one critic wrote, "the actors' voices, the noises, the whirlwinds of motion, the rumblings and the sounds of Creon's armoured 'robots' achieved superhuman power" (quoted in Nick Worrall); Bertolt Brecht's *The Threepenny Opera* (1930), using a set with doors reminiscent of Meyerhold's famous *The Inspector General* (this may have been the first non-German Brecht staging); and a notable version of Sophie Treadwell's *Machinal* (1933), viewed as a tract against dehumanization of life in Western urban society, with all of the characters but the heroine given puppetlike behavior. Tairov's three O'Neills were *The Hairy Ape* (1926), done expressionistically on a constructivist set showing all the locales simultaneously; *Desire Under the Elms* (1926), stressing the theme of possessiveness; and *All God's Chillun Got Wings* (1929), with Ella dying instead of regressing to childhood at the end (O'Neill approved). Shaw, J. M. Synge, and John Dos Passos were also represented.

Tairov's attempts at politically oriented Soviet plays usually went awry because of theatrically unimaginative writing. These included works by A. P. Globa, Mikhail Bulgakov, S. A. Semyonov, N. N. Nikitin, Nikolai Kulish, L. Pervomaisky, and others. Overtly experimental staging methods were minimalized, exposing dramaturgic weaknesses. Tairov's most successful Soviet drama was Vsevolod Vish-

nevsky's *Optimistic Tragedy* (1933), a spectacular, propaganda epic about the Russian civil war that became a modern classic and temporarily demonstrated that the aesthetic formalist director was a committed collectivist.

When Tairov got into trouble because of *The Epic Heroes,* he was forced to merge with Okhlopkov's Realistic Theater troupe, to which he was artistically opposed. The resultant clash ended the situation after 13 months. Tairov went on to stage plays such as the documentary *Stronger Than Death* (1938) and plays by A. N. Tolstoy and Maxim Gorky. He was spared Stalin's purges when he went on tour to the Far East, where he premiered Koonen's complex adaptation of *Madame Bovary* (1939), cinematically staged on tri-leveled settings placed on three revolves.

From 1941 to 1943, the Kamerny sat out the war uncomfortably in western Siberia and Kazakhstan, providing premieres of four Soviet plays. Back in Moscow, where Tairov was honored with the Order of Lenin in 1945, they offered an eclectic group of new productions, among them a gray-draped, evening-clothed, emotionally compelling, concert staging of Chekhov's *The Sea Gull* (1943), not revived by a major company since 1905. Gorky's 1915 *The Old Man* (1946), viewed in antifascist terms, is considered Tairov's final important production, although he staged several others. In 1949, the Kamerny was officially closed and Tairov was demoted to a subordinate position at another theater.

Unlike several of his autocratic colleagues, Tairov, despite his position at the Kamerny, was known for his kindness and diplomacy, although he had a magnetic, persuasive personality and reigned supreme over his company, who idolized him. His perfectly orchestrated productions revealed his meticulousness. Tairov's specialty lay in composing stage pictures; some said that his crowd work overshadowed his conversational scenes. Watching him, Norris Houghton observed that he seemed "passive. He does little acting, only once in a while shows an actor a move. Instead he walks about, talking his directions, beckoning or pulling his crowds into position." He could envision mass effects while in front of his cast, instead of having to direct them from the house. "He treats the crowd as one person, regulates its movement and tempo as though it were but one, and it reacts to his directions like one man." At his complex dress rehearsals, Tairov seemed like any Western director: "if . . . Russian . . . only sounded a little more like English, one could easily imagine himself in a theater on Shaftesbury Avenue!"

Alexander Tairov's influence at home was weaker than many of his contemporaries because of his relative lack of political commitment, but he was appreciated abroad and continues to be studied as one of Russia's most consistent innovators.

Further reading:

Tairov, Alexander. *Notes of a Director.* Coral Gables, Fla.: University of Miami Press, 1969.

Also: Houghton, *Moscow Rehearsals*; Rudnitsky, *Russian and Soviet Theater*; Slonim, *Russian Theater*; Worrall, *Modernism to Realism on the Soviet Stage.*

HERBERT BEERBOHM TREE (1852–1917)

HERBERT BEERBOHM was born in London, where his father was a successful corn merchant. Educated in England and Germany, Beerbohm worked as a clerk in his father's firm for eight years. He moved from amateur theatricals to a professional career, becoming a renowned character actor. When his father suggested that only those who reached the top of the theatrical tree succeeded, he appended Tree to his birth name.

After gaining experience in the provinces, Tree established himself in London in 1880. In 1883, he married Maud Tree, who became an important actress in her own right. By 1887, Tree's fame warranted his becoming an actor-manager at his own theater, where he maintained his own troupe, directed and produced all of the plays, and performed their juiciest parts. He soon rivaled London's leading actor-manager, Henry Irving. In 1888, after a brief tenure at the intimate Comedy Theater, Tree obtained the larger Haymarket Theater, which he renovated and provided with electricity. He proceeded to offer 34 classic and modern plays, many very successful, through 1896. Tree's first Shakespeare was *The Merry Wives of Windsor* (Tree as Falstaff, his greatest Shakespearean role; 1889). His others at the Haymarket were *Hamlet* (Tree as a Teutonic prince; 1892) and *Henry IV, Part I* (Tree as Falstaff; 1896). His overromanticized interpretation of *Hamlet* viewed the Dane as a sentimental lover, a quality exemplified by such touches as Hamlet's bestowing a silent kiss on Ophelia's hair after he has berated her. Hamlet's death was accompanied by choral music suggesting flights of angels. Instead of the traditionally somber graveyard, Tree used a cheerful springtime setting, with chirping birds and blooming flowers.

Of the modern plays, the most historically noteworthy were Oscar Wilde's comedy of manners, *A Woman of No Importance* (1893), Maurice Maeterlinck's symbolistic *The Intruder* (1890), and Henrik Ibsen's *An Enemy of the People* (Tree as Stockman; 1893), the Norwegian's first major West End staging. These choices were daring—especially the Ibsen (Tree gained Shaw's grudging respect)—and demonstrated that he was even more progressive than Irving.

Tree's directorial reputation grew following Haddon Chambers's melodramatic *Captain Swift* (1888), which used memorably detailed realistic scenery and furnishings for the interiors and was carefully staged in every particular. Many of Tree's hits were similarly meretricious crowd-pleasers, among them being Henry Arthur Jones's *The Dancing Girl* (1891; Tree eventually staged four Jones plays) and Paul M. Potter's adaptation of George du Maurier's *Trilby* (Tree's biggest commercial success; 1895), in which Tree was brilliant as the hypnotic Svengali. Tree's later productions, like his Shakespeares, were extremely lavish, especially those set in the distant past.

Tree's range was wider than most of his contemporaries and his selections were praised for their stylistic eclecticism. His breadth was exemplified at the Haymarket when he began the practice of offering a tryout series of Monday evening and Wednesday matinee showings of quality works with doubtful commercial appeal before putting them into his regular schedule. He believed that it was wiser to attempt raising the audience's standards than to play down to what they seemed likely to approve. When he did Shakespeare, he used a text that, although cut to accommodate scene changes, was far more reflective of the original than the mutilated, star-oriented versions then current. In 1895, his company made its first American tour.

One of the standards of Tree's theater that brought it success was that, unlike Irving's, it did not rely solely on the magnetism of its actor-manager but depended on a brilliant company. He did not cavil at taking supporting roles when necessary, and cast whomever he believed best suited to a role, even when it meant hurting his wife's feelings. Most of the best contemporary actors acted under Tree at one time or another. Another positive feature of Tree's taste was his employment of excellent orchestras and music to accompany the action. Some believe that Tree's contributions at the Haymarket were nearly as vital to the founding of the English repertory movement as the better-known ones of Harley Granville-Barker at the Court Theater.

In 1897, Tree opened the luxurious Her Majesty's (renamed His Majesty's after Queen Victoria's death in 1901). The playhouse, London's first to use a flat, instead of raked, stage, opened with Gilbert Parker's *The Seats of the Mighty*, a flop that Tree had originally staged in America.

Tree's greatest accomplishments at Her Majesty's were his Shakespeare revivals and, beginning in 1905, his creation of a series of Shakespeare Festivals. His first great Shakespeare staging (1898) was *Julius Caesar* (Tree as Antony). He followed with *King John* (Tree as the Bastard; 1899); *A Midsummer Night's Dream* (Tree as Bottom; 1900), *Twelfth Night* (Tree as Malvolio; 1901); *Richard II* (Tree as Richard; 1903); *The Tempest* (Tree as Caliban; 1903); *Much Ado About Nothing* (Tree as Benedick; 1905); *The Winter's Tale* (Ellen Terry as Hermione; 1906); *Antony and Cleopatra* (Tree as Antony; 1906); *The Merchant of Venice* (Tree as Shylock; 1907); *Henry VIII* (Tree as Wolsey; 1910); *Macbeth* (Tree as Macbeth; 1911); and *Othello* (Tree as Othello; 1912).

Tree was responsible for staging over 40 modern works and revivals at Her Majesty's, among them Stephen Phillips's once highly regarded blank verse historical dramas, *Herod* (1900), *Ulysses* (1902), *Nero* (1906), and *Faust* (1908), each sumptuously produced and each achieving over 100 showings; and David Belasco and John Luther Long's Japanese melodrama, *The Darling of the Gods* (1903), which enjoyed an extravagant presentation using authentic Japanese decor. Contemporary foreign stagings included playwrights Eugène Brieux, Octave Mirabeau, Leo Tolstoy, and Clyde Fitch (in one Fitch play Tree staged a boating scene with real water). His greatest non-Shakespearean revival was of Richard Brinsley Sheridan's *The School for Scandal* (1909).

Tree had a sharp eye for adaptable fiction and made much of works by novelists such as Dickens and Thackeray. He produced (in the American sense) Shaw's *Pygmalion* (1914), and interfered in its direction (to Shaw's dismay, he romanticized the ending), but the staging was mainly in the hands of its author.

Tree often participated closely in a playwright's work, and occasionally wrote scenes himself. His desire for total control sometimes led to violent disputes with dramatists, who might storm out during rehearsals. Henry Arthur Jones often fought with Tree and once ran from the theater, screaming that he would never come back. The fired-up Tree responded, "In that case we shall be able to get on with the rehearsals."

It is the 16 Shakespeare plays he staged (five more than Irving) for which Tree is best remembered. Tree's Shakespeare stagings gained acclaim for their spectacularly illusionistic visualizations, which, despite efforts to move the action along swiftly, occasionally necessitated long waits to shift the scenery. Although it sometimes led to illogicalities, given Shakespeare's nonspecific scenography, Tree called upon archaeological specificity to set scenes in locales deemed historically correct. Sometimes Tree rearranged Shakespeare's scenic order to create a desired visual or thematic effect, as when he ran the ghetto scenes in *The Merchant of Venice* together into a single unit. Tree was fond of interpolating tableaux and pantomimic actions, elaborating on textual hints to provide scenes of interesting, if not luxuriant, activity. Illustrative business was created, even to the point of introducing silent characters not in the script, to heighten thematic or character concerns. At times Tree might have a crowd of actors frozen in a tableau with numerous painted characters on a drop behind them. When appropriate, he cleverly alternated front scenes before a painted drop with built-up scenes behind the drop, sometimes even suggesting spatial continuity between the two as an exterior view shifted to an interior one. He was expert at using light to help convey mood, atmosphere, and the passage of time.

His *Julius Caesar*, designed by Lawrence Alma Tadema in archaeologically accurate fashion, was an epochal work, magnificently mounted (apart from certain infelicities noted by Shaw), and boasting a marvelously handled Forum crowd. Tree's pageant-mastery was evident as was his ability to get the most from his ensemble, each major role being superlatively handled in a play that Irving ignored because it has no single stellar character. Tree sought to create convincingly realistic effects, including having the supine corpse of Caesar visible (Tree refused to use a dummy) throughout the Forum scene, and Tree's own invention of hairy tights for the actors.

Equally renowned was *A Midsummer Night's Dream*, with its recreation of an Athenian forest so realistic that it had real rabbits. Some consider

Twelfth Night Tree's Shakespearean masterpiece, with its depiction of Olivia's exceedingly lovely English garden recreated from pictures in a contemporary magazine. To emphasize Malvolio's ego, the character was shadowed by four miniature, mirror-image Malvolios. Tree's Malvolio epitomized the actor's proclivity for creating comic business, as when he expressed a range of hilarious reactions to a nude statue as he inspected it through an eyeglass. In *Richard II* real horses were employed for a battle scene. Inspired by a brief speech in the play, Tree created an enthralling spectacle depicting Bolingbroke's entry into London on horseback as the crowd jeered and threw stones at the vanquished Richard, also on horseback. Tree's *Tempest* was bathed in eye-opening effects, including a realistic storm scene depicting the breakup of a ship at sea. At the end, Tree had Caliban, left alone on the island, looking wistfully at the ship departing with the other characters. *Antony and Cleopatra* was filled with opulent scenery and crowd scenes, especially that of Cleopatra's arrival, played with dancing flower girls, exotic music, crowds of onlookers, and religious practitioners. The Queen of the Nile was accompanied by her five children, an idea derived from Tree's research. His richest Shakespeare realization was *Henry VIII*, packed with pomp and pageantry.

At his Shakespeare Festivals Tree offered, miraculously, six fully produced plays in as many days. After several years the period lengthened to a fortnight and, by its last year, 1913, the series was expanded to a three-month period, during which others put their wares on display as well. Tree's accomplishment has been likened to the founding of a national theater.

Tree read extensively when preparing to stage Shakespeare. Although he liked to give the impression of being struck by inspiration, he took careful preparatory notes on the characters, business, blocking, milieu, sets, and costumes. His well-researched, insightful comments on *Henry VIII* were published. Although he had definite ideas about his effects, he was strangely ignorant of the theater's technical terms, and his technicians had to translate his requests into their own backstage language. "That one there—it gives no light," was a likely comment to a lighting specialist.

His rehearsals were typically chaotic and nerve-wracking. Tree was absent-minded, and was apt to walk off on some inconsequential business in the midst of rehearsal, leaving the actors to fend for themselves. He was surrounded by sycophants whose responsibilities were undefined, although they propped up Tree's ego by agreeing with him and laughing at his jokes. One can imagine the tension during the rehearsals and preparations for the yearly Shakespeare Festivals, which were held day and night for weeks. Rehearsals often were held after midnight, and might go on through the night, with meals taken on stage at free moments. Tree himself never seemed to flag. Despite the frenzy of rehearsals, his typically complex productions were marvels of efficiency once they opened.

At rehearsal, his irrepressible sense of humor was always on display as he fired off witticism after witticism (sometimes at the expense of his players); he even enjoyed keeping a record of the better ones. When an actress pronounced the word sky as "skay," he admonished her, "Oh, my God! Remember you're in Egypt. The 'skay' is seen only in Kensington." On being provoked unduly, he could be mercilessly snide, but he was likely to seek forgiveness if his words stung too sharply. To inspire an actor, he employed colorful analogies, saying, "I want you to play this part with a mauve voice," or offering similar hints. Often, he resorted to self-created aphorisms: "Keep your vowels and your bowels open"; "Judge an actress by the way she handles an artificial rose." If an actor failed to produce the desired results, Tree drilled him over and over until he got what he was after. When such a procedure caused an actress to break down in tears, Tree said, "Now, then, there is no more Constance Collier, let's find out how to act the part."

In addition to Tree's many famous productions, acting roles, and festivals, he founded, in 1904, the flourishing acting school now known as the Royal Academy of Dramatic Art. In 1909, he was knighted. The speeches he gave in America (where he acted in several films) during World War I made him a valuable ambassador. His achievements represent a transition between the 19th-century traditionalist mode and the twentieth's modernist method.

Further reading:

Bingham, Madeleine. *"The Great Lover": The Life and Art of Herbert Beerbohm Tree.* New York: Atheneum, 1979.

Pearson, Hesketh. *Beerbohm Tree: His Life and Laughter.* London: Methuen and Company, 1956.

Also: Mazer, *Shakespeare Refashioned.*

TOMMY TUNE (1939–   )

THOMAS JAMES TUNE was born in Wichita Falls, Texas, but was raised in Houston, where his father serviced oil rigs and trained horses. He began studying dance at five. During his youth, he staged amateur shows. The lanky, six-foot-six Tune received a theater degree from the University of Texas at Austin in 1962, two years after making his debut as a professional dancer.

Tune danced continually on Broadway, in tours and regional theaters, and in TV and films, including *The Boy Friend* (1971, costarring Twiggy). His first big break came as performer and cochoreographer to Michael Bennett (Tune's principal influence) on the musical *Seesaw* (1973). When his performing career stalled, he directed and choreographed *The Club* (1976), Eve Merriam's Obie-winning Off-Broadway satire on male chauvinism, set in a stuffy turn-of-the-century men's club whose members all were played by tailcoated women, with mustaches, canes, and cigars.

A musical he directed in Buffalo in 1977 was taken over by another director before flopping on Broadway (1978's *Platinum*, score by Gary William Friedman and Will Holt). While *The Best Little Whorehouse in Texas* (1978), score by Carol Hall, was going through a troubled workshop development, Tune was hired to choreograph and codirect it (with colibrettist Peter Masterson). The show, inspired by a true story about a Texas brothel and the political tempest surrounding attempts to close it down, moved from Off-Broadway to Broadway and became a hit. Tune's "Angelette March" stopped the show with its step-kicking chorus line of six vacuous, blonde, football cheerleaders, each linked on either arm to a life-sized, balloon-breasted, Slinky-legged dummy, bringing the line to 18. Tune won staging and choreography Tonys.

Following another out-of-town failure, Tune directed and shared the Tony-winning choreography with Thommie Walsh on his Broadway version of a two-part London hit, Frank Lazarus and Dick Vosburgh's *A Day in Hollywood/A Night in the Ukraine* (1980). It began with a spoof of 1930s Hollywood and ended with a wild, imaginary Marx Brothers farce. Tune's fondness for cross-gender casting was reflected in Harpo's being played by an actress. The Hollywood part was revised so that instead of a bare stage with singers against a simple drop, an approximation of Graumann's Chinese Theater was installed, with the six-member cast in fancy ushers' uniforms. His greatest idea was "Famous Feet," in which the dancers, performing on what *Time* described as "a narrow, mirror-backed bridge span of a stage high above the stage proper," revealed only their legs, seemingly floating on air, in duplications of the terpsichore of Judy Garland, Fred Astaire and Ginger Rogers, Charlie Chaplin, Minnie and Mickey Mouse, and others.

Tune directed his first nonmusical, Off-Broadway's *Cloud 9* (1981), Caryl Churchill's British political satire mingling themes of sexual liberation and repression with those of colonial exploitation. Moving across 100 years from a British settlement in 1880 Africa to a 1980 London park, it included bisexuality, homosexuality and heterosexuality, with seven actors playing 15 roles, many in drag in order to explore past and present gender confusion. Tune informed Jill Lynne: "In every play I've worked on, the sexual was always the hidden metaphor. In *Cloud 9* the hidden metaphor is not sexual. I think that the hidden metaphor—and this may sound so mundane—is life."

Federico Fellini's film *8½*, about a 40-year-old, woman-obsessed, Italian movie director and his creative block, inspired the unconventional *Nine* (1982), Tune's next hit, for which he won another directing Tony. The staging—which had barely any dance (no choreographer was credited)—was lauded over Arthur Kopit's book and Maury Yeston's score. The show had been developed in a workshop and went through extensive revisions; an entirely new ending was installed during previews. Set in a white-tiled Venetian spa dotted with symmetrically arranged cubes that Tune—without scene shifts—used to conjure up lagoons, canals, gondolas, beaches, and so on, *Nine* moved back and forth in time to project the hero's memories and fantasies. Twenty-one actresses served as choral instruments "conducted" by the hero and as the female influences in his life. The onstage orchestra sat in a tiled, half-moon shaped opening around which the women paraded on a walkway. At the end, white doves were released from balcony cages to flutter down upon the stage. The show was accused of being vulgar and empty of substance, but Tune's work was impressive. The *New York Daily News* trumpeted:

Nine is a Mardi Gras of technicolor images, sumptuous costumes, choreographed movements, creatively detailed performances . . . , dream sequence lighting effects . . . , stylish sets and arresting visual concepts that blend together brilliantly to create a cinematic form that fuses past, present, and future imaginings. . . .

The most talked-about moment was "A Call from the Vatican," performed by the sinuous, redheaded Anita Morris in a black lace body stocking: "she superbly executes a one-body simulation of two-body copulation," noted the *New York Times.*

Tune performed in Broadway's *My One and Only* (1983) in which he was reteamed with Twiggy. The show, loosely based on George and Ira Gershwin's 1927 *Funny Face,* was fraught with problems; the original director, Peter Sellars, who worked on it for 18 months, had an intellectual approach that clashed with Tune's show-biz style. Sellars was axed and four other directors involved before Tune and Walsh took over. Although trashed in advance, the show pulled off a miracle and ran for 767 performances. The campy show—its wobbly book about a 1920s aviator's romance with an English Channel swimmer—was saved by its clever, Tony-winning dances. The standout was "S'Wonderful," tapped in a shallow pool of water. "Kickin' the Clouds Away," another show stopper, was a tap ensemble set in a Harlem chapel: "Instead of the Busby Berkeley drill one expects," noted the *Times,* "the choreographers create a disjointed, centrifugal whirlwind of movement that sends individual dancers twirling into separate idiosyncratic versions of the overall 20's pattern."

Tune's first flop was his restaging of London's *Stepping Out* (1987), a realistic comedy with music about an adult tap dancing class. Tune thought it the hardest show he had ever tackled. To make the performances truthful, he cast nondancers and, like the play's teacher, trained them to do a chorus routine.

Tune clambered back with *Grand Hotel* (1989), a hit musical version of Vicki Baum's 1929 German play that revised a 1958 libretto by Luther Davis and a score by Robert Wright and George Forrest, with new tunes by Yeston. Like other Tune musicals, it was a triumph of style over substance, despite an attempt to bring in the Weimar Republic's problems by a Brechtian choral quartet of utensil-banging scullions. Tune's imagistic staging—which he said was an outgrowth of his *Nine* techniques ("I started with the *Nine* set and then dispersed it")—garnered

kudos, with the action progressing cinematically around two dozen gilded chairs that established new scenes by their rearrangement; good use was also made of the decadent hotel's transparent fluted columns and a revolving door.

The opening revealed Tune's genius, wrote the *Times,* as "phalanxes of performers crisscross the stage in everchanging configurations, the characters individually singing of their lots, until finally the audience sees the panorama of lives, upstairs and down, throughout the vast hotel." The onstage orchestra sat on a second level. Two adagio dancers who floated through the action representing, in Tune's words, "the romance and the decadence of the age," did a final number symbolizing Love and Death that was blasted as pretentious, but a hope-filled Charleston by the dying Jewish clerk Kringelein tore the house down; its subtext, Tune revealed, was AIDS.

Tune's recent staging of Peter Stone, Cy Coleman, Betty Comden, and Adolph Green's *Will Rogers Follies* (1991) was another show that went through trauma, opened to mixed reviews, and became a hit. Telling of Oklahoma humorist Rogers's life within the ghost-haunted, 1931 context of a *Ziegfeld Follies* rehearsal, this show—much of it staged on a stage-wide flight of translucent steps whose colors could be dramatically altered by interior lights—offered many chances for fireworks, beginning with the opening in which the large chorus kept entering down the steps, each time in new chaps, colors, and headdresses. In a notable routine, Rogers joined a seated, patriotically dressed chorus line in a rhythmical hand-clapping and leg-crossing routine.

Sheryl Flatow declared that Tune's fame accrues from his ability to transform "familiar material into fresh, new musicals of singular originality. . . . He combines the traditional showmanship of a bygone era with the unique perspective of a visionary, razzle-dazzling audiences with his bold, contemporary flights of fancy." Ross Wetzsteon added that Tune "not only . . . taps Broadway's roots but reinvigorates them with the hippest sense of irony, ambiguity and sophistication." A prevailing criticism is that he is attracted to featherweight material that allows him to show off his talents, making himself the star even when he does not perform. Tune insists that his dream is to have a meaningful show that will not require turning a sow's ear into a silk purse. His overarching purpose is to lift people's spirits and give them hope. In most of his productions, he

Keith Carradine in The Will Rogers Follies. *Directed by Tommy Tune. (1991)*   (Photo: Martha Swope)

tries to combine comedy with feeling, laughter with tears.

His shows typically employ unit sets that are not only cost-efficient but, in line with his "less is more" aesthetic, can imaginatively function for numerous locales; he is more interested in character than scenery. He told Ken Mandelbaum that he likes "to involve the audience as an imaginative co-partner."

Yoga plays a vital part in the spiritually inclined Tune's life and he practices daily. This influences his directing, too, as he begins rehearsals by engaging in 15 minutes of deep breathing exercises, as the actors stand with hands folded in prayer position. He told Carol Lawson, "I figure, if we all breathe the same air at the same rate, then our hearts are relatively in the same place." Casts also do these exercises during the run. Tune, seeking to meld them into a family, has the actors meet before each performance for what he calls "circle." The company sits on the floor holding hands, talks about the show, shares energy, and reminds itself of its commitment.

He holds definite acting opinions, believing that no one can play someone else. "I believe you are who you are," he stated to Leslie Bennetts. "You can bring all kinds of colors to that, but there's an overriding sense of humanity that comes from the heart, and you cannot and should not disguise that with character or costume or makeup."

Tune is boyishly friendly, willing to collaborate. Although he is a hard-driving perfectionist who likes to repeat business constantly to pare it down to its purest essence, actors usually adore him because of his vulnerability and positiveness. He differentiates between his directorial and choreographic personas. For the former, he told Don Shewey, "knowing when to shut up" is crucial, while the choreographer must be specific and demanding. Directing is "a much gentler thing and it requires a lot more concentration, more than just visual." The human element is predominant, and the actor's inner life and feelings, which are not as exact as movements, must be expressed: "The choreographer . . . can be quite bossy; the director has to coax. You can't demand somebody cry or 'feel *this*.' "

Everything on Tune's stage tells a story. To guarantee this, he closes his eyes and listens as if to the radio to judge the clarity of what is conveyed. He then plugs his ears and watches to see if the visual images alone are comprehensible.

Despite his accomplishments, he realizes that each show is a new adventure. Everything he has done must be forgotten and the show must be approached "with a clean slate," built one brick at a time. The actors are asked to begin "from square one." This sometimes means that the entire show is created during workshops and rehearsals. With *Grand Hotel* there was no finished script until shortly before the opening. Whatever does not work is discarded, no matter how much labor went into it, but Tune's velvet-glove personality helps collaborators to accept the loss.

While preparing *Will Rogers*, Tune was rehearsing for a national tour in a musical directed by someone else. In 1992, he was scheduled to direct *Busker Alley*, but backed out, explaining that there were problems with an investor; some claimed he was unwilling to cancel his tour. The producer sued. At the end of 1992, he starred in a revue, *Tommy Tune Tonite*, preparatory to a national tour that lasted well into 1993. In between, he staged a production with the all-female Takarazuka Theater Company in Japan. Among his coming projects is a musical about the *Titanic*, with a score by Yeston. This so-called last of the great director-choreographers, the only one to have won Tonys in four categories, will surely lead the Broadway musical pack through the 1990s.

Further reading:

Bennetts, Leslie. "*Stepping Out* Takes Shape." *New York Times,* January 11, 1987.

Flatow, Sheryl. "Ain't It Grand! " *Playbill,* February 28, 1990.

Gerard, Jeremy. "Keep on Dancin'." *Vanity Fair* (May 1991).

Lawson, Carol. "Fellini's 8½ Inspires a Musical." *New York Times,* May 9, 1982.

Lynne, Jill. "Tuned Up on *Cloud 9.* " *After Dark* (July 1981).

Mandelbaum, Ken. "*Auteur! Auteur!* Tommy Tune Talks about *Grand Hotel.*" *TheaterWeek,* November 20–26, 1989.

Shewey, Don. "Hoofers, Hookers and Hollywood Dreams." *Soho News,* July 2, 1980.

Wetzsteon, Ross. "Broadway's Triple Threat." *Saturday Review* 7 (May 1982).

Also: Kislan, *Hoofing;* Gottfried, *More Broadway Musicals;* Mordden, *Broadway Babies.*

EVGENY VAKHTANGOV (1883–1922)

EVGENY BAGRATIONIVICH VAKHTANGOV was born in the Caucasian city of Vladikavkaz (later Ordjonikize), in what became the Soviet Republic of Armenia, to a wealthy tobacco grower, and acted in local dramatics as a boy. Vakhtangov began math and physics studies at Moscow University in 1903 (he switched to law, but never graduated), while acting and directing with amateurs in Vladikavkaz and Moscow. Among his earliest assignments was Gerhart Hauptmann's domestic tragedy, *Holiday of Peace* (1904), for a hometown workshop. He directed and acted in plays by Maxim Gorky, Anton Chekhov, Henrik Ibsen, and Knut Hamsun, as well as others. From 1909 to 1911, he studied at I. A. Adashev's School of Drama, following which he was accepted into the Moscow Art Theater (MAT). Under its auspices he took a troupe of young actors to Novgorod-Seversk, where he staged a number of plays.

Vakhtangov was a serious Stanislavskian (the older man considered him his successor), and in 1912, he began teaching his master's system, most importantly at the Mansurov Studio. He taught there from 1913 until 1917, when it became the Moscow Dramatic Studio under his leadership. In 1920, it was renamed the Third Studio of MAT; in 1926, it became the Vakhtangov Theater. He also was linked with Moscow's Hebrew-speaking Habimah Theater.

He acted with the First Studio of MAT in 1913, studying with Studio head Leopold Sulerjitsky, whom he assisted on a Paris staging of *The Blue Bird*. Vakhtangov's first directing with the Studio, which operated in an intimate, proscenium-less theater, was another staging of *Holiday of Peace* (1913), notable not only for its cast's truthful feelings but for the introduction of a kind of nervous expressionism into the Studio's placid style of "sincere realism." He followed it with an overly naturalistic showing of Boris Zaitsev's *The Lanin Estate* (1914), before making a strong impact with Henning Berger's *Deluge* (1915), which reveals how a crisis brings out the best in people, only for them to revert to more cynical behavior when the danger passes. It was remarkably unified in combining psychologically penetrating characterizations and moderately heightened physical expressiveness in which every move and intonation served the theme.

While his early work was aimed at intensifying pyschological immersion, he increasingly attempted to go beyond Stanislavksy in search of more expressive theatricality; a major influence was Vsevolod Meyerhold. Vakhtangov came to be regarded as the finest synthesis of Stanislavskianism and Meyerholdianism (although critical of the extremes of both) in his blend of inner truth and theatricalized form. The term he gave to his artistic credo was "creative distortion," wherein nature's images are enhanced by artistic methods. He experimented in developing physical, vocal, and rhythmic approaches to a text, while always grounding characters in a psychological reality and eschewing impersonative portrayals. This led to his mature style of "fantastic realism."

Expressionism, grotesquerie, fantasy, circus, and commedia were among the techniques from which he borrowed to discover appropriate external means. Each production had to determine the correct form for the play at hand. Actors had to sing, dance, and improvise. Eventually, he established an approach that prefigured Bertolt Brecht by having the actors combine the subjective with the objective in demonstrating critical/ironical attitudes toward their characters. They often allowed the spectators to share their awareness that they were acting.

Vakhtangov was a firm supporter of the October Revolution, declaring that it was necessary to produce art for and with "the people." His first post-Revolutionary directorial work was a middling version of Henrik Ibsen's *Rosmersholm* (1918), for the First Studio. Then, from 1918 to 1922, while mounting several lesser works, including evenings of one-acts, he staged his five reputation-making works, Maurice Maeterlinck's *The Mystery of Saint Anthony* (1918; revised 1921), Anton Chekhov's *A Wedding* (1920; revised 1921), August Strindberg's *Eric XIV* (1921), S. Ansky's *The Dybbuk* (1922), and Carlo Gozzi's *Princess Turandot* (1922). Each sought theatrical means whereby the feelings and thoughts of the Russian people could be affected.

The first, a satirical fantasy about a tramplike saint who arrives at a funeral party to revive the deceased and meets with resistance from the family and friends who are glad to keep her dead, had been in preparation for two years before opening at the Moscow Dramatic Studio. The warm humor of the initial production expressed sympathy for the smug family. In 1921, Vakhtangov, under the U.S.S.R.'s spell, revised his staging for the Third Studio to derisively underscore the family's philistinism. With a black-and-white visual scheme based on the satiric drawings of Honoré Daumier, he used grotesquerie to give the bourgeoisie expressionistically stylized, rhythmic movements, with lifelikeness replaced by characteristic poses, gestures, and facial expressions. By contrast, the saint and a housemaid retained their humanity. Everything, particularly the crowd, was a unity designed to convey the central idea. Yet the internalized honesty of the acting prevented the work from becoming excessively formalistic or conventionalized. "Vakhtangov displayed inventive fantasy and affirmed the theatricality of a show, but he also stressed the intrinsic and human value of the master actor," wrote Marc Slonim. When Vakhtangov revived *The Wedding,* he gave it a similarly satirical, antibourgeois staging.

Eric XIV, Vakhtangov's last for the First Studio, was staged as the tragic story of a weak, mentally unbalanced, but human monarch (memorably played by Michael Chekhov) surrounded by lifeless, power-hungry courtiers, conceived as abstract, ghostly puppets distinct from the vitality of the king's subjects. Designer Ignaty Nivinsky's prisonlike palace set was cubistically distorted, suggesting a rust-corroded kingdom on the verge of collapse and reflective of the doomed king's aberrations. The symbolic costuming (Eric was all in white) and masklike makeups were strikingly exaggerated to instantly convey the nature of each character. Their topical relevance was instantly apparent.

The Dybbuk, produced in Hebrew, was problematic because of Vakhtangov's ignorance of the tongue and unfamiliarity with ghetto life, but it communicated the play's ritual mysticism as well as a class-oriented struggle seen by the director in the conflict of the wealthy and poor. The feelings of the young lovers (the bridegroom was played by an actress)—victims of a money-grubbing society—frequently burst through the morbid atmosphere of orthodox belief. Another black-and-white, hallucinatory, expressionistically disoriented production, set in an oppressively airless space, its characters wore mosaiclike painted faces and grotesquerie informed the acting. An unforgettable scene was the nightmarish wedding dance of the monstrously deformed, Goyaesque beggars. The white-garbed bride danced in their midst like a ray of light. Also outstanding was the way the Hasidic men moved synchronously but with bizarre, individualized arm and hand movements. The production remained a permanent part of the Habimah repertoire.

By complete contrast was the commedia-inspired *Princess Turandot*, a colorful, festive, romantic fantasia combining hilarity and lyricism, and Vakhtangov's most delightful, theatrically self-conscious staging. He did not forget its political purposes, telling the cast that the play was a picture of the future as they might see it in their dreams. "Let's show in our fairy-tale what people experience in their struggle against evil, for their future" (quoted in Nikolai Gorchakoff).

The show employed fourth wall–breaking conventionalism, often with great wit, including direct address, audience participation, and, in combination with formal evening dress, the donning of patently artificial costume pieces and beards before the spectators. A towel could be a turban, a scarf a beard. Actors displayed irony as they visibly stepped into and out of character. As the audience watched, stagehands busied themselves carrying symbolic props or carrying place-name signs. Familiar everyday props mingled with exotic ones. Nivinsky, asked to provide scenery that revealed China as seen through Italian eyes, provided an abstract, nonlocalized set of delightfully askew geometrical shapes, square, rectangular, and triangular overhead pennants, and raked platforms allowing for dynamic blocking and choreography. The actors kept strictly to the exactingly set movement, voice, and tempo while creating the sense that it was all being done for the first time. They were encouraged to perform with total sincerity, but when Barach started to cry, Tartaglia collected the tears in a basin and showed them to the audience to elicit respect for the other's feelings. Everything shouted, "This is theater, not life," and a sense of joy at the accomplishment tied actors and spectators together. The production is still played today.

During these years, Vakhtangov continued acting, while also finding the time to teach. Yet, he suffered from cancer (he died aged 39) and never got to see the completed *Princess Turandot*. On opening night, Stanislavsky visited the director's nearby sickroom during the intermission to inform him of the overwhelmingly favorable reception.

Much of Vakhtangov's rehearsal work featured improvisational methods because he felt that creativity arises from unconscious rather than—as Stanislavsky and the Marxists believed—conscious

sources. He liked to provoke his actors' imaginations by giving them hints ("traps" or "promoters") to ponder between rehearsals and to inspire them with the creative mood. One rehearsal thus built imaginatively on the other. Even the most complex, large-cast scenes could be created rapidly by preparing the actors' imaginations and allowing them to discover their own solutions. Despite the elegant precision of each moment in his stagings, they also bore an astonishing spontaneity; this resulted from considerable collaborative creativity. He wanted actors to work out their own business, while he served as stimulator and editor.

He was outstanding at helping actors by creating exciting improvisational situations (*études*) within the context of the action. Believing that directors must reveal "the grain" of their roles by demonstrative, not verbal, means, he often participated himself, changing characters like a chameleon as he encountered each player in turn. Fascinating physical and/or psychological obstacles were established in the improvisations for the actors to overcome in the process of developing vivid mise-en-scènes and sharply delineated performances. Sometimes, during an improvisation, he would shout out commands, or make sarcastic comments about sloppy or inaudible speech. Although he often showed what he wanted, he forbade blind copying.

Vakhtangov addressed his cast about the aims of a project when rehearsals began, but avoided intellectual discussions during the process, which was devoted to working the play out in action. His talks were more a stream of probing questions, aimed at both himself and his listeners, often answered by himself.

Rehearsals were models of discipline and respect for the space, which was holy and had to remain as clean as possible. He was a severe disciplinarian. Those who objected were not appreciated; an inopportune query could lead to dismissal from rehearsal. Vakhtangov's occasional tirades were occupational hazards his acolytes had to face. An indefatigable energy drove him, and he could begin a rehearsal at 8 P.M. and continue until 3 in the morning. He rehearsed for months before he was satisfied. Countless ideas were tried and discarded, and some of the best (such as the costume bits in *Turandot*) were accidental. Even the design evolved during the rehearsal period.

Vakhtangov was unusually well prepared, having done extensive research and knowing the characters intimately. He avoided minute analysis, however, for fear of corrupting the unity of a play. His knowledge was supplemented by wide-ranging study of the visual and performing arts, literature, and history. Music was a special love, and Vakhtangov used it abundantly both as a rehearsal stimulant for rhythm and feeling and as a performance accompaniment. He was adept at all aspects of technical theater and wished to employ the latest innovations to keep pace with the times.

Like Sulerjitsky, Vakhtangov was inspired by Leo Tolstoy's optimistic ethics, summarized by Slonim as "a negative attitude toward the upper classes and capitalist reality, affirmation of man's moral resurrection, pacifism, and belief in the forces of love and brotherhood." Also, from 1905 on he had leaned strongly toward revolutionary politics. Marxism—in its socialist rather than communist guise—was a powerful strain in his work, especially in his tendency to contrast politically positive characters with negative ones in terms of living people versus automatons or puppets. He hated propaganda, but believed that theatrical aesthetics were meant to be put at the service of their epoch—especially the time of ferment in which he was living—by making a play

socially important to a contemporary audience. "Our job," he said, "is to find the combination of form and content that will best capture the imagination of the spectator and remind him of contemporary problems" (quoted in Gorchakoff).

Vakhtangov's professional career lasted just a little more than ten years, but his presence was prolonged by the many top artists he trained, others he influenced, and his successful blend of theatricality and inner realism.

Further reading:

Gorchakoff, Nikolai. *The Vakhtangov School of Stage Art.* Edited by Phil Griffith. Moscow: Foreign Languages Publishing House, n.d.

Simonov, Ruben. *Stanislavsky's Protégé: Eugene Vakhtangov.* Translated and adapted by Miriam Goldina. Translation edited by Helen Choat. New York: DBS Publications, 1969.

Also: Houghton, *Moscow Rehearsals*; Rudnitsky, *Russian and Soviet Theater*; Slonim, *Russian Theater*; Worrall, *Modernism to Realism on the Soviet Stage.*

JEAN VILAR (1912–1971)

JEAN LOUIS CÔME VILAR was born in the port town of Sète, on the French Mediterranean, where his parents ran a millinery shop. He attended local colleges before deciding, at 20, to continue his education in Paris, where he worked for and studied under Charles Dullin for three years, absorbing his highly disciplined methods and respect for the theater as an art.

A military stint ended Vilar's work with Dullin in 1937. In 1938 he was part of a new leftist-oriented troupe called L'Equipe, which gave three 1939 programs before the army recalled Vilar. Discharged for health reasons in 1940, he joined La Roulotte, a troupe that played Molière, J. M. Synge, and Alfred de Musset to unsophisticated rural audiences.

In 1943, Vilar headed up his own small Paris art theater, La Compagnie des Sept, directing studio productions of uncommercial plays. Two were by August Strindberg and one was by Jean Schlumberger. The sets were starkly minimal and the acting was quiet and interiorized, with mesmerizing silences. After the liberation, he revived Strindberg's *The Dance of Death* (1945) in a highly successful production, also offered Molière, and gave the first French showing of Norwegian Sigurd Christiansen.

Vilar's breakthrough was T. S. Eliot's *Murder in the Cathedral* (1945), a production that abandoned the hermetic atmosphere of his earlier choices and starred Vilar as Becket. The strikingly simple sets and costumes were by Léon Gischia, a painter who remained Vilar's principal designer. The production even won the director a special one-time-only "Prix du Théâtre."

Vilar's Paris work had been confined to an elite audience of sophisticates. His place in modern theater history, however, was confirmed when he founded, in 1947, an outdoor festival at the papal palace in the medieval city of Avignon. The festival was a major development in the history of attempts to establish a so-called "popular theater" reaching audiences traditionally disenfranchised (by social, economic, and educational factors) from attending plays. Many others had sought such a theater, but Vilar was the first to make it work. It was also a critical step in the postwar process of decentralizing French culture.

The first season featured three Vilar productions, one each by Paul Claudel and Maurice Clavel, but most notably Shakespeare's *Richard II*, starring Vilar. *Richard II*, which typified Vilar's methods, was excitingly performed at a rapid pace as a political melo-drama. It was staged in the 1,500-seat Court of Honor. Although he came to doubt its possibilities in the philosophically fragmented modern world, united only by collective despair, Vilar sought to recapture the communal, ceremonial, even ritual effect of the Greek or Elizabethan theater, with audiences as much participants as observers. Preoccupied with the theater's educational function, he wanted the audience to respond as members of a concerned citizenry to the plays' historical, social, or ethical issues. The imposing brick walls surrounding the space remained undisguised and the stage was a large platform, 33 feet deep by 50 feet wide. (Later, the stage was shortened to accommodate more spectators.) The wall chosen to back the stage had four archways built into it; these could be incorporated into the staging. The walls were not lit, to neutralize their presence and to keep the focus on the play. Footlights and curtain were absent. Because only three stools were used as on-stage props, Vilar's functionalism came to be called the "three stools aesthetic." Banners and pennants, however, made an impressive sight blowing in the wind. Primary visual emphasis came from the actors moving about in boldly patterned and colored costumes, designed to instantly establish the characters who wore them, and from the simplified, nonrealistic spotlighting. (In some productions, the lighting conjured up locales, such as a forest or a tomb.) Vilar was a trained musician and made excellent, but selective, use of music and sound, especially after being joined by composer Maurice Jarre in 1951.

Early audiences were small, but they grew rapidly. Eventually the festival became a sold-out international event mingling people of all social and economic backgrounds. The number of performances grew to accommodate the attendance. Aiming to create a classless theater that could be as available to everyone as gas, water, and electricity, Vilar struggled to keep prices low.

During the festival's crucial first five years, non-French highlights included Georg Büchner's *Danton's Death* (1948), Shakespeare's *Henry V* (1950), and Heinrich von Kleist's *The Prince of Homburg* (1951). Among important French dramas were Pierre Corneille's *The Cid* (1949) and André Gide's *Oedipus* (1949). In 1951, the great film star, Gérard Philipe, who shared Vilar's social and aesthetic ideas, joined him and gave luminous performances in such plays as *The Cid* and *The Prince of Homburg*. Over the years, he also directed important productions

under Vilar's aegis. Vilar himself continued to play leads in many productions.

Some plays were revived in Paris after the festival season ended and many were redone in later Avignon seasons. Although he occasionally staged a well-known play, most Vilar choices were of plays hardly known to French theatergoers. He searched diligently for new French plays, but was rarely satisfied with them (Claudel, several of whose plays he staged, remained his favorite contemporary); most of his new plays failed. Consequently, it was his reluctant view that the modern theater's key figure was the director, not the dramatist. Vilar concentrated mainly on neglected classics and important but little-known (in France) modern foreign works. When he directed a familiar antique, like *The Cid* or Molière's *Don Juan,* it was to challenge the tired conventionality that had accrued to its usual presentations. Audiences used to stately presentations of the former were surprised by the heroic and lyrical panache he gave it.

Vilar's Avignon success led to his being named head of the nationally subsidized Théâtre National at Paris's Palais du Chaillot. He restored the organization's former name, the Théâtre National Populaire (TNP). Many of the same works were seen at both Avignon and the Chaillot, several remaining in the repertory for years. Vilar brought theater to a much more broadly based, responsive, and popular audience than had any of his predecessors; still, he failed to gain much working-class support. He also had to fight bureaucratic provincialism and tight budgets.

Half the year was spent in Paris, the other half in the provinces, the suburbs, and on foreign tours. Discussions between the artists and the public were regularly scheduled and the theater published materials (much of it by Vilar) to help patrons understand the repertory. Some of the worst excesses of the commercial theater were eliminated, such as allowing latecomers to interrupt a performance. By the time personal and professional reasons led him to resign the TNP in 1963, he had staged 30 of the 57 new productions offered under his leadership.

At the Chaillot, the TNP worked in a huge theater (up to 2,900 seats) whose Italianate features Vilar downplayed. The vast open stage (backed by black drapes) used ascetic sets, when there were any at all, consisting mainly of platforms and architectural units. The space was made even ampler by the removal of the curtain and proscenium and the addition of a thrust into the auditorium. Considerable use was made of sweeping choreographic movement. Vilar's masterful staging even made such intimate plays as Pierre de Marivaux's *The Triumph of Love* and Prosper Merimée's *The Coach of the Holy Sacrament* work on his expansive stages. Nevertheless, most TNP productions were of large-scale plays.

A number of Vilar's TNP productions were highly controversial. One of the most provocative was the French premiere of Bertolt Brecht's *Mother Courage* (1951). Vilar was vilified not only for staging a communist play with taxpayers' money, but for misconstruing Brecht's intentions and making the heroine tragic, thus weakening the play's antiwar message. But he kept the play alive and eventually got it right. Controversy also brewed over his choice of Büchner's *Danton,* because it was a German treatment, not a French one. Similar problems plagued him for years. Often, Vilar quieted critics by demonstrating the quality of his choices in the crucible of performance, although several years were sometimes necessary before a production satisfied him.

Vilar was not restricted to the TNP during these years, a good example of his outside work being Arthur Adamov's *The Invasion* (1950) at the Studio des Champs-Elysées. By 1963, Vilar had added to his TNP repertory stagings of foreign playwrights, including Anton Chekhov, Luigi Pirandello, Sophocles, Sean O'Casey, Pedro Calderón de la Barca, Carlo Goldoni, Aristophanes, and Robert Bolt (*A Man for All Seasons,* in 1963, was his farewell production), as well as plays by Shakespeare, Strindberg, and Brecht that he had not done before. French playwrights dominated these years, with new productions of lesser-known or rarely seen plays by such as Marivaux, Pierre de Beaumarchais, Molière, Honoré de Balzac, Victor Hugo, Jean Racine, Alfred Jarry, Merimée, Musset, and Jean Giraudoux, but only a few recent writers, such as Michael Vinaver, were staged amid the classics (some of them codirected).

From 1959 to 1961, he controlled the small Théâtre Récamier, to experiment with new modernist plays, but the project did not work out. The only play he actually staged (the rest were done by others under his producership) was Armand Gatti's first work.

In 1960, Vilar declared that he would henceforth direct only plays that bore vital lessons regarding contemporary social and political problems. His selections were classics and semiclassics. Several choices were inspired by France's current conflict in Algeria. Aristophanes' *Peace* (1961), which typified Vilar's hatred of war, was filled with topical references to the outside world. Several plays attacked

dictatorships, notably Brecht's *The Resistable Rise of Arturo Ui* (1960).

After leaving the TNP, Vilar freelanced, staging three plays, two in small Paris theaters and one in Geneva, but concentrating on opera and continuing to oversee the Avignon Festival, although no longer directing its plays. During the 1968 student uprisings, he was denounced for having betrayed the Marxist cause through his allegedly regressive and compromising ideas.

When directing, Vilar sought to be as faithful as possible to the dramatist and to make the play accessible to his diverse audience. It was his duty to uncover and reveal the spirit, not the letter, of the author's intentions. He did not desire to impose a personal view on the play, but to listen to its own voice, even if he disagreed with it.

He began with an extensive period of readings during which all were free to ask questions and offer ideas. If several versions of a play were available, the company would compare and discuss them. He deemphasized the director's role and refused to make his presence too clearly visible for fear of interfering in the communication of the playwright's work. Extensive freedom was given to all coworkers, from designers to composers to actors, with Vilar serving as a spiritual and artistic guide during the collaborative rehearsals. He worked gently, by suggestion rather than fiat, mingling closely rather than directing from the house. Actors marveled at his ability to find just the right phrase to illuminate a problem and stimulate their perceptions. He wished, above all, to keep his actors full of confidence.

Despite extensive preparation, Vilar never came to rehearsal with characterizations and business preordained. He had no written plan, although he declared that a director must make a written analysis of the play prior to rehearsals. Often, he revised his interpretations when restaging a work for a later production. Only when it came to insisting on stylistic unity was he likely to insist on specific results. This happened late in rehearsals, when it became imperative to take charge more vigorously.

Vilar's reliance on good acting was absolute. Clarity of diction and strength of projection were necessities, as was fluid and dynamic movement. He kept gestures to a minimum, seeking to make each one count. The guiding lights were simplicity and restraint in the interests of expressing a character's interior life.

Jean Vilar is remembered for establishing the Avignon Festival, for his development of the epic-scaled open stage, for his commitment to vibrant simplicity, for his TNP activities, and, among other things, for his view of the theater as an educational entity linked to the social conditions in which it exists.

Further reading:

Bermel, Albert. "Jean Vilar: Unadorned Theatre for the Greatest Number." *Tulane Drama Review* 5 (December 1960).

Bradby, David, and John McCormick. *People's Theatre.* London: Croom Helms, 1978.

Guicharnaud, Jacques. "Jean Vilar and the T.N.P." *Yale French Studies* 14 (Winter 1954–1955).

Hobson, Harold. "Jean Vilar and Others." *Drama* no. 117 (Summer 1975).

Vilar, Jean. "The Murder of the Director." *Tulane Drama Review* 3 (December 1958).

———. "Secrets." *Tulane Drama Review* 3 (March 1959).

Also: Cole and Chinoy, *Directors on Directing;* Whitton, *Stage Directors in Modern France.*

ANDRZEJ WAJDA (1926–   )

ANDRZEJ WAJDA was born in Suwalki, Poland. He studied painting at the Academy of Fine Arts in Cracow and filmmaking at the Lodz Film School. He was a film director before he entered the theater. He only began directing plays when the work of foreign artists, such as Peter Brook, Giorgio Strehler, and Bertolt Brecht demonstrated how theater could be socially and politically relevant. He started in Gdansk with Michael Gazzo's play about a drug addict, *A Hatful of Rain* (1959), which offered slice-of-life authenticity and unconventional subject matter. Wajda subsequently became internationally prominent via foreign festivals, tours, and works created abroad.

Although he never has been associated solely with one theater or ensemble, preferring to freelance, Wajda has most closely been connected with Cracow's state-subsidized repertory troupe, the Stary Theater. Stylistically, he is eclectic, although his productions normally have contemporary social and political resonances. While his film work was impeded by his liberalism (especially following his 1981 support of Solidarity, which led to his election to Poland's senate), he worked with relative freedom in the theater. His productions—which he frequently designs—have run the gamut from the visually exciting to the minimalist and cerebral, yet they invariably are emotionally powerful.

Wajda's textually faithful *Hamlet* (1960), in Gdansk, emphasized action over psychology, made the play and characters unmistakably Polish, and, apart from the pessimism evoked by introducing Fortinbras's army as cruel invaders, eschewed jarring surprises. The set employed a thrust stage and a three-tier scaffolding displaying various locales in small roomlike units. A less successful 1981 version (Wajda's third) at the Stary was taken over from the important director Konrad Swinarski after the latter died in an accident. Wajda recast Hamlet with a character actor known for his portrayal of nondescripts; the performance combined Hamlet's intellectualism with the qualities of an everyman confronted by an oppressive establishment. Each Wajda *Hamlet* bears an ordinal number to designate its place in the series.

William Gibson's two-character *Two for the Seesaw* (1967) was staged in an intimate Warsaw arena space. Shifting to large-scale theater, Wajda offered John Whiting's British drama *The Devils* (1963), produced in Warsaw on an operatic scale. His first native drama was Stanislas Wyspianksi's 1901 poetic, symbolistic satire on Polish society, *The Wedding* (1963), at the Stary.

After seven years of filmmaking (including *Ashes and Diamonds,* 1961, and *Gates to Paradise,* 1968), Wajda returned to theater with Friedrich Dürenmatt's *Play Strindberg* (1970), in Warsaw. This highly theatrical version of the dramatist's playful response to August Strindberg's *Dance of Death* used strobe and other special lighting and sound effects, a mirrored back wall reflecting the audience in a distorted, fun-house way, a boxing-ring-like central area, and an acting style combining a conventionalized "game-playing" quality with psychological depth.

In 1971, Wajda began his "Dostoyevsky trilogy" with *The Possessed,* loosely adapted from Albert Camus's episodic play of the novel. Premiered at the Stary, it was Wajda's first international success. (In 1974 he staged it at the Yale Repertory Theater in English.) As it took shape, he eliminated most of Camus's work, replacing it with scenes he wrote himself.

The setting was a bare, mud-covered stage backed by a cyclorama depicting the bleak and cloudy hori-

The Possessed. *Directed by Andrzej Wajda. (1971)*
(Photo: Stary Theater/Wojciech Plewinski)

zon. Interiors were established by selected pieces of furniture and imaginative lighting. The predominance of atmosphere over illusionism was fostered by vague and silent, black-shrouded figures, reminiscent of *kabuki* stage assistants, although Wajda used them not only to change props and sets, but to establish an ominous feeling; they participated in the wrenching finale's action. The acting, evolving from three months of rehearsal dominated by improvisations, had a frenzied, nervous pitch that created breathless tension.

Part two of the trilogy came with *Nastasya Filippovna* (1977), adapted from *The Idiot*, with the material evolving during rehearsals. The complex novel was greatly simplified so that its many themes could be explored by focusing on a small segment of the book involving only two characters, Prince Myshkin and Rogozhin. Nastasya, recently strangled by Rogozhin, was represented by her dress. The production was given in a dingy storage room at the Stary for 120 people surrounding the action on three sides. Wajda experimented with admitting the public to some rehearsals, thinking they might find this enjoyable, and that the company could learn from their responses. The experiment failed because the process

of showing unformed work proved unnerving, especially when their efforts were uncritically accepted as an end product.

Wajda discovered his final approach to the material following a lengthy rehearsal (rehearsals often were all-nighters) in which the actors themselves were allowed to be responsible for the script by performing material of their own choice from the novel within the framework he provided. The result was a kind of prepared improvisation that differed in dialogue and blocking from one performance to another.

The final Dostoyevsky installment was Wajda's adaptation of *Crime and Punishment* (1984), shown at the Stary. It focused only on Raskolnikov, the public prosecutor Porfiry, and the religious prostitute Sonya, the few others being little more than plot devices. This intimate staging was given in the same space as *Nastasya Filippovna,* with the audience watching the ultrarealistic production through panes of glass as if looking in from the street. Wajda pointed up the contemporary relevance of the theme, which confronts the notion that anyone— such as political terrorists—can claim theoretical justification for murder.

In 1972, Wajda directed David Rabe's anti-Vietnam war *Sticks and Bones,* in Moscow. He then did Wyspianski's *November Night* (1974) at the Stary. In this 1904 history drama about the abortive November 1830 anti-Russian Polish uprising, the historical figures mingle with Greek gods. Among Wajda's imaginative methods for unifying the mythological and historical levels was original music permitting the mythical scenes to be sung, the score serving

Crime and Punishment. *Directed by Andrzej Wajda.*
(1984) (Photo: Stary Theater/Stanislaw Markowski)

also to tie the work together. The finished production had an operatic quality. Highly selective means were used in the design, with lighting helping to change the many locales. Controversial portrayals of the Russian Grand Duke and his Polish wife, normally stereotypical villains, here displayed psychological complexity and a degree of sympathy. Through its original political interpretation, the production evoked powerful patriotic emotions while reenacting a national debacle.

In Warsaw, Wajda staged S. Przybyszewska's French Revolution drama, *The Danton Affair* (1975), with Robespierre and Danton retaining three-dimensional complexity despite their preoccupation with philosophical issues. Robespierre was treated more sympathetically than Danton, an attitude that was reversed in Wajda's 1985 film of the story. Opting for a minimalist approach, Wajda used a bare stage dominated by a table that could, with minor changes, assume multiple purposes. With the first few rows removed and replaced by a platform, the action moved into the auditorium to allow the spectators, some of whom also sat on the stage, to feel like participants. (Actors scattered among them furthered involvement.) Unlike most of Wajda's work, no use was made of music or special sound effects, and even the lighting was simplified. The focus was on ideas rather than aesthetics.

Wajda offered Antonio Buero Vallejo's *Abandoned by Reason* (1976) in Warsaw, and fellow Pole Slawomir Mrozek's *Emigré's* (1976) at the Stary. The first, dealing with Goya and concerned with art as a symbolic path to freedom from oppression, brought the audience and actors into close contact, borrowed blocking ideas from Goya's paintings, and created a perpetual state of menace by keeping on stage a band of "volunteers" who constantly were vigilant for some slip by which the liberal characters might be betrayed. Mrozek's two-character, allegorical piece, about a pair of nameless emigrants in a nameless state, was staged in a naturalistic environment behind a scrim set into a black frame that made the production look like a film. Each drama was concerned with ideas of freedom, a continual theme of Wajda's work.

Among Wajda's subsequent productions were Tadeusz Rozewicz's *White Wedding* at Yale (1977); Wajda's adaptation of Kazimir Moczarski's *Conversations with the Executioner* (1977) at the Kalisz Theater Festival; a dramatic amalgam called *As the Days Pass, As the Years Pass* (1978) at the Stary; Witkiewicz's *They* (1980) in Villeurbanne, France; Sophocles' *Antigone* (1984) at the Stary; Ernest Bryll's *Easter*

Vigil at Warsaw's Church of the Lord's Mercy (1985); Alexander Fredro's *The Vengeance* (1986); S. Ansky's *The Dybbuk* (1989), both at the Stary (also seen in Purchase, New York); the streamlined, two-hour, 10-minute *Hamlet IV* (1989), also seen at Purchase; and Wyspianski's *The Wedding* (1992, repeated in 1993), in German at the Salzburg Festival. In 1993, Wajda was developing a production of *Sansho the Bailiff*, with a script by screenwriter-director Terence Malick. It was based on Kenji Mizoguchi's classic Japanese film (1954) in which a decent provincial governor is exiled, his children put into slavery, and his wife sold into prostitution. A workshop production with an Asian-American cast opened late in the year at the Brooklyn Academy of Music, but only for an invited audience.

Of those seen in Poland, the Moczarski work was a naturalistically staged discussion of moral issues between a Polish resistance fighter and a Nazi war criminal forced to share the same cell. *As the Days Pass* was inspired by the work of director Robert Wilson and was a seven-hour presentation in three parts (seen separately or in a marathon showing) combining elements of great intimacy with epic scale, fictional with historical personages, and realism with symbolism. Within a theme concerning the passing of time, it presented a picture of cultural life in Cracow from the 1870s through World War I as depicted in fragmentary materials drawn from a variety of Polish writers.

Wajda turned up the heat in his controversial *Antigone*, fired by the declaration of martial law in Poland. Its modern dress reflected contemporary political attitudes, with Antigone an archetypal revolutionary confronted by an evil government. The chorus assumed multiple, socially pointed roles, from combat soldiers to establishment figures to Gdansk shipyard hardhats.

Easter Vigil was a religious dramatic poem staged at a ruined church because the radicalized author's work had been banned from theaters. Although its optimistic antigovernment message—inspired by the rise and fall of Solidarity—was disguised by a biblical tale about "doubting" Thomas, the Apostle, its metaphorical purpose was clear to the thousands who saw it despite the lack of advertisements. The presentation, in contemporary clothes, used the entire church space, including the street outside the main doors when a character entered through them leaving his car outside with the motor running.

The Vengeance was a 19th-century comedy often considered inaccessible; Wajda staged it in a straightforwardly neutral manner that barely betrayed the presence of a director. Its ultimate purpose, unlike almost all of Wajda's previous work, was to provide entertainment rather than subtextual allusions.

Wajda's post-1970 work often has demonstrated his ability to combine multiply layered images, beautiful tableaux, atmospheric lighting, original use of sound and music, expertly chosen props, and passionate acting, usually in episodic texts that allow for constantly fresh redeployments of his theatrical resources. He is fond of improvisational rehearsal techniques as a means of digging out the subtext and giving his actors a feeling of spontaneity, as if each performance was being given for the first time. Promptbooks and notes are not present, as he prefers collaborative measures in which decisions are arrived at by the company, under his guidance. He does not rehearse, however, without extensive preliminary preparation (sometimes covering several years), including research and cogitation so that the main outlines of his approach are roughly formed in his mind. Despite his preparation, he hopes to make new discoveries. He insists on an approximate idea of the set before he begins, although he favors the notion of ongoing revisions. As it is crucial that each prop and furnishing be perfect, he likes to choose them himself.

Wajda prefers to cast actors he knows, especially those who are intellectually sharp and artistically serious. A very patient man, he hates to rush those who are having difficulty but who he senses are emotionally committed. Because he works organically, he allows actors to discover their own blocking and gestures once they have determined the truth behind their actions. Actors must interact and always be "in the moment" while remaining aware of their work's larger social and political implications.

Wajda's rehearsals are inspiring, nonautocratic, and intellectually open. He strives to arrive at fitting images that will communicate the underlying meanings of a scene, and focuses on the best ways of expression. Actors must comprehend the meaning of everything they say and do and not be directorial puppets.

The director claims no interaction between his film and theater work. "Theater," he told Michael T. Kaufman, "is for words, for beautiful, complicated words and thoughts. . . . People will always go to the theater to hear words, dialogue, speeches and ideas, which are the basis of Western theatrical traditions." He is one of a group of Polish directors who have put their theater on the international map since the 1960s. His commitment to serious intellectual, social, and political themes, especially in the name of human liberty, makes his voice vitally important in Polish society, so very recently released from the shackles of a repressive political system.

Further reading:

Jacoby, Oren. "Wajda's Dostoevsky . . . Darkness Visible." *Theatre* 18 (Fall–Winter 1986).

Karpinski, Maciej. *The Theatre of Andrzej Wajda.* Translated by Christina Paul. Cambridge, England: Cambridge University Press, 1989.

Kaufman, Michael T. "Polish Director Finds Haunting Relevance in Dostoyevsky." *New York Times,* July 6, 1986.

Wajda, Andrzej. "Theatre versus Film." In *Twentieth Century Polish Theatre.* Edited by Bohdan Drozdowski. Translations edited by Catherine Itzen. London: John Calder, 1979.

MARGARET WEBSTER (1905–1971)

MARGARET WEBSTER was born in New York to renowned British actors Ben Webster and Dame May Whitty. She attended Queen Anne's School in Caversham, England, and acted in amateur theatricals. She later studied acting at London's Etlinger Dramatic School. From 1924 on she was a professional actress, and eventually played supporting roles in many plays she directed. Her directing career began in 1933, with amateur productions.

"Peggy" Webster's early professional stagings were showcases of revivals and new plays for small nonprofit groups. She moved into the commercial arena with Keith Winter's *Old Music* (1937), followed by her breakthrough, Shakespeare's *Richard II* (1938), staged for a record-breaking 171 Broadway performances with Maurice Evans in the lead. This was the first of a series of succesful Evans-Webster Broadway mountings of Shakespeare that made their reputations. They were essentially collaborative, although each later claimed responsibility for important ideas. Webster's hand was especially notable in the crowd scenes, where she provided three-dimensionality (including written "ad-libs") for the lowliest spear-carriers.

Webster continued to make her mark on Broadway, but her new play productions paled before her Shakespeares. Among her few modest victories in modern work was Lenore Coffee Cowen and William Joyce Cowen's biblical drama, *Family Portrait* (1939), starring Judith Anderson. Her Shakespeare productions with Evans continued with *Hamlet* (1938); *Henry IV, Part I* (1939), with Evans as Falstaff; *Twelfth Night* (1940), produced by the Theater Guild with Evans as Malvolio and Helen Hayes as Viola; and *Macbeth* (1941), costarring Anderson as Lady Macbeth. *Hamlet*, notable for being uncut, and based on the first folio version, ran three hours and 38 minutes, with a dinner break provided in the middle.

Webster believed that excessive study of the critical background of a Shakespeare play could confuse the director and that it was better to study the play itself than to rely on secondary accounts. Her goal was to bring out the story, for this is what keeps audiences interested. By producing the uncut *Hamlet* the presumed ambiguity in the title character (interpreted by Webster and Evans as an extroverted, action-loving hero) disappears, and marginal characters emerge as well rounded. *Hamlet* also demonstrated Webster's insistence that Shakespeare's characters be believable and humanly recognizable, which she achieved by downplaying the dialogue's rhetoric and by providing realistic byplay.

During this period, Webster published her acclaimed book, *Shakespeare Without Tears* (1942), and offered four 40-minute versions of Shakespeare comedies at the Flushing Meadows World's Fair (1939) in a modified Globe Theater. Her advocacy of providing out-of-work actors with showcase opportunities to gain experience led, in 1941, to her founding of the Experimental Theater, with the grudging support of Actors Equity. Her sole production was Euripides' *The Trojan Women* in a modern-dress staging that attempted to correlate the tragedy with the war in Europe.

In 1943, Webster did *Othello*, her first Shakespeare without Evans. Its 295 showings broke all records for the play. The production was controversial because Webster made the radical decision to cast African-American Paul Robeson as the Moor, whom she was convinced Shakespeare intended to be black.

In 1944, she successfully tackled Anton Chekhov's *The Cherry Orchard*, sharing the reins with Eva Le Gallienne, who played Madame Ranevskaya. It was the beginning of a close working relationship. Webster returned to the bard for *The Tempest* (1945), a production that featured several novelties, including the casting of black actor Canada Lee as

Caliban and Norwegian ballerina Vera Zorina as Ariel. The ingenious scenic plan, which employed a revolving stage, created the impression of a desert island.

Webster and Le Gallienne formed the American Repertory Theater in 1946, but it closed a year later after several unsuccessful revivals—including an opulent *Henry VIII*—that failed to generate the needed revenue. Unwilling to abandon her hopes for a repertory theater, Webster founded a bus-and-truck touring company in 1948, the Marweb Shakespeare Company, to bring stripped-down Shakespeare to towns around the country. It lasted for two years and, during its brief life of mostly one- and two-night stands, gave four plays on an easily transportable stage in every conceivable venue. Unlike Webster's earlier Shakespeares, these employed novel period choices, such as playing *The Taming of the Shrew* in terms of a troupe of strolling Victorian actors. Marweb's success in inspiring interest in classical drama was vital in the coming development of regional theater.

Webster, who was now also directing opera, reteamed with Evans in 1950 for a successful revival of George Bernard Shaw's *The Devil's Disciple.* They then reproduced their *Richard II.* Webster was responsible for a fine revival of Shaw's *Saint Joan* (1951), starring Uta Hagen. Her career ran into a roadblock in 1953, thanks to the House Un-American Activities Committee, which painted her pink. She did two flops in 1953, including *Richard III* with José Ferrer, her first Shakespearean turkey.

Subsequently, Webster found most of her jobs outside of New York. She gave lectures, acted in one-woman shows, and staged about a play a year. Her principal directing work took her to various British repertory companies, to Broadway, to the West End, to South Africa, to several large American universities, to Off-Broadway, and to another short-lived venture in repertory, the National Repertory Theater, starring Le Gallienne.

Webster staged 15 Shakespeare plays (including the World's Fair versions), nine on Broadway, and a good number of them commercial successes. By contrast to the then familiar heavily pictorial style, Webster's revivals were considerably simplified, although still leaning toward the picturesque. Her sets were normally spare yet beautiful, and devised to allow for rapid transitions. The sets provided basic Elizabethan elements, including minimal forestages, "inner belows," and rear galleries with "inner aboves." Props and furniture were minimal, and chosen to help establish locale. She was not in favor of a pure Elizabethan set, having discovered that its minimalism too often created dullness and inflexibility. In her eyes, a creatively managed proscenium stage—to which, perhaps, was appended a forestage—was the most satisfactory because its visual possibilities allowed most spectators to share the same picture. Her costumes were lovely and usually in a period either traditionally associated with the play or close to it (such as a Tudor *Hamlet*).

Webster worked closely with designers, and she always provided her own groundplan, believing only the director could truly appreciate the problems involved in moving actors about in a particular space. On occasion, she allowed her producer's or star's scenic ideas to take precedence over her own.

Webster, who normally believed in being faithful to the original, and who spent a great deal of time in selecting the best text (usually the folio versions), sometimes took creative liberties. In *Henry IV* she inserted at IV. ii. an edited version of the first Shallow scene from Part 2. The masque in *The Tempest* was excised. Her transposition of Prospero's "Our revels now are ended" from its original place to an epilogue was deemed radical but viable. She justified most of her cuts by claiming that Shakespeare himself did not write them, that the lines were archaic or too topical, the scenes were too expensive to produce, or simply, the play needed to be shortened.

The plays were her focus, not her own ingenuity. She normally sought to convey Shakespeare's universal concerns, not some tendentious attitude. The director serves the play, and not the other way around. Webster had little use for "gimmicky" interpretations, most of which she viewed as "adaptations." Her typical response to any play was to search for the reality of the characters and not a political or social hook. The director's function is to discover the psychological mechanism driving each character and to devise effective business to reveal these.

Webster prepared assiduously. She believed in knowing precisely what her goals were, from characterizations to pace to mood, while keeping the door open for change. Blocking was worked out on a groundplan using two-inch figures, and the skeletal results were entered in a promptbook that figured strongly, though not rigidly, in the rehearsals. Her purpose was to save time by not becoming bogged down in trial-and-error rehearsals. As her career progressed she became more precise in her jottings, using differently colored writing to set one type of cue off from another. Her blocking notes used lines

drawn from the dialogue to the margins, where shorthand notes described the moves.

A prime requisite in choosing Shakespearean actors was their ability to play with truth. This had to be combined with excellent speech, in which Webster found American players wanting, especially when it came to combining verbal imagery with internal honesty. She tried to get her actors to focus on their thoughts, not their words, and to put sense above beauty.

Webster's casting of blacks in roles for which others would not have considered them was pioneering. Her bus-and-truck company also included talented blacks, making her an early—if limited—advocate of nontraditional casting. She disliked the commercial system's auditions but did her best to make actors comfortable at them. When she auditioned elderly players for Noel Coward's *Waiting in the Wings* (1960), she read along with them to make them feel more comfortable. When she called back those who impressed her, she cautioned them to wear the same clothes to help her remember them better.

Leading roles in Webster's Shakespeare productions were often played by stars, because she did not trust lesser actors to handle the demands of such parts. This meant that she sometimes had to confront performers who had their own firm ideas. Unlike many other established directors, she was more likely to compromise than to insist on her own viewpoint, even when submission was painful. Her belief was that it was better to get an honest performance in which the performer believed than to have the latter produce an interpretation imposed by an autocrat.

Webster's first rehearsals saw her reading the entire play as clearly as possible to avoid the need to explicate the text. She knew that veterans could not find much value in this approach, but felt it aided less experienced actors. She thought that by taking the actors' minds off their own roles they would see the play in its totality. Webster then blocked, working from her prepared ideas, varying them only when something better arose. She believed that actors were more comfortable when working from a prearranged foundation and that they learned their lines more quickly under such circumstances. Her blocking went quickly, roughly an act a day. Despite such speed, she seemed relaxed and playful, although always businesslike.

Webster preferred a collaborative process, and was not a dictator or tyrant. She knew how to get actors to give their all and how to make them feel they were creative contributors. As a working actress, she understood their problems and how to address them in their own terms. She shied from demonstrations or readings, although the special requirements of movement and gesture in the classics often forced her to resort to such techniques, especially with Americans. To help actors playing classical roles, she explained the situations of the characters in contemporary terms to which the actors could respond. Webster also hated to get involved in talk-fests and favored actors who could trust their instincts rather than engage in verbal analysis.

Webster was generally reserved and she cautioned against undue directorial shouting, but there are stories of her losing her temper and screaming out of frustration. Tardiness was among the things that ticked off the compulsively punctual director.

Webster is important in the history of directing for her having succeeded in a male-dominated profession, for her unusually consistent triumphs with commercial productions of Shakespeare, for her advancement of nontraditional casting, and for her helping to prepare for the regional theater movement.

Further reading:

Downer, Alan. "The Dark Lady of Shubert Alley." *Sewanee Review* 54 (January 1946).

Evans, Maurice. *All This . . . and Evans, Too!* Columbia: University of South Carolina Press, 1987.

Heggie, Barbara. "Profiles: We." *New Yorker,* May 20, 1944.

Webster, Margaret. *Shakespeare Without Tears.* Rev. ed. New York: Globe, 1955.

———. *Don't Put Your Daughter on the Stage.* New York: Alfred A. Knopf, 1972.

Also: Johnson, *Directing Methods;* Leiter, *From Belasco to Brook.*

ORSON WELLES (1915–1990)

GEORGE ORSON WELLES was born in Kenosha, Wisconsin, but raised mostly in Chicago. An artistic and intellectual prodigy, he was the son of a wealthy businessman and a highly cultured woman. At the Todd School in Woodstock, Illinois, he was active in theatricals. Not long after his graduation, he and his mentor, Roger Hill, edited three Shakespeare plays, with a focus on the staging.

While on a 1931 walking tour of Ireland, the 16-year-old Welles talked himself into an acting job with Micheal MacLiammoir and Hilton Edwards's Gate Theater of Dublin. His exposure to their international repertory and to Edwards's theatricalist, antinaturalistic style played a vital part in his formation. Most of Welles's stage directing would consciously abandon conventional realism for overt presentationalism, exploiting rather than ignoring the presence of the audience.

After returning to America, he coached drama at Todd. In 1933, Welles began his American acting career with Katharine Cornell's company. That same year, he organized a theater festival at Todd, hiring professionals to play with local amateurs. Welles starred in and directed Gerald du Maurier's *Trilby.*

Welles's acting led to a radio career, where his contributions were multifaceted. His historic production and narration of H. G. Wells's *The War of the Worlds* on October 30, 1938, on RKO radio was so convincing it caused a mass hysteria in which listeners actually believed an alien invasion was occurring. While busy in radio he was simultaneously involved in stage work. In 1936, Welles, not yet 21, was hired by John Houseman to direct for the Negro unit of the WPA's Federal Theater Project (FTP). For his first assignment (at Harlem's Lafayette Theater) he set *Macbeth* in 1820 Haiti, with Macbeth based on the flamboyant leader Henri Christophe. Jack Carter's Macbeth was in the grip of otherworldly powers and not simply the victim of bloody ambition. The play featured impressionistic jungle foliage; the thump of native drums (the expressive use of sound was a Welles hallmark); mood-provoking lighting; a blues and spiritual score; and voodoo rituals for the witches, who were led by a male Hecate played as a priest bearing a huge bullwhip. For once, the presence of the witches seemed justifiable to a modern audience. The text was cut to 90 minutes and rearranged to emphasize melodramatic values.

Still under the FTP, Welles and Houseman created a classically oriented company, Project 891, at Maxine Elliott's Theater. They opened with a panned production of an 1851 French vaudeville farce by Eugène Labiche and Marc Michel called, in

Orson Welles (l) in Julius Caesar. *Directed by Orson Welles. (1937)*   (Photo: Theater Collection, Museum of the City of New York)

its new adaptation, *Horse Eats Hat* (1936). Welles's surrealistically farcical staging, which often broke the fourth wall, took extreme liberties, including moving the period to 1908 and midwesternizing the dialogue and characters. Welles appeared in a leading role.

More successful was his 75-minute version of Christopher Marlowe's *Doctor Faustus* (1937), with Welles in the title role. Carter played the seductive Mephistophilis, usually acted by a Caucasian. Imaginative lighting created a sense of limitless space on a seemingly bare stage. Boldly costumed characters stepped forth from black velvet hangings and were suddenly seen in pillars of light, some of them projected upward from the stage floor. The entertainment of the Seven Deadly Sins was a puppet show given in an upper box. One of several trapdoors served as the smoke-belching, sulfurous pit. A 20-foot thrust was used for more intimate scenes.

The next Welles 891 staging was Marc Blitzstein's radical political opera, *The Cradle Will Rock* (1937), an agitprop-influenced allegory about the conflict between trade unionism and reactionary capitalism. Welles provided an elaborately designed show, but it only lasted for a single preview. Not only did its

left-wing message rile powerful rightwingers, but the FTP was suffering a severe cutback in funds, necessitating the temporary postponement of various projects. The government closed the show on the night of its premiere. Choosing to interpret the action as censorship, they moved to another theater. There, with no sets or costumes, and with Blitzstein himself at an old piano rented at the last minute, the cast (forbidden by union rules from appearing on stage), sang from their seats as a spotlight operator struggled to pinpoint them.

Houseman and Welles quickly founded the Mercury Theater, which later revived *The Cradle Will Rock*. They recreated the barebones approach, but with the actors on stage, not in the house. The Mercury was a high-minded, popular-priced commercial organization that proposed to mingle political themes with aesthetic values. During their existence between 1937 and 1939, they produced five Broadway plays and two that closed out of town. *Julius Caesar* (1937), subtitled "The Death of a Dictator," and starring Welles as Brutus, was a swift-moving, 90-minute compression that twisted the drama into an antifascist statement. Caesar was a Mussolini-like tyrant, Brutus a well-meaning but ineffective liberal,

Cassius a fiery radical, and Antony a rabble-rousing demagogue. *Julius Caesar* did not really support Welles's political conception, but the international situation led many to accept it as a blow against totalitarianism. The mobs wore drab gangsterish overcoats and fedoras and the military dressed in fascistic uniforms. The sparsely decorated platform setting—backed by the exposed, blood-red-painted brick wall of the theater—was used for all locales, with shifts suggested by the lighting. Mote-filled beams projected upward by powerful lamps within the floor evoked Germany's Nuremberg rallies. Again, melodrama reigned over character and language. Welles's mob direction was remarkable, with emotions often evinced simply by the sound of footsteps.

Thomas Dekker's *The Shoemaker's Holiday* (1938) was a bawdy Elizabethan romp, filled with double-entendres, oversized codpieces, and four-letter comedy, depicting—in 90 minutes—the democratic society of old London. George Bernard Shaw's *Heartbreak House* (1938), with Welles as Capt. Shotover, proved a surprisingly straightforward—if prolix—interpretation, largely because Shaw refused to allow a single word to be cut. The Mercury's final New York production was of Georg Büchner's 1835 French Revolution drama, *Danton's Death* (1938). Again compressing a long play into 90 minutes, Welles (who played St. Just) stressed a nihilistic and antirevolutionary position, thereby muddying Büchner's political viewpoint. The most exceptional feature was a cycloramic surround to which thousands of Halloween masks were affixed to convey either the revolutionary masses or, perhaps, the heads of the guillotined thousands.

In the 1940s, Welles went to Hollywood and became a world-famous movie director (*Citizen Kane*, considered by some Hollywood's greatest film, 1941; *The Magnificent Ambersons*, 1942; *The Lady from Shanghai*, 1948; *Touch of Evil*, 1958; etc.) and actor (*Jane Eyre*, 1944; *The Third Man*, 1950; etc.). Over the years Welles suffered through numerous personal problems, including alcoholism, obesity, and several failed marriages. In spite of his sagging reputation, Welles continued to be known to the public as a bit player in films, a familiar face in television commercials, and a celebrity raconteur on talk shows. He also indulged in various other pursuits, including some political dabbling. For all his genius, however, he gained a reputation as an improvident, self-indulgent, self-destructive, and often impossible-to-work-with artist.

These traits also showed up in his stage work. An example was his version of William Gillette's 1894 comedy, *Too Much Johnson* (1938), staged at a Connecticut summer theater. Welles's impractical desire to use extensive film footage mingled with live action forced the Mercury to scuttle the work. Similarly doomed was his occasionally brilliant, but confusing and overlong, Shakespeare conflation, *Five Kings* (1939), coproduced with the Theater Guild, and combining five history plays in a multiscened, epic mélange. With its costly and unwieldy reliance on a huge, mechanically revolving set to bring all its locales into view, it had to be scrapped out of town.

Apart from several shows outside the legitimate theater realm, Welles—principally engaged in films—staged only eight more productions. Few compared to his commanding work of the thirties. The list includes his expressionistic *Native Son* (1941), an adaptation of Wright's socially conscious novel about a black man who accidentally kills a white woman; an overproduced musical extravaganza based on Jules Verne's *Around the World in Eighty Days*, with a mediocre score by Cole Porter (1946); another revival of *Macbeth* (1947), starring Welles, given at the Utah Centennial Festival in preparation for his movie of the play; a rushed, but oddly successful 1950 abbreviation of *Doctor Faustus* called *Time Runs* (with Eartha Kitt as Helen of Troy) given on the same bill with a critically panned Hollywood satire by Welles called *The Unthinking Lobster,* and staged in English for French audiences in Paris (it toured Germany in a different format); a disappointingly conservative 1951 London revival of *Othello* (with Welles as the Moor), given while Welles was in the midst of preparing his noteworthy movie version; Welles's Melville adaptation, *Moby Dick Rehearsed* (1955), staged in London; a sporadically worthwhile New York revival of *King Lear* (1956), which because of accidents he suffered, forced the grossly overweight Welles, who was playing Lear, to appear in a wheelchair; a brief run in Ireland of *Chimes at Midnight* (1960), a new adaptation of his *Five Kings,* based mainly on the two parts of *Henry IV,* with Welles as Falstaff, and staged as prelude to a film version; and, finally, the much-appreciated London premiere of Eugène Ionesco's *Rhinoceros* (1960), starring Laurence Olivier, but which proved a letdown to the director when he came to detest the play.

Welles thought his finest stage work was *Moby Dick,* an intriguing, stripped-down adaptation, staged as if a Victorian theater company were rehearsing it during the day, while playing *King Lear* at night. Welles was both the company's actor-manager and Ahab. In its extensive dependence on the audience's imagination (much pantomime was used), it was reminiscent of Welles's earlier theatricalist stagings.

Despite his obvious hatred of totalitarianism, Welles was the ultimate director-dictator. Even as a boy he rehearsed his fellow students by banging a big stick to assert himself. He believed the director was master of the entire production. His multiple talents (he was musically gifted as well as possessing excellent painting and sketching skills) prompted him to take a hand in every part of his productions. It was his firm conviction that only a single, over-arching conception of the play could be satisfactory; he denied theatrical creation as an act of collaboration. On occasion, he had disputes with his designers because he tended to claim responsibility for their work. He was more likely to have inspired the designs with his sketches and demands than to have designed them in the technical sense. His technical knowledge was considerable, though, and he even referred to instrument numbers in giving his lighting designers notes. "Production by Orson Welles," which suggested more than just direction, was his preferred billing.

Some actors remembered him as allowing them free expression and even improvisation, when he trusted them, but the bulk of Welles's actors considered him a tyrant who treated them like puppets. Welles had no truck with Stanislavsky, and was more concerned with getting something to look and sound right than with how an actor could summon up the proper feelings.

Because of his unruly but fertile imagination, he experimented endlessly to find precisely the right effect needed by a moment. It was not even important to explain his intentions, because his penchant for changing his mind might lead to a result at odds with his original plans; he felt it was unwise to be caught making an error of judgment. Moreover, he maintained, most actors are preoccupied with themselves and do not really care about knowing the "grand canvas." One of his oddest procedures was during the rehearsals for *Moby Dick,* for which—until just before the opening—he refused to rehearse on stage with the others, speaking his role over a booming public address system set up in the auditorium so that he could control the performances from out front and also save his voice. Even during a performance, he might sidle up to an actor and give him distracting, whispered directions. Nevertheless, he usually overwhelmed and charmed actors by the bravado, wit, enthusiasm, and force-of-nature charm of his oversized personality and Renaissance-man intelligence.

Welles had a ferocious temper and would often explode in gargantuan rages when displeased. Intimidation, as practiced by the towering Welles, who also owned famously resonant vocal cords, was an often successful device. Some of his tantrums were staged, but he occasionally overstepped his bounds and created long-lasting enmity with respected artists.

He controlled not only a production's look, but its text, cutting and transposing ruthlessly and, in Shakespeare, even interpolating dialogue from other plays to justify specific action. He was more concerned with the excitement he could create than with purist ideals of respect for the dramatist's script.

For various reasons, Welles, at least in his early days, preferred to direct late at night. When he worked with nonunion actors on his first productions, he was apt to begin at midnight and go on until daylight. To keep himself going during *Julius Caesar* rehearsals, he began to direct while seated on a high stool in the orchestra and eating a lavish meal from a fancy restaurant. He was also known to use stay-awake drugs such as benzedrine. It was a personal affront when actors, following union rules, left at five o'clock.

Few directors had as many talents or brought to Broadway the kind of artistic vision that Welles did during his early days, when most fare was conventionally representational. Had he chosen to do so, he might have revolutionized the American stage.

Further reading:

France, Richard. *The Theatre of Orson Welles.* Lewisburg, Pa.: Bucknell University Press, 1977.

Higham, Charles. *Orson Welles: The Rise and Fall of an American Genius.* New York: St. Martin's Press, 1985.

Leaming, Barbara. *Orson Welles.* New York: Viking Penguin, 1985.

McBride, Joseph. *Orson Welles: Actor and Director.* New York: Oxford University Press, 1977.

Also: Johnson, *Directing Methods.*

ROBERT WILSON (1941–   )

ROBERT WILSON was born in Waco, Texas, where his father was a prominent lawyer, and where, as a child, he was active in amateur theater. He studied business at the University of Texas at Austin before switching to interior design at Brooklyn's Pratt Institute, gaining a BFA in 1965. He painted, created (and/or designed) experimental dance and theater, and revealed unusual skills in aiding brain-damaged and otherwise impaired children.

Wilson's first large-scale project was Off-Broadway's *The King of Spain* (1969). Subsequently, his original pieces were oversized or chamber-sized. At times, he incorporates material from earlier work. Often, parts of longer works are produced as "prologues" or "overtures." Interpolations called "knee plays" or *entr'actes* are occasionally played alone. Wilson has branched out to stage established texts, primarily classics.

Among his famous large pieces are *The Life and Times of Sigmund Freud* (1969), which ultimately absorbed *Deafman Glance* (1970) and was the first Wilson work seen abroad; *KA MOUNTAIN AND GUARDenia TERRACE* (1972), performed on a mountain at Iran's Shiraz Festival; *The Life and Times*

Robert Wilson during the workshop for Alcestis. *(1986)* (Photo: American Repertory Theater/Paula Rhodes)

of Joseph Stalin (1973); *A Letter for Queen Victoria* (1974), Wilson's only Broadway production; *The $ Value of Man* (1975); *Einstein on the Beach* (1976; revived in Brooklyn, 1992), an "opera" (how Wilson often describes his musically dense work) with a hypnotic score by Philip Glass; *Death Destruction and Detroit* (1979), inspired by imprisoned Nazi Rudolf Hess, premiered in Berlin; *Edison* (1979), motivated by the inventor's life, premiered in Villeurbanne; *the CIVIL warS: a tree is best measured when it is down* (1984), each of its six sections created in a different country and intended for the Los Angeles Olympic Arts Festival, but—apart from individual components—unrealized because of the costs; *Death Destruction and Detroit II* (1987), premiered in Berlin and taking its inspiration from Franz Kafka's life; and *The Forest* (1988), premiered in Berlin and based on the Babylonian epic *Gilgamesh*.

Among his chamber pieces, usually employing from one to four players, are several differently subtitled works under the rubric of *Dia Log* (1973); *I Was Sitting on My Porch This Guy Appeared I Thought I Was Hallucinating* (1977); *The Golden Windows* (1982), premiered in Munich; and *Great Day in the Morning* (1982), with opera star Jessye Norman singing black spirituals.

Wilson began staging existing texts in 1984, when he directed back-to-back Medea operas. He later did Euripides' *Alcestis* and the Christoph Gluck opera version of it (1986), as well as controversial interpretations of other famous operas. One of these was his (for Wilson) unconventionally funny adaptation of Carl Maria von Weber's *Der Freischütz* (1990), adapted by Wilson, Tom Waits, and William Burroughs, as a musical comedy mixing German and English and coming off, according to one critic, as "a cross of *Cabaret, The Threeepenny Opera,* and *The Rocky Horror Show.*" It premiered in Hamburg and was seen in Brooklyn in late 1993. A year earlier (1992) he and Waits had collaborated on *Alice,* also premiered in Hamburg.

Anton Chekhov, Henrik Ibsen, and Shakespeare (a German *King Lear* in 1990 starring an octogenarian actress) have been explored. Wilson's newest works include Gertrude Stein's *Dr. Faustus Lights the Lights* (1992), seen in New York with German acting students, Georg Büchner's *Danton's Death* (1992), at Houston's Alley Theater, with Richard Thomas; Susan Sontag's *Alice in Bed* (1993); and *Orlando*

the CIVIL warS. *Directed by Robert Wilson. (1984)*   (Photo: American Repertory Theater/Richard Feldman)

(1993), a one-woman piece starring Isabelle Huppert. For the Büchner, the lengthy text was compressed and slightly rearranged, the formalistic images were crisply elegant, and the play's passion became more impressive by virtue of its contrast with the cool visual ambience. The *New York Times* described the scene in which Danton's wife, Julie, poisons herself:

> The back of the stage opens to reveal a flat rectangular box of light—pale green backdrop (almost white), a slightly darker shade of green for the floor. Julie . . . in a ravishing darker green silk dress . . . , reclining on a couch of black lacquered wood. Three vials, dark blue, ruby and black, lie on the floor bathed in a yellow light subtly warmer than its surroundings. The resonances with classical mythology are inescapable; the immediate esthetic impact profound.

Wilson's modern repertoire is exemplified by Heiner Müller, the Marxist German playwright. His open-ended, nonlinear, imagistic plays, *Hamletma-*

chine (1986) and *Quartett* (1987), found an ideal interpreter in Wilson, who shares Müller's distaste for fixed interpretation.

Bored by psychological realism, Wilson became a progenitor of the theater of images or visions, defined by Stefan Brecht as

> the staging, with live performers, movements and development in such a fashion as to appear a world or reality or the representation of one by an individual and seeming personally important and significant to him . . . independently of verbal, intellectual or discursive analysis. . . . [It] can not be construed as the making of a statement. . . . It is not an imitative or in any way a significative act; there is, for the maker, no question of meaning. The maker's intent is to impart the vision and a sense of its importance. [It] is a stage designer's theater. . . .

His earliest works grew out of workshops with a band of disciples known in 1968 as the Byrd Hoffman School of Byrds, a name derived from a therapist

Alcestis. *Directed by Robert Wilson. (1986)* (Photo: American Repertory Theater/Richard Feldman)

who had cured him of a speech impediment. Her name now refers to a foundation operating as a producing organization.

Wilson's momentous decors, which he usually designs himself or inspires others to design, reflect his artistic training, while, for years, the subjects and treatments of his shows were deeply enmeshed in his therapeutic concerns. Crucial to these concerns was his relationship with Raymond Andrews, a deaf-mute boy, and Christopher Knowles, an autistic youth. Rejecting the word "therapy" for his teaching, Wilson got these youths to confront the world by accepting them as unique individuals possessed of perceptive powers unknown to the average person. He believed that they were capable of communicating on levels that did not coincide with most people's conscious reality. He wished to capture their special visions. Thus, in developing *Deafman Glance,* in which Andrews appeared, very little of verbal import was employed (Wilson's earliest works were mostly nonverbal), only selected sounds somehow related to the hearing-impaired. The hearing actors learned how to communicate in an environment that recreated the inner workings of a deaf person's mind. Similar concepts were deployed in *Stalin,* which introduced Knowles doing verbal music he had composed using two tape recorders.

At first, Wilson was not concerned with traditional actors, favoring unself-conscious amateurs who could be themselves within his abstract schemes. Many were avant-garde artists; most lacked theater training and some had troubled personalities. To create a production he allowed the company to use their personal qualities; opening up to him their

natures during workshops, they participated in the shaping of the work. When he began to employ verbalization, much of it was composed by the performers.

Although responsible for almost everything heard and seen in his presentations, his collaborative tendencies are distinctive. Wilson's works are, to a great degree, evolved in rehearsal, although he begins from a certain vision. His effects may be closely merged with his fantasies and dreams, but their expression bears as much relation to his collaborators as to himself. From *The $ Value,* he worked with trained professionals, although many feel his work with amateurs was more interesting.

Most of Wilson's original work is considered anti-intellectual; themes are rarely clear and Wilson professes an inability to explain them, although critics have extrapolated certain broad ideas. While retaining an essential ambiguity, ideational content became somewhat more explicit in his more mature works. In *the CIVIL warS,* for example, Wilson confronted the ramifications of civil discord, from historical conflagrations to family strife. Some feel this to be a betrayal of his early works' mystery.

General images isolated include symbolic journeys through time and space, a fascination with mythic figures (Stalin, Freud, Edison, etc.), and the threat of violence where innocence exists. Lawrence Shyer notes, among other images, Wilson's recurrent use of icebergs, space ships, volcanoes, dinosaurs, planets, pyramids, flowers, lakes, the moon, and fire. These derive from many sources and artists. Often Wilson relies on a dramaturge's research (he admits to limited literary and historical knowledge), but he transforms everything into his unique expressive forms.

Plot and character do not function in Wilson's mathematically structured original work as they do in conventional drama. His collagelike accumulations of apparently illogically related images (occasionally on film or projections) present cryptic, symbolic, archetypal, fantastical, and familiar "characters" in an enigmatic blend of theatrical effects designed to be viewed objectively as pictures of allusive, if elusive, beauty. The material works on the unconscious, allowing the spectator to attach any meanings he prefers to the images. Wilson says that his texts—both originals and those culled from historical and literary sources, sometimes with several mixed in a single work—are often chosen more for aural values than ideas.

Wilson performances may be astonishingly slow; a simple gesture may take a half hour to complete. Several productions have been marathons. KA

MOUNTAIN lasted a week, nonstop, morning and night, and *Stalin* ran 12 hours, from evening to dawn. Audiences may daydream or come and go at their pleasure. As the images change imperceptibly, the audience perceives elements invisible when performed at a normal pace. This reflects Wilson's fascination with the Zen tranquility of *nō* theater.

Not everything is thus ritualistically attenuated, and some pieces conform closely to traditional time, even including fast-paced action. Dance is frequently employed, in particular a type of whirling movement. Choreographers Lucinda Childs and Andrew de Groat are closely associated with Wilson's pieces. The lanky Wilson himself often acts and dances in his productions.

Wilson's is preeminently a visual theater, which is one reason for its foreign success. Most of Wilson's works are created for the frontal view of a picture-frame stage. (A recent exception was the environmental staging of *Death Destruction and Detroit II.*) The actors—sometimes in great numbers—appear in artful tableaux against a variety of exceptional backgrounds that display conspicuous geometric shapes and range from the modernistically minimalist to the phantasmagorically spectacular. Wilson has moved progressively from illusionism to abstraction. The stage may be divided into multiple horizontal zones, each with its own activities and images, creating a magical layering. Although he occasionally uses bold color, Wilson favors cool monochromatism, making much use of grays, blacks, and whites. His intricate lighting, which frequently revels in geometric effects made visible by stage smoke, uses mainly white light. Wilson's design talents have been on display in many international exhibitions of his paintings, sculptures, and so on.

Actors may hang from the flies or swing on wires, like the spacemen floating "weightlessly" in *Death Destruction and Detroit.* (Props often fly as well.) They may wear realistic animal getups (one play had a chorus of ostriches), be made up to look like an army of black mammies, or be shown (on stilts) as giants.

All activity is set before a production opens, but a small degree of improvisational freedom is permitted during the execution, provided the precision of established timing, movements, entrances, and exits is followed. Speech was minimal in the early works, but—because of Wilson's interest in Knowles's language—verbal experiments using nondiscursive language played an increasingly vital part following *The $ Value.* Text is often amplified and distorted via body mikes, given an eerily disembodied effect, spoken in contradiction to physical behavior, deconstructed to prevent narrative logic, or otherwise made part of an intricately designed score employing unusual sounds. Words are sometimes appreciated for their structural components, which may be reflected in verbal patterns painted on the scenery.

Runs being brief and costs ruinously high, Wilson has found it difficult to get the funding to stage his noncommercial spectacles. Many have toured Europe, particularly to festivals. Because he was welcomed by well-subsidized foreign companies (especially in Germany), he became an expatriate in the 1980s.

Wilson has a reputation as both a self-controlled guru and a high-strung, demanding perfectionist given to screaming jags. He does not tell actors the meanings of their words, moves, or gestures, but offers suggestive instructions pertaining to the texture or relative weight of their behavior. They may be told to put their ideas aside for fear of providing an interpretation that will reduce the audience's imaginative participation. Many find this creatively liberating, as it allows them not only to make sense of the material for themselves, but even to let their concentration drift. The actors are not characters, but themselves, often being cast for the way they look. Improvisation is important, with Wilson refining what he likes. An assortment of graphic materials are placed on rehearsal walls, and their contents frequently become incorporated in the play. When he revives a work, Wilson aims for precise replication, and demonstrates the smallest movements, yet actors must seem at ease.

Robert Wilson is one of the world's most original and productive postmodernists, although some think him a naked emperor. While he continues to develop original pieces, he also has demonstrated conceptual talent in the direction of others' scripts, giving them surprisingly revelatory interpretations.

Further reading:

Brecht, Stefan. *The Theater of Visions: Robert Wilson.* Frankfurt am Main: Suhrkamp, 1978.

Robert Wilson: The Theater of Images. New York: Harper and Row, 1984.

Rockwell, John. "Staging Painterly Visions." *New York Times Magazine,* November 15, 1992.

Shyer, Lawrence. *Robert Wilson and His Collaborators.* New York: Theater Communications Group, 1989.

Also: Bradby and Williams, *Directors' Theatre;* Shank, *American Alternative Theatre.*

BRETAIGNE WINDUST (1906–1960)

ERNEST BRETAIGNE WINDUST was born in Paris,
France. His socially prominent, musically talented
American mother had met his British father, a noted
concert violinist, in Europe. Bretaigne eventually
settled with his divorced mother in New York after
World War I. He attended Columbia University
from 1924 to 1925 and entered Princeton University
in 1925. Originally interested in a diplomatic career,
he became enmeshed in campus theatricals with the
school club, the Theater Intime. He began as an
actor, started directing with an undergraduate-writ-
ten play in 1926, and soon staged various classic and
modern works.

In 1928, while still an undergraduate (he graduated in 1929), Windust and Harvard undergraduate
Charles Leatherbee—inspired by a talk with Konstantin Stanislavsky's partner, Vladimir Nemirovich-
Danchenko—cofounded the University Players (UP)
at Falmouth, Massachusetts, on Cape Cod, where
they recruited a summer stock company consisting
only of university-educated actors. (In 1932, they
called themselves Theater Unit, Inc.) The group
produced such luminaries as Joshua Logan, Henry
Fonda, Margaret Sullavan, Kent Smith, Norris
Houghton, and James Stewart. They played at Falmouth for five summers and produced at Baltimore's
Maryland Theater in 1931 and 1932. In the winter,
Windust was an assistant stage manager for the
Theater Guild.

Windust staged the majority of the UP's plays,
including works by A. A. Milne, Eugene O'Neill,
George S. Kaufman and Marc Connelly, Karel Capek, Philip Barry, and Ferenc Molnár, among many
others. Almost all were Broadway works of recent
vintage, and few were artistically daring. In Baltimore, however, after revivals of several of their
summer productions, the company found considerable success with Windust's direction of Aristophanes' *Lysistrata* (1932), given a delightfully bawdy,
yet tasteful, interpretation using 66 actors.

The company became affiliated with Broadway
producer-director Arthur Beckhard in 1932, staging
two plays for him as tryouts for New York. Windust
directed Allan Scott and George Haight's *Goodbye
Again*, starring guest actor Howard Lindsay, who
later played a big role in his career. After the Beckhard plays were shown on Broadway (where Beckhard staged *Goodbye Again* with Windust's assistance), the UP dissolved. However, Windust di-

rected several plays for a new management in Falmouth in 1933. His Broadway directing debut
arrived with a play premiered at Falmouth, a mediocre version of Gregorio Martinez-Sierra's 1911
Spanish drama, *Spring in Autumn* (1933). It flopped,
as did Windust's staging of Percival Wilde's *Little
Shot* (1935).

Windust returned to summer stock directing (and
occasional acting) in 1934, 1935, 1936, and 1938,
staging many plays (with one week of rehearsals
each) at the County Theater in Suffern, New York.
Helen Hayes starred in his revival of George Bernard Shaw's *Caesar and Cleopatra* (1935) and received more praise than for her 1925 Broadway
performance in the play.

Windust's big break was Robert E. Sherwood's *Idiot's Delight* (1936), a pacifist play about Europe on
the brink of war, starring Alfred Lunt and Lynn

Alfred Lunt and Lynn Fontanne in Amphitryon 38. *Directed by Bretaigne Windust. (1937)* (Photo: Theater
Collection, Museum of the City of New York)

Fontanne, America's great stage couple, for whom he earlier had been an assistant stage manager and actor. Lunt took a directorial hand in all his plays, so he and Windust actually collaborated on the works they did together. Lunt was credited with having "conceived and supervised" their presentations, Windust with having directed them. Windust had a minor acting role in this Pulitzer Prize-winner.

After Allan Scott's *In Clover* (1937), a disaster whose direction had to be handed to someone else, Windust and the Lunts followed up with S. N. Behrman's wordy, but successful, adaptation of Jean Giraudoux's fantasy-comedy of sexual dalliance between gods and mortals, *Amphitryon 38* (1937). Windust's expertise in French made a significant contribution to the polishing of the adaptation. One of the show's memorable visual effects was that of Lunt as Zeus and Richard Whorf as Mercury, their bare-bottomed bodies rising behind them as they reclined on their elbows in the clouds. The effect was produced by a cutout through which the actors placed their heads.

Continuing his specialization in comedies, Windust provided an expert revival of Somerset Maugham's *The Circle* (1938), starring Tallulah Bankhead. After doing a West Coast staging of Paul Osborn's fantasy about death, *On Borrowed Time* (1938), he directed his first Broadway musical, *Great Lady* (1938), score by Frederick Loewe and Earle Crooker. Despite giving the balletomane director a chance to present several ballets, it failed. He then offered his most famous production, Howard Lindsay and Russel Crouse's *Life with Father* (1939); its 3,224 performances remains the most for a nonmusical Broadway play. The director, distantly related to the Clarence Day family on whose late 19th-century lives the masterful drawing-room comedy is based, brought to it all his gifts for timing and business. Windust did extensive research on New York life in the 1880s in order to teach the cast the proper behavior, and every detail reeked of Victorian authenticity. He had the actors avoid playing for comedy, aiming instead for honesty and conviction. For the curtain calls, he eliminated individual bows in favor of posing the cast in a tintype tableau. Such pictorial calls became a trademark.

Yet another giant hit (1,144 performances) ensued, Joseph Kesselring's hilarious *Arsenic and Old Lace* (1941), about two kindly, but homicidal, old ladies. Again, Windust's comic genius helped the actors create risible but believable characters, such as a drama critic who kept referring to crumpled notes in his pocket, a mannerism stolen from playwright-producer Russel Crouse. Tiny Josephine Hull's mincing gait was made more ludicrous by Windust's giving her a dress that stopped just short of her ankles. For the curtain, 13 walk-ons were hired to file out of the cellar door, representing all of the old men the biddies had killed during the action. In 1956, Windust revived the play in Boston, with Gertrude Berg.

In 1942, Windust staged Lindsay and Crouse's modestly successful *Strip for Action*, an army comedy that included large doses of burlesque. Two flops followed before he tackled Dorothy and Howard Baker's controversial *Trio* (1944), which was strongly praised, but forced to close early because its lesbian theme offended certain city officials. John Patrick's *The Hasty Heart* (1945), about a dying Scottish soldier in Burma, proved worthy of 207 showings, but Jacques Deval's *Oh, Brother!* (1945) was a turkey. Windust redeemed himself with another terrific hit, Lindsay and Crouse's Pulitzer prize-winning comedy about presidential politics, *State of the Union* (1945), which starred Ralph Bellamy and ran 765 times.

Various physical problems kept him out of the service, but Windust was active in war-related activities and directed a comedy for presentation at military bases.

After *State of the Union*, Windust divided his energies among film, television, and theater. He staged six more plays on Broadway, the most successful being *Finian's Rainbow* (1947), with its now-classic Burton Lane and E. Y. "Yip" Harburg score. This was a 725-performance musical with fantasy elements concerning an Irish leprechaun; it contained crucial themes of political chicanery and racial bigotry. Windust's integration of book and musical numbers (choreography by Michael Kidd) was deemed exceptionally well done. His other popular productions of this period were both by his frequent collaborators, Lindsay and Crouse: *Remains to Be Seen* (1951)—a 198-performance comedy-mystery—and *The Great Sebastians* (1956), a vehicle for the Lunts, who played professional mind readers involved in espionage; their stunts, based on a code, baffled and delighted audiences for 174 showings. Less successful were William McCleery's *Parlor Story* (1947), *Gently Does It* (1953), and Howard Teichmann's *The Girls in 509* (1958), his final production. He also made notable contributions to Maxwell Anderson's *Anne of the Thousand Days* (1948), but during the troubled out-of-town period was hospitalized with fatigue and had to be replaced before the successful Broadway opening. He was replaced by librettist Preston Sturges (best known as a film director) on the cumbersome musical, *Carnival in Flanders* (1953). Windust play-doctored several shows and himself replaced the director of Andrew Rosenthal's troubled comedy, *Horses in Midstream* (1953), but the original director (Cecil Hardwicke) received the credit. Another Windust assignment closed out of town in 1957.

Windust was tall, slim, graceful, bespectacled, and stylishly dressed. He was admired for his drily subtle wit, intelligence, modesty, cool temperament and patience, fair-mindedness, boundless energy, artistic knowledge, ability to express himself clearly, and Continental savoir faire. He kept much of his tension hidden under a refined veneer of self-control, and frequently suffered from ulcers, an ailment that precipitated his early death. He was known for his ability never to be nonplussed by a problem or a question, to always have a positive attitude, and to have an answer at the ready, even if it later needed emendation. Actors puzzled by a direction or acting problem knew that, if asked, Windust could supply a definitive explanation based on a careful analysis of character and action, even in weekly stock. When an emergency threatened, he quickly handled it with aplomb. Once, when a UP actress could not find her prop baby for an entrance and started to behave hysterically, he removed a handkerchief from his head (he wore it to absorb perspiration) and immediately convinced her to pretend that it was the baby.

He was a meticulous preplanner, doing extensive background research and working out business and characterizations in advance. Norris Houghton called his approach "intellectual, analytical, deductive." His amateur painting skills helped him clearly visualize sets and costumes and to work closely with his designers, giving them the freedom to expand on the general ideas he provided and then editing the results. His ideas were firmly set and not easily changed, although he revised when he realized he was wrong. Some called him "Definite-minded Windy." His self-assurance, however, often led him to select less than worthy scripts that he thought he could make effective.

Windust created the blocking on a groundplan with toy soldiers or differently colored spools of thread to represent the characters. His preparation was so thorough that he practically memorized all lines and business and hardly needed notes or groundplans at rehearsal. He worked quickly, staging about 10 pages a day and beginning blocking as early as possible. He liked to have frequent run-throughs without interruption, and then to give general notes to the cast and individual notes privately. Windust's notes were respected for their exactitude.

A born leader with a notable air of authority, he ran a tight ship, expected and received disciplined behavior (punctuality was essential), and drilled his companies in a search for perfection. Even minor pieces of business, like making an army bed, were practiced repeatedly until performed with remarkable finesse. Only superficially was he a martinet, as most who worked with him detected his underlying humanity. "What do you think I am, a Nazi?" he would say to surprised players. He tried to avoid readings and demonstrations, but often had to provide them—although in very broad strokes—to save time. Still, he cautioned actors not to copy but to do it their own way. When something better than he had planned occurred, he happily scrapped his original ideas. Experienced actors were allowed more freedom than novices, but he was encouraging to all. Actors were often told not to speak to other actors' ears, but to their minds. He was a hands-on type of director, remaining physically close to the actors so that he could jump up and help them out of a tough situation. He regularly returned to his productions, calling special rehearsals to keep them fresh. He directed all of the touring companies of his Broadway productions.

One of Windust's drawbacks was as an improver of faulty scripts. He did not engage in rewriting himself, and limited himself to advising the playwright. He thought his job to be more that of an interpreter than an editor. Weak plays remained weak under his ministrations, but strong ones benefitted. In fact, in detailed letters to Lindsay, he made a number of crucial suggestions for improvements in *Life with Father,* including the way the first act reaches its climax. His analytical letters on the play reveal meticulous understanding of plot and characters.

Bretaigne Windust deserves recognition for his work with the University Players and as the director of a half dozen of the most popular American productions of mid-century, including the Great White Way's longest-running straight play ever.

Further reading:

Floyd, Harold Wayne. "The Directing Career of Bretaigne Windust." Unpublished Ph.D. diss. Bloomington, Indiana University, 1968.

Houghton, Norris. *But Not Forgotten: The Adventure of the University Players.* New York: William Sloane Associates, 1951.

Also: Houghton, "B. Windust and J. Logan."

JERRY ZAKS (1946–   )

JERRY ZAKS (*né* Byczek) was born in Stuttgart, Germany. His father eluded the Nazis but his mother survived a year at Auschwitz. The family moved to Omaha, Nebraska, then to the Bronx, New York, and finally to Paterson, New Jersey, where his father became a kosher butcher. Zaks abandoned premed at Dartmouth College for theater. He attended graduate school at Smith, and then gained recognition as a professional actor in plays and musicals.

He began directing with several short Neil Cuthbert plays at Off-Off-Broadway's Ensemble Studio Theater (EST). *Buddy Pals,* called by the *New York Times* "a knockabout comedy about television-dominated youth," was an amusing piece that gained its comic impact because its three characters "are sharply individualized by the author, the actors and the director, Jerry Zaks, who at every turn seems to emphasize the comic differences."

He did not turn to full-time directing until discovering Christopher Durang's *Sister Mary Ignatius Explains It All for You.* This irreverent, anticlerical spoof about a tyrannical Catholic-school nun whose hostile students challenge her hypocrisy, debuted as part of a 1979 EST one-act festival and moved to a long-run, 1981 Off-Broadway version at Playwrights Horizons. Zaks made the exaggerated piece work by reining the actors in to present a basically realistic performance. It was paired with Durang's *The Actor's Nightmare.*

By the time these one-acts were staged commercially, Zaks had introduced Durang's *Beyond Therapy* (1981), a flawed comedy about sexuality and psychiatry, starring Sigourney Weaver at Off-Broadway's Phoenix Theater. After directing a Philadelphia revival of Albert Innaurato's *Gemini* (1981), he mounted the national tour of *Tintypes* (1982), a revue of old American tunes he had performed in on Broadway. His New York career resumed at Playwrights Horizons with Durang's farce, *Baby with the Bathwater* (1983), which satirically slashes parents who foul up their children's happiness (and sexual identity). "Using jolly pop-out sets," wrote the *Times,* "Mr. Zaks summons up the flat look and slambang pace of 'I Love Lucy,' turned up to a deranged pitch."

Zaks directed Richard Dresser's one-acter, *At Home* (1984), for EST's "marathon," and guest-directed in Denver and Philadelphia. The 1984–1985 season witnessed a breakthrough as he undertook three Off-Broadway productions (and won an Obie for each of them). Larry Shue's long-run farcical hit, *The Foreigner* (1984), was set in a rural Georgia fishing lodge, and involved the Ku Klux Klan and a shy leading character who pretends not to know English. *The Marriage of Bette and Boo* (1985), Zak's fifth Durang, seen at the Public, was an angry, episodic, black comedy about an abrasive marriage, and the psychological scarring of a son (played by the author). According to the *Village Voice,* the expert performances—by players such as

Jerry Zaks directing Guys and Dolls.   (Photo: Martha Swope)

Mercedes Ruehl and Olympia Dukakis—were "a tribute to . . . Jerry Zaks, whose work has a matter-of-factness, akin to that of the writing, that similarly controls both the giddiness and the suffering." After Michael Zettler's *Crossing the Bar* (1985) closed rapidly, Zaks staged a series of excellent revivals (a word he dislikes), beginning with John Guare's semi-absurdist tragifarce, *The House of Blue Leaves* (1986). With a cast including Julie Hagerty, John Mahoney, Swoosie Kurtz, and Stockard Channing, this blockbuster moved from Lincoln Center's small Newhouse to the Vivian Beaumont, making it Zaks's Broadway directing debut and winning him a Tony.

Zaks's ability to mesh the surreal play's sudden transitions from Strindbergian bleakness to Feydeauesque hilarity and to keep the audience guessing was praised. He described the piece to Leslie Bennetts as tragedy, but declared that it was "ridiculous" to play it as such. "It denies the humanity of these people, because so much of their humanity is in their humor, and their Everyman quality." To incite immediate laughter, he played "Thus Spake Zarathustra" as the banal Queens setting came into view.

Zaks placed the play's importance before the director's. "If you are *truly* answering the questions, Is this right? Is this believable? Does this serve the play?—*then* you're directing," he noted to Lee Alan Morrow and Frank Pike. *Blue Leaves* exemplified his belief that comedy must be rooted in characters who "are concerned with affecting the people around them because of their own desperate needs." It is easy to make an audience laugh, he claims, but the laughter must derive from the "mystery" that arises from an audience's complete belief in and concern for the characters, no matter how heightened. Bennetts wrote that Zaks developed the appropriate tone by restraining any attempt to play for wackiness and constantly reminding "the actors to refer back to the characters' underlying emotional truths."

Zaks prods his actors to overcome their characters' obstacles, to make connections with others, and to fulfill their wants. When there is total commitment, laughter can be explosive. "Comedy," he told Ross Wetzsteon, "only works if the audience cares about the characters, if they believe that the characters' needs are *real.*" His credo, he asserts, is "only connect."

The Beaumont was home to Zaks's superlative, limited-run resuscitation of Ben Hecht and Charles MacArthur's rapid-fire, 1928 Chicago newspaper comedy, *The Front Page* (1986), starring Richard Thomas and John Lithgow. Zaks gave the cynical

comedy "a breeziness and split-second timing that make it fresh again," reported *New York Newsday.* His success led to his becoming a resident director at Lincoln Center, then run by Gregory Mosher and Bernard Gersten, who, with his assistance, were the first to bring a steady stream of notable successes to the institution's stages. Zaks demonstrated the workability of the Beaumont's huge thrust stage, frequently considered a white elephant.

Zaks offered Beaumont subscribers a sparklingly accomplished hit musical revival, Cole Porter's 1934 *Anything Goes* (1987), starring Patti LuPone. The director began his innovative reworking by opening with a recording of Porter himself singing the title tune. He interpolated five other Porter tunes into the score and commissioned a new libretto. It preserved the original's shipboard romance but made the old stock characters three-dimensional. Zaks, who went over every line and motivation as the authors (Timothy Crouse and John Weidman) wrote it, informed Stephen Holden, "The characters are people dealing with the ramifications of trying to fall in love." The Beaumont has no pit, so the costumed, 16-piece swing orchestra performed on a rear platform overlooking the art-deco luxury-liner setting. "A lighthearted burlesque," wrote Holden, "has been re-imagined as a sexy romantic comedy with music."

Next was Shue's *Wenceslas Square* (1988), seen at the Public shortly after the author died in a plane crash. Following it came Ken Ludwig's *Lend Me a Tenor* (1989), a Broadway hit with Victor Garber and Philip Bosco. This farcically complex treatment of an opera singer's private life was set in a sleek, white, art deco hotel room replete with many doors to slam. The *Voice* said this was an "impeccable, terrifyingly detailed production," packed with imaginative gags. Zaks, who won another Tony, provided "a silent-movie curtain call in which the best gags are seen fleetingly again as the cast tears in and out of the doors."

Early in 1990, Zaks directed Richard Thomas and Dianne Wiest in Steve Tesich's *Square One* Off-Broadway. He soon mounted Guare's *Six Degrees of Separation* (1990), starring Stockard Channing; this smash moved from the Newhouse to the Beaumont. A drawing room comedy-drama with socially relevant pretensions, it was based on a true story about a young black man—actually a homeless, homosexual hustler—who wormed his way into the homes of socially apathetic upper-class New York WASPs by claiming to be Sidney Poitier's son. Inspired by the notion of a bare stage to move the action from an to design a nonrealistic, multipurpose disk on the thrust. The somewhat stylized piece broke the fourth wall to assist the storytelling method Guare employed.

In 1991, Zaks directed Stephen Sondheim and John Weidman's controversial and unconventionally structured musical *Assassins* at Playwrights Horizons. Freely mingling time periods, ranging from farce to tragedy, and presented in many rhythms and styles, it concerned nine presidential assassins in American history. Noted *TheaterWeek*: "*Assassins* represents yet another Zaks staging that is awesome in its command and invention. . . . Zaks has come up with a seamless production that never falters." Among the "heartstopping" moments were two in the final sequence:

> eight assassins appear as if by magic from behind the cartons in the Texas Book depository, and, at the end of the scene, Booth sets fire to Oswald's suicide note, placing the note on the floor, and the note slowly revolves off into the distance, still aflame.

Zaks's most recent Broadway offering is Neil Simon's semiautobiographical comedy *Laughter on the 23d Floor* (1993), starring Nathan Lane as a character loosely based on comedian Sid Caesar. It opened to generally approving notices. Many of the same design personnel have worked often with Zaks, among them Walton, set designer Loren Sherman, lighting designer Paul Gallo, and costume designer William Ivey Long. He enjoys working with the same team from one show to another because he knows they will be able to translate his ideas into reality.

Zaks is famed for ensemble performances, perfect timing, and comic imagination. He often begins rehearsals by having the cast read the script "at table" for one or more days prior to blocking. This, he told Morrow and Pike, suggests what the actors' "impulses are going to be, what I have to watch for, and how each actor responds to the slightest bit of performance pressure."

Although he informed Wetzsteon that he is "an obsessive perfectionist," he hates to rush and likes to let the discovery process take its course. His acting years were invaluable in his formation as a director. Most actors like working with him, and, while he calls himself "ruthless," they consider him kind, collaborative, gentle, and caring. He tries to be open to suggestions. "People have to feel that they have the right to talk and suggest," he informed Morrow and Pike. When not satisfied that the actors are being truthful, he repeats material impatiently until they get it right. Zaks has little fondness for Method acting, but does not care how an actor prepares as long as the result has "the ring of truth." Talent means: "when they speak I believe them." But he also seeks totally committed actors brave enough to try anything, a quality he seeks at auditions by asking them to make improvised adjustments in their prepared material.

Recently, Zaks has gained notoriety for his tendency to replace leading players before a show opens. He does this when he realizes that his initial casting was a mistake. Two actors of note to whom this happened were Carolyn Mignini (*Guys and Dolls*) and Paul Provenza (*Laughter on the 23d Floor*). When questioned about this by the *New York Times*, Zaks said, "I never do this impulsively. . . . It's certainly not something I enjoy, and the only reason I do it is at the end of the day I want the show to be perfect."

In some productions he carefully staged certain scenes in his head before beginning to block, although giving the actors the impression that he was working spontaneously. But from *Lend Me a Tenor*, he told Gerard Raymond, he gained confidence and felt less threatened about letting the actors find things on their own. He therefore planned less diligently, counting on his understanding of "the basic vocabulary of how I am going to tell the story."

When, before becoming a director, Zaks appeared on Broadway in *Grease*, he found himself giving notes to the other actors (even while on stage), in order to keep the show's standards from slipping. He told Wetzsteon that "I was making the kind of suggestions I would have fired me for making." For one actor to be giving advice to another is disruptive, he insists, either in rehearsal or during a run.

Visitors are barred from rehearsals, because their presence is inhibiting to the actors as well as himself. Even playwrights cannot attend Zaks's early rehearsals so that when they do come they can bring an objective eye and provide useful feedback. Zaks occasionally does minor rewriting, but the author is told of all revisions. "It is not so much that I am tampering with the fabric but smoothing something out," he told Raymond.

In 1990, Zaks left Lincoln Center to become "director-at-large" for Broadway's theater-owning and producing firm of Jujamcyn, presumably the first time such an organization had hired a director to develop projects for its venues. He and Mosher, who quit Lincoln Center not long after, had developed a rivalry there following reports of a dispute over who

Guys and Dolls. *Directed by Jerry Zaks. (1992)*   (Photo: Martha Swope)

would direct *Six Degrees*. His first Jujamcyn project was an acclaimed $5.5-million revival of Frank Loesser's 1950 musical, *Guys and Dolls* (1992), with Nathan Lane, Peter Gallagher, and Faith Prince. Among the casting surprises was Walter Bobbie as Nicely-Nicely, much slimmer than his predecessors; a bit that had proved funny with fatter actors thus had to be killed. Prince told Wetzsteon that Zaks was

> the greatest director I've ever had at breaking down comedy and finding out why things work or don't work. . . . He's so precise. So specific. . . . Just one small example. In the carnation scene, where I say how I've been engaged for fourteen years and at last we're getting married and the next line is, 'Time certainly does fly.' People were laughing, but not very much, until Jerry had me speed up the first sentence and slow down the second one.

Jerry Zaks has been on a roll for over a decade, and his crowd-pleasing success shows every promise of continuing. He is eclectic enough to move from musicals to straight—mainly comic—plays, and even if he never does a serious drama—classical or new—his reputation is assured.

Further reading:

Bennetts, Leslie. "The Duality in *House of Blue Leaves.*" *New York Times*, April 9, 1986.

Holden, Stephen. "A Glimpse of Olden Days, Via Cole Porter." *New York Times*, October 18, 1987.

Raymond, Gerard. "Behind the Scenes at *Six Degrees of Separation.*" *TheaterWeek*, June 11–17, 1990.

Wetzsteon, Ross. "Zaks Appeal." *New York*, May 28, 1990.

———. "The Great New York Show." *New York*, May 4, 1992.

Also: Morrow and Pike, *Creating Theater.*

SELECTED BIBLIOGRAPHY

THIS BIBLIOGRAPHY IS, for the most part, limited to books that discuss two or more directors covered in the present work. Many—but not all—are mentioned in brief "Also" listings in the "Further reading" sections. See those sections for source material primarily concerned with each respective entry.

Addenbrooke, David. *The Royal Shakespeare Company: The Peter Hall Years*. London: William Kimber, 1974.

Bartow, Arthur. *The Director's Voice: Twenty-one Interviews*. New York: Theater Communications Group, 1988.

Beauman, Sally. *The Royal Shakespeare Company: A History of Ten Decades*. Oxford, England: Oxford University Press, 1982.

Bentley, Eric. *In Search of Theatre*. New York: Vintage Books, 1957.

Berry, Ralph. *On Directing Shakespeare: Interviews with Contemporary Directors*. London: Hamish Hamilton, 1989.

Bordman, Gerald. *American Musical Comedy: From Adonis to Dreamgirls*. New York: Oxford University Press, 1983.

Bradby, David. *Modern French Drama: 1940–1990*. 2d ed. Cambridge, England: Cambridge University Press, 1991.

Bradby, David, and David Williams. *Directors' Theatre*. New York: St. Martin's Press, 1988.

Braun, Edward. *The Director and the Stage: From Naturalism to Grotowski*. London: Methuen, 1982.

Brockett, Oscar, and Robert R. Findlay. *Century of Innovation: A History of European and American Theatre and Drama Since the Late Nineteenth Century*. 2d ed. Englewood Cliffs, N.J.: Prentice-Hall, 1991.

Brown, John Mason. *Dramatis Personae*. New York: Viking Press, 1965.

Browne, Terry. *Playwrights' Theatre: The English Stage Company at the Royal Court*. London: Pitman, 1975.

Brustein, Robert. *Reimagining American Theatre*. New York: Hill and Wang, 1991.

Carter, Huntley. *The New Theatre and Cinema of Soviet Russia*. London: International Publishers, 1924.

———. *The New Spirit in Russian Theatre, 1917–1928*. London: Brentano's, 1928.

Cheney, Sheldon. *The New Movement in the Theatre*. New York: Benjamin Blom, 1971.

Clurman, Harold. *Lies Like Truth*. New York: Grove Press, 1958.

———. *The Naked Image: Reflections on the Modern Theatre*. New York: Macmillan, 1966.

Cole, Susan Letzler. *Directors in Rehearsal: A Hidden World*. New York: Routledge, 1992.

Cole, Toby, and Helen Krich Chinoy, eds. *Directing the Play*. Indianapolis: Bobbs-Merrill, 1953.

———, eds. *Directors on Directing: A Source Book of the Modern Theatre*. Rev. ed. (of *Directing the Play*). Indianapolis: Bobbs-Merrill, 1963.

Cook, Judith. *Directors' Theatre*. London: George Harrap, 1974.

Croyden, Margaret. *Lunatics, Lovers and Poets: The Contemporary Experimental Theatre*. New York: McGraw-Hill, 1974.

Dickinson, Thomas H. *The Theatre in a Changing Europe*. New York: Henry Holt, 1937.

Eaton, Katherine Bliss. *The Theatre of Meyerhold and Brecht*. Westport, Conn.: Greenwood Press, 1985.

Eaton, Walter Prichard. *The Theatre Guild: The First Ten Years*. New York: Brentano's, 1929.

Findlater, Richard, ed. *25 Years of the English Stage Company at the Royal Court*. Derbyshire, England: Amber Lane Press, 1981.

Flanagan, Hallie. *Shifting Scenes of the European Theatre*. New York: Coward-McCann, 1928.

Fuerst, Walter René, and Samuel J. Hume. *Twentieth-Century Stage Decoration*. New York: Dover, 1967.

Gassner, John, ed. *Producing the Play*. Rev. ed. San Francisco: Rinehart, 1953.

Gielgud, John. *Early Stages: 1921–1936*. Rev. ed. London: Heinemann, 1974.

———. *Stage Directions*. New York: Capricorn, 1963.

———, with John Miller and John Powell. *Gielgud: An Actor and His Time*. New York: Clarkson N. Potter, 1980.

Gilman, Richard. *Common and Uncommon Masks: Writings on Theatre—1961–1970*. New York: Vintage Books, 1972.

Goldman, William. *The Season: A Candid Look at Broadway*. New York: Bantam, 1970.

Goodwin, Tim. *Britain's Royal National Theatre*. London: National Theatre, 1988.

Gorchakov, Nikolai. *The Theatre in Soviet Russia*. Translated by Edgar Lehrman. New York: Columbia University Press, 1957.

Gorelik, Mordecai. *New Theatres for Old*. New York: Samuel French, 1940.

Gottfried, Martin. *Opening Nights: Theatre Criticism of the Sixties*. New York: G. P. Putnam's Sons, 1969.

———. *Broadway Musicals*. New York: Harry N. Abrams, 1979.

———. *More Broadway Musicals: Since 1980*. New York: Harry N. Abrams, 1991.

Gregor, Joseph, and René Fulop-Miller. *The Russian Theatre*. Translated by Paul England. Philadelphia: Lippincott, 1930.

Guernsey, Otis, Jr., ed. *Broadway Song and Story: Playwrights, Lyricists, Composers Discuss Their Hits*. New York: Dodd, Mead, 1985.

Guicharnaud, Jacques, with June Beckleman. *Modern French Theatre from Giraudoux to Beckett*. New Haven: Yale University Press, 1961.

Houghton, Norris. "B. Windust and J. Logan." *Theatre Arts* 31 (April 1937).

———. *Moscow Rehearsals: An Account of Methods of Production in the Soviet Theatre*. London: George Allen and Unwin, 1938.

Innes, Christopher. *Holy Theatre: Ritual and the Avant Garde*. Cambridge, England: Cambridge University Press, 1981.

Johnson, Albert and Bertha. *Directing Methods*. South Brunswick, N.J.: A. S. Barnes, 1970.

Jones, David Richard. *Great Directors at Work: Stanislavsky, Brecht, Kazan, Brook*. Berkeley, Calif.: University of California Press, 1986.

Kiebuzinska, Christine. *Revolutionaries in the Theater: Meyerhold, Brecht, and Witkiewicz*. Ann Arbor, Mich.: UMI Press, 1988.

King, Bruce, ed. *Contemporary American Theatre*. New York: St. Martin's Press, 1991.

Kirby, E. T., ed. *Total Theatre: A Critical Anthology*. New York: E. P. Dutton, 1969.

Kislan, Richard. *Hoofing on Broadway: A History of Show Dancing*. New York: Prentice-Hall, 1987.

Knapp, Bettina. *Off-Stage Voices: Interviews with Modern French Dramatists*. Edited by Alba Amoia. Troy, N.Y.: Whitston, 1975.

———. *The Reign of the Theatrical Director, French Theatre: 1887–1924*. Troy, N.Y.: Whitston, 1988.

Kullman, Colby H., and William C. Young, eds. *Theatre Companies of the World*. 2 vols. Westport, Conn.: Greenwood Press, 1986.

Laufe, Abe. *Broadway's Greatest Musicals*. Rev. ed. New York: Funk and Wagnalls, 1977.

Leiter, Samuel L. *Shakespeare Around the Globe: A Guide to Notable Postwar Revivals*. Westport, Conn.: Greenwood Press, 1985.

———. *From Belasco to Brook: Representative Directors of the English-Speaking Stage*. Westport, Conn.: Greenwood Press, 1991.

———. *From Stanislavsky to Barrault: Representative Directors of the European Stage*. Westport, Conn.: Greenwood Press, 1991.

Lloyd Evans, Gareth, and Barbara Lloyd Evans, eds. *Plays in Review 1956–1980: British Drama and the Critics*. New York: Methuen, 1985.

Macgowan, Kenneth. *The Theatre of Tomorrow*. New York: Boni and Liveright, 1921.

———, and Robert Edmond Jones. *Continental Stagecraft*. New York: Benjamin Blom, 1964.

Marowitz, Charles, and Simon Trussler, eds. *Theatre at Work: Playwrights and Productions in the Modern British Theatre.* New York: Hill and Wang, 1977.

Marshall, Norman. *The Producer and the Play.* Rev. ed. London: Davis-Poynter, 1975.

Mazer, Cary M. *Shakespeare Refashioned: Elizabethan Plays on Edwardian Stages.* Ann Arbor, Mich.: UMI Research Press, 1981.

Miller, Anna Irene. *The Independent Theatre in Europe.* New York: Ray Long and Richard B. Smith, 1931.

Mitter, Shomit. *Systems of Rehearsal: Stanislavsky, Brecht, Grotowski, and Peter Brook.* New York: Routledge, 1992.

Mordden, Ethan. *Broadway Babies: The People Who Made the American Musical.* New York: Oxford University Press, 1983.

Morrow, Lee Alan, and Frank Pike. *Creating Theater.* New York: Vintage, 1986.

Novick, Julius. *Beyond Broadway: The Quest for Permanent Theatres.* New York: Hill and Wang, 1968.

Patterson, Michael. *The Revolution in German Theatre 1900–1933.* Boston: Routledge and Kegan Paul, 1981.

Robinson, Mary C., Vera Roberts, and Millie Barranger. *Notable Women in the American Theatre.* Westport, Conn.: Greenwood Press, 1989.

Roose-Evans, James. *Experimental Theatre: From Stanislavsky to Peter Brook.* 4th ed. rev. London: Routledge, 1989.

Rudnitsky, Konstantin. *Russian and Soviet Theater: 1905–1932.* Translated by Roxane Permar. Edited by Lesley Milne. New York: Harry N. Abrams, 1988.

Savran, David. *In Their Own Words: Contemporary American Playwrights.* New York: Theatre Communications Group, 1988.

Sayler, Oliver M. *The Russian Theatre.* New York: Brentano's, 1920.

Schevill, James. *Break Out! In Search of New Theatrical Environments.* Chicago: Swallow Press, 1973.

Shank, Theodore. *American Alternative Theatre.* New York: Grove Press, 1982.

Simon, John. *Uneasy Stages: A Chronicle of the New York Theater 1963–1973.* New York: Random House, 1976.

Slonim, Marc. *Russian Theater: From the Empire to the Soviets.* Cleveland and New York: World, 1961.

Speaight, Robert. *Shakespeare on the Stage.* Boston and Toronto: Little, Brown, 1973.

Styan, J. L. *The Shakespeare Revolution.* Cambridge, England: Cambridge University Press, 1977.

Van Gysegham, André. *Theatre in Soviet Russia.* London: Faber and Faber, 1943.

Waldau, Roy S. *Vintage Years of the Theatre Guild, 1928–1939.* Cleveland: Press of Case Western Reserve University, 1972.

Wiles, Timothy. *The Theatre Event: Modern Theories of Performance.* Chicago: University of Chicago Press, 1980.

Willett, John. *The Theatre of the Weimar Republic.* New York: Holmes and Meier, 1988.

Wills, Robert J., ed. *The Director in a Changing Theatre.* Palo Alto, Calif.: Mayfield, 1976.

Worrall, Nick. *Modernism to Realism on the Soviet Stage.* Cambridge, England: Cambridge University Press, 1989.

Ziegler, Joseph Wesley. *Regional Theatre: The Revolutionary Stage.* New York: Da Capo, 1977.

Zolotow, Maurice. *No People Like Show People.* New York: Random House, 1951.

INDEX